Praise for *A Companion to Catullus*

"This volume is strongly recommended to scholars and teachers for its sound exposition of a given Catullan problem and as a point of departure for any student starting out to explore the Catullan oeuvre."

Sjarlene Thom

"This *Companion* will be the best of companions to young Catullus scholars, as a strong starting point for work on the most important questions in Catullan studies."

New England Classical Journal

"The volume's 27 essays are the work of a team of internationally renowned scholars. It deserves a place in both the libraries of academic institutions as well as the well-stocked public library."

Reference Reviews

"Abounds with scholarship of a high order, state-of-the-art literary history and criticism, and, not least, solid practical advice for readers and instructors."

Choice

"This reviewer recommends the book without reservation not only to the Catullus specialist, but also and especially to all classicists and teachers."

Scholia Reviews

"Offers modern youth a direct hotline with an ancient author."

Journal of Classics Teaching

"It is a strong volume, to which the student meeting Catullus for the first time and the highly experienced reader can be sent with confidence."

Bryn Mawr Classical Review

BLACKWELL COMPANIONS TO THE ANCIENT WORLD

This series provides sophisticated and authoritative overviews of periods of ancient history, genres of classical literature, and the most important themes in ancient culture. Each volume comprises between twenty-five and forty concise essays written by individual scholars within their area of specialization. The essays are written in a clear, provocative, and lively manner, designed for an international audience of scholars, students, and general readers.

ANCIENT HISTORY

Published

A Companion to the Roman Army
Edited by Paul Erdkamp

A Companion to the Roman Republic
Edited by Nathan Rosenstein and Robert Morstein-Marx

A Companion to the Roman Empire
Edited by David S. Potter

A Companion to the Classical Greek World
Edited by Konrad H. Kinzl

A Companion to the Ancient Near East
Edited by Daniel C. Snell

A Companion to the Hellenistic World
Edited by Andrew Erskine

A Companion to Late Antiquity
Edited by Philip Rousseau

A Companion to Archaic Greece
Edited by Kurt A. Raaflaub and Hans van Wees

A Companion to Julius Caesar
Edited by Miriam Griffin

A Companion to Ancient History
Edited by Andrew Erskine

A Companion to Byzantium
Edited by Liz James

A Companion to Ancient Egypt
Edited by Alan B. Lloyd

A Companion to Ancient Macedonia
Edited by Joseph Roisman and Ian Worthington

In preparation

A Companion to the Punic Wars
Edited by Dexter Hoyos

A Companion to Sparta
Edited by Anton Powell

LITERATURE AND CULTURE

Published

A Companion to Classical Receptions
Edited by Lorna Hardwick and Christopher Stray

A Companion to Greek and Roman Historiography
Edited by John Marincola

A Companion to Catullus
Edited by Marilyn B. Skinner

A Companion to Roman Religion
Edited by Jörg Rüpke

A Companion to Greek Religion
Edited by Daniel Ogden

A Companion to the Classical Tradition
Edited by Craig W. Kallendorf

A Companion to Roman Rhetoric
Edited by William Dominik and Jon Hall

A Companion to Greek Rhetoric
Edited by Ian Worthington

A Companion to Ancient Epic
Edited by John Miles Foley

A Companion to Greek Tragedy
Edited by Justina Gregory

A Companion to Latin Literature
Edited by Stephen Harrison

A Companion to Ovid
Edited by Peter E. Knox

A Companion to Greek and Roman Political Thought
Edited by Ryan K. Balot

A Companion to the Ancient Greek Language
Edited by Egbert Bakker

A Companion to Hellenistic Literature
Edited by Martine Cuypers and James J. Clauss

A Companion to Vergil's *Aeneid* and its Tradition
Edited by Joseph Farrell and Michael C. J. Putnam

A Companion to Horace
Edited by Gregson Davis

In preparation

A Companion to the Latin Language
Edited by James Clackson

A Companion to Greek Mythology
Edited by Ken Dowden and Niall Livingstone

A Companion to Sophocles
Edited by Kirk Ormand

A Companion to Aeschylus
Edited by Peter Burian

A Companion to Greek Art
Edited by Tyler Jo Smith and Dimitris Plantzos

A Companion to Families in the Greek and Roman World
Edited by Beryl Rawson

A Companion to Tacitus
Edited by Victoria Pagán

A Companion to the Archaeology of the Ancient Near East
Edited by Daniel Potts

A COMPANION
TO CATULLUS

Edited by

Marilyn B. Skinner

A John Wiley & Sons, Ltd., Publication

This paperback edition first published 2011
© 2011 Blackwell Publishing Ltd

Edition history: Blackwell Publishing Ltd (hardback, 2007)

Blackwell Publishing was acquired by John Wiley & Sons in February 2007. Blackwell's publishing program has been merged with Wiley's global Scientific, Technical, and Medical business to form Wiley-Blackwell.

Registered Office
John Wiley & Sons Ltd, The Atrium, Southern Gate, Chichester, West Sussex, PO19 8SQ, United Kingdom

Editorial Offices
350 Main Street, Malden, MA 02148-5020, USA
9600 Garsington Road, Oxford, OX4 2DQ, UK
The Atrium, Southern Gate, Chichester, West Sussex, PO19 8SQ, UK

For details of our global editorial offices, for customer services, and for information about how to apply for permission to reuse the copyright material in this book please see our website at www.wiley.com/wiley-blackwell.

The right of Marilyn B. Skinner to be identified as the author of the editorial material in this work has been asserted in accordance with the UK Copyright, Designs and Patents Act 1988.

Library of Congress Cataloging-in-Publication Data

A companion to Catullus/edited by Marilyn B. Skinner.
    p.   cm. — (Blackwell companions to the ancient world)
  Includes bibliographical references and index.
  ISBN: 978-1-4051-3533-7 (hardback :   ) ISBN: 978-1-4443-3925-3 (paperback :   )
1. Catullus, Gaius Valerius—Criticism and interpretation.   I. Skinner, Marilyn B.
  PA6276.C66 2007
  874′.01—dc22
                                        2006025011

A catalogue record for this book is available from the British Library.

Set in 10/12pt Galliard by SPi Publisher Services, Pondicherry, India

1   2011

In memory of

James L. P. Butrica

attigit quoque poeticen, credimus, ne eius expers esset suauitatis

Cornelius Nepos, *Life of Atticus* 18.5

Contents

Illustrations

Acknowledgments

The editor of this volume, the contributors, and the publisher gratefully acknowledge the permission granted to reproduce the copyright material in this book:

Authorities of the Italian Air Force (Aeronautica militare) for fig. 4.2, photograph of the north end of the Sirmione peninsula (CODIC, SMA N. 356 – 12 August 1981). Thanks to the British Embassy in Rome for assistance in obtaining the photograph.
A. P. Watt Ltd for non-US English rights to reprint excerpts from W. B. Yeats' "The Scholars" and *The Autobiography of W. B. Yeats*. Permission granted by A. P. Watt Ltd on behalf of Michael B. Yeats.
Carcanet Press Ltd for world rights to reprint Robert Graves' "The Thieves," from *Robert Graves: The Complete Poems in One Volume*, edited by Beryl Graves and Dunstan Ward (2000). ©1995 by the Trustees of the Robert Graves Copyright Trust.
The University of Chicago Press, for permission to publish a synopsis of Brian A. Krostenko, *Cicero, Catullus, and the Language of Social Performance* (© 2001 by The University of Chicago. All rights reserved.).
Elisabetta Roffia, Soprintendenza per i beni archeologici della Lombardia, for photographs of fragment of fresco (Archivio Fotografico D 756) reproduced as fig.4.5.
David Higham Associates for world rights to reprint an excerpt from "Epitaph for Liberal Poets," by Louis MacNeice, included in E. R. Dodds, ed., *The Collected Poems of Louis MacNeice*. Copyright ©1966 by The Estate of Louis MacNeice.
Faber & Faber Ltd for UK and British Commonwealth (excluding Canada) rights to reprint excerpts from the following works by Ezra Pound:

"The Flame" and "To Formianus' Young Lady Friend" by Ezra Pound, from *Personae*, copyright ©1926 by Ezra Pound.
Selected Letters of Ezra Pound, copyright ©1950 by Ezra Pound.

Selected Prose of Ezra Pound 1909–1965, copyright ©1973 by The Estate of Ezra Pound.
"Canto IV" and "Canto V" by Ezra Pound, from *The Cantos of Ezra Pound*, copyright ©1934, 1937, 1940, 1948, 1956, 1959, 1962, 1963, 1966, and 1968 by Ezra Pound.
The Literary Essays of Ezra Pound, copyright ©1935 by Ezra Pound.
"Catullus: XXVI and LXXXV" by Ezra Pound, from *The Translations of Ezra Pound*, copyright ©1963 by Ezra Pound.

Faber & Faber Ltd for British Commonwealth and European rights to reprint an excerpt from *The Invention of Love*, by Tom Stoppard. Copyright ©1997 by Tom Stoppard.

New Directions Publishing Corporation for United States and Canadian rights to quote from the following works and authors:

"The Flame" and "To Formianus' Young Lady Friend" by Ezra Pound, from *Personae*, copyright ©1926 by Ezra Pound. Reprinted by permission of New Directions Publishing Corporation.
Selected Letters of Ezra Pound, copyright ©1950 by Ezra Pound. Reprinted by permission of New Directions Publishing Corporation.
Selected Prose of Ezra Pound 1909–1965, copyright ©1973 by The Estate of Ezra Pound. Reprinted by permission of New Directions Publishing Corporation.
"Canto IV" and "Canto V" by Ezra Pound, from *The Cantos of Ezra Pound*, copyright ©1934, 1937, 1940, 1948, 1956, 1959, 1962, 1963, 1966, and 1968 by Ezra Pound. Reprinted by permission of New Directions Publishing Corporation.
The Literary Essays of Ezra Pound, copyright ©1935 by Ezra Pound. Reprinted by permission of New Directions Publishing Corporation.
"Catullus: XXVI and LXXXV" by Ezra Pound, from *The Translations of Ezra Pound*, copyright ©1963 by Ezra Pound. Reprinted by permission of New Directions Publishing Corporation.
"Dear Little Sirmio: Catullus Recollected," by Stevie Smith, from *Collected Poems of Stevie Smith*, copyright ©1972 by Stevie Smith. Reprinted by permission of New Directions Publishing Corporation.

Pickering & Chatto Publishers Ltd for permission to quote an excerpt from Terry L. Meyers, ed., *The Uncollected Letters of Algernon Charles Swinburne, Vol. 3, 1890–1909* (London and Brookfield, VT: Pickering & Chatto, 2004). Reproduced courtesy of Pickering & Chatto Publishers.

Brian Read and the literary estate of Arthur Symons for permission to reprint Arthur Symons' translation of Poem 8, originally contained in *From Catullus – Chiefly Concerning Lesbia*, ©1924 by Arthur Symons.

Scribner, an imprint of Simon & Schuster Adult Publishing Group, for US rights to reprint excerpts from W. B. Yeats' "The Scholars" and *The Autobiography of W. B. Yeats*.

Every effort has been made to trace copyright holders and to obtain their permission for the use of copyright material. The publisher apologizes for any errors or omissions in the above list and would be grateful if notified of any corrections that should be incorporated in future reprints or editions of this book.

Abbreviations

Abbreviations of the names of ancient authors and their works follow, whenever possible, the practice of the *Oxford Classical Dictionary*, 3rd edition (1996), referred to as *OCD³*. Otherwise Greek authors and titles are abbreviated as in Liddell and Scott, *Greek-English Lexicon*, 9th edition, revised by H. Stuart Jones and supplemented by various scholars (1968), referred to as *LSJ*. Latin authors and titles are abbreviated as in the *Oxford Latin Dictionary* (1982), commonly cited as *OLD*. Names of authors or works in square brackets [—] indicate spurious or questionable attributions. Numbers in superscript following a title indicate the number of an edition (e.g., *OCD³*). Abbreviations and descriptions of works of secondary scholarship are also usually taken from *OCD³*.

General Abbreviations

ad; *ad loc.*	*ad locum*, at the line being discussed in the commentary
ap.	*apud*, within, indicating a quotation contained in another author
c., cc.	*carmen*, poem; *carmina*, poems
ca.	*circa*, about or approximately
cf.	compare
ch.	chapter
cos.	consul (date follows)
des.	*designatus*, appointed but not yet installed
suff.	*suffectus*, appointed to fill out a term
d.	died
def.	definition
esp.	especially

f.	*filius, filia*, son or daughter
ff.	and the following (lines, pages)
fig., figs.	figure, figures
fr., frr.	fragment, fragments
G	*Sangermanensis* (Paris codex of Catullus)
ibid.	*ibidem*, in the same work cited above
l.	*libertus, liberta*, freedman or -woman
m.	married
MS, MSS	manuscript, manuscripts
n., nn.	note, notes
no., nos.	number, numbers
O	*Oxoniensis* (Oxford codex of Catullus)
p., pp.	page, pages
passim	*passim*, throughout
pr.	praetor (date follows)
pref.	preface
pron.	*pronepos*, great-grandson
R	*Romanus* (Vatican codex of Catullus)
sc.	*scilicet*, namely
s.v.	*sub verbo*, under the word
test.	*testimonia*, mentions in later antiquity
tr. pop.	tribune of the people (date follows)
trans.	translated (by)
V	*Veronensis* (Verona codex of Catullus)
v., vv.	verse, verses
vel sim.	*vel simile*, or something similar

Roman *Praenomina*

First names of male Roman citizens, relatively few and handed down in families, are abbreviated on inscriptions and conventionally in modern works of scholarship. The following occur in this volume:

Ap.	Appius
C.	Gaius
Cn.	Gnaeus
D.	Decimus
L.	Lucius
M.	Marcus
P.	Publius
Q.	Quintus
Ser.	Servius
Sex.	Sextus
T.	Titus
Ti.	Tiberius

Greek Authors and Works

Aesch.	Aeschylus
Anth. Pal.	*Palatine Anthology*
App. *B Civ.*	Appian, *Bellum Civile*
Ap. Rhod. *Argon.*	Apollonius Rhodius, *Argonautica*
Arist. *Rhet.*	Aristotle, *Rhetoric*
Callim.	Callimachus
Aet.	*Aetia*
Epigr.	*Epigrams*
Democr.	Democritus
Dio Cass.	Dio Cassius
Hes. *Theog.*	Hesiod, *Theogony*
Hom.	Homer
Il.	*Iliad*
Od.	*Odyssey*
Joseph. *BJ*	Josephus, *Bellum Judaicum*
Pind. *Isthm.*	Pindar, *Isthmian Odes*
Pl.	Plato
Resp.	*Republic*
Plut.	Plutarch
Caes.	*Life of Julius Caesar*
Cat. Mi.	*Life of Cato the Younger*
Cic.	*Life of Cicero*
Galb.	*Life of Galba*
Nic.	*Life of Nicias*
Pomp.	*Life of Pompey*
Polyb.	Polybius
Strab.	Strabo
Theoc. *Id.*	Theocritus, *Idylls*

Roman Authors and Works

Apul. *Apol.*	Apuleius, *Apologia*
Asc. . . . C	Asconius, ed. A. C. Clark (OCT, 1907)
Aur. Vict. *Caes.*	Aurelius Victor, *Caesares*
Babr.	Babrius
Caes.	Caesar
B Civ.	*Bellum Civile*
B Gall.	*Bellum Gallicum*
Catull.	Catullus
Cic.	Cicero
Amic.	*De amicitia*
Att.	*Letters to Atticus*
Brut.	*Brutus*

Caecin.	*Pro Caecina*
Cael.	*Pro Caelio*
Cat.	*In Catilinam*
De or.	*De oratore*
Div.	*De divinatione*
Fam.	Letters to Acquaintances (*Ad familiares*)
Fin.	*De finibus*
Flac.	*Pro Flacco*
Font.	*Pro Fonteio*
Har. resp.	*De haruspicum response*
Inv. rhet.	*De inventione rhetorica*
Leg. Man.	*Pro lege Manilia*
Off.	*De officiis*
Orat.	*Orator*
Phil.	*Philippics*
Pis.	*In Pisonem*
Quinct.	*Pro Quinctio*
Sest.	*Pro Sestio*
Tusc.	*Tusculanae Disputationes*
Verr.	*In Verrem*
[Cic.] *Sall.*	[Cicero], *In Sallustium*
Dig.	Paulus, *Justinian's Digest*
Enn. *Ann.*	Ennius, *Annales* (ed. Skutsch)
Fest.	Festus
Gell. *NA*	Aulus Gellius, *Attic Nights*
Hirt. *B Gall.*	Hirtius, *Bellum Gallicum*
Hor.	Horace
Ars P.	*Ars Poetica*
Carm.	*Odes*
Carm. Saec.	*Carmen Saeculare*
Ep.	*Epistles*
Epod.	*Epodes*
Sat.	*Satires*
Isid. *Etym.*	Isidore, *Etymologiae*
Jer. *Chron.*	Jerome, *Chronica*
Just. *Epit.*	Justin, *Epitome* (of Trogus)
Juv.	Juvenal
Liv.	Livy
Luc.	Lucan
Macrob. *Sat.*	Macrobius, *Saturnalia*
Mart.	Martial
Men. Rhet.	Menander Rhetor
Nep. *Att.*	Cornelius Nepos, *Life of Atticus*
Ov.	Ovid
Am.	*Amores*
Met.	*Metamorphoses*
Tr.	*Tristia*

Paul. *Dig.*	Iulius Paulus, *Digesta Iustiniani*
Phaedr.	Phaedrus
Plaut.	Plautus
Bacch.	*Bacchides*
Men.	*Menaechmi*
Mil.	*Miles gloriosus*
Per.	*Persa*
Rud.	*Rudens*
Plin. *Ep.*	Pliny (the Younger), *Letters*
Plin. *HN*	Pliny (the Elder), *Natural History*
Prisc. *Inst.*	Priscian, *Institutes of the Art of Grammar*
Prop.	Propertius
Q. Cic. *Comment. pet.*	Quintus Cicero, *Commentariolum petitionis*
Quint. *Inst.*	Quintilian, *Institutes of Oratory*
Rhet. Her.	*Rhetorica ad Herennium*
Sall.	Sallust
Cat.	*Catiline*
Hist.	B. Maurenbrecher, ed., *C. Sallusti Crispi Historiarum reliquiae* (1893)
Jug.	*Jugurtha*
Sen. *Controv.*	Seneca (the Elder), *Controversiae*
Sen. *Ep.*	Seneca (the Younger), *Epistulae*
Serv.	Servius
Stat. *Silv.*	Statius, *Silvae*
Suet.	Suetonius
Calig.	*Life of Caligula*
Claud.	*Life of the Deified Claudius*
Gram.	*De grammaticis*
Iul.	*Life of the Deified Julius*
Ner.	*Life of Nero*
Vita Hor.	*Life of Horace*
Tac.	Tacitus
Agr.	*Agricola*
Ann.	*Annales*
Dial.	*Dialogus de oratoribus*
Hist.	*Historiae*
Ter. Maur.	Terentianus Maurus
Val. Max.	Valerius Maximus
Var. *Men.*	Varro, *Menippeae*
Vell. Pat.	Velleius Paterculus
Verg.	Vergil
Aen.	*Aeneid*
Ecl.	*Eclogues*
G.	*Georgics*

Works of Secondary Scholarship

AÉ	*L'Année Épigraphique*, published in *Revue Archéologique* and separately (1888–)
Blänsdorf	J. Blänsdorf, ed., *Fragmenta poetarum Latinorum epicorum et lyricorum praeter Ennium et Lucilium*, 3rd edn. (1995)
Bücheler	F. Bücheler, ed., *Petronii Saturae*, 8th edn. (1963)
Cèbe	J.-P. Cèbe, ed., *Varron, satires Ménippées* (1972–99)
CIG	A. Boeckh, ed., *Corpus Inscriptionum Graecarum* (1828–77)
CIL	*Corpus Inscriptionum Latinarum* (1863–)
CLE	F. Bücheler and E. Lommatzsch, eds., *Carmina Latina Epigraphica* (1825–1926)
Courtney	E. Courtney, ed., *The Fragmentary Latin Poets* (1993)
Diehl	E. Diehl, ed., *Anthologica Lyrica Graeca* (1925; 2nd edn. 1942; 3rd edn. 1949–52)
D-K	H. Diels and W. Kranz, eds., *Fragmente der Vorsokratiker*, 6th edn. (Berlin, 1952)
GLK	H. Keil, ed., *Grammatici Latini*, 8 vols. (1855–1923; rpt. 1961)
H.	R. Helm, ed., *Die Chronik des Hieronymus*, 2nd edn. (1956)
IG	*Inscriptiones Graecae* (1873–)
Inschrif. Eph.	H. Wankel, ed., *Die Inschriften von Ephesos*, 8 vols. in 10 (1979–84)
Inscr. Ital.	*Inscriptiones Italiae* (1931/2–)
LGS	D. L. Page, ed., *Lyrica Graeca Selecta* (1968)
Lindsay	W. M. Lindsay, ed.
DCD	*Nonii Marcelli De compendiosa doctrina*, 3 vols. (1903)
DVS	*Sexti Pompei Festi De verborum significatu quae supersunt cum Pauli epitome* (1913)
L-P	E. Lobel and D. L. Page, eds., *Poetarum Lesbiorum Fragmenta* (1955)
OCT	Oxford Classical Text
OLD	P. G. W. Glare, ed., *Oxford Latin Dictionary* (1968–82)
ORF	H. Malcovati, *Oratorum Romanorum Fragmenta* (2nd edn. 1955; 4th edn. 1967)
Pf.	R. Pfeiffer, ed., *Callimachus*, 2 vols. (1949)

P. Mil. Vogl. VIII 309	G. Bastianini and C. Gallazzi with C. Austin, eds., *Posidippo di Pella: Epigrammi*, Papiri dell' Universita degli Studi di Milano 8 (2001)
Radt	B. Snell, R. Kannicht, and S. Radt, eds., *Tragicorum Graecorum Fragmenta* (*TrGF*), 5 vols. (1971–85)
Sk.	O. Skutsch, ed., *The Annals of Q. Ennius* (1985)
S-M	B. Snell and H. Maehler, eds., *Pindari carmina cum fragmentis* (1987–8)
Supp. Hell.	H. Lloyd-Jones and P. Parsons, eds., *Supplementum Hellenisticum*, Texte und Kommentare no. 11 (1983)
TLL	*Thesaurus Linguae Latinae* (1900–)

Notes on Contributors

Ronnie Ancona is professor of classics at Hunter College, CUNY, and in the PhD program of the CUNY Graduate Center. She received her PhD in classics from the Ohio State University in 1983. Her publications include *Time and the Erotic in Horace's Odes* (1994); *Horace: Selected Odes and Satire 1.9*, student text with accompanying teacher's guide (1999, 2nd edition 2005); *Writing Passion: A Catullus Reader* with accompanying teacher's guide (2004); *Gendered Dynamics in Latin Love Poetry*, co-edited with Ellen Greene (2005); and *A Concise Guide to Teaching Latin Literature*, forthcoming. She is the series editor for the Bolchazy-Carducci college-level Latin Readers and, with Sarah B. Pomeroy, the co-editor of a series on women in antiquity for Routledge. Current projects include a monograph, *Contextualizing Catullus: Literary Interpretation and Cultural Setting*.

Brian Arkins is professor of classics at the National University of Ireland, Galway. He was educated at Clongowes Wood College and at University College Dublin, where he obtained an MA in classics and a PhD in Latin. His main research interests are in Latin poetry and in reception studies, with special reference to modern Irish literature. His books include *Sexuality in Catullus* (1982); *An Interpretation of the Poems of Propertius* (2005); *Builders of My Soul: Greek and Roman Themes in Yeats* (1990); *Greek and Roman Themes in Joyce* (1999); and *Hellenising Ireland: Greek and Roman Themes in Modern Irish Literature* (2005). He has also published over a hundred journal articles.

William W. Batstone is professor of Greek and Latin at the Ohio State University. He received his PhD from the University of California at Berkeley in 1984. His research interests include literary theory and philosophical hermeneutics as well as both the prose and poetry of the Roman Republic and early Empire. He is the author with Cynthia Damon of *Caesar's Civil War* (2006) and has written on reception theory, Bakhtin, rhetoric, and metatheatre as well as on Plautus, Catullus,

Cicero, Sallust, and Vergil. He is currently working on articles for companions to Roman history and Roman rhetoric and a book on comedy, ancient and modern, and the vicissitudes of Hegel's concrete universal.

J. L. Butrica, who passed away while this book was in press, received his BA from Amherst College in 1972, and his MA and PhD from the University of Toronto in 1973 and 1978 respectively. Besides a few articles on Greek drama, most of his work was concerned with the textual criticism of Latin poetry (most notably *The Manuscript Tradition of Propertius* [1984]). More recently he began to publish reviews and articles on Roman sexuality. He also translated Erasmus' "Ecclesiastes" for the "Collected Works of Erasmus" series (due to appear in 2006–7). Currently he has two substantial articles awaiting publication in *Phoenix* and *Rheinisches Museum* arguing that *Epigrammata Bobiensia* 37 and 36 respectively are works of the Domitianic poet Sulpicia (a traditional attribution, now generally rejected, in the first case, a new attribution in the second).

Jeri Blair DeBrohun is associate professor of classics at Brown University. She received her PhD from the University of Michigan in 1992 and taught in the Classics Department at Florida State University for three years before joining the Brown faculty in 1995. Her research specializations are Hellenistic and Roman poetry, with particular emphasis on Republican and Augustan poetry at Rome. Her publications include *Roman Propertius and the Reinvention of Elegy* (2003) plus articles on Propertius, Catullus, Ovid, and Lucretius. She also has an interest in cultural studies, and she is currently writing a book on *Greco-Roman Dress as an Expressive Medium*.

Julia T. Dyson Hejduk is associate professor of classics at Baylor University. She received her PhD from Harvard University in 1993. Before taking up her present post in 2003, she worked for ten years at the University of Texas at Arlington. Her research interests include Latin poetry, Roman religion, and women of ancient Rome. She has written one monograph, *King of the Wood: The Sacrificial Victor in Virgil's Aeneid* (2001), a sourcebook in translation with commentary, *Clodia: Readings in Roman Passion, Politics, and Poetry* (forthcoming), and several articles on Vergil and Ovid. She is currently at work on a monograph involving religion and intertextuality in Ovid, *Ovid and His Gods: The Epic Struggles of an Elegiac Hero*.

Andrew Feldherr is professor of classics at Princeton University. He received his PhD from the University of California at Berkeley in 1991. His research concentrates on Latin literature in several genres with a special emphasis on historiography (*Spectacle and Society in Livy's History* [1998]) and epic. He is currently completing a monograph on the *Metamorphoses* entitled *Playing Gods: The Politics of Fiction in Ovid's Metamorphoses* as well as editing the *Cambridge Companion to the Roman Historians*.

Julia Haig Gaisser is Eugenia Chase Guild Professor in the Humanities Emeritus at Bryn Mawr College, where she taught from 1975 to 2006. She received her PhD in Greek from the University of Edinburgh in 1967. Her research interests lie in three principal areas: Republican and Augustan poetry, the transmission and reception of

Roman literature, and Renaissance humanism. She is the author of *Catullus and His Renaissance Readers* (1993) and *Pierio Valeriano On the Ill Fortune of Learned Men: A Renaissance Humanist and His World* (1999) and the editor of *Catullus in English* (2001), an anthology of Catullus translations. Forthcoming are *Oxford Readings in Catullus* and *The Fortunes of Apuleius: A Study in Transmission and Reception*.

Daniel H. Garrison is professor of classics at Northwestern University. He received his PhD from the University of California at Berkeley in 1968. His dissertation work was rewritten as a monograph, *Mild Frenzy: A Reading of the Hellenistic Love Epigram* (1978). His editions of Horace's lyrics, *Horace Epodes and Odes: A New Annotated Latin Edition* (1991), and Catullus, *The Student's Catullus* (3rd edition, 2004), grew out of his classroom work with these poets at Northwestern. He has also written on Greek and Roman sexual culture in *Sexual Culture in Ancient Greece* (2000). He is now completing an annotated translation of the first comprehensive anatomy book in Europe, Andreas Vesalius' *De humani corporis fabrica* (1543, 1555), and is editing a volume on constructions of the human body in the ancient world.

Ellen Greene is the Joseph Paxton Presidential Professor of Classics at the University of Oklahoma. She received her PhD from the University of California at Berkeley in 1992. Her research specialization is Greek and Roman lyric poetry, with an emphasis on issues in gender and sexuality. She is the author of *The Erotics of Domination: Male Desire and the Mistress in Latin Poetry* (1999), and has edited or co-edited four collections of essays: *Reading Sappho: Contemporary Approaches* (1996), *Re-Reading Sappho: Reception and Transmission* (1996), *Women Poets in Ancient Greece and Rome* (2005), and *Gendered Dynamics in Latin Love Poetry* (with Ronnie Ancona, 2005). She has also published numerous articles on Greek and Latin love lyric, and is currently working on a book-length study of Sappho for Blackwell.

Judith P. Hallett is professor of classics at the University of Maryland at College Park. She received her PhD from Harvard University in 1971, and has been a Mellon Fellow at Brandeis University and the Wellesley College Center for Research on Women as well as the Blegen Visiting Scholar at Vassar College. Her major research specializations are Latin language and literature; gender, sexuality, and the family in ancient Greek and Roman society; and the history of classical studies in the United States. Author of *Fathers and Daughters in Roman Society: Women and the Elite Family* (1984), she has also co-edited a special double issue of *Classical World* on *Six North American Women Classicists* (1996–7), a special issue of *Arethusa* on *The Personal Voice in Classical Scholarship* (2001), and a special issue of *Helios* on *Roman Mothers* (2007). Her co-edited volumes include *Roman Sexualities* (1997); *Compromising Traditions: The Personal Voice in Classical Scholarship* (1997); and *Rome and Her Monuments: Essays on the City and Literature of Rome in Honor of Katherine Geffcken* (2000). In addition, she has published over sixty articles, chapters in books, and translations, as well as speeches (*ovationes*) and songs in classical Latin. Finally, she contributed the essays on Cornelia, Sulpicia the elegist, Martial's Sulpicia, and the women of the Vindolanda tablets to *Women Writing Latin*, Volume I (2002).

W. R. Johnson is John Matthews Manly Distinguished Service Professor of Classics and Comparative Literature, Emeritus, at the University of Chicago. He received his PhD from the University of California at Berkeley in 1967. He has taught at Berkeley and Cornell and at the University of Chicago and has been visiting professor at the University of Michigan and UCLA. He gave the Martin Lectures at Oberlin in 1984, the Townsend Lectures at Cornell in 1989, and the Biggs Lectures at Washington University in 2004. In 1984 his monograph *The Idea of Lyric* won the Christian Gauss Award for Literary Criticism. He has written several books and numerous articles on Latin poetry, most recently *Lucretius and the Modern World* (2000) and the introduction to Stanley Lombardo's translation of *The Aeneid* (2005).

Peter E. Knox is professor of classics at the University of Colorado in Boulder. He received his PhD in 1982 from Harvard University, where he also taught briefly before moving to faculty positions at Columbia University and his present post. His research interests focus on Roman literature of the late Republic and early Empire, as well as Greek poetry of the Hellenistic period. He is the author of *Ovid's* Metamorphoses *and the Traditions of Augustan Poetry* (1986) and *Ovid,* Heroides: *Select Epistles* (1986), and has published widely in scholarly journals on topics in Greek and Latin literature, ranging from Sappho to Nonnus. In addition he is known as co-editor of *Style and Tradition: Studies in Honor of Wendell Clausen* (1998) and as editor of *Oxford Readings in Ovid* (2006) and a *Companion to Ovid*, forthcoming in this series.

David Konstan is the John Rowe Workman Distinguished Professor of Classics and the Humanistic Tradition, and Professor of Comparative Literature, at Brown University. He holds a BA in mathematics, and a PhD in classics, from Columbia University. Prior to coming to Brown in 1987, he taught for 20 years at Wesleyan University in Connecticut. He has held visiting appointments at the University of Otago in New Zealand, the University of Edinburgh, the Universidade de São Paulo, the University of La Plata in Argentina, the University of Natal in Durban, the University of Sydney, Monash University in Melbourne, the American University in Cairo, and the Universidad Nacional Autónoma de México. His books include *Roman Comedy* (1983); *Sexual Symmetry: Love in the Ancient Novel and Related Genres* (1994); *Greek Comedy and Ideology* (1995); *Friendship in the Classical World* (1997); *Pity Transformed* (2001); and *The Emotions of the Ancient Greeks* (2006). He was president of the American Philological Association in 1999.

Brian A. Krostenko is associate professor of classics at the University of Notre Dame. He received his PhD from Harvard University in 1993 and has held faculty positions at the University of California at Berkeley and the University of Chicago. His research interests are the culture of the late Roman Republic, Cicero, rhetoric, and Latin linguistics. He is the author of *Cicero, Catullus, and the Language of Social Performance* (2001), which explores the problem of aestheticism in Roman culture by means of historical semantics.

Sven Lorenz received his PhD from Ludwig-Maximilians-Universität in Munich in 2001. His doctoral dissertation on Martial's depiction of the emperors (*Erotik und*

Panegyrik: Martials epigrammatische Kaiser) was published in 2002. Since then, he has published articles on Martial, Juvenal, and the *Appendix Vergiliana*. Recently he has completed a full annotated bibliography on Martial scholarship from 1970 to 2003 (part 1: *Lustrum* 45, 2003, 167–277; part 2: forthcoming). He teaches Latin and English at a secondary school near Munich.

Elizabeth Manwell is the Sally Appleton Kirkpatrick Assistant Professor of Classical Studies at Kalamazoo College in Kalamazoo, Michigan. She received her PhD from the University of Chicago in 2003. Her research interests encompass the literature and culture of the Roman Republic, theories of gender, and classical reception.

Randall L. B. McNeill is associate professor of classics at Lawrence University in Wisconsin. He received his AB *summa cum laude* from Harvard University in 1992 and his PhD from Yale University in 1998. His research focuses on techniques of self-presentation and the depiction of social relationships in Latin poetry of the late Republican and Augustan periods. He is the author of *Horace: Image, Identity, and Audience* (2001) and articles on Horace, Catullus, and classical Greek art.

Paul Allen Miller received his PhD in comparative literature from the University of Texas at Austin (1989). He is currently Carolina Distinguished Professor of Classics and Comparative Literature at the University of South Carolina, and the editor of *Transactions of the American Philological Association*. He is the author of *Lyric Texts and Lyric Consciousness: The Birth of a Genre from Archaic Greece to Augustan Rome* (1994); *Latin Erotic Elegy: An Anthology and Reader* (2002); *Subjecting Verses: Latin Love Elegy and the Emergence of the Real* (2004); and *Latin Verse Satire: An Anthology and Critical Reader* (2005). He has edited or co-edited 11 volumes of essays on literary theory, gender studies, and topics in classics, including *Rethinking Sexuality: Foucault and Classical Antiquity* (1998). He has published articles on Latin, Greek, French, and English literature as well as theory. He is currently finishing work on *Spiritual Practices: The Reception of Plato and the Construction of the Subject in Postmodern France*.

Christopher Nappa is associate professor of classics and chair of classical and Near Eastern studies at the University of Minnesota. He is the author of *Reading after Actium: Vergil's Georgics, Octavian, and Rome* (2005) and *Aspects of Catullus' Social Fiction* (2001) as well as a number of articles on Latin poetry. His interests include Republican and Augustan Latin literature, satire, and intertextuality.

Vassiliki Panoussi is assistant professor of classical studies at the College of William and Mary. She received her PhD from Brown University in 1998. Previously she held a visiting position at the University of Virginia and a faculty post at Williams College. Her research focuses on Roman literature of the late Republic, the age of Augustus, and the early Empire as informed through the study of intertextuality, cultural anthropology, and sexuality and gender. She has published articles on Catullus, Vergil, Ovid, Seneca, Lucan, and Statius. She is currently completing a book-length study of Vergil's *Aeneid* and its intertextual and ideological relationship to Greek tragedy. She is also at work on another book project on *Women's Rituals in Roman Literature*.

George A. Sheets is associate professor at the University of Minnesota, and associate professor of law in the University of Minnesota Law School. He received his PhD from Duke University in 1974, and his JD from the William Mitchell College of Law in 1990. His research and teaching interests include comparative Indo-European linguistics, the application of linguistic pragmatics to literary texts, the history of the Greek and Latin languages, and comparative law. Currently he is working on a study of jurisprudential issues associated with tombs, corpses, and deceased persons as legal subjects and objects in Roman law.

Marilyn B. Skinner is professor of classics at the University of Arizona in Tucson. She received her PhD from Stanford University in 1977. Before taking up her present post in 1991, she held faculty positions at Reed College, the University of California at Los Angeles, and Northern Illinois University, and visiting appointments at the University of Texas in Austin and Colgate University. Her research specialization is Roman literature of the Republican and Augustan eras. She has authored two monographs, *Catullus' Passer: The Arrangement of the Book of Polymetric Poems* (1981) and *Catullus in Verona* (2003), and has co-edited a collection of scholarly essays, *Vergil, Philodemus, and the Augustans* (2004). She is well known for her work on sexuality and gender in antiquity, as both co-editor of *Roman Sexualities* (1997) and author of *Sexuality in Greek and Roman Culture* (2005). Finally, she has published numerous articles on the Greek female poetic tradition, including Sappho and her successors Korinna, Erinna, Anyte, Moero, and Nossis.

W. Jeffrey Tatum is Olivia Nelson Dorman Professor of Classics at Florida State University. In 2005 he was De Carle Distinguished Lecturer in the Humanities at Otago University. His research concentrates on the Roman Republic. He is the author of *The Patrician Tribune: Publius Clodius Pulcher* (1999) and numerous articles on Roman history and Latin poetry.

Elena Theodorakopoulos has been a lecturer in classics at the University of Birmingham since 1994. She received her PhD from the University of Bristol in 1996 and her research specialization is Roman literature of the Republican and Augustan ages. She has written on Vergil, Ovid, and Catullus, as well as Apollonius of Rhodes. She has also edited *Attitudes to Theatre from Plato to Milton* (2004) and co-edited *Advice and its Rhetoric in Greece and Rome* (2006). In addition she has an interest in filmic representations of Rome, on which she has just completed a book, *Story and Spectacle* (forthcoming). Currently, she is at work on a book on Catullus and performance.

Elizabeth Vandiver is the Clement Biddle Penrose Associate Professor of Latin and Classics at Whitman College in Walla Walla, Washington. She received her PhD from the University of Texas at Austin in 1990. Before coming to Whitman in 2004, she held several visiting appointments, including positions at Rhodes College, the University of Maryland, and Northwestern University. Her research specializations include historiography, Latin lyric, translation studies, and the classical tradition. She has published a monograph, *Heroes in Herodotus: The Interaction of Myth and History* (1991), and the first English translation of Johannes Cochlaeus' biography of Martin Luther in *Luther's Lives: Two Contemporary Accounts of Martin Luther* (2002). She is currently at work on a third book, which examines the importance of the classical tradition in British poetry of World War I. She has published articles on a variety of topics, including Catullus, Livy, the classical tradition, and translation.

T. P. Wiseman is Emeritus Professor of Classics at the University of Exeter; he was lecturer and then reader at the University of Leicester before going to Exeter in 1977. His Oxford DPhil thesis was published as *New Men in the Roman Senate 139 BC–AD 14* (1971); his other books include *Catullan Questions* (1969), *Cinna the Poet and Other Roman Essays* (1974), *Clio's Cosmetics* (1979), *Catullus and His World* (1985), *Roman Studies Literary and Historical* (1987), *Historiography and Imagination* (1994), *Remus: A Roman Myth* (1995), *Roman Drama and Roman History* (1998), and *The Myths of Rome* (2004), which won the American Philological Association's Goodwin Award of Merit for 2005. He is a Fellow of the British Academy, and an honorary DLitt of the University of Durham. In 1996 he received the silver griffin award of the Comune di Sirmione for his work on Catullus.

CHAPTER ONE

Introduction

Marilyn B. Skinner

Catullus, as William Fitzgerald acutely observes, is a poet whom "we have taken rather too much to our hearts" (1995: 235). For a considerable part of the nineteenth and twentieth centuries, both lay and academic audiences reacted to the lyric voice in the Catullan collection as that of a friend and contemporary, whose grief over a brother's death and anger at betrayals of trust struck us as candid, universally human responses to circumstance. Yet treating Catullus sympathetically as one of ourselves greatly impeded efforts to appreciate his literary achievement as a whole and to locate his poetry within its particular cultural and historical milieu. New Criticism finally taught readers to value the longer works of the learned "Alexandrian" Catullus and even to relish displays of erudition in the love poetry, but only at the price of dismissing his barbed invective and his coarsely funny occasional pieces as material supposedly displaying a "lower level of intent" (Quinn 1959: 27–43). Appreciation of the Catullan corpus, obscenity and all, in its entirety and within its proper context had to wait for the rise of New Historicism in the 1980s and the subsequent impact of the cultural studies movement on the humanities.[1]

It is just since the 1980s, then, that wide-ranging research has succeeded in grounding Catullus firmly in the socio-historical world around him – by investigating his provincial North Italian background, his family connections, and his dealings with the Roman elite; by observing his interactions with fellow provincials seeking advancement; by teasing out references to matters of everyday life in his poems; by studying, lastly, the circumstances under which his works were produced and disseminated and what they might have conveyed to the audiences at which they were aimed. This historicizing approach has proved unusually fruitful; since Wiseman's *Catullus and His World* (1985), influential articles and entire monographs on Catullus have appeared with increasing frequency. Such recent critical studies have employed a variety of incisive tools, including those of anthropology, cultural studies, gender theory, Lacanian psychology, performance theory, reader-response theory, and sociolinguistics, to delineate the basic cultural and rhetorical frameworks within which the poetry operates. They have given us a more nuanced grasp of Catullus' language and poetics and his standing among his contemporaries.

Unfortunately, this ferment in present critical discourse seldom trickles down to high-school or even undergraduate college classrooms, although on both levels of Latin instruction Catullus is now one of the three ancient authors most commonly encountered. As Ancona and Hallett demonstrate in this volume, his current peda-gogical popularity is likewise a nascent phenomenon. Within the living memory of many North American teachers, Catullus was a text assigned only on the college level, and then with some trepidation: despite their relatively easy syntax and their imme-diate emotive appeal, the poems were deemed simply too racy for the young. Incorporation into the Advanced Placement syllabus (for examinations usually taken in the senior year of high school, approximately age 17) gradually furthered Catullus' secondary-school canonicity, though he was not finally accepted as a core AP author until 1994. Consequently, although annotated teaching texts and mater-ials on the poet have proliferated over the past few years, and good general introduc-tions, such as those of Martin (1992) and Hurley (2004), are available, students and teachers looking for more detailed summaries of current scholarly opinion find nothing really suitable in English. Hence the Blackwell *Companion to Catullus* appears to be a timely project. Containing essays on a range of topics by recognized and emerging authorities and drawing together two decades' worth of research into a collection adaptable for classroom use, this volume is intended to present C. Valerius Catullus to a wider public as a writer who was very much a man of his time and a perceptive eyewitness to the last troubled decade of the Roman Republic.

Unlike most studies of literary figures that attempt to reach out to non-specialist readers, the Blackwell *Companion to Catullus* does not begin with a chapter on the author's life, for the very good reason that we know almost nothing about it. Texts, translations, surveys, and entries in reference works dating from earlier periods do contain short biographies of Catullus. Most have been based, directly or indirectly, upon Ludwig Schwabe's 1862 reconstruction of his career, known to those of us in the field as the *Catullroman* ("Catullus novel"). As that term of art hints, Schwabe's account is quite speculative, and prior biographies that leaned on it wove the scant data into highly imaginative scenarios. They focused on Catullus' affair with the pseudonymous "Lesbia," generally assumed to be Clodia, wife of Metellus Celer (*cos.* 60 BC) and sister of the radical demagogue P. Clodius Pulcher (*tr. pop.* 58). Drawing heavily on the first-person statements in the poetry, and treating artistic utterances as confessional pronouncements, they represented their subject as the disillusioned lover of a corrupt and degenerate noblewoman and attributed his purported early death to the suffering caused by that experience (or, alternatively, to tuberculosis, on no evidence whatsoever).

Here, too, the new socio-historical approach results in a changed emphasis. We can still start with the few external facts. Following earlier authorities, the late-antique chronicler Jerome reports Catullus' birth at Verona in 87 BC (*Chron.* 150 H.) and assigns to 58–57 BC his death at Rome during his thirtieth year (*XXX aetatis anno*, *Chron.* 154 H.). The latter date is demonstrably incorrect: all the poems in the collection to which dates can be ascribed were written during the period 56–54 BC, though we find no unambiguous reference to events subsequent to 54. Most scholars, accordingly, have treated Catullus' life-span of 29 years as fixed and moved the date of birth down to 84; there has been a recent tendency to shift the death-date as well, down to 52 or even 51 (Granarolo 1982: 19–30; Wiseman 1985: 191; Thomson 1977: 3–4). But there is a possibility that the number *XXX* could be a scribal error; might Catullus have instead lived almost to the age of forty (*XXXX*) and thus seen the outbreak of civil war? Cornelius Nepos, to whom he dedicated his *libellus*, confirms that by 32 BC he was dead (*Att.* 12.4), but we have no idea how long before that he died, or what, if anything, he might have been doing after 54 BC.[2]

In his *Life of the Deified Julius* (73), the biographer Suetonius records: *Valerium Catullum, a quo sibi uersiculis de Mamurra perpetua stigmata imposita non dissimulauerat, satis facientem eadem die adhibuit cenae hospitioque patris eius, sicut consuerat, uti perseuerauit* ("[Caesar] had not denied that Valerius Catullus had put a lasting mark of shame against his name by his lampoons concerning Mamurra, but, on the same day Catullus apologized, Caesar invited him to dinner and continued to accept the hospitality of Catullus' father, just as he had been accustomed to do"). In this volume, T. P. Wiseman unpacks what this sentence tells us about the social standing of Catullus' family, and David Konstan explores its implications for Catullus' view of politics. I have elsewhere noted (Skinner 2003: xxi) that, with a father still alive, Catullus would have been a *filiusfamilias*, or son subject to paternal authority (*potestas*), legally unable to own property and dependent upon others for his living expenses in Rome. That would make his vitriolic personal attacks upon his father's guest, no less a personage than the military governor of Cisalpine Gaul, all the harder to explain. In the absence of extenuating circumstances, about which we know nothing, one wonders how on earth Catullus thought he could get away with embarrassing the family so blatantly.

The last bit of information contained in other sources is Apuleius' testimony (*Apol.* 10) that "Lesbia" was a cover name for a woman named Clodia. That statement is corroborated by internal evidence, for in poem 79 Catullus informs us that "Lesbius" (who, in accordance with Roman nomenclature, must be some paternal relation of "Lesbia") is "Pulcher," a broad hint at the notorious Clodius Pulcher. As Dyson Hejduk explains (below, pp. 254–5), the identification of Clodia Metelli as Catullus' mistress is not wholly certain, but there is a reasonable probability that it is correct, given her own social and political visibility. These days, though, historians are less interested in the details of the affair (if it was real) and more concerned with their implications for Catullus' contemporary Roman audience. In the poems, a married woman associated with a powerful aristocratic clan is not only adulterously involved with the speaker, a young Transpadane, but accused of indiscriminate relations with named and unnamed others and figuratively branded in cc. 37 and 58 a common prostitute. Few today would accept this as a realistic picture of a noblewoman's life. The cruel beloved is a standard generic component of ancient erotic verse (Dixon 2001: 137–40), and libelous charges of sexual immorality were part of the orator's and the politician's rhetorical gear, unscrupulously deployed against female as well as male opponents. Is the construction of "Lesbia" in the corpus just an assemblage of literary *topoi*, though, or does it also pass a harsh judgment upon the social scene in which she moved? There would be little point to the poet's dramatic revelation that "Lesbia" was the aristocratic Clodia if the world of Roman politics were not somehow relevant to her literary and symbolic function. W. Jeffrey Tatum in this volume consequently finds a telling parallel between her lack of personal integrity and the high-handed way in which the nobility, in Catullus' eyes, was exploiting the municipal equestrian class, and Konstan provocatively analyzes her insatiable promiscuity in c. 11 as a trope for Rome's wars of imperial expansion and plunder.

From the poems themselves we learn a few additional facts: that Catullus served for a year in Bithynia on the personal staff of the propraetor C. Memmius, probably in 57–56 BC (cc. 10, 28, 46); that the loss of an elder brother, who died and was buried in the Troad, was a devastating blow (cc. 65, 68a–b, 101); that his family owned property on the peninsula of Sirmio, near Verona (c. 31), and also an estate (most likely a working farm) somewhere between upscale Tibur and the rustic Sabine district (c. 44); that he formed close ties at Rome with numerous other poets and intellectuals (Cinna, Cornificius, his great friend Licinius Calvus, the brothers Asinii, Nepos, probably Valerius Cato) and was acquainted with several distinguished Roman senators, members of the nobility, and key players, including Cicero, Gellius Publicola, Hortensius Hortalus, Manlius Torquatus, and Cicero's influential ally P. Sestius. For a young unknown provincial, Catullus must have climbed the social ladder in Rome very quickly. Did he simply make the most of good connections, or were other talents brought to bear?

More and more Catullan scholarship is embracing a theory of performativity: that many of Catullus' poems were originally scripts for live recital by their author, most likely at banquets to which he had been invited, and that in those scripts the speaker fashions a self-image that will further his goals and ambitions. Critics emphasize various and sundry elements implicated in Catullan performance: Selden (1992) considers it a form of rhetorical, and Krostenko (2001a) a mode of linguistic, critique; Fitzgerald (1995) studies it as a tool for controlling and manipulating audience response; Wray (2001) analyzes it as a display of competitive masculinity; more pragmatically, I have suggested (1993a, 2001) that live performance was a tactic allowing a talented outsider to curry favor with those able to help him advance socially, economically, and perhaps politically.[3] Several chapters in this volume acknowledge the likelihood of convivial recitation, but it is Elena Theodorakopoulos' reading of poem 68 in light of that assumption that reveals how postulating a "back story" of performance on private occasions may clarify old Catullan questions. Consequently, imagining the presence of the poet as a guest, a well-known artist and entertainer, in the dining rooms of leading Roman personages allows us to view him as someone not only having access to privileged information about the workings of power but also very much concerned about its concrete use and abuse.

Contributors to this volume examine current developments in traditional, as well as new, areas of Catullan research. In part I, "The Text and the Collection," J. L. Butrica reviews the transmission of the Catullan text from antiquity to the present day, while I myself offer an account of the debate over the vexed question of authorial arrangement (a chore I hesitated to impose on any colleague). Part II, "Contexts of Production," then introduces us to the numerous ways in which Catullus' poetry can be regarded as reflective of its times. T. P. Wiseman, who pioneered investigation of the poet's family and its later fortunes (Wiseman 1987), provides a history of the Valerii Catulli and their presence in Northern Italy. David Konstan examines the contemporary political scene in Rome, offers an explanation for Catullus' direct attacks on Caesar and Mamurra, and, most interestingly, finds political reverberations in other ostensibly non-political poems. Andrew Feldherr locates Catullus' studied appeal to a learned coterie in the context of larger intellectual debates over Hellenization and shows how he and his fellow provincials employed learning to their advantage as they jockeyed for status within the circles of the Roman nobility. Elizabeth Manwell provides an overview of research on gender and masculinity and then analyzes contradictory paradigms of masculinity in Catullus, a matter that has received considerable attention in recent years.

Later generations habitually characterized Catullus as *doctus*, "learned," in tribute to his impressive acquaintance with the earlier poetic tradition. Although numerous predecessors exercised influence on his work, he himself recognizes Sappho and Callimachus as his primary poetic models. In part III, "Influences," Ellen Greene shows how Catullus' appropriation of the "Sapphic voice" enables him to express his private erotic subjectivity – yet, by disrupting conventional gender polarities, likewise destabilizes his own sense of male identity. Peter E. Knox provides a concise introduction to Callimachus, including a review of his most important works and an explanation of the innovative features of Callimachean poetics; Knox then surveys the far-reaching effects of "Callimacheanism" on the Roman poetic tradition, from Ennius through Catullus and his fellow neoterics, down to the Augustan Age.

Catullan language and style are distinctive. In part IV, "Stylistics," three authorities investigate those formal aspects of the poetry. We still speak of the "Catullan revolution" as an abrupt break with previous artistic techniques. W. R. Johnson wittily elucidates Cicero's grumpy reactions toward the poets he christened the "neoterics" and considers possible reasons why Catullus and his colleagues might have developed their innovative poetics. George A. Sheets analyzes the elements of Catullan style—diction, rhythm and meter, pragmatics—that endow it with its characteristic flavor, while Brian A. Krostenko shows that Catullus' deployment of the vocabulary that connotes "elegance" (or the reverse) plays upon ambivalent cultural attitudes toward displays of aestheticism in the political arena.

The Catullan corpus is by no means homogeneous – indeed, no other Latin poetic collection manifests such diversity in genre, meter, tone, and subject matter. Critics therefore frequently treat thematically related groups like the "Lesbia poems" as coherent elements of the collection and approach some of the "longer" poems, cc. 64 and 68 in particular, as independent compositions worthy of monographs. In part V, "Poems and Groups of Poems," we find studies of thematic categories, as well as in-depth readings of those two major works. William W. Batstone considers a set of poems commonly labeled "programmatic pieces" and boldly inquires what the label means and whether it can justifiably be applied: what makes verses programmatic, and is the program in the author's eye or the eye of the reader? Julia T. Dyson Hejduk examines the large body of poems thought to relate to the poet's affair with "Lesbia," finding, intriguingly enough, not one but three distinct "Lesbias," with contrasting poetic functions. Vassiliki Panoussi rereads the wedding compositions, 61 and 62, from an anthropological perspective. As re-enactments of ritual activity, each examines weighty cultural issues: tensions between male and female, conflict of personal desires and societal demands, continuation of the family line, sexual fidelity – all topics privately meaningful to the Catullan speaker as well.

Current work on Catullus 64, the short epic known today as "The Wedding of Peleus and Thetis," concentrates upon its intertextual relations with predecessors and uncovers the implications of allusions to earlier Greek and Latin masterpieces. Jeri

Blair DeBrohun's chapter on this epyllion specifically analyzes its use of Apollonius of Rhodes' *Argonautica*. This Hellenistic poem, she concludes, underlies Catullus' text in unsuspected ways: it determines the essential structure of the narrative and, through ominous reflections of the suppressed tale of Jason and Medea, tropes the poet's indebtedness to the past as intergenerational conflict. Elena Theodorakopoulos carefully walks the novice through the massive array of textual and interpretive problems associated with Catullus 68, which, for her, becomes an exceptional attempt to achieve permanence by overcoming the limitations of time and mortality. Finally, W. Jeffrey Tatum considers the function of Catullan invective: beginning with a consideration of the role of polemic in Roman political debate, he examines the conventions of political abuse as they are reflected in Catullus' poetry and analyzes the hidden messages in Catullan obscenity, showing that the concerns expressed are of a piece with the ethical stance of the speaker throughout the corpus. Despite the apparent diversity of the collection, then, certain leitmotifs emerge that provide an overall impression of engaged social commentary.

How did Catullus' subsequent readers view his poems, and how have their reactions to the author shaped the ways in which we read him? Reception theory – which studies how later perceptions, products of their own time, are mapped onto the original poem and become part of the text we confront – is represented in this volume by the series of chapters grouped under the rubric of part VI, "Reception." Four of these essays deal with responses to Catullus in antiquity. For Randall L. B. McNeill, the great problem is Horace's apparent dismissal of Catullus as a precursor and model: was the later lyric poet really as ungenerous as he seems? Vergil, on the other hand, makes sophisticated and often poignant reference to certain poems; going beyond a mere listing of passages, Christopher Nappa's chapter seeks to envision "Catullus" as Vergil might have perceived him. In Paul Allen Miller's view, Catullus, not Gallus, is the real inventor of Latin love elegy and poem 68 the single text that gave birth to it; Miller's reading of 68b complements and complicates Theodorakopoulos's in taking it as the expression of a polarized subjectivity. Martial, according to Sven Lorenz, redefines Catullus as primarily a composer of iambics and invokes his practices to justify the use of aggressive obscenity, meanwhile insisting that his own joking verses do no harm. This section concludes with two studies of Catullus' reception in later periods. Julia Haig Gaisser tells of the rediscovery of the text at the beginning of the Renaissance and the slow process of purging its most egregious errors; her account spells out the debt Catullus owes to his earliest editors and commentators. Brian Arkins surveys his assimilation by Romantic, Victorian, and twentieth-century poets and critics, who together created a sentimental image of Catullus still lingering as a ghostly presence in our classrooms.

We come then to the question of how Catullus is to be presented to students, as explored by veteran instructors in part VII, "Pedagogy." Ronnie Ancona and Judith P. Hallett discuss problems stemming from the relatively recent adoption of Catullus as a high-school author. Given the short tradition of teaching Catullus in the United States, they find that Latin instructors are less advantaged than their colleagues in the United Kingdom, where his poetry has been on the syllabus for decades. Ancona and Hallett also discover that British and American pedagogical treatments of Catullus differ considerably: in Britain, the "biographical" approach to the poet is still in vogue, while in the American classroom that method is no longer popular. Acquainting students with the sexually explicit poems is still a controversial matter; teachers may benefit from the authors' suggestions on that point. Ancona and Hallett's chapter is followed by that of Daniel H. Garrison, who offers practical strategies for teaching Catullus in college. This juxtaposition of chapters reveals that articulation between levels of instruction is a major educational problem. The poems of Catullus that AP students have read in the high-school classroom were, in Garrison's words, "a thoughtfully chosen subset of his work that was tailored to their youth rather than the complexity of Catullus' actual oeuvre" (p. 516), and their experience of him in college will consequently involve learning to read him in a more sophisticated way. The question Ancona and Hallett pose – "Whose Catullus?" – is therefore a pertinent one: is he the intellectual property of scholars, kindergarten through twelfth-grade teachers, college teachers, or their respective students? Each category of readers, it seems, views him from a distinct perspective not easy to reconcile with those of the others.

Lastly, there is the Catullus many readers confront only through the medium of an English translation. In part VIII, "Translation," Elizabeth Vandiver explains just how difficult rendering Catullus into another language can be. It is hard to find equivalents for both meter and vocabulary, and obscene words pose their own particular difficulties, for Roman cultural assumptions are not the same as ours. Some poems depend on an equivalence of sound and meaning, and others, the longer "Alexandrian" poems, derive weight from the learned obscurity of their mythological references; how can these effects be replicated in an idiom and a poetics as alien as those of English? As Vandiver finally shows, Catullus' own ventures in translating from Greek to Latin opt for free adaptation rather than strict fidelity to the language and meaning of the original. Perhaps there is solace in knowing that the poet had at least some inkling of his modern translator's dilemma.

Although the *Companion to Catullus* was intended as a reference work, authors were encouraged to go beyond summarizing received critical attitudes and urged to supply the reader with original insights into their subject matter. These chapters can therefore be regarded as innovative contributions to the field. Some break new methodological ground when attempting to offer solutions to long-standing problems. Others frankly acknowledge the controversies that swirl around an author whose surviving text is so lacunose and problematic and whose life is very much a mystery; while they do not reach a definite conclusion on a particular topic, then, they seek to present a balanced survey of all the evidence bearing upon it. Researchers may find it expedient to refer to such essays for capsule accounts of the state of a given question. Students and teachers, for their part, should feel confident that this volume contains the most reliable and up-to-date opinion on Catullus and his unique place in Roman intellectual and literary history. Finally, each of our contributors is at pains to demonstrate that the poet's artistry, despite its embeddedness in its own cultural milieu, will perpetually speak to the current generation in the form of a *lepidus nouus libellus*, as a fresh new voice.

NOTES

1 For an assessment of how these two approaches have affected present critical investigations of literature, see Klein (2005: 83–106).

2   In Skinner (2003: 181–3), I tentatively advanced the idea that the historical Catullus might have married and continued the family line. Wiseman, thinking in similar fashion, now calls attention to the small fragment of fresco recovered from the imperial-age villa at Sirmio that depicts a young man holding a scroll. As the scroll could indicate someone distinguished in the literary realm, it may, he suggests, represent Catullus himself (below, pp. 65–6). One other clue to the figure's identity is his barefoot state, for the analogous bare feet of the Prima Porta Augustus are a symbol of heroization (Müller 1941: 496–7; Galinsky 1996: 161). Deceased ancestors were objects of familial cult: in a letter dubiously attributed to Cornelia, mother of the Gracchae, the writer envisions her son C. Gracchus paying her posthumous rites: *ubi mortua ero, parentabis mihi et inuocabis deum parentem* ("when I am dead, you will make ritual offerings to me and call upon your parent as a divinity," *ap.* Nep. fr. 2). As a recipient of cult, the young man must be a recognizable and not a generic individual, conceivably the ancestor of the person responsible for the décor of the villa. That is not conclusive proof, of course, but perhaps it is evidence enough to permit serious consideration of the hypothesis.

3   Although some still adhere to the older view that Catullus rejected politics to devote himself to a life of art and enjoyment (e.g., Miller 1994: 134–6), we now see increasing consideration of his use of poetry to negotiate his cultural identity and his provincial status among members of the Roman elite (Fitzgerald 1995: 185–211; Habinek 1998: 94–6) and to critique Roman society from that perspective (W. J. Tatum 1997; Nappa 2001). Because employment on a provincial governor's staff was one recognized way to launch a political career, Catullus' term of service abroad with Memmius may also have been undertaken for motives beyond his (ironically) professed hope for self-enrichment.

WORKS CITED

Dixon, S. 2001. *Reading Roman Women: Sources, Genres, and Real Life*. London.

Fitzgerald, W. 1995. *Catullan Provocations: Lyric Poetry and the Drama of Position*. Berkeley, Los Angeles, and London.

Galinsky, K. 1996. *Augustan Culture*. Princeton, NJ.

Granarolo, J. 1982. *Catulle, ce vivant*. Paris.

Habinek, T. N. 1998. *The Politics of Latin Literature: Writing, Identity, and Empire in Ancient Rome*. Princeton, NJ.

Hurley, A. K. 2004. *Catullus*. London.

Klein, J. T. 2005. *Humanities, Culture, and Interdisciplinarity: The Changing American Academy*. Albany, NY.

Krostenko, B. A. 2001a. *Cicero, Catullus, and the Language of Social Performance*. Chicago and London.

Martin, C. 1992. *Catullus*. New Haven, CT, and London.

Miller, P. A. 1994. *Lyric Texts and Lyric Consciousness: The Birth of a Genre from Archaic Greece to Augustan Rome*. London and New York.

Müller, V. 1941. "The Date of the Augustus from Prima Porta." *American Journal of Philology* 62.4: 496–9.

Nappa, C. 2001. *Aspects of Catullus' Social Fiction*. Frankfurt.

Quinn, K. 1959. *The Catullan Revolution*. Melbourne. Rpt. Cambridge 1969; Ann Arbor, MI, 1971. 2nd edn. London 1999.

Schwabe, L. 1862. *Quaestiones Catullianae*. Vol. I. Giessen.

Selden, D. L. 1992. "*Ceveat lector*: Catullus and the Rhetoric of Performance." In R. Hexter and D. Selden, eds., *Innovations of Antiquity*. New York and London. 461–512.

Skinner, M. B. 1993a. "Catullus in Performance." *Classical Journal* 89: 61–8.

Skinner, M. B. 2001. "Among Those Present: Catullus 44 and 10." *Helios* 28: 57–73.

Skinner, M. B. 2003. *Catullus in Verona: A Reading of the Elegiac* Libellus, *Poems 65–116.* Columbus, OH.

Tatum, W. J. 1997. "Friendship, Politics, and Literature in Catullus: Poems 1, 65 and 66, 116." *Classical Quarterly* n.s. 47: 482–500.

Thomson, D. F. S., ed. 1997. *Catullus. Edited with a Textual and Interpretative Commentary.* Toronto.

Wiseman, T. P. 1985. *Catullus and His World: A Reappraisal.* Cambridge.

Wiseman, T. P. 1987. *Roman Studies Literary and Historical.* Liverpool.

Wray, D. 2001. *Catullus and the Poetics of Roman Manhood.* Cambridge.

PART I

The Text and the Collection

CHAPTER TWO

History and Transmission of the Text

J. L. Butrica

Every work of classical literature extant today has survived through its own unique textual tradition, usually involving copies on parchment or paper of various dates from late Antiquity to the Renaissance, sometimes even papyrus copies from Antiquity itself. The poetry of Catullus is one text of all too many whose survival into the modern world depended upon a single copy – a fact with significant and often unfortunate consequences for our understanding of this author and his work.

Tom Stoppard's play *The Invention of Love* deals in part with A. E. Housman's work on the textual tradition and textual criticism of another Roman poet, Propertius. To clarify the scholarly basis of that work for his audience, and classical textual criticism in general, Stoppard used Benjamin Jowett, the famous translator of Plato, as an unlikely mouthpiece for a speech dealing with the transmission of Catullus:

> This morning I had cause to have typewritten an autograph letter I wrote to the father of a certain undergraduate. The copy as I received it asserted that the Master of Balliol had a solemn duty to stamp out unnatural mice. In other words, anyone with a secretary knows that what Catullus really wrote was already corrupt by the time it was copied twice, which was about the time of the first Roman invasion of Britain: and the earliest copy that has come down to *us* was written about 1,500 years after that. Think of all those secretaries! – corruption breeding corruption from papyrus to papyrus, and from the last disintegrating scrolls to the first new-fangled parchment books, with a thousand years of copying-out still to come, running the gauntlet of changing forms of script and spelling, and absence of punctuation – not to mention mildew and rats and fire and flood and Christian disapproval to the brink of extinction as what Catullus really wrote passed from scribe to scribe, this one drunk, that one sleepy, another without scruple, and of those sober, wide-awake and scrupulous, some ignorant of Latin and some, even worse, fancying themselves better Latinists than Catullus – until! – finally and at long last – mangled and tattered like a dog that has found its way home, there falls across the threshold of the

Italian Renaissance the sole surviving witness to thirty generations of carelessness and
stupidity: the *Verona Codex* of Catullus; which was almost immediately lost again, but not
before being copied with one last opportunity for error. And there you have the foundation of the poems of Catullus as they went to the printer for the first time, in Venice 400
years ago. (Stoppard 1997: 24–5)

"Jowett" can be criticized on some minor points: he neglects causes of corruption
other than scribal error, ignores the "secondary" tradition, elides the considerable
scholarly activity that intervened between rediscovery and first publication, and in
general downplays the element of sheer uncertainty that surrounds the whole enterprise of recovering an ancient text: not to mention that, if "Christian disapproval"
was ever a factor, it seems to have left some of Antiquity's most flagrantly obscene
poetry unmolested. On the whole, however, though the last century and a quarter of
scholarship allows us to refine this picture to a considerable extent, it is accurate in its
essence: about the transition in Antiquity from papyrus roll to codex, about certain
causes of scribal corruption such as unfamiliar scripts, about interpolation, about the
alteration of archaic forms, about that single manuscript at Verona, now lost, known
as the "Verona codex" or Veronensis (*V*), from which all the complete copies of our
Catullan corpus derive, and about the vast temporal gulf between Catullus himself
and the earliest extant complete text – though 1,400 years would be more accurate
than 1,500.

The Text in Antiquity

To understand how our extant MSS of Catullus reflect what Catullus wrote, how he
might have arranged his works, and how they circulated in Antiquity, we begin of
course by studying the text as attested in Antiquity itself. It might seem an obvious
starting point to say that the history of the text begins with the author himself and his
own publication of his work, but "publication" is still a nebulous concept at this
point in the Roman Republic, a generation before the first booksellers known by
name (see, in general, Starr 1987). It is hard to believe, however, that a literary
culture like that of the neoterics (the "newer" or "modern" poets, comprising
Catullus, Licinius Calvus, Helvius Cinna, and others) – a culture that was, like that
of the Greek Alexandrians whom they followed in so many respects, dependent upon
both literary and scholarly texts – relied solely upon books made by the poets' own
slaves from copies that their friends happened to own. In fact, Catullus himself refers
to "running to the booksellers' cases" in search of bad poetry with which to avenge
himself upon his friend Calvus (c. 14.17–18, *ad librariorum/curram scrinia*).
Whatever the involvement of the book trade, however, the "publication" of short
or occasional works in particular (the majority of Catullus' poems) is still likely to
have been largely a matter of distributing handwritten copies to friends or to influential *grammatici* like Valerius Cato (the closest thing then to literary critics), or
allowing others to have their own scribes make copies. But at some point, with or
without the cooperation of the authors, booksellers were apparently able to offer the
(presumably) collected *Epigrammata* or *Poemata* of the neoterics; and Catullus
himself became a standard text in the book trade, not only as a part of the common

literary heritage of the educated Roman who read for pleasure but – fittingly for a neoteric "scholar-poet" – as a learned authority whose practice mattered in establishing correct Latin usage.

Since there are no ancient copies of Catullus extant (not even among the *graffiti* of Pompeii), our knowledge of the text in Antiquity depends upon the evidence of what is called the "secondary tradition," references and quotations in ancient writers and glossaries as opposed to the "primary tradition" represented by extant manuscripts of the text itself. The relatively extensive secondary tradition of Catullus sometimes reveals or corrects errors of the primary tradition and casts light upon how the text has been corrupted since Antiquity; it also supplies evidence bearing on the all-important question of how the poet himself arranged his works for circulation, though it comports some awkward problems as well. (The very full collection of *testimonia* in Wiseman 1985: 246–62 can be supplemented occasionally from Manzo 1967, on the glossarial tradition.)

An excellent starting point for understanding how the reliance on handwritten copies affected the condition of the text and how ancient copies of Catullus relate to the text of our MS tradition is the passage where the second-century AD author Aulus Gellius discusses the text of Catullus 27.4 (*NA* 6.20.6). He quotes the poem's first four lines, with the last reading (in modern editions of Gellius like Marshall's OCT) *ebria acina ebriosioris* ("drunkener than the drunken grape"). Gellius maintains that this is the correct reading: "though [Catullus] could have said *ebrio*, and could have employed the more customary neuter form *acinum*, nevertheless he said *ebria* out of a fondness for the sweetness of that Homeric hiatus, because of the harmony with the following letter *a*. Moreover, those who think that Catullus said *ebriosa* or *ebrioso* – for this too is found written by accident – have of course encountered books written from corrupted originals." Gellius' argument, then, is that some writers like the aesthetic effect of what is called "hiatus" (in particular when the same vowel ends one word and begins the next without the first being elided and thus, in effect, eliminated; he has already praised its use in Homer), and that Catullus employed it here, writing *ebria acina*, with hiatus and without the normal elision.

At best, Gellius only implies that the reading is attested in copies of the poem; one could be forgiven for thinking that he was perversely trying to justify a corrupt reading in a copy he had seen or even for suspecting that it was in fact a conjecture of his own. In any case, he notes that two other readings, *ebriosa (acina)* and *ebrioso (acino)*, are also found in contemporary copies: disconcerting though it is to find three different readings attested within only two centuries of composition, the situation is not surprising in a world of handwritten books, sometimes produced without the "quality control" of correction from the exemplar or from other copies, and with an almost inevitable proliferation of fresh errors in each new version. It is also disconcerting that the archetype of the Catullan tradition transmitted yet another corruption, *ebriose acino*. Few editors nowadays accept Gellius' argument, and Fordyce (1961: 158) has explained why Gellius' reading should be rejected: hiatus does not certainly occur elsewhere in Catullus' hendecasyllabics, while the use of an adjective in both its base and comparative forms within a short span (here *ebriosus* and *ebriosior*) appears with some frequency. Of course the claim that *ebrioso (acino)* is found in copies from corrupt exemplars should be taken with the grain of salt it deserves, since it is presumably determined solely by the desire to champion *ebria acina*.

One obvious difficulty in dealing with the secondary tradition is the fact that, like primary sources, secondary sources also survive through textual histories in which accidental corruption may occur; in fact, in the passage just discussed, the reading *ebria acina* that Gellius' discussion presupposes had to be restored by the nineteenth-century scholar Moritz Haupt from the corrupted version given by the MSS of Gellius' work, which have *ebriose ac in* or *ebriose ac me* – and those MSS also corrupted every word that Gellius subsequently quoted here as known to him from copies of Catullus! (Again the corrections printed in modern editions are due to Haupt.) Incidentally, there just might be evidence here for interaction between primary and secondary sources. Certainly it is curious that both the corrupt archetype of the Catullan tradition and the corrupt text of Gellius agree in the clearly erroneous reading *ebriose*; this could be coincidental, of course, since the *-e* may have been influenced by the endings of *Postumiae ... magistrae* in the previous line, but it could also be evidence that someone in the Middle Ages compared his text of Gellius with a text of Catullus or vice versa (there are no extant MSS of Book 6 of Gellius made before the twelfth century).

Another difficulty of the secondary tradition is uncertainty over whether an author has cited from a text or simply from memory. For example, when Pliny the Younger cites Catullus 16.5–8 at *Ep.* 4.14.5, he reads *et* instead of *ac* in both 7 and 8, which could be a fault of his memory, a fault of his copy of Catullus, or a corruption in the MSS of Pliny. Similar considerations apply when Quintilian (*Inst.* 9.3.16) quotes Catullus 62.45 with *innupta* instead of *intacta*. Responsible editors resolve such cases not by blindly following the primary or secondary tradition in preference to the other but by judging which reading is likely to be right on criteria of sense, style, and content, though a decision might not always be easy.

This is only the beginning of the challenges presented by the secondary tradition. It is unexciting but comforting when primary and secondary sources agree. Disagreements are more interesting, though not of course the ones where the secondary tradition is easily dismissed as erroneous (even if it is not possible to identify whether the erroneous reading is what the ancient writer found in his text or a corruption introduced in the transmission of his work). Some places where a secondary source offers a clearly erroneous reading include: Gellius' discussion (*NA* 7.16) of Catullus 92, where the MSS have apparently corrupted *dispeream* (92.2) to *dis spereat* (*sic*) and *sunt mea* (92.3) to *sin ea* (as it happens, however, while one branch of the Catullan tradition has omitted nearly the whole of 92.2–4, the other, like the MSS of Gellius, reads *ea*, and *mea* is a conjecture of Isaac Vossius); Macrobius' citation of Catullus 64.327 and 171–2 (*Sat.* 6.1.41–2) with the corruptions *ducenti subtemine* [*vel sim.*] for *ducentes subtegmina* and *non* for *ne* respectively; and Priscian (*Inst.* 5.77, 7.22), where the MSS read *Celtiberosae* [*Celtiberiae*] in Catullus 37.18 instead of *cuniculo-sae*. Of course the secondary tradition is of real value when it offers a clearly correct reading where the primary tradition is in error, even if the corruption is one easily healed. Whether or not Gellius was right about *ebria acina*, he correctly cited 27.2 with *inger* as its first word, while the Catullan archetype gave the morphologically "normal" but metrically impossible form *ingere*. The MSS of Pliny the Younger, which wrongly read *et* for *ac* in 16.7–8, correctly give *sunt* in 8, where the MSS of Catullus give *sint*, and Quintilian, though he mistakenly quotes Catullus 62.45 with *innupta* instead of *intacta*, correctly reads *dum* [*cara*], corrupted in the archetype to *tum*. Unfortunately, not all cases are decided so easily. Priscian (*Inst.* 1.22) quotes 2b.3

in the form *quod* [sc. *malum*] *zonam soluit diu ligatam* ("[the apple] that undid the sash long tied"), while the authoritative MSS read *negatam* ("the sash long denied"); most editors, but not all, trust the MSS of Priscian over those of Catullus. In 97.6 modern editions of Catullus print the Celtic word for "carriage-body" that he uses as *ploxenum*, the form apparently used by Quintilian when he noted (at *Inst.* 1.5.8) that Catullus found the word in the region of Padua. Festus (p. 260 Lindsay *DVS*) also cites the line, but gives the word as *ploxinum*. Since the principal MSS of Catullus have the corruptions *ploxnio* (*O*) and *ploxonio* (*GR*), it may be that Festus, not Quintilian, was right about Catullus' spelling.

The secondary tradition is particularly awkward when it attests something not found in the primary tradition. For example, Catullus 64.23–4 was long printed in the form given by the Veronensis:

> heroes, saluete, deum genus! o bona mater!
> uos ego saepe, meo uos carmine compellabo.

Then the publication in the early nineteenth century of the so-called Verona scholia to Vergil's *Aeneid* yielded the following defective quotation in a note on *Aen.* 5.80: "Catullus: Saluete deum gens o bona matrum progenies saluete iter...." While editors do not follow Madvig and the scholion in reading *gens* rather than *genus*, they do accept the remainder of the citation as genuine, and *progenies saluete iter<um>* is now printed as a defective line, numbered 23b to avoid disturbing the traditional numeration. (This case also reveals the presence of interpolation [a kind of mistaken correction] in the Catullan archetype, since it can be presumed that someone consciously altered *matrum* to *mater* once *progenies* was no longer present to justify the genitive grammatically.)

Many editors trust the secondary tradition against the primary tradition at 1.2. According to Servius (author of a fifth-century commentary on the works of Vergil) in a note on *Aen.* 12.587, Catullus treated *pumex* as a feminine rather than masculine noun, but our Catullan corpus contains no example of feminine *pumex*, though it does offer one of apparently masculine *pumex* in 1.2 (*arido...pumice*). Editors who emend to *arida* do so despite the fact that, elsewhere in the secondary tradition, this line is quoted no fewer than six times, always with *arido* (except in a single MS of Isidore of Seville's *Etymologiae*), and despite the possibility that Servius refers to a lost line (or was simply mistaken).

In other cases where a secondary source mentions a grammatical form, a line, or a whole poem absent from the MSS, editors often include these among the fragments of Catullus. Earlier editors were more generous in this regard than recent ones; in 1889 Ellis printed 13 fragments and Postgate 10, but Mynors (1958) gives 5, and Thomson (1997) only 3.

Mynors's frr. 1–3 are the three printed by Thomson. Fr. 1 comprises four lines addressed to Priapus in the meter called priapean, quoted from Catullus by the metrical writer Terentianus Maurus (the first is cited by six other ancient authorities as well, and Terentianus comments that "we know that Catullus wrote more such lines this way"). Fr. 2, *de me<r>o ligurrire libido est*, is another line apparently quoted from a *priapeum*, this time by the grammarian Nonius Marcellus exemplifying the rare verb *ligurrire*, a synonym of *degustare*. Fr. 3, *at non effugies meos iambos*, is a hendecasyllabic line quoted by Pomponius Porphyrio, a commentator on Horace, in a note on *Carm.* 1.16.3. If all these quotations are genuine, they imply that as many as three poems of Catullus (conceivably even an entire collection of *Priapea*) have been lost from the corpus that we have (or perhaps were never there, whether by accident or by deliberate omission).

The two fragments printed by Mynors but not by Thomson are really "*testimonia*," i.e., statements about Catullus' poetry rather than quotations from it. Fr. 4 is the remark by Pliny the Elder (*HN* 28.19) to the effect that Catullus wrote "an erotic imitation of spells" such as is found in Theocritus and Vergil. This has been dismissed (cf. Gaisser 1993: 278 n. 19), but Pliny knew Catullus far too well for us to assume an erroneous reference: since he twice appeals to poems of Catullus as evidence for historical persons, and begins his encyclopedia not only quoting Catullus 1.3–4 but explicitly "softening" the meter in line with contemporary practice, he surely deserves to be taken seriously as a witness to the existence of a *Pharmaceutria*, presumably in hexameters like Pliny's other examples, Theocritus *Id.* 2 and Vergil *Ecl.* 8. Fr. 5 is the statement by Servius (on Vergil *G.* 2.95) to the effect that Catullus "criticized" the Rhaetian grape as useless for any purpose and wondered why Cato had praised it; he even claims that Vergil wrote *G.* 2.95 in awareness of both Cato's praise and Catullus' criticism. This too has been dismissed, but caution is suggested by Martial 14.100, an epigram on a *panaca* (presumably a vessel for storing wine) that connects Catullus with Rhaetian wine. These *testimonia* give us two more poems of Catullus absent from our corpus, one of them perhaps substantial (Theoc. 2 and *Ecl.* 8 comprise 166 and 109 lines respectively).

As to the citations or *testimonia* ignored by recent editors, Servius asserts in a note on *Aen.* 4.409 that Catullus treated *cauere* as a third- rather than second-conjugation verb; many scholars (including Mynors) have thought that this reflects the scansion of the imperative *cave* with a short *-e* at 50.18 (or possibly 61.145), but such commonplace shortenings do not necessarily prove that Catullus conjugated the verb *cauo, cauis, cauit*, etc., as Servius suggests. Servius also asserts (on *Aen.* 5.610) that Catullus used *arcus* as a feminine noun and (on *Aen.* 7.378) that he used the neuter noun *turben* instead of its masculine equivalent *turbo*; but is it not illogical to dismiss these while accepting the claim about feminine *pumex* simply because *pumex* does occur in our text of Catullus while *arcus* and *turben* do not? (Masculine *turbo* is certainly found at 64.107; it is impossible to say with certainty whether *turbine* in 64.149 and 314 and 68.63 is from *turbo* or *turben*, but 64.107 favors the former.) A defective passage of the metrical writer Caesius Bassus cites *Catullus in anacreonteo* (*GLK* 6.262.19); the Catullan archetype has transmitted no poem in anacreontics, but Bassus is in general a credible source. If these further references are reliable, they could bring the total of "lost" poems to nine.

Only one alleged citation can be dismissed with complete confidence, the phrase *et Lario imminens Comum*, supposedly cited from Catullus in Vibius Sequester's compilation of bodies of water named in literature; it occurs, however, only as an addition to a fifteenth-century MS of the work (British Library Add. 16,986) and is therefore likely to be a forgery based on Catullus 35.3–4, *Noui ... / Comi moenia Lariumque litus.*

Two final examples will further illustrate the degree of uncertainty that the secondary tradition can entail. The Veronensis gave Catullus 64.65 as *non tereti strophio lactentis uincta papillas.* Isidore of Seville, in defining *strophium*, says "de quo ait Cinna *strofio lactantes cincta papillas*" (*Etym.* 19.33.3). This is normally assumed to be an erroneous citation of Catullus under Cinna's name, though some scholars think that both deviations from our text of Catullus (*lactantes* for *lactentis, cincta* for *uincta*) are in fact what Catullus wrote (cf. Manzo 1967: 155). On the other hand, given the personal association and stylistic affinities of Catullus and Cinna, as well as the tendency of Roman poets to imitate each other very closely, there is at least a chance that Isidore is citing a line of Cinna that Catullus imitated – or one in which Cinna imitated Catullus. Similar considerations apply in the case of Cinna fr. 2, attributed to Cinna by Isidore (*Etym.* 19.2.9) in the form *lucida confulgent alti carchesia mali* but usually edited with *cum fulgent*, as quoted in a scholion to Lucan 5.418 (which, by the way, reads *summi* for *alti*). The same or a similar line is quoted by Nonius Marcellus (p. 546 Lindsay *DCD*) from "Catullus Veronensis" in the defective form *lucida qua splendet carchesia mali*. Again it is uncertain whether misquotation or imitation is involved; but it was on Nonius' authority that, well into the nineteenth century, *lucida qua splendent summi carchesia mali* sometimes appeared in editions of Catullus as 64.235b. Of course, simple misattribution is a possible explanation.

In addition to being witnesses to the text of Catullus, for good or for ill, ancient secondary sources also serve as witnesses to the arrangement of Catullus' poetry as it circulated in Antiquity; indeed, they are virtually the only witnesses to this, since (as will be argued below) only a single ancient title survived into the Middle Ages, in a single authoritative MS and in corrupted form. How Catullus himself arranged his works has been discussed extensively in recent years, with scholars divided between what might be called the "one-roll" theory – that Catullus designed all the extant poetry to stand as a single unified collection – and the "three-roll" theory – that our corpus represents a combination of three different ancient rolls that respectively contained poems 1–60, 61–8, and 69–113. The ancient citations, however, suggest something different.

Unfortunately for our purposes, standard practice in the "literary" tradition and often in the "grammatical" tradition as well was to cite by author's name alone, with works rarely specified; nevertheless, some clues remain. We can come within a century or so of Catullus' own lifetime with the *Controversiae* of the Elder Seneca (ca. 50 BC – ca. AD 40), who says at 7.4(19).7 that Catullus *in Hendecasyllabis* called his friend Calvus *salaputium disertum* (= c. 53.5). This surely implies knowledge of a collection called *Catulli Hendecasyllabi*: when something more specific than an author's name appears with a citation, it identifies a work, not a meter. (On the other hand, when Priscian notes [*Inst.* 1.22] that Catullus *inter hendecasyllabos Phalaecios posuit* the line *quod zonam soluit diu ligatam* [c. 2b.13], he *is* referring simply to the meter, since the scansion is his evidence for the treatment of *soluit* as a trisyllable; perhaps the presence of *Phalaecios* is the "clue" that shows that the hendecasyllabic meter is meant and not a collection of poems.) Some decades later, Quintilian (*Inst.* 1.5.20) refers to the poem on Arrius (c. 84) as a *nobile epigramma*; it *is* an epigram, of course, and the existence of the collected *Catulli Epigrammata* is not necessarily implied, though of course it is not excluded. But when he cites c. 62.45 from *Catullus in Epithalamio* (*Inst.* 9.3.16), this surely is evidence for the independent circulation of Catullus 62 under that title, since there is no parallel for citing a poem within a collection by a title; moreover, the ninth-century copy of this poem discussed below confirms the title by calling it *Epithalamium Catulli*. Later still, Aulus Gellius refers to c. 92, which we would call an epigram, as a *carmen* (*NA* 7.16); this must surely be a generic reference of some sort, since it would be otiose to observe that Catullus had written something *in a poem*. The only possible title in the grammatical tradition occurs in Charisius, who quotes Asinius Pollio "Against Valerius, Book I" as saying that the masculine noun *pugillares* is the correct form of this word for writing-tablets, then adds "but Catullus *in Hendecasyllabis* quite often uses the neuter *pugillaria*" (*GLK* 1.97.12–13; in fact it occurs only once, at 42.5, and it is not clear whether this is further evidence of lost poems). If Charisius' statement derives (as some believe) from an invective against Catullus by Asinius Pollio, it is, like Seneca's reference to c. 53, a near-contemporary witness to the collected *Hendecasyllabi*. (I do not regard fr. 3, *at non effugies meos iambos*, as evidence for a collection of *Iambi*; the line, which is a hendecasyllabic, refers rather to the poet's hendecasyllabics, which were regarded as a form of iambic verse.)

Ancient authorities, then, acknowledge cc. 42 and 53 as part of the collected *Hendecasyllabi* and c. 62 as an autonomous *Epithalamium*. A collection of *Epigrammata* seems possible, though far from certain, and the same could be said of a collection of *Carmina* containing c. 92. Fortunately, the fragments of Catullus' friends Calvus and Cinna (collected in Courtney 1993: 201–24) provide valuable *comparanda* for interpreting this meager evidence; they are cited by title more frequently, and with little ambiguity; and, like Catullus, they too wrote short poems in hendecasyllabics and other meters, longer poems like epyllia or epithalamia, mostly in hexameters, and epigrams.

Nine ancient citations of or references to Calvus' poetry specify a source. Gellius (*NA* 9.12.10) quotes one hendecasyllabic as representing the usage of "C. Caluus in poematis" (fr. 2). (Asconius cites fr. 1 as *hendecasyllabus Calui elegans*, but this does not constitute evidence for *Hendecasyllabi* as a book title.) A fragment which "must come from an epithalamium in glyconics and pherecrateans" comparable to c. 61 (Courtney 1993: 203) is cited by Charisius from "Licinius Caluus in poemate" (fr. 4). Priscian cites a portion of a hexameter from "Caluus in epithalamio" (fr. 5). Two authorities (pseudo-Probus and "Servius Danielis" [a term designating material added to certain MSS of Servius' commentary on Vergil from a second ancient source, generally thought to be another ancient Vergilian commentator named Aelius Donatus]) cite hexameters from "Caluus in Io" (frr. 9–10, 12–13). A partial dactylic hexameter plus a complete pentameter are cited by Charisius from "Caluus in carminibus" (fr. 15); Nonius Marcellus cites the partial hexameter in a slightly different form without naming a work. Finally, a scholion on Juvenal 9.133 cites an *epigramma* of Martial against Pompey, but a partial citation of the poem in Seneca the Elder (*Controv.* 7.4.7) allows it to be attributed correctly to Calvus (fr. 18). For Calvus, then, we have collected *Poemata* that include one in hendecasyllabics and one in glyconics and pherecrateans; an *Epithalamium* in hexameters; the epyllion *Io*; a collection of *Carmina* containing elegiac couplets; and a possible collection of *Epigrammata*.

In the case of Cinna, there are eight such references. In Charisius we have four hexameters cited from "Cinna in Propemptico Pollionis" (fr. 1) and a reference to Hyginus' commentary "in Cinnae Propemptico<n>" (fr. 4). "Servius Danielis" cites two hexameters from "Cinna in Smyrna" (fr. 6); Priscian cites the same source for masculine *aluus* (fr. 7), Charisius for the genitive form *tabis* (fr. 8). Gellius cites two hendecasyllabics to show that the word *nani* can be found "in poematis Helui Cinnae" (fr. 9), and cites a choliambic from "Cinna in poematis" (fr. 10). Finally, Nonius quotes the end of a dactylic hexameter from "Cinna in epigrammatis" (fr. 12). For Cinna, then, we have collected *Poemata* that include one poem in hendecasyllabics and one in "limping" iambics; the *Propempticon* for Pollio; the epyllion *Smyrna*; and a collection of *Epigrammata*.

Thus, apart from the *Carmina* attested for Calvus alone, the output of both poets follows the same pattern: a collection of hendecasyllabics and other lyric verses called *Poemata*, long poems in hexameters called by individual titles (epyllia, epithalamia, a propempticon), and a collection of epigrams. And it is impossible not to be struck by how closely this pattern resembles what we find within our Catullan corpus: a grouping of hendecasyllabics, choliambics, and other meters; a series of long poems, mostly in hexameters, including both an epithalamium and an epyllion; and poems in elegiac couplets, first long ones, then epigrams. There is one clear discrepancy, of course: Catullus' lyrics are called his *Hendecasyllabi*, while those of Calvus and Cinna are called *Poemata*, but the difference is unlikely to be important. Discussing his own light poetry in emulation of Catullus, Pliny the Younger reveals the diversity of titulature possible for such collections: "The one thing that seems to need stating in advance is that I'm thinking of inscribing these trifles of mine *Hendecasyllabi*, a title limited by meter alone. So, if you prefer to call them *Epigrammata* or *Idyllia* or *Eclogae* or, as many do, *Poematia*, you may call them that; I offer only *Hendecasyllabi*" (*Ep.* 4.14.8). The Greek diminutive *poematia* is a close enough equivalent of *poemata* to show that the *Hendecasyllabi* of Catullus could have been called his *Poemat(i)a*, just as the *Poemata* of Calvus and Cinna could presumably have been called their *Hendecasyllabi*.

However, while the titles of the longer poems (which need titles to distinguish them) are certainly authorial, titles like *Hendecasyllabi/Poemata* or *Carmina* need not be. Indeed, I would be reluctant to attribute them to the authors rather than to booksellers, or perhaps to *grammatici* who prepared editions that were then offered for sale by *librarii*. There are no explicit aesthetic signs of unity or structure in Catullus' collections at least (which is not to say, of course, that scholars have not attempted to find them – see Skinner, chapter 3 in this volume), and Catullus may well have died before he could even have contemplated a definitive compilation of his lyrics or elegiacs. Moreover, the purely generic nature of the titles *Hendecasyllabi* and *Carmina* suggests an origin in commerce or in literary classification – the intervention of an editor or a bookseller, in other words. If that is the case, then it is impossible to feel certain that "standard" collections existed, or that every copy of *Poemata* or *Carmina* contained the same selection of *poemata* or *carmina*, or in the same order.

On the basis of the ancient citations of Catullus and this comparison with Calvus and Cinna, I would suggest that Roman readers of the first century AD knew at least five or six separate works of Catullus and/or collections of his verse, each originally occupying its own papyrus roll (perhaps even more if the *Pharmaceutria* existed and if there was a separate collection of *Priapea*). One of these is the *Hendecasyllabi*, presumably coinciding more or less with what are now called the "polymetrics" (certainly as far as c. 53), though I would conjecture that it comprised 1–61 rather than 1–60: the work that Calvus composed in the same meter as 61 circulated among his *Poemata*, not on its own (Jocelyn 1999 makes the same suggestion, without reference to Calvus). The three long works that followed in the Veronensis – the *Epithalamium* (62), the *Attis* (63), and the epyllion often identified now as the "Wedding of Peleus and Thetis" but perhaps called the *Ariadne* in Antiquity, to judge by the analogy with the *Io* and the *Smyrna* (64) – would each have occupied its own roll. (Some scholars, such as Clausen 1976, hypothesize a *libellus* containing 61–4; it may well be that some papyrus rolls in Antiquity contained 61–4 [or rather 62–4], but there is no reason to think that Catullus "published" them together, or that whoever compiled the ancestor of the Veronensis found them already united in a single roll or volume.) The only substantial uncertainty is whether the remaining poems represent a collection of *Carmina* in elegiac couplets (65–8) and a collection of *Epigrammata* (69–116) or simply a single collection of *Carmina* (65–116). The latter is more likely if we can argue by analogy with Charisius' "Licinius Caluus in poemate," which evidently means "in one of the *Poemata*," that Gellius' phrase *in Catulli carmine* (i.e., c. 92) means "in one of the *Carmina*"; but if these collections were indeed created by *grammatici* or *librarii*, then perhaps both formats coexisted in Antiquity.

Modern scholars have largely neglected these ancient citations (the exception is Giardina 1974, which E. A. Schmidt 1979 tries to refute) while pursuing instead the possibly chimerical collection which they call the *Passer* ("Sparrow") of Catullus, despite the lack of any allusion to it among the ancient citations. Some may, of course, wish to see this as a "popular" alternative title for the *Hendecasyllabi*, others as the title of a smaller collection that has been subsumed within the collected *Hendecasyllabi*. While the former hypothesis can probably be discounted, the latter cannot, since any titles that Catullus himself gave to individual lyrics or to small collections of them, even if they persisted in the collected *Hendecasyllabi*, would have been lost in the transmission along with all the other titles; a similar argument could be mounted to defend the search for "cycles" or "garlands" within the *Carmina* and/or *Epigrammata* as well.

The notion that Catullus himself published a *libellus* of some description rests of course upon c. 1, which speaks of giving a "charming new *libellus*" to a man named Cornelius who had somehow expressed respect for Catullus' *nugae*, or "trifles." As others have observed, Catullus 1 is unlikely to have introduced our entire Catullan corpus: a poem like Catullus 64 could hardly be termed *nugae*, and some later poems bear dedications to other persons. If it did introduce something, this is likely to have been the *Hendecasyllabi* or perhaps some smaller group subsumed within that collection, but it may not even be an introductory poem at all. The only other *libellus . . . nouus* in Latin literature is a book (of indeterminate contents) finished so recently that the ink is not yet dry (see Martial 4.10, clearly written with Catullus 1 in mind). This is plausible for a single poem or even a slim collection but not for a corpus of thousands of lines or even for a collection of several hundred; of course the flexibility with which *libellus* is used is yet another complicating factor. Perhaps a bookseller took a poem that originally concerned the gift of a single poem to Cornelius and put it at the head of the *Hendecasyllabi* to pose as a dedication. (If this is the case, it may have happened by the second half of the first century AD, since

Pliny the Elder, who quotes c. 1 when dedicating his own *Natural History* to the emperor Titus, may have read it as such a dedication.) The idea that Catullus' supposed *libellus* was entitled, or simply known as, his *Passer* (i.e., "Sparrow") is based on two poems of Martial (1.7; 4.14) in which Catullus' sparrow is clearly a work of literature, but there is no reason to believe that these refer to a collection rather than specifically to c. 2, the celebrated poem on Lesbia's sparrow. Those who believe in the *Passer* point out that literary works were sometimes identified by their opening words (*arma uirumque* often stands for the *Aeneid*, for example), but they must then engage in special pleading to exclude c. 1 from the collection, since in this case *passer* would be the first word of the *second* poem (cf. Clausen 1976: 39 n. 7; Gaisser 1993: 11). It is also possible to argue that Martial himself was unaware of an alleged Catullan *Passer*. Book 14 of Martial, known as the *Apophoreta* ("Things to be taken away"), comprises epigrams on gifts that might be given to guests to take home at Saturnalia, with headings composed by Martial himself, not by medieval scribes (as is more often the case with ancient poetry-books). Within the work is a series (183–96) on gift-books, with the label "Catullus" applied to 195:

> Tantum magna suo debet Verona Catullo
> quantum parua suo Mantua Vergilio.
>
> Great Verona owes as much to her Catullus
> as little Mantua [owes] to her Vergil.

Unfortunately, neither epigram nor title gives any clear indication of the precise contents. It is probably a safe bet, however, that this was not the whole corpus as we have it, for two reasons. First, the book is presumably a papyrus roll rather than a parchment codex, and a roll long enough to hold the corpus contained in the Verona codex is a theoretical possibility but rarely attested – and not very practical when reading for pleasure. Moreover, when Martial mentions an unusually large book here, he acknowledges its size; see 184 (a complete Homer), 186 (a complete Vergil), and 192 (Ovid's *Metamorphoses*). If Martial's "Catullus" is only a portion of Catullus' total output, the likeliest candidate is surely the *Hendecasyllabi*, since those were clearly the best known of his poems in Antiquity, to judge by frequency of citation, or perhaps some portion of them; Martial's use of "Catullus" for his lemma, rather than, say, "Catulli Passer," would suggest that he did not know *Passer* as the title of the *Hendecasyllabi* or even as the title of a "garland" within the *Hendecasyllabi*.

To sum up: it is highly improbable that the Verona codex directly reproduced any single earlier Roman papyrus roll. Rolls long enough to contain all that we have of Catullus were the exception, not the norm, and unlikely to have been used for works read for pleasure. Nor is Catullus likely to have collected the entire corpus himself and prefaced it with c. 1. Instead, the Catullan corpus as we have it is far more likely to be a compilation and consolidation of the kind that followed naturally in the transition from roll to codex that led to (for example) single-volume copies of Vergil. It was probably created no earlier than the third or fourth century, and its components included a copy of the *Hendecasyllabi*, copies of autonomous longer works (whether all that he wrote or only some we cannot say), and either a copy of the *Carmina*, comprising all the works in elegiac couplets, or else a copy of the longer elegiac works plus a copy of the epigrams. If Catullus did indeed write a *Pharmaceutria* and/or a collection of *Priapea*, their absence could have several explanations: the compiler lacked access to a copy; the compiler disliked the contents and consciously omitted them; they were once included, but subsequently deleted in a later, more censorious age; they were once included, but have since been lost through physical damage. Nor can we be certain that the components, especially the two (or three) collections, were not already damaged when combined into our corpus or that they did not suffer damage after compilation, especially at the end of the *Carmina*. Since each of the elements of the corpus originally existed independently of the others, there is no reason to suspect authorial intent behind the order of the components.

Apart from any accidents of transmission that occurred after the components were assembled, what we have is simply "one man's Catullus," a collection of whatever the compiler could find, or perhaps of whatever he chose to include, not necessarily a corpus recognized as a definitive *opera omnia* or even the result of conscious "editorial" intervention. The same consideration applies to the quality of the text preserved in that corpus; the individual books that were compiled were only random representatives of the hundreds or perhaps thousands of copies once scattered throughout the Empire, and need not have been used for any reason of supposed "accuracy." On the contrary: in terms of contents, text, and annotation, our Catullan corpus is simply whatever the Verona codex happened to contain, rightly or wrongly.

The Text in the Middle Ages

The history of the text in the Middle Ages is the history of who read Catullus, where, when, and how; potentially, therefore, it is an important element of cultural history. However, though Catullus continued to be known through late Antiquity and is mentioned casually by the likes of Ausonius in the fourth century, Martianus Capella in the fifth, and Boethius in the sixth, he is essentially unknown in the so-called Dark Ages and after till nearly 1300, apart from the ninth-century copy of Catullus 62; for nearly everyone in Europe during the Middle Ages Catullus was merely a name and a few citations, no more accessible than his contemporaries Calvus and Cinna are to us today, and no extant library catalogue names him. Thus Stoppard's Jowett is off the mark in referring to "a thousand years" or "thirty generations" of copying, for the copying of Catullus was a rare occurrence indeed.

Nevertheless, numerous claims have been made on the basis of alleged "echoes" that Catullus was known to some medieval author or other, but this is a precarious category of evidence that cannot be used effectively without carefully considering alternative sources, or possible intermediaries (especially in the poetry of late Antiquity or the early Middle Ages, seldom taken into account by classicists) – or even the role of mere coincidence. Past claims that are now largely rejected or at least ignored are discussed in Ullman (1960: 1029–35). More recently, Giuseppe Billanovich has claimed (1974: 46ff.) that a Brescian monk named Hildemar shows familiarity with Catullus in a poem composed around the middle of the ninth century, but this is rightly disputed at Tarrant (1983: 43 n. 1), and the other claims advanced by Billanovich in the same work are no more persuasive. No more certain is the alleged imitation of Catullus 68 in a work of Agius of Corvey composed in 874 alleged in Nisbet (1978: 106–7). As to the claims of Guido Billanovich (1958) that

Catullus was known to and imitated by Lovato Lovati near the end of the Middle Ages, these were greeted with skepticism in Ullman (1960) and conclusively refuted in Ludwig (1986).

The history of the text in the Middle Ages is also a matter of practical interest to the editor, and therefore of at least slight importance to the reader. Italian scholars were consulting *V* for as much as a century before any extant MS was copied, and their quotations and references to Catullus therefore constitute a fresh "secondary tradition" that can occasionally be used along with the principal MSS to reconstruct *V*. However, they are less reliable for this purpose than the MSS, since they worked in a tradition of excerpting that allowed quotations to be adapted to specific, often moralistic, purposes, and the collections that contain them of course have their own MS traditions in which accidental errors can occur.

Our chief evidence for what happened to the text of Catullus in the Middle Ages lies of course in the manuscript tradition. Nearly 150 MSS containing some or all of Catullus exist today in libraries and private collections (for a full enumeration see Thomson 1997: 72–91), but it is likely that only three of them have independent value for reconstructing the text (i.e., only these three do not appear to derive directly or indirectly from another MS that survives). The three MSS, all written in northern Italy near the end of the fourteenth century, are:

O (= Oxford, Bodleian Library, Canonici class. lat. 30);
G (= Paris, Bibliothèque Nationale lat. 14137, dated 1375, and probably written by Antonio da Legnano);
R (= Vatican library, Ottobonianus lat. 1829).

G was the first of these to be used by editors, but because they had no way to appreciate its importance, they used it along with a number of fifteenth-century MSS of no value at all except as the occasional source of emendations. *O* was first used by Robinson Ellis, but he had no inkling of its value, which it was left to Emil Baehrens to appreciate (Stoppard has Jowett taunt him over this in a memorably humorous sequence that is inspired by Housman's ridicule of Ellis as having "the mind of an idiot child"). *R* (the source of most of the fifteenth-century copies, which were only rarely influenced by *O* or *G*) was discovered in 1896 by W. G. Hale, who soon realized that a fresh proliferation of errors shared by *GR* but not by *O* showed that they derived from the Veronensis through a lost copy, which editors designate *X*. The reconstruction of *V* from these witnesses is not entirely straightforward; while it is true that the agreement of *O* with either *G* or *R* against the other will normally give the reading of *V*, disagreements of *O* against *GR* are more difficult to resolve, and the entire enterprise is complicated by the corrections, conjectures, and variant/alternative readings that arose at various stages. Even the exact relationship between *V* and *OGR* has been disputed. Though it was long thought that *O* and *X* were copied directly from *V* itself, McKie (1977) and Thomson (1997) have argued convincingly that another lost copy (I shall use Thomson's *siglum* and call it *A*) must lie between *O* and *X* and the Veronensis (Thomson 1997: 26–7). Moreover, the very nature of *V* is also disputed. This was formerly assumed to be a MS of late Antiquity in some script such as semiuncial (see, for example, Thomson 1997: 23; I wonder whether an even more difficult script such as a North-Italian pre-Carolingian minuscule might be involved), but Billanovich and Thomson now use *v* to designate that copy, employing *V* to identify a hypothetical MS in Gothic script copied from it about 1280 (Giuseppe Billanovich 1988; Thomson 1997: 24–5). Thomson defends this view on the grounds that certain errors of *OGR* were induced by the misreading of Gothic script or of late abbreviations, but the former were argued away in Clausen (1976), and for the latter see Tarrant (1983: 45 n. 17); hence the hypothesis that a Gothic *V* was copied from *v* and served as the source from which *A* was later copied may be unnecessary – we need no more than a single intermediary, *A*, between the early Veronensis and *OX*.

At only two points in the Middle Ages can knowledge of Catullus be documented securely in the form of an actual copy, at (probably) Tours in the ninth century, and at Verona in the thirteenth or fourteenth. The evidence for Tours is the text of Catullus 62 contained in Paris, Bibliothèque Nationale lat. 8071, cited by editors of Catullus as *T. T* was copied in the third quarter of the ninth century, probably at Tours; it is an anthology, but contains nothing else by Catullus (there is an unresolved scholarly controversy as to how *T* is related to the eighth-century MS Vienna 277, with similar contents but no Catullus). The lines in which *T* and *V* either share an error or contain two variations of the same error show beyond a doubt that they have a common source (for the former cf. 9 *uisere*, 45 *tum*, 58 *cura*, 59 *nec*, for the latter 7 *imbres T: imber V*, 8 *certes. i. T, certe si V*, 63 *patris T: pars patri V*).

As to Verona, the earliest evidence for the presence of Catullus there is in the writings of Rather, a bishop of Verona, around 966. Again "echoes" of Catullus have been alleged in his writings, but those adduced in Reece (1969) in his *Index citationum* do not survive critical inspection, not even the claim that Catullus 58b.2–3 served as the source of *non angelico...subvectu, non pennigero, ut poeticus ille noster,...volatu* (30.2.7ff.): there is no reason to take *pennigero...uolatu* as an echo of Catullus' *Pegaseo...uolatu* when neither *penniger* nor *uolatus* is a rare word and (as Gaisser 1993: 283 n. 68 notes on the authority of a colleague), "a more likely source for Rather is Jerome: 'et quasi *pennigero volatu* petulcam animal aufugit' (*Vita Pauli* 8)." Thus the only evidence that Rather read Catullus is his own claim that he did so: in an awkwardly long sentence in a sermon on Mary and Martha (too long to quote in full), he refers to reading both *Catullum numquam antea lectum* ("Catullus, never before read") and *Plautum...iam olim...neglectum* ("Plautus long neglected"). It is far from certain whether Rather meant that Catullus had been read by no one at all or only by himself, or that Plautus had long been neglected by everyone or only by himself; but the context does imply that these readings distract Rather from his pastoral duties, suggesting that they are not simply a hypothetical possibility but a factual one.

Of course scholars have tried to explain how an identical strain of text could be found in both ninth-century Tours and tenth- and/or thirteenth-century Verona: was it originally at or near Tours, then taken to Verona after *T* had been copied? Was it originally at Verona? And if it was, does *T* derive its text of Catullus 62 from the Veronensis itself (on some unexplained westward journey) or from a copy of it, or perhaps from a copy of Catullus 62 alone? Such questions are intimately tied up with the notorious epigram by Benvenuto Campesani of Vicenza (d. 1323) that is found in MSS *G* and *R*. Entitled "On the resurrection of Catullus, Veronese poet," it appears to claim that, thanks to a fellow countryman, Catullus has now returned to his homeland "from a distant country," his "paper" no longer shut up beneath a bushel basket:

> Ad patriam uenio longis a finibus exul:
>   causa mei reditus compatriota fuit,
> scilicet a calamis tribuit cui Francia nomen
>   quique notat turbe praetereuntis iter.
> quo licet ingenio uestrum celebrate Catullum,
>   cuius sub modio clausa papirus erat.

> An exile, I come to my homeland from a distant country:
>   the cause of my return was a compatriot,
> namely a scribe to whom France assigned a name
>   and who marks the route of the passing crowd.
> Celebrate with whatever talent you can your Catullus,
>   whose paper was shut up under a bushel-basket.

Thomson (1997: 26) well remarks that "The meaning of Campesani's epigram, and the facts underlying it, are the greatest puzzles in this whole question of the *resurrectio Catulli*." The traditional literal reading takes it to convey that a notary (*a calamis*) named Franciscus discovered a copy of Catullus under a bushel-basket somewhere (perhaps in France, since that is where *T* was copied), then brought it to Verona. More fancifully, some scholars in the twentieth century entertained the notion that the words *scilicet a calamis tribuit cui Francia nomen* refer not to a notary but to Can Grande, a fourteenth-century lord of Verona, via a pun on French *canne*, meaning much the same as Latin *calamus*, and even that *quique notat turbe praetereuntis iter* refers to an equestrian statue of him set up in public (for these theories see, conveniently, Zaffagno 1975). A conspicuous weakness of such views, however, is that there was no need for an Italian to pun on French *canne* when his own language offered *canna*, with exactly the same meaning. Most recently, Giuseppe Billanovich (1988) has tried to solve the enigma (and to keep Catullus in Verona) by reference to contemporary Italian politics: the MS involved is not *V* but *X*, and the "distant country" is no further from Verona than nearby Padua.

Whatever Campesani meant to convey, any understanding of the epigram must surely take into account its clearly metaphorical and indeed humorous nature: after all, if the rebirth is literally true, then the return from exile is not, and if the return is literally true, then the resurrection is not – it is surely not implied that Catullus was resurrected *and* repatriated *and* rescued from under a bushel-basket. In fact, the "resurrection" of the title is only a metaphor, and applied with a light touch, since the concept does not recur within the poem. Instead, this begins with a fresh metaphor, the return from exile, which is itself supplanted by a third metaphor (the only one that has been recognized for what it is), the biblical notion of "hiding one's light under a bushel" – hence the invitation now to celebrate Catullus' genius (cf. Matthew 5:15, Mark 4:21, Luke 11:33; *papirus* often means "wick" rather than "book" in medieval Latin). In the end, only the allusively identified notary seems "real"; it may be relevant that Guglielmo da Pastrengo praised Campesani himself as a "remarkable poet *and notary*" (*poeta et scriba mirabilis*). I suggest that Campesani's "riddle" commemorates a notary named Francesco who metaphorically restored Catullus to life for his home-city by undertaking the challenge of copying the ancient Veronensis into a script comprehensible to his contemporaries – in other words, creating *A*, the copy of *V* from which *OX* and thus all the other MSS derive, metaphorically taking the text out from under the bushel that had concealed it and making it accessible to readers and potential admirers. As to *T*, there seems to be no evidence to establish which is more likely, that a complete or partial copy of Catullus was taken from Verona to Tours, or that both *T* and *V* derive independently from an archetype that was originally found in France and only later made its way to Verona.

Whatever the truth behind the epigram, the text of Catullus was indeed restored to European civilization in Verona not long before the year 1300, but in a seriously corrupted and somewhat confused condition in which many words had been mis-copied, divisions between poems blurred, and (nearly) all titles lost. The very earliest medieval allusions clearly presuppose a text without titles. Giuseppe Billanovich (1988: 38) has drawn attention to a MS of Terence closely connected to one belonging to Petrarch (London, British Library Harley 2525) in which c. 52.1 is cited "apud Catullum prope finem primi operis" ("in Catullus near the end of the first part of his work"); instead of confirming the theory that Catullus circulated on three rolls in Antiquity (cf. Heyworth 1993: 132), this merely shows that this medieval reader lacked titles to cite but noticed the sequence lyrics/long poems/epigrams and used it as the basis of his citation, with the lyrics being the obvious "first part" of the corpus. When Hieremias de Montagnone, working between 1275 and 1320, quotes Catullus, his text again seems to lack titles and is instead divided into 12 large sections that he calls *capitula* – a division that, according to Ullman's persuasive arguments, Hieremias introduced himself (Ullman 1973; Ullman also demonstrated that the remains of these divisions can be traced in *O*). Around 1310, Benzo of Alessandria quotes Catullus 35.1–4, in the corrupt version of the Veronensis, in his *Cronica* (cf. Clausen 1976: 41 f.); he introduces the quotation with "Catullus writes to his friend Aurelius," which Ullman has shown derives from 21.1, the first line of the large block in which 35.1–4 appeared. A florilegium compiled in Verona in 1329 quotes 22.19–21 under "Catullus ad Varum," but Ullman again has shown that this is another deduction from a faultily divided text.

These citations by *capitulum* or by improvised title suggest a shortage or, more likely, total absence of titles in *V*. The issue of whether titles were present in the Veronensis or were invented exclusively in its descendants is not merely an academic matter of reconstructing a lost MS; it is vital to the entire question of how Catullus arranged his poetry. For example, an assumption about the antiquity of the titles in the MSS is fundamental to Wiseman's claim that the entire corpus as we have it was assembled in its current order by Catullus himself: "One might expect, *a priori*, that a collection entitled *Catulli Veronensis liber* and beginning with a dedication poem ought to be Catullus' own arrangement" (Wiseman 1985: 265–6). But what if *Catulli Veronensis liber* (found in *O* only as an addition by a later hand) is nothing but the improvisation of a thirteenth- or fourteenth-century Italian?

Certainly there is no compelling reason to believe that the titles found in the descendants of *V* derive from Catullus himself. For one thing, ancient poetry collections seem not to have given titles to their individual components, but medieval and Renaissance MSS often supplied them, and those in *OGR* most frequently conform to the patterns "To *X*" and "About *X*" characteristic of those late inventions. For another, they occur only in places where the MS tradition indicates a division between poems and never elsewhere, no matter how clear it is that a new poem is beginning. These misdivisions are a relatively common phenomenon, and what we now know as a corpus of (more or less) 113 poems comprised no more than 53 in the archetype, and quite probably fewer. Mynors's OCT (pp. xiv–xv) offers a "Carminum in archetypo discriptio" which is supposed to tabulate the poem-divisions and titles of the Veronensis, but it really represents a compilation of the divisions and titles marked in one or more of *OGR* (see the rightly skeptical observations of Heyworth 1993: 133 n. 46); many of these – conceivably even all of them – were introduced first in *A*, in *O*, in *X*, or in *G* or *R*. In any case, at the most generous estimate, *V* indicated new poems only at (the first line should be understood when no further indication is given) 2, 4, 5, 6, 7, 8, 9, 11, 12, 13, 14, 15, 17, 21, 22, 23, 25, 26, 27, 28, 29, 30, 31, 32, 34, 35, 36, 37.1, 37.17, 40, 49, 50, 51, 52, 53.5, 54.6, 56, 59, 61, 62, 63, 64.1, 64.323, 65, 68, 69, 72, 76, 80, 89, 92, 100, and 101.

Some of the most revealing titles, of course, are those that cannot possibly be authentic under any interpretation. One class of these comprises titles introduced at incorrect divisions, such as "Ad Egnatium" at 37.17 at the head of a poem that combines 37.17–20, addressed to Egnatius, with 38, addressed to Cornificius, and 39, addressed again to Egnatius; "De Octonis capite" at 53.5; and "Ad Camerium" at 54.6. Other clearly inauthentic titles misidentify the contents. The title "Argonautia" bestowed on 64.1–322 is based on the same hasty misunderstanding of the poem's opening as the note that stands in *O* stating that "here he tells the story of the golden fleece" (*narrat hic ystoriam aurei velleris*); probably the same thirteenth- or fourteenth-century scholar was responsible for both. Most revealing of all, however, is the title to Catullus 36, "Ad lusi cacatam" (i.e., "Ad lusicacatam," "To Lusicacata"), based on its opening line as corrupted in *V*, *anuale suo lusi cacata carta* (modern editions read *annales Volusi, cacata carta*).

Beyond confirming that we have lost any ancient titles that *V* contained, *OGR* have little or no value for the debate over how Catullus' poetry circulated in Antiquity. It has been claimed that the unusually large gap that follows Catullus 60 in *O*, where it ends near the bottom of f. 14ᵛ and 61 starts afresh at the top of f. 15ʳ, is "a survival perhaps of the ancient division of Catullus' work into *libelli*" (Thomson 1997: 7), but the gap is not substantially larger than some others left by this scribe, who may simply have been unwilling to leave a "widow" comprising only a line or two on f. 14ᵛ. It has also been observed that, while *O* has very few decorated initials early in the corpus (only at 1 and 2, in fact), they have been supplied fairly consistently in the elegiac parts of the corpus (65, 68, 69, 72, 77, 80, 89), and it has been suggested that this too reflects the construction of the corpus from different sources. Another explanation, however, is that the owner of *O* simply took a greater interest in the epigrams than in the polymetrics, perhaps because the meter was more familiar.

The only title of significance is "explicit epithalamium," which is found between the end of Catullus 61 and the beginning of 62, though only in *O*, where it is written not as a heading but as just another line of text in a single unbroken poem comprising both 61 and 62. The obvious interpretation – that this is the remnant of an ancient title identifying 61 as an epithalamium – is unlikely to be correct, though we are certainly dealing with a survivor from Antiquity. As we have seen, the title "epithalamium" belongs to 62, not to 61: it is 62 that Quintilian cites as the *Epithalamium*, 62 that bears that title in *T*. Hence I suggest that "explicit epithalamium" combines scraps of two originally separate notices: "explicit" survives from a heading such as "explicit liber hendecasyllaborum" that stood at the end of 61, "epithalamium" from "incipit epithalamium" at the head of 62 (an arrangement like "liber hendecasyllaborum explicit epithalamium incipit" could explain even better what we find in *O*). (*G*, on the other hand, calls Catullus 62 "exametrum carmen nuptiale"; this is not ancient, being the definition of "epithalamium" found in the medieval *Vocabularium* of Papias.)

Editing Catullus is, in effect, the process of repairing the damage that befell the text during Antiquity and the Middle Ages. It begins with the reconstruction of *V*; then, once the readings of the archetype are known, with whatever variants or notes were present, editors must evaluate them and judge whether they are authentic or corrupt. As to the quality of the text offered by *V*, it had clearly suffered considerably from scribal error in its transmission, chiefly (one expects) in the copying of *V* itself from some difficult older script (see Thomson 1997: 23 for speculation about these early stages) and in the copying of *A* from *V*. The text of Catullus 62 in *T* shows that much of the corruption was already present in the ancestor of both *T* and *V* and had occurred before the ninth century, and allows us to judge how much additional corruption was introduced in *V*. An idea of the total extent of corruption in *V* can be gained by examining an edition such as Mynors's OCT, the standard text of Catullus for the English-speaking world, with Thomson (1997) its only possible rival, for its more accurate *apparatus criticus*. In some respects, the picture can look quite rosy to the unwary. For one thing, Mynors rejects no lines as interpolations, though such interpolations have occurred in other authors, including Ovid and Propertius. This probably reflects both the infrequency with which Catullus was read and copied and the difficulty of reproducing the largely unfamiliar metrical schemes of the lyrics. In addition, Mynors regards only two passages as involving a disruption in the order of lines (58b.2–3; 64.377–80). In three passages, he supplies a refrain omitted by the archetype, and in one passage he omits a refrain transmitted erroneously by the archetype (64.378); in 12 other places he indicates lines lost either within a poem or between poems. In 26 passages, a line is noted as metrically deficient, with the missing word(s) supplied by conjecture when possible. In 17 lines, Mynors prints the transmitted text with one or more obeli (†) to show that it is hopelessly corrupted, with no convincing remedy yet proposed. That these cases total under 100 will perhaps convey an impression of optimism for a corpus of well over 2,000 lines. But these cases are greatly outnumbered by the passages where Mynors acknowledges an error in the archetype and replaces it with a correction that he regarded as certain. In the first 100 lines (1.1–7.2), for example, he corrects 36 such errors – just over one in every third line – while in the last 100 lines (99.11–116.8) he corrects 45 – nearly one in every second line. The text of Catullus clearly suffered from substantial corruption on the infrequent occasions when it was copied; among ancient Latin poets, perhaps only the text of Propertius was corrupted to a comparable degree.

The Text in the Renaissance and Beyond

The interdependent processes of correction and study began hand in hand as soon as Catullus became available to the so-called "proto-humanists" of the fourteenth century. Giuseppe Billanovich (1988) has done the most speculating about the role that these scholars might have played in the "resurrection" of Catullus (his views are conveniently summarized in Thomson 1997: 24–33 along with Thomson's own and McKie's); Billanovich's most plausible suggestion is that Albertino Mussato may be responsible for early annotations like the metrical notes found in *G* and even for some early conjectures, even if he did not commission the copying of the MS that Thomson designates *A*. Petrarch is sure to have had a role somewhere; the most likely places are either as an annotator of *A* or as the owner of *X* (Thomson 1997: 27–8). Those who were responsible for the restoration of poem-divisions that took place in the near descendants of *V* (and it was surely a cumulative, collaborative effort) were the first modern textual critics of Catullus, just as the authors of the numerous annotations in *O* and *G* were the first interpreters and rudimentary commentators.

Neither this annotation nor the impulse to improve the transmitted text was in any way unusual; in fact, both were entirely natural parts of "manuscript culture" as practiced from Antiquity through to the Renaissance, necessitated by the unreliability of handwritten copies. The correction of scribal errors (such as corruptions and misdivisions) normally involved two processes. A scholar could correct his own copy by searching for better readings in other copies, or he could correct by conjecture, in effect "guessing" the author's original intention (or sometimes by reasoning from the content of some other ancient text: for example, Quintilian's paraphrase of 93.2 at *Inst.* 11.1.38 obviously facilitated the restoration of the line as Catullus wrote it). Naturally conjecture was the more fruitful activity in the earliest days of Catullan scholarship; as we have seen, there were numerous errors, many of them superficial, awaiting correction, and fifteenth-century scholars corrected hundreds of these, representing the vast majority of the corrections now accepted into the text. The first scholar whose corrections to the text of Catullus we can identify with any certainty is Colluccio Salutati (1331–1406), chancellor of Florence, who commissioned the copying of *R* and was its first owner; his conjectures can be found among the readings that editors designate with the symbol *r* (see, for example, 3.16, where *o [factum male]* is Salutati's correction of the transmitted *bonum*). Collating other copies was more difficult; there were very few MSS at all in existence (a note in *G* complains of this very fact, and apologizes to the reader for not offering a better text), and none not descended from *V*, so that consultation inevitably involved closely related MSS: for example, the MS that editors designate *m* (Venice, Bibl. Naz. Marciana XII.80 [4167]) was copied from *R*, then subsequently collated against *R* at a later stage (enabling editors to distinguish between earlier and later stages of annotation by Salutati), and at some point supplied a set of variant readings recorded in *G*.

In the fifteenth century, as corrections proliferated, inspection of other copies was increasingly profitable, though of course readers of this period lacked the knowledge of the tradition that we possess today and could not distinguish authoritative readings from conjectures. The corrections of (mostly) anonymous fifteenth-century humanists remind us of the notable service that they performed for classical texts, in contrast to the image perpetuated in modern scholarship. Though Mynors's *apparatus criticus* bears testament to their achievement (in addition to those identified by name, every reading there designated by a Greek letter is the conjecture of some anonymous humanist), he nonetheless followed the standard view in his preface and denounced the supposed "befouling" of texts by the men known scornfully as the *Itali*. It ought to be clear, however, that no one can evaluate how a scholar practiced the art of textual criticism without knowing the texts on which he worked; yet such knowledge was non-existent in the nineteenth century, and no one who denounced the *Itali* really had any idea of what they had done. In fact the accusations of excessive and irresponsible emendation that nineteenth- and twentieth-century scholars have repeated from Karl Lachmann are simply part of a rhetorical tradition that can be traced as far back as the fifteenth century, in which someone (often a scholar who emends heavily) criticizes another group of scholars for emending either too carelessly or too heavily. With the increasingly improved texts and advancing knowledge of Latin language and literature and Roman history came the opportunity for the writing of commentaries (catalogued and described in Gaisser 1992; see also Gaisser 1993: 24–108 for discussion of some of the early printed commentaries), and for Catullan influence in literature as well. It would be fair to say that the single most important figure in the reception of Catullus is Giovanni Gioviano Pontano, a virtually unique combination of scholar, poet, and emender who practiced every one of his arts at the highest level. It is unfortunate that his own MS of Catullus does not survive (though his copies of Tibullus and Propertius, for example, do) and that we are therefore poorly informed about his no doubt extensive conjectural activity (the six occasions on which his name appears in the *apparatus criticus* of Mynors's OCT are surely the proverbial "tip of the iceberg"). As an emender of the text, Pontano earned the scorn of nineteenth-century scholars, who saw him as the worst (or perhaps the best) of the *Itali*. But he was widely recognized in his own day and for centuries after as a scholar of importance and as an authority on the Latin language; and, while many of the humanists who emended Catullus were poets at least to the extent of being able to spin out hexameters or elegiac couplets with varying degrees of fluidity, Pontano was not only prolific – he was good as well, and his reputation as a poet remained as strong as his reputation as a scholar until the nineteenth century, and no doubt contributed, like his scholarship, to his abilities as an emender. It was through such early works of Pontano as the *Liber Parthenopaeus* that Catullus was restored not only to the world of scholarship but to the world of literature as well (cf. Gaisser 1993 and this volume).

Catullus first appeared in print in 1472, in an edition published in Venice by Vindelino de Spira (Hain *4758; *BMC V* 161–2); for the subsequent publication history see Thomson (1997: 43–60). Of course attempts at correcting the text did not cease, and perhaps reached a peak in the nineteenth century with the efforts of such indefatigable emenders as Baehrens and Ellis; nevertheless, many problems still remain, though their impact on interpretation is minimal. Modern textual criticism continues to follow the same lines as in the Renaissance. Scholars continue to propose new conjectures or resurrect old ones, or they defend passages against conjecture, and of course questions of poem-division are still debated: whether 2.11–13 are a fragment or follow on from 2.10, whether 14.24–6 are a fragment or the conclusion of 14, whether 51.13–16 are the conclusion of 51.1–12 or a fragment of another poem in Sapphics, whether "58b" should be separated from 58, whether 68 is one poem or two, whether a new epigram should begin at 76.13. The text of Catullus remains a work in progress, 700 years after its resurrection and repatriation.

GUIDE TO FURTHER READING

Those who wish to explore the aesthetic arguments for Catullus' supposed involvement in the arrangement of his surviving works should consult the literature cited by Skinner in the next chapter. For the history of the text, the publications of B. L. Ullman are still of value, while accessible English-language accounts can be found in Tarrant (1983) and especially in Thomson (1997: 22–38). There is some value in comparing the introduction to Thomson's 1997 edition with that to his 1978 edition to see how the opinions of a leading Catullan scholar have evolved. For the reception of Catullus in Antiquity and the Renaissance, one can do no better than explore the pages of Gaisser (1993); see also her chapter in this volume. For those who read Italian, the articles and books of Giuseppe Billanovich listed in the "Works cited" can all be recommended as the products of a scholar with an unmatched knowledge of the reception of classical culture in medieval Italy.

WORKS CITED

Billanovich, Giuseppe. 1959. "Dal Livio di Raterio al Livio di Petrarca." *Italia medioevale e umanistica* 2: 103–78.

Billanovich, Giuseppe. 1974. "Terenzio, Ildemaro, Petrarca." *Italia medioevale e umanistica* 17: 1–60.

Billanovich, Giuseppe. 1981. *La tradizione del testo di Livio e le origini dell'umanesimo.* Padua.

Billanovich, Giuseppe. 1988. "Il Catullo della Cattedrale di Verona." In *Scire litteras = Bayerische Akademie der Wissenschaften, Philosophisch.-historische Klasse, Abhandlungen* 99. Munich. 37–52.

Billanovich, Guido. 1958. "*Veterum vestigia vatum* nei carmi dei preumanisti padovani." *Italia medioevale e umanistica* 1: 155–243.

Clausen, W. V. 1976. "*Catulli Veronensis Liber.*" *Classical Philology* 71: 37–43.

Courtney, E., ed. 1993. *The Fragmentary Latin Poets.* Oxford.

Ellis, R. 1878. *Catulli Veronensis Liber.* Oxford.

Fordyce, C. J., ed. 1961. *Catullus: A Commentary.* Oxford.

Gaisser, J. H. 1992. "Catullus." In V. Brown, ed., *Catalogus Translationum et Commentariorum* 7. Washington, DC. 197–292.

Gaisser, J. H. 1993. *Catullus and His Renaissance Readers.* Oxford.

Giardina, G. 1974. "La composizione del liber e l'itinerario poetico di Catullo: contributi alla sistemazione del problema." *Philologus* 118: 224–35.

Heyworth, S. J. 1993. "Dividing Poems." In O. Pecere and M. D. Reeve, eds., *Formative Stages of Classical Traditions: Latin Texts from Antiquity to the Renaissance.* Spoleto. 117–48.

Jocelyn, H. D. 1999. "The Arrangement and the Language of Catullus' So-Called *polymetra* with Special Reference to the Sequence 10–11–12." In J. N. Adams and R. G. Mayer, eds., *Aspects of the Language of Latin Poetry* = Proceedings of the British Academy 93. Oxford. 335–75.

Keil, H. 1961. *Grammatici latini* (*GLK*). 8 vols. Hildesheim. Rpt. of the 1855–80 Leipzig edn.

Ludwig, W. 1986. "Kannte Lovato Catull?" *Rheinisches Museum* 129: 329–57.

Manzo, A. 1967. "Testimonianze e tradizione del 'liber' catulliano nella letteratura esegetico-scolastica antica." *Rivista di Studi Classici* 15: 137–62.

McKie, D. S. 1977. "The Manuscripts of Catullus: Recension in a Closed Tradition." Dissertation. Cambridge University.

Mynors, R. A. B., ed. 1958 (rev. 1960). *C. Valerii Catulli Carmina recognovit brevique adnotatione critica instruxit.* Oxford.

Nisbet, R. G. M. 1978. "Notes on the Text of Catullus." *Proceedings of the Cambridge Philological Society* n.s. 24: 92–115 (= R. G. M. Nisbet, *Collected Papers on Latin Literature*, ed. S. J. Harrison [Oxford 1995] 76–100).

Reece, B., ed. 1969. *Sermones Ratherii Episcopi Veronensis.* Worcester, MA.

Schmidt, E. A. 1979. "Das Problem des Catullbuches." *Philologus* 123: 216–31.

Starr, R. J. 1987. "The Circulation of Literary Texts in the Roman World." *Classical Quarterly* n.s. 37: 213–23.

Stoppard, T. 1997. *The Invention of Love.* New York.

Tarrant, R. J. 1983. "Catullus." In L. D. Reynolds, ed., *Texts and Transmission: A Survey of the Latin Classics.* Oxford. 43–5.

Thomson, D. F. S., ed. 1978. *Catullus: A Critical Edition.* Chapel Hill, NC.

Thomson, D. F. S., ed. 1997. *Catullus, Edited with a Textual and Interpretative Commentary.* Toronto.

Ullman, B. L. 1960. "The Transmission of the Text of Catullus." In *Studi in onore di Luigi Castiglioni.* 2 vols. Florence. II.1027–57.

Ullman, B. L. 1973. *Studies in the Italian Renaissance.* 2nd edn. Rome.

Wiseman, T. P. 1985. *Catullus and His World: A Reappraisal.* Cambridge.

Zaffagno, E. 1975. "L'epigramma di Benvenuto di Campesani: *de resurrectione Catulli poetae Veronensis.*" In *I classici nel medioevo e nell'umanesimo.* Università di Genova. Pubblicazioni dell'Istituto di filologia classica e medievale. Genoa. 289–98.

CHAPTER THREE

Authorial Arrangement of the Collection: Debate Past and Present

Marilyn B. Skinner

No one can deny that the collection before us is a wild chaos.
> B. Schmidt, "Die Lebenszeit Catulls und die Herausgabe seiner Gedichte"

He has arranged his poetry book with the most careful consideration; if someone can't see that, so much the worse for him.
> U. von Wilamowitz-Moellendorff, *Sappho und Simonides*

After a full century and a half, the question of authorial design in the corpus of Catullus' surviving poems – occasionally designated *die Catullfrage*, "the Catullan question," as though it were the *only* one – continues to prove intractable. Yet, like Freud's exasperated "What does a woman want?" it may be a question so framed as to discourage consensus. Although it appears to be one of fact – does the present order of the poems in the collection reflect the intentions of their author? – it is in actuality one of *import* based upon an observer's subjective response to the *liber Catulli*: if the corpus is seen as coherent in whole or part, design is present, and such design presumably must be authorial. Perceptions of coherence, however, are largely determined by ideas of aesthetic propriety common to the larger culture, which in turn shape value-judgments. Is this an effective introduction/closure? Are the relationships (quantitative, thematic, verbal) among contiguous items significant enough to exclude chance placement? How much of a "fudge factor" is permissible in the case of elements that do not fit the pre-existing critical paradigm? The answers to such inquiries change over time, as expectations of art change. An account of the Catullan question offers a history in miniature of aesthetic reception in the West from the middle of the nineteenth century to the present. Not surprisingly, growing willingness to observe purposeful assignment where none was admitted previously accompanies a growing appreciation of complexity, polyvalence, and dissonance in the literary product.

When scholars speak of "authorial arrangement," they generally have in mind the internal order of poems within one division of the corpus, though many, particularly in recent decades, have extended their investigations to the entire collection. The existence of c. 1, the dedication of a *lepidus nouus libellus* ("charming new book") to Cornelius Nepos, indicates that during his life Catullus did assemble at least one volume of poetry. Length, however, discourages us from assuming that that solitary *libellus* can be identified with our present *liber Catulli*, which seems instead to have been compiled into codex form from independently circulating smaller units (although those units, some maintain, might have constituted an original tripartite edition). Specific references by the elder Pliny (*HN* 28.19), and by Servius in his commentary on line 2.95 of Vergil's *Georgics*, to works not in the present collection imply that some pieces thought to be by the poet did not make it into the codex. As Butrica demonstrates (above, pp. 20–1), the generic divisions within the *liber Catulli* conform to the practice of Catullus' contemporaries: the neoterics grouped their shorter pieces into collections of hendecasyllabics and lyrics or elegiac epigrams but issued their longer poems as solo works. Later *testimonia* refer to collections generically (*poemata*, *epigrammata*) or by title, in the case of individual pieces, but do not cite book number – as one might expect had an author published his complete works all at once. At first glance, then, the external evidence is indecisive; some of it points one way, some the other.

In the chapter that follows I provide a history of this dispute and an assessment of the relevant arguments. While space set firm limits on the number of studies I was able to discuss, I have tried to take sufficient note of the most crucial ones. Although I have made several contributions of my own to the literature on the topic (Skinner 1981, 1988, 2003), I will refrain from advocating a specific position here, since it is essential for students of Catullus to acquaint themselves with the problem and its implications before drawing conclusions.

Emergence of the Question

The arbitrariness of the *liber Catulli* scandalized nineteenth-century readers. If the poet ordered and published his poems himself, why was their chronology so muddled? Johann Fröhlich was the first to propose that the authentic edition, which did observe chronological order, had been disturbed after Catullus' death and the pieces rearranged by a later hand (1843: 700–1, 712–13). Credit for casting the strongest doubts upon belief in Catullan arrangement is usually awarded, however, to Eduardus a Brunér (Edouard-Jonas-Guillaume de Brunér), whose 1863 study "De ordine et temporibus carminum Valerii Catulli" (first given in 1861 as a presidential address to the Finnish Society of Sciences and Letters) anticipated many of the points raised by other scholars in subsequent decades. In that paper Brunér formulated the basic grounds for postulating that the present corpus is an assemblage put together by a posthumous editor (pp. 602–12):

- The length and diversity of the collection argue against the premise that it was contained in a single volume, especially one designated by the author as a *libellus*.
- The size of that hypothetical scroll would have been larger than comparable poetry collections by later authors, particularly if we assume some of the contents were afterward lost.

- The dedication poem was not composed for the whole *liber Catulli*, because the poet would not have characterized his more ambitious works as *nugae*, "trifles" (1.4).
- While Catullus indeed published *libelli* in his lifetime, the poems in each were arranged in the order in which they were written, with thematically related pieces, whether hendecasyllabics, iambs, or elegiac epigrams, grouped together, as in Martial's collections. The present order is owed to a redactor who knew little about the poet and who capriciously decided, when the scrolls were being transcribed into codex form, that a metrical arrangement would be more desirable.[1]

Brunér's argument for following Fröhlich in assuming a chronologically ordered authorial arrangement is revealing: Catullus' verses were so bound up with immediate experience that the sole thread unifying them was the life of their author. Hence they would be intelligible to a reader only if presented in autobiographical sequence (p. 612). That assertion depends upon a view of the Catullan poem as a spontaneous expression of personal feeling – a Romantic notion all but abandoned today.

Out of the spirited discussion of these issues that ensued during the next half-century, three stances emerged (Beck 1996: 13–14). Although the idea of an original chronological arrangement was eventually discarded, some scholars continued to insist that the collection was put together after the poet's death and showed no traces of meaningful design whatsoever. Bernhard Schmidt's sweeping denial (1914: 278), cited as the first epigraph to this chapter, is an exemplary statement of that position. Others, however, rallied to the defense of authorial editorship, grounding their case on perceived systematic placement of individual poems within the corpus. Soon after the appearance of Brunér's article, Rudolf Westphal observed a consistent pattern of separating two poems of related content with one or more of heterogeneous content and identified five thematic or tonal *Zyklen* ("cycles") based on that scheme, which organized the whole group of polymetrics. The most important (and convincing) of these was the "Lesbia cycle," poems 2–12, six pieces chronologically arranged so as to give a brief history of the affair with Lesbia, interspersed with cordial poems addressed to male friends. Such patterning could not be found in the second and third sections of the corpus, however – on the one hand, there were too few of the longer poems; on the other, the pagination of the epigrams in the codex had, in Westphal's view, been disturbed (1867, 1870[2]: 1–13).

Could other traces of planning be found in the collection? In a doctoral dissertation published in 1877, J. Süss argued that each of the three parts of the *liber Catulli* was introduced by a dedication: poem 1 to Nepos, poem 61 to Manlius Torquatus, and poem 65 to Hortensius (pp. 23–4). Nepos' *libellus* could be identified with the hendecasyllabics 1–60, which had contemporary Rome as their background. Poems 61 through 64, based on Greek models, featured wedding themes and were appropriately presented to a bridegroom. Finally, 65–116 formed a self-contained unit, marked off by the repeated phrase "poems of Battus' descendant" (*carmina Battiadae*, 65.16 and 116.2) and thereby identified as imitations of Callimachean elegy and epigram. Süss further explained the juxtaposition of dissimilar poems as a manifestation of the principle of *uariatio*, or avoidance of repetition (p. 28), and pointed out that adjoining poems, such as 49, 50, and 51, clarified one another by evoking relationships among the parties mentioned (pp. 30–1). His insistence that the ordering of the poems, though carefully planned, followed no rigid principle ("steifes Prinzip," p. 31) allowed flexibility in fitting the individual pieces into a larger scheme. Accordingly, he concluded that the arrangement of the poems was wholly authorial. Similar impressions of underlying clarity in the midst of apparent disarray elicited Wilamowitz's supporting declaration, pontifical but unfortunately sadly cryptic, which stands as the second, contrasting epigraph above (1913: 292). But even Wilamowitz's authority was unable to convince unbelievers. Weighing up the arguments on both sides, Wilhelm Kroll pronounced the question insoluble (1968 [1923]: ix–x).

Many critics sought middle ground between the extreme views of Schmidt and Wilamowitz. The most influential of these was Theodor Birt, who in 1882 published a comprehensive treatment of the material and formal features of the ancient book. After surveying the length of extant books of poetry and calculating the probable dimensions of fragmentary papyrus editions, Birt concluded that Brunér was correct: because of its size, the Catullan corpus could not have been transmitted in just one roll (pp. 401–13). Containing perhaps 2,400 lines when complete, it would have been more than double the size of the longest surviving Augustan poetic volume, Book 2 of Horace's *Satires* (1,083 lines). The collection as it stands, however, might have been assembled out of separate *libelli* issued by the poet himself, with their contents becoming disarranged during the process: this would account for coherent sequences, such as the opening cluster of Lesbia poems, while also explaining the presence of apparent fragments and the sections where groupings seemed arbitrary. These conclusions had a decisive impact on Anglo-American scholarship, for they were accepted by Robinson Ellis in the second edition of his commentary on Catullus (1889: 4–5) and became the starting point for Arthur Leslie Wheeler's "History of the Poems," the first of his 1928 Sather Lectures on Catullus.

Wheeler was, however, more conservative than Birt in his approach to the question of authorial editorship. When he gauged the likely size of a papyrus roll containing the entire corpus, he arrived at an "inconvenient and unwieldy" length of 38 feet, well beyond the upper limit for extant rolls (1934: 16).[2] Like Birt, he assumed that the *liber Catulli* as we have it was compiled at a later date, but he also conjectured that many of the pieces then gathered together had been disseminated among friends but never included in any published collection, surviving independently instead. The *libellus* dedicated to Nepos, which, judging from the epithet *nugae*, contained light verse, and poem 64, issued as a *monobiblos* or "single volume," were probably in the hands of booksellers at the time of the poet's death. There may also have been a volume of elegiac verse in circulation. Beyond that it was impossible to say (pp. 21–4). Finally, Wheeler differed pointedly with Wilamowitz in denying the presence of order throughout the collection. At best, there were some "twelve or fifteen" instances of either contiguous grouping or separative patterning, "rather simple devices of arrangement" that might be attributed to Catullus, but planlessness was the rule. The text had suffered too much in the course of transmission during the first two hundred years to preserve more than those few sequences (pp. 26–31). For English-speaking critics during the middle years of the twentieth century, Wheeler's negative conclusions set limits to further discussion; Fordyce's popular school edition reiterates them without real argument (1961: 409–10). To doubt such a competent appraisal may well have seemed intellectually irresponsible.

Charting the *liber Catulli*

As the foregoing remarks reveal, early attempts to grapple with *die Catullfrage* were burdened with preconceived notions about the way in which poems in an authorially ordered *libellus* would be set out. When scholars began investigating how ancient writers did organize their poetry books, using Augustan *libelli* as evidence, they discovered strategies of arrangement that seemed to hold as well for parts of the *liber Catulli*.

Variatio, according to Kroll (1924), was the primary aim of all Roman compilers, even those putting together collections not their own, like the *Catalepton* attributed to Vergil. Genre permitting, metrical diversity was a basic organizing principle, as indicated by the display of lyric meters at the beginning of Horace's *Odes* Book 1, the 12 so-called "*Paradeoden*." Single-meter collections, such as those of the elegists, strove for contrasts in mood and situation. The tendency, beginning in Hellenistic times, to combine motifs from previously distinct genres ("*die Kreuzung der Gattungen*") made variety possible even in prose collections, such as the letters of the younger Pliny, and allowed thematic complexity in poetic arrangements.

Wilhelm Port asserted the aesthetic integrity and harmony of Augustan poetry collections, whose individual pieces were bound together "like flowers in a garland" (1926: 280). His survey of representative works – Vergil's *Eclogues*; Horace's *Satires*, *Odes*, and *Epistles*; Tibullus' elegies; Ovid's *Amores* – called attention to certain recurrent formal features (pp. 456–61):

- Ensembles (*libelli*) comprised of multiples of five or ten poems.
- Partition of poetry books into two symmetrical halves.
- The close relationship and function of the *Einleitungsgedicht* (opening poem) and the *Schlußgedicht* (closing poem). The former often dedicates the book to a designated individual. At the same time, it makes a programmatic statement about the contents, sometimes including a defense of artistic principles. The latter can echo, or otherwise allude to, the opening poem; it may contain biographical information about the author, as a kind of signature.[3]
- Ring-composition as a structuring principle of the whole, with the most significant pieces usually located at the beginning or end of the book.
- The midpoint of the book as yet another location where major statements, especially of a dedicatory or programmatic nature, can be situated.[4]
- *Variatio* in form, meter, and/or content as a determining factor in the placement of individual poems: through separation of related pieces, the arrangement strives for the greatest possible degree of counterpoint.
- In lengthier poetry books, collection of poems into shorter groups and *uariatio* among groupings. Two adjacent poems may be closely connected; sets of three usually follow the principle of separative patterning (A-B-A); sets of four can alternate (A-B-A-B) or be chiastic (A-B-B-A).

Twenty-five years later, Bruno Heck sought to apply Kroll's and Port's findings to the *liber Catulli* by attempting to produce, for the first time, a complete schematic plan of the entire corpus. In his Tübingen dissertation (1951), proposed patterns are first explained verbally and then laid out in complicated visual diagrams. Although critics have objected that the resulting taxonomies are capricious and far too involved to serve as feasible schemes of organization (Coppel 1973: 157; Most 1981: 110; Beck 1996: 66 and n. 199), the various approaches employed have been widely adopted.

Heck begins with observations on the tripartite arrangement of the collection. Pieces linked by meter, diction, or length are grouped together (1–60; 61–8; 69–116), and the most ambitious works, poems 61–8, occupy a position of honor at the center, flanked by two subgroups of closely related poems. The goal of his investigation is to determine whether these aesthetic principles governing the layout of the whole *liber Catulli* also obtain for sequences within the three parts (p. 31). In the polymetric section one prevailing objective is metrical variety, with the poems in other meters distributed strikingly among the hendecasyllabics. This section is subdivided into two parts, poems 2–31 and poems 32–60, which correspond to each other in approximate number of lines and in similar metrical arrangements. Within the whole section, Heck also traces out four successive clusters of poems in which patterns of thematic response are reinforced by the controlling placement of non-hendecasyllabic poems. The first of these, poems 2–13, depicting the progress of the Lesbia affair, is succeeded by three other groups organized around other key concerns of the author's life, their mood edging toward distress in the closing poems. Poems 29–31, three consecutive pieces in exceptional meters (the only sequence of this kind in the polymetrics), stand midway between the first two and the last two groupings, articulating a range of Catullan preoccupations: political corruption, failed friendship, the frustrations of the journey to Bithynia. *Variatio*, finally, is in evidence throughout: "Within units and groups, Catullus sometimes applies the principle of interruption ('Sperrung'), then again that of symmetrical placement; sometimes he puts related poems next to each other, and then again poems of heterogeneous content," so as to convey the story of his life without becoming tedious (p. 61). Heck's scheme for the polymetrics thus sweepingly integrates metrical, mathematical, thematic, and biographical/chronological models of organization.

The epigrams in the third section accord in content and style with the poems of the initial section (p. 65), although metrical distribution is of course no longer a factor. Within this section, too, Heck finds a structural and thematic division. Poems 69–92 are a well-integrated group of epigrams, set out in formal patterns of contrast and correspondence, which analyze Catullus' combined love and hate for Lesbia with growing urgency while mounting scathing attacks on her lovers. Some humorous pieces, such as poems 78 and 84, are interjected to provide relief from tension. Poems 88–91, successive thrusts at Gellius, build to a climax that unites the previously distinct themes of Lesbia's infidelity and of betrayal by false friends. The next quatrain, poem 92, last of the epigrams in this group, looks back to the *odi et amo* ("I hate and love") dilemma, closing the ring (p. 72). In contrast, poems 93–116 seem more disparate thematically, but Heck points out the unusual number of poems linked by similar motifs in this group, both juxtaposed as a pair (e.g., 93 and 94, 110 and 111) and separated by a contrasting poem (e.g., 107 and 109). As his visual diagrams indicate, Heck's model of arrangement for the first subgroup of epigrams is sequential, following the development of thought and emotion as it unfolds from one poem to the next (p. 73); for the second subgroup it becomes architectonic, defined by consecutively matched and separated poems (p. 80a).

The arrangement of the *carmina maiora* ("longer poems") in the middle of the *liber Catulli* is relatively straightforward. There are eight poems (68 counts as one poem): an epithalamium in glyconic stanzas, another in hexameters, a short mythic epyllion in galliambics, a long epyllion in hexameters, and four poems of assorted content in elegiacs. The change from the shorter polymetrics to the lengthier pieces is aptly bridged by poem 61, since glyconics are related metrically to hendecasyllabics and other lyric verse forms, while the two hexameter poems are separated by one in the rare galliambic meter. Poems 61–4 are associated thematically as well as metrically, two wedding hymns – one vividly Roman and personal, one Hellenizing and artificial – followed by two mythic narratives. Poem 64, Catullus' most ambitious work, returns to the theme of marriage by describing Peleus and Thetis' wedding; it is set off from the first two epithalamia by the tale of Attis, who rejects physical love and manhood. The second, elegiac half of the *carmina maiora* is dominated by the two verse epistles 65 and 68, preoccupied with the loss of a brother and the desire to send a poem to a deserving friend. Poem 66, a translation of Callimachus' *Lock of Berenice*, follows 65, its transmittal letter; this elegy is in turn connected to 67 through the device of an inanimate speaker, in the first poem a lock of hair and in the second a house door. The juxtaposition of 66 and 67 points an ironic contrast between the Alexandrian court and the daily life of a Roman town; by returning us to the present, the latter prepares us for Catullus' confessions of private feeling, his grief over his brother and his continued passion for Lesbia, in the second verse epistle, 68 (pp. 83–9). For the whole collection of poems, Heck concludes, the Lesbia affair, with its simultaneous experience of love and hate, is the governing concept creating thematic unity.

This analysis, it is obvious, is indebted both to Kroll's insistence on *uariatio* as an aesthetic rule of Augustan poetic collections and to Port's remarks on other formal features of those collections. Clusters of poems, symmetrical distribution, architectonic structuring, placement of major poems in a central or pivotal position, ring-composition, thematic and metrical parallelism – all these theoretically available patterns of arrangement are integrated into Heck's explanations. Such a barrage of abstract models brought into play all at once could not help but produce outcomes of questionable complexity. Yet, whether or not we deem Heck's results plausible, it will repay us to take a closer look at the models themselves and how they dictated the internal mapping strategies of the next generation of researchers seeking to establish Catullan editorship.

Aesthetic Axioms

Investigation of meaningful patterns within the *liber Catulli* requires the researcher to postulate one or more principles of organization. Chronological arrangement has been ruled out ever since critics stopped regarding Catullus' work as a kind of poetic blog. As we saw, one model that took its place was that of the cycle or cluster: the polymetric collection, and perhaps the epigrams as well, might be organized as sequences of poems linked by subject matter though not necessarily juxtaposed. Heck perceived clusters only in the polymetrics, but Barwick (1958) defined five cycles organized around main characters, three in the polymetrics – Lesbia (cc. 2, 3, 5,

7, 8, 11); Furius and Aurelius (cc. 15, 16, 21, 23, 24, 26); Veranius and Fabullus (cc. 9, 12, 13, 28, 47) – and two in the epigrams, Gellius (cc. 74, 80, 88, 89, 90, 91, 116) and Mentula (cc. 94, 105, 114, 115). Other scholars subsequently chimed in with several additional cycles and mini-cycles built upon themes and tropes as well as persons.[5] Objections soon followed. Since the notion of "cycle" is ill-defined, any repetition of name or coincidence of motif is easily pressed into creating a cyclic linkage, however strained. Furthermore, this formula fails to account for the placement of poems *within* a series or the presence of extraneous pieces in the collection that appear to have no relationship to others. It has been pronounced too fuzzy, then, to serve as a controlling principle of organization (Wiseman 1969: 3–4). While the presence of clearly structured sequences at the beginning of the polymetric collection – the "Lesbia" and the "Furius–Aurelius" cycles – is now, as we will see, generally accepted, various attempts to project such patterns onto the rest of the corpus have not earned the same degree of recognition.

For the polymetric section, arrangement by meter seems a hypothetical possibility, and investigators have accordingly put forth metrically based schemes of organization. H. J. Mette (1956) proposed that pieces in alternating aeolic and iambic measures were set out in three unequal concentric circles around the core-poems 11, 31, and 51 – two compositions in Sapphic strophes and one in choliambs. The correlations he drew, though, appeared more ingenious than convincing, since his quasi-symmetrical units differed in number of lines and colometric structure. Placement of non-hendecasyllabic pieces is also essential to Dion's (1993) analysis of polymetric design, as her "ensembles" are marked off, frequently but not always, by the occurrence of an iambic poem in the final position. Again, though, her groupings might appear more ingenious than natural. Jocelyn (1999) recently revived the notion of a purely metrical arrangement. He divides the meters of poems 1–61[6] into three distinct groups: the "Phalaecian" (hendecasyllabic) epigrams, the poems in iambs, and the *melē*, or poems in lyric measures (cc. 11, 17, 30, 34, 51, 61). Linguistic and stylistic features of the latter poems, belonging to a higher register, deviate markedly from the more conventional language of the Phalaecian verses and the iambs. These six pieces are distributed at regular intervals among the other items in what Jocelyn believes to be a formal arrangement obvious to an ancient reader. Yet he leaves the question of the designer open, stating that "a scholarly editor aware of the generic distinctions of verse writing would seem at least as likely as the poet" to have been responsible (p. 341). Since Jocelyn excludes considerations of meaning from his discussion, and indeed seems to doubt whether thematic coherence is present at all in the corpus, his observations on the disposition of poems, though tantalizing, remain inconclusive.

With Otto Skutsch's discovery of metrical variations in the first foot of the hendecasyllabic line (1969), a different scheme of arrangement emerged. The opening foot of the hendecasyllable, termed the "aeolic base," is normally spondaic; in Catullus' successors, such as Martial, spondees are the rule. Greek metrical practice, however, permitted the substitution of an iamb or trochee, and the poets of Catullus' generation allowed themselves the same freedom.[7] In the polymetric section of the *liber Catulli*, the position of poems having at least one non-spondaic, or "lighter," base is unexpected, as they are not scattered throughout. If the dedication to Nepos is excluded, this section falls into two parts: the first, poems 2 through 26, contains 263 hendecasyllabic lines, of which only three have an iambic, and none a trochaic, base;[8] in the 279 lines of the second part, poems 27 to 60, there are 33 iambic and 30 trochaic bases. The dedicatory poem has one iambic and three trochaic bases in ten lines, conforming to metrical practice in the second half of the polymetrics. Since the dedication would have been composed later than the rest of the poems, the roughly chronological placement of the hendecasyllabics suggests a change in technique. For this part of the collection, there seems to be a correlation between metrical and thematic arrangements; the shift to lighter bases occurs after poem 26, reinforcing Barwick's contention that a cycle of poems ends there.

Two other Latinists immediately perceived the implications of this find. Kenneth Quinn noted that the dedication to Nepos must therefore have introduced a volume containing *both* groups of hendecasyllabics: "That the arrangement of the hendeca-syllabic poems is due to an editor, who sandwiched 2–26 in between 1 and 27–58, or hit upon the idea for himself of arranging the poems in accordance with this minor variation in metrical usage, can be ruled out" (1972b: 14; cf. 1973b: 387). T. P. Wiseman took conjecture a step further: poems apparently written just after Catullus' return from Bithynia in the spring of 56 BC contain no lighter bases, but those datable to 55–54 BC do. In the first half of the polymetrics, all three instances of a non-spondaic base occur in the "Lesbia cycle" (at lines 2.4, 3.17 and 7.2). Wiseman accordingly dates the affair itself to the period between late 56 and early 54 BC (1974: 109–10). When the book was compiled, certain Lesbia poems were placed at the beginning for special emphasis, at the price of metrical uniformity.

Skutsch's observation strengthened existing belief that the poems at the beginning of the collection were disposed in architectonic patterns that contribute to meaning. According to Barwick, the course of the affair is reflected in the positioning of the matching poems that constitute the Lesbia cycle, as the spacing between the elements of each pair increases (1958: 312). Segal (1968) elaborated on this insight by tracing out the progression of the six Lesbia pieces from lightheartedness to disillusionment and rejection. He noted, moreover, that poems 2–11 could also be divided into two pentads in which the poems *not* concerned with Lesbia still corresponded to and cross-referenced each other. Barwick likewise pointed out formal correspondences between the triad of poems attacking Aurelius (15, 16, 21) and those directed at Furius (23, 24, 26), apparently intended to drive home resemblances between the two cronies (p. 315). E. A. Schmidt drew thematic parallels between the poems that made up the Furius–Aurelius cycle and the intervening poems 17, 22, and 25 (1973: 220–1). Finally, Schmidt asserted that the arrangement of poems 9, 12, and 13, which feature Catullus' friends Veranius and Fabullus, associates those figures with Lesbia but also mirrors the triadic layout of the Aurelius and Furius sequences, serving as a structural pivot (pp. 224–5). Coincidence of metrical disposition and architectonic design thus induced perceptions of tight logical patterning, which have convinced many that Catullus indeed arranged this one section of his *libellus* – but have also prompted recent attempts to truncate the whole.

The structures of Catullus' longer poems have frequently been analyzed as speci-mens of ring-composition (Thomson 1961; Wiseman 1974: 59–76; Traill 1988). Search for circular configuration has also been extended to parts of the corpus: for example, Most (1981) explains Catullus' *carmina maiora* as a series of concentric rings balanced symmetrically around poem 64, which through its mythic vignettes recapitulates the themes of the poems that surround it. Others have sought to trace annular patterns from first poem to last. Helena Dettmer published her master-plan of the collection in 1997. That scheme consists of nine successive rings of thematically related pieces – five rings in the polymetrics, one ring of longer poems, three rings in the epigrams – and a five-poem tag at the end. Associations between related items are determined by a variety of factors: dramatis personae, verbal echoes, thematic parallels or inversions, lesser motifs. Structural design is reinforced by a network of mathematical symmetries; corresponding units are shown to have equivalent numbers of lines. Dettmer's blueprint, though unlike Heck's in its configurations, is just as complicated and, according to critics, labors under the same constraints. Three polymetric items (cc. 17, 30, and 48) find no counterpart in the plan and their presence has to be explained away (1997: 49–50, 63–4, 100–1). To make the numerical totals in the polymetrics come out, lacunae for which we have no evidence must be posited (pp. 246–7). "Themes" of certain poems are elastically defined in order to forge a contrived correspondence (Forsyth 1993: 495; Claes 2002: 22). Finally, as I myself have wondered (2003: 189 n. 24), how could the reader of a scroll, who would encounter just a portion of the text at any time, be in a position to grasp the intricacies of this layout?

New attention to the mechanics of the ancient reading process has encouraged the application of a linear strategy to the analysis of Greco-Roman poetry collections.[9] Although the possibility of concentric patterning is by no means excluded, in this model the underlying frame of reference is sequential, entailed by the physical act of unrolling and stretching out the papyrus scroll and the experience of assimilating exposed content one column at a time. As the reader peruses the collection, she relates each poem encountered to the preceding and following ones, imposing narrative unity on the whole by ascribing it to a single subjectivity, that of the first-person speaker.[10] For any one poem, though, a variety of potential narrative associations is possible, so each "can only be interpreted in terms of its dialogical relations with the other poems in the collection" (Miller 1994: 51). Accordingly, multiple readings of the text are admissible and the case for meaningful positioning can be presented as likely, but not certain.

Beck, as we saw, applied a linear strategy of reading to part, not all, of the corpus. Subsequent advocates of Catullan editorship used this method to trace lines of thematic development in other sections of the *liber Catulli*, such as the Lesbia cycle (Segal 1968; Rankin 1972), the polymetrics as a group (Clausen 1976;[11] Skinner 1981),[12] and, most notably, the longer poems. Godo Lieberg's pioneering study proposed to uncover the scheme of arrangement in 61 through 68 "passando di carme in carme," noting formal and thematic connections along the way (1958: 23). Relations among 61 through 64 were evident: three of the four poems deal with marriage and love between spouses, while 63, in contrast, depicts a young man seized by religious, as opposed to sexual, passion. There are, nevertheless, striking situational parallels between Attis in 63 and Ariadne in 64: both are overcome by *furor*; both stand on a beach lamenting their lost homelands; the emotional state of each figure is described in similar terms (pp. 32–4). While the elegiac poems 65 to 68 differ from the epithalamia and mythic narratives metrically and thematically, marriage is touched upon briefly in 66 and 67 and resurfaces as a motif at 68.143–6 when Catullus distinguishes his illegitimate union from genuine wedlock (pp. 46–7).

Starting at this point, Schäfer (1966: 73–7) proposed that the marriage theme runs continuously through *all* the longer poems, with the sole exception of 63; following him, Wiseman (1969: 20–5) argued that it was the main criterion of arrangement, since it builds to the crucial opposition of marriage and adultery in 68b. Lastly, Sandy's demonstration (1971) that Attis' fanatic self-surrender to Cybele is akin to a conjugal pledge has now fully justified, for some interpreters, the inclusion of 63 among the matrimonial poems: "it is a kind of anti-epithalamium" (Ferguson 1988: 34).

Is it possible to read the entire *liber Catulli*, from beginning to end, as a meaningful ensemble? Since the publication of *Catullan Questions* in 1969, T. P. Wiseman has been the most consistent and passionate advocate of that position and is responsible, more than any other scholar, for persuading the field of Catullan studies to reconsider Wheeler's arguments. After a theoretical consideration of the issues, Wiseman began his first Catullan monograph by dividing the polymetrics into three subsections: the Lesbia cycle (2–14); the Juventius cycle (15–26); and a set of primarily invective verses (28–60). The Juventius cycle was introduced by the programmatic poem 14a, warning the reader that poems of an "avowedly homosexual nature" would follow, the invective section by another programmatic poem, 27, which promised *calices amariores*, "bitterer cups" (1969: 7–8). Two subsidiary themes punctuate the Lesbia and Juventius cycles: urbanity and its opposite, vulgarity, and foreign travel, the latter providing a wider perspective on the poet's world. In the invective section, however, the reader is summoned back from such exotic places as Bithynia and Adriatic ports of call to Rome and its corrupt politics. Following the *carmina maiora* and their preoccupation with marriage, the epigrams fall into two divisions. Like Beck, Wiseman perceives an obvious break between 69–92, which combine the compulsively recurring topics of Lesbia's infidelity and betrayal of friendship with accusations of incest and oral sex, and 93–115, largely political, culminating in furious digs at the poet's arch-enemy "Mentula."[13] Interlocking sequences in the first half terminate in revelations that the invective target – Rufus, Gellius – has been Lesbia's lover, but the political squibs in the second half are more casually associated and interspersed with unrelated occasional poems (25–9). In this way, Wiseman showed it was possible to follow a plausible unfolding line of narrative in the *liber Catulli*.

Although insisting that Catullus had published all three parts of the collection himself, Wiseman admitted certain difficulties with that hypothesis. The volume containing the *carmina maiora*, 61 through 68, would have been considerably longer than the other two. Moreover, several verbal similarities in the putatively independent epigram book seemed to be explicit cross-references to poem 68. Three years later, Kenneth Quinn's *Catullus: An Interpretation* offered an alternative scenario. Once Süss had pointed out the dedicatory aspects of poem 65 and the repetition of *carmina Battiadae* in 65 and 116, some critics preferred to separate 65–8 from the *carmina maiora* and regard them as a prologue to the epigrams. Quinn made the case for that more balanced division of the *liber Catulli*. He also drew a correspondence between Cornelius Nepos' three volumes of world history, "learned and labored" (*doctis . . . et laboriosis*, 1.7), and a hypothetical three-volume collected edition of Catullus' poems, which the dedication to Nepos would have introduced (1972b: 9–20). In the last chapter of *Clio's Cosmetics*, Wiseman espoused that solution, reinforcing it with the observation that one or more of the Muses would then receive mention in each of the three opening poems (1.9, <o> *patrona uirgo*, "patron virgin"; 61.2, *Uraniae genus*, "child of Urania"; 65.2, *doctis...uirginibus*, "learned virgins"). Furthermore, the continuity between the marriage theme as developed in the second book and its resumption in the elegies might give even more reason to suppose that these volumes were published together (1979: 176–9).

Catullus and His World: A Reappraisal contributed a more detailed sequential reading of the Lesbia poems. At the outset, Wiseman distinguishes between two stages of linear comprehension: "that of the first-time reader of the collection, recognising the 'Lesbia' relationship as a major theme and having his insight into it progressively developed as he proceeds; and that of the returning reader, who knows what comes afterwards, and can use his knowledge to pick up cross-references in both directions" (1985: 137). The stance he himself adopts is that of the first-time reader gradually learning more about Lesbia, and about Catullus' psychological and emotional involvement with her. As the poems unfold, they tell a story of self-delusion and bleak realization. The cycle on Lesbia provides a narrative framework; the polymetrics from 28 to 60 reveal the scope of her degradation. In 68b, the most extended treatment of the love affair, Catullus gives full expression to his fantasies, casting his mistress as goddess and bride. The epigrams proceed to expose the futility of his hopes through a "long fugue of love, hate and self-justification" (p. 171). Near the end of the epigram collection, however, poem 107 surprisingly hints at reconciliation, and poem 109 appears to depict Lesbia at last "offering love on Catullus' terms" (p. 174). The poet has therefore chosen to leave the story open-ended, something we as readers must accept. This is, of course, one man's private construction of a "plot" (and one with which I would partly disagree), but it nevertheless shows again that sense can be made of the Lesbia poems read in order. We must ask ourselves, then, whether such an imaginative exercise was a task that Catullus the author might have set his readers. Would it have been possible for a Roman artist to have conceived of a poetry book laid out as a Borghesian "garden of forking paths,"[14] or, to use a more familiar analogy, a hypertext? That is a question that goes beyond the conventional debate over *die Catullfrage*.

New Directions

The old posthumous editor – at least, the one who supposedly put together the entire Catullan collection, or reorganized it from scratch – has not been much in evidence since the mid-1970s.[15] Apart from Jocelyn, who straddles the fence, the last firm denials of Catullan arrangement in its entirety were those of Coppel (1973: 141–84) and Goold (1973: 8–10), both of whom mainly reiterated the arguments of Brunér and Wheeler.[16] We find instead an increasing willingness to harbor the notion that some parts of the *liber Catulli* may indeed preserve authorial arrangements. Syndikus, for example, describes the opening sequence as an "Ouvertüre" sounding major themes and recognizes other key groupings in the polymetrics and epigrams, even though he dismisses as misguided efforts to find cyclic patterning throughout the corpus (1984: 52–62). In D. F. S. Thomson's view, Heck's arguments for planned order "faltered" as they approached the end of the *liber Catulli*, and those of his successors "have tended to induce in those who follow them a similar feeling of *decrescendo.*" Yet he adds, "All the same, who has not been struck, independently, by the tight coherence and pleasing balance of the first few poems when they are read together? This surely must be C.'s doing" (1997: 6–7). Where, then, is the author's hand no longer evident, and what considerations might enable us to draw the line?

In 1983, T. K. Hubbard attempted to scale back the size of the Catullan *libellus*. He contended that the volume dedicated to Nepos was a *libellus* in the true sense, containing only poems 1 through 14, whose tone and structure were unified in a manner distinct from the other polymetra.[17] Poems 1 and 14 balance each other as *Einleitungs-* and *Schlußgedicht*, each involving the presentation of a book of verse, framing the collection "with positive and negative paradigms of [Catullus'] poetic doctrine" (p. 227). Pieces in between are set out in concentric patterns both thematic and metrical. On the assumption that 2b was a fragment of a separate poem, the book would have contained 15 pieces, arranged in multiples of five, each with its own prevailing subject matter and tone. Numerous verbal cross-references can be traced among the texts in each pentad. Read sequentially, moreover, both the six Lesbia poems and the occasional poems that punctuate them display "a very tight linear unity," organized around themes of foreign travel and gift-giving (p. 230). As for 14b, Hubbard at that time regarded it as the fragmentary prologue to a second *libellus* ending with poem 50, but did not inquire closely into the design of that further volume.

Hubbard's article is undoubtedly the chief contribution to the debate since Skutsch's metrical discovery and Wiseman's *Catullan Questions*, for numerous subsequent studies take its thesis as a point of departure. Stroh (1990) modified Hubbard's scheme, extending the *libellus* to incorporate fragment 14b and the Juventius poems 15–26; those poems, he argued, replicate the concentric arrangement of the preceding sequence so exactly that they must balance it. The paradigmatic edition of Catullus' verse therefore presents us with two equivalent and contrasting love affairs, one sentimental and earnest, the other coarse and trifling.[18] Jan-Wilhelm Beck advanced an opposing hypothesis. He put forth arguments for *two* published Catullan *libelli*, one featuring Lesbia (poems 2–14) and the other Furius, Aurelius, and Juventius (poems 14a–26); the latter volume is an ironic and self-parodic response to criticism of the former (1996: 154–223). While Scherf preserves the integrity of the entire polymetric group, he posits 2–14 as the first and 14a–26 as the second of four hendecasyllabic sequences defined by treatment of the aeolic base (1996: 78–81). Dettmer, though envisioning a somewhat different configuration of the poems, agrees with Hubbard in maintaining that the first 14 poems are connected by simultaneous schemes of concentric responsion and linearity (1997: 13–40). Holzberg, like Scherf, designates poems 1–14 and poems 14a–26 as the first two "blocks" of the polymetric segment, although he bases these divisions on thematic, rather than metrical, grounds (2002a: 73–7). Hubbard's reconstruction of the *libellus* was heavily influenced by Skutsch's demonstration of a break in metrical technique between 2–26 and 27–58, and most of these corollary investigations also cite that phenomenon as evidence. The presence of uniformly spondaic aeolic bases (apart from three admitted exceptions in the Lesbia cycle) in combination with annular patterning, then, is the one significant feature that, in the minds of conservative critics, now serves to define the limits of Catullan editorship.

Attempts to curtail the part(s) of the collection arranged by the author – to reduce the *Passer* to a hummingbird, as it were – have been countered by proposals from those who continue to search for order throughout the collection, or in other sections of the *liber Catulli*. In two short articles (1986a and 1986b), Ferguson essayed sketchy linear readings of the polymetrics and epigrams, illustrating them with diagrams of cyclic and thematic linkages.[19] King (1988) argued that poems 65 through 116 were an assortment of elegies and shorter epigrams inspired by "Callimachean" themes. For Scherf (1996), metrical organization of those two sections establishes Catullan editorship: the hendecasyllabics are grouped according to frequency of lighter bases, while the longer elegiac poems 65, 66, and 68, which differ from the epigrams in terms of greater metrical refinement, precede the latter because they are more closely associated with the "neoteric" epyllia 63 and 64.[20] Claes contends that the fundamental principle of arrangement in the corpus is "extreme variation" (2002: 23–4) and relies upon "concatenation," a combination of linear reading and pursuit of thematic and lexical parallelism, to establish unity. Holzberg (2002a) presents a linear reading of the entire collection as a "voyage of discovery." Skinner (2003) sequentially reads the elegiac poems 65 through 116 as a virtually intact second *libellus* whose dominant theme is valedictory. In the introductory suite of five longer poems, Catullus writes from Verona to friends in the metropolis, justifying his poetic silence by his bereavement; the epigrams cite the corrosion of politics and language to explain why he is taking leave of Rome, his readers, and his art. Lastly, Hubbard (2005) reconsiders the possibility that the poet might have issued other *libelli*. Hubbard studies poems 14b to 51 as an arranged collection in which homoerotic and invective themes predominate and poems 65 through 116 as a *libellus* with an internal movement analogous to that of 68b, where the speaker's lament for his dead brother becomes the emotive turning point of the composition.

Conclusion

On the matter of Catullan arrangement, scholarly progress has moved glacially and without the impetus of global warming. Yet, after a century and a half, some limited consensus seems to have been reached. Whether they stipulate that the *libellus* ended with poem 14 or extend it to include the Juventius poems, Catullan scholars now appear to agree that the opening sequence(s) of the polymetric section are elegantly structured according to a combination of metrical and thematic principles, and that Catullus himself is responsible for that design. We may, accordingly, identify this segment of the corpus with the *libellus* dedicated to Nepos, as a whole or in part. Dispute continues over the layout of the remaining polymetric poems; there is certainly no agreement on whether they continue the *libellus*, represent another organized volume or volumes, or were gathered together and added posthumously. The *carmina maiora* probably circulated first as independent poems, but who compiled them may never be known. Finally, the elegiac poems are beginning to receive the same amount of attention formerly directed toward the polymetrics. They too seem to display interesting features: stylistic and metrical contrasts between the longer opening elegies and the epigrams, and patterned arrangement of the first

25 epigrams succeeded by looser correlations among the remaining ones. Recent papyrus discoveries, particularly the new Posidippus (*P. Mil. Vogl. VIII* 309), contribute to the debate – by providing evidence of how published Hellenistic poetry collections were structured (Hutchinson 2003) and, more disturbingly, by perhaps calling the notion of a "controlling author as editor and architect" into question (Barchiesi 2005: 341). In the next 150 years we may finally see a satisfactory resolution of *die Catullfrage*. Or not.

NOTES

1 Brunér postulates two *libelli*, one issued in 58 BC containing most of the Lesbia poems, the other – identified with the *libellus* dedicated to Nepos – which came out in 54, shortly before the poet's death. The longer poems, he believes, were published later by the poet's friends (pp. 651–2).

2 Wheeler calculated this figure using hypothetical columns of 8 by 5 inches containing 25 verses each. Though his estimate stood for a long time as the last word on the issue, it was recently reconsidered on the basis of further papyrus discoveries. Because those papyri indicate that both column width and number of verses per column were variable, Minyard thinks that the Catullan *Liber* might have been held in a roll "of little more than 20 feet" (1988: 345).

3 Kranz would later term the closing poetic self-reference a *sphragis* (1961).

4 See further Conte on "proems in the middle" (1992).

5 Thus E. A. Schmidt designated poems 31, 35, 36, 37, 42, 44 as a cycle of apostrophes to inanimate objects (1973: 221–4); Forsyth identified 41–3 as an "Ameana cycle" (1977a) and 82, 100, 110, and 111 as a "Quintius and Aufillina" cycle (1980–1); poems 4, 10, 31, and 46 are thought by some to form a "return from Bithynia" cycle (Thomson 1978: 213). The fact that the same poems can be assigned to different cycles betrays the subjectivity of the criteria applied.

6 Despite its length, Jocelyn includes the epithalamium for Manlius Torquatus in this first part of the corpus, since its metrical system is almost identical to that of poem 34: both are written in stanzas of glyconics followed by a pherecratean. For supporting evidence from the *testimonia* to Calvus, see Butrica in this volume (pp. 20–2).

7 See Loomis (1972: 60–1) and Scherf (1996: 75–6).

8 The MS reading *illud* admits a trochee into the first foot of 3.12, but Skutsch, for other reasons, prefers spondaic *illuc* (pp. 39–40)

9 See the special issue of *Arethusa* 13.1 (1980) on Augustan poetry books and, in particular, Van Sickle's influential article "The Book-Roll and Some Conventions of the Poetic Book" for how the concrete features of the scroll shape content and arrangement.

10 Lee-Stecum (1998: 1–6) connects the sequential reading approach with the theory of the reader's gradual construction of meaning (and re-evaluation of perceptions through rereading) advocated by the "reader-response" school of literary criticism; on this pregnant affiliation, see also Skinner (2003: xxxi).

11 On the basis of what seems to be Martial's citation of a Catullan book title at 4.14.13–14 (*sic forsan tener ausus est Catullus/magno mittere passerem Maroni*), Clausen (1976: 39) suggested that the title of the volume dedicated to Nepos was the *Passer*. This possibility was strongly endorsed by Skinner (1981: 12–13) and W. R. Johnson (1982: 108–23) and has been accepted by other researchers (Hubbard 1983: 236; Syndikus 1984: 55; Gratwick 1991). For a more skeptical view, see Butrica, this volume.

12 Sequential reading of the polymetrics as a *libellus* created doubt that the final, somewhat mixed group of poems in the MSS (51 or 52 to 60) had been included in the original volume. Clausen (1976: 40) thought the book ended with 50, while Skinner, taking 51 as a poetological statement rather than a love poem, interpreted the problematic fourth stanza as a *sphragis* (1981: 85–91). Assuming that the last few poems were later tacked on to the complete volume accounts for their heterogeneity and for the fragmentary quality of 58b and 60; on the other hand, it requires us to suppose that 57 was suppressed by the author, while 29 was not, and that 55 and 58 – both of which we would be sorry to lose – were also excluded for some unknown reason. I confess that I am still not completely comfortable with either option.

13 Because of its metrical anomalies, Wiseman dismissed poem 116 as a spurious addition to the epigram book, but was later convinced (by Macleod 1973) that it is in fact an "inverse dedication" and thus a suitable piece with which to end the collection.

14 The title of a well-known story by Jorge Luis Borges, which envisions a novel in which all the possible outcomes of any one decision are realized. Miller (1994: 75–6) applies this metaphor to the Catullan collection.

15 Micaela Janan contributes a fresh approach to the discussion: her denial of rational order in the collection is not based on philological grounds but dictated by the theoretical perspectives of Lacanian psychoanalysis, which postulate a fluid and amorphous Catullan "subject" (1994: ix–x).

16 Ten years later, Goold attempted to have it both ways, now attributing the layout of the hendecasyllabics 2–26 to Catullus himself, but claiming that the poems in other meters were inserted posthumously (1983: 236).

17 Pulbrook (1984) independently arrived at the conclusion that cc. 1–14 form the nucleus of a "Lesbia *libellus*," but theorized that the original volume would also have contained elegiac poems on Lesbia that were later extracted. One can object that the perceived coherence of this group of poems, which justifies making them the core of a *libellus*, would certainly have been disrupted by the hypothetical insertion of numerous epigrams.

18 Reconstruction of the poet's "erotisches Liederbuch" is ancillary, however, to Stroh's real pedagogical point: Catullus' enshrinement as a school author in German *gymnasia* preserves a distorted and misleading image of our author as an exponent of "das romantische Ideal einer Monogamie der freien Liebe" (1990: 148). For corollary issues surrounding the teaching of Catullus in North American and British schools, see Ancona and Hallett in this volume.

19 Ferguson gives a condensed plan of these arrangements in his 1998 survey of Catullan scholarship (pp. 12–16).

20 Here Scherf follows Ross's seminal demonstration of technical differences between "the neoteric elegiacs and the epigrams proper" (Ross 1969: 115–37); cf. Duhigg (1971).

GUIDE TO FURTHER READING

Students wishing to pursue this topic might begin by reading the initial chapter of Wheeler's *Catullus and the Traditions of Ancient Poetry* (1934: 1–32) and the first part of Wiseman's *Catullan Questions* (1969: 1–31), which present the two sides of the dispute in readily accessible form. Other contributions that have influenced present views include Clausen (1976), Dettmer (1997), Hubbard (1983), Skutsch (1969), and the special issue of *Classical World* 81.5 (1988). Barchiesi (2005) hypothesizes a multiplicity of Catullan *libelli* circulating in antiquity, including non-authorial compilations arranged to suit personal taste – a model far murkier than that assumed in this chapter, but one with which Butrica (this volume) might have agreed.

WORKS CITED

Barchiesi, A. 2005. "The Search for the Perfect Book: A PS to the New Posidippus." In K. Gutzwiller, ed., *The New Posidippus: A Hellenistic Poetry Book*. Oxford. 320–42.

Barwick, K. 1958. "Zyklen bei Martial und in den kleinen Gedichten des Catull." *Philologus* 102: 284–318.

Beck, J.-W. 1996. *"Lesbia" und "Juventius": Zwei libelli im Corpus Catullianum. Untersuchungen zur Publikationsform und Authentizität der überlieferten Gedichtfolge*. Göttingen.

Birt, T. 1882. *Das antike Buchwesen in seinem Verhältnis zur Litteratur*. Berlin. 2nd impression Aalen 1959.

Brunér, E. a. 1863. "De ordine et temporibus carminum Valerii Catulli." *Acta Societatis Scientiarum Fennicae* 7: 599–657.

Claes, P. 2002. *Concatenatio Catulliana: A New Reading of the* Carmina. Amsterdam.

Clausen, W. V. 1976. "*Catulli Veronensis Liber.*" *Classical Philology* 71: 37–43.

Conte, G. B. 1992. "Proems in the Middle." In F. M. Dunn and T. Cole, eds., *Beginnings in Classical Literature*. Yale Classical Studies vol. 29. Cambridge, MA. 147–59.

Coppel, B. 1973. *Das Alliusgedicht: Zur Redaktion des Catullcorpus*. Heidelberg.

Dettmer, H. 1997. *Love by the Numbers: Form and the Meaning in the Poetry of Catullus*. New York.

Dion, J. 1993. "La composition des 'carmina' de Catulle." *Bulletin de l'Association Guillaume Budé* 2: 136–57.

Duhigg, J. 1971. "The Elegiac Metre of Catullus." *Antichthon* 5: 57–67.

Ellis, R. 1889. *A Commentary on Catullus*. 2nd edn. Oxford.

Ferguson, J. 1986a. "The Arrangement of Catullus' Poems." *Liverpool Classical Monthly* 11.1: 2–6.

Ferguson, J. 1986b. "The Arrangement of Catullus' Poems." *Liverpool Classical Monthly* 11.2: 18–20.

Ferguson, J. 1988. *Catullus. Greece & Rome* New Surveys in the Classics No. 20. Oxford.

Fordyce, C. J., ed. 1961. *Catullus: A Commentary*. Oxford.

Forsyth, P. Y. 1977a. "The Ameana Cycle of Catullus." *Classical World* 70: 445–50.

Forsyth, P. Y. 1980–1. "Quintius and Aufillena in Catullus." *Classical World* 74: 220–3.

Forsyth, P. Y. 1993. "The Fearful Symmetry of Catullus' Polymetrics." *Classical World* 86: 492–5.

Fröhlich, J. 1843. "Über die Anordnung der Gedichte des Q. Valerius Catullus." *Abhandlung der königl. bayerische Akademie der Wissenschaften*, Philosophisch.-philologischen Kl. 3.3 (Munich). 691–716.

Goold, G. P. 1973. "Interpreting Catullus." Inaugural lecture delivered at University College, London. London.

Goold, G. P, ed. and trans. 1983. *Catullus*. London.

Gratwick, A. S. 1991. "Catullus 1.10 and the Title of His 'Libellus'." *Greece & Rome* 38.2: 199–202.

Heck, B. 1951. "Die Anordnung der Gedichte des Gaius Valerius Catullus." Dissertation. Tübingen.

Holzberg, N. 2002a. *Catull: Der Dichter und sein erotisches Werk*. Munich.

Hubbard, T. K. 1983. "The Catullan *Libellus.*" *Philologus* 127: 218–37.

Hubbard, T. K. 2005. "The Catullan *Libelli* Revisited." *Philologus* 149: 253–77.

Hutchinson, G. O. 2003. "The Catullan Corpus, Greek Epigram, and the Poetry of Objects." *Classical Quarterly* n.s. 53: 206–21.

Janan, M. 1994. "*When the Lamp Is Shattered*": *Desire and Narrative in Catullus*. Carbondale and Edwardsville, IL.

Jocelyn, H. D. 1999. "The Arrangement and the Language of Catullus' So-Called *polymetra* with Special Reference to the Sequence 10–11–12." In J. N. Adams and R. G. Mayer, eds., *Aspects of the Language of Latin Poetry* = Proceedings of the British Academy 93. Oxford. 335–75.

Johnson, W. R. 1982. *The Idea of Lyric: Lyric Modes in Ancient and Modern Poetry.* Berkeley.

King, J. K. 1988. "Catullus' Callimachean *carmina*, cc. 65–116." *Classical World* 81: 383–92.

Kranz, W. 1961. "SPHRAGIS: Ichform und Namensiegel als Eingangs- und Schlußmotiv antiker Dichtung." *Rheinisches Museum* 104: 3–46 and 97–124.

Kroll, W. 1924. *Studien zum Verständnis der römischen Literatur.* Stuttgart.

Kroll, W., ed. 1968 [1923]. *C. Valerius Catullus, herausgegeben und erklärt.* 5th edn. Stuttgart.

Lee-Stecum, P. 1998. *Powerplay in Tibullus.* Cambridge.

Lieberg, G. 1958. "L'ordinamento ed i reciproci rapporti dei carmi maggiori di Catullo." *Rivista di Filologia e di Istruzione Classica* 36: 23–47.

Loomis, J. W. 1972. *Studies in Catullan Verse: An Analysis of Word Types and Patterns in the Polymetra. Mnemosyne* Supplement 24. Leiden.

Macleod, C. 1973. "Catullus 116." *Classical Quarterly* 23: 304–9.

Mette, H. J. 1956. Review of E. V. Marmorale, *L'ultimo Catullo. Gnomon* 28: 34–8.

Miller, P. A. 1994. *Lyric Texts and Lyric Consciousness: The Birth of a Genre from Archaic Greece to Augustan Rome.* London and New York.

Minyard, J. D. 1988. "The Source of the *Catulli Veronensis Liber.*" *Classical World* 81: 343–53.

Most, G. 1981. "On the Arrangement of Catullus' *Carmina Maiora.*" *Philologus* 125: 109–25.

Port, W. 1926. "Die Anordnung in Gedichtbüchern augusteischer Zeit." *Philologus* 35: 280–308, 427–68.

Pulbrook, M. 1984. "The Lesbia *Libellus* of Catullus." *Maynooth Review* 10: 72–84.

Quinn, K. 1972b. *Catullus: An Interpretation.* London.

Quinn, K. 1973b. "Trends in Catullan Criticism." In H. Temporini, ed., *Aufstieg und Niedergang der römischen Welt.* Vol. I.3. Berlin and New York. 369–89.

Rankin, H. D. 1972. "The Progress of Pessimism in Catullus, Poems 2–11." *Latomus* 31: 744–51.

Ross, D. O., Jr. 1969. *Style and Tradition in Catullus.* Cambridge, MA.

Sandy, G. N. 1971. "Catullus 63 and the Theme of Marriage." *American Journal of Philology* 92: 185–95.

Schäfer, E. 1966. *Das Verhältnis von Erlebnis und Kunstgestalt bei Catull. Hermes* Einzelschriften 18. Wiesbaden.

Scherf, J. 1996. *Untersuchungen zur antiken Veröffentlichung der Catullgedichte. Spudasmata* 61. Hildesheim, Zurich, and New York.

Schmidt, B. 1914. "Die Lebenzeit Catulls und die Herausgabe seiner Gedichte." *Rheinisches Museum* 69: 267–83.

Schmidt, E. A. 1973. "Catulls Anordnung seiner Gedichte." *Philologus* 117: 215–42.

Schmidt, E. A. 1979. "Das Problem des Catullbuches." *Philologus* 123: 216–31.

Segal, C. 1968. "The Order of Catullus, Poems 2–11." *Latomus* 27: 305–21.

Skinner, M. B. 1981. *Catullus' Passer: The Arrangement of the Book of Polymetric Poems.* New York.

Skinner, M. B. 1988. "Aesthetic Patterning in Catullus: Textual Structures, Systems of Imagery and Book Arrangements. Introduction." *Classical World* 81: 337–40.

Skinner, M. B. 2003. *Catullus in Verona: A Reading of the Elegiac* Libellus, *Poems 65–116.* Columbus, OH.

Skutsch, O. 1969. "Metrical Variations and Some Textual Problems in Catullus." *Bulletin of the Institute of Classical Studies of the University of London* 16: 38–43.

Stroh, W. 1990. "Lesbia und Juventius: Ein erotisches Liederbuch im Corpus Catullianum." In P. Neukam, ed., *Die Antike als Begleiterin*. Klassische Sprachen und Literaturen Band XXIV. Munich. 134–58.

Süss, J. 1877. *Catulliana*. Erlangen.

Syndikus, H. P. 1984. *Catull: Eine Interpretation. Erster Teil: Einleitung, Die kleinen Gedichte (1–60)*. Darmstadt.

Thomson, D. F. S. 1961. "Aspects of Unity in Catullus 64." *Classical Journal* 57: 49–57.

Thomson, D. F. S., ed. 1978. *Catullus: A Critical Edition*. Chapel Hill, NC.

Thomson, D. F. S., ed. 1997. *Catullus, Edited with a Textual and Interpretative Commentary*. Toronto.

Traill, D. A. 1988. "Ring Composition in Catullus 63, 64, and 68b." *Classical World* 81: 365–9.

Van Sickle, J. 1980. "The Book-Roll and Some Conventions of the Poetic Book." *Arethusa* 13: 5–42.

Westphal, R. 1867. *Catulls Gedichte in ihrem geschichtlichen Zusammenhange übersetzt und erläutert*. 2nd edn. 1870. Breslau.

Wheeler, A. L. 1934. *Catullus and the Traditions of Ancient Poetry*. Berkeley and Los Angeles.

Wilamowitz-Moellendorff, U. von. 1913. *Sappho und Simonides*. Berlin.

Wiseman, T. P. 1969. *Catullan Questions*. Leicester.

Wiseman, T. P. 1974. *Cinna the Poet and Other Roman Essays*. Leicester.

Wiseman, T. P. 1979. *Clio's Cosmetics: Three Studies in Greco-Roman Literature*. Leicester.

Wiseman, T. P. 1985. *Catullus and His World: A Reappraisal*. Cambridge.

PART II

Contexts of Production

CHAPTER FOUR

The Valerii Catulli of Verona

T. P. Wiseman

The Transpadanes

aut Transpadanus, ut meos quoque attingam

or a Transpadane, to mention my own folk too
(39.13)

The lands beyond the Padus had once been the territories of the Insubres, the Cenomani, and other Gallic peoples, but in 101 BC they were overrun by the invading Cimbri, a disaster which effectively wiped out the Gallic communities. After the Cimbri had been defeated the lands were settled by ex-soldiers, whose status was regularized 12 years later by a grant of the *ius Latii*. The old tribal *oppida* were now *coloniae*, with full Roman citizenship conferred on their ex-magistrates (Asc. 3C; Caes. *B Civ.* 3.87.4).

The colonists worked hard to make their raw frontier towns something to be proud of; we get a glimpse of the process in Catullus' poem 17, about the *colonia* (not Verona) that needed a new bridge over the marsh. Verona itself was a stronghold in a bend of the river Athesis, guarding the point where the great military road from Genua to Aquileia – the Via Postumia, built in 148 BC – crossed the north–south route over the Brenner pass by which the Cimbri had come. But we know that its walls, gates, and sewers were not finished until after 49 BC, when Caesar granted all the colonists full Roman citizenship (Wiseman 1987: 328–34).

In Catullus' time the colonists were subject to a proconsul, for until 42 BC all the land between the Apennines and the Alps was the province of Gallia Cisalpina (the province that thought "Ameana" beautiful, 43.6). But their lands were wide and proverbially fertile (Polyb. 2.15.1–3), and many of them, including the poet's father, were rich and influential people. The candidates for office who made the journey to ask for their votes still referred to the territory as Gallia (Cic. *Att.* 1.1.2, *Phil.* 2.76) – or perhaps *Gallia togata*, if you wanted to be polite (*Phil.* 8.27; Hirt.

B Gall. 8.24.3) – but that was only how it looked from Rome. The colonists themselves knew that they were Romans, not Gauls, and that their lands belonged to Italy, not a mere province. Caesar, who knew them well and recruited his Fifth Legion from them (Suet. *Iul.* 24.2), always supported their claim for full citizenship and granted it as one of his first acts as dictator. In the meantime, however, they defined themselves geographically as "those across the Padus," *Transpadani,* a term whose earliest attestation is Catullus' reference to his "own folk" (Fig. 4.1).

The great river that defined and fertilized the region also provided a highway to the Adriatic and the Greek world (Plin. *HN* 3.123). Verona's river-port was Hostilia (Tac. *Hist.* 3.9.1), where the road to Bononia and the south crossed the Padus by either a pontoon bridge or a ferry. From there one sailed via the southern branch of the Padus delta (Catull. 95.7; cf. Polyb. 2.16.11), by stages down the eastern coast of Italy, stopping perhaps at Ancona (c. 36.13) and "open Urii" on the Gargano peninsula (c. 36.12, with Wiseman 1969: 43–4), and across to Dyrrhachium, "the tavern of the Adriatic" (c. 36.15). It was by a familiar route that the *phaselus* brought Catullus home from the Cyclades (c. 4.6–7). In the other direction, the Via Postumia to Genua provided good communications with the western Mediterranean and the coast road to Narbonensis and Spain (Strab. 4.1.12).

Sharing a common origin and a common prosperity, the cities of Italia Transpadana seem to have thought of themselves not as rivals or natural enemies but as members of the same family ("Brixia, beloved mother of my Verona," c. 67.34). That sense of kinship was strong enough to survive Augustus' division of the area into two regions, *Transpadana* (*XI*) and *Venetia et Histria* (*X*); Brixia and Verona were in *regio X*, but

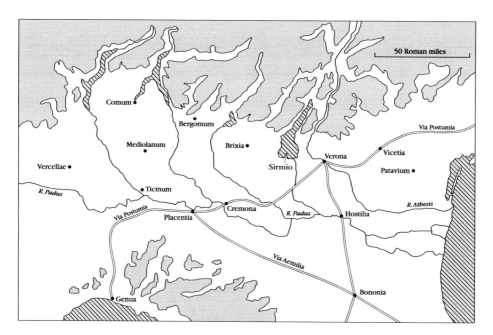

Figure 4.1   Transpadane Italy. The contour level is at 3,000 feet (910 m).

in AD 77 C. Plinius Secundus of Comum could refer to C. Valerius Catullus of Verona as his "fellow-landsman" (*HN* pref. 1, *conterraneum meum*), implying a Transpadane *terra* not defined by mere administrative boundaries. What the younger Pliny referred to as *regio mea* (*Ep.* 7.22.2) and Sir Ronald Syme liked to call "the Pliny country" (Syme 1979: 694–8) – evidently extending from Vercellae to Verona, and perhaps beyond – represented a traditional consciousness of identity that can already be detected in Catullus' references to friends and acquaintances at Comum (35.1–4) and Brixia (67.31–6).

Sirmio lay about half way between Verona and Brixia. At the extremity of a long peninsula projecting four kilometers out from the south shore of Lake Garda (*lacus Benacus*), today's little town is on the island created by a channel across the narrowest point. (See Fig. 4.2, p. 60.) Since it is called *insula* in a document of AD 774, five hundred years before the Scaligeri built their castle, I think we can assume that it was already an island in Roman times. Certainly it was one of the finest villa sites in the whole of Italy. It was surely there that Catullus' father entertained Caesar (Suet. *Iul.* 73), and there is no reason to doubt that the great villa whose remains survive today at the very tip of the island replaced in sumptuous style the home to which Catullus came joyfully back in 56 BC (Wiseman 1987: 335–6).

What exactly was Catullus doing in Bithynia? What was his brother doing in the Troad? What were Veranius and Fabullus doing in Spain? It's clear from poems 10 and 28 that they were hoping to make serious profits, and that they expected the proconsuls of those provinces to help them do it. But there is no hint of military service. These young men were not getting booty from conquest, as Mamurra so spectacularly did (c. 29.11–20), but exploiting the economic opportunities of long-pacified provinces. It is possible to detect in Catullus' poems the traditional values of a man who cared about profit and loss and balancing the accounts – a set of attitudes which may have been characteristic of a Transpadane upbringing (Wiseman 1985: 96–115).

Catullus settled in Rome (c. 68a.34–5), and died there (Jer. *Chron.* on 58–57 BC), but we don't know when. There is no reason to suppose that the surviving collection of poems is posthumous, and there is ample but neglected evidence for other poems, and plays, that may have been published later (Wiseman 1985: 189–98). At his brother's death the poet grieved "our whole house is buried with you" (c. 68b.94). We know how much the family meant to him (cc. 61.204–23, 68b.97–8, 72.4), and the implication is that at that point there was no one else to carry on the line. If we take seriously what he says about the brother's death making "the whole business" of love poetry impossible (c. 68a.19, *totum hoc studium*), we are entitled to infer a conscious change of life. My guess is that he married and had children.

The Valerii Catulli

We know of 12 individuals, besides the poet and (presumably) his father and brother, who bore the names Valerius Catullus or Valeria Catulla. Together they offer the possibility of a very fragmentary family history – and provide as well an object lesson in the variety of source material from which Roman social history must be constructed.

Figure 4.2   The north end of the Sirmione peninsula; the remains of the first-century villa are visible at the very tip. Photo by courtesy of Aeronautica militare (SMA n. 356–12 August 1981).

1   C. Valerius Catullus was named on the painted *titulus* of a Dressel type 7–11 amphora found in Rome in 1878 (*CIL* 15.4756); the lettering perished long ago, but the record of it is enough to attest an exporter of *garum* from southern Spain at some date between about 40 BC and AD 60 (Wiseman 1987: 340).
2   A reused third-century BC statue base on the Athenian acropolis (*IG* II² 4159) records the honorific statues put up by the Athenian *demos* to L. Valerius L. f. Catullus, "for the sake of his *arete* and *sophrosune*," and to his mother Terentia Cn. f. Hispulla. The Terentii Hispones were a family from Milan, active as *publicani* in Asia and Bithynia in the 50s BC (Cic. *Att.* 11.10.1, *Fam.* 13.65.1), and senatorial at least by the time of Tiberius (*AÉ* 1986.259).

3   One of the colleges of moneyers who struck *quadrantes* under Augustus consisted of P. Betilienus Bassus, C. Naevius Capella, C. Rubellius Blandus, and L. Valerius Catullus. The date of the college is difficult to determine, but the revised edition of *The Roman Imperial Coinage* puts it in 4 BC (Sutherland 1984: 78), which is consistent with Rubellius Blandus' consulship in AD 18 (Syme 1988: 183–4).

4   The suffect consuls who took office on May 9, AD 31, were Faustus Cornelius Sulla and Sex. Tedius Valerius Catullus (*CIL* 14.2466, *Fasti Ostienses*). The latter's name is spelt "Teidius" in the *Fasti Nolani* and the *Fasti* of the Arval Brethren, and that is probably the correct version; a late Republican senator Sex. Teidius is known, and another Sex. Teidius was patron of Cyme in the province of Asia (Syme 1991: 492–3). A dedication inscription from Lanuvium, now lost but reliably reported in the seventeenth century (*CIL* 14.2095), gives the consul the filiation L. f. and allows the inference of a son [L(?). Valerius] Catullus who was a *pontifex* (Fig. 4.3).

5   Suetonius (*Calig.* 36.1) reports "Valerius Catullus, a young man of consular family" as boasting that he had been an active sexual partner of Caligula, and quite worn himself out on him.

6   L. Valerius Catullus Messallinus was consul *ordinarius* with Domitian in 73 (*CIL* 5.7239), consul II *suffectus* in 85 (*Fasti Ostienses*), and a notorious member of Domitian's advisory council (Tac. *Agr.* 45.1; Plin. *Ep.* 4.22.5; Juv. 4.113–22).

7   Valeria Catulla was the wife of a distinguished Hellene called Ti. Claudius Marcellus, *Helladarches* of the Delphic Amphictiony, which authorized her to put up a statue to him at Delphi, no doubt in the first or second century AD (*AÉ* 1991.1458).

8   The records of the Arval Brethren for May 17, 105, list their boy attendants as follows (*CIL* 6.2075.1.47–51):

> [*. . . pueri matrimi patrimi prae*]textati cum pu
> blicis ad ara[*m rettulerunt . . . Cornelius Dola*]bella Verania
> [*nus*] D. Valer[*ius. . . . . Valeriu*]s Catullus Mes
> [*sallinu*]s T. Vini[. . . . .*spo*]rtulis cenatum
> [*est denaris centenis.*]

Since there were always four boys serving, we can hardly infer a single polyonymous D. Valerius (. . .) Catullus Messallinus as no. 2. They must be

(a)   (P.?) Cornelius Dolabella Veranianus
(b)   D. Valerius (. . .)
(c)   (L.?) Valerius Catullus Messallinus
(d)   T. Vinius (. . .) or Vinicius (. . .)

```
                          DIVO·AVG
SACRVM·SEX·TEIDIVS·L·F·VALERIVS·CATVLLVS·COS
      L·VALERIVS·CATVLLVS·PONTIF
```

Figure 4.3   Schematic reconstruction of a lost inscription from Lanuvium (*CIL* 14.2095); the right-hand part was reported by Lucas Holstenius (1596–1661), whose notebooks survive in Dresden.

9   In 108 the proconsul of Asia was M. Lollius Paullinus D. Valerius Asiaticus
     Saturninus, who had been suffect consul in 94. His son was honored in Samos
     and Ephesus, and from the latter inscription (*Inscr. Eph.* 3.695B) his name can
     be reconstructed as (D.? Valerius D. f. D. n.) D. *pron.* Vol. Taurus Catullus
     Messallinus Asiaticus; the Voltinia tribe is that of Vienna in Narbonensis, home
     of the Valerii Asiatici.

10   Late in the second century AD a Valerius Catullus (no *praenomen* given) is
     attested on brickstamps as *negotiator* – presumably marketing manager – for a
     brick factory that belonged first to the *clarissimi uiri* who were heirs of the
     clarissima femina Passenia Petronia (*CIL* 15.419), and then to the *clarissimus
     uir* Hortensius Paulinus (*CIL* 15.416). No doubt Paulinus was himself one of
     Passenia's heirs; he was evidently from Verona (*CIL* 5.3338), but all the brick-
     stamps come from Rome and its immediate environs.

11   A handsomely inscribed statue base in Brixia attests the honor paid to
     L. Valerius Catullus (no details given) by decree of the *decuriones* of the city
     (*Inscr. Ital.* 10.5.273). The inscription is dated to the late second or early third
     century.

12   Also in Brixia, a third-century inscription in honor of Sex. Valerius Poblicola
     Vettillianus and his wife Nonia Arria Hermionilla was put up by their grandson
     M. Annius Valerius Catullus (*CIL* 5.4484). Nonia was the daughter of a consul
     of 201, granddaughter of a consul of 154, and great-granddaughter of a consul
     of 138; both her family and that of her husband were prominent in Verona as
     well as their native Brixia (Wiseman 1987: 363–6).

The constant use of the *praenomen* L. (nos. 2, 3, 4, 6, 11) suggests the possibility that
Catullus the poet and his homonym the *garum*-exporter (no. 1) may have been
younger sons. Success in the capital evidently did not cause the Valerii Catulli to
forget their Transpadane origin: no. 2 was married to a lady from Milan, no. 10
worked (in Rome) for a Veronese senator, and nos. 11 and 12 attest the continued
prominence of the family in Brixia. Business interests (nos. 1, 10) are another
continuing feature, as are connections in the Greek East, inferred already from the
travels of the poet and his brother and further attested by nos. 2, perhaps 4 (through
his adopted father), and 9.

   Nos. 2–5 are easy to put together in a conjectural stemma (Syme 1991: 493–4):

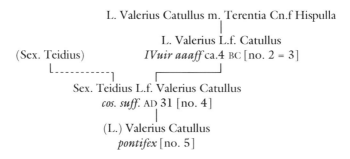

The *garum*-exporter (no. 1) could be a brother of any of these four Lucii. It would be pleasant if an inscription turned up one day to reveal the parents of the first of them; for the moment, we can only guess that the L. Valerius Catullus who married Terentia Hispulla may have been the poet's son.

The *pontifex* must be Caligula's friend, possibly father of the Catullus who was proconsul of Crete and Cyrene in 72 or 73 (Joseph. *BJ* 7.437–53), though it is not absolutely certain that he was a Valerius. The *pontifex* was more certainly the father of no. 6, L. Valerius Catullus Messallinus, consul in 73; however, Messallinus' second *cognomen* involves a quite intricate complex of aristocratic connections.

A tombstone in Rome records a baby girl called Statilia Catulli f. Messallina (*CIL* 6.26789). Her name is explained by the marriage of Valeria Messallina, daughter of the great orator Messalla Corvinus, to T. Statilius Taurus, consul in AD 11 (implied by Suet. *Claud.* 13.2). They had two sons, consuls in 44 and 45, one of whom had a daughter, Statilia Messallina, who became Nero's third wife (Suet. *Ner.* 35.1). Syme has convincingly revived Borghesi's nineteenth-century conjecture that the two consuls had a sister, also Statilia Messallina, and that she married a Valerius Catullus, our no. 5; the dead baby was their daughter, and their son was L. Valerius Catullus Messallinus (Syme 1991: 494–5).

Another sibling might be inferred from *CIL* 6.6467, the funerary inscription of *Heracla Catulli Tauri L. seruos*, if that enigmatic formula means "slave of L. Catullus Taurus." (Reading the *L* not as a *praenomen* but as *l(iberti)* would make it either "slave of Catullus, freedman of Taurus" – unlikely, since Catullus is not a plausible *cognomen* for a freedman – or else "slave of a freedman of Catullus Taurus" – even more unlikely, with the master not even named.) Whether our no. 7, the Valeria Catulla married to the *Helladarches*, belongs in this generation or later is impossible to say.

No. 8, the altar-boy (L.?) Valerius Catullus Messallinus, cannot be the son of no. 6, because he is a *puer matrimus patrimus*, with both parents alive, and Domitian's notorious adviser was already dead by 98 (Plin. *Ep.* 4.22.4–6). His father could conceivably have been the Catullus whose escape from shipwreck is celebrated in Juvenal's twelfth poem – a man with wealth like that of Maecenas, who saved his life by jettisoning it (Wiseman 1987: 361–2). The boy's colleague D. Valerius (. . .) is probably identical with our no. 9, who was honored in his father's province three or four years later. His distinctive *praenomen* brings in another important aristocratic connection, since both the inscriptions of no. 9 pointedly include his tribe and three generations of his forebears (*D. pron.*), thus emphasizing his descent from the great D. Valerius Asiaticus who was honored and then destroyed by Claudius (Tac. *Ann.* 11.1–3). He also bore the name Taurus, a reminder of the consuls of 44 and 45, neither of whom survived Claudius' reign (Suet. *Claud.* 13.2; Tac. *Ann.* 12.59). Under Trajan, it was safe to boast of martyred ancestors (Plin. *Ep.* 3.16).

The following stemma is offered merely *exempli gratia*, since there are too many unknowns to allow any confident hypothesis. But it does at least provide an economical explanation of the data:

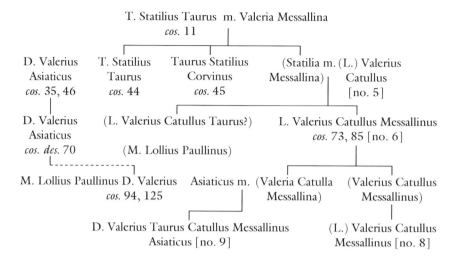

We need not be surprised at these grand connections. Back in the late Republic, the poet had patrician friends (e.g., Manlius Torquatus, c. 61.209) and a patrician mistress (c. 79.1, alluding to the Claudii Pulchri); he was uninhibited about attacking Caesar and Pompey (c. 29.23–4), and his politeness to Cicero shows the irony of a social equal (c. 49.6–7). When the Valerii Catulli became senatorial under Augustus, and consular under Tiberius, they lost what residual stigma equestrian status still had in those circles (Tac. *Ann.* 6.27.1, referring to one of the colleagues of no. 3 above); the sexual relations reported between Gaius Caesar and no. 5 were explicitly between equals.

Friends of emperors could afford grand palaces. (See Fig. 4.4, p. 65.) The great villa at Sirmio, with its huge peristyle garden and long porticos with views over the lake, was built in the Augustan period – replacing a much smaller earlier house – and modified in the late first century AD to include a sumptuous bath complex (Roffia 1997: 146–8, 159–61). That fits very well with the prosopographical evidence for the fortunes of the Valerii Catulli.

Syme convincingly described the years 60–110 as "the acme of Transpadana" (1991: 635–46). Oddly, though, he thought that our no. 6, Domitian's friend, didn't really fit into his picture (Syme 1991: 640 n. 34, 480):

> The present exposition segregates L. Valerius Catullus Messallinus (*cos.* 73, II *suff.* 85). His northern links had now grown remote, his extraction blended with aristocratic lineage. . . . The aristocrat who could trace descent from Messalla Corvinus and from the great Statilius Taurus stands apart from northern consuls of his time, and he is not normally assessed in their context and rubric.

It seems to me that the great villa is enough to refute this idea. An entertainingly symmetrical misconception is that of the archaeologists who rule out *a priori* any connection between the villa and the poet's family, because it must have belonged to "some military or senatorial family of the time, possibly even an imperial personage" (McKay 1975: 133). In fact, the villa was *not* too grand for the Valerii Catulli, and Catullus Messallinus was *not* too grand for the villa. He must surely have lived there.

Figure 4.4 Hypothetical reconstruction of the Sirmio villa, drawn by Sheila Gibson RIBA FSA, 1981.

His descendants, however, the young cousins who served the Arvals in 105 (our nos. 8 and 9), did not grow up to be consuls and imperial advisers. The second-century Valerii Catulli seem to have been less ambitious, their eminence now merely local (nos. 10–12). There were indeed senatorial Valerii Catullini, including a consul under Commodus, but what relationship they had with the Transpadane family is not known (Wiseman 1987: 363).

Remembering Catullus

Tantum magna suo debet Verona Catullo
quantum parua suo Mantua Vergilio.

Great Verona owes as much to her Catullus as little Mantua does to her Vergil.

Mart. 14.195

Verona was always proud of her poet (Ov. *Am.* 3.15.7; Mart. 1.61.1, 10.103.5), and Transpadane gentlemen liked to write in his style (Plin. *Ep.* 4.14, 4.27). One of the fragments of wall-painting recovered from the Sirmio villa in the 1950s shows a young man holding a scroll, barefoot, with a narrow-stripe tunic beneath his toga (Fig. 4.5); the context is unknown (a matching piece shows an athlete with his trainer), but who else is it likely to be?

The year after Catullus Messallinus' second consulship, Martial presented himself to the Roman reading public as a Catullan epigrammatist (*sic scribit Catullus*, Mart. 1 pref.). There are countless references and allusions to Catullus in Martial's work, and one form of homage was to choose appropriate names like "Fabullus" and "Lesbia" for the imagined or anonymous victims of his satirical observations. "Most of the imaginary names were doubtless chosen at random, but now and again they relate to their context" (Shackleton Bailey 1993: 325); "Fabullus" first appears in a poem about the host at a party providing perfume, just as the real Fabullus did in Catullus 13 (Mart. 3.12).

One of the most interesting of these allusions comes in the eighth book of epigrams, where Martial is on his best behavior; the book is formally dedicated to Domitian, and inspired by the emperor's own virgin goddess. Here is the poem (Mart. 8.1.4), in Shackleton Bailey's text and translation:

> Formosissima quae fuere uel sunt,
> sed durissima quae fuere uel sunt,
> o quam te fieri, Catulla, uellem
> formosam minus aut minus pudicam!

Fairest of women that ever were or are, but cruellest of women that ever were or are, oh, how I would have wished you, Catulla, to become less fair or else less virtuous!

The unmistakable Catullan echo (cf. c. 49.1–2, *Disertissime Romuli nepotum/quot sunt quotque fuere*) might suggest that the virtuous lady is imaginary, and that Martial has simply invented an appropriate name for her (Shackleton Bailey 1993: 347, indexed with an asterisk) – but in 94, the date of Book 8, "Catulla" was not a name you could use for just anyone. I think it is much more likely that this is a compliment to a real woman, and the Catullan echo is a graceful tribute to her famous ancestor.

In Juvenal's satires, written 20 years later about the people of Martial's time (Syme 1984: 1135–57), Catulla appears as a highly sexed lady who can deny her lover nothing (Juv. 10.322). She is cited at another point (Juv. 4.49–50) for the argument that women, unlike men, refrain from homosexual relationships:

> Tedia non lambit Cluuiam nec Flora Catullam:
> Hispo subit iuuenes et morbo pallet utrique.

Tedia doesn't lick Cluvia, Flora doesn't lick Catulla; Hispo submits to young men, and is pallid from both vices.

These are all elite names: Mestrius Florus was consul in about 75, Cluvius Rufus in 80. And three of them, Catulla, Hispo, and Flora (Syme 1991: 489 on the Mestrii), are Transpadane. It could be just an accident that Juvenal juxtaposes Catulla with Te (i)dia and Hispo, whose names recall the grandmother and adoptive father of the Valerius Catullus who was consul in 31 (no. 4 above); but he also brings a lady called Hispulla rather gratuitously into the poem about the Catullus who escaped

Figure 4.5 Fragment of wall-painting from the villa at Sirmione (fig. 4.4 above), showing a young man with a scroll. Photo by courtesy of the Soprintendenza per i beni archeologici della Lombardia (Archivio Fotografico D 756).

shipwreck (Juv. 12.11). For whatever reason, the names were associated in the author's mind.

I offer another guess: that the Catulla mentioned by Martial and Juvenal and the Catullus featured in Juvenal 12 were daughter and son of L. Catullus Messallinus, mother of one of the Arvals' attendants and father of the other.

Catullus Messallinus was blind as well as hateful. In the famous scene of Domitian's council about the giant turbot, Juvenal introduces him as Catullus *mortifer*, the bringer of death,

> qui numquam uisae flagrabat amore puellae,
> grande et conspicuum nostro quoque tempore monstrum,
> dignus Aricinos qui mendicaret ad axes
> blandaque deuexae iactaret basia raedae.

who burned with love for a girl he could never see, a great monster conspicuous even in our times, fit to beg and blow flattering kisses at the wheels of a carriage descending the hill at Aricia.

(Juv. 4.114–17, with Courtney 1975: 157–8)

The carriage is a *raeda*, a Transpadane term (Quint. *Inst.* 1.5.56–7); the kisses are not *oscula* but Catullan *basia*; and the mocking line about his mistress is a complex allusion to Catullus' poem about the bride from Brixia, whose father-in-law, *blind* with passion, had taken her virginity first (*impia mens caeco flagrabat amore*, c. 67.25).

As Tacitus' *Dialogus*, Suetonius' *De uiris illustribus*, and Plutarch's *Parallel Lives* are enough to show, this was an age that looked back with particular interest to the great men of the late Republic and the early years of Augustus. A personal link with a classic author was particularly valued: the Transpadane Silius Italicus (Syme 1988: 380), consul in 68, orator and epic poet, owned an estate that had belonged to Cicero, and bought and restored the tomb of Vergil (Mart. 11.48; Plin. *Ep.* 3.7.8); Passennus Paullus, a distinguished *eques* from Asisium, was descended from Propertius, and praised by Pliny as a poet in his own right (Plin. *Ep.* 6.15.1, 9.22; cf. *CIL* 11.5405). The Valerii Catulli, still sumptuously established at Sirmio, could make a better case than either of those.

In the very first sentence of his *Natural History*, C. Plinius Secundus of Comum deliberately misquoted Catullus' first poem, and excused the liberty with the following explanation to his princely dedicatee (pref. 1):

> Ille enim, ut scis, permutatis prioribus syllabis duriusculum se fecit quam uolebat existimari a Veraniolis suis et Fabullis.

> For as you know, by putting the first syllables [of 1.4] in a different order he made himself a bit harder than he wanted to be thought by his "dear Veranii and Fabulli".

The inseparable Veranius and Fabullus (cc. 12.15–17, 28.3, 47.3) also had a resonance in Flavian Rome. Fabullus found a fictitious afterlife in Martial (see above), but Veranius was still a real name, and a significant one.

Catullus' friend Veranius, a scholarly young man (c. 9.8, *ut mos est tuus*), may or may not be identical with the Veranius who wrote about religious antiquities (Syme 1988: 634–6). He was no doubt father, or uncle, of the Q. Veranius who served as an equestrian officer in the fourth legion and was then tutor to Livia's younger son Claudius Drusus in the 20s BC (*AÉ* 1981.824). That man's son, also Q. Veranius, was legate to Drusus' son Germanicus in AD 18, and prosecuted Cn. Piso two years later (Tac. *Ann.* 2.56.4, 3.10.1); his grandson, Q. Veranius the consul of 49, was adlected into the patriciate by Claudius and served as imperial legate in Britain under Nero (*CIL* 6.41075).

Like the Valerii Catulli, the Veranii achieved senatorial status under Augustus, rose to consular rank in the next generation, and were on close terms both with the old aristocracy of Rome and with the imperial house itself. The consul's daughter Verania Gemina married L. Piso Frugi Licinianus, who was chosen by Galba as his heir (*CIL* 6.31723); after the butchery in the Forum on January 15, 69, she had to beg the soldiers for her husband's head (Plut. *Galb.* 28.2). The Veranii were also related to the patrician Cornelii Dolabellae; for instance, a Verania may have married the Dolabella who was consul in 86, the year after Valerius Messallinus. That would account for the name of another of the boys who served the Arvals in 105 (p. 61 above), Cornelius Dolabella Veranianus.

Who chose the boys for this duty? Whoever it was will have known his Catullus –
not only the kiss-poems and the sparrow-poems, so constantly referred to by Martial,
but also the joyful greeting of a dear friend: *Verani, omnibus e meis amicis/antistans
mihi milibus trecentis....* (c. 9.1–2). That was the ancestor of young Dolabella
Veranianus, hailed by the ancestor of young Catullus Messallinus and his cousin.
What made those boys aristocratic was not just their patrician descent from the
Cornelii Dolabellae and the Valerii Messallae; they had also inherited a longer-lasting
kind of nobility.

In that very year, 105, Pliny the Transpadane wrote to old Vestricius Spurinna
(*Ep.* 5.17.1):

> Scio quanto opere artibus faueas, quantum gaudium capias si nobiles iuuenes dignum
> aliquid maioribus suis faciant.

> I know how much literature matters to you, and what pleasure it gives you when our
> young nobles do something worthy of their ancestors.

Writers had always borrowed the language of glory, like Horace with his monument
more lasting than bronze (*Carm.* 3.30.1), or Livy on the *nobilitas* and *magnitudo* of
his competitors (pref. 3); the *aemulatio gloriae* (Just. pref. 1) was as real in literary
achievement as in the traditional aristocrat's pursuit of consulships and triumphs. It
was natural that one's descendants should inherit that glory too.

When Catullus prayed that his work might last more than one *saeculum* (c. 1.10),
the poem was addressed to Cornelius Nepos, a fellow-Transpadane (Plin. *HN* 3.127).
How the goddess granted his prayer can be seen in two of Martial's gift-tag poems
(14.100 and 152), written well over a *saeculum* later:

> Si non ignota est docti tibi terra Catulli,
> > potasti testa Raetica uina mea.

> If the land of learned Catullus is not unknown to you, you have drunk Rhaetian wines
> from my jar.

> > Lodices mittet docti tibi terra Catulli;
> > > nos Helicaonia de regione sumus.

> The land of learned Catullus will send you blankets; we [rugs?] are from the region of
> Helicaon [son of Antenor, founder of Patavium].

The Transpadane region was synonymous with the name of a poet – but why wasn't it
Vergil? Perhaps because Vergil belonged to everyone: he was the bard of Latium and
the *gens togata* (*Aen.* 1.6, 282), familiar from school wherever Latin was spoken.
Catullus was more locally specific. Besides, Mantua was a small place, and the obscure
village of Andes could hardly compete with Sirmio; one couldn't imagine senatorial
or consular Vergilii still living there.

Catullus symbolized the Transpadana because his family kept the name conspicuous, right down to M. Annius Valerius Catullus (no. 12 above), who honored his
grandparents in Brixia about three centuries after the poet's time. Let us hope that he
survived the invasion of the Alemanni, which shattered the peace of the Transpadana
in the 260s. It was close to Lake Garda that the Alemanni were defeated ([Aur. Vict.]

Epit. de Caes. 34.2); *uenusta Sirmio* must now have been a military site, the villa abandoned and in ruins (Roffia 1997: 162–3).

Ausonius in the fourth century still knew Catullus as "the Veronese poet" (1.4.2), and it seems that his works were preserved in Verona throughout the long centuries of Ostrogothic, Lombard, and Frankish rule; a monk in Brixia evidently knew them in the 840s, and a learned bishop of Verona refers to them in the 960s (Gaisser 1993: 17; see Butrica, this volume). But some time after that, Verona lost her poet. It was only in the early fourteenth century that a manuscript of the *Catulli Veronensis liber* was brought back to the city, celebrated by an epigram on the poet's "resurrection". It begins:

> Ad patriam uenio longis a finibus exul;
> causa mei reditus compatriota fuit.

An exile, I come to my native land from distant parts; a compatriot was the cause of my return.

We don't know who it was who brought Catullus home, but it's fitting that it was one of his "own folk."

GUIDE TO FURTHER READING

T. P. Wiseman, "The Masters of Sirmio" (Wiseman 1987: 307–70), is an attempt to explore the history of the Valerii Catulli in parallel with that of the Sirmio site. For the senatorial families of the Transpadane region, see Sir Ronald Syme's series of studies, designed as a book on "Pliny and Italia Transpadana" but published posthumously as volume 7 of *Roman Papers* (Syme 1991: 473–646). For the villa at Sirmio, see the excellent new guide by Dr Elisabetta Roffia, director of the Museo delle Grotte di Catullo, Sirmione (Roffia 2005).

WORKS CITED

Courtney, E. 1975. "The Interpolations in Juvenal." *Bulletin of the Institute of Classical Studies of the University of London* 22: 147–62.

Gaisser, J. H. 1993. *Catullus and His Renaissance Readers.* Oxford.

McKay, A. G. 1975. *Houses, Villas and Palaces in the Roman World.* London.

Roffia, E. 1997. "Sirmione, le 'grotte di Catullo'." In E. Roffia, ed., *Ville romane sul lago di Garda.* Brescia. 141–69.

Roffia, E. 2005. *Le "grotte di Catullo" a Sirmione: Guida alla visita della villa romana e del museo.* Milan.

Shackleton Bailey, D. R. 1993. *Martial: Epigrams. Edited and Translated.* 3 vols. Vol. 3. Cambridge, MA, and London.

Sutherland, C. H. V. 1984. *The Roman Imperial Coinage.* Vol. 1. Rev. edn. London.

Syme, R. 1979. *Roman Papers.* Vols. 1–2. Oxford.

Syme, R. 1984. *Roman Papers.* Vol. 3. Oxford.

Syme, R. 1988. *Roman Papers*. Vols. 4–5. Oxford.
Syme, R. 1991. *Roman Papers*. Vols. 6–7. Oxford.
Wiseman, T. P. 1969. *Catullan Questions*. Leicester.
Wiseman, T. P. 1985. *Catullus and His World: A Reappraisal*. Cambridge.
Wiseman, T. P. 1987. *Roman Studies Literary and Historical*. Liverpool.

CHAPTER FIVE

The Contemporary Political Context

David Konstan

The latest datable allusions in Catullus' poems are to events in the latter part of the year 54 BC. This does not mean, of course, that Catullus died in that year, or ceased composing poetry, or that there are no later poems in the surviving collection. Most of the poems give little or no clue as to when they might have been written. But the political poems can all be safely assigned to 54 or earlier, and this is a reasonable terminus for a discussion of their context.

Catullus' family was from Verona, and he was undoubtedly born and educated there (cf. Ov. *Am.* 3.15.7). He must have been a Roman citizen, since he served on the staff of Memmius when the latter was provincial governor in Bithynia; but since Transpadane Gaul only acquired full Roman status in 49 BC – prior to this, it had only "Latin rights" – it is likely that his father had been a magistrate in Verona, and had thereby acquired citizenship for himself and his immediate family (see Wiseman 1969: 59–60, 1987: 331; Skinner 2003: xxii).

At some point, Catullus came to Rome, but it is hard to say just when. It was surely in Rome that he became friends with C. Licinius Calvus, the distinguished orator and poet, a relationship so loyal that Ovid (*Am.* 3.9.61–2) imagines them as bosom companions even in the underworld. In Rome, too, Catullus made other friends and enemies, or at least came to know people he could plausibly represent as such in his verses. These were among the most distinguished figures of his day, including Caesar and Pompey, Cato, Cicero, Cicero's rival in oratory Hortensius, and the historian and biographer Cornelius Nepos, to whom the dedicatory poem (c. 1) is addressed. Rome, finally, was the locus of his passionate affair with the woman he calls Lesbia, possibly to be identified with Clodia (Apul. *Apol.* 10), the wife, as many scholars suppose, of Q. Metellus Celer, the scion of a prominent noble family.[1]

All this could have happened over a period of two or three years in the life of an intense young man (there is reason to think that Catullus died young, perhaps at the age of 30 or so). The earliest datable references in the poetry may be assigned to the year 56 or 57 BC (Wiseman 1969: 47), though of course he must have begun writing poems earlier, perhaps even as a boy. Nevertheless, the political context of the poetry would appear to be determined by events in the early 50s, beginning more or less with the formation, in 59, of what is called the First Triumvirate, that is, the informal alliance between Julius Caesar, Pompey the Great, and Crassus, the wealthiest man in Rome, under the terms of which they reigned supreme in the state until 54 and beyond.

With hindsight, the triumvirate may seem to be the beginning of the end of the Republic, and thus a crucial moment in Roman history. And yet, despite the threat that the alliance might have posed to traditional aristocratic institutions and dominance in Rome, it appears that the last generation of the Republic, in Erich Gruen's apt phrase (Gruen 1974), continued to practice politics as usual in this decade, whatever their private misgivings. In any case, to determine how Catullus responded to the dramatic events of this period, our evidence must be first and foremost the poems themselves. And these, I believe, reveal a complex and profound view of the contemporary political scene.

We may begin with the most obviously political statement in the corpus, Catullus' ferocious attack on Pompey and Caesar in poem 29.[2] One can infer the approximate date of this poem from several references. First there is the allusion to the conquest of Britain. Caesar mounted two invasions, the first of which took place in the summer of 55, the second in the summer of 54: the poem, then, is no earlier than 55, but may well have been composed in the following year. Second, we know that Julia, Caesar's daughter and Pompey's wife, died in September 54; while it is not impossible that Catullus should have referred to Caesar and Pompey as father-in-law and son-in-law after her death, it is perhaps unlikely, since the marital bond that had been so important in uniting the two rivals was now ended. It is reasonable, then, to assign the poem to some time between the autumn of 55 and the spring of 54.

The poem refers also to other recent military campaigns, in Gaul, in the area of the Black Sea, and in Spain. Caesar had, of course, been active in Gaul since 59, when he was assigned command of the province for five years. The wealth from Pontus was brought back to Rome by Pompey after the long war against Mithridates, which culminated in Mithridates' suicide in 63 (Pompey arrived in Italy in December of 62). Finally, it was Caesar, again, who fought in Spain, when he was propraetor there in 61. Catullus is conjuring here, as he does again (as we shall see) in poem 11, with the geographical breadth of Rome's reach: from Asia in the East, to Spain in the West, to Britain at the extreme North. All the inhabitable world, bounded by the Atlantic Ocean or by the African desert, must have seemed poised to fall under Rome's dominion. The time had not yet come when Crassus would be defeated and slain in his expedition against the Parthians on June 9, 53, his head to be used in place of Pentheus' in a performance of Euripides' *Bacchae* (the Parthians were apparently thoroughly Hellenized). Indeed, the absence of any allusion to this event in the corpus of Catullus' poetry goes some way to confirming, in my mind, the supposition that the collection as we have it ends prior to that date.

The Mamurra who so enriched himself through the campaigns of Caesar and Pompey was a Roman knight from the town of Formiae (cc. 41.4, 57.4), who had served with Pompey in the East and with Caesar in Spain; in Gaul, Caesar appointed him *praefectus fabrum* or head of the engineer corps (Plin. *HN* 26.48); he perhaps returned to Rome after Caesar's first crossing into Britain. Catullus is not the only contemporary who attests to the vast wealth that Mamurra amassed. Cicero, writing to Atticus in 50 (7.7.6), speaks of his fortune, and comments in another epistle (*Att.* 13.52.1) on his self-indulgent and profligate pursuits, while the elder Pliny, a hundred years later, still can mention his house on the Caelian hill as an example of luxury (*HN* 36.48). That Catullus felt a profound disgust at the thought of this wastrel cornering all the wealth accumulated through Rome's military campaigns is obvious, and he resents Caesar and Pompey equally for their condoning of it.

But what is it precisely that Catullus objects to in Mamurra's behavior and the connivance of Rome's two greatest generals? More precisely, does his strident attack on the three men amount to a condemnation of their politics? Kenneth Quinn (1972b: 267) thinks not: "Catullus is not a political satirist. His verse expresses no political ideas, no political attitudes as such, except perhaps a general disgust with politics," or at the most "disgust with the establishment and those who manipulate the establishment for their own ends." Quinn finds the ostensibly political poems repulsive (p. 269): "For most readers of Catullus the poems of political invective occupy one of the less attractive corners of the background. The attacks on Caesar are probably the most interesting, because of their victim – and also because of the anecdote preserved by Suetonius."

In his *Life of the Deified Julius* (73), Suetonius observes that Caesar was always ready to be reconciled with his opponents when the opportunity presented itself, no matter how nasty the attack. Thus, he forgave Catullus' friend Gaius Calvus, of whose "famous epigrams," as Suetonius calls them, there survive some fragments, and "when Valerius Catullus, whose verses concerning Mamurra – as Caesar admitted – had left an indelible stain on him, apologized, he invited him to dinner that very day, and continued to accept the hospitality of Catullus' father, as he always had done." With due caution, we may perhaps infer from this report "that Catullus' invective verse had been circulating widely enough in Rome to come to Caesar's attention while he campaigned in Gaul," and that the apology, if it really happened, "must have taken place while Catullus was at home in Cisalpine Gaul and Caesar was wintering there, sometime between late 55 and early 52" (Skinner 2003: xxi), the winter of 54 being the most likely occasion.[3]

It is possible that c. 29 was the very poem that had so offended Caesar, although there are, as we shall see, other candidates. The language is certainly calculated to sting: Caesar is directly addressed as a *cinaedus* or receptive homosexual, one who enjoys playing the female role in a homoerotic relationship – a grave insult in macho Rome.[4] In addition, he is called shameless and voracious.[5] These are vile epithets, but Mamurra himself comes off even worse; indeed, the chief offense with which Caesar and Pompey are charged is that of letting Mamurra get away with appropriating booty beyond measure and rampant adultery (cf. Asper 1997: 68). Is Catullus expressing anything more than pique at the conspicuous wealth of a henchman of the generals, or, worse still, resentment that he and his circle are not getting their share of the loot?

Catullus levels a stronger charge, in fact. He accuses Caesar and Pompey, the two most powerful men in Rome, of having ruined everything for the sake of this greedy underling. The plain meaning is that the wars they waged in remote parts of the world, culminating in the invasion of Britain, were undertaken for the sake of enriching Mamurra and people like him, lackeys, comrades, or even sexual partners (hence the label *cinaedus*) who stood to benefit from such predatory campaigns. For the rest, there was only destruction. But can this be intended seriously as a commentary on Roman imperial politics – that the wars to extend or reaffirm Rome's control over Spain and the Pontus, Gaul and Britain, were launched in the service of a limitlessly avaricious and corrupt faction of knights and nobles, who found in them a source of endless wealth and opportunities for debauchery? Is this not hyperbole, the real point being merely that Mamurra and a few lieutenants like him should not be allowed to run riot?

I believe that Catullus' critique of Roman imperial politics is serious and sophisticated, even if it does not fully coincide with modern interpretations of the causes of Rome's wars.[6] The motive for subduing Gaul and Britain may well have seemed to contemporaries to be personal enrichment on the part of the commanders, driven by a hollow lust for power, display, and sex.[7] Epicureanism, one of the leading philosophical currents of the time, explicitly characterized political ambition and avarice as empty desires, motivated by an irrational fear of death; Lucretius, who dedicated his didactic poem *On the Nature of Things* to a Memmius who in all likelihood was the same man with whom Catullus served in Bithynia, brought the message of Epicurus home to Romans at the very moment when Catullus was composing his last poems (there is reason to believe that Lucretius died around the year 54, and there are signs that he knew Catullus' verse, or Catullus his). There is nothing inherently absurd about explaining foreign wars as a consequence of the dissoluteness of a ruling caste.

In the next-to-last poem in the collection as we have it (115), Catullus again attacks Mamurra, here under the nickname Mentula, "Prick" or "Cock" (Catullus makes the equation clear in 29.13). On the surface, the epigram seems contradictory. On the one hand, Mamurra is said to own 70 acres or *iugera* of arable land plus an undetermined amount of marsh; this is hardly a huge domain by contemporary Roman standards, though doubtless it was a valuable piece of property.[8] On the other hand, he is described as richer than Croesus, at least potentially, and his holdings are said to extend northwards to the mythical territory of the Hyperboreans and westward to the Atlantic Ocean. The whole thing is then capped by the claim that Mamurra himself is bigger than all his lands, since he is not a human being but rather, as Catullus dubs him, a giant penis – presumably stretching to the ends of the earth.

One way to understand the point of this puzzling poem is to take the comparison with Croesus and the exaggerated statement of Mamurra's holdings not so much as ironic as metaphorical: such a property should be enough to satisfy any man's wants, and its owner would be equal to Croesus, if riches are measured by normal needs. To a rational or moderate person, such an estate is as good as one that extends to the limits of the world. Mamurra, however, is not such an individual, but rather someone driven by limitless lusts. That is the implication of the name Mentula or "Cock," and the allegation that this organ represents the whole of Mamurra's identity.[9] The cock is described as gigantic because it is insatiable: even if Mamurra's lands did reach the boundaries of the Roman Empire, they would not be enough for a man whose essence was pure desire. Mamurra's cupidity, symbolized by his sexual lust, surpasses all bounds – even those of the Roman Empire itself.[10]

Once again, then, Catullus has associated Mamurra's appetites with the need for territory as far away as Spain or Britain or the regions beyond Scythia, traditionally the homeland of the Hyperboreans. The motif is not casual but considered, and can be exploited with subtlety.

In the preceding poem (c. 114), Catullus once more homes in on Mamurra's greed. The property mentioned here is presumably the same as that in c. 115; but in this poem, Catullus states in straightforward economic terms the reason why it does not suffice for Mamurra's needs. Rich as the estate itself is, Mamurra's conspicuous consumption (*sumptus*) exhausts its profits.

There is a textual problem in the first line that bears on the interpretation of the poem, and it is worth a brief notice. The renaissance scholar Avancius proposed the reading *Firmanus saltus non falso, Mentula, dives, / legitur*, that is, "Mentula, your estate in Firmum is rightly called rich" (Mynors's text follows the Aldine edition). On this reading, which is adopted by Kroll, line 4 must be rendered: "for its costs outstrip its yield" (so Kroll 1968: 285: "[a holding] der trotz aller möglichen guten Eigenschaften doch mehr kostet als er einbringt").[11] But this can hardly be said of a property that is truly fruitful, as Mamurra's surely is. The point is not that Mamurra has made a poor investment, despite the apparent value of the land. It is rather, as in c. 115, that no amount of property, whatever its productivity, would cover Mamurra's expenditures (for full discussion, see Syndikus 1987: 136–8). Again, in line 5, it must be Mentula, not his estate, that lacks everything, since he inevitably exceeds his resources, however great they may be. Hence he is poor in the midst of plenty.[12] Or so I understand it.

To meet his outlays, Mamurra must continually acquire more land, the chief symbol and source of affluence in Roman culture. But because his appetites are limitless, he can never have enough, even if he were to possess an estate the size of Rome's entire Empire. This is why he is not just a wastrel, but rapacious as well: he must always be adding more to compensate for what he has squandered. The plunder brought in by war is essential to him.

In poem 57, any distinction between the characters of Caesar and Mamurra is erased, as Catullus brands them equally as pathic homosexuals and seducers. If Caesar was referring to a single epigram of Catullus when he declared that his verses concerning Mamurra had marked him with undying blots (*perpetua stigmata imposita*), this one is a fair contender for the honor; apart from the directness of the calumny, the reference to stains (*maculae*) imprinted (*impressae*) on the two reprobates might have motivated Caesar's own turn of phrase.

Here again, Caesar, along with Mamurra, is labeled a *cinaedus* or pervert.[13] There is no doubt that this term, like *pathicus*, indicates the passive role in sex between men, at least for Catullus (compare his use of the term in cc. 25.1–3, 16.1–2). At the same time, they are both characterized as sexual predators, friendly rivals in the pursuit of married women (*adulter* in classical Latin refers to a man who has sex with another citizen's wife) and young girls, presumably virgins. We have already seen that Mamurra is attacked as being all phallus, and in c. 29 (lines 5 and 9) he was said to be circulating among all the bedrooms in Rome. So too, in c. 94, Catullus quips:

> Mentula moechatur. moechatur mentula? certe.
>   hoc est quod dicunt: ipsa olera olla legit.

> Cock screws wives. "Screws wives? Cock?" Of course.
>   It's the old saying: the pot collects the greens.

For us, there is a certain tension, not to say outright contradiction, between the role of passive homosexual and that of hyperphallic womanizer. Thus, Thomson, in his recent commentary (1997: 340–1), remarks of poem 57:

> This lampoon . . . perfectly illustrates the needlessness, and indeed the impossibility, of supposing that sexual slanders . . . are meant as anything more than an elaborate form of abuse. . . . If one wished to reproach someone for immoral behavior, one would of course take care not to seem implausible by accusing him simultaneously of passive homosexuality and the seduction of other men's wives – both of which were standard topics of triumph verses. If, however, the real object was to express dislike of, or opposition to, a person in the public eye, Roman custom dictated that all kinds of bizarre charges might be added to the burden of the indictment.

Suetonius, indeed, reports, in his life of Julius Caesar (52.3), the quip of C. Curio to the effect that Caesar was "every woman's husband and every man's wife." Now, it is true that classical Greek and Roman views of sexuality were predicated on a disjunction between the active lover (*erastês, amator*) on the one hand, and the receptive beloved (*erômenos/ê, amatus/a*) on the other. This opposition, moreover, was coordinate with status roles: as Marilyn Skinner (1979: 142) has put it, "the adult male who allows himself to be used as the passive partner automatically becomes womanish and despicable."

But we must beware of projecting a Victorian conception of the sexes onto ancient Greeks and Romans. The passivity attributed to women was not impassiveness; on the contrary, men imagined women to be as vulnerable to sexual desire as they themselves were, if not more so, and at the same time less capable of self-control, which was a supremely masculine virtue. Seen this way, the phallic pursuit of women and the pathic submission to other males are two sides of the same coin: both are expressions of a sexual impulse run wild. The middle to which both extremes are opposed is sexual restraint or moderation.

Poem 57 appears to be a purely personal smear, void of political content. But in fact it picks up the theme of Catullus' other poems about Caesar, Pompey, and Mamurra, in which unchecked licentiousness and greed are seen as ruinous to the Republic (in c. 113, probably composed in the year 55 when Pompey was embarking on his second consulship, Catullus attacks Pompey as an aging adulterer who has long shared his mistress with another man).[14] The immensely powerful generals who controlled Rome's fate were sexually and economically rapacious, and this in turn provided the motive for the campaigns that confirmed their supremacy. Moral corruption in the ruling caste was a political question.

We have no way of knowing the precise date of c. 57. Quinn (1973a: 256) speculated that it was written between 61 and 58, but it could well have been composed two or even three years later (see Wiseman 1969: 35–6). I do not wish to enter into the game of constructing a narrative of the quarrel between Catullus and Caesar and its aftermath, which is, in my view, as risky a business as tracing the story line of Catullus' affair with Lesbia. What we can say is that around the same time that Catullus was composing c. 29 on Caesar and Mamurra, and very possibly c. 115 on Mamurra's estate as well (with its reference to Ocean and the far North), he wrote his famous farewell poem to Lesbia (c. 11), which can be dated pretty securely on the basis of the reference to Caesar's excursion – presumably the first, in the summer of

55 – into Britain.[15] Structurally, the most extraordinary feature of the poem is the long preamble in which Catullus lauds, with apparent sincerity, the readiness of Furius and Aurelius to follow him as far as India, Arabia, Persia, Egypt, Gaul up to the border with Germany, and even Britain: four stanzas of geographical prelude before Catullus gets to the point, which is to deliver his bitter message to Lesbia – presumably: it is well to remind ourselves that she is not named in this poem. That the task has been assigned to Furius and Aurelius has seemed all the more odd, since in other poems by Catullus they are treated with suspicion or downright hostility.[16] Rather than inquire into their function here, however, I should like to call attention to the fact that once again, as in cc. 29 and 115, Catullus conjures up the distant reach of Roman armies, which are here imagined as marching into Egypt, beyond Bactria or Afghanistan, and all the way to India – as far east as Alexander the Great himself had gone. Why should Catullus have introduced this dimension of Roman imperialist activity so emphatically into this poem, the ostensible purpose of which is to terminate an amorous relationship?

We have seen that, in his attacks on Caesar and Mamurra, Catullus associates the drive to territorial expansion with the exaggerated sexual impulses of the Roman elite. Caesar's and Mamurra's perversity takes the form both of phallic aggression against married matrons and young girls and of pathic receptivity: both are evidence of wantonness, even though the one may be seen as hypermasculine, while the other is a sign of feminization. Catullus is indifferent here to the distinction between behavior appropriate to men and to women.

In the penultimate stanza of c. 11, Catullus complains that Lesbia loves no one truly, but rather seizes and crushes her innumerable adulterous partners (*moechis*). Although she is a woman, her behavior resembles Caesar's and Mamurra's: like them, she is sexually predatory and violent. So too, in c. 58, Catullus describes Lesbia as "skinning" (*glubit*) Roman citizens – the descendants of Remus – in the back alleys of Rome. Despite the hopes Catullus had entertained of a bond of eternal friendship with Lesbia (c. 109), she is as bad as the men whom he attacks in his invectives, all of whom are compulsively driven by lust. She is an overly masculine woman, just as Caesar and Mamurra (and Furius and Aurelius in c. 16) are represented as rapacious and yet feminized men: common to both extremes is sexual voracity.

Caesar and Mamurra, according to Catullus, waged wars for the expansion of the Roman empire in order to feed their limitless appetites for wealth and sex. As one begins to read c. 11 one might imagine, for a moment, that Catullus intends to join one of these expeditions. In the final stanza, however, the perspective is suddenly reversed. In comparing himself to a flower at the edge of a field, Catullus locates himself at the periphery, like the populations that Roman armies will conquer. It is not he who will penetrate (*penetrare*) the soft (*molles*) Arabians;[17] he is rather one more victim of the inexorable plow, which, like Rome's legions, cuts down everything in its path.[18] Here again, Catullus has subtly connected Roman imperialism with sexual excess and depravity. Although he does not intimate here, as he does in the poems concerning Mamurra, that the wars have been incited in order to finance the sexual license of Rome's decadent leaders, Catullus nevertheless sees boundless military aggression and sexual dissipation as two manifestations of a single perverse drive.[19] Like the more direct attacks on Caesar, Pompey, and their henchmen, c. 11 too is a poem about Roman politics, from which Catullus seems profoundly estranged.[20]

There is in Catullus' poetry-book, I believe, one more reference, albeit an oblique one, to Rome's imperial ventures and to the toll they take on Rome's victims, both abroad and at home. It is in a poem where few scholars have recognized a topical allusion, namely, the miniature epic known as the epithalamium for Peleus and Thetis (c. 64), although the wedding song proper is an inset piece of some 59 verses toward the end. The poem begins with the voyage of the *Argo*, in which Peleus participated. As Catullus tells it, Thetis and other sea nymphs emerged from the sea to gaze at the extraordinary vessel, and this was the occasion on which Peleus and Thetis fell in love (14–21). The context for their enamorment is thus a naval expedition to the far end of the Black Sea.[21]

In some versions of the myth, Jupiter obliges Thetis to marry a mortal because of a prophecy that her son will be greater than his father, and she is sometimes represented as abandoning her husband's bed after the first night.[22] In Catullus, however, Jupiter (if it is he who is identified as "father") simply gives his sanction (*tum Thetidi pater ipse iugandum Pelea sensit*, 21). The wedding itself takes place in Peleus' mansion in Pharsalus, which Catullus models on a Roman villa, complete with atrium and marriage chamber.[23] The hero and his immortal bride assume the guise of Roman notables, joined in wedlock with the pomp of great aristocratic families. At the same time, Catullus expresses his surprise at Peleus' good fortune in marrying the granddaughter of the world-encircling Ocean, whom Jupiter himself had desired (25–30). There may be an element of allegory here: Thetis' union with the mortal Peleus seems analogous to the conquest of the oceans by mankind, which has just been achieved by the invention of seafaring.

The preparations for the marriage are interrupted by a long description of the coverlet on the wedding couch, on which are embroidered scenes from the story of Theseus and Ariadne, including his desertion of her on a barren island. The theme of abandonment is in apparent counterpoint to the happy nuptials of Peleus and Thetis, and Catullus signals the contrast between the frame story and the embedded tale in the transition to the ecphrasis (47–52). Although the lines are commonly rendered neutrally – the couch is "spread with woven purple dipped in rosy murex dye," and the coverlet "reveals . . . the virtues of heroes," in the version of Guy Lee (1990: 83) – the word *indicat* often has the significance "expose," and is used, for example, of uncovering the truth behind the testimony of a witness or defendant in court.[24] The tapestry is said to be tinged, moreover, with *fucus*, literally a purplish dye but very commonly used in the sense of "deceit."[25] Finally, while the word *uirtus* in Catullus' time connoted ethical goodness in addition to the older meaning of martial courage (*OLD* s.v., def. 3), the plural form *uirtutes* retained the primary sense of valiant deeds or accomplishments, with an emphasis on success rather than on the morality of the means.[26] A tapestry dyed in fraudulence that exposes the achievements of heroes is a good medium for the tale of Theseus' thoughtless betrayal of Ariadne.[27]

The song of the Parcae predicts the achievements of Peleus and Thetis' great son-to-be, Achilles (338–70), in the war that will devastate Troy (346). The hallmark of Achilles' success is carnage, fields flowing with blood (344), bodies cut down like wheat (353–5), heaps of corpses choking the river Scamander (359–60).[28] Bereaved mothers will bear witness to his glorious deeds (348–51). Here again, the collocation of *uirtutes* with *clara facta* makes evident the martial reference of the word "virtues": they are achievements on the battlefield, irrespective of the pain they bring to aged women.

The final witness to Achilles' "great virtues" (*magnis uirtutibus*, 357) is Polyxena, the Trojan princess who will be slain at his tomb as a sacrifice to his ghost (362–70) – an episode that might well seem a macabre travesty of a marriage union.[29] "Come therefore [*quare*]," the Parcae continue, "and consort in long-imagined love" (trans. Lee 1990) – it takes a moment to realize that the Parcae have returned to Peleus and Thetis as their subject, and the juxtaposition of the brutal sacrifice with the joy of the wedding ceremony is jarring.[30]

Catullus concludes the epyllion with an epilogue contrasting the piety of bygone days with the perversity of present times, when brothers slay each other, sons do not mourn the death of fathers, a father looks forward to his son's funeral so that he can enjoy his daughter-in-law, a mother deliberately seduces her son (399–404).[31] This is clearly a commentary on the morality of the age, but what has it to do with politics?

In 1930, L. Herrmann proposed that Peleus and Thetis in the epyllion were in fact stand-ins for Pompey and Julia, the daughter of Julius Caesar whom Pompey married in 59. Herrmann imagined the occasion for the poem to be Julia's pregnancy, and the song of the Parcae was intended to celebrate the child to come. Julia, as we have noted, died, either in childbirth or soon after the birth of a daughter, in September 54 (Vell. Pat. 2.47.2; Suet. *Iul.* 26; Plut. *Caes.* 23, *Pomp.* 53; Dio Cass. 39.64). There are no certain indications of when c. 64 was composed, though some scholars have taken apparent echoes of Lucretius to point to the year 54, when *On the Nature of Things* may have been published. It is conceivable that the address to Peleus as *Emathiae tutamen*, "bulwark of Emathia," with which the Parcae begin their song, would have evoked Pompey to a contemporary audience (323–4).

Emathia was a poetic name for Macedon, the home of Alexander the Great, whose image Pompey imitated to the point of styling himself Magnus (cf. Sall. *Hist.* 2.88 M.; Plut. *Pomp.* 2.1–2; Syme 1958: 2.770). Krebs (unpublished) takes *Caesaris... Magni* in 11.10 as a sign that Caesar has now taken over from Alexander, the subject of the first stanza, and Pompey, the subject of the second, the title of "Great." What is more, Catullus describes the bond between Peleus and Thetis in distinctly political language: no lovers were ever joined in such a pact (*tali foedere*, 335) as the alliance (*concordia*, 336) of these two. The conquest of the sea (think of Pompey's clearing the Mediterranean of pirates), the expedition to far Pontus, the extraordinary opulence of Peleus' villa, the reminiscence of a bygone age of valor already tainted by opportunism, the moral corruption of the present, and the evocation of a future war in Troy, with violence and destructiveness parading as heroism – might this not reflect Catullus' feelings toward the father-in-law and son-in-law who had ruined the entire world in the pursuit of wealth and power?[32]

Among the supporters of Caesar was P. Vatinius, to whom Catullus alludes wittily in c. 53. Vatinius had been responsible for Caesar's securing a five-year command in Gaul in 59, but the trial in which Calvus attacked him for illegitimately canvassing for office very likely took place in 54 (so Gruen 1966; 58 and 56 have also been proposed), when Vatinius was defended by none other than Cicero (Tac. *Dial.* 21.2; cf. Gruen 1974: 317). If so, the poem may take its place as a light-hearted outrider of the anti-Caesar invectives. The humor is in the coarse appreciation on the part of a bystander at the edge of the crowd for Calvus' precise delineation of Vatinius' crimes. Perhaps Catullus meant to suggest that Calvus was reaching the masses with his oratory; Vatinius is said to have remarked that he ought not to be condemned simply because Calvus was such a fine speaker.[33] A late date is perhaps confirmed by the parallel mention of Vatinius in c. 52. Vatinius had boasted he would be consul, and had achieved the praetorship in 55; perhaps that is the moment when his confidence would have run high. The formula, "why, Catullus, do you delay to pass away," of course means, in effect, "Now you've seen the worst – why go on living," but it is not impossible, I suppose, that Catullus really was, or believed himself to be, near the end of his life when he wrote these verses. If so, it is another reason to date them to 54, the year in which he may well have died. Conceivably, too, the ironic verses on Cicero's eloquence (c. 49) were occasioned by this same trial, especially since Cicero had attacked Vatinius in 56 in his most personal and malicious manner – his rapid about-face might well have earned Catullus' backhanded praise.

I have been suggesting that during the years 55 and 54, that is, the time of the latest poems in the surviving collection, Catullus saw Caesar and Pompey as driven by greed and lechery – their own and that of their underlings – to launch wars in Gaul and the East, spreading destruction abroad and corruption at home to satisfy their petty lusts. And yet, so high-minded a contempt for self-enrichment at the expense of the provinces seems inconsistent with Catullus' own apparent disappointment with his year of service (57–6) in Bithynia on the staff of C. Memmius, who, on Catullus' evidence, "screwed" his officers and left them unexpectedly impoverished at the end of their tour of duty. In c. 10, for example, Catullus recounts how he was embarrassed by a girlfriend of his pal Varus, when he pretended that, despite Memmius' stinginess – "a bugger of a praetor who didn't give a damn for his cohort" (12–13: *irrumator praetor, nec faceret pili cohortem*) – he had at least acquired in Bithynia eight sturdy slaves to carry a sedan-chair, and was then forced to confess that he did not even make off with that much.

Catullus is still more explicit about his discontent in c. 28, where he commiserates with his friends Veranius and Fabullus, who are suffering hunger and cold on the staff of Piso – presumably the Piso who was Caesar's father-in-law – while he was governor, in all likelihood, of Macedonia in 57–55; Catullus complains that he too has been "screwed over" by Memmius, and has not earned a penny. "Get lords for friends!" he petulantly exclaims, and concludes by cursing Piso and Memmius alike as a disgrace to Romulus and Remus. Catullus himself was, at this time, either still in Bithynia or recently returned to Rome.

It is, of course, possible that Catullus was the kind of person who is fiercely partisan toward his friends and antagonistic toward his enemies, and that his indignation at the excesses of Mamurra was, in the end, motivated more by a petty resentment that others were prospering while he and his friends were being left out in the cold than by a more properly political revulsion at the policies of Caesar and Pompey, which were leading to the ruin of the world. In c. 47, he attacks Piso simply for preferring two other men over Veranius and Fabullus, who have to scrounge for dinner invitations while their rivals enjoy sumptuous banquets. But the difference between Catullus' expectations of profit and Mamurra's extravagance may rather have been a matter of degree. Like others of his class, Catullus counted on being rewarded appropriately by the nobility, receiving preference and remuneration in exchange for service.[34] It was one thing to entertain elegantly in Rome and treat your staff handsomely in the provinces, another to wage wars as far as Britain and Parthia for the sake of enriching one's cronies beyond all measure. Catullus' hostility to Caesar and Pompey was, after all, that of an aristocrat, not a modern egalitarian.

But I would like to suggest that there may have been a development or change in Catullus' view of the triumvirs over the brief, three- or four-year period to which his political poems are plausibly dated.[35] If we are right to believe that he served in Bithynia with Memmius in 57, returned to Rome in 56, and composed his most bitter attacks on Caesar and Pompey in 55 and 54, it may be because he came to perceive their policies and behavior in a different light in that final couple of years. It is easy – too easy – to invent reasons for such a shift. Relations among the triumvirs were always tense, but they patched up a particularly dangerous rift in 56, at a meeting in Luca; as a result of this deal, Caesar's proconsulship in Gaul was extended for another five years in 55, while Pompey and Crassus also obtained proconsular commands, Pompey choosing Spain as his sphere of action, and Crassus Syria, with a view to a campaign in Parthia. All three had numerous legions at their disposal. Foreign wars might well have seemed to be motivated by the private ambitions of the generals.[36] What is more, Vatinius, who had been responsible for the law that granted Caesar his first command in Gaul, was now being prosecuted by Catullus' best friend, Calvus, who might have influenced his views. It was a likely moment for Catullus to lash out against Caesar's and Pompey's ambitions, even if the former had been his father's guest.

The problem with the above argument is that it is circular: the supposition, based on a certain reading of Catullus' poems, is that his intense opposition to the triumvirs was motivated by circumstances pertaining specifically to the years 55 and 54, and the events of those years are invoked in turn to confirm the reading. One could equally well adduce earlier misdeeds of Caesar and Pompey if one had reason to antedate Catullus' antagonism to them. All depends on the chronology of Catullus' verses, and this is both notoriously difficult to establish and based largely on inference from evidence internal to the poems themselves. It would seem safer, in respect to Catullus' politics as in the affair with Lesbia, to abandon attempts to construct a historical narrative.

That said, and with all due hesitation, I should like to introduce one last bit of evidence for such an alteration in Catullus' views – this the least secure of all, let the reader be warned. Poem 65 is a reply to a request by the great orator Hortensius Hortalus for some original verses of Catullus; Catullus explains that the recent death of his brother has paralyzed his creativity, but he offers instead to send him a translation he has made of Callimachus. There is no reason to doubt that the poem in question is precisely c. 66, a rendition into Latin of the Lock of Berenice, which Callimachus appended as the conclusion to the four books of his *Aitia*.

When did Catullus compose cc. 65 and 66? There is no way of knowing. If we suppose that c. 101 represents an actual visit on Catullus' part to the grave of his brother near the region of ancient Troy, and that he made the voyage while he was serving in Bithynia, then his brother's death will have occurred before the spring of 57, when Catullus set out for the province. He may well have written c. 65, then, while in Verona, as he did the first part of c. 68, where again he refers to a lapse in his poetic activity as a result of his brother's death (68.19–40). By this time, at all events, Catullus considered his home to be in Rome, not Verona (*Romae uiuimus: illa domus,/illa mihi sedes, illic mea carpitur aetas*, 68.34–5). Catullus could have written these words in the year 58 (which would mean he had moved to Rome in that year or sooner); but the date might be earlier, conceivably much earlier, despite the absence of reliable allusions in the poems to events of the time. Let us, merely for the sake of the argument, place the date of c. 65 in 58 or 59, and that of c. 66 – the translation of Callimachus – around the same time or a little before.

That Catullus should have studied Callimachus closely, and gone so far as to try his hand at rendering his verses into Latin, is no cause for surprise. Callimachus was the model of the learned, precisely crafted, and pithy style of poetry that Catullus and his circle affected. One must not forget, however, that Callimachus was not just a practitioner of a refined aesthetic technique, but also a court poet who, like Theocritus and other contemporaries, composed panegyrics to the royal family in Alexandria. No poem of his was more political than the Lock of Berenice, which he wrote in celebration of Berenice's dedication of a lock of her hair which she had promised on condition that her husband, Ptolemy III (Euergetes), return safely from his military expedition against Syria – a campaign that had brought him all the way to the borders of Bactria in the East. Berenice fulfilled her vow in the summer or autumn of 245, and when the offering disappeared a short while afterwards, the court astronomer Conon purported to discover a new constellation in the heavens, which he identified with the shorn tress of the queen (details in Marinone 1997: 19–21).

Late in 62, as we have seen, Pompey returned from the East, where he had finally eliminated the threat of Mithridates and restored Roman control over the Seleucid kingdom of Syria. The analogy with the campaign of Ptolemy Euergetes in the same region is not far to seek. Within two years, moreover, Pompey would marry Caesar's daughter Julia, thus securing an alliance between Rome's most powerful leaders that might well remind one of the wedding of Berenice and Ptolemy: for with her ascent to the throne of Egypt on January 27, 246, Berenice, queen of Cyrene, had effected the union of two domains whose relations had been marked by rivalry and animosity. Of course, Julia had not made vows for Pompey's return. But a Greek poem celebrating a dynastic marriage and the safe completion of military operations against a grave threat arising in Syria might well have had political resonance in the Rome of 60 or 59.[37] And who would be a better recipient of the translation of this eulogy than Hortensius, who had vehemently opposed the Lex Gabinia in 67, by which Pompey was granted almost limitless powers to rid the Mediterranean of piracy? By way of a learnedly allusive poem, Catullus helps to reconcile a fellow poet to the new situation in Rome.

Fanciful? Absolutely. But if we are to imagine the political context in which Catullus may have written both his jibes against the leading figures in Rome and other kinds of topical verse, some such exercise of the historical imagination is required, and the one proposed may serve some heuristic function. What is more, there may be a clue in the poem itself that hints at this interpretation, much as *Emathiae tutamen* in poem 64 suggested the identification of Peleus with Pompey. I mean the use of the term *caesaries* to indicate the lock (8) – a term which elsewhere in Latin literature always and only refers to a complete head of hair: might this not have evoked the name Caesar, Julia's own cognomen?[38] The pun would not be unique to Catullus; in the *Einsiedeln Eclogues* (probably dating to the reign of Nero), we read (1.43–7): "His thick beard and white hair [*caesaries*] shone with full dignity…and he duly covered his Caesarian head [*Caesareumque caput*] with his cloak."[39]

In c. 66.41–50 there is also a connection between the ruthlessness of imperial expansion and a cruel indifference to a lover's sentiments that may, I am inclined to believe, have inspired the similar association in c. 11. Just as steel cut a path through the promontory of Athos for Xerxes' armies when they were invading Greece, so it divides the lock of hair from the beloved head of Berenice. Catullus may have found in Callimachus' rather extravagant image something that resonated with his own sense that Rome's violence in war was not unrelated to cruelty in love.[40]

We have cited above the passage in which Suetonius reports that Catullus apologized for the slurs on Caesar's reputation. Is there any evidence in the poems of a more conciliatory posture toward Caesar on Catullus' part? One possible candidate is c. 93, consisting of a single distich – although everything depends on how one punctuates the first line:

> Nil nimium studeo, Caesar, tibi uelle placere,
> nec scire utrum sis albus an ater homo.

On the traditional reading (with the above punctuation), the sense is:

> I don't try very hard, Caesar, to wish to please you,
> nor to know whether you're a white person or a black.

While the meaning of the second verse is not altogether perspicuous – it is apparently a way of expressing Catullus' indifference – the thrust is hardly amiable, and the poem might be read as a rejection of a friendly initiative by Caesar rather than as a gesture of contrition. S. Koster (1981: 131– 2), however, has argued in favor of placing a full stop after *nimium*:

> "Nothing in excess." I'm trying, Caesar to wish to please you,
> and not to know whether you're a white person or a black.

This sounds more like an effort at compromise, although Ernst Schmidt (1985: 65–6) has suggested that the second verse, in this case, means that only by ignoring whether Caesar is good or bad can Catullus refrain from criticizing him.

There is one last poem – or rather, the very first in the collection – that has not usually been read as political in character, but which, nonetheless, may also express, however indirectly, a positive view of Rome's imperial expansion. C. 1 is a dedicatory piece, whether or not the collection it introduced was precisely the one we have today. The book by Cornelius Nepos that Catullus mentions is his *Chronica*, a historical account of the world beginning at least as early as the time of Homer (cf. Gell. *NA* 17.21.3), with a special emphasis, apparently, on establishing a reliable comparative chronology of Greece and Rome. Nepos was also, incidentally, another member of Catullus' circle who found Mamurra's mansion outrageously luxurious for being the first to be lined entirely with marble (Plin. *NH* 36.48).

Whatever the personal relationship between Catullus and Nepos, who was also something of a poet, might have been, why did Catullus single out his historical work for special mention? It may, of course, be simply a matter of one writer complimenting another, and indicating by the way that the man who appreciated Catullus' own early efforts himself had literary credentials. The compact and studied character of Nepos' work may also have commended itself to a neoteric poet, who admired these qualities in Alexandrian scholar poets such as Callimachus (cf. W. J. Tatum 1997: 485;

Rauk 1997: 319–20; Wiseman 1979: 27–40). But Nepos' work just may have had a further significance in its time. Andrew Wallace-Hadrill (1997) has described the process by which local knowledge, which is traditional and specific to particular communities, was replaced by a universal *scientia* in the period of the transition from the Republic to the Empire in Rome. Part of the reason for the change, according to Wallace-Hadrill, was the expansion of Rome and the corresponding responsibilities of administering a far-flung Empire. Fixing the date of a religious festival or other public event across the entire realm demanded an accurate year and a universal sense of time, as opposed to the random intercalations that had served the needs of a small city. It may be that the impulse to standardize world chronology, like that of establishing a consistent calendar, was a reflex of Rome's new sense of itself as the center of a vast territory, and that, in paying homage to Nepos' achievement, Catullus was subtly acknowledging Rome's hegemonic place in the new world order.[41]

Catullus was witness to a dramatic moment in Roman politics, when a few powerful rivals teamed up briefly and turned their energies to foreign wars and plunder. As Catullus saw it, their military and sexual lust for conquest was of a piece – not an eccentric view among Romans – and his poems testify, I believe, to an increasing awareness, during the course of the 50s, of how ruinous these passions were to the world he knew.

ACKNOWLEDGMENT

My thanks to Regina Höschele for her perceptive comments on an earlier draft of this chapter, and to the editor of this volume for her helpful suggestions.

NOTES

1 Any biographical reports concerning Catullus – even those that seem confirmed by his own verses – must be taken with a large grain of salt; see Holzberg (2002a). Little of the discussion that follows depends on more than the assumption that some, at least, of the political poems were composed in, or not much before, the year 54. For thumbnail sketches of the figures to whom Catullus refers – or seems to refer – see Neudling (1955). For an ingenious but ultimately quixotic attempt to organize Catullus' poetry into periods according to the vocabulary employed, see Stoessl (1977).
2 The text used throughout this chapter is Mynors's 1958 OCT (revised 1960); departures from Mynors are noted. In c. 29, I read *ante* instead of *uncti* in v. 4, and *urbis potentissimi* instead of †*urbis opulentissime*† (obelized in Mynors) in v. 23. Badian (1977) proposes reading *nunc Gallicae timetur et Britannicae* (sc. *praedae*) in v. 20, i.e., "we now fear for the Gallic and British loot"; but would one fear for the loot, or for the province that will be looted?
3 Skinner notes too that, since his father was still alive, Catullus would have been *in patria potestate*, that is, legally a minor, at the time.
4 C. A. Williams (1999: 172–8) argues that *cinaedus* suggests any kind of sexual deviance, as opposed to *pathicus*, which refers specifically to the receptive adult male. Catullus, however, seems freely to equate the two; cf. poems 25.1–3 and 16.1–2.

5   I assume, with the majority of scholars, that these slurs are addressed to Caesar; Quinn
    (1973a: 176–7) and some others suppose that the first ten lines of the poem are directed to
    Pompey, the second ten to Caesar, while the final four speak to both. For discussion, see
    Syndikus (1984: 178–9); Asper (1997: 67–8).

6   W. J. Tatum (1997: 484) observes that Catullus' poetry "is conspicuously unfurnished
    with straightforward and obvious political formulations. Yet . . . one can hardly fail to
    recognize Catullus' invective against Caesar and Pompey . . . as a political attack."

7   See Sall. *Cat.* 10–13, where dissoluteness is explicitly identified as the motive for war, and
    cf. *Jug.* 41–2, where Sallust retrojects the same motives into an earlier war. W. J. Tatum
    (1993: 37) notes, in connection with c. 79: "A Roman politician attacked his rivals as
    perverts not because they actually were depraved but because he hoped to persuade
    someone that they were actually depraved and consequently unworthy of credence or
    loyalty or honour. Such rhetoric was a supplement to, but not a substitute for, genuine
    political argument." I am suggesting that certain kinds of personal excess were in fact
    perceived as having decidedly political consequences. Butrica (2002) argues that c. 79
    need not refer to incest at all, but rather to decadent behavior generally and the feminized
    associations of the term *pulcher* = *exoletus*.

8   P. B. Harvey (1979) argues that such an estate would have constituted a large holding at
    the time; contra Thomson (1997: 552). Thomson suggests that "*Pratum* and *arvum*
    are well-known agricultural-sexual metaphors for the female *pudenda*," but even if this is
    so, it fails to explain why Catullus should ascribe to Mentula a small estate rather than a
    large one.

9   In classical antiquity, a large sexual organ was commonly thought of as signifying a bestial
    excess of sexual appetite; thus Priapus was customarily depicted as macrophallic; cf. Dover
    (1978: 125– 6); Winkler (1990: 28–9, 34); Fredrick (1995: fig. 15) on the statue of
    Priapus in the House of the Vettii in Pompeii.

10 Catullus' *mentula magna minax* echoes Ennius *Annales* fr. 620 Skutsch = 621 Vahlens,
    machina multa minax minitatur maxima muris, and there may be some intertextual
    play between the image of Mamurra's sexual organ and the battering ram that threatens
    city walls; there is no context for the Ennian fragment, however, and interpretation is
    hazardous.

11 Cf. Ellis (1889: 496): "the profits derived from it [i.e., the estate] were less than the
    necessary outlay."

12 The idea is commonplace; cf. Democr. fr. 219 D-K: "The desire for money, if it is not
    limited by sufficiency [*koros*], is much worse than extreme poverty, for greater desires
    produce greater needs."

13 This is one reason to suppose that the first part of c. 29 is addressed to him, although, as
    Quinn remarks (1973a: 177), "it is a word with which C[atullus] is pretty free."

14 At least, this is the charge if we accept Pleitner's emendation of *Maeciliam* to *Mucillam*, a
    diminutive of Mucia, Pompey's third wife; but even if *Maeciliam* is retained, the poem
    suggests an association between Pompey and the spread of adultery. Marmorale's argu-
    ment (1957: 60–1) that Pompey is named here only to identify the year renders the
    reference rather flat.

15 Reading *horribilesque ulti-* in v. 11, instead of *horribile aequor ulti-* with Haupt, followed
    by Mynors.

16 Fernández Corte (1995) argues that the offer by Furius and Aurelius is intended to be
    read as insincere, and that Catullus' exposure of their false pretensions to friendship is
    analogous to his rejection of Lesbia's dishonest love in the concluding stanzas. Holzberg
    (2002a: 38) suggests that both Furius and Aurelius are made-up names, and that it would
    be wrong to seek either historical personages behind them or a consistent representation
    of their characters. Maleuvre (1998: 161) suggests that Aurelius stands for Caesar, a view

only slightly less implausible than the same author's claim that the brother whom Catullus laments in c. 65 is Calvus (75–86). For my own view of the relationship between c. 11 and the characterization of Furius and Aurelius in other poems of Catullus, see Konstan (2000); it is worth mentioning that both are treated as sexually rapacious, and that Aurelius is described as the father of all hungers, present, past, and future, in c. 21.

17 On *penetrare*, cf. Janan (1994: 64–5).

18 Fitzgerald (1995: 181) affirms that "Lesbia is seen as a threatening monster on the edge of the empire, that is, beyond the pale of civilization, and also, by association with the plough, as a manifestation of the ruthless indifference that characterizes Roman imperial might"; but if Lesbia is at the boundary, it is because she, like Furius and Aurelius, has arrived there from the center; Catullus, on the contrary, is located there from the beginning, a helpless figure on the fringe. Fitzgerald adds: "Bringing together the 'friends' and the lover, Catullus allows them to cancel each other out as they merge into a generalized and indifferent violence on whose periphery he locates, very precisely, himself" (p. 182).

19 E. Greene (1997: 153) observes that Catullus "casts both Caesar's and Lesbia's conquests in a similar light of moral degradation as against his own poetic rendering of himself as a delicate, fragile flower that is victimized by the brutality of the world."

20 For Mamurra as a foil for or counter-image of Catullus himself, see Deuling (1999).

21 For Catullus' Greek sources, see Braga (1950: esp. p. 160). In Apollonius' account, Peleus and Thetis are married and Achilles is born prior to the voyage.

22 Cf. Harmon (1973: 325); for a possible hint in vv. 379–80 of a future separation between Thetis and Peleus, see Konstan (1977: 81–2).

23 Vv. 43–6, with Kroll (1968) and Fordyce (1961).

24 See Konstan (1977: 40); *OLD* s.v., defs. 2, 3; Kinsey (1965: 916) takes *indicat* ironically.

25 Cf. Konstan (1977: 40); *OLD* s.v., def. 4.

26 See Earl (1961: 28; 1967: 83).

27 This interpretation, which I have defended in Konstan (1977, 1993), has not won universal consent; for the contrary view, see, e.g., Syndikus (1990: 139 n. 162).

28 Cf. E. A. Schmidt (1985: 85): "Die Charakteristik der Taten Achills is nach Auswahl und Sprache eindeutig negativ."

29 See Curran (1969: 190–1); Bramble (1970: 25–7).

30 On the harsh transition, see Hutchinson (1988: 308). Boës (1986) sees no irony in the collocation of festive joy and images of wartime brutality; cf. also Syndikus (1990: 184–6).

31 On the perversions described in the epilogue, see Arkins (1982s: 152); Jenkyns (1982: 96–7); P. A. Watson (1984); Forsyth (1987a).

32 A Roman audience might expect to detect political allegory in mythological narratives; see Leach (2000) for discussion of such allusions in dramatic performances.

33 Weiss (1996) argues, perhaps rightly, that *salaputium* in fact refers to Calvus' wit ("salt"), and is Catullus' way of defending his friend's effectiveness as a popular orator, against Cicero's criticism (*Brutus* 283, 289) that his style went over the heads of the masses.

34 Nevertheless, there were limits; Braund (1996) suggests that Memmius might well have had reason to be scrupulous in administering the province, given his tense relationship with Caesar, who himself had connections in the area, and would be prepared to prosecute him for malfeasance. If so, Catullus' snideness in respect of Memmius may be a sign that he was not yet, in 56, personally at odds with Caesar. Pizzone (1998: 284) suggests, on the contrary, that Memmius must have known of Catullus' hostility to Caesar as early as 58 (cf. E. A. Schmidt 1985: 67–8), or he would never have taken along with him a young man whose family had such close ties with his arch-enemy; on this hypothesis, it is necessary to posit a break between Catullus and Memmius after the return from Bithynia (286–7).

35 Cf. Pizzone (1998: 288): "È dunque plausibile che una certa diversità di toni e di modi all'interno del gruppo di carmi contro Cesare e Mamurra sia da ricollegare a differenti momenti di composizione, a differenti contesti storico-cronologici."

36 Catullus might have observed that Bithynia and Macedonia were both settled provinces, in which Roman military power was employed to maintain order, whereas Caesar's and Pompey's campaigns were plainly wars of aggression (I owe this observation to Marilyn Skinner).

37 I am indebted for this interpretation to a conversation with Susan Stephens; she must not be held responsible, however, for the view expressed here.

38 I am indebted to Regina Höschele for this idea. The term *caesaries* was imagined to derive from *caedere*, "cut" (Serv. on *Aen.* 1.590, 8.659), and hence was of course appropriate as a description of the shorn lock. For the connection between *caesaries* and Caesar, cf. Fest. p. 50 Lindsay *DVS*, and Nadeau (1982), who finds the same pun in Ov. *Met.* 1.180 and, indirectly, in Vergil by way of Catullus (I owe this last reference to Damien Nelis).

39 Cf. also Luc. 1.183–9 for a possible association of *caesaries* with Caesar.

40 There are other echoes in c. 66 of earlier motifs in the Catullan collection, e.g., the description of Berenice's other locks as "sisters" in mourning (51) may evoke the mention of Catullus' own brother's death in c. 65, and the positioning of the lock in the heavens alongside Ariadne's crown (59–61) may recall Ariadne's apparent divinization in c. 64. It is possible that Catullus recognized a remarkable combination of themes in Callimachus' poem, which he exploited in various works of his own; either he or a canny editor then arranged them in such a way that c. 66 appeared as a reprise or confluence of motifs that it may well have inspired in the first place. I owe these observations to Regina Höschele; we plan to discuss the question further in a future publication.

41 Contra Rauk (1997: 322), who describes Nepos' *Chronica* as "traditional."

GUIDE TO FURTHER READING

On economic and other motives for Roman imperialism during the Republic, an excellent source is Harris (1985). A good overview of Roman value terms may be found in Earl (1967). Lintott (1999) gives a sense of the rough nature of Roman politics. For Roman social and political history, Crawford (1993) is balanced and clear; also useful is Brunt (1971). Caesar has his admirers as well as detractors; see Meyer (1995). For political interpretations of particular poems, see the articles by Braund (1996), Butrica (2002), and Tatum (1993, 1997); also Skinner (1989). For more general appraisals of Catullus in a political context, see Konstan (2000/2), Skinner (1979), and Wiseman (1985). The relationship between politics and desire, a complex topic in modern theory, is explored in Janan (2001).

WORKS CITED

Arkins, B. 1982a. *Sexuality in Catullus*. Altertumswissenschaftliche Texte und Studien 8. Hildesheim.

Asper, M. 1997. "Catull, Mamurra und Caesar: Eine öffentliche Auseinandersetzung?" In T. Baier and F. Schimann, eds., *Fabrica: Studien zur antiken Literatur und ihrer Rezeption*. Stuttgart and Leipzig. 65–78.

Badian, E. 1977. "Mamurra's Fourth Fortune." *Classical Philology* 72: 320–2.

Boës, J. 1986. "Le mythe d'Achille vu par Catulle: importance de l'amour pour une morale de la gloire." *Revue des études latines* 64: 104–15.

Braga, D. 1950. *Catullo e i poeti greci.* Messina and Florence.

Bramble, J. C. 1970. "Structure and Ambiguity in Catullus LXIV." *Proceedings of the Cambridge Philological Society* 16: 22–41.

Braund, D. C. 1996. "The Politics of Catullus 10: Memmius, Caesar and the Bithynians." *Hermathena* 160: 45–57.

Brunt, P. 1971. *Social Conflicts in the Roman Republic.* New York.

Butrica, J. L. 2002. "Clodius the 'pulcher' in Catullus and Cicero." *Classical Quarterly* n.s. 52: 507–16.

Crawford, M. 1993. *The Roman Republic.* 2nd edn. Cambridge, MA.

Curran, L. C. 1969. "Catullus 64 and the Heroic Age." *Yale Classical Studies* 21: 171–92.

Deuling, J. K. 1999. "Catullus and Mamurra." *Mnemosyne* ser. 4 52: 188–94.

Dover, K. J. 1978. *Greek Homosexuality.* London and Cambridge, MA.

Earl, D. C. 1961. *The Political Thought of Sallust.* Cambridge.

Earl, D. C. 1967. *The Moral and Political Tradition of Rome.* London and Ithaca, NY.

Ellis, R. 1889. *A Commentary on Catullus.* 2nd edn. Oxford.

Fernández Corte, J. C. 1995. "Parodia, *renuntiatio amicitiae* y *renuntiatio amoris* en Catulo XI." *Emérita* 63: 81–101.

Fitzgerald, W. 1995. *Catullan Provocations: Lyric Poetry and the Drama of Position.* Berkeley, Los Angeles, and London.

Fordyce, C. J., ed. 1961. *Catullus: A Commentary.* Oxford.

Forsyth, P. Y. 1987a. "Catullus 64.400–402: Transposition or Emendation?" *Échos du monde classique/Classical Views* 31: 329–32.

Fredrick, D. 1995. "Beyond the Atrium to Ariadne: Erotic Painting and Visual Pleasure in the Roman House." *Classical Antiquity* 14: 266–88.

Greene, E. 1997. "Journey to the Remotest Meadow: A Reading of Catullus 11." *Intertexts* 1: 147–55.

Gruen, E. 1966. "Cicero and Licinius Calvus." *Harvard Studies in Classical Philology* 71: 215–33.

Gruen, E. 1974. *The Last Generation of the Roman Republic.* Berkeley, Los Angeles, and London.

Halperin, D. M. 1990. *One Hundred Years of Homosexuality and Other Essays on Greek Love.* New York.

Harmon, D. P. 1973. "Nostalgia for the Age of Heroes in Catullus 64." *Latomus* 32: 311–31.

Harris, W. V. 1985. *War and Imperialism in Republican Rome 327–70* b.c. Oxford.

Harvey, P. B. 1979. "Catullus 114–15: Mentula, Roman Agricola." *Historia* 28: 329–55.

Herrmann, L. 1930. "Le poème 64 de Catulle et Vergile." *Revue des études latines* 8: 211–21.

Holzberg, N. 2002a. *Catull: Der Dichter und sein erotisches Werk.* Munich.

Hutchinson, G. O. 1988. *Hellenistic Poetry.* Oxford.

Janan, M. 1994. *"When the Lamp is Shattered": Desire and Narrative in Catullus.* Carbondale and Edwardsville, IL.

Janan, M. 2001. *The Politics of Desire: Propertius IV.* Berkeley.

Jenkyns, R. 1982. *Three Classical Poets: Sappho, Catullus and Juvenal.* London.

Kinsey, T. E. 1965. "Catullus 11." *Latomus* 24: 537–44.

Konstan, D. 1977. *Catullus' Indictment of Rome: The Meaning of Catullus 64.* Amsterdam.

Konstan, D. 1993. "Neoteric Epic: Catullus 64." In A. J. Boyle, ed., *Roman Epic.* London. 59–78.

Konstan, D. 2000/2. "Self, Sex, and Empire in Catullus: The Construction of a Decentered Identity." In V. Bécares Botas, F. Pordomingo, R. Cortés Tovar, and C. Fernández Corte, eds., *La intertextualidad griega y latina*. Madrid. 213–31. (Also available online at http:// zeno.stoa.org/ cgi-bin/ptext?doc= Stoa:text:2002.01.0005.)

Koster, S. 1981. "Catull beim Wort genommen." *Würzburger Jahrbücher* n.F. 7: 125–34.

Krebs, C., unpublished. "Caesar Magnus: Alexander, Pompey, and Caesar in Catull. 11."

Kroll, W. 1968 [1923]. *C. Valerius Catullus, herausgegeben und erklärt*. 5th edn. Stuttgart.

Leach, E. W. 2000. "Cicero's Pro Sestio: Spectacle and Performance." In S. K. Dickison and J. P. Hallett, eds., *Rome and Her Monuments: Essays on the City and Literature of Rome in Honor of Katherine A. Geffcken*. Wauconda, IL. 329–97.

Lee, G., trans. 1990. *The Poems of Catullus*. Oxford and New York.

Lintott, A. 1999. *Violence in Republican Rome*. 2nd edn. Oxford.

Maleuvre, J.-Y. 1998. *Catulle ou L'anti-César: perspectives nouvelles sur le "Libellus."* Paris.

Marinone, N., ed. 1997. *Berenice da Callimaco a Catullo: testo critico, traduzione e commento*. Rev. edn. Bologna.

Marmorale, E. V. 1957. *L'ultimo Catullo*. Naples.

Meyer, C. 1995. *Caesar*. Trans. D. McLintock. New York.

Mynors, R. A. B., ed. 1958 (rev. 1960). *C. Valerii Catulli Carmina recognovit brevique adnotatione critica instruxit*. Oxford.

Nadeau, Y. 1982. "*Caesaries Berenices* (or the Hair of the God)." *Latomus* 41: 101–3.

Neudling, C. L. 1955. *A Prosopography to Catullus*. Iowa Studies in Classical Philology 12. [London.]

Pizzone, A. M. V. 1998. "Memmio e i carmi catulliani contro Mamurra: una proposta di cronologia." *Maia* 50: 281–9.

Quinn, K. 1972b. *Catullus: An Interpretation*. London.

Quinn, K., ed. 1973a. *Catullus: The Poems*. 2nd edn. London and Basingstoke.

Rauk, J. 1997. "Time and History in Catullus 1." *Classical World* 90: 319–32.

Schmidt, E. A. 1985. *Catull*. Heidelberg.

Skinner, M. B. 1979. "Parasites and Strange Bedfellows: A Study in Catullus' Political Imagery." *Ramus* 8: 137–52.

Skinner, M. B. 1989. "*Ut decuit cinaediorem*: Power, Gender, and Urbanity in Catullus 10." *Helios* 16: 7–23.

Skinner, M. B. 2003. *Catullus in Verona: A Reading of the Elegiac* Libellus, *Poems 65–116*. Columbus, OH.

Stoessl, F. 1977. *C. Valerius Catullus: Mensch, Leben, Dichtung*. Meisenheim.

Syme, R. 1958. *Tacitus*. 2 vols. Oxford.

Syndikus, H. P. 1984. *Catull: Eine Interpretation. Erster Teil: Einleitung, Die kleinen Gedichte (1–60)*. Darmstadt.

Syndikus, H. P. 1987. *Catull: Eine Interpretation. Dritter Teil: Die Epigramme (69–116)*. Darmstadt.

Syndikus, H. P. 1990. *Catull: Eine Interpretation. Zweiter Teil: Die grossen Gedichte (61–68)*. Darmstadt.

Tatum, W. J. 1993. "Catullus 79: Personal Invective or Political Discourse?" In F. Cairns and M. Heath, eds., *Papers of the Leeds International Latin Seminar 7*. Leeds. 31–45.

Tatum, W. J. 1997. "Friendship, Politics, and Literature in Catullus: Poems 1, 65 and 66, 116." *Classical Quarterly* n.s. 47: 482–500.

Thomson, D. F. S., ed. 1997. *Catullus, Edited with a Textual and Interpretative Commentary*. Toronto.

Wallace-Hadrill, A. 1997. "*Mutatio morum*: The Idea of a Cultural Revolution." In T. Habinek and A. Schiesaro, eds., *The Roman Cultural Revolution*. Cambridge. 3–22.

Watson, P. A. 1984. "The Case of the Murderous Father: Catullus 64.401–2." *Liverpool Classical Monthly* 9: 114–16.

Weiss, M. 1996. "An Oscanism in Catullus 53." *Classical Philology* 91: 353–9.

Williams, C. A. 1999. *Roman Homosexuality: Ideologies of Masculinity in Classical Antiquity.* New York and Oxford.

Winkler, J. J. 1990. "*Phallos politikos:* Representing the Body Politic in Athens." *differences* 2.1: 28–45.

Wiseman, T. P. 1969. *Catullan Questions.* Leicester.

Wiseman, T. P. 1979. *Clio's Cosmetics: Three Studies in Greco-Roman Literature.* Leicester.

Wiseman, T. P. 1985. *Catullus and His World: A Reappraisal.* Cambridge.

Wiseman, T. P. 1987. *Roman Studies Literary and Historical.* Liverpool.

CHAPTER SIX

The Intellectual Climate

Andrew Feldherr

Yeats's notorious challenge to Latinists, "Lord, what would they say/Did their Catullus walk that way?" distinguishes a vigorous Catullus in the flesh from the poet as object of research by academics not especially at home in their own. By the early 1980s, though, scholars could answer that they might not walk the walk, but Catullus himself sure talked the talk. New Criticism had cast its spotlight on "the text itself" as an autonomous entity uninflected by the swagger of its historical author; "Alexandrianism," with its imagined ideal of the refined poem that spoke through other poems to an elite audience informed by a vast and detailed literary knowledge, was seen as the foundation of Roman poets' understanding of the aims and nature of literature. Catullus was as bookish as we (Latinists), had always aspired to live on the page, and we were always his ideal readers, as well as being essential interlocutors for any informed understanding of his work. Richard Thomas's (1982) analysis of the opening of Catullus' epic celebration of the wedding of Peleus and Thetis provides the most dazzling glimpse of Catullus the scholar-poet at work. Thomas shows that the first 15 lines of that poem, describing the voyage of the *Argo* on which the mortal hero Peleus first catches sight of the sea goddess he will wed, contain allusions to and corrections of no fewer than five previous literary versions of the scene. Above all, the lines figure as a polemical refinement of the second-century BC poet Ennius' Latin adaptation of the beginning of Euripides' *Medea*: Catullus corrects Ennius' imprecise rendering of the type of tree from which the ship was built and, while citing the earlier author's idea that the ship was called the *Argo* because its crew came from Argos, lets his reader know that he prefers a more obscure derivation of the name, probably found in Callimachus, from a long-obsolete Homeric adjective meaning "swift." To add insult to injury, Catullus recovers a threefold alliteration to be found in Euripides but not in Ennius. This kind of poetry, then, is already literary scholarship, and modern scholars must use all their skills to recover the intellectual background that would have made it comprehensible to its original Roman audience.

Such a picture of the role of learning in Catullan poetry seduces for many reasons. The sort of learnedness Catullus values looks in kind a lot like the learning valued by philologists, and the "polemical" edge to the Catullan art of reference bears comparison to the way professional academics put their knowledge on display by building on and correcting the work of predecessors. But it is precisely the recognizability of this Catullus that ought to put us on our guard, not simply because it raises the suspicion that Latinists have followed a long tradition of finding someone like themselves in the infinitely accommodating diversity of the Catullan oeuvre, but because what seems to need no explanation is often the most important thing to explain. My aim in this chapter therefore is to expand the picture of Catullan learning that emerges from the works of critics like Thomas by considering why such learnedness matters in Catullus' poetry and what work these displays of the mastery of Greek letters perform in the construction of his self-image. Not only was Catullus the most learned of Roman poets – *doctus* even in the eyes of the hyper-refined Ovid – but also his verses are explicitly embedded in contemporary social transactions. Yet for the most part the "social" Catullus of the polymetrics and epigrams and the "learned" Catullus of the longer poems move in different scholarly circles today. The former attracts the greatest share of attention from historically minded critics and the latter from formalists. By accepting this division, however, we risk both missing a rich and subtle document in the history of Rome's engagement with Hellenic culture and underplaying an important area of contention and complexity within the poet's work. For, as I hope to show, learnedness forms much more than a mode of poetic expression for Catullus; it is a subject his poetry explores in its own right, and its role in shaping the position and status of its author is made explicitly ambiguous. I want to begin, therefore, with a brief discussion of the social dynamics of Catullan poetry as they emerge from the shorter poems: how the work constructs its author as a social actor, "performing" friendships and enmities. This discussion will pay particular attention to the various functions of learnedness, as a criterion of judgment and an almost talismanic shared possession that defines Catullus' community of *amici* and shields their exchanges from the comprehension of outsiders. However, this analysis also exposes a potential contradiction in Catullus' depiction of learning: it serves as a tool and mark of social distinction in the eyes of both insiders and outsiders, yet sets the community it engenders apart from social business as usual. The second part of the chapter relates this contrast between the inward-facing and outward-facing aspects of literary culture to the thematization of Hellenism in Catullus 64, where it appears both as the cause of a contemporary moral downfall and as an elusive refuge from the social corruption it engenders. The final section then suggests some historical contexts for understanding these contradictory attitudes.

Material Culture?

Let me begin with the reminder that this is a poet for whom knowledge, in a variety of forms, matters. The dedicatory epigram that begins our Catullan book performs the physical gesture of handing over an objectified volume to its dedicatee before a larger audience. One likely context for such a public exchange, and the explicit subject of many other Catullan verses, was the *conuiuium*, a drinking party which imitates the Greek symposium as an arena in which one may win praise by putting on display a range of valued skills and qualities – wit, elegance, learning, and restraint – but also in which one may be shamed for being seen to lack them.[1] Such qualities emerge from a relentlessly repeated aesthetic vocabulary: *lepidus*, *uenustus*, *urbanus*, and their opposites, including especially *ineptus* and *rusticus*. Catullus' attacks on napkin-stealers like Asinius, depicted as a scion of the crude tribe of Marrucini (12), as well as compliments like that offered a Calvus (50) or a Caecilius (35), make it clear that the *conuiuium* was a competitive place, where behavior was being refined as it was subjected to criticism. But the evaluative criteria applied there suggest a context conspicuously apart from the many other places where a Roman male expected to make himself known: those quintessential Roman qualities of *uirtus* and *honos*, for which a reputation was won on the battlefield or through political success, nowhere appear in Catullus' discussion of his contemporaries. Nor is there any praise of a more ambiguous, but no less powerful, personal asset: wealth. The Catullan speaker cheerfully admits his poverty – at least he does so to the audience for his poetry: his purse is full of cobwebs (13), he has no battery of Bithynian litter-bearers, though he is not above boasting that he does (10). But if Catullus' poetry enacts a battleground of wits whereby players will try to put one another in their places for not knowing how to act, it also grants its audience inclusion in this privileged world by its vicious attacks on real outsiders whose faults are much worse than napkin-stealing: indeed the typical targets of Catullus' wildest invective are generally tagged with one of two kinds of offence – gross sexual indulgence and importunate greed. Both are tried and true subjects of Roman invective, but they help draw attention to what is special about Catullus' privileged readers: the restraint and tact with which they manage their desires.

But alongside "knowledge" as a criterion for judgment – knowing how to act or speak, for example – Catullus' poetry also puts in play a process of knowing one another that is no less competitive. Each "performer" – and Catullus, whose poetry becomes material testimony to his own urbanity and wit, is very much a performer too – presents his own knowledge of aesthetic codes as a clue to the kind of person he is, and expects to be known for it in a way that will gratify his vanity and increase his status. Arrius believes that he has spoken "marvelously" the more chances he has had to pronounce words with false aitches – apparently a rustic habit and a sign of poor education which Arrius foolishly affects (84). Egnatius is similarly attached to his inept smile (39), and Suffenus is never happier than when he writes bad poetry (22). But unlike the poems in which Catullus' friends like Nepos and Calvus are praised for their accomplishments, for these impostors the danger is rather that their true selves will become known through the particular mirror Catullus holds up to their habits. Thus Catullus applies his own "ethnographic" knowledge of the habits and peculiarities of provincials to convert Egnatius' smile from a mark of urbane wit to one of Spanish urine-drinking. The play of knowledge at work in Catullan poetry then involves calculated revelation and concealment, with each participant aiming to know his fellows at the same time as he makes known his own judgment and skill. We may imagine that such poetic wit initiates yet another level of social differentiation among its audience, as those who appreciate and understand Catullus' own wit will stand apart from those who do not. And yet this outwardly directed, exclusionary view of the *amicitia* Catullus' poetic performance sustains also implies a more positive, and quite different, way of thinking about friendship. For his work grants a kind of "behind-the-scenes" view of the creation of his self-image, showing how Catullus himself can be caught out in his role-playing (10), bested in his erotic encounters (8), and vulnerable to misunderstanding of his persona, especially when measured against more traditionally Roman canons of conduct (16). Thus at the same time as Catullus claims the upper hand through his mastery of *urbanitas*, this other dimension of Catullan self-revelation invites his audience to a more intimate level of acquaintance, as though the very exposure of weakness implied a trust that such weakness would not be exploited.

As a transition to a more explicit consideration of where the sort of specialized literary scholarship Thomas describes fits into this picture, I want to take a closer look at another "convivial" poem about etiquette; Catullus' reproof of the napkin-stealing Asinius (12). In short order, Catullus explicates a trivial *faux pas* in ways that make it clear why it is not in the least trivial. The work begins with a loading of value-laden terms that separate Asinius completely from the values of Catullan society. In this urbane world he is emphatically an Italian tribesman, one of the East Italian hill people called the Marrucini.[2] In his own eyes, napkin-stealing makes up the kind of witty gesture that should win approval, but, thanks to Catullus, it is made to signify his ignorance of right behavior. Yet the napkin itself, we realize, functions not only as an instrument for gaining admission to this privileged world, but, in a double sense, as a symbol of belonging. First, its exotic provenance, sent back by two young friends of Catullus serving with a Roman administrator in the provinces, and its fine work-manship make it a general image of refinement itself. But it is also more directly symbolic of the intimate bond that links the giver and recipient. In trying to appro-priate it, Asinius lays claim both to abstract qualities and to membership in the circle of friendship its possession implies. The poem strips him of both; in place of a woven object, he receives a "text" testifying to his boorishness that also circulates among friends.[3] The reciprocity of text and textile, which we will see at work in other Catullan poems as well, invites even closer scrutiny of the napkin's qualities, and here two motifs within the poem are especially important. First is the contrast between the small, enclosed space of the *conuiuium*, where the napkin is first seen changing hands, and the breadth of the Empire separating Catullus from his *amici*, who operate in what was for the Romans the last place on earth, bounded by the endless Western Ocean. Such a small object can encompass such a vast space only if we neglect to measure its merely material properties. Thus the poem also packs its own slightness, of both form and occasion, with many references to wealth and abun-dance, which are in turn rejected as criteria of value. Possession of the napkin for Asinius entails receipt of 300 hendecasyllables, the sort of threat that should impress someone who so misunderstands the napkin. Asinius' brother Pollio is "stuffed with wit"[4] but would give much more of his wealth than the napkin is worth, a whole talent, to undo the consequences of his brother's actions. And finally the poet makes clear that the napkin does not matter to him because of its *aestimatione* ("worth"), itself a word of some substance in the poem, whose five syllables take up almost half of one of those hendecasyllabi. This lumpen prosaic word, expressing a prosaic subject, is replaced by a very different word of almost equal size in the next line, *mnemosynum* ("memento"), which shows the right appreciation of the napkin. An object from the far West of Rome's empire is to be defined by a word that is itself a foreign import, now from its eastern, Greek half. And the spatial vistas Catullus' napkin unfolds are matched by temporal expansion, for as a memory this token of *amicitia* acquires a meaning that looks to the future as well as to the present. A similar programmatic transformation of another important Catullan text happens in the first poem of our collection, where the poet's polished little book begins as an offering to a friend at a *conuiuium* but then becomes something that "will live for more than one age," and thus reciprocate if not surpass the historical work of Nepos for which it is offered in exchange, if "the protecting maiden" intervenes.[5] The "protecting maiden" is almost certainly a Muse, and the Muses, whose very name suggests remembering, were the daughters of Mnemosyne.

One would not have had to be very learned to understand *mnemosynum* as it's used in Catullus 12, any more than a profound knowledge of French is required to understand the English "souvenir." But if this poem doesn't quite display specialized literary knowledge, it nevertheless provides us with some useful terms for describing and understanding its place in the social context of Catullan poetry. And here I want to apply three elements from the description of the napkin to Catullan learning. First, like the napkin, Catullus' knowledge of Greek literature is far from dematerialized. It is physically present in the world of his original audience both in the form of the polished and exquisite texts in which he displays it and also in the material resources required to develop it. Fabullus and Veranius may have sent Catullus a napkin, but we know that elaborate manuscripts of Greek texts function in precisely the same way, as gifts that can be sent back to friends in Italy by affluent young Romans on the make in the provinces. Thus Catullus' friend Helvius Cinna, who served with him in Bithynia, sent a deluxe edition of the fashionable Greek poet Aratus to one of his *amici*.[6] But even beyond giving such gifts, it would have been impossible to develop the kind of knowledge required to compose a poem like Catullus 64 without wealth and access to the resources of other wealthy men. The first public library was not built in Rome until a quarter century after Catullus' death. Books, even if they were not of the opulence of Cinna's Aratus, had all to be copied by hand, and were never cheap in antiquity. Even if one had as much wealth and manpower as Cicero, there were still likely to be volumes one could only consult or copy if an acquaintance lent them to one. Nor do problems end with the acquisition of the text. For all that we stress the bilingualism of the Roman upper classes, understanding contemporary spoken Greek, as Nicholas Horsfall has pointed out (1979), was not the same as understanding Thucydides or Callimachus. And while many manuscripts would have had marginal notes to help with difficulties in vocabulary or obscure references, there was no such thing as a Greek-to-Latin dictionary in this period. Hence another essential "material" support for learning: a Greek scholar, quite often a slave, who could explain and interpret obscurities for you. And, coincidentally, that very same Cinna who sent back a text of Aratus also seems to have imported from his Bithynian expedition the learned Parthenius, an enslaved Greek who taught many of the greatest poets of the next generation.[7]

However, it would give a very incomplete picture of the cultural significance of Catullan scholarship to consider it only in terms of its material supports, and as an epiphenomenon of the networks of *amicitia* within which so much of his poetry operates. For like the Spanish napkin sent by Veranius and Fabullus, the textuality of Catullan verse extends and transcends the rituals of *amicitia*. The extensions allowed by the mere fact of writing are obvious – written texts preserve ephemeral moments of conversation, translating them into something not just long-lasting but eternal; they extend their audience outward beyond the privileged conversational group, and they allow the rituals of friendship to include those made absent by journeys, or by death itself, which Catullus memorably figures as a sort of sea journey that allows no return: "for just now in the whirlpool of Lethe, the flowing wave has washed over the slight pale foot of my brother" (65.5–6). And, as Catullus knows, his own works' immortality – in which so much is invested – depends on the "learned virgins," on the care and learning necessary to give his poetry importance not only within the synchronic sphere of social negotiations but in the diachronic literary history which the opening of poem 64 maps for us.

This gives rise to essential contradictions and uncertainties affecting Catullus' attitudes toward the relationship between learning and the social practice of poetry, a sense of the incompleteness, even of the incompatibility, of the different horizons in which his poetry moves that provides no small part of the energy of his best work. Thus we find this supreme poet of social presence aspiring to relationships that strip away the worldliness of the *conuiuium*, inviting that same friend who gave him the napkin to a dinner at which he will provide no wine or food, but only salt and the savor that the love gods feast on (13). Literary exchange occurs in the competitive context of the banquet, as his verse-duel with Calvus records (50), but its effects extend to the solitary Catullus after he leaves the banquet, and precisely reverse the imagery of leisured abundance conjured up by such a scene. In remembering Calvus – as he showed himself in literary play – Catullus now can neither eat nor sleep, prey to a madness and desire quite out of place among the *delicati*. However good the jokes were yesterday, this work is not among them. It proclaims itself a *poema*, and again the Greek word, made conspicuous by its Latin gloss *feci*, suggests the wrought product of a different space entirely, one that pulls the protagonists into a new plot, a love story or perhaps a little *Iliad* in which the hero tosses sleepless on his bed out of longing for an absent friend, and Calvus is warned to fear the Greek goddess Nemesis if he neglects a suppliant's prayers.[8] But of course, for all the private passions that seem to set the *amici* apart from others, Catullus' verses would not be out of place at a *conuiuium*; indeed we may, but are not compelled to, regard their move outside as simply the best joke of all, so that the social frame of competitive versification from which the *poema* removes its own creation and its subjects always threatens to enclose them again.

Another dimension of the contrasting contexts in which his learning places the poet emerges from the complex dedication to the first of two longer elegiac poems, his "translation" of Callimachus' poem on the catasterism (transformation into a star) of a tress from the head of the poet's royal patron, Berenice II.[9] While the original survives only in very incomplete form, Catullus seems to have followed his Greek predecessor extremely precisely, so precisely that the significance of the work within his own oeuvre is hard to pinpoint. Some have found in the lock's separation from its "brothers" a telling echo of the personal grief foregrounded in poem 65 (esp. Clausen 1970), but it is at least as plausible to relate the poem not to the inner emotional state of the poet but to the social circumstances of the poetry. For the prefatory poem 65 ensures that we see this Callimachean adaptation in terms of the social work it does, as recompense for the obligation the poet owes to the dedicatee, and in such a context there could be no more appropriate poem in the Hellenistic canon than this grand celebration of patronage.[10] But it is less important to privilege one way of reading the translation as Catullan than it is to recognize that the contradiction engendered by these contrasting ways of interpolating an author into this text follows precisely from the paradoxical way the dedicatory epistle presents the learning of which this is the fruit. For the poet begins by lamenting his own separation from the cultivation of the Muses brought about by the sorrow he feels for the death of his brother. Here the Muses represent an industry placed at the service of his friends, the tools of the poet's *amicitia*, and the translation an attempt to maintain connections with this outer world. And yet for all his claims to have lost his learning, it is precisely Greek literary and mythical allusions that give Catullus the language in which to describe the death of his brother; his grief insures that his songs will always be sad, like those the Daulian nightingale sung lamenting her lost Itylus (Hunter 1993c). It is a commonplace of New Criticism to wonder how someone torn by sorrow can turn such a neat allusion. But the mismatch between content and expression seems to me less important than the ambiguity about where we "place" learning in relation to the author's life. For it seems at once to adorn the compositions that bind him to a world of social exchange and (as in the Calvus poem, or the suggestion that the poet's love for Lesbia comes from her Sapphic "exemplar") to define the more intimate space whither he withdraws from it.

The dualism I have suggested in this poem's configuration of literary culture implies a deep uncertainty about the significance of Greek learning in the context of elite Roman culture. This uncertainty *per se* is nothing surprising at any historical period in Rome, and we shall shortly sketch some of the reasons why Romans felt so ambivalent about the place of Greek modes of expression in their new Empire. First, though, I want to look more closely at how Catullus' poetry stages the relationship between Greek literature and Roman realities. For viewing Rome through the lens of Greek myth – and it is important to realize the extent to which Greek myth did define a worldview especially associated with literary and artistic expression – at once amplifies Rome's successes and castigates them, exposes its losses and restores them. As Greek learning testifies to the wealth and prestige of individual members of the elite, so, most noticeably in the art of the late Republic, the grandiloquent visual language of the Hellenistic kingdoms, with its giants, nereids, and heroes, becomes incorporated into the monuments of Roman conquest. Among the most striking visual transformations of the Roman city in Catullus' lifetime would have been the great theater complex in which Pompey the Great literally staged his own conquest of the East as Agamemnon's victory over Troy (Kuttner 1999). But victory, especially eastern victory, while an unmistakable sign of Roman supremacy, always potentially threatened to undermine that success by making the Romans less themselves. Indeed the very material abundance for which the paraphernalia of learning becomes a synecdoche was perceived as breaking the spirit of the Romans with avarice, and corrupting the conduct of individuals toward one another, an area of particular concern to a poet so engaged in preserving *amicitia*.

Catullus and the Golden Fleece

With this ambiguity about the public face of Roman Hellenism in mind, let us return to the work with which we began, Catullus' elaborate miniature epic on the wedding of Peleus and Thetis which Thomas especially has made a showpiece of Catullan learning (see DeBrohun, this volume). Indeed Thomas suggests that the poet's motive for beginning with the construction of the *Argo* was the opportunity it gave him to show off his mastery of its abundant literary manifestations. I want to turn that argument around by suggesting that the *Argo* story, rather than simply offering a *corpus uile* for the display of literary scholarship, provides a framework for contextualizing and exploring the nature of that scholarship. For the story's significance in the world of Greek myth closely meshes with the poet's treatment of his own personal story. Jason's objective was a golden fleece that would allow him to obtain the kingship in his native city of Iolcos, an object that easily symbolizes the wealth and power that Roman armies were winning for themselves in the very same geographical regions of Asia Minor during Catullus' lifetime. But, like all great mythical blessings, the fleece comes accompanied by a more ambiguous possession: the woman Medea, whose cunning, knowledge, and sorcery will be both Jason's salvation and his destruction as, again in pursuit of golden wealth and kingship, he violates his promise to her and she avenges herself on him by killing his children.[11] The Medea myth, like the story of Ariadne that appears within the poem's ecphrastic core, thus bears a close connection to the themes of betrayal and oath-violation that feature prominently in Catullus' elegiac poetry. This mythical voyage to the East elsewhere provides the imagery in which Catullus describes his own expedition to Bithynia in the entourage of the governor Memmius (4), an adventure from which Catullus professes not to have brought back heroic riches. The second great eastern expedition mentioned in the poem, the campaign against Troy, features as well in the poet's personal story to emblematize the loss of his brother, the tragic reverse of the light-hearted mock epic of how Catullus and his friends failed to strike it rich in the provinces.

The links between the mythical content of poem 64 and these significant themes from elsewhere in the poet's work have often been observed,[12] but not as much attention has been given to how these narratives relate to contemporary anxieties about the social effects of Hellenization. In sketching this stage in my argument, I want to turn from the beginning of the poem to its conclusion. Here the poet moves from the Fates' prophecy of the birth of Achilles, which paints the Trojan War in the blackest terms, to draw the explicit contrast between the mythical past and the contemporary Roman present.[13] In those long-ago times the gods showed themselves directly to man (64.384–6) – a point the poet supports with a brief catalogue of the contexts of divine epiphany in Greek myth. Now, however, we have all "put justice to flight from our greedy minds" and rejected any bounds that obligations to the gods or one another place on the fulfillment of our desires (398). And so the gods "do not deign to look upon such intercourse and do not allow themselves to be touched by clear light" (407–8).

The first thing to notice about this ending is how it links the ills of contemporary Roman society to the problems arising from empire, specifically greed, the avarice that, as the historian Livy will describe (pref. 12), comes from the increase of wealth.

And that golden fleece has brought with it countless reminders of Medea in the form of murderous fathers and incestuous mothers. The intellectual legacy of conquest figures here in two ways, as a metonym for material riches that cause decline, and as a consequence of our fallen state. For the first, Asia Minor, Jason's route to the mythical Colchis, was the source for many of the instruments of Roman learning. We have already discussed Cinna's Aratus manuscript from Bithynia, and its human interlocutor Parthenius: other literary treasures, from the library of the Attalids and the dynasts of Asia Minor, were making their way to Rome at the same time. And, as texts were an important element of eastern riches, so the initial sign of those riches in the poem looks very much like a text. This is not so much because of the specific properties of the fleece itself – though animal skins were a physical medium of writing particularly associated with Asia Minor: the Greek word for them derives from the city of Pergamum – but through the intermediary of another textile which appears in the poem as a source of mythical knowledge. For the tapestry that adorns the nuptial couch, and does closely approximate Catullus' written text in the narrative it bears, also resembles the golden fleece in its opulence and especially in its association with products of the East. The cloth is dyed with luxurious scarlets: the couch is wrought of "Indian ivory" (64.48–9).

But if Greek learning becomes a sign of wealth, and indeed provides the mythical language in which to paint Rome's decline as elsewhere it provides the language for adorning its triumphs, that decline in turn gives a new urgency to learning. The last lines of the poem describe the obscurity in which the gods have cloaked themselves, in striking contrast to the luminous moment at the poem's beginning when men and divinities gaze upon one another. And the explicit display of literary learning with which the poem commences highlights another important feature of those now lost epiphanies: the gods Catullus mentions wear forms made familiar by earlier literary works. His Mars and Athena appear as if in the *Iliad*, and his Dionysus – though the Delphic context most directly suggests his sculptural representation in the pediment of Apollo's temple (Thomson 1997: 435) – seems to have stepped out of the *Bacchae*. Through texts, then, we escape to a place where we can see the gods in clear light. Or rather where we can imagine seeing them, for the important corollary to Catullus' exaltation of the mythical past over the historical present is the fictional nature of that past. Catullus describes the age when heroes beheld nymphs with their own eyes merely as an epoch "too much hoped for" (*nimis optato saeclorum tempore*, 64.22). And the poem is full of little contradictions reminding the audience of how difficult it is to fit this past into authentic history. The *Argo* appears as the first ship, yet the coverlet makes us see an even earlier ship fading into the distance from the perspective of someone betrayed by false promises; the song that the Fates sing at the wedding prophesying the glory of Achilles also raises overlapping issues about the truth of myth: in a lost drama of Aeschylus, Thetis accuses Apollo of lying for singing a similar song on the same occasion precisely because he never mentioned the death of her son, and Plato in turn upbraids Aeschylus for the intimation that the gods could lie (Aesch. fr. 350 Radt = Pl. *Resp.* 2.383b). Thus Catullus has here "corrected" the myth by falsifying the tradition that preserves it – or perhaps the problem was that Apollo, like the Fates, always told the truth but that Thetis, like so many other figures in this poem, just didn't understand his meaning.[14] Indeed even the desirability of that golden mythical world appears questionable, for, as many commentators have realized, the precise charges against contemporary Roman society are but permutations of the crimes of myth, and no greater exemplum of the devastating qualities of forgetfulness of duty can be found than Theseus.

Thus retreat into Greek textuality as an escape from the present is a strategy that the poem itself questions even as it embraces it. What one learns when "entering the text," as the central ecphrasis, focalized through another "seeing" character, Ariadne, compellingly invites the reader to do, is how chancy a thing reading is, and how bound up with the present circumstances of a text's reception. Sometimes, misunderstanding comes from the partial perspective of interpreters like Ariadne, who simply looks the wrong way and therefore doesn't notice that her narrative is not a tragedy of abandonment but a triumphal tale of apotheosis to be realized at the arrival of the approaching Dionysus. (Is Catullus' narrator himself an "Ariadne" in his view of contemporary morality in the greatest age of conquest Rome was ever to know?) Sometimes the authors themselves are negligent, like Theseus who simply forgets to change the sails (another deceptive cloth) and so causes his father to kill himself in despair. In either case the image of a scholar-poet dealing corrections to his predecessors and uncovering true etymologies seems less likely in such a context than a revelation of the kaleidoscopic power of texts to distort the past and mislead the present.

This deceptiveness of verbal and visual signs is intimately connected with their status as the products of foreign cultures and as clues for interpreting overseas conquest. For, like the golden fleece, many of the crucial hermeneutic moments in the poem are prompted by or refer to foreign expeditions. The tapestry is an eastern product, representing a god coming from the East. Theseus' sails – dyed with "Spanish" rust – are designed to show whether he has succeeded or failed in his expedition against the Cretan Minotaur. The Fates' song raises the question of whether the Trojan War should be seen as glorious or destructive. Nor can the hermeneutic problems such texts raise be separated from their materiality. The tapestry that presents a glorious vision of how the union with the East exalts (*amplifice*, 265) the West also seduces with an almost sexual physicality. It "embraces" the nuptial couch with its image of a partly clothed bride sexually available to another internal viewer (266). Not surprisingly, the Thessalian observers look on desirously (*cupide*, 267); yet the very same adjective describes the frame of mind that has driven a divine maiden, "justice," away from the *coetus* ("assembly")[15] of present-day men. Thus the physical presence of this foreign artistic product creates the corrupt desire which for the narrator makes the past represented in those images all the more desirable as an alternative to the present.

How this legacy of Hellenic culture becomes both Medea and Muse, an import at once indispensable and corrupting and an immortal refuge and escape from contemporary society, emerges especially from the epigram that most explicitly comments on poetic preferences for Alexandrian refinement, the praise of yet another monument (*monimenta*) of the poet's friend Cinna (95.9).[16] The "monument" in question, a formidably learned poem telling how Zmyrna, having consummated her incestuous desire for her father, is transformed into a myrrh tree and gives birth to Adonis, is contrasted with three other verbal productions: the poems or speeches of Hortensius, the annalistic poems of a certain Volusius, and the notoriously long-winded bad boy of Hellenistic literary criticism, Antimachus. The terms and imagery Catullus deploys in this comparison testify to his own learning, for they reproduce closely those of Callimachus in the association of bad poetry with a muddy river, but, as translated here, direct attention to the role of such Hellenized preferences in Roman culture. Learning again becomes a criterion for social winnowing, positioning Catullus closer to his *amicus*, farther from those who oppose his tastes, and "monumentalizing" both moves through a text that itself, as in poems 1 and 50, participates in a socialized network of reciprocal composition, a text returned for a text.[17]

But Cinna and Catullus are not the only characters whose words make social claims. Whatever Hortensius produced a thousand of in so short a time – the lost line may have alluded to erotic Hellenized poetry spewed out at a banquet, a logorrheic epic, or the voluminousness of Hortensius' oratory – he, like Suffenus, thinks well of his fluency and was indeed among the most distinguished aristocrats of his day. Volusius was not so prominent a figure, but if he personally lacked the prestige of a Hortensius, his work was almost certainly an account of Rome's public history, a record of military triumph like its great antecedent the *Annales* of Ennius. With the last comparand, Antimachus, we move from the present to the past, and yet this Greek figure's popularity is expressed in Roman political terms. Nothing like as broad a swath of the Roman population as *populus* implies read any Antimachus. The characterization of his reception as "popularity," though, helps to clarify a symbiosis of the social and the literary diametrically opposite to the one put into practice by Catullus' poem. Hortensius' words and Volusius' in different ways offer textual manifestations of Roman prestige; Antimachus' literary reputation appears as political success.

If we assume Catullus is doing more here than mechanically applying Callimachean aesthetic criteria, what, precisely, sets Cinna's poem apart from those other works? If it is primarily its separation from what we may conveniently call public life, why and on what terms is this good to reject? Our best resource for approaching these questions comes from the imagery of the poem itself. As we saw in the napkin poem, a rejection of physical abundance coincides with vast expansion in time and space. The nine winters Cinna has labored over the *Zmyrna* contrast with Hortensius' monstrous fertility, but also with the annalistic scope and structure of Volusius' poem, which would similarly have unrolled over the course of years. But Hortensius' celebrity will perhaps be limited to a single season, as Volusius' works will "die" at the shores of his native Po. The "people" who rejoice in Antimachus too are a notoriously fickle lot. Ease of birth implies ease of death, and the more any literary work has invested in popular success, the emptier it is.

But if Hortensius' and Volusius' works move from somethings to nothing, Cinna's poem seeks throughout an abiding material presence: to become a monument, a term that implies at once a preservation of the past and a reminder of its passing away. Indeed Cinna's poem, as Catullus' presents it, seems bred in the same world as that described at the end of poem 64. The very plot of the poem begins with a tale of incest. And the illicit sexuality of its content becomes, thanks to Catullus' brilliance, a metaphor for its own production. As Kenneth Quinn observes, the ninth harvest (*messem*) of the first line easily suggests the ninth month (*mensem*) of gestation (1973a: 431). If the poem is born, not made, Cinna becomes at once Zmyrna, going through labor like his protagonist, and the begetter of *Zmyrna*, assuming that the poem as product is like the child, a doubling of roles not far from incest. However, the story that begins in corruption ends with a birth – the birth, moreover, of a figure associated with the futility of sexuality and with mortality, yet also a quasi-divine figure ritually reborn every year.[18] Hence the next reference to the *Zmyrna*, which will be sent to the "channeled streams of the Satrachus," the Cypriot river in which Aphrodite bathed the young Adonis, a gesture perhaps to be connected with his immortalization.[19] Thus Catullus' celebration of the poem tracks its progress toward immortality as a *monumentum* in terms that recall the mythical content of Cinna's own text.

This link between obscure Hellenistic learning and transcending a single age at once reminds us of the similar connection between erudition and permanence in poem 1 and suggests a way of contextualizing Catullus' rejection of the teeming poetic products he uses as foils. In those other cases, as we have seen, the cultural accomplishment appears subordinated to the adornment of empire, to the verbal forms within which success measured in conventional Roman terms was won and expressed. From this perspective, the poem recalls not only Callimachean concerns but Ciceronian ones as well, most particularly those explored at the conclusion of the *De re publica*, where, in the dream of Scipio, the temporal and spatial limitations of Roman power and of the fame earned through political victory are made plain through the vision of true immortality revealed by Greek philosophical constructs. Here too, Cinna's escape into a mythical past opened by literary scholarship seems to break free of the socialized and materialized culture of a Hortensius or Volusius. But just as Scipio's instruction only makes him a wiser and more dedicated statesman on his return, so too Cinna's monumentalization, as accomplished through the poetic compliment offered by his *sodalis* Catullus, brings him back to earth, re-placing him within a temporal social network, but one whose difference and specificity we now more clearly recognize.

Between Verona and Rome

I want now to conclude by suggesting some overlapping historical contexts that make sense of the ambivalence about Hellenic literary culture manifested in Catullus' poetry. I offer them not as explanations of Catullan attitudes but rather as backgrounds against which the poet's manipulation of these issues can take on an extra-textual significance for contemporaries and for us. The male figures who emerge most prominently as Catullus' *amici* often share similar geographical and social origins. The offspring of the wealthiest citizens of the towns of Cisalpine Gaul, a region whose prosperity and political importance increased dramatically after the civil wars of the 80s BC, these young men followed a similar career trajectory, which brought them, via a period of service in the retinue of a provincial administrator, to the metropolis. There, as the dramatis personae of the Catullan corpus shows, they enjoyed connections within the urban political elite. Because their position was so new, members of this remarkably successful generation had great flexibility in defining their own social identity within overlapping but not concentric social circles. Catullus never entirely abandoned his native Verona for Rome, and we can imagine that the friendship his father cultivated with Julius Caesar greatly enhanced his family's prestige locally. Conversely, a Catullus' status at home, no doubt together with his family's wealth, provided not only the fuel for his social journey but also an alternative social context within which he could enjoy a pre-eminence greater than that he could achieve in the capital.[20] Hence, as Emma Dench's recent work on Romanization (2005) suggests, this group of young men enjoyed the possibility of "triangulating" their social position by playing up either their urbanity or their provincial status.

The display of literary culture plays a significant role in the complex social negotiation we are imagining. First, a sophisticated literary education provided a Catullus, or a Cinna from nearby Brescia, with an important prerequisite for advancement. We know that some of the most important *grammatici* (professional teachers of literature) sought employment in Northern Italy at this time (Suet. *Gram.* 3.6) – and that thus there was a good market for their services among men who could afford to pay them. Those who won literary distinction in Rome over the next fifty years came from this region in disproportionate numbers. But beyond being an instrument of advancement, the literary distinction Catullus' circle claims for itself possessed, I suggest, an ambiguity that at once paralleled and facilitated the construction of overlapping urban and provincial identities. On one level, there was an obvious connection between such knowledge and the urbanity prized in the polymetrics, the poetry through which Catullus publicizes his connections among the Hellenized elite of Rome – one of the alternative social roles available to him. But, as a close reading of the poetry has shown, learning also offered a retreat from social obligations as well as an autonomous context for Catullan self-expression that transcended its social impetus. In this sense the split in the manifestations of Catullan learning map a set of alternatives similar to his contrasting geographic identities. Dench makes this particularly clear in her analysis of another Catullan dedicatory poem, the opening of the intensely learned 68. As in poem 65, Catullus stages a withdrawal from Roman society that opposes his ability to compose a learned tribute to a noble friend. This withdrawal is again connected with Catullus' mourning for his brother, but here it assumes a geographical dimension as well. The poet has left Rome and therefore has no library at hand as a compositional resource: only one case of book rolls has followed him to Verona (68.36). And yet the slightness of his literary apparatus implies the opposite of a renunciation of abilities; on the contrary, according to the Callimachean aesthetic, the single *capsula* ought to have a value surpassing mere quantity (Dench 2005: 337–8). Here, very neatly, Catullus' redefinition of his cultural knowledge through an emphasis on refinement corresponds to a return to the place of his own origin and prestige. This retreat is only partial – the very existence of poem 68 signifies his maintenance of social connections – but it allows the poet to highlight the independent terms on which he does participate.

The ambiguities of Catullus' social position also help to explain the thematic opposition his poetry establishes between literary culture and material abundance. As we have seen, the moralizing tone of Catullus 64 with its identification of cupidity as the source of Roman social disruption helps define literary culture as an escape from the corruption brought by riches. However conventional such a condemnation of wealth as a source of corruption may be in Latin literature, we should not miss its special importance in Catullus. No age witnessed a greater increase in the material goods of empire, or of the social and political disruption they fueled, than the final decades of the republic. And, on a more intimate scale as well, Catullus' poetry undoes the consequence of economic desire. For his work portrays the pursuit of gain through provincial service – and we should not forget that cultural capital in the form of manuscripts and *grammatici* were among the spoils to be won – in terms of its negative effects on the solidarity of *amicitia*. The "napkins" and texts fetishized in the epigrams and polymetrics are necessary because Fabullus and Veranius are in Spain, or Catullus is in Bithynia. Most tellingly, in Catullus' poetry the very route that took him eastward as the up-and-coming member of a governor's staff merges geographically with the voyage to his brother's tomb, superimposing on his path to success reminders of the irrecoverable loss of the figure with whom he shared the closest of bonds. It is in these terms that we should understand Catullus' connection between literary refinement and poverty – which was itself a Callimachean convention. And the other face of literary culture, its inevitable connection to material success, always stood in contrast to the surface meanings of Catullus' claim to have a purse full of spider webs.

The opposition sketched between learning and economic prosperity, then, cannot be securely explained either in terms of a "countercultural" opting out of the career track that mattered, or as sour grapes. Catullus' *amici* were neither dropouts nor failures. Cinna went on to hold the tribunate; Calvus was as successful an orator as he was a poet; and, had Catullus lived another decade, perhaps we would hear of him too as tribune or senator.[21] Rather, the decoupling of wealth from culture helps define the terms of a generation's success. It was wealth that gave Catullus his learning, and wealth that placed him in the urban context in which he particularly delights to display it. Yet wealth *per se*, however essential to accruing status, was also a very ambivalent possession. It always paled in comparison to the prestige aristocratic families acquired from political success. The material products of empire, then, offered a social standard that would always qualify the position of a Cinna or a Catullus, defining them in terms that would insure their subordination. But a "culture" that opposes itself to materiality at once testifies to social position and makes it unquantifiable. It also gives the poet a great measure of autonomy, revealed by the implicit rejection of any social superior as *patronus*. The *amici* define their own society; the poetic skill with which they realize their small monuments becomes the secret of their reputation and makes their words matter within the larger realms of political discourse, as Catullan invective probably did.

The question of culture's materiality relates to another important and long-lived Roman anxiety about the role of Hellenic cultural accomplishments in their own society. Livy has Cato the Elder express a fear of the first Greek works of art brought to Rome as plunder: "these statues may have taken us captive rather than we them" (Liv. 34.4.3). Within the moralizing content of Livy's work, this statement reflects the avarice the sight of such marvels engenders – itself a very Catullan attitude. But the image of Greek learning reversing the roles of master and slave has even greater resonance in Roman culture; hence Horace's famous formulation about "Captive Greece making her fierce conqueror captive" (*Ep.* 2.1.156). Throughout the history of the Republic, the literary culture of Greece was carefully managed to differentiate Rome from its Italian rivals without assuming the subordinate position that merely participating in Greek literature as Hellenized outsiders would have implied.[22] The very existence of a poetic literature in Latin results from such a careful negotiation of status, reconfiguring the Greek elements, omnipresent within Latin poetry from its inception, within the language of Rome. And such issues manifest themselves on a personal as well as a national scale; for one important way in which Greek literature was always "domesticated" at Rome was through the slave status of its teachers and masters. The position of these rhetoricians served as a constant reminder that it was really Rome that had taken Greece captive: it at once makes literary knowledge servile and yet makes access to it a mark of the highest social prestige.

Catullus' accomplishment forms very much a part of this story. The first printed edition of Catullus' work mistakenly claims that Catullus was born on the very day rhetorical instruction in Latin first began in Rome (Wiseman 1985: 207–8). Though useless as fact, the error provides a helpful reminder for gauging the cultural significance of Catullus' work. As Corbeill (2001) has shown, the professionalization of Latin rhetoric helped consolidate the "separate but equal status" of Roman culture; but it also meant that the prestige of that culture was open to anyone who could pay for it. For Catullus to write the kind of poetry he does, in Latin, was remarkable. His work did not consist of the self-evidently trivial, transparently Hellenizing trifles of an aristocrat like Catulus or Hortensius, nor did it, like Volusius', peg its value to its Roman content. It assumes the triviality that marks Hellenizing verse as something that adorns but does not define the status of a great noble, but invests it with a social role that would not be possible if his work were only to be measured by the position of the Greek relative to the Roman. The possibility that Catullus' achievement could be denigrated by being treated simply as a Greek literary production emerges from one of the few remarks that Cicero makes about contemporary poetry that stylistically resembled Catullus'. Cicero dubs those who affected Hellenistic tastes and rejected the Latin classics like Ennius "singers of Euphorion" (*Tusc.* 3.45; see Johnson, this volume), making them follow in the path of Greek poets, and perhaps even comparing them to the performing slaves who sang at public festivals. Tellingly, in the only place where Catullus advertises his work as derivative of a specific Greek poet, in the dedication to the "Lock of Berenice," he creates an opposition between the "translation," which fulfils Catullus' social obligations, and the nightingale song he sings for his brother's death. In an important sense, then, he advertises that Callimachus' words are not spoken in his own voice.

Cicero's gibe reveals a final dimension of Catullus' uses of literary culture. From one perspective, literature may have defined a space for displaying excellence and cultivating *amicitia* operating alongside the traditional practices of the elite, one where status was measured by learned qualities like *lepos* and *elegantia* as opposed to ancestral prestige or mere wealth. But from another it was perhaps precisely the embeddedness of literary culture within the manifestations of elite status that mattered. Without it, Catullus' learning makes him look very like another class of person who would possess the kinds of knowledge on display in poem 64: the professional *grammatici*. They too could amass great wealth and reputation and often wrote as well as taught poetry. But their background was entirely different, for they were often expensive slaves or freedmen.

One of these figures in particular offers a useful foil to the Catullus that emerges from his poems – P. Valerius Cato. The two were born at roughly the same time – Cato was probably a few years older – and in the same region of Italy. Indeed they practically share the same name – Catullus is a diminutive of Cato – and may well have been related.[23] Cato too wrote exquisitely learned poems, which probably shared many themes and even a couple of characters with Catullus 64, at least one on a mythological subject treated by Callimachus. Cinna predicts, in very much the language of Catullus 1 and 95, that it "will endure the ages" (*saecula permaneat*, fr. 14 Courtney).[24] But for all his role as a trainer of nobles and poets, Cato's own position was quite distinct from theirs. He was a freed slave, although he cared enough about escaping the stigma of this status to write a poem claiming to have been freeborn but illegally enslaved during the civil wars. And though his skills brought him enough wealth to buy a property of his own in the Alban hills, it was eventually auctioned off, and he apparently ended his life in poverty.

We know this from a pair of epigrams attributed to Furius Bibaculus advertising his deprivations. The tone of these poems is a little unclear and, like so many Catullan poems, depends on the social story we read into them. The first runs as follows (Suet. *Gram.* 11.3): "If by chance someone sees the home of my friend Cato, three vermilioned woodchips, and that little garden guarded by Priapus, he wonders by what arts he acquired such great wisdom that three cabbages, a half measure of spelt, and two grape clusters have nourished him, huddled under his roof tile, until great old age." Catullus too claims a poverty that strips him of everything but poetic salt, but such language in his case seems all the more transparently conventional in contrast to the realism with which Bibaculus depicts someone else's poverty. Here there is no dematerializing, no obscuring of social position, but rather an all-too-vivid portrait, which, far from reducing Cato to an essential *sapientia*, links *sapientia* itself to destitution. For the point in both epigrams is that Cato, despite his learning, is merely a bankrupted freedman. This demystification of learning to demote its possessor forms a precise and illuminating obverse to Catullus' own deployment of knowledge.[25]

NOTES

1 The traditional institutions of the Roman *conuiuium* were in many respects opposed to those of the archaic symposium. In particular, Roman dining practices could highlight a social hierarchy antithetical to that of the ideal symposium. However, the *conuiuium* was a complex and flexible institution capable of instantiating Hellenistic distinctions based on behavior and skill as well as Roman ones of social status. For the role of Hellenized symposia in the formation of Roman lyric poetry, see especially Murray (1985).

2 Even if "Marrucinus" was adopted as a cognomen by the Asinii, as most recent commentators suggest, its striking prominence in this poem still mobilizes the frequent Catullan contrast between city and country. For a reading of how Asinius' Marrucine origins color the poem, see especially Dench (2005: 336).

3 On the metaphorical relationship between weaving and verbal composition, see Scheid and Svenbro (1996: 131–55).

4 *Differtus*, "stuffed", is a generally accepted emendation but not a certain one.

5 The reading of 1.10 on which this argument has been based, *patrona virgo* ("patron muse"), while accepted in almost all current editions of Catullus, is not textually secure and has recently been challenged again by Gratwick (2002).

6 We know this from the surviving epigram Cinna wrote to accompany the gift (fr. 11 Courtney); the text was copied on mallow bark. For a fuller reading of Cinna's epigram as an introduction to Catullus' literary culture in relation to its material underpinnings, see Hinds (2001).

7 See Courtney (1993: 212–13) for a summary of evidence and scholarly opinions.

8   For a somewhat different reading of what's at stake in the shift from playfulness to poetic composition, see Habinek (2005: 133–4).

9   An even richer treatment of the same themes can be found in the parallel dedication that opens the second of Catullus' explicitly if more ambiguously derivative long elegies, poem 68. In the interest of economy, I concentrate here on poem 65.

10 This is not to argue that the particular relations between the upper-class Catullus and the non-regal Hortalus approximated in any way the kind of debt Callimachus owed to Berenice. Indeed the implied difference between the two provides another important avenue for reading the poem with reference to patronage and social relations.

11 Konstan (1977) describes the prominent allusions to Medea in the poem's narrative.

12 Putnam (1961) is the classic treatment.

13 Among the most influential "darker" readings of Catullus 64 are Curran (1969), Bramble (1970), and Skinner (1984).

14 So indeed in Catullus 64 there is nothing specific to indicate that Achilles does die, and it is possible to understand 361–70 as implying nothing about the hero's mortality.

15 64.407. For *coetus*' occasional ability to assume the sexual connotations of its close cognate *coitus*, see J. N. Adams (1982: 179).

16 The following analysis assumes the unity of 95a and 95b; for the philological issues, see Thomson (1997: 525).

17 By this I don't mean that Catullus 95 was necessarily a response to a gift of the *Zmyrna* on Cinna's part. Rather, inasmuch as Cinna's text was the necessary prerequisite for Catullus', his own work as poet/friend is called into being by Cinna's.

18 For the complex myth of Adonis and its combination in different ritual enactments of differing measures of mourning and festive celebration, see Detienne (1994: 133–45).

19 Bathing infants in rivers in other myths serves as a device to immortalize them (most notably in the case of Achilles), and elsewhere among the myths of Adonis' infancy, Aphrodite is represented as contesting possession of the infant Adonis with Persephone, the underworld goddess to whom she had entrusted him. The Cypriot locale of the river is also relevant to this argument, for, as Detienne makes clear, it was in Cyprus above all that ritual emphasis fell on the rebirth of Adonis as opposed to his early death.

20 On the history of Catullus' family, see esp. Wiseman (1987: 324–42, and this volume).

21 For the identification of this Cinna with the figure killed by mistake at Caesar's funeral, see Wiseman (1974: 44–58). The biographical information about both figures will be conveniently found in Courtney (1993: 201–24).

22 For a survey of the social factors possibly impinging on the invention of Latin literature, see Feeney (2005).

23 Catullus addresses a poem, 56, to a "Cato." If this person is to be identified with Valerius Cato, it suggests that the two were closely acquainted. See Thomson (1997: 339).

24 Courtney *ad loc.* attractively suggests that Cinna's poem on Cato's poem was the inspiration for both Catullus' compliment to Cinna's own *Zmyrna* and his own dedicatory poem (perhaps with a hint of rivalry in Catullus' *perenne*?).

25 On Valerius Cato, see especially Kaster (1995: 148–61), who, however, adopts a more upbeat reading of Bibaculus' poems.

GUIDE TO FURTHER READING

Rawson (1985) gives the best introduction to Roman intellectual life in Catullus' time. The evidence for Catullus' background, life, and connections is treated most fully in the works of Wiseman, esp. (1985). Clausen (1964) has been the most influential presentation of Roman literary Alexandrianism. Fantham (1996) provides an excellent overview of the nature of Roman literary production (on the circulation and production of books, see especially Starr 1987). Dupont (1998) and Habinek (1998, 2005) have now advanced a very different view of what Latin literature was for. On the cultural politics of Hellenization, see the essential new work of Dench (2005) and the illuminating observations of Hinds (2001).

WORKS CITED

Adams, J. N. 1982. *The Latin Sexual Vocabulary.* Baltimore and London.

Bramble, J. C. 1970. "Structure and Ambiguity in Catullus LXIV." *Proceedings of the Cambridge Philological Society* 16: 22–41.

Clausen, W. V. 1964. "Callimachus and Latin Poetry." *Greek, Roman, and Byzantine Studies* 5: 181–96.

Clausen, W. V. 1970. "Catullus and Callimachus." *Harvard Studies in Classical Philology* 74: 85–94.

Corbeill, A. 2001. "Education in the Roman Republic: Creating Traditions." In Y. L. Too, ed., *Education in Greek and Roman Antiquity.* Leiden. 261–87.

Courtney, E., ed. 1993. *The Fragmentary Latin Poets.* Oxford.

Curran, L. C. 1969. "Catullus and the Heroic Age." *Yale Classical Studies* 21: 169–92.

Dench, E. 2005. *Romulus' Asylum: Roman Identities from the Age of Alexander to the Age of Hadrian.* Oxford.

Detienne, M. 1994. *The Gardens of Adonis.* Trans. J. Lloyd. Princeton, NJ.

Dupont, F. 1998. *The Invention of Literature: From Greek Intoxication to the Latin Book.* Trans. J. Lloyd. Baltimore.

Fantham, E. 1996. *Roman Literary Culture: From Cicero to Apuleius.* Baltimore.

Feeney, D. C. 2005. "The Beginnings of Latin Literature." *Journal of Roman Studies* 95: 226–40.

Gratwick, A. S. 2002. "*Vale patrona virgo*: The Text of Catullus 1.9." *Classical Quarterly* 52: 305–20.

Habinek, T. N. 1998. *The Politics of Latin Literature: Writing, Identity, and Empire in Ancient Rome.* Princeton, NJ.

Habinek, T. N. 2005. *Roman Song Culture.* Baltimore.

Hinds, S. 2001. "Cinna, Statius, and 'Immanent Literary History' in the Cultural Economy." *Entretiens Fondation Hardt* 47: 221–57.

Horsfall, N. 1979. "*Doctus sermones utriusque linguae.*" *Échos du monde classique/Classical Views* 23: 85–95.

Hunter, R. 1993c. "Callimachean Echoes in Catullus 65." *Zeitschrift für Papyrologie und Epigraphik* 96: 179–82.

Kaster, R. A. 1995. *C. Suetonius Tranquillus: De Grammaticis et Rhetoribus.* Oxford.

Konstan, D. 1977. *Catullus' Indictment of Rome: The Meaning of Catullus 64.* Amsterdam.

Kuttner, A. L. 1999. "Culture and History at Pompey's Museum." *Transactions of the American Philological Association* 129: 343–73.

Murray, O. 1985. "Symposium and Genre in the Poetry of Horace." *Journal of Roman Studies* 75: 39–50.

Putnam, M. C. J. 1961. "The Art of Catullus 64." *Harvard Studies in Classical Philology* 65: 165–205.

Quinn, K., ed. 1973a. *Catullus: The Poems.* 2nd edn. London and Basingstoke.

Rawson, E. 1985. *Intellectual Life in the Late Roman Republic.* Baltimore.

Ross, D. O., Jr. 1973. "*Uriosque apertos*: A Catullan Gloss." *Mnemosyne* 26: 60–2.

Scheid, J., and J. Svenbro. 1996. *The Craft of Zeus: Myths of Weaving and Fabric*. Trans. C. Volk. Cambridge, MA.

Skinner, M. B. 1984. "Rhamnusia Virgo." *Classical Antiquity* 3: 134–41.

Starr, R. J. 1987. "The Circulation of Literary Texts in the Roman World." *Classical Quarterly* n.s. 37: 213–23.

Thomas, R. F. 1982. "Catullus and the Polemics of Poetic Reference (Poem 64.1–18)." *American Journal of Philology* 103: 144–64.

Thomson, D. F. S., ed. 1997. *Catullus, Edited with a Textual and Interpretative Commentary*. Toronto.

Wiseman, T. P. 1974. *Cinna the Poet and Other Roman Essays*. Leicester.

Wiseman, T. P. 1985. *Catullus and His World: A Reappraisal*. Cambridge.

Wiseman, T. P. 1987. *Roman Studies Literary and Historical*. Liverpool.

CHAPTER SEVEN

Gender and Masculinity

Elizabeth Manwell

Not long ago, at a local county fair, I found myself consuming a sticky mess of French fries under a tent that abutted a Marine recruitment kiosk. The young male soldiers (and they were exclusively male) had no need to hail passersby, since most of the adolescent boys who happened along tended to stop. The Marines lured the boys with two pieces of equipment, one high tech and one low – a Humvee and a chin-up bar. Though men and women alike ogled the massive tank-like vehicle, it was the simple metal bar that attracted the kids. All of them wanted to test themselves against the Marines, and I witnessed a number of spontaneous competitions – between friends, younger teens, and older professional soldiers and aspirants.

I was somewhat surprised, since I assumed that the allure of a machine – especially a large, technologically sophisticated, cherry-red machine – would hold much more appeal than an unadorned iron pipe. The fascination, however, lay not in the apparatus itself, but in the competition that it inspired. The contests allowed the boys to perform or reinforce their toughness, strength, competitiveness (what made them masculine in their eyes), offered a way to create community among themselves, and provided a forum for them to emulate and identify with men they found heroic. Where the Humvee was merely an accidental marker of masculinity, the chin-up bar offered a tangible way for these boys to engage in a performance of manhood.

The way that the ancients performed masculinity and the structures that reinforced male gender identity are not the same as those of the twenty-first century in the United States. This example is instructive, however, because it brings to light issues that scholars have attempted to address as they examine the nature of male gender identity in ancient Rome and the societal structures that codified it, such as markers of masculinity, the importance of competition in male public life, the value of *uirtus* (virtue, manliness), and the public nature of gender performance. This chapter will consider two studies found in this large body of scholarship, both of which examine these issues in Catullus, specifically, a Foucauldian reading of Catullus by Marilyn Skinner and a postmodern interpretation by David Wray. Both address how Catullus fashions a masculine subjectivity for himself, and how his notions of masculinity conform to or challenge our ideas of what it meant to be a Roman male in the first century BC. It will first, however, be profitable to consider the origin of the study of masculinity and, more specifically, what it meant to be a man in Rome.

Studying Masculinity, or Why Should We Care about Men?

Even to talk about masculinity is a fairly recent phenomenon, a notable outgrowth of feminism and feminist studies. Feminist interrogations of the subordination of women in the 1960s and 1970s (what is commonly called "second-wave feminism") questioned the political and social possibilities of women's lives under patriarchal culture. The concerns that feminist women expressed led to a revision of what many perceived to be a "natural" social order and exposed women's concerns about the myriad ways that society discouraged autonomous behavior and the adoption of what were commonly held to be male-gendered traits. In addition, feminism rightly encouraged a more inclusive examination of women as a part of culture – as active agents in the production of culture, whether in history, society, politics, or art.

The influence of feminist theory has extended, however, beyond the mere recovery of historical women or the articulation of women's subordination and has given birth to more sophisticated analyses of gender and sexual identity. Indeed queer theory, postcolonial theory and the field of cultural studies (among others) are indebted to the ways in which second-wave theorists and activists questioned the way that women were made Other.[1] One of the most influential changes in feminist work lies in a shift from an emphasis on "woman" to one on "gender" (R. Adams and Savran 2002: 4). In addition, theories that postulated sexuality as a historical construct (e.g., Foucault 1978) and gender not as an essence but a compulsory performance in which individuals enact socially accepted and mandated gender roles (e.g., Butler 1990, 1993) have effectively moved feminism beyond the feminine and have allowed scholars and researchers to reconsider gender subject positions for men, women, transvestites, transsexuals, and the intersexed.

Though some semblance of a men's movement appeared as early as the 1970s, masculinity studies perhaps can be said to have emerged as a distinct discipline or subfield of gender studies in the 1980s. Early works focused on masculinity studies as complementary to feminist work, in an attempt to articulate the sympathy many men felt with the women's movement while simultaneously feeling excluded from it (Fasteau 1975; Pleck and Pleck 1980). Other work explicitly focused on homosexuality and homosocial bonds between men.[2] Since the 1980s, the study of masculinity and male subjectivity has grown to be a large and healthy topic of scholarly interest: if male and female are genders that are performed, they must both be interrogated in order to come to a sophisticated and complex understanding of gender relations and the place of gender within culture, both being "historically constructed, mutable, and contingent" (Adams and Savran 2002: 2). As with feminism, there is no single definable approach or topic for the study of masculinity; the lack of an orthodoxy may be in part attributable to the fact that masculinity studies came into its own when postmodernism was at its apex, but the favorable result is the abundance of approaches to male identity and culture as they reveal themselves in the social sciences, hard sciences, arts, and humanities. While the study of masculinity does not replace the need for feminism or queer theory, it frequently offers a compelling or illuminating counterpoint.

Studying Roman Masculinity or Why Should We Care about Dead White Men?

The study of male relationships and male identity, then, has been welcomed by many classicists engaged in studies of gender. In particular, feminist scholars, whose earlier work focused on the rare bits of literature left by women or on representations of women in male-authored texts, have found new ways to explore gender dynamics and the social structures that inform normative and non-normative gender identities. Thus, studies of the construction and performance of masculinity in ancient Greece and Rome have emerged in recent years as a "new" field, or perhaps a very old field with a new perspective.

While studies of Greek masculinity, and in particular pederastic relations between males, have been an integral part of scholarly discourse for many years (e.g., Dover 1978; Halperin 1990), the study of Roman manhood is a comparatively recent phenomenon. Those who have tackled the subject have considered a variety of contexts and content; authors have focused on homosexuality as represented in literary and historical texts or performed by individuals, the use of oratory to provide a homosocial forum for male experience, and transformations that male identity undergoes under Christianity, among others (Richlin 1992; Gleason 1995; C. A. Williams 1999; Burrus 2000; Gunderson 2000).

The study of Roman masculinity, irrespective of approach or subdiscipline, begins with the articulation of the Roman values that had to be instilled and nurtured in any Roman man.[3] Core values enable the constitution of a *uir* (man); indeed not only are they the building blocks of manhood, but one proves that he is a *uir* through the demonstration or performance of these qualities. As Eric Gunderson has observed, *uir* is appropriately translated not only as "man" but also as "husband" and "soldier" (2000: 7). Thus, not only are marriage and military service intimately tied to male identity, but the word *uir* itself indicates not merely sex, but also gender, "a manly man," one who has fully achieved manhood. Ethical terms associated with *uir* express both moral and corporeal fitness, though these categories for the Romans are interrelated; moral turpitude shows in one's actions, physical weakness reveals ethical lapses (C. Edwards 1993: 20–2). Thus, a good man (*uir bonus*) is recognizable by distinctive, positive, traditional attributes that are taken to be normative: he is Catonic, stoic, self-controlled, self-sacrificing, strong, and excelling in manly deeds. Roman male behavior is prescribed by a complex matrix of positive moral qualities, including *disciplina* (discipline), *pietas* (dutiful respect), *fides* (loyalty), *continentia* (self-restraint), and, of course, *uirtus* (manly excellence). Although this list provides only a brief survey of an array of terms, the conservatism inherent in these values is obvious.[4] Those terms expressing physical soundness likewise conjure an image of immobility; a real *uir* is *fortis* (strong), *durus* (hard), *sanus* (sound), and *integer* (whole). The soldier/farmer/statesman model of behavior that Romans held up to each other (and that we often hold up to our students) represents the ideal male – traditional, unchanging, and beyond reproach.

Manhood, then, for the Romans was an achieved state, not one automatically conferred, since men had to prove their virility and might well lose it. Thus, much of Roman literature illuminates the tension between the achievement of manhood and its potential loss (Gleason 1995: 59, 80–1; Gunderson 2000: 96). Ancient texts reveal anxiety about an individual's fitness as a man, though expression of this concern varies depending on author, genre, and historical period. Livy's Mucius Scaevola, for example, demonstrates traditional stoic virility dependent upon its performance, whereas the elegiac poets pose as being enslaved to and in perpetual conflict with their mistresses (*dominae*). Youths and old men in particular struggle to achieve manhood, since both are at a vulnerable time of life, due to their inability to exhibit the potency of the ideal Roman *uir* (Skinner 2005: 213–14). Consequently, not only proper ethical values are critical to a *uir*, but also potency – physical, mental, and sexual. For Romans, the performance of masculinity involves a demonstration of hardness, where the term "hard" (*durus*) obtains both morally and physically. A *uir durus* demonstrates his hardness both through his presentation of a stoic exterior (à la Scaevola), and by acting as an active, penetrative partner in all his sexual encounters, whether with males or females (C. Edwards 1993: 174; C. A. Williams 1999: 163).[5]

Those who fail to exhibit the requisite "hardness" are vulnerable to charges of *mollitia* (softness). Unsurprisingly, softness, an attribute of women, marks men as effeminate and not truly male. The *mollis mas* (soft male) has failed in his attempt to achieve the status of a "real" man, and this failure is often attributable to sexual failings. Yet, just as virility is performed, so too is *mollitia*: references to men who scratch their heads with one finger or walk with a hasty or lively gait depict such individuals as womanly (C. Edwards 1993: 63; Gleason 1990: 392–3). *Mollitia* denotes a matrix of behaviors and preferences, including gesture, demeanor, and physical prowess. Connotations of sexual passivity, however, are never completely divorced from the notion of softness, which comprises part of a larger nexus of aberrant (to the Romans) behaviors that conflict in a demonstrable way with the male ideal articulated above.

Accusations of *mollitia*, then, can often be translated as allegations that a man is or behaves as a *cinaedus*. There is no easy translation for this term; appropriated from the Greek (*kinaidos*), it indicates a man who prefers to be penetrated in sexual encounters.[6] In sexual practice, to be male was to be the active partner (Richlin 1992; Parker 1997). Thus, the *cinaedus* represents a willful abdication of the role of *uir* through deliberately engaging in "softening" behavior. In a world in which manhood must be achieved and demonstrated, and in which virility though once claimed can be lost, the *cinaedus* occupies a distinctly countercultural position. Though vilified for his complete lack of manly virtues,[7] he can also be read from the outside as a revolutionary figure who opts out of the system (cf. C. Edwards 1993: 96–7).

If reality matched the paradigm, there might be little more to say about the nature of masculinity in Roman culture, but the perfection of Roman manhood remained as elusive as any other ideal. While true *cinaedi* may well have existed, accusations of *mollitia* tend to appear as attempts to injure one's standing. Cicero himself was criticized by his contemporaries for deporting himself in an effeminate way while speaking (Tac. *Dial.* 18.5) and Caesar was suspect for wearing his toga loosely belted (Dio Cass. 43.43.1–4).[8] These examples demonstrate the instability of masculinity – even a man such as Cicero was vulnerable to allegations that his behavior was insufficiently manly, and one needed to be ever-vigilant in order to preserve one's integrity. It is more useful to think of *cinaedus* and *uir* as end marks on an axis along which men chart a course rather than distinct categories into which one fits.

These examples, however, also illustrate the perceived efficacy of charges of *mollitia*. Indeed, charges of softness are common expressions of derision for one's opponents and frequent forms of slander in the public world of Roman life. The Romans (as well as the Greeks) were a public people, and when we speak of the ethical and physical tokens of masculinity, we are in large part describing public behavior and discourse. That is, Romans did nearly everything in the public eye (including activities that we regard as our most private, such as bathing). For these men, accusations of *mollitia* are not merely components of a public discourse, but the fabric of a competition that is visible to all. Consider, for example, Cicero's accusation against Marc Antony (*Phil.* 2.44):

> uisne igitur te inspiciamus a puero? sic opinor; a principio ordiamur. tenesne memoria praetextatum te decoxisse? 'patris,' inquies, 'ista culpa est.' concedo. etenim est pietatis plena defensio. illud tamen audaciae tuae, quod sedisti in quattuordecim ordinibus, cum esset lege Roscia decoctoribus certus locus constitutus, quamuis quis fortunae uitio, non suo, decoxisset. sumpsisti uirilem, quam statim muliebrem togam reddidisti. primo uulgare scortum, certa flagitii merces, nec ea parua; sed cito Curio interuenit, qui te a meretricio quaestu abduxit et, tamquam stolam dedisset, in matrimonio stabili et certo collocauit.

> Therefore do you want us to examine you from boyhood? Yes, I think so; let us begin at the beginning. Do you remember that you went bankrupt as a boy? You will say, "that is my father's fault." I agree. Truly your defense is full of piety. Nevertheless, it was typical of your boldness, that you sat in the 14 rows [of the knights], although a specific place was designated by the Roscian law for the bankrupt, even if one had gone bankrupt by fault of fortune, and not of his own. You took up the toga of manhood, which immediately you rendered a toga of womanhood. At first you were a common whore, the price of your disgrace was fixed, and not small. But quickly Curio intervened, who took you away from your whorish pursuits and, just as if he had given you an apron, settled you into a stable and sure marriage.

This charge, which would read as libelous in our own culture, offers Cicero a way to insult and explain simultaneously. His portrayal of Antony as decadent and soft is tied inextricably to what Cicero sees as his moral and political failings. *Mollitia* is not an excuse, but an analysis: surely a man this degenerate and wrong-headed must desire to engage in the worst of sexual depravities. His status as *cinaedus* is deftly tied to lack of piety and financial profligacy. A more light-hearted example appears in this epigram by Calvus about Pompey:

> Magnus, quem metuunt omnes, digito caput uno
>   scalpit; quid credas hunc sibi uelle? uirum.
>   (Scholiast on Juv. 9.133)

> Magnus, whom everyone fears, scratches his head with one
>   finger. What do you think he wants? A man.

Here the accusation reads less as an ongoing dispute than as a playful jab at a public figure. Yet, as in the previous example, Calvus mocks Pompey for his inferior gender performance, which the public observes and evaluates. Competition is a crucial aspect of the performance of masculinity, for men in Rome always display themselves with the knowledge that they will be judged, evaluated, and critiqued by the populace. It is in this way that that populace assesses the effectiveness of the performance.

For the Romans, then, masculinity is never truly fixed, but a male body must always be dressed with a convincing performance of manhood. The slippage between status as a *uir* (in its fullest sense) and a soft man means that a man is potentially always renegotiating his gender status. Moreover, those who seek to challenge the definition of what is normative, to separate a performance of masculinity from the male himself, can find numerous cracks in which to insert the lever.

Catullus' Masculinity

An attempt to assess or contextualize masculinity within the Catullan corpus may initially seem to be futile. Anyone who has read Catullus' rather effete and playful poetry might well consider it more appropriate to interrogate his femininity, as indeed scholars have.[9] The diction of the *carmina*, however, to my mind does not reflect a poet in drag (or, perhaps, not merely a poet in drag), but rather a writer trying to articulate a series of complex relationships about the nature of power, subjectivity, love, loss, and art. One exceedingly effective tool at his disposal is to play with and reformulate gendered subjects in his work. That is, it is not sufficient to expose the feminine voice of the poet; Catullus' poetry shows a distinct and original conceptualization of male subjectivity, which is in dialogue with but distinct from normative Roman male gender identity.[10] We have already examined the discourses of hardness and softness, and the way that allegations of the latter were employed to defame and degrade. These concepts are important also when we consider the issue of Catullus' interpretations of gendered subjects.

Softness

Perhaps the ultimate marker of *mollitia* is castration. The irrevocability of the state directs attention to what has been lost and to the negotiation of a new state or way of being in the world. Consider the final stanza of poem 11 (21–4), often considered Catullus' valedictory to Lesbia (Quinn 1973a: 125):

> nec meum respectet, ut ante, amorem,
> qui illius culpa cecidit uelut prati
> ultimi flos, praetereunte postquam
>   tactus aratro est.

> Don't let her look back on my love as before,
> which because of her has fallen just like the flower
> at the edge of the field, after it's been touched by
>   a passing plow.

T. P. Wiseman likens this image to rape (1985: 146), and given the Sapphic meter and the loss of the "flower," this is a perfectly plausible reading, one which compels us to read Catullus as a woman violated by his *puella*. Yet, knowing that the narrator represents himself as a man who has been wronged by and eagerly desires to separate himself from his unfaithful, ball-breaking girlfriend (11.16–20), one should juxtapose feminine Catullus alongside poorly masculine (i.e., castrated) Catullus (Miller 1994: 102–19; E. Greene 1995: 82). In this stanza the poet imagines a complex subjectivity, one that binds the virgin (as Wiseman and others rightly note) to the eunuch. Even softness is multivalent, and the poet's claim of effeminacy here cannot be evaluated without considering his artistry: the impact and effect of the Sapphic meter; its resonances with the other Sapphic poem, 51; its invective content; and the absurdity of the juxtaposition of this meter and its subject.

Another poem, 63, deals directly and explicitly with castration. In it Attis, a devotee of the goddess Cybele, castrates himself in a moment of religious ecstasy. Upon realizing fully what he has done, he expresses regret for his act of self-mutilation, for which offense the goddess drives him mad. Though he refers to himself as a *notha mulier* ("faux-woman," 63.27), the narrator marks him as female the moment the brutal act is completed (4–8):

> stimulatus ibi furenti rabie, uagus animis,
> deuolsit ili acuto sibi pondera silice,
> itaque ut relicta sensit sibi membra sine uiro,
> etiam recente terrae sola sanguine maculans,
> niueis <u>citata</u> cepit manibus leue tympanum.

> there goaded by a maddening rage, out of his mind,
> he severed the weights from his loins with sharp flint,
> and as he noticed his limbs were separated from his manhood
> staining the earth with recently shed blood,
> with snow-white hands <u>she</u> hastened to take up a light tambourine.

In short, Attis occupies an ambiguously gendered position, no longer male, not truly female, but more *mulier* than *uir*.

One of the most striking aspects of this poem is how Attis defines the masculine world that he has left behind (58–61):

> egone a mea remota haec ferar in nemora domo?
> patria, bonis, amicis, genitoribus abero?
> abero foro, palaestra, stadio et gyminasiis?
> miser a miser, querendum est etiam atque etiam, anime.

> Shall I be borne from my home into these distant woods?
> Will I be separated from my country, belongings, friends and parents?
> From the forum, the wrestling floor, the races, the gymnasium?
> Wretched, o wretched soul, you must complain again and again.

His catalogue of loss shifts from the personal (his friends and family) to male-gendered activities that take place in the public eye (athletics and public discourse). Becoming a "woman" has obvious and drastic implications for one's public self – s/he will never compete with his peers in the same way or in the same place again – but the personal conflicts are critical here too. Attis forfeits the stability of identity that humans (or humans in the West) crave, the knowledge that one has a definable place within a country, a family, and a peer group. *Mollitia* requires abandonment of the past and the redefinition of subjectivity, and, as in poem 11, the subject must create a space for himself that is neither fully male nor fully female.

The complications of *mollitia* are further amplified by the commingling of Greek and Roman motifs. Though this is a Roman poem written in Latin (about a man's longing for the forum), Attis is recognizably a Greek who travels to the East (Phrygia, 2) to take part in rituals for a distinctly foreign goddess. As Catharine Edwards has observed, *mollitia* has associations too with Greek or eastern luxury-loving prodigality, and thus the confusion of culture mimics that of gender (1993: 92–7). Recognizing this, Marilyn Skinner has offered a provocative reading of this poem ("*Ego mulier*: The Construction of Male Sexuality in Catullus"), which moves beyond reading it as a simple case of gender confusion, and instead offers an interpretation which illuminates both the constraints of Roman society and the power dynamics inherent in the performance of gender. She structures her argument upon a Foucauldian social constructionist model of gender identity development, beginning with the notion that gender is not fixed or essential, but rather that "semiotic fields structured upon the putatively natural polarity of 'male' and 'female' must . . . be treated as products of cultural systems" (1993b [1997 edn.]: 130). Given the Greek/Roman confusion in this poem, the cultural difference between the Greek *erômenos* (beloved) and the Roman *puer delicatus* (boy toy) are of special import. Unlike the Greeks, who perceived of citizen youth as appropriate love objects within a socially encouraged system of pederasty, the Romans were to focus their attentions exclusively on youths who were slaves or freedmen (Dover 1978; Richlin 1992: 220–6; Skinner 1993b [1997 edn.]: 135). The deportment of these two types of youths is distinct: the Greek youth is courted, and is expected to behave demurely, to refuse initial passes by an older man, and never to appear too eager for contact; a Roman slave boy or former slave would necessarily occupy a more vulnerable position. In both cultures the boy occupies a liminal space between youth and adulthood and between the female and the male, and, as Skinner observes, the Romans are concerned with not only his physical but also his moral vulnerability (1993b [1997 edn.]: 136).

For Skinner, then, Attis occupies a singularly precarious position even prior to his self-castration, and his act of self-mutilation can be read as a vain attempt to hold off the course that biology would compel him to take, allowing him to remain "fixed" as a boy, a passive sexual partner, an object of desire (1993b [1997 edn.]: 137). His rejection of the active sexual role (63.64) reflects his ambivalence about the desirability of making the transformation from *puer delicatus* to *uir*, and denotes an attempt to carve out a sexual identity for himself. Unlike other ancient authors who treat this story, Catullus transforms it into a tale of "an irrevocable abdication of male cultural responsibility," in that Attis deliberately aligns himself with the female and rejects through his emasculation the life of the forum and the law courts, or the agora and the assembly (1993b [1997 edn.]: 139).

Yet the most intriguing and innovative part of Skinner's argument is the connection she makes between the poetic and the political. Others have argued that later elegiac poetry employs a vocabulary of sexual domination and erotic contest to create a discourse about political power and social disenfranchisement (Cahoon 1988; E. Greene 1999b; Wyke 2002), and what we might gain by reading the poem as a response to the contemporary political atmosphere merits consideration. Skinner, examining the climate in Rome, both political (as the Republic long embattled drifts into civil war) and cultural (as Romans simultaneously demonstrate fascination with and disgust at the exoticism of eastern culture) reads Attis' castration in light of Foucault's theory:

> Now, the isomorphism of ancient social and sexual relations induces Foucault (1986: 81–95) to posit a causal connection between changes in Roman political conditions and new modes of subjectivity. Tighter restrictions on freedom of action in the public sphere and graver risks for both large and small players in the political game resulted, he argues, in a more intense absorption with oneself as ethical subject, ultimately leading to modifications in sexual values and practices. . . . I submit, then, that the monstrous inversion of gender relations contained in the asymmetrical partnership of *minax Cybebe*, "threatening Cybele," and her emasculate consort Attis reflects elite alarm over perceived restrictions on personal autonomy and diminished capacity for meaningful public action during the agonized death throes of the Roman Republic. (1993b [1997 edn.]: 141–2)

Skinner finds Catullus' use of gender imagery – and in particular the effeminate or emasculated male – a potent symbol of the political castration felt by Catullus and his compatriots. Softness does not merely reflect one's bodily state or sexual preference; rather, it works metaphorically to designate the symbolic space where political and cultural criticism is performed. As Skinner observes, Attis' refusal to participate in the socially sanctioned gender system reflects a deliberate choice. His reluctance to make the transition from *puer delicatus* to *uir* certainly shows a hesitancy to adopt the trappings of manhood and its attendant responsibilities. The ambiguity of Attis is also evident elsewhere, however, which Skinner observes. Attis, as a Greek youth, highlights the conflict between Greek and Roman, and how that conflict is mapped upon the male body. Reading the (fe)male body of Attis as a Roman body and a Catullan body compels a re-evaluation of gender categories both within and beyond the text.

By reading other Catullan verses in light of this analysis, Skinner suggests that we can think of Catullus' elegiac poems about Lesbia not as love poems, but as statements of political disenfranchisement (1993b [1997 edn.]: 143–4). These are verses that have struck some critics for their privileging of political or friendship vocabulary (terms such as *fides*, *foedus*, *pietas*, and the like) over traditional erotic diction (Reitzenstein 1912; Ross 1969; Lyne 1980). The poet's focus on his lack of faith in Lesbia, his immobility as he attempts to remove himself from a hopeless situation, and his loss of power to a woman of means can thus be read as a statement of disillusionment with a political system gone awry (Skinner 1993b [1997 edn.]: 144–5).

By using Foucault's work to frame her argument, Skinner proves *mollitia* to be more than a marker of the male body. Instead, it works as a tool to question the power structure of the late Roman Republic, a mouthpiece for articulating a growing sense of disenfranchisement and male anxiety. Through *mollitia* we can observe that sexual and political powers are homologous. Softness is not a vice, but rather a medium through which the poet can articulate a political position.[11]

Hardness

While softness represents a crucial component of Catullus' view of masculine identity, hardness is an equally, if not more, important part of this pairing. As mentioned above, the Romans considered hardness as normative, and a critical quality in the competitive world of Roman males, especially among the elite. Like other writing of the Republic, Catullus' poetry offers a window on these male-dominated contests of one-upmanship, where the goal is to prove one's manhood both by asserting one's own hardness and by revealing the opponent's effeminacy.

It is perhaps easiest to think of the importance of hardness to Catullus by considering his invective poetry, of which poem 16 remains one of his most famous and most obscene examples:

> Pedicabo ego uos et irrumabo,
> Aureli pathice et cinaede Furi,
> qui me ex uersiculis meis putastis,
> quod sunt molliculi, parum pudicum.
> nam castum esse decet pium poetam   5
> ipsum, uersiculos nihil necesse est;
> qui tum denique habent salem ac leporem,
> si sunt molliculi ac parum pudici,
> et quod pruriat incitare possunt,
> non dico pueris, sed his pilosis   10
> qui duros nequeunt mouere lumbos.
> uos, quod milia multa basiorum
> legistis, male me marem putatis?
> pedicabo ego uos et irrumabo.

> I, yes, I will fuck your mouth and fuck your ass,
> slack-jawed Aurelius and loose Furius,
> because you think I am low on modesty
> since my verses are quite yielding.
> For a devout poet is appropriately pure   5
> himself, but his verses need not be.
> In the end they possess a piquancy and charm,
> since they are quite yielding and low on modesty
> and may excite an itch –
> I don't mean in boys, but in those hairy guys   10
> who can't stir their heavy loins.
> Because you read "many thousand kisses,"
> do you think that I'm less than a man?
> I, yes, I will fuck your mouth and fuck your ass.

Hardness and softness, sexual potency and passivity, delicacy and brutality – the binaries along which one could read this poem are obvious, and certainly accord with Roman notions of the *uir* and the *cinaedus* or *pathicus*. The poet answers charges of *mollitia* with threats of sexual violation thought by the Romans to be among the most disgraceful acts one might perform. In addition, there is an ethical dimension to his attack – Furius and Aurelius seem to have alleged that a soft man cannot exhibit modesty or piety. In return this "pious poet" issues a particularly vituperative stream of invective. Yet, the more closely we examine the poem, the more the lines between hardness and softness blur. The poet suggests that performing *mollitia* (for example, in the poems where he mentions the hundreds of kisses) is not evidence that one is soft. Is a poetic performance of hardness, then, proof that one is a *durus uir*? Does Catullus find that enacting softness can be appropriate, even manly? Catullus appears interested in questions of a man's integrity – bodily and moral – but a poem like 16 reveals that his notion of masculine identity is neither monolithic nor easily defined.

The attack on Furius and Aurelius also exhibits the poet's investment in competition. Certainly, the poem is a rejoinder (and an open one, upon its publication), to an ongoing dispute. In a poem like 16 the importance of competition in defining a male subject is obvious (as it is in numbers of his other invective poems, e.g., 15, 21, 25). Yet, competition may be just as critical to other verse, as David Wray has recently argued. In his book *Catullus and the Poetics of Roman Manhood* (2001), Wray attempts to shift our focus toward an unsentimental, rarely sincere poet whose primary concern is his status among his male peers. Using an anthropological model (based on that of Michael Herzfeld 1985) Wray looks to the poems to see what they can tell us of the other Catullus, the *uir durus*, who delights in besting his friends and enemies alike.

To Wray we owe perhaps the most comprehensive explication to date of how Romantic and Modernist theories of poetic reception compel our reading of the Catullan corpus. Despite the best efforts of many scholars to eschew a biographical reading of the poems, most of his readers persist in a belief that Catullus offers us a window into his life, a sincere emotional outpouring of love or disgust. The source of anxiety for many lies in an attempt to reconcile (or more frequently, to ignore) those aspects of the Catullan poetic identity that do not accord with the persona of the sincere lover (e.g., the tormenter of Gellius). In response to this, Wray proposes a postmodern poetics for Catullus, where "postmodern" is carefully defined: "A preference for the performative and ludic over the sincere and introspective; for emotional volatility over emotional intensity; for erudition, verbal wit, invention and allusivity over immediacy and 'originality'; for encyclopedic collage over meditative lyric . . . the discovery of a new formalism" (2001: 39). What we might read as dissonance (e.g., the introduction of a playful allusion or the correction of an earlier poet's error into a lament) instead betokens a different system of valuation and appropriate behavior (2001: 51–2; see above, poem 11). And, indeed, if vying with one's comrades (or the western poetic tradition) is acceptable in a poem of mourning, then competition may well be valued for its own sake.

Many scholars have noted the importance of performance in Catullus' verse (e.g., Newman 1990; Fitzgerald 1995; Krostenko 2001a), but it is Wray's distinct contention that what is being performed in these poems is masculinity. In particular, the form that manhood took involved a "free exchange of spoken and written invective" (2001: 58–9) that during the late Republic in no way imperiled the issuer of the insult (though this would change under the Principate). Whether the social structure engendered competitive invective, or such banter was an element in creating a system that solidified the importance of the masculinity/effeminacy axis, such play emphasizes the fact that a man's performance of his virility was observed publicly and constantly evaluated. As noted above, manhood was not a state that, once achieved, remained static. Rather, a man was continually appraised by his peers, and the effectiveness or authenticity of his performance was ever subject to revision and comment.

Wray introduces his analysis of Catullus' performance of manhood through a discussion of Herzfeld's "poetics of manhood." Herzfeld's anthropological fieldwork concerns Cretan men, for whom manhood is a performance that foregrounds the performance itself, creating meaning by tying the speaker to larger systems of ideology or identity through his boasts (Herzfeld 1985: 10–11, 23). Herzfeld explains this concept:

> In Glendiot [Cretan] idiom, there is less focus on "being a good man" than on "being good at being a man" – a stance that stresses *performative excellence*, the ability to foreground manhood by means of deeds that strikingly "speak for themselves." . . . What counts is . . . effective *movement* – a sense of shifting the ordinary and everyday into a context where the very change of context itself serves to invest it with significance. Thus, instead of noticing *what* men do, Glendiots focus their attention on *how* the act is performed. (Herzfeld 1985: 17)

It is Wray's aim to introduce the concept of a poetics of manhood into the discussion of Catullan poetics as a "third term" to disrupt or "triangulate" the binarism that dominates so much of Catullan criticism. In a poem like 16, considerations of "performative excellence" can offer insight into the problems inherent in reading a text that superficially presents a clear line along which to plot facets of masculinity. Rather than focusing on the active/passive axis in the poem, we may instead concentrate on the performance of masculinity in this poem, its audience, and how it shapes or reshapes male subjectivity.

It is important to note that Wray does not argue that sincere emotion, personal reflection and political commentary are wholly absent from Catullus' verse (though his skepticism is palpable), but he does strongly suggest that we should not assume that every "Catullus" is the same (2001: 86–7). Indeed, one of his most provocative readings – and one that illustrates well the way that a poetics of manhood can disrupt readings that posit a sincere, meditative, and knowable poet – is of a pair of poems tied closely to narratives of the Lesbia affair and Catullus' male friendships, poems 50 and 51.

Poem 51, the translation of Sappho 31, is one of Catullus' most famous verses because of its meter, the masterful reconceptualization of the original, and the prominence it has in the "Lesbia cycle." This poem has been read as the starting point in the affair with Lesbia, potentially a missive that he sent to Clodia to reveal his passion without fully disclosing his intentions, should the poem be intercepted or the message displease its recipient (Quinn 1973a: 241, 1972b: 57–60; Wray 2001: 90). The delicacy of the language, and the fact that Catullus writes himself as the second coming of Sappho, in thrall to the vision of a woman, has made this poem fodder for those who interrogate Catullus' feminine side, but seems an odd choice for one who desires to examine Catullus' instantiation of manhood as prioritizing the "performative over the ethical" (2001: 67, 92–3).[12]

The poem itself includes self-referential qualities that one might not anticipate in a translation. The first two lines exhibit perfect assonance (as does the first part of the third), and the anaphora of *otium* at the end of the lyric recalls the repetitions of *ille*,

ille, and *qui* at its inception (Wray 2001: 92). This ludic quality – the playful structure that calls attention to its playfulness – suggests a focus on the poetic craftsman (or a very stylized articulation of his mastery), which accords with the final stanza, a deliberate departure from the Greek original. In those final lines, rather than focusing on things feminine, as Sappho might and often does, Catullus expresses regret for his "womanish" pursuits:

> otium, Catulle, tibi molestum est:
> otio exsultas nimiumque gestis:
> otium et reges prius et beatas
> > perdidit urbes.
>
> Leisure, Catullus, is your trouble,
> you exult in leisure and are too unrestrained.
> Leisure has been the ruin of kings and blessed cities
> > before you.

While this non-Sapphic postscript may not have been as jarring or seemingly emphatically Roman as it appears to us (Wray 2001: 93–5), one way to account for the emphasis on *otium* is to read it in conjunction with the preceding poem 50, addressed to his friend and fellow poet, C. Licinius Calvus:

> Hesterno, Licini, die otiosi
> multum lusimus in meis tabellis,
> ut conuenerat esse delicatos:
> scribens uersiculos uterque nostrum
> ludebat numero modo hoc modo illoc,   5
> reddens mutua per iocum atque uinum.
> atque illinc abii tuo lepore
> incensus, Licini, facetiisque,
> ut nec me miserum cibus iuuaret
> nec somnus tegeret quiete ocellos,   10
> sed toto indomitus furore lecto
> uersarer, cupiens uidere lucem,
> ut tecum loquerer, simulque ut essem.
> at defessa labore membra postquam
> semimortua lectulo iacebant,   15
> hoc, iucunde, tibi poema feci,
> ex quo perspiceres meum dolorem.
> nunc audax caue sis, precesque nostras,
> oramus, caue despuas, ocelle,
> ne poenas Nemesis reposcat a te.   20
> est uemens dea: laedere hanc caueto.
>
> Yesterday, Licinius, at our leisure we
> Fooled around a great deal in my notebooks,
> As we had agreed to be charming:
> Each of us writing little verses
> Messed about now with this meter, now that,
> Passing them back and forth in jest and wine.
> And I left there inflamed by your charm,

Licinius, and your wit, so that food
Could not help me in my wretched state,
Nor could sleep close my eyes with stillness,
But untamed in a furor I tossed and turned upon
The whole bed, longing to see the dawn,
So that I could speak with you and be with you.
But after my limbs, exhausted by their efforts,
Lay half-dead in my bedlet,
Darling, I wrote this poem for you,
In which you can perceive my pain.
Now, don't be impudent, I beg,
Don't refuse my prayers, dear pet,
Or else Nemesis might require a penalty from you.
She's a vicious goddess: make sure you don't wound her.

Wray suggests that we read these two poems as a pair, which is framed by the experience of leisure (*otiosi*, 50.1, and *otium*, 51.13–15), the first as a "cover letter" for the second (2001: 97).[13] The case for taking these two poems as a pair is compelling: They share not only the aforementioned concern with leisure, but the speaker ("Catullus" in both) evinces a palpable erotic distress, which he characterizes as a disease. His experience of the love object is similar as well: he merely desires to be in the presence of and to speak with the one he desires, where conversation stimulates desire and it absence causes illness (2001: 98). Finally, the speaker refers to himself as *miser* (50.9, 51.5). Wray perceptively observes that this has no counterpart in the Sapphic original; it is a Catullan introduction, and, apart from the self-address in the final stanza, is the only place where the speaker's gender is noted: "It is here that the reader first becomes aware that Poem 51 is not so much a translation, one might say, as a performed imitation of Sappho's original poem, an appropriation or ventrilo-quizing of her words in the male (Catullan) speaker's own voice" (Wray 2001: 98).

The "cover letter" poem has parallels in the Catullan corpus, most notably in poem 65, though Wray argues persuasively that other instances of "poetic epistolarity" (namely poems 30, 38, 66, 68, 116, and perhaps 13) are similar to 50 in that "the epistolary commerce they represent and imply is transacted exclusively between men" (2001: 105). Read in this way, the poem becomes the thing (*hoc*, 50.16) – that is, the translation is the item exchanged – and the purpose is not to reflect upon personal relations or to woo, but to demonstrate those postmodern qualities that Wray so carefully articulated. Catullus' playful "I made this for you" creates a matrix of learned jokes: that he has crafted an original poem, when he has not; that he is playing with gender roles (that he *is* Sappho); that he is making a made-thing, playing on *poiéô*, the Greek word for "make" from which *poema*, "poem," is derived (Wray 2001: 99). The verses become more an erudite exercise and are further removed from their ostensible purpose of demonstrating a man's painful loss. Indeed, Wray reads the poet's overblown hyperbole at the end of 50 (the somewhat jarring invocation of Nemesis) as part of his "self-consciously outrageous performance" that will compel Calvus to pay attention to him, to laugh, to approve, and to respond in kind (2001: 107).

Furthermore, competition between men emerges as a salient feature of this type of poetic composition. If the poem that Catullus sends Calvus is the poem that follows, then Catullus has accomplished a remarkable *coup*. His bits of "fooling around" are a polished translation, which has been altered to cast the spotlight ever more on the poet himself and his talent. As Wray observes, this poem (and the other epistolary poems like it) make sense only as a response or an invitation "in the form of specifically poetic performance" (2001: 106). What else we can read into poem 51 is unclear – is Catullus slyly valuing an unnamed female above Calvus? Is he playing with Sapphic homoeroticism in an effort to say something (playful? sincere? outrageous?) about his own relationships? Regardless, what becomes obvious when read in this way is that the female (that is, Lesbia or her equivalent) is effectively erased from the equation. She is reified in the process of being an object of exchange between men (Wray 2001: 108–9). Rather than the focus of an erotic liaison that colors our reading of poem 50, the interpretation of Sappho's verse is stripped of its femininity. Or rather, its femininity is in service to a masculine competitive discourse.

It is perhaps misleading to subtitle this portion of my chapter "Hardness," for it leaves one with the impression that Wray is impervious to the allure of Catullan *mollitia* and has no interest in the topic.[14] Yet, it is the aggressive, brash, and witty accuser of poem 80 and the subtler but no less devious gossip of poem 6 who remain the focus of this work. By reintroducing the importance of the *uir durus* – or in Catullus' case perhaps the *uir lepidus durusque* – Wray has offered up a potent corrective. Given the emphasis on Catullus' femininity, his introspection or his adoption of a soft persona for hard goals (as with Skinner, above), it is requisite that some attention be paid to what is a critical aspect of the performance of masculinity – the hard surface and the hard center, even if, as Wray suggests, it is all a performance – and merely a piece of the performance at that.

Rewriting Masculinity

It is no surprise that Catullus reflects aspects of the traditional male ideal. As noted by Skinner, his poetry has been remarked upon for its inclusion of political vocabulary (emphasizing the importance of *pietas, amicitia*, and the like), though often in places where one would not expect to find it (e.g., poems 73, 76, 87). In fact, he notes his own piety and modesty in poem 16 and expresses a longing for the forum and other typical masculine activities in poem 63, showing at the very least that he has learned the diction of Roman virility. It is also obvious that Catullus has successfully internalized cultural values regarding hardness and softness, since these concepts occur as opposites in his verses, much as they do in Cicero's attack on Antony or Calvus's jibe at Pompey. Yet, while a matrix of traditional values and behaviors associated with the *uir* are present in these verses, they are not valorized as in the foundation legends of Livy or anecdotes about Cato. Rather, Catullus uses concepts and language that define the Roman male to redefine masculinity.

The analyses of Catullus' poetry by Skinner and Wray deftly show two different ways that Catullus can be seen to accomplish this. For Skinner, the poetic register is not merely literary but also political. The anxiety about the stability of a male identity observable in his verses may reflect alienation from the political and social roles that were traditionally available to men. Reading poem 63 (or other verses about male anxiety) should cause us to rethink other poems that seem transparent to us; if Lesbia is not a lover (or not merely a lover), but a sign of a particular kind of power relationship, we need to re-evaluate the way we have read the corpus to date.

Like Skinner, Wray wants us to question the orthodoxy of Catullan scholarship by shifting the focus. If our Catullus is not the sincerely enraptured, emotionally broken lover of Lesbia, what Catullus should take his place? The postmodern Catullus that Wray proposes permits a re-evaluation of the corpus as well, since he introduces a self-consciously playful and voluble poet who never loses sight of his own performance of manhood. Virility is performed not only in competition between Catullus and his friends and enemies; he seems to delight in trying on other masculine identities or crashing two subjectivities into one another (as in poem 11), as he further destabilizes what masculinity might signify. Wray does not necessarily ask us to abandon our love-sick Catullus, but he does insist that we consider the multiple masculine identities the poet wears simultaneously.[15]

For all this, the elusiveness of the poet may be what is most appealing about Catullus, and attempts to say something meaningful about his conception of the male subject are greatly restricted by the sliver of poetry he has bequeathed to us. We lack much of the context for his poetry and should bear in mind that the Catullus we read and the performance of virility we witness are in large part ones we have created. Any performance of gender is necessarily colored by one's knowledge of the culture, the performers themselves, and one's own vantage point. My seat at the county fair showed me only one brief moment in a performance that those boys will continue to refine and replay throughout their lives. What I did not see that evening – their pallor or delight on the Tilt-o-Whirl, their prowess at winning a stuffed animal at a midway game, whom they kissed in the shadows of the poultry barn – might tell me much more about the effectiveness of their performance, but we can only interpret what we see.

NOTES

1   Though it is a term of widespread use in philosophical, critical, and psychoanalytic contexts, I use the term "Other" much as does Luce Irigaray, who argued that signification and identity are based in the masculine, whereas the feminine is other in relation to male sameness, and does not signify on its own (1985).
2   The term "homosocial" denotes social affinities between members of the same sex, as distinct from homosexual desire. On the distinction between the homosexual and the homosocial, and the ways that homosociality can structure men's lives, see Sedgwick (1985).
3   See in particular Richlin (2000), on the way that the public life of the forum shaped a "boy's transition to manhood."
4   A fuller discussion of Roman values can be found in Hellegouarc'h (1972).
5   For a structuralist reading of Roman sexual activity and passivity, see Parker (1997).
6   This is a generalization. On the specific differences between *cinaedus, pathicus, scultimoni-dus,* and boys, see C. A. Williams (1999).
7   The vilification of the *cinaedus* is evident in many works: see, for example, Juv. 2 and 9 and Catull. 112.
8   Caesar perhaps shows best the danger of being either too soft or too hard. He was famously said to have been "a man to every woman and a woman to every man" (Suet. *Iul.* 52.3), which illustrates the danger not so much of softness as of excess.
9   Catullus' femininity is best articulated and analyzed by Adler (1981).

10 Christopher Nappa makes a similar argument, in which he distinguishes between a Catullan critique of masculinity and virility (2001: 42 and *passim*).

11 Skinner's argument has been critiqued by Paul Allen Miller, who also examines Catullus' subjectivity in light of Foucault (1998). Miller's conclusions are radically different but equally provocative.

12 Wray does deal at length with poetry that would seem, perhaps, more suitable to discussions of an aggressively hypermasculine performance. See esp. ch. 4, "Towards a Mediterranean Poetics of Aggression," and ch. 5, "Code Models of Catullan Manhood."

13 As Wray observes, this is not a new suggestion, but it is one that has not been given much attention of late (2001: 97 n. 75).

14 See, for example his discussion of the "kiss" poems (5 and 7), where he notes an often missed Catullan effeminacy (2001: 145–51).

15 Miller perhaps articulates best what he calls "the vertiginous flux of a complex multi-leveled and multi-temporal subjectivity" (1998: 192).

GUIDE TO FURTHER READING

Those interested in the history and breath of the study of masculinity might begin with Rachel Adams and David Savran's *The Masculinity Studies Reader* (2002). Excellent treatments of the performance and meaning of masculinity in Roman culture are found in Barton (1992), Gleason (1995), Gunderson (2000), Skinner (2005) and Williams (1999). In addition to Skinner (1993b [1997 edn.]) and Wray (2001), important studies of Catullan masculinity include Miller (1998), and Skinner (1982 and 1989).

WORKS CITED

Adams, R., and D. Savran, eds. 2002. *The Masculinity Studies Reader*. Malden, MA.

Adler, E. 1981. *Catullan Self-Revelation*. New York.

Barton, C. 1992. *The Sorrows of the Ancient Romans: The Gladiator and the Monster*. Princeton, NJ.

Burrus, V. 2000. *Begotten, Not Made: Conceiving Manhood in Late Antiquity*. Stanford, CA.

Butler, J. 1990. *Gender Trouble: Feminism and the Subversion of Identity*. New York.

Butler, J. 1993. *Bodies That Matter: On the Discursive Limits of "Sex."* New York.

Cahoon, L. 1988. "Bed as Battlefield: Erotic Conquest and Military Metaphor in Ovid's *Amores*." *Transactions of the American Philological Association* 118: 293–307.

Dover, K. J. 1978. *Greek Homosexuality*. London and Cambridge, MA.

Edwards, C. 1993. *The Politics of Immorality in Ancient Rome*. Cambridge.

Fasteau, M. 1975. *The Male Machine*. New York.

Fitzgerald, W. 1995. *Catullan Provocations: Lyric Poetry and the Drama of Position*. Berkeley, Los Angeles, and London.

Foucault, M. 1978. *The History of Sexuality*. Vol. 1, *An Introduction*. Trans. R. Hurley. New York.

Foucault, M. 1986. *The Care of the Self*. Vol. 3, *The History of Sexuality*. Trans. R. Hurley. New York.

Gleason, M. W. 1990. "The Semiotics of Gender: Physiognomy and Self-Fashioning in the Second Century C.E." In D. Halperin, J. Winkler, and F. Zeitlin, eds., *Before Sexuality*. Princeton, NJ. 389–415.

Gleason, M. W. 1995. *Making Men: Sophists and Self-Presentation in Ancient Rome.* Princeton, NJ.

Greene, E. 1995. "The Catullan Ego: Fragmentation and the Erotic Self." *American Journal of Philology* 116: 77–93.

Greene, E. 1999b. *The Erotics of Domination: Male Desire and the Mistress in Latin Love Poetry.* Baltimore.

Gunderson, E. 2000. *Staging Masculinity.* Ann Arbor, MI.

Hallett, J. P., and M. B. Skinner, eds. 1977. *Roman Sexualities.* Princeton, NJ.

Halperin, D. M. 1990. *One Hundred Years of Homosexuality and Other Essays on Greek Love.* New York.

Hellegouarc'h, J. 1972. *Le vocabulaire Latin des relations et des partis politiques sous la République.* 2nd edn. rev. and corr. Paris.

Herzfeld, M. 1985. *The Poetics of Manhood: Contest and Identity in a Cretan Mountain Village.* Princeton, NJ.

Irigaray, L. 1985. *This Sex Which Is Not One.* Trans. C. Porter. Ithaca, NY.

Krostenko, B. A. 2001a. *Cicero, Catullus, and the Language of Social Performance.* Chicago and London.

Lyne, R. O. A. M. 1980. *The Latin Love Poets from Catullus to Horace.* Oxford.

Miller, P. A. 1994. *Lyric Texts and Lyric Consciousness: The Birth of a Genre from Archaic Greece to Augustan Rome.* London and New York.

Miller, P. A. 1998. "Catullan Consciousness, the 'Care of the Self,' and the Force of the Negative in History." In D. H. J. Larmour, P. A. Miller, and C. Platter, eds. *Rethinking Sexuality: Foucault and Classical Antiquity.* Princeton, NJ. 171–203.

Nappa, C. 2001. *Aspects of Catullus' Social Fiction.* Frankfurt.

Newman, J. K. 1990. *Roman Catullus and the Modification of the Alexandrian Sensibility.* Hildesheim.

Parker, H. N. 1997. "The Teratogenic Grid." In Hallett and Skinner (1997: 47–65).

Pleck, E., and J. Pleck, eds. 1980. *The American Man.* Englewood Cliffs, NJ.

Quinn, K. 1972b. *Catullus: An Interpretation.* London.

Quinn, K., ed. 1973a. *Catullus: The Poems.* 2nd edn. London and Basingstoke.

Reitzenstein, R. 1912. "Zur Sprache der lateinischen Erotik." *Sitzungsberichte der Heidelberger Akademie du Wissenschaften* 12: 1–36.

Richlin, A. 1992 [1983]. *The Garden of Priapus: Sexuality and Aggression in Roman Humor.* Rev. edn. New York and Oxford.

Richlin, A. 2000. "Gender and Rhetoric: Producing Manhood in the Schools." In W. Dominik, ed., *Roman Eloquence: Rhetoric in Society and Literature.* London. 90–110.

Ross, D. O., Jr. 1969. *Style and Tradition in Catullus.* Cambridge, MA.

Sedgwick, E. K. 1985. *Between Men: English Literature and Male Homosocial Desire.* New York.

Skinner, M. B. 1982a. "Pretty Lesbius." *Transactions of the American Philological Association* 112: 197–208.

Skinner, M. B. 1989. "*Ut decuit cinaediorem*: Power, Gender, and Urbanity in Catullus 10." *Helios* 16: 7–23.

Skinner, M. B. 1993b. "*Ego mulier*: The Construction of Male Sexuality in Catullus." *Helios* 20: 107–30 (= Hallett and Skinner 1997: 129–50).

Skinner, M. B. 2005. *Sexuality in Greek and Roman Culture.* Malden, MA.

Williams, C. A. 1999. *Roman Homosexuality: Ideologies of Masculinity in Classical Antiquity.* New York and Oxford.

Wiseman, T. P. 1985. *Catullus and His World: A Reappraisal.* Cambridge.

Wray, D. 2001. *Catullus and the Poetics of Roman Manhood.* Cambridge.

Wyke, M. 2002. *The Roman Mistress: Ancient and Modern Representations.* Oxford.

PART III

Influences

CHAPTER EIGHT

Catullus and Sappho

Ellen Greene

Although only two poems of Catullus, 11 and 51, are specifically written in the
Sapphic stanza, the figure of Sappho and the love lyric tradition he inherits from
her occupy a privileged status within Catullus' body of work. Ever since she composed her poems on the island of Lesbos at the end of the seventh century BC, the life
and lyrics of Sappho have haunted the western imagination. Indeed, Sappho's provocative images of homoerotic desire have disturbed readers through the ages, and
have given rise to a multitude of fantasies, fictions, and myths about both her poetics
and her persona.[1] Not only is Sappho the earliest surviving woman writer in the West,
but she is also one of the few and certainly one of the earliest woman writers before
the twentieth century to express overtly in verse the (erotic) desire of one woman for
another.[2] Even in poems that do not deal explicitly with love, Sappho often depicts
herself as part of a world in which the emotional and/or erotic bonds between
women take center stage. Since ancient Greek society was largely male-dominated,
Sappho's ostensible focus on a "woman-centered" world in her poetry has, at least in
part, made her a fascinating yet vexing subject of speculation and fantasy. In Latin
texts, the Sapphic tradition becomes reconfigured as a vehicle for expression of
heterosexual love. As a number of scholars have shown, this heterosexualization of
Sapphic desire, the appropriation of feminine (homoerotic) desire by the male poetic
voice, can be traced throughout the tradition of love lyric in the West.[3]

Like a number of Roman poets writing in the late Republic and early Principate,
Catullus, quite self-consciously, attempts to bring into Latin the tradition of love lyric
inherited from the ancient Greeks.[4] Sappho is arguably one of the most widely read
poets of Greek and Roman antiquity. Although only approximately 40 fragments of
her work are long enough to be intelligible, her influence on the western poetic
tradition is undeniable.[5] For many male writers in ancient Rome, notably Catullus,
Horace, and Ovid, Sappho represents the paradigmatic poetic voice of feminine
desire and sexuality. Catullus' adaptation of Sappho's poems and literary tropes,
Ovid's depiction of Sappho in the *Heroides*, his collection of fictional letters from

abandoned heroines, and Horace's allusions to Sappho in his *Odes* show some of the attempts by Roman male poets to "translate" a feminine discourse within a male-dominant cultural context.

While Horace claims to have been the first to bring into Latin the verse written in the Aeolic dialect of Greek, produced at the close of the seventh century BC on the island of Lesbos, Catullus is the only Roman poet whose poetic affiliation with Lesbian poetry is exclusively focused on Sappho. Horace makes it clear that the poetry of Alcaeus, Sappho's contemporary on Lesbos, is as critical to his lyric self-presentation as is Sappho's verse. But that is not the case with Catullus. The world of feminine desire and poetic imagination evoked in Sappho's poetry is an integral feature of Catullan love lyric, and, more specifically, serves as a vehicle for Catullus' implicit critique of aspects of Roman social and aesthetic values. Owing mainly to the homoerotic features of her verse and her powerful expressions of erotic desire, Sappho's literary reputation in Rome is often associated with sexual impropriety and degeneracy.[6] Catullus exploits that association to challenge, albeit implicitly, conventional Roman attitudes toward desire, masculinity, and a life devoted to artistic endeavor.

In general, the Romans had, at best, an ambivalent attitude toward the ancient Greeks. On the one hand, Romans admired and emulated the great achievements of the Greeks in the areas of philosophy, art, and literature. On the other hand, the Romans of the late Republic regarded the Greeks as morally decadent and excessively pleasure-seeking. In that context, the overt feminine sexuality and immersion in a life of beauty and imagination portrayed in Sappho's poems would have been viewed as threatening to many of the values the Romans of Catullus' era held most dear: manly virtue, duty, and obligation to the state. Catullus often expresses a commitment to a life of passion and poetic imagination through an identification with Sappho's poetics and persona. In doing so, he flouts many aspects of Roman values and conventions, primarily the expectation that a Roman male citizen would maintain his dignity and social standing by exercising self-control with respect to emotions and desires. Giving in to personal pleasures and the unruly emotions associated with love would have been considered both un-Roman and un-masculine.[7]

One of the primary ways Catullus represents his identification with Sappho and her feminine-dominant world is by naming his female beloved "Lesbia." Approximately 26 of Catullus' poems are associated directly with Lesbia. In 13 of those poems, Catullus mentions Lesbia by name. But in at least 12 more poems Catullus refers to an unnamed mistress whom most readers assume to be Lesbia. Who is this Lesbia, whose presence clearly dominates Catullus' work? On the most literal level, the name Lesbia may be a pseudonym for Catullus' actual mistress. Many scholars believe that Lesbia refers to a woman named Clodia, generally thought to be either Clodia Metelli, a consul's wife, or one of her sisters. Since the name Clodia is metrically equivalent to the name "Lesbia," it could easily have been substituted for "Lesbia" if the manuscript circulated privately, as was often the case (Miller 1994: 102). But a more important reason for the use of this particular pseudonym is that *Lesbia* is the Latin adjective denoting a woman from Lesbos, and in the context of erotic poetry this appellation would most certainly refer to Sappho. Thus, direct and indirect references to Lesbia in Catullus' poetry evoke the values represented in Sappho's work as well as her iconic status as love poet.

For the most part, readers of Catullus have regarded Sappho as his poetic muse, his inspiration for carrying on a tradition of love lyric. Some readers, however, have emphasized the ways in which use of the pseudonym "Lesbia" allows Catullus to explore sex-role reversal in the context of heterosexual love relationships. In Latin texts women desiring other women are typically portrayed as masculine. Horace, for example, referred to Sappho (*Ep.* 1.19.28) as *mascula* ("mannish" or "strong"). Since Sappho's powerful expressions of active erotic desire contravene the conventional amatory ideal of women as subordinate and men as dominant, it made sense for Latin authors to characterize Sappho as usurping the traditional masculine role. This is especially relevant to Catullus' Lesbia poems. In those poems Catullus often assumes the subordinate, feminine role and, for the most part, depicts his mistress Lesbia as cruel, unfaithful, and domineering. While we certainly cannot equate the figure of Lesbia with Sappho, it is nonetheless fair to say that allusions to Lesbia in Catullus' poetry evoke in varying ways the poetics and persona of Sappho.

My discussion of specific poems in which Catullus incorporates Sappho into his own work will be organized according to the three main stances he adopts toward Lesbia in his poems. The first part of my chapter will deal with poems 5 and 7, the two poems of Catullus in which he expresses a sense of joy at the blissful happiness of his union with Lesbia. In these two poems Catullus implicitly celebrates an identification with the world of erotic fulfillment and imagination that we see in a number of Sappho's surviving poems. But, in addition, Catullus uses the celebration of his union with Lesbia, and implicitly his association with Sappho, to reject the crass commercialism and mercantilism of Roman society.

In the second part, I will examine poem 51, Catullus' translation/adaptation of Sappho's poem 31, which expresses Sappho's anguished passion and feelings of powerlessness at the sight of her (female) beloved. Sappho 31 is perhaps her most famous poem, possibly because of Catullus and many subsequent poets who imitated it, but more importantly because it is arguably her most powerful articulation of desire for the ever-elusive beloved. It is in this poem that Sappho conveys so poignantly the bittersweet nature of love (Carson 1986). Catullus' adaptation of Sappho's poem provides a striking illustration of how his incorporation of her work in general is shaped both by his cultural distance from her and by his gender; in particular, by conceptions of masculinity prevalent in Roman culture. It also expresses most dramatically the characteristically Catullan conflict between the demands of *negotium*, that is, the world of business and male power relations, and the attractions of Sappho's apparently feminine, private world. It must be understood that, despite Catullus' clearly strong identification with Sappho, he does not appropriate the homoerotic elements in Sappho's poetry. Rather, he attempts to reconstruct many aspects of Sappho's poetic world as expressions of *male* heteroerotic desire. This has especially important implications with regard to Catullus 51, a poem in which Catullus tries to adopt Sappho's poetic voice in the context of describing his emotions upon seeing Lesbia.

The third part of this chapter will focus on poem 11, in which Catullus expresses anger, disappointment, and bitter sarcasm toward Lesbia. Catullus berates himself for his attachment to a woman he usually portrays as perpetually unfaithful. Lesbia is depicted as not only unworthy of Catullus' love but also morally degenerate. This negative portrayal of Lesbia would seem to contradict Catullus' positive identification with the Sapphic poetic tradition. How is it that Lesbia can evoke Catullus' poetic muse and all that she represents and, at the same time, be characterized as a figure who is so reprehensible? My view is that these seemingly opposite portrayals of Lesbia in Catullus' poems encapsulate the difficulties of translating Sappho's discourse of feminine desire and poetic imagination into a Roman, masculine context.

Celebrating Lesbia, Celebrating Love

As mentioned above, in two of his best-known poems, poems 5 and 7, Catullus rejoices in his love for Lesbia. Given that the name Lesbia evokes Sappho, Catullus would seem to be implicitly celebrating not only his specific love for his mistress but in more general terms a life devoted to *eros* and the poetic imagination. It may also be argued that in poems 5 and 7 Catullus celebrates the poetic relationship he has with Sappho. In other words, he is paying homage not only to his love for Lesbia but also to his "love" for the poet Sappho.

> Let us live, my Lesbia, and let us love,
> and value at one cent the talk of crabby, old men.
> Suns may set and rise again.
> For us, once the brief light has set,
> night is one continuous sleep.
> Give me a thousand kisses, then a hundred,
> then another thousand, then a second hundred,
> then yet another thousand, then a hundred.
> Then, when we have made many thousands,
> we will confuse our counting, so that we may not
> know, nor will anyone be able to cast an evil eye,
> when he knows that our kisses are so many.
>
> (poem 5)

> You ask, Lesbia, how many kisses
> would be enough, and more than enough.
> As many as the huge number of the Libyan sands
> in the desert near silphium-bearing Cyrene,
> between the oracle of lusty Jove
> and the sacred tomb of Battus,
> or as many as the stars, when the night is silent,
> that watch the furtive loves of mortals.
> To kiss you with so many kisses would be enough
> and more than enough for mad Catullus,
> kisses which neither the gossips could count up,
> nor an evil tongue bewitch.
>
> (poem 7)

The two poems translated above are Catullus' most emphatic expressions of his erotic and aesthetic ideal. He defiantly asserts that, for him, life and love are inextricably entwined and that the woman whose name evokes Sappho is the focal point of that assertion. He implies not only that Sappho is his creative muse but also that his identification with her serves as a vehicle for him to challenge traditional Roman values. Like Sappho, who often represents love as transcending the contingencies of time and circumstance, Catullus' passionate, hypnotic expression of love's power also refuses to acknowledge limits, at least in the poems cited above. The world, for the moment, is blotted out and all that exists is the energy generated by the lover's kisses, which have no practical use in the world, but rather exist as an end in themselves. This is analogous to Sappho's repeated demonstrations that memory and the poetic imagination have the power to overcome the intrusions of the exterior world (Stehle [Stigers] 1979, 1981; Burnett 1983; E. Greene 1994). In Sappho's case, these intrusions usually take the form of either forced separations between lovers or erotic rejection and loss. For a Roman male, the poetic expression of a commitment to passion and imagination as a way of life means not only an encounter with potential loss and abandonment, but also a confrontation with a masculine-dominated culture that on the whole values duty over pleasure, stoic fortitude over emotion, industry over leisure. We can see that confrontation played out in Catullus' attempts to defy the crabby old men who disapprove of the passionate life he so confidently advocates.

By applying monetary standards to human worth, Catullus implicitly negates the world to which the old men belong, which makes money – numerical quantification – the primary means of human exchange and validation. In exposing the absurdity of rendering human worth accountable, he subverts the mechanism of accounting altogether. Although he uses numerical reckoning to "count" the number of kisses, his use of repetition has a spellbinding effect that contradicts the practical, controlled discourse of the commercial world. Not only does Catullus imagine the lovers becoming confused by their number of kisses, but the mixing of the languages of love and money confounds the narrow expectations of the old men. Catullus not only exposes the "bankruptcy" of their world, but also shows how the calculative impulse is, in itself, a kind of death, a way of making things static, frozen in meaning and possibility. The limits set by numerical calculation, by the rational knowledge of things, are overturned in Catullus' contravention of numerical restraints, his discourse of passion – in which finite, arithmetical calculations explode into the realm of the incalculable and unknowable – the "many thousands of kisses" and the infinite grains of sand.

Although Catullus formally addresses Lesbia in both 5 and 7, his focus of attention is on the shadowy presence of the men whose hostile gaze and uncomprehending perspective threaten to negate the value of his erotic ideal and poetic identity. His address to Lesbia in both poems is merely a dramatic means of asserting the value of the passionate life. While we cannot be sure that she will respond to his request for kisses and that their union will be consummated, that scarcely matters. What is most striking in these poems is the fact that Catullus' request for kisses takes on a life of its own. His passionate utterance of unmediated desire in its expression of "infinite potency and energy" seems to stand on its own, an end in itself rather than a means to an actual, consummated erotic union. In *these* poems, at least, the realities of the external world become subordinated to the poet's imaginative vision of idyllic, "mad" passion. Similarly, in one of her best-known surviving poems, fragment 94, Sappho creates a vivid picture of idyllic erotic union, despite impending separation from her beloved and questions about whether the other woman even remembers what they experienced together.[8] For both Sappho and Catullus, what matters most is the capacity of their poetic voices to transform the disappointing realities of the external world, whether those realities take the form of separation, rejection, or a society that devalues a life of passion and poetic imagination.

Although Catullus imagines blissful passion with Lesbia, whose name evokes Sappho, it is really he, rather than Lesbia, who more nearly approximates the legendary Greek poet. It is highly ironic that the name "Lesbia" should call Sappho to mind, given Catullus' mostly negative depiction of his mistress throughout the corpus. Even in poems 5 and 7 Lesbia seems more like a catalyst for, rather than a mutual participant in, his unbounded desire. Indeed, the fact that in poem 7 Lesbia asks Catullus to quantify their kisses seems to align her with the materialistic values associated with the crabby old men – the very values he scorns. As Micaela Janan puts it, Lesbia "pulls the request (for kisses) back from infinity by asking Catullus to number infinity" (1994: 62). Moreover, since Catullus is addressing Lesbia when he refers to himself as "mad Catullus," one can infer that his passion and his imaginative flights from the mundane and practical seem as "mad" to her as to the crotchety, evil-tongued scandalmongers. The irony here is that the female beloved, Lesbia, is implicitly associated with the material and practical concerns of conventional Roman males while the male lover, Catullus, is identified with the "un-masculine" realm of beauty, imagination, and the pursuit of erotic fulfillment, a realm that we may also associate with Sappho's feminine poetic world. We can see that association most dramatically in Catullus' adoption of the Sapphic persona in his translation and adaptation of Sappho's famous poem 31. In his version, c. 51, he assumes a woman's voice, yet at the same time expresses the conflict this poses for him as a Roman male.

Catullus Translating Sappho

Numerous poets through the ages, both male and female, have translated and imitated Sappho's fragment 31. Catullus' translation, however, is generally considered to come closest to the original.[9] A central theme of both poems is the exploration of a conflict between the experience of the poet as someone who can speak about his or her desire and is, therefore, an integrated self, and the experience of the poet as a lover who, when faced with desire for the beloved, undergoes a nearly total collapse of the self. The power of both the Sapphic and Catullan versions, in large part, depends on the paradox of being able to speak so eloquently about the inability to speak in the presence of the beloved.

The narrative situation in the two poems is quite similar; both Sappho and Catullus describe a scene in which they observe the female beloved with a male rival. Although both poems at the outset describe an erotic triangle, Catullus pictures himself rivaling another male for the attentions of Lesbia, while Sappho appears to compete with a man for the affections of an unnamed woman. While the figure of woman in Sappho's poem is both subject and object of desire, in Catullus' version the woman, Lesbia, is only in the object position (cf. Miller 1994: 102). Insofar as Lesbia's name evokes Sappho, it is quite plausible to think that Catullus' object of desire is Sappho herself: in addition to describing the effects of desire on him when he sees Lesbia, he is also describing the effects that Sappho's poetry has on him (i.e., it renders him "speechless"). I will return to this conceivable subtext of Catullus 51 when I discuss the representation of Lesbia in poem 11 below. Nonetheless, by making the speaker of the poem male, Catullus recontextualizes Sappho's poem as heterosexual; he replaces Sappho, the speaking, desiring subject, with himself. This creates a paradoxical situation. On the one hand, it serves to feminize Catullus by identifying him with Sappho in her role as the female lover and pursuer of a beloved and, on the other, it erases the "feminine signature" of the poem by turning a female homoerotic situation into a conventional love triangle where two males compete for one woman. In what follows I will explore this paradox, focusing on the ways Catullus appropriates the Sapphic paradigm of erotic desire to express his own ambivalence about Roman ideals of masculinity and sexuality.

> That man seems to me to be equal to the gods,
> who sits opposite to you and near by
> hears you sweetly speaking
>   and charmingly laughing,
>
> something which truly   5
> excites the heart in my breast;
> for whenever I see you suddenly,
> then it is no longer possible
>   for me to speak,
>
> But my tongue is broken in silence   10
> and at once a thin flame runs under my skin,
> and there is no sight in my eyes,
>   and my ears hum,
>
> and cold sweat possesses me, and
> trembling seizes me completely,   15
> and I am greener than grass,
>   and I seem to myself to be little short of dying.
>
> But everything must be ventured,
> since even a needy person. . . .
>   (Sappho 31)
>
> That man seems to me to be equal to a god,
> that man, if it is allowed (*si fas est*), seems to surpass the gods,
> who sitting opposite you again and again
>   looks at you and hears you
>
> sweetly laughing, which steals away   5
> all senses from wretched me; for as soon
> as I have seen you, Lesbia, nothing
>   remains for me.
>
> But my tongue is numb, a thin flame
> flows down under my limbs, my ears ring   10
> with their own sound, my eyes are covered
>   with a double night.
>
> Leisure (*otium*), Catullus, is troublesome for you;
> you revel in leisure and you desire excessively;
> leisure before has destroyed both kings   15
>   and blessed cities.
>   (Catullus 51)

Both Sappho and Catullus present opening scenarios in which they are external observers of their beloved, who is seemingly engaged in intimate, though non-sexual, contact with a male rival. And both refer to this rival as god-like, partly because he can claim the beloved's attentions, but more importantly because he appears to remain miraculously unmoved in the presence of the desired woman. In both poems, the man is unnamed and rapidly fades out of sight. In Catullus' translation, however, this figure (*ille*) dominates the first stanza of the poem, whereas, in Sappho's original, the man serves primarily to point up the contrast between the impassivity he exhibits and Sappho's highly charged emotional responses to her female beloved. Indeed, the opening phrase in Sappho's poem, "it seems to <u>me</u>" (*phainetai moi*), focuses attention on the speaker herself rather than on her object of desire, thus suggesting that from the beginning Sappho is primarily engaged with her own perceptions and imagination rather than the presence of potential or actual rivals.

By contrast, Catullus begins his poem by repeatedly mentioning "that man." This suggests that the speaker's main focus of attention is not the object of desire, the woman, but the presence of another man. Indeed, the second line in Catullus' poem, "that man, if it is allowed, seems to surpass the gods," has no equivalent in the Sapphic original. Like Sappho, Catullus compares the unnamed man to a god, but in the second line goes further by saying that the man in fact *surpasses* the gods. This emphasis on a hierarchical relationship between man and god reinforces an ambiance of rivalry and competition between the man who can gaze at Lesbia without any apparently disruptive effects and the wretched lover (Catullus) who cannot. Moreover, the phrase *si fas est* in the second line invokes a social and political context almost entirely absent from Sappho's poem. Although Catullus links himself, through his translation, to the Sapphic tradition of presenting *eros* as both disabling and disruptive to the lover, he nonetheless situates the voice of the lover in relation to male public culture. "If it is allowed" not only diverts attention from the dramatic situation of erotic encounter, but also evokes the moral hierarchies and responsibilities associated with the socio-political order, an order from which Roman women were largely excluded.

Furthermore, by giving so much prominence to the presence of "that man" and to the power the "other" seems to have in contrast with himself, Catullus adds an important dimension to the situation of erotic triangulation envisioned in Sappho's original. In Sappho's poem, the man and the exterior world in general are subordinated to the sweet sound and lovely laughter of the desired woman. The poem quickly turns away from the opening scene of heterosexual courtship to Sappho's intense engagement with her own emotional responses. In Catullus' poem, however, the masculine world of business and power politics (*negotium*) serves as a backdrop against which the speaker depicts his private passions. In other words, the primary relationship in the poem is not between Catullus and his beloved, but between the speaker and "that man" – the figure who embodies not only the contingencies of the exterior world for the lover (as in Sappho's poem) but the pressures of *negotium* in general. The man who rivals Catullus for Lesbia's attentions is apparently able to withstand the temptations of love. In the context of Roman culture, the fact that "the man" can gaze at Lesbia without any unsettling effects means that he is free to attend to his duties to the community; thus, his imperviousness to Lesbia's charms attests to his "manliness." The contrast between "that man" and the unhappy lover (Catullus), then, represents a way for Catullus to explore not merely different responses to amatory experience but, more importantly, uncertainties and anxieties about pursuing the erotic life in the context of a culture that values duty over private pleasure.

On the surface, the descriptions of the loss of voice and identity brought on by the sight of the beloved appear to be quite similar in the two poems. The Sapphic and Catullan narrators are both robbed of their faculties, both seem to experience a sense of dissolution and bodily fragmentation at the sight of their beloveds. Like "that man," Catullus too gazes at the woman. Thus we can see a direct contrast between the power of the other man to gaze and the weakness that overwhelms Catullus at a mere glance. In Sappho's poem "the man" loses definition almost immediately, whereas Catullus sustains the image of the man's distinct identity by referring to him with a much greater degree of specificity. The presence of Catullus' male rival persists in the contrast implicitly maintained throughout the poem between the man who can resist Lesbia's charms – and is thus a *man* in the Roman sense of not indulging in excessive emotion – and Catullus, who cannot help giving into his unruly emotions (thereby becoming feminized). In a number of the poems about Lesbia (see in particular cc. 8 and 76), Catullus admonishes himself for his over-indulgence in pleasure and his attendant lack of moral resolve. In those poems, he tells himself to stop behaving like a woman, that is to say, like a person who feels victimized by love and desire. And that is precisely what appears to happen to Catullus in poem 51 – he, like Sappho in poem 31, is robbed of his senses when he sees his mistress.

Sappho describes her breakdown at the sight of her beloved by cataloguing the fragmentation of her own body. While Catullus says that his wretched condition leads to *all* his senses being stolen from him, Sappho refers only to her separate body parts. She describes herself as a collection of disparate parts that have "wandered off from herself." Near the end of the poem, Sappho's declaration that she appears to herself to be little short of dying reinforces the sense of bodily alienation and fragmentation that seems to characterize her experience of self. Indeed, the four complete stanzas of the poem are framed by the verb "to seem." The opening line, "he seems to me," refers to the man as the object of the speaker's gaze, while in stanza 4 the speaker uses the verb "seem" in the first person (*phaínom'*). *She* now becomes the object of her own gaze; her expression in line 16, "I am greener than grass," reinforces the sense in which the speaker sees herself as if from outside. This suggests increased emotional control on Sappho's part, which culminates in her ability to address herself in a voice of confident self-assertion when, in line 18, she tells herself that all her symptoms can be endured. The imperative tone of that statement (G. Wills 1967: 190) implies that Sappho has not only achieved some sort of recovery but also reconstituted herself out of the experience of being broken by love.

While Catullus also pictures himself robbed of his faculties, he does so in a way that is markedly different from Sappho. He begins by saying that all his senses have been stolen from him and that nothing remains for him. Although Catullus appears to imitate Sappho's description of emotional and bodily disintegration, his use of *omnis* and *nihil* seems rather to suggest the persistence of an integral identity. In Sappho's poem, on the other hand, the self is systematically broken down into its component parts. The most striking image of bodily disintegration there is the image of the broken tongue. Catullus, however, describes his physical symptoms, including his vocal rupture, in a way that suggests, at most, only partial disintegration. In the first place, he describes his tongue not as broken but as merely sluggish or numb (*torpet*). While Sappho says in line 11 that "at once a thin flame runs under my skin," Catullus describes the fire as flowing down under his limbs. The change from "runs under" (*upadedrómêken*) to "flows down" (*demanat*) and the omission of the adverbial phrase "at once" diminish the sense of urgency in the dislocation of self brought on by the sight of the beloved. Moreover, while Sappho declares that "there is no sight in my eyes," and that her "ears hum," Catullus tells us that his "ears ring / with their own sound" and that his "eyes are covered / with a double night." Employment of hyperbole in both these images, intensifying the Sapphic references to lack of sight and humming ears, not only calls attention to his own self-conscious artistry but also draws us away from the immediacy of erotic encounter. The self-reflexiveness in the image of ears ringing "with their own sound" (*sonitu suopte*) and the fact that a distinct obstruction to sight has closed over him in the image of the double night reinforce the way in which Catullus is cut off from the world, more absorbed in his own image-making than in the effect of the beloved's presence on him.

Sappho's images of disintegration, on the other hand, have an immediacy and vitality that constantly remind us of the unsettling effect the beloved's presence has on her. While Catullus begins his description of his physical symptoms by saying that all senses are taken from him and that nothing remains in him, Sappho tells us only that "*something*" has excited or stirred the heart in her breast. Moreover, her emphasis on the general nature of her desire, reflected in her statement about how she feels "whenever" (*ôs ... idô*) she sees her beloved, evokes the repetition and regeneration of desire. While desire has shattered Sappho and brought her to a place near death, it has also engendered the awareness of continuity, of the potential for the renewal of erotic experience through recollection of the beloved. From the outset, Sappho presents herself as being in a heightened state of sensual arousal in the presence of the loved one, whereas Catullus in the same situation describes himself as *devoid* of his faculties: "nothing/remains for me." Further, the specificity in naming his beloved and in describing his gaze in the historic perfect tense, *nam simul te ... aspexi* ("for as soon/as I <u>have</u> seen you"), implies a temporality that distances the speaker from the immediacy of erotic encounter, and suggests that desire in Catullus' poem is for him not completely debilitating, nor does it offer potential for erotic renewal in the face of abandonment or separation.

Sappho's description of her "breakdown" involves a breathless piling up of symptoms that goes on for nearly three stanzas. Despite the fact that she is describing how desire has robbed her of her powers, of her very control over her bodily functions, she exhibits intense erotic control in affirming the degree to which her senses are aroused by the sight of the beloved. Sappho's images of speechlessness, sweat, trembling, fire under the skin, and in general an overwhelming of the senses leading to near death suggest the completion and climax of the sexual act. By contrast, Catullus condenses the description of his symptoms into one stanza, beginning with the image of his sluggish tongue and ending with the image of eyes covered with a double night. Nothing in Catullus' description of his responses to Lesbia's presence evokes the vitality of erotic encounter. Rather, the images in his description have a gloomy self-referentiality that emphasizes the way in which desire turns the speaker in on himself and separates him from the world of *negotium* evoked in the opening stanza.

In the last stanza of his poem,[10] Catullus turns abruptly away from his interior world of poetic images and back toward male public culture.[11] After describing the devastating effect of Lesbia's presence upon him, and in particular how it seems to separate him from the outside world, he then awakens suddenly as if from a bad dream and warns himself about the dangers of *otium* ("leisure, idleness"). *Otium* was considered to be directly opposed to *negotium*; it constituted an antithesis to the public life and meant living a life free from the burdens of official duties and responsibilities. More than that, *otium* is associated with the "frivolous," un-Roman pursuits of love and poetry.[12] The implication in Catullus' apparent rejection of a life devoted to such matters is that *otium* has caused him harm because it has led him to abandon not only his duties to the community but also his rationality. Catullus' words to himself in line 14, "you revel in leisure and you desire excessively," recall Cicero's description (and implicit condemnation) of a man conquered by emotion.[13] Succumbing to private passions was considered not only "unmanly" but morally weak as well. As Catharine Edwards points out, "those who could not govern themselves, whose desires were uncontrollable, were thought to be unfit to rule the state" (1993: 26). Capacity for self-regulation was thought to be crucial if one were to maintain *dignitas* or social standing – without which a Roman male could not function adequately in the world of Roman politics and power relations.

Indulgence in *otium*, therefore, is an indulgence in the pleasures of love and poetry, pleasures associated with the world of beauty and imagination evoked in the poems of Catullus' literary model, Sappho. Catullus implies in the last two lines of the poem that *otium* destroys the speaking subject in the same way that it has caused the downfall of kings and "blessed cities." But *otium* does not destroy the lover; rather, it creates the conditions that make love and love poetry possible. By linking erotic desire with the destructive force attributed to *otium*, Catullus reveals the extent to which the experience of erotic desire provokes conflict in him. He is clearly attracted to the Sapphic ideal – a life devoted to love, beauty, and the poetic imagination – yet this ideal opposes traditional Roman values associated with the publicly committed military or political life of a Roman male citizen (Ancona 2002: 173). The last stanza of Catullus' poem does not, in my view, resolve these oppositions between Sapphic and Roman ideals. At most, he may implicitly be expressing the hope at the end that an adherence to traditional Roman ideals will enable him to get over not only his indulgence in love but also his identification with the more private, feminine world epitomized by Sappho. His poem, however, does raise the issue of whether *otium*, and by extension the poet-lover, has any place in the world of empire. Indeed, Catullus' concern about the potential dangers of *otium* may be regarded as an inquiry into the possibilities of living a life of passion and imagination in a culture that values *negotium* more than *otium* and, at the same time, considers virtue synonymous with masculinity. The unresolved disjunction between masculine and feminine, public and private, business (*negotium*) and leisure (*otium*) reminds us, at the end, not of the comparison between the nameless, powerful "other man" and the anguished lover, but of Catullus' own conflict in resolving the contradictions between desire and the normative conceptions of Roman masculinity (i.e., duty, rationality, honor). That conflict gets played out even more dramatically in Catullus 11, the only other poem written in the Sapphic meter.

Catullus 11 and Sappho's "Erotic Flowers"[14]

The issue of how Catullus can maintain a sense of self, a sense of masculine power in the face of desire, comes to the forefront in poem 11. He imagines a fictive potential journey with two male companions, a journey permeated with imagery of both Roman military conquest and aggressive male sexual activity. On the surface, it would seem that he is attempting to reconstitute the fractured, feminized self we saw in poem 51 and recuperate his sense of masculinity by aligning himself with traditional Roman male values. Catullus' imagined journey to the sites of Roman imperial domination, combined with his vilification of Lesbia, would seem to suggest that he wants to regain his power, in part, by rejecting his identification with the feminine vulnerability and "near-death" experience of love and passion expressed in his "translation" of Sappho. But the complexity of poem 11 only intensifies the sense of conflict over his commitment to both Sapphic and Roman ideals that he expresses in poem 51 and elsewhere. Thus his self-presentation and his alignment with competing values and commitments are, in my view, much more difficult to sort out. On the one hand, Catullus appears to identify himself with the masculine world of adventure and action as he imagines himself on a journey with his companions to current theaters of Roman military aggression. On the other hand, he portrays himself as a fragile flower cut down by the violent, masculine plow, a symbol of Lesbia's inhuman cruelty to him and of a dehumanized imperial culture that seems to have no room for love and love poetry. In what follows I will discuss these competing identifications expressed in poem 11, and how Catullus incorporates Sappho's work into his poem, to explore his conflicting attitudes toward Rome's imperial values and his own place within them.

Furius and Aurelius, companions of Catullus,
whether he will penetrate into the farthest Indi,
where the shore is pounded by the far-resounding
    eastern wave.   4

or into the Hyrcani or the soft Arabians,
whether to the Sagae or arrow-bearing Parthians,
whether into the waters which sevenfold
    Nile dyes,   8

whether he will cross over the lofty Alps,
viewing the memorials of mighty Caesar,
the Gallic Rhine, the horrible and
    remotest Britons,   12

all these things, prepared to test together,
whatever the will of the gods shall bring:
announce a few words to my girl,
    words not pleasant.   16

Let her live and flourish with her adulterous lovers,
whom three hundred at once she holds in her embrace,
loving no one of them truly, but again and again
    breaking the strength of them all.   20

And let her not look, as before, at my love,
which by her fault has fallen like a flower
at the furthest meadow, after it has been touched
    by a passing plow.   24

                    (poem 11)

In the first four stanzas of the poem, Catullus seems to be attempting to recover his sense of masculinity by embracing a male world of action and repudiating his former life of private passion. I believe, however, that his attitudes and allegiances cannot be mapped out so clearly; he undercuts his apparent acceptance of conventional Roman male values in a number of ways. The most obvious of these is the comparison of his love for Lesbia to a flower that has been mowed down by an indifferent plow. It is quite likely that Catullus models this flower image on Sappho's use of flowers as symbols of female sexuality and vulnerability. I will discuss the implications of the flower image in Catullus a bit later. For now I would like to focus on the ways his imagined journey and his message to Lesbia reveal a conflict between his masculine and feminine personas, between the Sappho-identified Catullus we saw in poem 51 and the attempt by him in the last stanza of that poem to align himself with traditional Roman values.

The world depicted in Catullus' imagined journey with Furius and Aurelius is consummately Roman. In language of epic grandeur, the speaker imagines them in a wide sweep of geographical locales corresponding to the military expeditions of Caesar, Pompey, and other Roman generals. Yet Catullus' description of the journey is charged with eroticism.[15] The images of the men "penetrating" the places they visit and of the shore being "pounded" linguistically evoke male sexual aggression. Moreover, the images of venturing into the farthest Indies and crossing over the lofty Alps imply a transgressive crossing of boundaries. In the context of "penetration" of conquered landscapes, this crossing of boundaries suggests a link between sexual violation and unbounded imperialistic conquest (see Konstan, this volume, pp. 77–8). On one level, to be sure, Catullus identifies himself with vigorous manly activity that links him with Caesar's own exploits. But the erotic character of Catullus' description of his imagined journey cannot be considered simply "masculine." When he imagines himself and his companions as "penetrators" of the landscape, the speaker simultaneously becomes carried away with his own grandiose visions of travel. In other words, the geographical catalogue in lines 1–12 seems like a flight of imagination permitting him impossibly to cross boundaries of time and space – reminiscent of his transgression of numerical restraints in poem 5. While Catullus puts himself in the role of "penetrator," thereby living up to normative Roman conceptions of masculinity, his hyperbolic description of his journey also reveals a retreat into a world of poetic imagination and thus a movement away from the masculine realm of power and practicality. The erotic atmosphere of his description of his journey, then, undercuts the idea that he is simply rejecting his identification with Sappho's world of desire and imagination and attempting to regain a masculine sense of self. It would be more accurate to say that Catullus' fictive journey serves to heighten the impression of him as profoundly conflicted in regard to the appeal Sapphic and Roman values have for him. That ambivalence can also be observed through the way he refers to Lesbia in his message to her.

Catullus' depiction of Lesbia as a grotesque monster, as quite literally a "ball-buster," invokes male stereotypes about female sexuality. In this poem (and others), Lesbia epitomizes the image of the wayward woman inherited from a tradition of invective against women – particularly with regard to their inability to restrain their sexual impulses. Since the wanton Lesbia, who circulates her body indiscriminately, evokes Sappho, it is certainly possible to think that Catullus might be expressing his own sense of awe at (and perhaps powerless envy of) Sappho's literary prominence, dependent in large measure on her poetry being accessible to the widest possible audience. Might the vulgarity of Lesbia's availability as a lover suggest that Catullus, at least on one level, feels overpowered by Sappho as a poet? We might take into account his description in poem 51 of his speechlessness and near paralysis at the sight of Lesbia. In addition, Sappho, like Lesbia, expresses active erotic desire and was also thought to have presided over a community of young women.[16] It was not uncommon for Romans of Catullus' era to consider a woman who expresses and acts upon such desire as masculine, and therefore as monstrous[17] to some degree. Although Catullus clearly pays homage to Sappho in many ways, he might also have a certain ambivalence toward her, given his identification, however conflicted, with traditional Roman male values. I mentioned earlier that Sappho's reputation in Rome was mixed. The depiction of Lesbia as morally degenerate in Catullus 11 does, to a degree, correspond with the way many Romans thought of Sappho. Therefore, we ought not to think of Catullus' identification with Sappho and the world depicted in her poetry as unproblematic or entirely straightforward. His connection to the Sapphic tradition is mirrored in his ambiguous attitudes toward both Lesbia and Rome. We can see those ambiguities in the last two stanzas of the poem.

In his request to Furius and Aurelius, in lines 15–16, to announce a few "not pleasant" words to Lesbia, Catullus describes his mistress as an epic monster with as much hyperbole as he described his epic journey.[18] Yet his transformation of Lesbia into an entity as awe-inducing as one of Caesar's monuments depersonalizes her, and thus objectifies her in much the same way as she herself dehumanizes her nameless lovers. Thus, one can argue that Catullus' verbal abuse of Lesbia reinforces his identification with conventional masculine, and here misogynistic, attitudes. Yet, through his retreat into poetic images and his devaluation of the excesses of conquest and domination, he shows an alienation from male culture. That alienation is reinforced in the poem's final images of Lesbia as a cold, utilitarian plow and Catullus as a fragile flower crushed by what seems like an inhuman killing machine. This concluding image of Catullus certainly seems to emphasize his identification with feminine sexuality and vulnerability. Indeed, it is quite possible that he draws on Sappho as a source for his image of a cut flower. In general, flower imagery is used by Sappho to suggest female sexuality and intimacy and to convey a feminine world of beauty and imagination set apart from the male world of business and politics.[19] Most pertinent to Catullus 11 is Sappho's fragment 105c, in which she is thought to compare a young girl to a purple flower trodden upon by shepherds:[20]

> Like a hyacinth in the mountains that the shepherd men
> trample with their feet, and its purple flower
> falling to the ground. . . .

On the basis of references to flowers and fruit in Greek archaic poetry, scholars generally interpret the flower, the hyacinth, in Sappho's fragment as representing youth, beauty, innocence, and virginity. Some readers of the fragment have thought it to be part of a wedding-song in which Sappho or a chorus of young women laments a bride's impending "deflowering." But there is no way to reconstitute the context for Sappho's fragment. What is important for our purposes here is how reading the fragment helps us to grasp the implications of Catullus' possible appropriation of the image of the trampled hyacinth. In a way similar to his adoption of the Sapphic, feminine persona in poem 51, Catullus here implicitly puts himself in the feminine position, where he is vulnerable to external forces that threaten his autonomy as both lover and love poet.

In her fragment Sappho makes the masculine identity of the shepherds clear by referring to them as *ándres*, "shepherd men" (my emphasis). Given the association (in Sappho and in other poets) of flower images with the "blossoming" of feminine sexuality, the trampling of the shepherds points to the destructiveness of the male world. Like the plow image in Catullus' poem, which functions as a symbol of the triumph of male industriousness over leisure, the image of the shepherds in Sappho's poem points to the mundane masculine world of work. The shepherds go about their work, heedless of the beauty of their surroundings. Likewise, the plow carries on its utilitarian function in conformity with the goals of the inexorable will of the "fatherland." Both Sappho and Catullus show, implicitly, that the flower and the men who destroy it belong to very separate worlds. Sappho's flower is associated with an ideal realm of beauty, a realm portrayed as unattainable in the larger world (outside the protected sphere of her circle). In a number of fragments she uses flower imagery to connote female eroticism and innocence within a segregated female world of erotic and social affiliation. She depicts this world as separate from normal community life and therefore apart from the world of men. Similarly, Catullus' position, as a flower at the edge of a meadow, places him on the margins of mainstream, male Roman society – seemingly helpless in the face of an impersonal machine that symbolizes the dehumanizing effects of culture.

The plow's indifferent mowing down of nameless living things parallels Caesar's violent subjugation of foreign lands. Although the shepherds in Sappho's fragment cannot be associated with the grandiose and, arguably, self-serving purposes of a Caesar, they are nonetheless part of a consumerist social fabric that is undeniably male. Both the shepherds and the plow exploit nature for "civilized" purposes. To be sure, the plow represents a higher degree of civilization than does herding, but both are forms of a civilizing exploitation of the natural environment. Moreover, the plow image in Catullus is a common symbol for the masculine phallus in Greco-Roman literature, while the flower often connotes female virginity.[21] Catullus thus implies that female submission to the male is inevitable, that a life devoted to passion and imagination will ultimately have to give way to the demands of duty.

This idea is especially relevant to Sappho. The pathos in the image of the hyacinth being trampled, at least in part, derives from the notion that this fragment may have been part of a wedding-song. In that context, the flower may be a metaphor for female virginity. Sappho's depiction of the hyacinth's destruction by heedless shepherds may thus express a sense of sadness and regret at not only the girl's loss of virginity but also the realization that on entering the realm of marriage, she must subordinate herself to her husband. The hyacinth's fall can be seen as a metaphor for a young woman's inevitable descent from an ideal realm of passion and imagination to the mundane realities of married life. Throughout her surviving poetry Sappho portrays herself as part of what one scholar calls "magical space,"[22] a realm in which female homoerotic desire, beauty, and imagination flourish. Whether this "space" was actual or imagined we will probably never know. But it is quite clear that Sappho wants to celebrate *eros*, imagination, and the enjoyment of beauty as crucial to a fulfilling life. In poem 11 Catullus implicitly acknowledges Sappho's understanding of the difficulties of pursuing a life of passion and imagination within the practical constraints of the world. While marriage, for her, is not necessarily portrayed as evil, it is nonetheless a political and social institution that severely limits female autonomy. For Catullus the masculine plow is associated with the ruthless conquest embodied in both Caesar and Lesbia. In identifying himself with Sappho's flowers Catullus expresses not only his sense of himself as a victim of a corrupt social system but also his quest to find his own "magical space," however marginal, where love and poetic imagination can thrive.

Despite the fact that Sappho's trampled hyacinth suggests loss and regret, one may argue that her flower image also has a "self-justifying intensity," in the sense that the flower image serves to celebrate beauty for its own sake.[23] Likewise, the pure, aesthetic beauty of Catullus' flower image seems to outstrip the images of destruction associated with Caesar and Lesbia. While Catullus cannot stop the mechanisms of conquest and destruction, he can, through his image-making, turn our attention to the pristine beauty of a singular, nameless, and isolated flower. In its suggestions of failure, his fallen flower may remind us of the questions implicitly raised in the last stanza of poem 51 about the difficulty for Roman man in occupying himself with the pleasures of beauty and imagination – occupations considered both "trivial" and feminine and therefore unworthy of an "upstanding" Roman male citizen. Yet Catullus demonstrates the worth of his erotic and aesthetic ideal, in part, by representing both Caesar's and Lesbia's conquests as morally degraded, in opposition to his poetic rendering of himself as a delicate, fragile flower victimized by the brutality of the world. We naturally sympathize with that flower, whose innocence and beauty have immediate, sensual appeal as well as, and perhaps more importantly, moral superiority.

Yet it is difficult to reconcile Catullus' identification in the poem with the feminine Sappho and his aggressive, masculine stance toward Lesbia. Perhaps we have to be content with considering him as, ultimately, conflicted with regard to the Sapphic tradition. In the end, I think, he tries to have it both ways, and in many respects he succeeds. One may argue that Catullus' attempts to distance himself from Lesbia may be his strategy for regaining a sense of a masculine self in the face of desire. It may also be plausibly argued that his verbal abuse of Lesbia allows him to assert his poetic independence from Sappho. Indeed, his difficulty in speaking when he looks at "Lesbia" in poem 51 may be read as an expression of his own sense of inadequacy with regard to Sappho's powerful legacy of lyric passion. At the same time, however, the "aesthetically compelling" image of the flower at the end of poem 11 connects Catullus in a powerful way with a Sapphic sensibility – in particular, with the belief in passion and poetic imagination as intrinsically worthy, though often marginalized, cultural values.

NOTES

1   For recent discussions of Sappho's reception and transmission in both the literary and scholarly traditions, see DeJean (1989); Williamson (1995: 5–33); Most (1996); Parker (1993); Prins (1996).

2   For discussions of the debate concerning Sappho's sexual proclivities, see Hallett (1979); DeJean (1989); Lardinois (1989); Williamson (1995: esp. 5–33, 90–132); Snyder (1997).

3   For a discussion of the ways in which male poets have appropriated the Sapphic voice, see especially Jacobson (1974: 277–99); Lipking (1988: 57–126); Stehle [Stigers] (1977); E. Harvey (1989); E. Greene (1999a).

4   See Ancona (2002) for an analysis of Sappho's influence on Horace.

5   In 2004 two German scholars, Michael Gronewald and Robert Daniel, published two new fragments of Sappho recovered from Egyptian mummy cartonnage (2004a, 2004b). Dated to early in the third century BC, the papyri are believed to be the earliest known text of Sappho. Naturally, this new find has generated a great deal of interest among Sappho scholars and has already provoked much discussion about how these fragments fit into the rest of Sappho's surviving work.

6   See Holzberg (2002a: 33–9) for an account of Sappho's personal reputation in antiquity and the salacious connotations of the proper name "Lesbia."

7   See C. Edwards (1993) for an illuminating discussion of Roman moralizing discourses.

8   On Sappho 94, see especially McEvilley (1971); Burnett (1983); E. Greene (1994).

9   There have been a number of important studies comparing Sappho 31 and Catullus 51. See especially: Wormell (1966); G. Wills (1967); Lipking (1988); O'Higgins (1990); Miller (1994); Janan (1994); E. Greene (1999a).

10 On this much-debated last stanza, see especially: Fredricksmeyer (1965: 153–63); R. I. Frank (1968: 233–9); Segal (1970: 25–31); Copley (1974: 25–37); Itzkowitz (1983: 129–34); Finamore (1984: 11–19); Wiseman (1985: 152–3); Vine (1992: 251–8). For *otium* in Latin literature, see André (1966) and Laidlaw (1968: 42–52).

11 This fourth stanza, which has no equivalent in Sappho's original, has been the subject of much controversy. The sudden shift from the speaker's absorption in his disintegration to his apparent rejection of the erotic and imaginative life has led many scholars either to consider the fourth stanza spurious or to construct elaborate explanations of poetic unity. My reading of Catullus' departure from Sappho's original in this stanza will do neither. What seems to concern scholars most is the apparent lack of coherence between the debilitated voice of Catullus in stanza three and his voice in the final stanza, a voice that seems to be identified with the very un-Sapphic concerns of politics and empire. These disjunctive voices, however, are entirely consistent with the multi-voiced self presented in a number of Catullus' poems, particularly those about Lesbia. In the Lesbia poems, Catullus sometimes either addresses himself as "Catullus" in the second person or refers to himself in the third person. The effect of this multi-voiced speaker is often to dramatize the conflict not only between "loving" and "hating" Lesbia, but also between what he knows to be "right" – according to Roman conceptions of duty and rationality – and what he feels.

12 See Platter (1995: 218–20). Platter rightly observes that "*Otium* creates a space both oppositional and imaginative within which the poet can rhetorically resist the ideological demands of Roman society for business and duty in their conventional sense" (p. 218).

13 R. I. Frank (1968: 235) points out that Catullus' words (*exsultas nimiumque gestis*) closely parallel Cicero's description of a man overcome by emotions: "reveling and desiring thoughtlessly" (*exsultans et temere gestiens, Tusc.* 5.6.16). Further, Frank argues that both Cicero and Lucretius condemn love (*amor*) as a form of mental illness.

14   I take the title of this section, in part, from Stehle [Stigers] (1977). In that essay, Stehle discusses, among other things, the association of flower imagery with feminine vulnerability, virginity, and unattainability in Sappho's poetry.
15   See Putnam (1982: 15); Kinsey (1965: 540–1); Sweet (1987: 520); and Yardley (1981: 143) for an interpretation of the images in the catalogue as erotic.
16   For different views of Sappho's "circle" of female companions and the importance of her female affiliations in general, see especially: Hallett (1979); Parker (1993); Skinner (1993c); Calame (1994); Lardinois (1994); Stehle [Stigers] (1997).
17   She would be thought of as "monstrous" because such flagrantly sexual behavior would pervert what Romans considered to be desired feminine virtues: modesty, compliance, and a willingness to be subordinate to men.
18   Scott (1983: 41) points to the mythological figure of the monster Scylla as Catullus' "ultimate source" for his description of Lesbia: "Thus it seems to me, Catullus drew on the fluid tradition concerning Scylla to shape the imagery and invective of his message to Lesbia. His picture deftly combines throughout the primordial, epic beast and the later, sexually wanton woman."
19   See in particular Stehle [Stigers] (1977); Snyder (1997).
20   We can only guess what the context for this poem might have been. Scholars have speculated, on the basis of Sappho's other fragments, that the flower represents a young girl whose beauty and innocence have been destroyed through the loss of her virginity.
21   See Miller (1994: 104–6) for a discussion of Catullus' flower image in poem 11.
22   See Snyder (1997: 18–19, 58–9) for discussions of how Sappho "constructs a private world of intimate physical intimacy," especially in fragment 2.
23   Both duBois (1995) and Snyder (1997), two eminent Sappho scholars, suggest that the image of the hyacinth in her fragment does not ultimately point to its utter destruction. DuBois asserts: "The destruction of the mountain flower at the feet of the herdsmen is accomplished even as the integrity of the hyacinth is reinvoked" (p. 45). Similarly, Snyder argues that "it is just possible that the image of the hyacinth . . . performed in some way the role of celebrating a woman's beauty" (p. 105).

GUIDE TO FURTHER READING

Anyone wishing to pursue this topic further might consult Lipking (1988: 57–67). Much of the scholarship on Catullus' identification with Sappho focuses on comparisons between Sappho 31 and Catullus 51. Some useful studies on the two poems in combination include E. Greene (1999a), Janan (1994: 71–6), Miller (1994: 101–19), O'Higgins (1990), Stehle [Stigers] (1977), G. Wills (1967), and Wormell (1966).

WORKS CITED

Ancona, R. 2002. "The Untouched Self: Sapphic and Catullan Muses in Horace, *Odes* I.22." In E. Spentzou and D. Fowler, eds., *Cultivating the Muse*. Oxford. 161–86.
André, J. M. 1966. *L'otium dans la vie morale et intellectuelle romaine*. Paris.
Burnett, A. 1983. "Desire and Memory (Sappho Frag. 94)." *Classical Philology* 74: 16–27.
Calame, C. 1994. *Choruses of Young Women in Ancient Greece*. Trans. J. Orion and D. Collins. Lanham, MD.
Carson, A. 1986. *Eros the Bittersweet*. Princeton, NJ.

Copley, F. O. 1974. "The Structure of Catullus C. 51 and the Problem of the *otium* Strophe." *Grazer Beiträge* 2: 25–37.

DeJean, J. 1989. *Fictions of Sappho, 1546–1937*. Chicago.

DuBois, P. 1995. *Sappho is Burning*. Chicago.

Edwards, C. 1993. *The Politics of Immorality in Ancient Rome*. Cambridge.

Finamore, J. 1984. "Catullus 50 and 51: Friendship, Love and *otium*." *Classical World* 78: 11–19.

Forsyth, P. Y. 1991. "Thematic Unity of Catullus 11." *Classical World* 84: 457–64.

Frank, R. I. 1968. "Catullus 51: *otium* vs. *virtus*." *Transactions of the American Philological Association* 96: 233–9.

Fredricksmeyer, E. 1965. "On the Unity of Catullus 51." *Transactions of the American Philological Association* 96: 153–63.

Greene, E. 1994. "Apostrophe and Women's Erotics in the Poetry of Sappho." *Transactions of the American Philological Association* 124: 41–56.

Greene, E., ed. 1996. *Re-Reading Sappho: Reception and Transmission*. Berkeley, Los Angeles, and London.

Greene, E. 1999a. "Re-Figuring the Feminine Voice: Catullus Translating Sappho." *Arethusa* 32: 1–18.

Gronewald, M., and R. W. Daniel. 2004a. "Ein neuer Sappho-Papyrus." *Zeitschrift für Papyrologie und Epigraphik* 147: 1–8.

Gronewald, M., and R. W. Daniel. 2004b. "Nachtrag zum neuen Sappho-Papyrus." *Zeitschrift für Papyrologie und Epigraphik* 149: 1–4.

Hallett, J. P. 1979. "Sappho and Her Social Context: Sense and Sensuality." *Signs* 4: 447–64.

Harvey, E. 1989. "Ventriloquizing Sappho: Ovid, Donne, and the Erotics of the Feminine Voice." *Criticism* 31.2: 115–38.

Holzberg, N. 2002a. *Catull: Der Dichter und sein erotisches Werk*. Munich.

Itzkowitz, J. B. 1983. "On the Last Stanza of Catullus 51." *Latomus* 42: 129–34.

Jacobson, H. 1974. *Ovid's Heroides*. Princeton, NJ.

Janan, M. 1994. *"When the Lamp is Shattered": Desire and Narrative in Catullus*. Carbondale and Edwardsville, IL.

Kinsey, T. E. 1965. "Catullus 11." *Latomus* 24: 537–44.

Konstan, D. 2000/2. "Self, Sex, and Empire in Catullus: The Construction of a Decentered Identity." In V. Bécares Botas, F. Pordomingo, R. Cortés Tovar, and C. Fernández Corte, eds., *La intertextualidad griega y Latina*. Madrid. 213–31. (Also available online at http://zeno.stoa.org/cgi-bin/ptext?doc=Stoa:text:2002.01.0005.)

Laidlaw, W. A. 1968. "*Otium*." *Greece & Rome* 15: 42–52.

Lardinois, A. 1989. "Lesbian Sappho and Sappho of Lesbos." In J. Bremmer, ed., *From Sappho to de Sade: Moments in the History of Sexuality*. London. 15–35.

Lardinois, A. 1994. "Subject and Circumstance in Sappho's Poetry." *Transactions of the American Philological Association* 124: 57–84.

Lipking, L. 1988. *Abandoned Women and Poetic Tradition*. Chicago.

McEvilley, T. 1971. "Sappho, Fragment 94." *Phoenix* 25: 1–11.

Miller, P. A. 1994. *Lyric Texts and Lyric Consciousness: The Birth of a Genre from Archaic Greece to Augustan Rome*. London and New York.

Most, G. 1996. "Reflecting Sappho." In E. Greene (1996: 11–35).

O'Higgins, D. 1990. "Sappho's Splintered Tongue: Silence in Sappho 31 and Catullus 51." *American Journal of Philology* 111: 156–67.

Parker, H. N. 1993. "Sappho Schoolmistress." *Transactions of the American Philological Association* 123: 309–51.

Platter, C. 1995. "*Officium* in Catullus and Propertius: A Foucauldian Reading." *Classical Philology* 90: 211–24.

Prins, Y. 1996. "Sappho's Afterlife in Translation." In E. Greene (1996: 36–67).

Putnam, M. C. J. 1982. "Catullus 11: The Ironies of Integrity." In *Essays on Latin Lyric, Elegy, and Epic*. Princeton, NJ. 13–29.

Scott, R. T. 1983. "On Catullus 11." *Classical Philology* 78: 39–42.

Segal, C. 1970. "Catullan *otiosi* – The Lover and the Poet." *Greece & Rome* 17: 25–31.

Skinner, M. B. 1993c. "Woman and Language in Archaic Greece, or, Why is Sappho a Woman?" In N. S. Rabinowitz and A. Richlin, eds., *Feminist Theory and the Classics*. New York. 125–44.

Snyder, J. M. 1997. *Lesbian Desire in the Lyrics of Sappho*. New York.

Stehle [Stigers], E. 1977. "Retreat from the Male: Catullus 62 and Sappho's Erotic Flowers." *Ramus* 6: 83–102.

Stehle [Stigers], E. 1979. "Romantic Sensuality, Poetic Sense: A Response to Hallett on Sappho." *Signs* 4: 464–71.

Stehle [Stigers], E. 1981. "Sappho's Private World." In H. Foley, ed., *Reflections of Women in Antiquity*. New York. 45–61.

Stehle [Stigers], E. 1997. *Performance and Gender in Ancient Greece*. Princeton, NJ.

Sweet, D. 1987. "Catullus 11: A Study in Perspective." *Latomus* 46: 510–26.

Vine, B. 1992. "On the 'Missing' Fourth Stanza of Catullus 51." *Harvard Studies in Classical Philology* 96: 251–8.

Williamson, M. 1995. *Sappho's Immortal Daughters*. Cambridge, MA.

Wills, G. 1967. "Sappho 31 and Catullus 51." *Greek, Roman, and Byzantine Studies* 8: 167–97.

Wiseman, T. P. 1985. *Catullus and His World: A Reappraisal*. Cambridge.

Wormell, D. E. 1966. "Catullus as Translator (C. 51)." In L. Wallach, ed., *The Classical Tradition: Literary and Historical Studies in Honor of Harry Caplan*. Ithaca, NY. 187–201.

Yardley, J. C. 1981. "Catullus 11: The End of a Friendship." *Symbolae Osloenses* 56: 63–9.

CHAPTER NINE

Catullus and Callimachus

Peter E. Knox

We do not know for certain the contents of the book that Catullus introduces with a short, dedicatory poem, describing it as "pretty" and "new":

> cui dono lepidum nouum libellum
> arida modo pumice expolitum?
> Corneli, tibi.

> To whom do I give my pretty new book, freshly polished with dry pumice? To you, Cornelius.

On the face of it, this dedication does not pose many stumbling blocks to interpretation, but with reflection the questions grow. Who is the Cornelius to whom Catullus presents his little book, and why is he a particularly appropriate recipient? What is there about this book that is new and pretty, and does Catullus merely refer to the physical appearance of a brand new papyrus roll? The answers to these other questions, which would surely have occurred to an ancient reader as well, are not immediately deducible from the context. Some answers, such as the identity of the addressee, require a bit of familiarity with the literary culture of the mid-first century BC, for instance the fact that a certain Cornelius Nepos, who hailed from Catullus' native Cisalpine Gaul, composed a historical work known as the *Chronica*. Other answers can only emerge more gradually, from the perspective of a profound engagement with Catullus' writings, which will inevitably draw in other figures from among his literary antecedents and contemporaries.

The book that Catullus offers to Nepos is a *libellus*, not a full-fledged book, that is, but the diminutive form. The circumstances of the transmission of Catullus' text do not allow us to know what poems were included in it, but the reader will inevitably notice the emergence of patterns of arrangement, and most modern critics are persuaded that the short poems (1–60), known as the "polymetrics," formed a single collection, whether as a separate book or one part of a larger collection (Wiseman 1969: 1–31). This grouping of poems on diverse themes, like the collection of epigrams (69–116), recalls the practice of Greek poets of the Hellenistic period, and is particularly associated with the name of Callimachus of Cyrene, active in Alexandria in the third century BC. The diminutive form of *libellus* will also come to be familiar to readers, as this linguistic usage is characteristic of Catullus' verbal style (Ross 1969: 22–6), but the associations that it evokes, both in its colloquial tone and in its depreciative effect in calling this a "little book," emerge upon closer engagement with Catullus' contemporaries. And again, the name of Callimachus comes into play. That the book is new will not surprise in this setting, but again as the reader moves further into the Catullan corpus the idea of "novelty" in a poetic context will take on other associations. And finally, while *lepidus* and related terms will be found to have prominence in what one might call Catullan ethics, they will also be found to carry an aesthetic charge. In each instance the reader will be challenged to look beyond the text of Catullus to intertexts among contemporary Roman and Greek poets, but more particularly to the works of the Greek poets of the Hellenistic period who transformed the world of letters two centuries earlier.

Callimachus

Callimachus was not only the most influential poet in the Greek world of the third century BC, he was one of the age's most compelling intellects. His writings can be dated roughly from 285 to 245 BC, although these dates are only approximate and his literary career may well have begun earlier than this. What little we know, or think we know, of his life is derived primarily from inferences drawn from his poetry and the biography contained in the Byzantine encyclopedia known as the *Suda* (*Test.* 1 Pf.). Although his family originated in Cyrene, he spent much of his life in Egypt at Alexandria, where he worked in the great Museum and its Library. He never headed the Library, but he was intimately connected with it and was known at the court of the Ptolemies, where he may have served in his youth as a royal page (Cameron 1995: 1–11). Much of his most influential poetry celebrates members of the dynasty.

According to the *Suda* Callimachus authored more than 800 books (i.e., papyrus rolls) in poetry and prose, of which the following is a partial list (*Test.* 1 Pf.):

> *The Coming of Io; Semele; Founding of Argos; Arcadia; Glaukos; Hopes;* satyric dramas; tragedies; comedies; lyric poems; *Ibis...; Museum; Pinakes of the Illustrious in Every Branch of Literature and of What they Wrote,* in 120 books; *Pinax and Register of the Dramatic Poets Arranged Chronologically from the Beginning; Pinax of the Glosses and Compositions of Democrates; Names of Months According to Tribe and Cities; Foundations of Islands and Cities and their Changes of Name; On the Rivers of Europe; On Marvels and Curiosities in the Peloponnesos and Italy; On Changes of Names of Fish; On Winds; On Birds; On the Rivers of the Inhabited World; Collection of Wonders of the Entire World According to their Locations.*

What emerges from the bare essentials of his biography is a portrait of a polymathic scholar with an extraordinary range of interests. These scholarly interests inform his poetry as much as – some would say more than – the divine inspiration of the Muse, and it is one of the features of his poetry that modern readers find most difficult to appreciate. As W. Clausen once observed (1982: 182), "it is impossible to read much of Callimachus...without being impressed, or depressed, by his multifarious learning."

Callimachus' most famous work of poetry was the *Aetia*, which more than any of his other works, more so indeed than any other single work of Greek literature after Homer, impressed itself upon the minds of the Roman poets of the first century BC. The work no longer survives intact and until the twentieth century it had to be reconstructed from scattered quotations in other ancient authors. Papyrus finds in the last century have significantly increased our understanding of the poem's composition, narrative content, and style. There is general agreement about the basic outlines of the *Aetia*, which was composed in two parts. At the beginning of the poem (fr. 2 Pf.), Callimachus imagined himself transported in a dream from Alexandria to Mount Helicon in Greece, the place where Hesiod famously encountered the Muses while herding his sheep (*Theog.* 22–34). There Callimachus engages in a lively question-and-answer session with the Muses as he asks about the origins of rituals and numerous other topics. The answers that he receives from them form the etiology that gives the work its title. This structure was not carried over to Books 3 and 4, which were probably composed later and added to the original two-book version. In these last two books etiological stories are straightforwardly juxtaposed and we do not know how Callimachus endowed this part of his point with narrative unity, or if he did so at all.

Beyond this general outline, there is considerable controversy over many of the details of the *Aetia*, particularly concerning the Prologue to the work (fr. 1 Pf.), in which Callimachus addresses his critics, whom he refers to as "Telchines," a mythical race of troglodytes dwelling on the island of Rhodes. This important programmatic statement is open to conflicting interpretations both because of the fragmentary state of the text and because of the cryptic terms in which Callimachus states the fundamental premises of his approach to poetry (fr. 1.1–6 Pf.):

> [Often] the Telchines mutter at my song, ignorant as they are and no friends of the Muse, because I did not accomplish one continuous poem on [the deeds] of kings or heroes [of old] in many thousands of lines, but instead like a child [steer] my poetry into a small compass, though the decades of my years are not few.

This opposition between two types of poetry, the long and turgid versus the short and refined, is a consistent theme throughout the Prologue. The device of contrasting one with the other is reproduced with concrete examples in an important passage, where Callimachus refers to two predecessors in the genre of elegy, one the much earlier Mimnermus, the other his near-contemporary Philetas. Unfortunately, the papyrus that preserves this text is damaged at key points; addressing his critics, the Telchines, Callimachus asserts (fr. 1.9–12): "[...] of a few lines; but bountiful Demeter by far outweighs the big [lady?]. And [of his] two [works], not the big woman, but the small-scale [verses] teach us that Mimnermus is sweet." The interpretation of these lines is much disputed and the brackets indicate how speculative is the reconstruction of text, but an ancient commentary on these lines that is also preserved on papyrus probably points in the right direction in explaining that a long poem by Philetas is being compared unfavorably with a shorter work known as the "Demeter." Likewise, a longer poem by Mimnermus, identified as "the big woman," is being unfavorably contrasted with his shorter poems (Cameron 1995: 307–9).

Sixty-three epigrams attributed to Callimachus are preserved in the *Palatine Anthology*, and surviving fragments (frr. 393–402 Pf.) suggest that he wrote many more. The selection preserved in the *Anthology* covers a wide range of topics, including erotic, sympotic, funerary, and dedicatory. In many epigrams literary themes are intertwined with the personal, most notably in a poem that makes a connection between the poet's erotic interest in a handsome youth and his tastes in literature (*Epigr.* 28 Pf.):

> I loathe the Cyclic poem, nor do I like
>   the road that carries many to and fro;
> I also hate a gadabout lover, nor do I drink
>   from the fountain: I detest all common things.
> Lysanias, you are so, so handsome – but before I get
>   the words out clearly, Echo says "he's another's."

The first four lines of the poem have often been read as a separate statement of Callimachus' poetic creed, but it is important to consider his programmatic pro-nouncements in their entire context: that is how Catullus and the Roman poets read them, however they may have adapted their readings to their own purposes. This is an erotic poem, in which Callimachus first lists four things he does not like, while in the last couplet he describes what he does like, the boy Lysanias. The final twist comes in the last line when it turns out that he cannot have what he likes after all (Cameron 1995: 387–402). The Cyclic poems that he does not like and the imagery of the crowded road echo themes raised in the *Aetia* Prologue, but they are adapted here to the amatory purposes of the epigram. For his association of his personal affairs and Lesbia with literary values, Catullus found an influential precedent in Callimachus.

Callimachus' antipathy to long poetry on heroic themes has sometimes been considered at odds with his other major narrative work, a hexameter poem of more than a thousand lines known as the *Hecale*. It is usually classed by scholars as an "epyllion," a modern critical term used to describe a wide range of poems from the Hellenistic period to Roman times containing narrative of less than epic proportions. Although the term is not ancient (W. Allen 1940), it serves a practical utility in discussing the common characteristics of a number of Hellenistic works, some largely lost, such as Callimachus' *Hecale* or the *Hermes* of Eratosthenes, others such as Theocritus' *Idylls* 13 ("Hylas") or 24 ("Heracliscus") surviving but differing con-siderably in scale (Hollis 1990: 23–6). Although the *Hecale* survived the wreck of ancient literature only in papyrus scraps and later quotations, from the reputation it enjoyed in antiquity it is clear that, for most later Greek and Roman writers, this poem provided the prototype for the short narrative poem. It recounts the story of Theseus' defeat of the great bull that was ravaging the countryside around Marathon. But the most prominent feature of Callimachus' narrative was not the actual heroic feat: most of the poem told of his visit with an old peasant woman from whom the poem takes its title. Theseus rests overnight in her hut when he seeks shelter from a sudden rainstorm. Much of the poem seems to have been taken up with their conversation and her hospitality to the hero, and although most of this part of the *Hecale* has been lost, some appreciation of its characteristics may be gleaned from Ovid's imitation in his description of the visit by Jupiter and Mercury to the peasant home of Baucis and Philemon (*Met.* 8.624–724). A key trait that this poem shares with Catullus, as we shall see, is a narrative focus that deviates from the ostensible theme of the poem.

Papyrus discoveries have also restored some portions of a collection of 13 poems in iambic meters apparently designed as a coherent collection (Kerkhecker 1999: 271–95). The first of the *Iambi* represents the figure of Hipponax, the sixth-century poet who, together with Archilochus, was most closely identified with the origins of the genre. Hipponax returns from the dead to lecture the philologists of the Museum in Alexandria, warning them against envy. The collection is a miscellany, with invective playing a reduced role and including poems on a variety of topics, among them fable, epinician, and ecphrasis. In the framing poem (13), Callimachus again invokes Hipponax in defending himself against criticisms for writing in a variety of forms (*polyeideia*). In a central passage, he denies that there is a "one poet, one genre rule" (fr. 203.30–4 Pf.): "who said . . . you compose pentameters, you the heroic, it is your lot from the gods to compose tragedy? In my opinion, no one. . . ." Callimachus has softened the invective tone of iambic poetry to include a wider range of admonitory discourse, and adapted it to literary programmatic purposes in defense of a more sophisticated approach to literary genre (Acosta-Hughes 2002: 82–9).

Six hymns survive in a medieval manuscript tradition, reviving the traditional form of the Homeric hymns. It is a matter of dispute whether these hymns actually formed part of a ritual performance (Cameron 1995: 63–7) or, as most critics believe, were entirely literary creations designed to create the illusion of a performance. The *Hymn to Apollo* (2) concludes with another important programmatic statement that strikes many of the same notes already heard in the *Aetia*, the Epigrams, and the *Iambi* (105–13):

> Envy spoke secretly in Apollo's ear: "I do not admire the poet who does not sing like the sea." Apollo gave Envy a kick and said: "Great is the stream of the Assyrian river, but it carries much filth and refuse in its water. The bees do not bring water from everywhere to Demeter, but only the pure and undefiled stream that rises up from a holy spring, the supremely best." Hail, lord; but let Blame go where Envy dwells.

Many critics have seen in this passage a further statement of Callimachus' antipathy to narrative epic, including even Homeric epic (F. Williams 1978: 85–9). The passage closely parallels the *Aetia* Prologue in its denunciation of the big and crude, but it also serves a function within the hymn in cutting short what the poet had promised would be a performance of the god's virtues that would last for days. Callimachus' pronouncements on literary values were enormously influential, both among his contemporaries and eventually at Rome; but they are never cut-and-dried statements to be taken as prescriptive. Catullus and Callimachus' other readers at Rome for the most part knew how to read his works in context and adapted his aesthetics to their own.

Callimachus in Rome

From its beginnings in the third century BC, Roman literature was, in the strictest sense of the term, derivative: the earliest poets writing in Latin took their bearings from the dramatic and narrative poetic traditions of Greece. Indeed, the most important of these poets, Livius Andronicus and Ennius, were themselves Greek, and the Latin literary culture that they initiated was, in many respects, an extension of the Greek (Mayer 1995). Roman writers in every genre, with the exception only of satire, saw themselves as carrying on a live tradition extending back to the authors of the Greek canon. The earliest works of Latin poetry were translations and adaptations of Greek masterpieces, like Livius Andronicus' translation of the *Odyssey* and Plautus' adaptations of Greek New Comedy. Indeed, Ennius portrayed himself, and in turn was viewed by later generations, as another Homer (*Ann.* 3–11 Sk. Skutsch 1985: 147–67). And Terence was seen by later critics as a "knock-off" (*dimidiate*, Caes. fr. 1 Blänsdorf) of Menander. But the role of Callimachus in Latin poetry was somewhat different from these classic models, and it was Catullus who was largely responsible for his disproportionate influence on succeeding generations of Roman poets.

To be sure, Callimachus was not unknown in Rome before the 50s BC. Ennius certainly knew enough of his *Aetia* to allude to the famous dream at the beginning of his *Annals* (Skutsch 1985: 147–50), although the extent to which it influenced his approach to poetry is difficult to gauge because of its fragmentary state. We know even less about the composition of Ennius' *Saturae* and so it is impossible to evaluate how much the origins of the quintessentially Roman genre of satire might owe to Callimachus' reconfiguration of iambic poetry. The same observations apply to the *Satires* of Lucilius later in the second century BC (Puelma-Piwonka 1949). An adaptation of one of Callimachus' epigrams (41 Pf.; Courtney 1993: 75–6) by Lutatius Catulus (*cos.* 102 BC) is an indication of the reading interests of the cultured Roman elite of this period, rather than of a literary movement taking its inspiration from Callimachus. Catulus was a learned man, a respected orator, and the friend of Greek poets such as Archias and Antipater of Sidon. When the next generation adapted Callimachean poetics, there was now a readership capable of recognizing it. The intense engagement with Callimachus that begins in the generation of Catullus has often been attributed to an external stimulus associated with the contemporary Greek poet Parthenius of Nicaea. Parthenius was brought to Rome in the late 70s or early 60s BC, probably by the poet Cinna or a close relation (Lightfoot 1999: 9–16). Almost every aspect of Parthenius' relations with Cinna, Catullus, Gallus, and the "neoterics" is disputed, but the cumulative weight of the abundant circumstantial evidence strongly suggests that, while he may not have played the dramatic role sometimes ascribed to him (Clausen 1964), Parthenius was clearly heavily implicated in the increasingly sophisticated engagement of Catullus and his contemporaries with the poetry of the Hellenistic world (Lightfoot 1999: 50–76). Callimachus was "the chief classic of an unclassical art," as one of the greatest critics of Hellenistic poetry referred to him (Wilamowitz 1924: I.170), and it was inevitable that as the Romans came to know the works of Parthenius, now present in Rome, and the corpus of Hellenistic epigrams recently assembled by Meleager of Gadara (Gow and Page 1965), they would also want to know more about the inspirational source of this poetry in his works.

Callimachus in the Polymetrics and Epigrams:
Callimachean Poetics

The dedication poem at the head of Catullus' surviving works evokes a literary and social background, establishing the tone in which the following poems might be read:

> cui dono lepidum nouum libellum
> arida modo pumice expolitum?
> Corneli, tibi: namque tu solebas
> meas esse aliquid putare nugas
> iam tum, cum ausus es unus Italorum
> omne aeuum tribus explicare cartis
> doctis, Iuppiter, et laboriosis.
> quare habe tibi quidquid hoc libelli
> qualecumque; quod, <o> patrona uirgo,
> plus uno maneat perenne saeclo.

> To whom do I give my pretty new book, freshly polished with dry pumice? To you, Cornelius, for you already thought my that my trifles were of some value when you, the only one among the Italians, dared to unfold the whole of history in three rolls, learned ones, by Jupiter, and laborious. So have for yours, this trifle of a book, such as it is; and may it, o patron Muse, last more than one age.

The poem is addressed to the polymath Cornelius Nepos, some fifteen to twenty years Catullus' senior, with a question and response in the same manner as the opening poem of the nearly contemporary collection of Greek epigrams prepared by Meleager of Gadara (*Anth. Pal.* 4.1.1–4; Gow and Page 1965: II.593–7). The physical description of the book, which some commentators have taken to refer only literally to its outward appearance (Kroll 1968; Fordyce 1961), is now generally recognized as programmatically reflecting the qualities of the poetry (see Batstone, this volume, p. 236). It is likely that Catullus' first readers might have recognized a good deal more of the associations established in this brief proem to the collection, but even against the loss of so much contemporary Latin poetry, as well as Hellenistic antecedents, the literary affiliations declared by Catullus resonate for modern readers. In particular, the role of Callimachus as a formative influence on Catullan aesthetics is clear (Elder 1966). In *lepidus* the reader may well detect a phonetic, as well as a semantic, echo of the adjective *leptós / leptaléos* "slender" (Wiseman 1979: 169–70), used to distinctive effect by Callimachus in the *Aetia* Prologue in describing Apollo's injunction to him "to keep your Muse thin." The connotations of *lepidum* "charming, pretty" and *nouum* "new, fresh" suggest the qualities espoused in Callimachus' poetics, not to follow the beaten track. This, too, is reflected in the book, not a *liber*, but the diminutive *libellus*, a small book that exemplifies the self-depreciation of the poet who was admonished to nurture a slender Muse. For a Roman reader, who would be literate in Greek as well, this background is further underscored in the precocious feminine form *arida* in the following line, modifying *pumice*, which is elsewhere always masculine. Such variations of gender are found elsewhere in Latin poetry, often to draw attention to Greek models

(Wiseman 1979: 167–8); in this case, Catullus performs the gender switch to recognize that the Greek for pumice is *kíséris* (f.). Thus the polish applied to his roll is, in a sense, Greek, and the verbal markers in the descriptive terms point to Callimachean aesthetics.

In poem 95, Catullus treats poetic quality by contrasting the short epic *Zmyrna* of his friend Helvius Cinna with two long poems by other poets; one identified as Hortensius, perhaps identical with the addressee of c. 65, the other as Volusius, whose *Annales* were the target of a hendecasyllabic squib in c. 36:

> Smyrna mei Cinnae nonam post denique messem
>   quam coepta est nonamque edita post hiemem,
> milia cum interea quingenta Hortensius uno
>
>   . . . .
> Smyrna cauas Satrachi penitus mittetur ad undas,
>   Smyrnam cana diu saecula peruoluent.
> at Volusi annales Paduam morientur ad ipsam
>   et laxas scombris saepe dabunt tunicas.

My Cinna's *Zmyrna* is finally out, nine summers and nine winters after it was begun, while in the meantime Hortensius . . . five hundred thousand . . . in one . . . *Zmyrna* will be sent all the way to the hollow waves of Satrachus, the grey centuries will long peruse *Zmyrna*. But Volusius' *Annals* will perish at Padua itself, and often will provide loose wraps for mackerel.

Catullus formulates his aesthetics in concrete terms by setting good poetry against bad (Syndikus 1987: 83–4), by comparing the short narrative poem by Cinna with the presumably much longer *Annales* of Volusius, who came from Hatria in the region of Padua (Solodow 1987). In this he clearly evokes the difficult passage in the *Aetia* Prologue (fr. 1.9–12 Pf.), where Callimachus describes his poetics by contrasting the short (good) poems of Philitas and Mimnermus with their longer (bad) works. Catullus incorporates this contrastive manner with another characteristically Hellenistic form, the encomiastic epigram in praise of an admired author. Callimachus had written a brief, aesthetically charged epigram praising the *Phaenomena* of his near-contemporary Aratus (*Epigr.* 27 Pf.):

> The song is Hesiod's in theme and style, but it isn't
>   Hesiod to the last drop: No, the man of Soloi
> has skimmed the sweetness and left the rest. Hail,
>   delicate discourses, token of Aratus' vigilance.

Key terms in characterizing Aratus' poetry are *leptaí* "delicate," echoing Apollo's injunction to Callimachus in the *Aetia* Prologue and an important term for Aratus as well (Kidd 1997: 445–6), and *agrupníē* "vigilance," denoting the intense care needed in producing poetry up to Callimachus' standards.

Little survives of the poetry of C. Helvius Cinna, but from the fragments and testimonia (Courtney 1993: 212–24), we may gauge some sense of his importance for contemporaries, which extended into the next generations as well (Vergil *Ecl.* 9.35). Cinna was closely associated with the contemporary Greek poet Parthenius, whom he brought to Rome as a captive, probably after the Mithridatic war in 66 BC.

Some scholars have seen Parthenius as a pivotal figure in the dissemination of Callimachean poetry to Rome, because of his own very clear Callimachean affiliations (Clausen 1964). While this may be to attribute too much significance to a single person, it is likely that he was largely influential with Cinna. The poem to which Catullus alludes told the story of the story of Smyrna (also known as Myrrha or Zmyrna), the daughter of Cinyras, king of Cyprus, who conceived an uncontrollable passion for her father. The offspring of their incestuous union was Adonis, Aphrodite's lover. The poem was notorious for its obscurity (Courtney 1993: 219–20) and its sexual content (Ov. *Tr.* 2.435). Something of the poem's manner and thematic disposition can probably be inferred from the pseudo-Vergilian *Ciris*, which may have borrowed passages from it (Lyne 1978a: 39–45) and Ovid's retelling of the story in the *Metamorphoses* (10.298–502). In its focus on a somewhat obscure myth and the stylistic elaboration implied in the long period of composition, Cinna's *Zmyrna* exemplifies the Callimachean aesthetic embraced by Catullus and his contemporaries: stylistic refinement coupled with narrative innovation.

Catullus does not only draw on Callimachus in programmatic statements within the shorter poems; his embrace of Callimachean aesthetics is integrated into the subject matter of the polymetrics and epigrams, including poems that strike the modern reader as most personal and intense in dealing with Lesbia. In this respect it is possible to trace a more intense engagement with Callimachean resources than is found in the earlier reception by the likes of Lutatius Catulus, who adapted one of Callimachus' erotic epigrams a generation earlier (Ross 1969: 152–3). In a well-known epigram, Callimachus light-heartedly describes his wandering affections (*Epigr.* 41 Pf.):

> Half my soul still breathes, but the other half, I don't know
>   if it's Love or Death that's taken it: only it's gone.
> Is it off again to one of the boys? And yet I told them
>   many times, "Young men, don't take in that runaway."
> Help me to look for it, for I'm sure of one thing: somewhere,
>   love-sick, that good for nothing is hanging about.

Catulus' adaptation is in many ways characteristic of Roman translation, importing themes that are then turned into a more personal framework. Where Callimachus' epigram is playful, turning on the intellectual conceit of his soul's splitting, Catulus focuses on the more concrete image of the runaway slave (fr. 1; Courtney 1993: 75–6):

> aufugit mi animus; credo, ut solet, ad Theotimum
>   deuenit. sic est; perfugium illud habet.
> quid si non interdixem ne illunc fugituum
>   mitteret ad se intro, sed magis eiceret?
> ibimus quaesitum. uerum, ne ipsi teneamur,
>   formido. quid ago? da, Venus, consilium.

My soul has run away; to Theotimus, I think, as usual, it has fled. So it is: it always has him as sanctuary. It's not as if I hadn't forbidden him to admit that runaway to his home, but to throw him out. We shall go in search. But I'm afraid we'll be caught as well. What to do? Venus, advise.

With Catulus' epigram we have a sense that real emotions are at stake, signaled at a minimum by the foregrounding of the love interest's name, Theotimus. No equivalent is found in Callimachus' poem, unless a name is concealed there by textual difficulties. In the process of adaptation, however, the stylistic balance of Callimachus' epigram is sacrificed for "a series of brief, jerky utterances" (Courtney 1993: 76). When Catullus translates one of Callimachus' erotic epigrams, however, a feel for maintaining the stylistic focus is evident (70):

> Nulli se dicit mulier mea nubere malle
>   quam mihi, non si se Iuppiter ipse petat.
> dicit: sed mulier cupido quod dicit amanti,
>   in uento et rapida scribere oportet aqua.

My woman says that she prefers to wed no one other than me, not if Jupiter himself should ask her. So she says, but what a woman says to an eager lover should be written on wind and running water.

Catullus' skeptical reflections on Lesbia's sincerity are rendered in an idiom derived from Callimachus' ironic epigram on the fickle lover (*Epigr.* 25 Pf.):

> Kallignotos swore to Ionis he would never love
>   anyone, male or female, more than her.
> He swore, but it's true, what they say: the vows
>   of lovers never reach the ears of the gods.
> Now he burns for a boy, and the poor girl
>   (as they also say) is out in the cold.

While condensing and otherwise intensifying the sentiments in transferring the theme to Lesbia, Catullus preserves the smoothness and balance of the Callimachean original (Syndikus 1987: 4). The repeated *dicit* underscores the disillusionment, recovering the effect of Callimachus' repeated "he swore" (*ômose[n]*), which in the original is in the emphatic opening position in each of the first two couplets. Catullus' poem begins with the emotionally charged *nulli*, and eliminates Callimachus' last couplet, which comes as something of an intellectual cap, but an emotional anti-climax. The interplay of stylistic elegance and emotional complexity is at the heart of Catullus' shorter verse. Simple themes are expressed in extravagant language, while complex emotions might be condensed in the simplest language (*odi et amo*...), an aesthetic that he learned from Callimachus and imported, with appropriate and original modifications, into Latin verse.

Catullus and the *Aetia*

Catullus' most conspicuous engagement with the heritage of Callimachus is found in the closely linked pair of poems 65 and 66. The first poem takes the form of a dedicatory address to a friend identified as Q. Hortensius Hortalus, a famous orator and early rival of Cicero's who was by the time of this poem's writing largely retired from the public scene (W. J. Tatum 1997: 488–97), but was still recognized as a literary figure sympathetic to the poetics of the new generation

(Courtney 1993: 230–2). The poem is Catullus' response to Hortensius' request (65.17–18), whether for the specific poem that follows or simply for a specimen of verse we cannot say. In reply, Catullus writes that even though he is overwhelmed by grief at his brother's death, he is sending Hortensius "these translated verses of Battus' son" (*haec expressa tibi carmina Battiadae*, 16). What follows in poem 66 was recognized as long ago as the fifteenth century by Angelo Poliziano as a Latin translation of a work by Callimachus; only in the twentieth century, however, did the recovery of substantial fragments of the original in papyri make possible some assessment of the relationship of Catullus' version to the Greek original (Bing 1997). Callimachus' poem, known familiarly as "The Lock of Berenice," is the last narrative in the fourth book of the *Aetia*, although many scholars hold that it was originally produced as a separate poem and only later incorporated into the expanded *Aetia* (Pfeiffer 1953: xxxvii).

The subject of Callimachus' poem makes for an unusual Latin work. The original was composed to celebrate Berenice, the young queen of Ptolemy III Euergetes, who succeeded to the throne of Egypt in 247 BC. Shortly after their marriage he departed for the wars in Syria and Berenice dedicated to the gods a lock of her hair for his safe return. When the lock disappeared the astronomer Conon identified it in a group of stars located between Leo, Virgo and the Bear. The catasterism (new constellation) thus forms the subject of an elegant piece of court poetry, which Catullus translates into correspondingly elegant Latin. The opening of the poem is devoted to the earthly events that form the background to the lock's elevation; the second half provides a hair's-eye view of its translation to the heavens, allowing the lock to express its own feelings about this state of affairs. It is in this part of Catullus' poem that we are best able to compare his version with the Callimachean original, and critics differ on the effects Catullus has achieved.

A much discussed example occurs at a point where the lock laments that it will no longer be able to partake of Berenice's exquisite hair ointments (Callim. fr. 110.75–6 Pf.):

> "I am not brought pleasure by my being a star so much as I am brought distress that I shall not any more touch Berenice's head, from which I drank, when she was still a maiden, many ordinary oils and did not taste womanly perfumes."

In part because of the poor transmission of the text, Catullus' rendition was scarcely interpretable before the discovery of the papyrus (66.75–8):

> non his tam laetor rebus quam me afore semper,
>   afore me a dominae uertice discrucior,
> quicum ego, dum uirgo quondam fuit, omnibus expers
>   unguentis, una uilia multa bibi.

> "I do not so much rejoice at these things as I grieve that I shall always be parted, always be parted from my mistress' head, with which, while she was formerly a maiden, not enjoying perfumes, I drank many frugal scents."

In substituting *dominae* "mistress" for Callimachus' neutral "that one's" (*ekeínēs*), Catullus highlights the opposition between the experiences of the maiden and the adult woman. For some critics this is part of an overall strategy in this poem and

the introductory epistle to Hortensius to inject more pathos into the experience of
the lock, drawing on themes of separation and disillusionment found elsewhere in
Catullus in depictions of his relationship with his brother (Clausen 1970). Others find
in Catullus' version a more faithful rendition of Callimachean burlesque in the dishar-
mony between the lock's passionate discourse and the humorous content (Hutchinson
1988: 322–4). The question assumes some importance because of two issues of direct
relevance to Catullan intertextuality and its reception by later Roman poets.

    The first arises with 10 lines in Catullus' poem that were clearly not present in the
papyrus fragment of Callimachus. In this passage Catullus instructs all wives to make
an offering of ointments prior to marriage (79–88):

> nunc uos, optato quas iunxit lumine taeda,
>   non prius unanimis corpora coniugibus
> tradite nudantes reiecta ueste papillas,
>   quam iucunda mihi munera libet onyx,
> uester onyx, casto colitis quae iura cubili.
>   sed quae se impuro dedit adulterio,
> illius a mala dona leuis bibat irrita puluis:
>   namque ego ab indignis praemia nulla peto.
> sed magis, o nuptae, semper concordia uestras,
>   semper amor sedes incolat assiduus.

> Now you, whom with its longed-for light the marriage torch has joined, do not first hand
> over your bodies to your harmonious spouses, baring your breasts with opened robe,
> before the perfume jar offers me pleasant gifts, the jar that belongs to you who observe the
> laws in a chaste bed. But she who has given herself to impure adultery, ah, let the light dust
> drink up her wicked gifts and nullify them: for I seek no rewards from the unworthy. But
> rather, o brides, always may harmony, always may love dwell continually in your homes.

No trace of these lines is to be found in the papyrus that preserves this part of
Callimachus' *Coma*, and for a long time most scholars subscribed to the hypothesis
that Catullus is following a different version of the *Coma*, which Callimachus integrated
into the *Aetia* (Pfeiffer 1949: *ad* fr. 110.79–88). In recent years, however, most critics,
but by no means all (e.g., Hollis 1992; Marinone 1997: 41–9), have pursued a different
explanation of these lines as an addition to the original by Catullus (Putnam 1960;
Hutchinson 1988: 322–4). Some critics have interpreted this insertion as one way in
which Catullus introduces his personal signature on this translation, by infusing the
poem with images of separation and the intense feelings that accompany it (Clausen
1970: 90–4). Others make more restrained claims for this innovation, with the solemn
language addressed to the brides marking a contrast with the fanciful situation that
"makes the interplay with the fantasy the more preposterous" (Hutchinson 1988: 323).

    Our reading of this insertion has some bearing on the interpretation of another
couplet, which presents a celebrated crux in Vergil's reception of Catullus (and
Callimachus). Earlier in the poem the lock proclaimed its reluctance to be separated
from Berenice (39–40):

> inuita, o regina, tuo de uertice cessi,
>   inuita: adiuro teque tuumque caput.

> "Unwillingly, O queen, I left your crown, unwillingly, I swear by you and by your head."

Only a part of the pentameter survives from Callimachus' poem: "I swear by your head and by your life" (fr. 110.40 Pf.). We cannot tell whether the pathetic repetition of *inuita* represents something of the Callimachean original, although it is been persuasively argued that this kind of rhetorical intensification is more likely to be a Catullan innovation (Clausen 1970: 91–2). It may then follow that here Catullus may be read as interpreting his model by injecting a stronger emotional element that evokes the images of youthful separation, drawing on such familiar themes in, for example, the poetry of Sappho (Vox 2000). Some critics would counter that Catullus has simply reproduced and at best exaggerated the element of playfulness in the original *Coma*. The question then arises: how did Vergil read this passage? For in a context of presumed seriousness, Aeneas' encounter with Dido in the Underworld, his hero quotes from Catullus, *inuitus, regina, tuo de litore cessi* ("unwillingly, queen, I left your shore," *Aen.* 6.460), substituting "shore" for "head" with only a slight further change to accommodate Aeneas' masculine gender. Commentators on the two passages take a variety of positions on the significance of this obvious imitation. Some (e.g., Norden 1957: 254) merely note the echo without comment on its possible interpretative consequences; others (e.g., Fordyce 1961: 334) insist that Vergil's attribution to Aeneas of a near-quotation of a talking lock of hair can only be unconscious; while others (e.g., Austin 1977: 164) recognize that the allusion is deliberate and see it as part of Vergil's ability to elevate even the trivial to his grander purposes. More recently, some critics (e.g., Clausen 1970) have interpreted Catullus' *Coma* on a higher plane, not inconsistent with the serious theme of Aeneas' separation from Dido. It may just be possible that all of this is beside the point, and that in alluding to Catullus' adaptation of Callimachus, Vergil refers to both the proximate (Catullus) and more remote (Callimachus) models. It may then be the case that Vergil's reader, like Dido, may respond to Aeneas' rhetorical strategy of quoting from Callimachus' court poem by wondering if this is the best he can do.

Catullus and the *Iambi*

The final poem in Catullus' corpus as it has come down to us (116) opens with an explicit reference to Callimachus:

> saepe tibi studioso animo uenante requirens
>   carmina uti possem mittere Battiadae,
> qui te lenirem nobis, neu conarere
>   tela infesta meum mittere in usque caput,
> hunc uideo mihi nunc frustra sumptum esse laborem,
>   Gelli, nec nostras hic ualuisse preces.
> contra nos tela ista tua euitabimus acta:
>   at fixus nostris tu dabis supplicium.

Often with my mind earnestly hunting I sought how I might send you poems of the Battiad, that I might soften you towards me and you might not try to land deadly shafts upon my head. But I now see that I have undertaken this toil in vain, Gellius, and that my prayers have not availed in this matter. I shall evade those shafts of yours launched against me; but you shall be pierced by mine and pay the penalty.

The reference to "poems of the Battiad" recalls the poem addressed to Hortensius (65), which is the first in elegiacs in the collection. Whether this placement is deliberate, as it seems, and whether this was the work of the poet or an editor are a matter of speculation. This poem has generally been read as an opening shot in Catullus' vituperative relationship with Gellius, who is lampooned in several epigrams (74, 80, 88–91), but that it makes an important statement about Catullus' relationship with Callimachus has only lately been the focus of critical inquiry. Allusion to Callimachus is signaled by the opening word of the first couplet, in which he is also named. That the lost first word of the *Aetia* was *polláki* "often" has only recently been established (Pontani 1999), opening the door to recognizing the *Aetia* Prologue as an active intertext here (Barchiesi 2005: 333–6). Catullus thus signals the programmatic purpose of the poem in contrasting one kind of poetry (*carmina . . . Battiadae*), which he cannot write, with another associated with the invective of archaic iambic (*tela infesta*). Callimachus himself had notably attempted a renovated form of iambic verse, one that was distinguished from Hipponactean iambus, by toning down the note of personal invective, scoring hits in "a devious and urbane manner" (Macleod 1973: 306). The opening iambus in his collection makes the point by having Hipponax himself return from the dead and announce a form of iambic verse that does not torment his opponent Bupalos (fr. 191.1–4 Pf.):

> Listen to Hipponax. For indeed I have come from the place where they sell an ox
> for a penny, bearing an iambus which does not sing of the Bupalean battle. . . .

This form of iambus is characterized by the familiar Callimachean values of refinement, as Catullus hints at in describing the great concentration (*studioso animo uenante*) and effort (*laborem*) involved in composition (Syndikus 1987: 144). Catullus composed 12 poems in iambic meters (4, 8, 22, 25, 29, 31, 37, 39, 44, 52, 59, 60), but there is little in these poems to suggest an association with archaic iambos; rather, it is a Callimachean background that is evoked (Heyworth 2001: 117–25). The turn to invective announced in the final line thus treats iambos in terms of tone and content rather than meter.

This accounts for the exceptional circumstance that Catullus only uses the word *iambus* in his hendecasyllabics, in cc. 36, 40, 54, and fragment 3 (Heyworth 2001: 125). In giving the term a wider generic application Catullus stretches ancient definitions of genre tied to meter. In one case (40) he uses the term to characterize hendecasyllabics deployed as personal invective, in a context that clearly alludes to the iambics of Archilochus (Heyworth 2001: 127). In another poem directed at Julius Caesar (54), the term refers both to an earlier poem actually written in iambics (29) and to the politically charged hendecasyllabics in which it appears. In poem 36, Catullus merges the Archilochean and invective associations of iambics with an attack on a literary target, the epic *Annals* of Volusius (1–10):

> Annales Volusi, cacata charta,
> uotum soluite pro mea puella.
> nam sanctae Veneri Cupidinique
> uouit, si sibi restitutus essem
> desissemque truces uibrare iambos,
> electissima pessimi poetae

> scripta tardipedi deo daturam
> infelicibus ustulanda lignis.
> nec uos pessima se puella uidit
> iocose ac lepide uouere diuis.

Annales of Volusius, crappy paper, discharge a vow for my girl. For she made a vow to Venus and Cupid that, if I were restored to her and ceased to hurl fierce iambics, she would give the choicest writings of the worst poet to the limping god for him to burn with ill-omened timber. But the naughty girl did not see that it was you she was wittily and charmingly vowing to the gods.

The iambics that Catullus has been hurling at Lesbia can hardly be limited to c. 37 and the end of c. 8, the only two poems in that meter directed against Lesbia in any sense (Thomson 1997: 298), and with most commentators we should see here another instance of *iambos* referring to the content of the verses, not the meter. Within this context of Callimachean aesthetics, deprecating pretentious epic poetry, Lesbia makes a vow to burn Catullus' non-Callimachean, old-fashioned invective; Catullus interprets this vow, however, in a most Callimachean manner (*iocose ac lepide*) as an injunction to burn Volusius' *Annals*.

Callimachean Narrative in Catullus

Catullus' longest and most ambitious work is the narrative poem in hexameters known as "The Wedding of Peleus and Thetis," a work at once "learned and laborious, a specimen of strictly premeditated art" (Clausen 1982: 187). The story of Peleus' marriage to Thetis serves to provide a frame for the inset story of Theseus' abandonment on Naxos. This story is couched in an ecphrasis (or digression), describing the scenes embroidered on a cover for the marriage bed (76–264). In its elaborate structure and emotional pyrotechnics, the poem resembles nothing surviving from previous Greek literature, but its debt to Hellenistic precedents in inspiration and execution has never been doubted. In its elaborate construction, the artificial connections between tapestry and wedding, and its use of lexical and metrical Grecisms, the poem has always been recognized as closely connected with the Hellenistic background (Lefèvre 2000a). Indeed, for long it was thought to have been a translation of some lost original, like poem 66 and the *Coma Berenices* (Kroll 1968, 1st edn.: 142). Few, if any, would now subscribe to that view, which was debunked long ago (Perrotta 1931), but it can hardly be doubted that some important sources for the narrative of Ariadne that were known to Catullus have been lost and their recovery might explain much of the poem's intertextual nature (Knox 1998).

Among Catullus' contemporaries we know of works in the same vein, although they exist for us practically only as titles: Cinna's *Zmyrna*, Valerius Cato's *Dictynna*, Calvus' *Io*, and Caecilius' *Magna Mater* (Courtney 1993: 189–227). Some information about the style and manner of these poems can be gleaned from the later poems mistakenly attributed to Vergil, the *Culex*, a mock narrative about the descent of a gnat into the Underworld, and the *Ciris*, which tells the story of the daughter of Nisus who fell in love with Minos (Lyne 1978: 32–6). But the most significant surviving example of the form is Catullus' poem, and its relationship with contemporary or earlier exemplars of the genre can only be estimated from careful analysis of Catullus' language measured against the few surviving fragments.

The opening lines of the poem establish a formal tone and a distancing from the narrator's present, but they do so in a way that summons up recollections of a literary pedigree as well (64.1–7):

> Peliaco quondam prognatae uertice pinus
> dicuntur liquidas Neptuni nasse per undas
> Phasidos ad fluctus et fines Aeetaeos,
> cum lecti iuuenes, Argiuae robora pubis,
> auratam optantes Colchis auertere pellem
> ausi sunt uada salsa cita decurrere puppi,
> caerula uerrentes abiegnis aequora palmis.

Once on Pelion's summit long ago pine-trees were born, and swam (people say) through Neptune's liquid waves to the waters of Phasis and the borders of Aeetes, when chosen youths, the flower of Argive manpower, desiring to carry off from the Colchians the golden fleece, ventured in a swift ship to speed over the briny seas, sweeping with blades of fir the azure plains.

In the first line Catullus evokes the stylistic background of Hellenistic narrative, with *quondam* ("once long ago"), "an adverb to summon up the dateless past" (Clausen 1982: 187). The mannerism is common in other Hellenistic narrative poems (Bühler 1960: 47), but it evokes most directly the opening of Callimachus' *Hecale*, the first line of which has been preserved for us by an ancient commentator (Call. fr. 230 Pf. = 1 H):

> Once, in the uplands of Erechtheus, lived
> an Attic woman

The reader's apprehension of other literary presences here is confirmed in *dicuntur* "people say," echoed elsewhere in lines 19 *fertur*, 76 *perhibent*, 124 *perhibent*, 212 *ferunt*. The use of such terms, which serve to distance the narrator from the events related in the poem, is also a lexical marker to signal an intertextual connection with other accounts, sometimes called an "Alexandrian footnote" (Ross 1975: 77–8; Hinds 1998: 1–2). The densely allusive and learned fabric of these opening lines has been closely examined by commentators, with its points of contact to early poetry in Euripides, Apollonius, Callimachus, and Ennius duly explicated (R. F. Thomas 1982; Clare 1996).

It has been suspected that Callimachus' *Hecale* exerted a powerful influence on other parts of the poem, as well as contributing to its general thematic structure and tone. It is possible, but only possible, that Catullus' use of the ecphrastic narrative on the tapestry is itself an imitation of such a device used by Callimachus in the opening of the third book of the *Aetia* (R. F. Thomas 1983: 105–13; Hutchinson 1988: 302). But the influence of Callimachus' story of Theseus in the *Hecale* has been detected in Catullus' poem in the portion that also deals with Theseus. An unattributed Greek hexameter quoted by Cicero (*Att.* 8.5.1), "vainly venting the rage in its horns on the air," has long been suspected as belonging to the *Hecale* (Hollis 1990: 323–4). It is the merest chance that this line (fr. 723 Pf. = 165 Hollis), which must have been easily recognizable to Cicero's correspondent, is clearly the model for Catullus' description of Theseus' struggle with the Minotaur (110–11):

> sic domito saeuum prostrauit corpore Theseus
> nequiquam uanis iactantem cornua uentis

so, overpowering its body, Theseus laid low the monster as it vainly tossed its horns at the empty air.

In transferring details from Callimachus' celebrated account of one of the labors of Theseus to another, Catullus is likely to have utilized other parts of the narrative than this one line. One fragment of the *Hecale*, recently restored (238 Pf.; *Supp. Hell.* 281; 17 Hollis), preserves part of a conversation between Theseus and his father Aegeus, with Theseus asking to be sent out against the Marathonian bull: "so let me go, father: you'll get me back safely." We know from the *Diegesis* of the *Hecale* that Aegeus was not persuaded. His situation in Catullus 64 is very similar and he is there represented as reluctant to send out his recently rediscovered son on a potentially fatal mission (215–17):

> gnate, mihi longe iucundior unice uita,
> gnate, ego quem in dubios cogor dimittere casus,
> reddite in extrema nuper mihi fine senectae.

"Son, only son, sweeter by far to me than life; son, whom I am forced to send off on perilous ventures, restored to me but recently at the extreme limit of old age."

And just as Athena is invoked as Theseus' hope against the bull in that fragment, so Aegeus reposes his hopes for success against the Minotaur in the patron goddess of Athens (228–30):

> quod tibi si sancti concesserit incola Itoni,
> quae nostrum genus ac sedes defendere Erecthei
> annuit, ut tauri respergas sanguine dextram.

"But if the tenant of holy Itonus, she who consents to defend our people and the seat of Erectheus, grants you to steep your right hand in the blood of the bull."

The hypothesis that this motif has been transferred from the *Hecale* (Hollis 1990: 151–2) gains some support from Catullus' reference here to the Minotaur as a "bull" (*tauri*). The word *Minotaurus* is in fact attested no earlier than Catullus in Latin or Greek literature (Clausen 1988: 15–17), so it is unsurprising that he should have associated Theseus' two great bullfights.

Another experiment by Catullus may also have been inspired by his experience of reading Callimachus' narratives. Poem 63 describes the self-castration by a Greek youth named Attis, caught up in the fervor of the cult of Cybele, the Great Mother of Asia Minor. The exotic features of the poem, its obvious Greek affiliations, and the unusual meter have all suggested a translation or close adaptation of some lost original. That is, of course, far from a certain conclusion, but that the poem draws on the same sources of inspiration in the Callimachean tradition seems clear even from our meager evidence (Wilamowitz 1924: II.291–5; Fantuzzi and Hunter 2004: 477–85). The galliambic meter was associated with Callimachus by ancient metricians, who cite from a "famous" work by him two verses on the Gallai, adherents of the Great Mother (fr. 761 Pf.):

> The Gallai, thyrsus-loving runners of the mountain Mother,
> whose utensils of bronze and castanets resound.

There is no telling if these lines actually belong to Callimachus (they probably do), or if he ever treated the story of Cybele and her mythical attendant Attis at any length (he probably did), but there are enough traces of it in the fragments to suggest he had an interest in the story (Knox 2002: 168–70) and that Catullus is alluding to that general ambience. But it is also likely that he is drawing on other post-Callimachean forms of dramatic monody, such as the so-called *Fragmentum Grenfellianum* (Fantuzzi and Hunter 2004: 485). What this illustrates is that Catullus is best seen as part of a continuum that stretches from the third-century Greek culture of Alexandria to Rome of the first century, an uninterrupted tradition that spans time, language, and cultural boundaries.

After Catullus

No Roman poet of the succeeding generations was unaffected by the shift in Latin poetics attributable to Catullus and his contemporaries. The loss of their work leaves him as the sole representative of this sea change in Latin poetry. Had Catullus not entered so deeply into the literary world of Callimachus, it would have been inconceivable for Vergil, to take only one example, to couch his famous declaration of pastoral poetics (*Ecl.* 6.3–5) in terms of the *Aetia* Prologue:

> cum canerem reges et proelia, Cynthius aurem
> uellit et admonuit: "pastorem, Tityre, pinguis
> pascere oportet ouis, deductum dicere carmen".

> When I was singing of kings and battles, Cynthian Apollo tweaked my ear and warned me, "Tityrus, a shepherd should raise his sheep to be fat, but sing a slender song."

Every poet of Vergil's generation seems clearly to have taken his critical bearings from Callimachus, whose considerable influence extends also into the next generation and Ovid. That is a much longer story to be told elsewhere, but it is only a possible story because Catullus prepared the way.

GUIDE TO FURTHER READING

The standard text of Callimachus remains Rudolph Pfeiffer's magisterial two-volume edition (1949, 1953), but it must now be supplemented by additional fragments found in Lloyd-Jones and Parsons (1983: 89–144). For Books 1 and 2 of the *Aetia* these are incorporated into the edition by Massimilla (1996); in addition, for the fragments of the *Hecale*, Hollis's edition (1990) should be consulted. The recent studies by Kerkhecker (1999) and Acosta-Hughes (2002) have injected new life into the study of the *Iambi*. The translation by Nisetich (2001) makes Callimachus' works accessible to the Greekless, including many fragments not translated in the Loeb edition and several new papyri. A major re-evaluation by Alan Cameron (1995) has called into question many prevailing assumptions about Callimachus' views on literature, the circumstances of the composition of his works, and his influence on the Roman poets.

Since the publication of Wimmel's seminal study (1960), there has been a steady flow of books and articles on Callimachus' influence on Roman poetry. Since Wilamowitz's important book on the subject (1924), there has also been a tradition of appending a brief treatment of the Roman poets to studies of Hellenistic poetry; recent contributions by Hutchinson (1988) and Fantuzzi and Hunter (2004) contain much of interest on Catullus. Clausen (1964) exercised considerable influence upon its first appearance and is still worth consulting, as is his later paper (1970) dealing exclusively with Catullus and Callimachus. In fact, most studies of Callimachean influence on Catullus are to be found in journal articles or in commentaries on his works, but special mention might be made of the running commentary on all his poems by Syndikus (1984, 1987, 1990). Lehnus (2000) provides a full annotated bibliography for all matters Callimachean, with special sections for the reception of Callimachus' works in Rome, including Catullus (421–9).

WORKS CITED

Acosta-Hughes, B. 2002. *Polyeideia: The* Iambi *of Callimachus and the Archaic Iambic Tradition*. Berkeley.
Allen, W. 1940. "The Epyllion: A Chapter in the History of Literary Criticism." *Transactions of the American Philological Association* 71: 1–26.
Austin, R. G. 1977. *P. Vergili Maronis Aeneidos Liber Sextus*. Oxford.
Barchiesi, A. 2005. "The Search for the Perfect Book: A PS to the New Posidippus." In K. Gutzwiller, ed., *The New Posidippus: A Hellenistic Poetry Book*. Oxford. 320–42.
Bing, P. 1997. "Reconstructing Berenike's Lock." In G. W. Most, ed., *Collecting Fragments: Fragmente sammeln*. Göttingen. 78–94.
Bühler, W. 1960. *Die Europa des Moschos*. Wiesbaden.
Cameron, A. 1995. *Callimachus and His Critics*. Princeton, NJ.
Clare, R. J. 1996. "Catullus 64 and the *Argonautica* of Apollonius Rhodius: Allusion and Exemplarity." *Proceedings of the Cambridge Philological Society* 42: 60–88.
Clausen, W. V. 1964. "Callimachus and Latin Poetry." *Greek, Roman, and Byzantine Studies* 5: 181–96.
Clausen, W. V. 1970. "Catullus and Callimachus." *Harvard Studies in Classical Philology* 74: 85–94.
Clausen, W. V. 1982. "The New Direction in Poetry." In E. J. Kenney and W. V. Clausen, eds., *The Cambridge History of Classical Literature. Vol. II: Latin Literature*. Cambridge and New York. 178–206.
Clausen, W. V. 1988. "Catulliana." In N. Horsfall, ed., Vir Bonus Discendi Peritus: *Studies in Celebration of Otto Skutsch's Eightieth Birthday. British Institute of Classical Studies* Supp. 51: 13–17.
Courtney, E., ed. 1993. *The Fragmentary Latin Poets*. Oxford.
Elder, J. P. 1966. "Catullus I, His Poetic Creed, and Nepos." *Harvard Studies in Classical Philology* 71: 143–9.

Fantuzzi, M., and R. Hunter. 2004. *Tradition and Innovation in Hellenistic Poetry.* Cambridge.

Fordyce, C. J., ed. 1961. *Catullus: A Commentary.* Oxford.

Gow, A. S. F., and D. L. Page, eds. 1965. *The Greek Anthology: Hellenistic Epigrams.* 2 vols. Cambridge.

Heyworth, S. J. 2001. "Catullian Iambics, Catullian *Iambi.*" In A. Cavarzere, A. Aloni, and A. Barchiesi, eds., *Iambic Ideas: Essays on a Poetic Tradition from Archaic Greece to the Late Roman Empire.* Lanham, MD, Boulder, CT, New York, and Oxford. 117–40.

Hinds, S. 1998. *Allusion and Intertext: Dynamics of Appropriation in Roman Poetry.* Cambridge.

Hollis, A. S. 1990. *Callimachus: Hecale.* Oxford.

Hollis, A. S. 1992. "The Nuptial Rite in Catullus 66 and Callimachus' Poetry for Berenice." *Zeitschrift für Papyrologie und Epigraphik* 91: 21–8.

Hutchinson, G. O. 1988. *Hellenistic Poetry.* Oxford.

Kerkhecker, A. 1999. *Callimachus' Book of* Iambi. Oxford.

Kidd, D., ed. 1997. *Aratus: Phaenomena.* Cambridge.

Knox, P. E. 1998. "Ariadne on the Rocks." In P. E. Knox and C. Foss, eds., *Style and Tradition: Studies in Honor of Wendell Clausen.* Stuttgart and Leipzig. 72–83.

Knox, P. E. 2002. "Representing the Great Mother to Augustus." In G. Herbert-Brown, ed., *Ovid's Fasti: Historical Readings at its Bimillennium.* Oxford. 155–74.

Kroll, W., ed. 1968 [1923]. *C. Valerius Catullus, herausgegeben und erklärt.* 5th edn. Stuttgart. (1st edn. Leipzig.)

Lefèvre, E. 2000a. "Alexandrinisches und catullisches im Peleus-Epos (64)." *Hermes* 128: 181–201.

Lehnus, L. 2000. *Nuova bibliografia callimachea (1489–1998).* Alessandria.

Lightfoot, J. L. 1999. *Parthenius of Nicaea.* Oxford.

Lloyd-Jones, H., and P. Parsons. 1983. *Supplementum Hellenisticum.* Berlin.

Lyne, R. O. A. M., ed. 1978a. *Ciris: A Poem Attributed to Vergil.* Cambridge.

Macleod, C. W. 1973. "Catullus 116." *Classical Quarterly* 23: 304–9.

Marinone, N., ed. 1997. *Berenice da Callimaco a Catullo: testo critico, traduzione e commento.* Rev. edn. Bologna.

Massimilla, G. 1996. *Callimaco: Aitia, Libri Primo e Secondo.* Pisa.

Mayer, R. G. 1995. "*Graecia Capta*: The Roman Reception of Greek Literature." *Papers of the Liverpool Latin Seminar* 8. Liverpool. 289–307.

Nisetich, F. 2001. *The Poems of Callimachus.* Oxford.

Norden, E. 1957. *P. Vergilius Maro: Aeneis, Buch VI.* 4th edn. Stuttgart.

Perrotta, G. 1931. "Il carme 64 di Catullo e i suoi pretesi originali ellenistici." *Athenaeum* 9: 177–222, 371–409.

Pfeiffer, R., ed. 1949. *Callimachus.* 2 vols. Oxford.

Pontani, F. 1999. "The First Word of Callimachus' ΑΙΤΙΑ." *Zeitschrift für Papyrologie und Epigraphik* 128: 57–9.

Puelma-Piwonka, M. 1949. *Lucilius und Kallimachos: Zur Geschichte einer Gattung der hellenistisch-römischen Poesie.* Frankfurt.

Putnam, M. C. J. 1960. "Catullus 66.75–8." *Classical Philology* 55: 223–8.

Ross, D. O., Jr. 1969. *Style and Tradition in Catullus.* Cambridge, MA.

Ross, D. O., Jr. 1975. *Backgrounds to Augustan Poetry: Gallus, Elegy and Rome.* Cambridge.

Skutsch, O. 1985. *The Annals of Quintus Ennius.* Oxford.

Solodow, J. B. 1987. "On Catullus 95." *Classical Philology* 82: 141–5.

Syndikus, H. P. 1984. *Catull: Eine Interpretation. Erster Teil: Einleitung, Die kleinen Gedichte (1–60).* Darmstadt.

Syndikus, H. P. 1987. *Catull: Eine Interpretation. Dritter Teil: Die Epigramme (69–116).* Darmstadt.

Syndikus, H. P. 1990. *Catull: Eine Interpretation. Zweiter Teil: Die grossen Gedichte (61–68).* Darmstadt.

Tatum, W. J. 1997. "Friendship, Politics, and Literature in Catullus: Poems 1, 65 and 66, 116." *Classical Quarterly* n.s. 47: 482–500.

Thomas, R. F. 1982. "Catullus and the Polemics of Poetic Reference (Poem 64.1–18)." *American Journal of Philology* 103: 144–64.

Thomas, R. F. 1983. "Callimachus, the *Victoria Berenices*, and Roman Poetry." *Classical Quarterly* 33: 92–113.

Thomson, D. F. S., ed. 1997. *Catullus, Edited with a Textual and Interpretative Commentary.* Toronto.

Vox, O. 2000. "Sul genere grammaticale della *Chioma di Berenice*." *Materiali e Discussioni* 44: 175–81.

Wilamowitz-Moellendorff, U. von. 1924. *Hellenistische Dichtung in der Zeit des Kallimachos.* 2 vols. Berlin.

Williams, F. 1978. *Callimachus,* Hymn to Apollo*: A Commentary.* Oxford.

Wimmel, W. 1960. *Kallimachos in Rom. Hermes* Einzelschriften 16. Wiesbaden.

Wiseman, T. P. 1969. *Catullan Questions.* Leicester.

Wiseman, T. P. 1979. *Clio's Cosmetics: Three Studies in Greco-Roman Literature.* Leicester.

Wiseman, T. P. 1985. *Catullus and His World: A Reappraisal.* Cambridge.

PART IV

Stylistics

CHAPTER TEN

Neoteric Poetics

W. R. Johnson

If it were not for three brief passages scattered in the corpus of Cicero, the idea (and the name) of neoteric poetics might never have come into existence. At the opening of a letter to Atticus (7.2, November 26, 50 BC) Cicero announces his safe passage back to Italy from Cilicia with a florid and funny hexameter: *flavit ab Epiro lenissimus Onchesmites*, "it was the gentlest of South Eastern breezes that blew me hither from Epirus." He is here apparently parodying the – to him – overly exquisite style of certain poets whose recent success in the poetry world somewhat irks him and whom he therefore lumps together (and dismisses with amused contempt) by affixing to them a Greek label: *hoi neoteroi*, "the newer poets," that is, the trendy newer poets.

Four years later, their vogue still rankling him, he identifies them (in *Orat.* 161) with a Latin phrase, *poetae novi*, "the new poets." Finding the metrical practices of their predecessors primitive and uncouth (*subrusticum*), they have devised refinements in meter that seem to annoy Cicero, who had once thought of himself as a modern sort of poet but who now finds himself relegated, in his own eyes and perhaps in the eyes of the newcomers, to the junk heap to which the outmoded find themselves consigned. Cicero now discovers, it would seem, that he prefers untaught tradition (*indocta consuetudo*), which naturally produces euphony, to the contemporary artifice (*ars*) and theory (*doctrina*) that seek to replace the venerable practices of the great old poets.

Finally, a year later, in his *Tusculan Disputations* (3.45), in a passage where he quotes Ennius to refute Epicurus, he breaks off his recitation of the verses in question, whose style and sound and sentiments he believes to be incomparable (*praeclarem carmen*), to bless the wonderful old poet (*o poetam egregium! quamquam ab his cantoribus Euphorionis contemnitur*, "o peerless poet! despite all the rotten things Euphorion's warblers may say of him"). In his two previous barbs at them, Cicero was mostly aiming at the stylistic pretensions of the new poets (their boast that they were "making it new" by scrapping the decrepit poetic styles and worn-out versification of those who had written in the grand tradition). Here, though he is insisting on the excellence of Ennius' manner, it is also the greatness of his matter and its significance that engage his admiration and elicit his praise – and his scorn for the grand old poet's detractors. Ennius, in the present context, is presented as a monumental moral poet in the supreme (moral) tradition of classical Greek tragedy. What he writes about Andromache's tragic recognition of her doom and its meaning is, in equal measure, aesthetically pleasing and philosophically illuminating. But these parvenus of Parnassus, what are they, with their pretty twitterings, what are they saying about Fate and Life and Truth – if, that is, they are really trying to say anything at all?

We know little of substance about Euphorion except that he flourished in the third century BC, wrote a number of poems that we possess only in scraps, and ended as the head librarian at Antioch. He was, then, a Hellenistic poet-scholar who, like other of his poetic contemporaries and poetic heirs, had a special fondness for the cultivation of refined, intricate style, for obscure myths or obscure versions of popular myths, for "the criminal-love story" (see Crump 1931: 99–102), and for recondite allusions and unfamiliar diction. He was, in short, a consummate poet-scholar and a committed (obsessive) craftsman in whom *ars* and *doctrina* had systematically uprooted any trace of *indocta consuetudo* that he might have been born with. He was, for Cicero's purposes in the passage in question, the exact opposite of Ennius (and of poets like him: Homer, Aeschylus, Sophocles, and, of course, Cicero). Which meant that Euphorion was an exact marker for everything that Cicero found rebarbative and threatening in the productions of the poets whom he variously called *neoteroi* and *poetae novi* and *cantores Euphorionis*.

What was clear to Cicero and his first readers – what kind of poetry Euphorion wrote, what characterized his choices of style, theme, genre – is only tantalizingly vague to us. Cicero's phrase is vivid by virtue of its mockery and malice, but our sense of Euphorion is so dim that it offers little help in defining for us the identities of the irritating new kids on the block who goaded Cicero into inventing it in order to categorize them and to dismiss them. Who were these warbling epigones, what kind of poetry did they write?

Their names and what little is left of their poems have been carefully assembled and painstakingly scrutinized in the pages of Edward Courtney's *The Fragmentary Latin Poets*. Having rounded up the usual neoteric suspects (in addition to Catullus these are: M. Furius Bibaculus, C. Licinius Calvus, C. Helvius Cinna, Q. Cornificius, L. Ticida, and P. Terentius Varro Atacinus), and having sifted, with exemplary patience, both their meager fragments and the bits and pieces of information about what there is to "know" about them, he is driven to conclude that "neoterics" is "a word we should cease to use" (1993: 189). This term, he decides, like *poetae novi* and *cantores Euphorionis*, does not indicate "a unified school of poets" or even "a group of poets in the terms which have become conventional (since, as far as I can find, about the turn of this [the twentieth] century)." He allows that "most of these poets, like Vergil, came from Cisalpine Gaul" and further admits "that we can trace personal links between some of them." But beside these frail similarities he can discover no evidence – so many pieces of the jigsaw are missing – that the poets in question show enough homogeneity to warrant their being gathered together into any sort of meaningful group.

Courtney's skepticism is as robustly nourished as it is devastating, and, after reviewing his arguments, one is almost tempted to assent to his suggestion that the notion of a "school" of neoterics needs to be allowed to fade away. Nevertheless, something or someone had become for Cicero a source of sustained if minor irritation. To explain this irritation we don't need to invent a conspiracy composed of a crowd of bright young things whose essential purpose was to rattle the cage of an aging and thin-skinned poetaster, or to imagine, more charitably, a loose confederation of poets who gathered on a fairly regular basis (think, for instance, of Mallarmé's evenings at home) to reaffirm their shared conviction that the course of Latin poetry needed changing and that they alone knew how to go about transforming its styles, its meters, its themes. Our instinct for tidiness, our penchant for classifying our artists and periodizing them, marking them off by generations or, more neatly, by decades, easily leads us into identifying schools of poets and painters and actors when we are trying to characterize (in order to understand) the nature of a given kind of artistic production whose features (and intentions) we find at once distinctive and in some ways elusive. One need only recall here the once fervent and still lingering efforts to provide a definitive pigeonhole for The Romantic School and to reduce a vast, dynamic explosion of revolutionary forms and feelings into some semblance of unity of origin, evolution, and signification. Yet the spectrum of differences in literary product (in national variation, in diversity of individual temperament and talent, in shifts in direction from year to year and decade to decade) has thus far precluded any final judgment about the nature of Romanticism. "Schools" or even "groups" of artists, if they are possessed of genuine vitality, are so violent in the rejection of the status quo they end by destroying, are so volatile in terms of the powerful, unique egos that fuel their vision and their energies, that anything like the stability we want to impose on them ends in being a bit too fragile, too tenuous, and always just beyond our grasp, our yearning for a satisfying fixity.

Nevertheless, such poetic entities do find their way into the world. They come into being, whatever the degree of their cohesion, whatever their duration, in the way that other fashions (in dress or food or dance) make their often mysterious appearances and disappearances. They come into being because, at certain times and in certain places, our human need "to make things new" wins out over our human need to cling to what we were born into and fear to lose. At some uncertain time in the history of Rome and its poetry (over a period of years or decades) some readers and some perspective writers of Latin poetry found themselves saying to themselves or to each other, muttering at first, then more vociferously and more frequently: "That stuff we learned at school, those corny, moldering idiocies our teachers made us explicate and memorize, the sort of antiquated crap that Cicero and his pals keep churning out, let's just toss it in the Tiber, let's get rid of it for good and all. Let's just admit it, let's say it loud and clear: Ennius is a long-winded, pompous, blubbering halfwit. We want, we deserve, something fresher, funnier, more titillating. We want some chills and thrills. We want something we can wrap our brains around. We want – for godsake – we want to feel alive."

It matters little who (which, if any, of our usual suspects) was the first to have such an imprecation against the classic Latin poetic norm burst into his mind. This disenchantment will have proceeded from its hidden origins incrementally toward the moment (or year or decade) when it became too frequent to ignore, too manifest not to demand, first utterance, then action: the deliberate effort to reject the style or styles that had begun to be felt as intolerable or to reconcile them with a style or styles that felt more comfortable, more in tune with what the disenchanted reader/writer found himself experiencing in the world around him, with what he had come to feel was "natural" for him in that time and place. When the voice of Ennius and the voices derived from his ceased to be meaningful (in this context, less resonant, less satisfying), new voices had to be fabricated – fabricated out of other voices, voices that were heard as alien to the Ennian voice and its offspring, voices as different from it, as opposed to it, as possible. What E. M. Cioran says of the aftermath of the Romantic revolution in French literature is perhaps useful here:

> For two centuries, all originality has been manifested by an opposition to classicism: no new form or formula has not reacted against it. To pulverize the *acquired*, such seems to me the essential tendency of the modern mind. In whatever section of art you consider, every style asserts itself against *style*. It is by undermining the idea of reason, or order, of harmony, that we gain consciousness of ourselves. . . . The classical universe no longer being viable, we must shake it up, introduce it into it a suggestion of incompletion. (1998: 133)

In describing this process of "fecund dissolution," Cioran mingles style and substance in what at first seems a peculiar way, in that he appears to be insisting that how something is said is more central to the process of writing than what is being said, appears to be privileging form over feeling, surface over depth, manner over matter. He does so, I think, because when we attempt to disentangle the mysterious fusion of words with the things and thoughts and feelings we desire those words to represent, it is the surface sheen of that fusion that we first experience and attend to, that we are, whether we admit it or not, first attracted to or repelled by.

In his dismissal of the new poets, Cicero believed, apparently, that what offended him about them was the way they wrote. Even in his reference to Euphorion, though it is unclear whether it is really the manner or the matter of the Greek's Roman epigones that disturbs him, his tone – we catch it in his choice of the derisive *cantores* – suggests that what he thinks he wants to express is his dislike of their style, namely, of a frivolous, perhaps effete, manner that seeks to hide a poverty or even an absence of genuine matter behind a repertoire of glittering verbal tricks (the exact opposite of what is recommended in Cato the Elder's famous solution to the problem of style: *rem tene, uerba sequentur*, "grab hold of what needs saying and the words you need will automatically pop out of your mouth"). Yet the passionate contrast he designs between the supreme, deathless poet of old Rome and the tiresome whippersnappers who rush off to Greeklings for their inspiration and their technique suggests that, beyond the affront they offer to his sense of stylistic decorum, it is their dereliction of the true purpose of poetry that disgusts or perhaps frightens him. When they are busy giggling over Ennius' primitive versification and barbaric diction, when they are devising subtler rhythms and searching out astonishing vocabularies and contriving amazing new feats for old tropes and figures to perform, they are also bent on pulverizing (to use Cioran's apt word) the core of the moral universe which the poetry of Ennius incorporates even as they flagrantly disavow any responsibility for preserving, enlarging, and passing on the ethical codes and the spiritual disciplines that make Romans Romans and that make Romans great, in war, in peace, throughout the known world.

I'm not unaware that I'm constructing a response by Cicero to the new poets out of meager materials. In doing so, in sketching this cartoon of him as he might have appeared at this pivotal moment (to the new poets at least) just when the shift was occurring from Ennian classicism to the poetry world in which Catullus began operating, I'm trying to imagine the kind of world that Catullus and the poets contemporary with him lived in and wrote in, the kind of world that came into being when the traditions that Ennius represented – and not to Cicero alone – first began to seem, and then obviously became, irrelevant. To replace it what was needed was a new poetics that could help make sense of the confusion and the exhilaration of living in a world where Cicero and Catiline, Sempronia and Servilia and Fulvia and Clodia, were all doing their things, the world that we find reflected, now dimly, now vividly, in the pages of Sallust and Appian.

In his life of Cicero, Plutarch, drawing on what was probably the received opinion of his day, affirms that Cicero, in the period just before the arrival of the new poets on the scene, was regarded – and not by himself alone – as the "best poet in Rome." Having begun to compose poetry when he was only a boy, "as he grew older [he] gave his attention more fully to the refinements of this art" (*Cic.* 2.3, trans. Warner). It may be impossible to decide what it was that most irked Cicero about the new poetry, its manner or its matter, but given his devotion to the cultivation of poetic technique, one is tempted to begin with the difficulties he might have experienced when confronted with what he perceived as the abrupt break with the stylistic tradition (its handling of versification, diction, word order, figures, and tropes) that he had inherited from his cherished poetic predecessors and that, over the years, he had worked steadily to perfect. What we have of Cicero's poetry clearly shows not only formidable technical mastery of traditional styles but also some effort at smoothing out some of its rough edges and a certain interest in and flair for modernizing tendencies. Nevertheless, when we learn (again from Plutarch) that if Cicero "set his mind to it, he could compose five hundred lines of verse in a night" (41.3, trans. Warner), we may be excused from wondering whether his expertise was less artistic than mechanical. That is to say, what he meant by writing poetry was not what, say, Catullus or Calvus or Cinna meant when they thought of themselves as writing poetry. We know from Catullus 95, for instance, that Cinna spent nine years working on his *Zmyrna* as compared with a hapless hack whose yearly quota of verses reached the half-million mark; it would be too good to be true if the real target that lay hidden behind this malicious comparison was not Volusius, the victim Catullus names, but the egregiously prolific Cicero, who is tenderly savaged in 49. As far as one can tell, Cicero thought the process of making verses (or writing poetry) consisted of the poet's imposing on his material (its stated subject and its intellectual, moral, and spiritual content) certain verbal patterns (rhythm, diction, figures) whose function it was to heighten (by way of aesthetic effects) his readers' pleasure in and understanding of what his material meant (what he intended it to signify). In this (classicizing) poetics, a poem's manner was thought of as being, essentially, ancillary to its matter, it was a means to an end, it was by way of being a baited hook, or, to borrow a figure from one of Cicero's most powerful poetic competitors (Lucretius, who was also not one of the new poets), it was the honey smeared on the rim of a medicinal cup. This is hardly to say that Cicero had no aesthetic sense, that he did not enjoy poetry (almost, perhaps, as much as he enjoyed composing and performing the prosaic cola that graced and steeled his highly original, his incomparable orations). But in writing his verse (unlike his prose) he did not, so far as we can tell, concern himself with the interdependence of his matter and his manner, he did not seek to invent new stylistic modes which could evoke or represent new feelings, new ideas, new modes of being.

Something is going on in the longer poems of Catullus (61 through 68), a host of new feelings in search of new forms, that is not going on in what is left to us of Cicero's poetry, where what is being said is framed with and overlaid by a venerable, if freshly refurbished, way of saying it. Catullus (and presumably those of his contemporaries who shared something of his stylistic proclivities) does not content himself with remodeling and updating Ennian language and Ennian versification; he totally transforms that Ennian tradition by subjecting it to the pressures, newly rediscovered, made newly fashionable, of Alexandrian, or, more specifically, of Callimachean, passion for stylistic experimentation and stylistic innovation.

That Alexandrian need for stylistic transformation, like the Catullan need which is in large measure derived from it, came about (again, much like the Catullan revolt from Ennian poetic authority and its Ciceronian reflection) because of the world Callimachus lived in and wrote for (I here take the liberty of allowing Callimachus to represent the central features of the poetry written in the era we call Alexandrian). Callimachus, master librarian, the guardian and disciplined connoisseur of archaic and classical Greek literature, could not fail to be specially impressed by the fact that the language and the spirit of Homer no less than the language and spirit of Sophocles were radically – and in some ways painfully – different from the language and spirit of the world he was born into and lived and worked and wrote in. His own time was, to be sure, vital, was sufficiently varied and fascinating enough to engender poetry plentifully, but he and his contemporaries could hardly be unaware that, though they clearly knew more – about almost everything – than Homer or Sophocles knew or could have known, they felt less, or rather felt big things more feebly, than had the poets of those heroic ages (but small, ephemeral, ordinary, trivial things they felt exquisitely): grandeur, in short, had somehow leaked out of existence as Callimachus and his contemporaries and their successors experienced it. The boundaries of Greek culture had expanded immensely since the heroic eras, but the Greek psyche had somehow shrunk (they had, the Alexandrians, no Achilles or Odysseus, they had no Oedipus or Electra).

This contradiction attracted their interest and produced in them the habit of a sort of squinting irony. They saw themselves diminished; they turned from epic panoramas and tragic meditations to small embroideries and comic parodies. They had catalogued all the books and had read most of them, and their own usually shorter books became rich and crowded with delicate allusions to vanished grandeurs (nor could their well-tempered irony sometimes refrain from wondering how real that fabled grandeur had been – they were, after all, becoming adept at textual criticism, historical research, and literary theory). They could not compete with their adored predecessors and "the large-mannered motions of their mythy minds" (Wallace Stevens, "Sunday Morning"), but, in addition to repairing the disarray into which the texts of the old poems had fallen, they could correct some of their stylistic and metrical crudities, and, adding to the tradition something of their own, they could cherish elegance and promote it zealously. If style could not exist to serve Eternal Truth, it could serve itself: there could be a poetics of style for style's sake. The word that gathers all this tumult of artistic anxiety and resilience and ambition into a program and a creed is *leptos*, which, according to the 1994 Liddell and Scott *Abridged Greek-English Lexicon*, means (1) peeled, cleaned of the husks; (2) thin, fine, slender, delicate; (3) thin, lean, meager; (4) strait, narrow; (5) slight, small, insignificant; (6) fine, subtle, refined, ingenious. If we compress all these connotations into a single thought, we have some grasp of the complexity of what Callimachus and his Alexandrians felt about their place in the Greek poetic tradition, and we also have the core of the poetics that they constructed for themselves. As so often occurs in the history of culture (think here of what Nietzsche does with "good and bad" in his *The Genealogy of Morals*), what was strength is now weakness and what was weakness is now strength. And what was a vice becomes a virtue.

Bred from this stylistic transvaluation of the norms and practice of classical, heroic styles, there arose a rejection of the moral and civic ideals that had, in different ways and in different eras, underwritten those styles. This rejection, this cluster of rejections, manifested itself in two ways, the one, so to speak, negative, the other, positive. The negative reaction was against the kinds of actions and people that Homer and Sophocles were interested in imagining and also against the values and ideas, the hopes and fears, that prompted those imaginings and sustained them. In reacting against Homeric and Sophoclean matter, the Alexandrian poet-librarian and the poets who in various ways were influenced by his artistic creed, by his stylistic and moral innovations, found themselves mocking the old, unattainable grandeurs, perhaps in exact proportion as they envied those grandeurs, cherished them, subverted them, and, in a way, preserved them by mutating them. This process of trivializing the antique splendors they could not hope to recover was constantly accompanied by a reverence of whose ironies these modernizers were never forgetful. Every time they echoed a phrase or a line they had filched from the Past, every time they parodied (seriously or not) an iconic hero or a grand type-scene or a simile, dazzling in its archaic perfection, every time they smiled wittily at a solemn moment in the old poetry where brave truths and larger-than-life confrontations with elemental adversaries of the human spirit met with thrilling, incomparable representation, they recognized and, in their tone and their gestures, they admitted that they and the present they were writing in were somehow dwarfed by the powerful tradition they were busily looting, dissecting, ironizing, and, inevitably, helping to propagate.

These poets tend to dislike what they regard as the oversized. "A big book is a big bore," states the essence of Callimachean poetics as well as it can be stated. He and his like-minded contemporaries and their descendants did not despise epic poems; they liked reading epics (mostly Homer's) and commenting on them and improving the texts in which they read them. But they did object to writing them or to being showered with requests to write long heroic poems that they knew could no longer be written well. They did not object to the heroic figures of the great tradition, but they had no interest in attempting to clothe modern men in heroic costume because they had learned, in their libraries, too much about how myth and history are fabricated to be tempted into participating in that enterprise. So they wrote short poems (of varying lengths, of various sorts), ones whose language could be polished and trimmed with a joyous severity that even a Flaubert might envy. And in those shorter poems, if some sort of hero was necessary, they reinvented the old heroes or rather they sketched cartoons of them (a strategy that Lyne 1978b: 182–3 defines as

"Callimachean narrative alternatives") and made them enact some curtailed segment snatched from their entire careers, some snippet from their total repertoire of man-liness (e.g., the Theseus in Callimachus' *Hecale* or the Heracles of Theocritus' *Hylas*). In these stories, whether the tone is semi-serious or outright burlesque, the hero sometimes dwindles to almost a bit player, and the heroic ideal is subjected to wry scrutiny both in order to emphasize the fissures in the worldview the hero represents and in order to cast a flash of ironic light on the flaws and illusions of the modern world in which a Heracles or an Achilles or a Jason is distinctly out of place.

So much for this parodic mode whose initial purpose is to demonstrate the utter pastness of the irretrievable past in order to illumine and define what might otherwise seem the poverty of modern poetry and the shrunken boundaries and failing energies of the world in which these modern poets and their readers endeavor to pursue the poetic enterprise. But Callimachus is not ashamed of not being, of not being able to be, Homer. It was his destiny to live in the debris of the post-classical world, and he made marvels of the orts and shards his Muses had hoarded for him in the library where he lived his real life. He redefined, if he did not in fact invent, the idea of *leptos*, and he put the craft back in craftsmanship. He (and his kind) remade the meaning of poetry by acknowledging the end of heroism and of the heroic styles that expressed it by inventing counter-ideals and the counter-styles that they required.

If Callimachus invents a new idea of the poet (an elitist, disdainful of the vulgar throng, a skeptical, perfectionist dandy), it is – so far as we can tell from the fragments of Alexandrian poetry – his heirs who discover what amounts to a new clustering of materials. In dismissing the classical hero and the legends out of which he was fabricated, what kind of people, what kind of stories were there left to write about? One solution to this problem, as we've just seen, is on view in the single Hellenistic epic that is extant: Apollonius Rhodius' *The Voyage of the Argonauts*. In this poem (which by the Homeric standard is considerably truncated, thereby meeting the Callimachean requirement for brevity), the adventures of the poem's heroic protag-onist, Jason, are all but reduced to a framing device for what seems to most interest the poet (and his intended readers) about this hero and his exploits: namely, how Medea, virgin princess and witch, struggles vainly against her sudden and over-whelming passion for Jason, how she comes to decide to help him steal the golden fleece, thus betraying her father and her country and choosing Love over Patriotism. Poets had written of the power of Eros before Apollonius, but in this god's archaic and classical avatars his assault on human beings was violent but mostly brief, a sudden fit of insanity that vanished as quickly as it had come – in any case, something one wanted desperately to avoid or to be liberated from as soon as possible. It was not something that easily permitted detailed representation (though Apollonius' best model, Euripides, had managed to do it splendidly in his portrait of Phaedra in the *Hippolytus* and, as Aristophanes tells us, elsewhere) because this dreadful madness extended beyond reason's reach and reason's vocabulary. It needed, then, no descrip-tion (if that were possible), it needed only, at all costs, to be shunned. Whatever it was, it was not (as would be the case with Medea and the lovers who took their descent from her) something that one was willing to sacrifice everything (life itself) to gain. It was not something, a rapture, a torrent, that dissolved the lover's identity and permanently transformed her (or him, but it was usually a her) into something new, something rich and strange.

This fascination with erotic tribulation – overwhelming and possibly fatal passion viewed not from the passion's outside but from inside it, from its very core – becomes, increasingly, a frequent theme in Hellenistic poetry. It is brilliantly imagined in Theocritus' portraits of Simaetha (*Id.* 2) and Polyphemos (*Id.* 11) as desperate lovers and superbly glimpsed at the end of *Idyll* 13 where a love-crazed Heracles searches for his vanished Hylas. But it reaches what is perhaps its most fully realized potential (until Catullus gets hold of it) in the closing moments of Bion's *Lament for Adonis* where Aphrodite, the love goddess herself, attempts vainly to put her grief for the death of her beloved into words. What is going on here has been described as the operation of a new sentimentality, and that patronizing nod to the poem's peculiar strength points the poem's readers in the right direction. But the perspective on erotic obsession that is responsible for this poem's imaginative force and the depth of its feeling is not sentimental; rather, it is haunted – by a realization that the power of Eros is as far beyond comprehension (and hence, verbalization) as it is, for this representation of Aphrodite, beyond remedy. A Homeric Aphrodite would grieve for her Adonis magnificently perhaps, but she would then gather herself together and speed off on the hunt for a new favorite, another boy toy. This Aphrodite is both frozen in her limitless sorrow and consumed by the purity and intensity of the erotic fulfillment that assured its inescapable permanence.

In a well-ordered society, one in which the person's familial and civic duties define his identity and help shield it from irrational impulses and dangerous temptations that might otherwise overwhelm it, this kind of poetry is a diversion merely, a minatory entertainment, a cautionary tale whose representations of alien and risky delights can be safely, vicariously tasted. But when the social fabric endures unusual strain, when politics have turned turbulent and individuals feel their lives disordered by that strain and that turbulence, tales of erotic distress take on a different shade, assume a different function. When Parthenius of Nicaea arrived in Rome – the exact date of his arrival is the subject of debate – he did not find himself in a city uncorrupted by high Greek culture or entirely innocent of Hellenistic poetry, its charms, its seductive (and un-Roman) inducements to unnecessary leisure and relaxation. Roman poets had long since had some acquaintance with Hellenistic poetry and, more recently, they had encountered the work of Meleager, another purveyor of the "new sentimentality" that espoused the truth of true love and privileged passion over duty; but they did not, apparently, know all there was to know about the poetic possibilities afforded by stories that centered on truly neurotic erotic entanglements. Stowed away in his luggage when he came to Rome, Parthenius brought the materials (the poems of Euphorion among them) that he would eventually publish as the *Erotika Pathemata*, a volume he would dedicate to the elegiac poet Gallus. But even before he offered the volume to Gallus (sometime in the 40s BC), he had, it seems, exercised some influence (in the late 60s and the 50s) on the young (new) poets who were looking for new subjects to write about and new styles with which to represent them. In addition to nourishing their regard for Alexandrian poetics, he shared with them his own fascination with legends of ruinous and ruined love.

The only extant examples of this new perspective on eros (new, that is, to Rome) are to be found in some of Catullus' longer poems (to which we will presently turn), but this pervasive erotic mentality shaped the focus of several other works that are now lost to us: Cornificius' *Glaucus* (which was probably about his hero's love for Scylla); Cinna's *Zmyrna* (about her incestuous love for her father); Calvus' *Io* (about her sufferings after she had encountered an amorous Zeus?); a later imitation of neoteric matter and manner, the *Ciris* (about Scylla's betrayal of her father and her country for King Minos, with whom she had become infatuated); and, not of least importance, Varro Atacinus' rendering of Apollonius and his Medea.

What links most of these stories together and gestures toward the attraction they held for the new poets is the power of transgressive love (the escape it offers from tradition, from, Romanly speaking, the implacable demands for total submission to the code and the culture of Duty). Nor did the new poets fail to grasp the capacity of that transgressive love to institute transformations (some of them good, some of them not good), to confer new identities, new ways of being in the world. In the poems of Cinna and of the epigonic writer of the *Ciris*, their amorous heroines, Zmyrna and Scylla respectively, are, like Medea and like the Ariadne of Catullus 64, guilty of a love that compels them to transgress against their fathers' authority. All four of these princesses become fugitives from their societies, and each of them finds herself, having given "all for love," taking on a new and problematic identity. In the cases of Zmyrna, Scylla, and Ariadne, their isolation and their abjection end in radical transformations, glorious (Ariadne becomes a goddess, Myrrha becomes a fragrant tree much used in religious rituals) or dismal (Scylla becomes an immortal sea monster). Though she undergoes no bodily transformation, Apollonius' Medea (and doubtless Varro's), after having shed her girlish innocence, develops a new – and perhaps immortal? – identity of sorts: changed into something at once less and more than human. (This complex transformation, from loving maiden to monstrous witch, will later be elegantly represented by Ovid, who offers his own version of all these heroines – though he gives short shrift to Ariadne [*Met.* 8.172–9].) The stories of Io and Glaucus (to complete this survey of the neoteric preference for Alexandrian "alternative narratives" over heroic legends) differ from the ones we've just glanced at in that they do not make use of the theme of transgression. Both of them, however, are informed by erotic suffering that issues in transformations – in both cases the protagonists become divine beings (she becomes Isis, he a sea god). When Catullus takes up this material (this version of eros and the values and the worldviews that nourish it), he tends to fuse transgression and transformation, but he is invariably concerned with some shift in identity, the place and moment in which a new experience with eros, a new awareness of sexual power, brings with it a new sense of selfhood.

This constant theme in Catullus' own poetry manifests itself strikingly in the Callimachean text for which he decided to provide a Latin rendition, *The Lock of Berenice*. Newly wed to King Ptolemy when he went off to war, his anxious bride had vowed a lock of her hair to the gods in hopes they would grant him a safe return. It is the lock of hair that speaks of its desolation and its sense of having been unselved from Berenice when it was translated into the heavens, but that transformation and the sense of privation the lock feels and tries to express seem to mirror the feelings of Berenice when she felt, despairingly, bereft of her bridegroom: she was not so much, at the time of his departure, a wife, but a bride – no longer a virgin – and a bride in danger of becoming a widow, a fearfully divided consciousness, a psyche that finds itself held in a bewildering zone between its vanished past and its clouded future. This liminal mood, this growing sense of the mind's crossing an unfamiliar threshold and entering into an unknown mode of being, gives shape to the terrifying poem about Attis (63), to the central panel of the poem about the wedding of Peleus and Thetis which depicts Ariadne on Naxos (64), and to the strange complexities that mark the long elegy (68) about the poet's own psychic confusions – whether fact, fictions, or a mixture of the two – over several separations he is suffering: his brother's death, his unexplained absence from Rome where his poetic life (and self) flourishes, his gnawing uncertainty about his place in the affections of the radiant woman who has apparently changed his life.

Having emasculated himself to become a priest of Cybele, the speaker of the Attis poem rushes into the forest that surrounds her temple, then, having joined with other devotees in celebration of their goddess, he/she falls into a deep sleep and wakens, with horror, to find what he has done and what and who he has become. Apparently he had been a typical young Greek male (athletic, admired, and courted), but he had somehow become involved in the worship of Cybele and had chosen to become one of her priests, a decision he now regrets when he confronts what he has done to himself. The frame of the poem (beginning with his self-emasculation and ending with his being pursued by the goddess, angered by his remorse) is frightening enough, but the center of the poem, his terrified and angry recognition of the ruined selfhood that he has brought upon himself, chills the bone. He describes himself not just as a Maenad but as *ego mei pars, ego uir sterilis*, "I only a part of myself, I, a sterile male" (63.69). These phrases, and the sense of alienation and abjection that they introduce as the speaker realizes that he will spend the rest of his life in a place far distant from his homeland as a crazed creature he cannot understand and cannot accept being, are as far from the kind of poetry that Cicero and his admirers would want as can be imagined: the poem, with its strange, sinister, "oriental" music and its subtle, unflinching contemplation of rejected manhood, is the antithesis of the model for masculine identity in Rome. But it represents an ideal subject and an ideal treatment of that subject for Catullus' neoteric project: it reaches far down into what we might want to call the Roman national subconscious during the frenzied decades when Catullus and his kind were at work. What it finds there, and represents with maximum attention to a delicate artistry appropriate to it, is a blurred and threatened sense of identity.

The world these young men had been educated for, the careers and lives their fathers had promised them, were more than in doubt as the Roman oligarchs busily tried to ruin each other and succeeded, soon after Catullus was dead, only in ruining themselves and wrecking Rome. The Rome in which Clodius and Cicero and their respective partisans occupied themselves in their fatal feud had no need of more ideological fanatics; it needed, its good poets needed, a different set of preoccupations. They settled on investigating styles of interiority that would have baffled their grandfathers and doubtless caused their fathers many sleepless nights. They opted for mannered erudition and Alexandrian gestures, they learned the argot suitable to a *jeunesse dorée*. They began to imagine the feelings of Myrrha and Io and Scylla and Glaucus, of creatures who were ejected, like them, from the worlds they had been born into, and, who were, like them, between selves, unselved, reselved.

What Catullus imagined, in addition to Attis, was what it was like to be Ariadne when she was abandoned by Theseus on Naxos. Ariadne, in poem 64, is the central image on the tapestry that will cover the wedding couch of Peleus and his goddess-bride. She is flanked on one side by the magnificent preparations for the wedding and on the other by the sumptuous finale that takes the form of an epithalamium announcing the coming birth of Achilles, greatest of the Greek heroes. The figure of Ariadne, then, is framed by forceful memories of the heroic world, but she herself, caddishly deserted by the hero Theseus, belongs to and speaks like one of the lost ladies who are the hallmark of Alexandrian-neoteric poetics. Towards the end of the section that depicts her comes a brief intimation (251–64) of the off-stage moment when she will be rescued by Bacchus and transformed into his goddess-bride, but what the poem focuses on is her abjection and anxiety, her abandonment, and her despair. Those emotions, mirrored in the pessimism and anger of a brief and bitter coda, the epilogue with its sudden glance at the horror of contemporary times, are the poem's core.

And, in his long elegy (68), Catullus depicts himself, or a poet perhaps not unlike himself, in the grip of conflicting and confused emotions. This poem seems to have no core, or to have several cores that are constantly in motion, shifting about, clashing, reverberating, fading. But something like a core, in any case a major thematic marker, is the figure of Laodamia, like Berenice another anxious bride, but less lucky than she, worried that her husband, Protesilaus, will not return from the war at Troy. Coming to her wedding, she set her foot on the threshold of her husband's house, just as the poet's faithless mistress (faithless to him, faithless to her husband) had memorably crossed the threshold of the house that a friend had lent them where they could consummate their adultery (so the bride in the poet's first wedding-song also crosses her bridegroom's threshold [61.159–61], but timorously, fearful of this transition, this step into maturity and mortality). The poet thinks of Laodamia and her despair, fixates on it, because her husband's death at Troy reminds him of his brother's death there. He and Laodamia have these deaths in common, but Laodamia, who is also linked to the poet's *femme fatale*, was, unlike her, a doting and faithful wife. It is the poet who is finally like Laodamia because another grief he shares with her, after his brother's death, is the grief he feels as he contemplates the likelihood of losing the heartless creature he adores. It is hard – or perhaps it isn't – to imagine Cicero trying to read this poem, with its tangled self-absorption, its swirling moods, its determination to eschew any trace of public virtue and to plumb the depths of interiority.

The neoteric fascination with an eros unsanctified by Roman family values and the traditional Voice of the Paterfamilas is powerfully exemplified by Catullus not only in the narratives we've looked at but also in the shorter poems that flank them, those poems where his – or his speaker's – passions for Lesbia and Juventius communicate the pervasive rejection of old Rome and its poetry that most exactly characterizes his poetic productions (and very probably those of the poets contemporary with him, whom, for want of a better term, we call neoteric). But the poetics of this generation of poets did not die out with them. The Alexandrian sensibility they inherited and then naturalized in Roman verse continued its evolution, splendidly, in the next generation with the work of Gallus and the elegists, Propertius and Tibullus, who quickly followed where he led; and it lingers, hauntingly, in the endless variations that Ovid manages to coax from it in his *Metamorphoses*, that massive, tender, and ironic "epic" where "alternative narratives" and exquisite artistry of the Callimachean kind take possession of heroic matter and manner, fuse with them strangely, and demolish them. But it finds what may be its culmination, its incomparable perfection, in its most famous and influential incarnation – the figure of Dido.

She brings with her, in what quickly came to be regarded as Rome's national epic, all the ungovernable erotic passion and all the scorn of propriety and of duty that the epic genre (by its very nature) and Roman epic (in particular) seek to minimize or to exclude (recall Helen's attempt to spurn Aphrodite, and remember how easily Calypso's desires are terminated). Different though he was in the scope of his ambitions from the new poets who went before him, Vergil was, from his first work until his last, steadily inspired by the example of Catullus and his contemporaries. His vision was larger than theirs had been (or could have been), his materials were endlessly more complex, but his achievement is unthinkable without theirs.

Although Catullus and his kind had not despised Homer or Ennius, they, like their Alexandrian masters before them, had found the great epic tradition unsuitable to the zeitgeist that in part they were born into and in part they – disaffected, bewildered, bored, a truly lost generation – helped to widen and enrich. They devised for themselves and for their audiences a smaller scale of feelings and thinking, a narrower horizon of hope, a further turning inward, away from civic failure and public catastrophe – inward, to a private world of immense, exciting emotions and of extraordinary pleasures (and pains), to a place of fantasy that had nothing to do with what duty demanded and everything to do with a pure concentration on the individual psyche and what it feared and desired. What they lacked in traditional sweep and grandeur and patriotism they more than made up for with their interest in experimenting with new genres, with their efforts to master new styles and new meters as well as new emotions. Yet this expansiveness was held in check by the demand for elegance: the neoterics were zealous in their search for artistic precision, for the restraint and constant revision (recall, again, those nine years it took Cinna for his short counter-epic) that an obsession with craftsmanship imposed on the production of their poems. Linked with this exact artistry was a habit of irony, for in constructing his alternative narratives and small counter-epics, as he sifted through various disparate versions of a given myth, the neoteric poet learned that the truths he was after were, more often than not, as elusive as they were fractional.

When Horace and Vergil came on the scene (but not Propertius, who was more truly loyal to his neoteric fathers) they kept the passion for craftsmanship, and they did not abandon the irony. But times had changed. The craftsmanship had become almost subordinate to, no longer quite equal with, the larger and more complicated materials it was now framing and embellishing, and the irony was tempered by a steadier reverence for Rome's past (poetic and political) and by a habit of hope (or wishful thinking) for its cultural and political future. What the new poets had discovered about style, carefully integrated with classical modes, was transferred by Vergil and Horace into what would end by being a genuinely Augustan poetry. What they invented, as Roman equivalents to Alexandrian small stories about unheroic lives, seemed to disappear into the more spacious canvases that Vergil and Horace decided to work with. But as Horace's versions of Pindar mostly border on something like counter-epinician, so Vergil's version of Homer (and Ennius) is, because Dido is so central to his total pattern, heavily tinged with the spirit of the new poets, with not a little of their distrust of the heroic and with much of their disenchantment with the Roman Way. The elaborate, exquisite, and luminous manner by means of which she is represented derives in large measure from the manner that Catullus had devised to represent his Ariadne. But the figure of Dido, doomed queen who is willing to risk her realm and her life for a supreme happiness that cheats her of itself, has its origin not only in Ariadne but also in Attis. Like all of these, Dido's story is fed by a vision of a profound, transmuting love that alters the consciousness of the individual it fastens upon (whether happily or unhappily does not matter). What only matters is that Dido (the consummate lover still, though Emma Bovary and Anna Karenina, Werther and Humbert Humbert give her a run for her money) becomes larger than herself, larger than the life (and the city) that had tried to contain her. She has made herself meaningful in a world that seemed to her drained of all meaning by virtue of her limitless passion, which is paradoxically at once creative and destructive, salvific and ruinous. Her style and her substance are both of them indebted to Catullus and his coevals: that fusion of manner and matter was the gift of the neoterics to world literature.

GUIDE TO FURTHER READING

Courtney's (1993) skepticism about the name and nature of neoteric poetry is shared by Crowther in his brief, impressive article (1970). The older tradition about "the new poets" is clearly stated in Wheeler (1934) and Mendell (1962). Lyne supplements his persuasive article (1978b) with his edition of the *Ciris* (1978a). Other useful views on various aspects of neoteric poetics are to be found in Traglia (1962), Wiseman (1974), Ross (1969), Krostenko (2001a), and Wray (2001). For Cicero, see Ewbank (1933). For the Alexandrians, in addition to Crump (1931), see Clausen (1964), Cameron (1995), and Lightfoot (1999).

WORKS CITED

Cameron, A. 1995. *Callimachus and His Critics*. Princeton, NJ.

Cioran, E. M. 1998. *The Temptation to Exist*. Trans. R. Howard. Chicago.

Clausen, W. V. 1964. "Callimachus and Latin Poetry." *Greek, Roman, and Byzantine Studies* 5: 181–96.

Courtney, E., ed. 1993. *The Fragmentary Latin Poets*. Oxford.

Crowther, N. B. 1970. "OI NEωTEPOI, Poetae Novi, and Cantores Euphorionis." *Classical Quarterly* 20: 322–7.

Crump, M. M. 1931. *The Epyllion from Theocritus to Ovid*. Oxford.

Ewbank, W. W. 1933. *The Poems of Cicero*. London.

Krostenko, B. A. 2001a. *Cicero, Catullus, and the Language of Social Performance*. Chicago and London.

Lightfoot, J. L. 1999. *Parthenius of Nicaea*. Oxford.

Lyne, R. O. A. M., ed. 1978a. *Ciris: A Poem Attributed to Vergil*. Cambridge.

Lyne, R. O. A. M. 1978b. "The Neoteric Poets." *Classical Quarterly* 28: 167–87.

Mendell, C. W. 1962. *Latin Poetry: The New Poetry and the Augustans*. New Haven, CT.

Ross, D. O., Jr. 1969. *Style and Tradition in Catullus*. Cambridge, MA.

Traglia, A., ed. 1962. *I Poeti Nuovi*. Rome.

Warner, R., trans. 1972. *Plutarch: Fall of the Roman Republic*. London.

Wheeler, A. L. 1934. *Catullus and the Traditions of Ancient Poetry.* Berkeley and Los Angeles.

Wiseman, T. P. 1974. *Cinna the Poet and Other Roman Essays*. Leicester.

Wray, D. 2001. *Catullus and the Poetics of Roman Manhood*. Cambridge.

CHAPTER ELEVEN

Elements of Style in Catullus

George A. Sheets

The Catullan corpus encompasses a great variety of poetic compositions: epigrams, lampoons, "occasional" poems, hymns, dramatic dialogues, an "epyllion," translations, verse-letters, and at least one poem (63) that defies classification under any conventional rubric. The meters too are very diverse: hexameters and elegiacs, various iambic periods, the rare galliambic and priapean periods, Aeolic measures in both strophic and stichic schemes, and the distinctively Hellenistic "book" lyric that the poet calls his "hendecasyllables." This variety and formal virtuosity are qualities that the "new" poetry of the late Republic owed to Hellenistic Greek influence. One of the most salient characteristics of the latter was the breakdown of traditional correlations between style and genre. As the genres became more artificial, they all tended to become more alike in their eclecticism (Kroll 1924: 202–24). Nevertheless, formal differences did remain, and indeed proliferated, once genre itself became just another color among the available choices on the poet's stylistic pallet. This is particularly evident in the poetry of Catullus, in which many of the same stylistic artifices are found across the collection, but often in greatly different concentrations and put to very different effects. Similar themes are handled in diverse forms, and identical forms are deployed to the exposition of widely dissimilar themes. Individual poems range in length from 2 to over 400 lines, and together they cover many different subjects – love, friendship, betrayal, literature, politics, travel, personal triumphs and defeats, and death. The tonal range is equally broad: playful, contemptuous, celebratory, intimate, bitter, resigned, introspective, vulnerable, aloof. In most poems the authorial presence is emphatically foregrounded; in some it is minimized or suppressed entirely. A similar variety exists with respect to the presence, prominence, and ostensible familiarity of explicit addressees. Likewise the knowledge and attitudes imputed to a "preferred" reader or listener, in effect the audience constructed by the poetry, change from one poem to another and among groups of poems. In sum, the single most characteristic aspect of Catullan "style" is its protean character.

It should be noted at the outset that examples of stylistic features to be discussed in this chapter do not always fit into discrete categories. Our consideration of diction, for example, will begin with archaisms; yet a particular archaic usage may be conventional in the Latin poetic register as Catullus found it, in which case it could be considered as much "literary" as "archaic." Rhythm will be discussed in connection with meter, yet rhythm is constituted by factors that include alliteration, assonance, anaphora, rhyming, etc., all of which are figures of speech. Moreover certain rhythmic effects are traditionally associated with an archaic style of poetry and prayer. Thus rhythm too can be an archaism. Vernacular usage, Grecism, and diminutives will all be treated as separate categories of diction, yet there is considerable overlap among these three categories and between them and archaism. It follows that the stylistic categories used in this chapter are not mutually exclusive.

Diction

It is well known that the Roman literary tradition came into being in response to, and as an ongoing appropriation of, the highly evolved conventions of Hellenic literature. The starting point was a native tradition of stylized language associated with the *concepta verba* of Italic religious traditions and Roman law (Conte 1994: 15–23; Palmer 1954: 95–109). The synthesis of these native and borrowed traditions quickly developed into something approaching a normative style of elevated poetry in Latin. In the late Republic the Latin poetic register remained strongly tied to Roman literary models of the past, especially the epic poetry and tragedy of the second century BC. An enduring characteristic of this style was the use of archaic and traditionally poetic diction. Catullus, despite his critical attitude toward old-fashioned poetry (*Annales Volusi, cacata charta*, 36.1), selectively borrows from this traditional register. At the same time Catullan diction evinces numerous characteristics that are alien to the tradition of elevated Latin poetry. Particularly in the polymetrics, but not only there, Catullus uses a vernacular idiom studded with vulgarisms, neologisms, and argots.

Archaism

The term "archaism" in this chapter refers to any formal, lexical, or syntactic feature that appears to be obsolete or obsolescent in general usage when Catullus was writing. Archaic language was commonly found in Roman religious, legal, and other socially privileged texts, including the tradition of elevated literature. When found elsewhere, it presumably tended to evoke these traditional associations. In principle the effect might be one of grandeur, solemnity, and distance from everyday life or, if the usage were parodic, of pomposity, irony, fustiness, or ridicule. Occasionally, however, an archaic feature in verse will have been motivated by little more than metrical utility. Dactylic verse, for example, does not admit a cretic ($-\smile-$) and therefore cannot accommodate words that contain that sequence of syllabic quantities. This constraint will have been a factor in Catullus' use of the morphologically archaic *custōdībant* (64.319), *scībant* (68.85), and *audībant* (84.8), for classical *custōdiēbant*, etc. The same factor can account for the archaic consonant stem ending

in the adjective *Veronensum* (genitive plural, 100.2) and the substantive *caelestum*
(64.191). In the participle *sonantum* (34.12), however, the unconventional formant
is presumably a stylistic choice, since the pherecratean verse does admit a cretic.
Moreover, even when metrically motivated, such morphological oddities will have
imparted to dactylic verse a traditional color.

   Archaic diction takes various forms. Phonological archaisms are the least capable of
proof because of orthographic uncertainties in the textual tradition. For example, the
archaism *tuos* for *tuus* at 63.92 (*tuo V*) is Ellis's conjecture, accepted by Mynors,
Fordyce, and Quinn. The archaic spelling of *adolescens* (63.63) is the reading in *V*, but
Thomson (1997: 149) emends to the classical *adulescens*. Other archaic spellings in *V*
are the ablative *aureis* (46.3) for *auris* and *ni* for *ne* (61.146) to introduce a final
clause, on the accuracy of which editors again disagree. Editorial disagreement is less
likely where the phonological feature affects a syllabic quantity or the number of
syllables in a word, as in *veluti* (63.33) and *uti* (116.2) for *velut* and *ut*. The long
ultima in *tibī* (51.13), trisyllabic *sŏlŭit* (2b.3), and tetrasyllabic *pervŏlŭent* (95.96) are
all examples of archaic phonology (Coleman 1999: 35), as is the lenition of post-
vocalic /s/ at word-end, reflected in the meter by its failure to "make position":
dăbĭs supplicium (116.8).

   Morphological archaisms are generally easier to confirm, and Catullus makes
frequent use of them. The sigmatic perfect stem representing an old "aorist" subjunctive and optative respectively in *recepso* (44.19) and *ausit* (61.65) are archaic
(Heusch 1954: 117–19). Lachmann's widely accepted conjecture *siris* (66.91), a
word commonly found in early prayer, would be another example of the same
formation (Fordyce 1961: 340). The present stem in *senet* (4.26) for *senescit*, the
perfect stem in *tetulit* (63.47) for *tulit*, and the original perfect stem of *deposīvit*
(34.8) for *deposuit* are all archaic; so too the short root-vowel perfect stem in *iŭverint*
(61.18), although the latter is necessitated by the dactylic meter. Other morphological archaisms include adverbs in -*iter* derived from o-stems: *puriter* (39.14,
76.19) and *miseriter* (63.49), the inherited genitive plural formant in *deum*
(63.68), *divum* (64.134), and *Hiberum* (9.6), the present passive infinitive formant
in *citarier* (61.42), *compararier* (three times, all occurring in a refrain of poem 61 at
lines 65, 70, and 75), *nitier* (61.68), and *componier* (68.141), the non-apocopated
imperative *face* (36.16), the feminine plural pronoun *haec* (64.320), nominative *labos*
(55.13) for *labor*, the thematic conjugation of *lavit* (39.14) for *lavat*, the consonant
stem *grates* (44.16) for *gratias*, the mock-legal "future" imperative *moveto* (15.11)
for *move*, etc.

   Lexical archaisms include both old words and traditionally "poetic" usages of still
current words. Examples of the former include: *caelitum* and *caelites* (11.14, 61.49,
61.190), *autumant* (44.2), *prognatae* (64.1), *consanguineae* (64.118), *Mavors*
(64.394), *senecta* (64.217), *auctet* (67.2), *postilla* (84.9), and *simplex* verbs that by
the late Republic had been replaced in common usage with compounds: e.g., *apisci*
(64.145) for *adipisci*, *crevi* in the sense of "decide" (64.150) for *decrevi*, *dicet*
(64.227) for *indicet* (additional examples at Heusch 1954: 66–8). Traditional
"poetic" usages of words that are not archaic *per se* include: *pubis/pubes* (64.4,
64.267) in the sense of "men in their prime," *freta* (4.18) and *aequor* (in various
cases at 4.17, 11.8, 64.7, 64.12, 64.17, 66.20, 68.3, 101.1) to mean "sea," *puppi/
puppes* (64.6, 64.172) as a metonymy for "ship(s)," *vada salsa* (64.6) to mean the

"sea," *tempestate* for *tempore* (64.73, 66.11), and *genitor* for *pater* (63.59, 64.27, 64.117, 64.401, 88.6).

Catullus uses words drawn from sacral and legal language. In most cases the original associations are more salient than any "literary" valence that such words might otherwise carry: e.g., *sospites/sospes* (34.24, 64.112), *dapem/dape* (64.79, 64.304), *fata* (64.321) in the sense of "oracular words," and *praefantes* (64.382). Various forms of *sanctus* occur 11 times, but always in the context of worship, prayer, or divinity: 34.22, 36.3, 36.12, 63.24, 64.95, 64.228, 64.268, 64.298, 68.5, 76.3, 109.6. On the other hand, a powerful religious word that seems to have escaped from its original orbit is *sacer* (with its denominative verb *sacrare*), which occurs 10 times in various forms and thematic contexts across the entire corpus: *sacer*, 7.6, 14.12, 17.6, 61.71, 63.24, 64.388, 68.75, 71.1; *sacrare*, 55.5, 102.3. Legal words, particularly those charged with ethical implications, are another staple of Catullan vocabulary: *culpa* (11.22 and six other occurrences), *iniuria* (72.7), *fidem* (30.6 and eight other occurrences), *fido* (64.182, 102.1), *foedus* (109.6 and four other occurrences), *violasse* (67.23, 76.3), *iure* (62.16 and four other occurrences).

Another category of traditionally poetic words is comprised of Greek-style compound epithets and substantives borrowed from early Latin epic and tragedy: e.g., *sonipedibus* (63.41), an adjective attested twice in fragments of Accius; *flexanimo* (64.330), found twice in Pacuvius; the Ennian substantive, later reused by Vergil, *caelicolis* (30.4), *caelicolae* (64.386), *caelicolum* (68.138), the last of these also showing the archaic genitive plural formant of the first declension; *horrificans* (64.270), cf. *horrificabili* in Accius, etc. A number of other such compounds are not attested before the generation of Lucretius and Catullus, although their "poetic" status is clear then and thereafter: e.g., *clarisonas, clarisona* (64.125, 64.320), *letifero* (64.394), *raucisonos* (64.263), *unigena* (64.300, 68.53). Still other compound nouns and adjectives appear to be Catullan coinages and are not attested elsewhere: e.g., *lasarpiciferis* (7.4), *sagittiferos* (11.6), *septemgeminus* (11.7), *tardipedi* (36.7), *hederigerae* (63.23), *properipedem* (63.34), *erifugae* (63.51), *nemorivagus* (63.72), *silvicultrix* (63.72), *amplifice* (64.265), *inobservabilis* (64.115), *fluentisono* (64.52); *falsiparens* (68.112), *multivola* (68.128), *omnivoli* (68.140), etc. All of these compounds are confined to the polymetrics and the longer poems. They constitute one of several traits that distinguish these more neoteric compositions from the stylistically less innovatory epigrams (Ross 1969: 17–22).

Archaisms can also take the form of non-normative syntax, although in some instances the usage in question might equally well be considered vernacular rather than archaic, for the two sometimes overlap. For example, Catullus occasionally uses an indicative verb in place of a subjunctive in indirect questions (e.g., 61.77, 62.8, 62.12). He sometimes uses an indicative in causal relative clauses (62.14, 64.157, 68.5, 68.32, 114.2). The preposition *cum* appears in instrumental phrases where the classical norm would call for a simple ablative: *celeri cum classe* (64.53), *ista cum lingua* (98.3–4). As an alternative to classical *potest/possit* Catullus admits the archaic *potis est* (65.3, 72.7, 76.24) and *potis sit* (115.3).

The presence of archaic and traditional diction in the hymns and long narrative poems on mythological subjects (63, 64) is perhaps unsurprising. More interesting is the use of such diction in the iambic and hendecasyllabic poems, where the subjects are ostensibly commonplace and realistic, and the style is generally more vernacular.

Here the effect of archaic diction tends to be ironic or parodic. A typical example is the conspicuously archaic *recepso* (44.19), in place of *recipiam* or *recepero*, which the poet uses in reference to the frigid oratory of his acquaintance Sestius. The word in this context constitutes an ironic reference to the old-fashioned or perhaps over-wrought compositions of Sestius. As noted in the commentaries, the same poem includes the archaic and grandiloquent *autumant* (2), the archaic and solemn *grates* for *gratias* (16), and, if Muretus' conjecture is accepted, an archaic prosody in *ultu'* with dropped final /s/ in verse 17. Although common in early Latin verse, and still present in the poetry of Lucretius, the failure of final /s/ to make position was conspicuously rejected by the neoterics and later poets. We have already seen one secure example in Catullus, however, in poem 116.8 (*dabi' supplicium*), a parting shot directed at Gellius. This valedictory epigram faults Gellius for his lack of appreciation of Catullus' Callimachean compositions (*carmina…Battiadae*). In this context the dropped /s/ has an ironic effect (Coleman 1999: 34): Gellius, who apparently cannot broaden his taste beyond the poetry of the past, will suffer the punishment for this philistinism in his own distinctive way.

A few additional examples of the ironic use of archaism in Catullus can be mentioned, though space will not permit a thorough treatment of this subject. We have seen that the archaic passive infinitive formant in *-ier* is used six times by Catullus, of which five are found in poem 61, a wedding hymn, where such diction is consistent with generic convention. The sixth example is at 68.141, in a ribald context where the word *componier* appears in a moralizing aphorism with tongue clearly in cheek: *atqui nec divis homines componier aequum est*. A similar effect is created by the imperative formant associated with legal language at 15.11, where *moveto* lays down the law in another ribald context. The archaic adverb *puriter* occurs twice in Catullus, once at 39.14 and a second time at 76.19. Both poems contain additional archaisms, but whereas poem 76 is anguished and serious in tone, poem 39 is a humorous epigram. Krostenko (2001b: 246–51) suggests that this and other archaisms in 39 are a device that Catullus uses to characterize an "old man's voice" of reproof.

Finally, it should be noted that even in elevated contexts an archaism might have an ironic shading. Given the neoteric fondness for subtle allusion and polysemy, the use of archaic language can sometimes carry multiple connotations. For example, the verb *sospites* "preserve, defend" in the hymn to Diana (34.24) is an ancient liturgical term with powerfully religious associations (Ernout and Meillet 1967: s.v. *sospes*; Fordyce 1961: 176). Poem 34 is a highly formal composition that contains other archaisms (*deposivit* for *deposuit*; *sonantum* for *sonantium*) and *concepta verba* of traditional sacral language (*sumus in fide*; *sis…sancta*; *bonis frugibus*; *bona…ope*). (Sheets 2001: 14–20). Yet even in so solemn a context there is perhaps the hint of a smile in this reference to the goddess' previous benefactions upon the *gens Romuli*. Adapting a formula traditional in Greek prayer (Fordyce 1961: 175) the poet introduces *sospites* with the clause *antique ut solita es*. Old deeds seem to put a wry gloss on an old word, or vice versa.

Vulgarism

If archaic literary diction represents one end of the stylistic spectrum, at the other end is "vulgar" idiom, meaning vernacular language associated with common people in the eyes of status elites. The vulgar register of Latin is sometimes called the *sermo plebeius*, to distinguish it from the *sermo cottidianus*.[1] The latter term describes the informal register of cultivated speakers, to whatever extent that language differs from idiom otherwise stigmatized as unacceptably coarse. Despite this distinction a well-attested sociolinguistic phenomenon is the appropriation of vulgar idiom into the informal register of status elites. Indeed it appears that language change over time originates "from below" and percolates upward through the mechanism of "style shifting" in high-status groups (Labov 2001: 85).[2] This accounts for the high degree of overlap between attested "vulgar Latin" and reconstructed "proto-Romance."

Vernacular usage was already exploited as an element of style in the earliest Greek personal poetry. Whether taking the form of slang, regional dialectism, or coarse vocabulary on scabrous topics, vernacular usage complemented the interest of personal poetry in describing the poet's realities and expressing private feelings with strong emotion. What Palmer (1980: 106) says of Archilochus, writing in the seventh century BC, applies equally well to Catullus, writing in the first: "The very note of his poetry is individualism, and self-expression with cynical and flippant rejection of heroic ideals, unconcealed surrender to erotic passion, ferocious attacks on enemies and gross obscenity." Vernacular usage was also associated with the literary traditions of comedy and mime. It suited the focus of both these genres on humble figures and the mundane vicissitudes of daily life. Vulgarisms in Catullus are predominantly found in the iambic and hendecasyllabic poems and, to a lesser extent, in the epigrams. The vital, edgy idiom that results from his synthesis of vulgar, polite, and poetic language enhances the illusion of candor. The vernacular component probably also imparted a vaguely subversive or contrarian quality to those compositions which exploit it, since research suggests that socially defined stylistic registers function as expressions of ideologies and manifestations of political values (Irvine 2001: 42–3). A subversive aesthetic would suit the intense subjectivity of Catullan poetry and complement the poet's expressions of affection for friends, anger at rivals and enemies, and lampoons of the socially and politically prominent.

Where elite speech tends to manifest a sense of restraint and conformity to convention, vernaculars typically exploit slang, neologisms, oaths, ellipses, repetition, and various other forms of pleonasm as means of intensifying the affectivity of language (Palmer 1961: 168–73). Catullus makes use of all of these devices, along with other vernacular features like the cliché and the aphorism. For example, in place of the positive degree of adjectives, he frequently uses a redundantly emphatic superlative: *cognitissima* (4.14), *lividissima* (17.11), *insulsissimus* (17.12), *viridissimo* (17.14), *piisimi* (29.23), *electissima pessimi poetae* (36.6), *dissertissime* (49.1), *optimus omnium* (49.7), *lepidissima* (78.1), *pulcerrima* (86.5). Intensifying adverbs are used to the same effect: e.g., *non sane illepidum* (10.4), *longe plurimos* (22.3), *maxime… profunda* (17.11), *mala valde* (69.7). Another intensifying device is morphological expansion by means of prefixes and suffixes that add little or nothing to the semantic content of the underived form: e.g., *comesse* (23.4), *comesset* (29.14) formed upon *comedo* in place of *edo* "eat" (cf. Sp. *comer*), *persaepe* (64.340) for *saepe*, *perluciduli* (69.4) for *lucidi*. Note that the last is doubly marked with the prefix *per-* and the diminutive suffix *-lo-*. Diminutives form an entire class of affective derivatives in Catullus that will be discussed separately below. Here we may note, however, that while diminutives are not vulgar *per se*, the vulgar character of many of them in Latin is independently attested by their descent into the standard vocabulary of Romance languages: e.g., Catullan *oricilla* (25.2)[3] – cf. Italian *orechio*, French *oreille*; *vetuli* (27.1) – cf. Italian *vechio*, French *vieux/vielle*. Catullus sometimes uses vulgar expansions of words for humorous effect. For example, adopting the already colorful verb *futuit* "screw" in his epigrams (71.5, 97.9), in the iambic and hendecasyllabic poems he freely coins derivatives of the same verb to intensify its force: *ecfututa* (6.13), *diffututa* (29.13), *confutuere* (37.5), *defututa* (41.1).

Lexical vulgarisms in Catullus take many forms. One set consists of subliterary words that later emerge in Romance as normative for the concepts they denote: e.g., *basium, bellus, formosus, comparare* with the meaning "to buy" (cf. Spanish *beso, bello, hermoso, comprar*). Another set of vulgar words consists of scurrilous metaphors: e.g., *verpa* "prick," to refer to a person (28.12); *cacata* "shitted," to refer to books (36.1); *scabies* "rash" (47.2) to refer to a person. A third category of vulgar usage is slang: e.g., *beatiorem* meaning "richer" (10.16–17); *uncti* as a metaphor for "wealth" (29.4); *solebant* meaning "used to screw" (113.1–2), and other sexual slang like *tunderetur* "got banged" (59.5); *perdepsuit* "thoroughly kneaded" (74.3); *trusantem* "thumped" (56.6), which is also a morphological vulgarism in the form of the frequentative from *trudo*; etc. (J. N. Adams 1982: 219–21). Foreign words that refer to the common realia of daily life are subliterary and vulgar: e.g., *grabatus* "cot" (10.22) < Greek *krábatos*; *ploxeni* (97.6), perhaps a Celtic word meaning some kind of common cart or part of a cart; *carpatinus* "leather" (98.4) < Greek *karbátinos*. The vulgar, as opposed to simply informal, use of such words is often evident from the context. For example, Catullus uses the Greek word *platea*, ancestor of Italian *piazza*, at 15.7 to refer to the place where would-be seducers go trolling for action. The *crepidas... carpatinas* in poem 98 are some sort of footwear, which are said to be the objects that "stinking Victius" is quite willing to lick, along with "assholes" (*culos*). Finally some words are not vulgar in themselves, but their usage is: e.g., the adverbs *repente* in the sense of "on first impression" (10.3); *bene* in the sense of *multum* (3.7 and *passim*); *male* in the sense of *valde* (10.33 and *passim*); *sane* meaning "to be frank" (10.4, 43.4); the adjective *molestus* (five times in various forms) meaning something like "a pain in the ass."

Vulgar syntactic constructions, including several which descend into Romance, are common in the iambic and hendecasyllabic poems: e.g., *unus caprimulgus* (22.10), where *unus* is the equivalent of an indefinite article;[4] *une de capillatis* (37.17), where *de* is used partitively in place of *ex* or a genitive without preposition;[5] *ad solam dominam usque pipiabat* (3.10), where *ad* anticipates the Romance preposition to introduce an indirect object. The verb *velle* is sometimes used pleonastically with little or no modal force (Loefstedt 1911: 207–9): e.g., *velles dicere nec tacere* (6.3), *dum volo esse conviva* (44.10). The ablative of *mens* modified by an adjective is on its way to becoming the Romance adverbial formant: *obstinata mente* (8.11), *liquidaque mente* (63.46), *constanti mente* (64.209/238), *lymphata mente* (64.254). The nominative personal pronouns *ego* and *tu* are sometimes used pleonastically on their way to becoming mere subject pronouns in Romance: e.g., *ultro ego deferrem* (68.40), *tu, quod promisti, mihi quod mentita inimica es* (110.3) (Hofmann 1926: 100–1 for the phenomenon in general; but see J. N. Adams 1999: 118, arguing that many apparently "unemphatic" uses of these pronouns are motivated by pragmatic factors and are not necessarily "colloquial" in character).

At the discourse level too Catullus incorporates vernacular conventions. He is fond of using stereotyped phrases of the kind familiar in Roman comedy to function as affective particles (Hofmann 1926: 125–34 for the phenomenon in general): *quaeso* (10.25, 103.3), *inquam* (13.6), *amabo* (32.1), *sodes* (103.1), etc. Colloquial oaths are used to similar effect: *Juppiter* (1.7), *me hercule* (38.2), *si placet Dionae* (56.6), *me divi iuverint* (66.18), *ita me di ament* (97.1). Aphorisms are another characteristic of vernacular discourse: *suus cuique attributus est error* and *non videmus manticae quod in tergo est* (22.20–1), *nam risu inepto res ineptior nullast* (39.16), *ipsa olera olla legit* (94.2). Gigante (1978) collects all the examples.

Grecism

Despite a few bold experiments by Ennius, elevated poetry in Latin was traditionally averse to admitting Greek words and morphology. Proper nouns and adjectives and, to a lesser extent, the case-endings attached to both were exceptions. Since Greek toponyms and the names of figures from Greek myth and legend often had no equivalent in Latin, their presence tended to connote an exoticism that reinforced the aesthetic of removal from everyday life. For the neoterics, the rich literary and cultural associations of such words will have added to their appeal. Catullus accordingly uses Greek proper names and case-endings in abundance: e.g., in the long narrative poems (63 and 64) and in poem 66: genitive *Cybeles* (63.12), *Cybebes* (63.20), *Arsinoes* (66.54); accusative *Attin* (63.42), *Thesea* (64.53, 64.239, 64.245), *Minoa* (64.85), *Amphitriten* (64.11), *Pelea* (64.21), *Booten* (66.67); accusative plural *Tempe* (64.287), *Thyiadas* (64.391), *Athon* (66.46); vocative *Theseu* (64.69, 64.133), *Peleu* (64.26). The well-traveled little boat of poem 4 lists among his distant ports of call *Cycladas* (4.7), *Propontida* (4.9), and (using a Greek vocative) *Amastri* (4.13). In poem 11, in which the *comites Catulli* are prepared to accompany Catullus to the ends of the earth, the ethnics *Arabas* (11.5) and *Sagas* (11.6) bear Greek endings. In poem 36, in a mock dedication to Venus that celebrates her cult sites with neoteric *doctrina*, two of the places appear with Greek endings: *Ancona* (36.13) and *Amathunta* (36.14). A learned and highly allusive mythological excursus within the story of Laodamia refers to Hercules by means of the Greek patronymic *Amphytrioniades* (68.112). Callimachus, when named, also appears only through his Greek patronymic: *Battiadae* (65.16, 116.2). All these examples are in addition to numerous Greek proper nouns and adjectives bearing Latin endings: e.g., *Libyssae* (7.3), *Eoa* (11.3), *Eurotae* (64.89), *Oceanus* (64.30, 88.6).

Apart from proper names, only a few of the Greek words in Catullus have any "poetic" pedigree: e.g., *pelagus* for "sea" (63.16, 63.88, 64.127, 64.125), *aether* for "sky" (63.40), and *carbasus* (64.227) for "sail." Otherwise, conspicuously Greek words[6] in Latin literature tended to have a very different aesthetic. On the one hand, as we have seen, they were associated with vulgar idiom in comedy, mime, and satire. On the other hand a sprinkling of Greek *mots justes* was part of the vernacular register of the cultivated Roman, as richly documented by Cicero's correspondence. In Catullus they suggest the urbane conversational style of the *scurra*, and are chiefly confined to the polymetrics and elegies (Ross 1969: 100–4). Some examples: *phaselus* (4.1), *moechus* (10 times in various forms), *cinaedus* (8 times in various forms), *hendecasyllabos* (12.10), *mnemosynum* (12.13), *palimpseston* (22.5), *catagraphos* (25.7), *zephyri* (46.3), *epistolium* (68.2). Neither informal nor vulgar is the use by Catullus of Greek words that are motivated by the Hellenic setting of the poems in which they appear. In poem 63, Attis' Greek identity and its loss are emphasized with an abundance of Greek words: onomatopoetic *reboant* (63.21); *notha* (63.27);[7] *thiasus* (63.28); *palaestra, stadio, gyminasiis* (all in 63.60, where they are oddly grouped with the seemingly out-of-place Latin *foro*); *ephebus* (63.63); etc. Here the effect is not one of informality but instead an activation of the cultural associations of Greekness. The same can be said of *strophio* (64.65) and *calathisci* (64.319) in poem 64.

Catullus makes only sparing use of Greek syntactic constructions. Commentators often note the nominative predicate adjective at 4.2: *ait fuisse navium celerrimus*, where the personified Greek boat seems to speak Latin with a Greek accent. Quinn (1973a: 67) considers Catullus' use of an adverbial accusative with a passive participle to be another syntactic Grecism: e.g., twice in *non contecta levi velatum pectus amictu, non tereti strophio lactentis vincta papillas* (64.64–5); but Coleman (1999: 82–3) makes a good case that this is an archaic usage: e.g., Ennius, *perculsi pectora Poeni* (*Ann.* 310 Skutsch). If recognizably archaic, the aesthetic force of the usage would presumably be more to elevate than to innovate in the neoteric manner. Conversely, the locative use of *ut* at 11.3 seems to be patterned after Greek *hina*, but Jocelyn (1999: 353) is not persuasive in characterizing this as an elevated feature, in light of the same usage at 17.10. A number of other oddities in Catullan syntax could be Grecisms. The subjunctive *vellet* in *Chommoda dicebat, si quando commoda vellet* looks like the Greek past general conditional construction (with subjunctive for optative, of course; cf. Fordyce 1961: 375–6, who takes a different view). The cumulative use of negatives without re-negation in *respondi id quod erat, nihil neque ipsis/nec praetoribus esse nec cohorti* (10.9–10) is very natural as Greek idiom, but inconsistent with normative Latin (Kühner and Stegmann 1976: II.1, 825). If nothing else, these unconventional constructions exemplify the eclectic possibilities of the neoteric style and its freedom to experiment.

Diminutives

One of the most distinctive aspects of Catullan diction is the poet's use of diminutives. In this respect Catullus goes well beyond the practice of any Hellenistic models, regardless of genre. Something of the same inventiveness appears in Plautine comedy, but even there neither the frequency nor the affective range of diminutives equals what one finds in Catullus. We have seen that diminutives are characteristic of both the *sermo cottidianus* and the *sermo plebeius*, yet in Catullus they are found also in the more elevated poems, where vulgarisms are otherwise avoided. Conversely in the epigrams, despite the frequency of vulgarisms there, diminutives are rare. The explanation for this distribution is that diminutives were used by Catullus as a neoteric feature. In this respect, as in several others, the epigrams reflect a different stylistic tradition (Ross 1969: 22–6).[8]

True diminutives should be distinguished from words that are diminutive in form but have ceased to carry any diminutive meaning. For example, a word like *puella*, originally a diminutive of *puera*, had replaced its source word in common Latin usage. True diminutives connote that the referent is in some sense small, insignificant, weak, or otherwise should evoke feelings of affection, intimacy, or contempt. Not infrequently multiple associations are suggested at the same time. All of these pragmatic overtones are well suited to the passionate and sentimental persona that Catullus constructs, even if the dominant force of specific examples is not always transparent through the layers of irony. The translations that follow are merely approximations of the likely connotations.

One common function of diminutives in Catullus is to express affection: e.g., *flendo turgiduli rubent ocelli* (3.18) "[those sweet] eyes are all swollen and red from crying"; *flosculus . . . Iuventiorum* (24.1) "tender little blossom of the Iuventii." Another function is playful informality: *gemelle Castor et gemelle Castoris* (4.27), cf. "Pete and Repeat"; *femellas omnes* (55.7) "all the chicks." A third is to connote delicacy: *floridulo ore* (61.186) "little bud of a mouth," *brachiolum teres* (61.174) "smooth and slender forearm." Sometimes Catullus uses diminutives ironically to soften or attenuate the underlying meaning of the source word: *scortillum* (10.3) "a bit of a tart," *molliculi* (16.4) "a tad queer," *lucelli/lucello* (28.6–8) "some sort of profit." A related but different usage is to express contempt for the person or topic at issue: *turpiculo naso* (41.3) "foul little nose," *uno in lecticulo erudituli ambo* (57.7) "both of them sophomores in the same cozy seminary" (Quinn 1973a *ad loc.* for justification of the pun). Still another function, this one even more alien to English usage, is to suggest empathy or arouse pathos in the serious and elevated poems: *pallidulum pedem* (65.6) of the poet's brother; *amiculi* (30.2) of the poet himself, following a betrayal; *frigidulos . . . singultus* (64.131) of Ariadne's sobbing, following her abandonment.

Meter, Rhythm, and Sound

Genre and meter

Since stylistic experimentation and the mixing of genres were typical of Hellenistic Greek poetry, it is unsurprising that both are to be found in Catullus too. In order for innovation in itself to have had any aesthetic significance, the mixing must have been perceptible to informed readers of the new poetry. This section examines the traditional generic associations of the meters Catullus uses.

Meter was a marker of genre in both the Greek and Roman poetic traditions. Most of the meters used by Catullus carried traditional literary associations that were, so to speak, activated by default. An informed Roman reader would have known these associations and filtered the poetry through them. For example, the dactylic hexameter, long associated with epic poetry and hymnody, was a meter of ostensibly serious and elevated verse. The circumscribed narrative episodes that constituted little narrative epics on mythological subjects in the hands of Callimachus and Theocritus owed their generic novelty to the fact that they stood within, while departing from, a very familiar tradition and set of conventions. Catullus 64 does not, of course, stand in the same position of innovation with respect to Hellenistic epyllion (a modern term) as the latter does to Homer, but the principle is the same. Likewise poem 62, the hexameter wedding-song, stands in a tradition running back through Theocritus to Sappho, but it also departs from that tradition by the idealization of the subject and conflation of Greek and Roman elements (Fraenkel 1955: 6–8). The departures are all the more salient because they run against the generic expectations.

The traditional associations of the elegiac distich were more varied. In early Greek literature this was the meter of choice for relatively brief, non-narrative "wisdom" poems on public themes (e.g., Tyrtaeus, Solon) and personal relationships (e.g., Theognis, Mimnermus). Later (ca. 400 BC) the *Lyde* of Antimachus of Colophon revived the form and launched it in a new direction. The *Lyde*, said to have been named after the poet's mistress, was a long narrative poem on a variety of topics that were unified by a common theme, perhaps that of "unhappy love." The poem was much admired by Hellenistic poets, even if criticized by Callimachus as "fat" and "hardly clear."[9] Catullus (95.10) partially echoes that criticism. Yet Callimachus seems to have approved of at least the generic innovation of Antimachus, for his own *Aetia* is a long narrative in the elegiac meter on a variety of topics unified by a common theme. Callimachus also wrote miscellaneous shorter elegies on different topics, such as the *Kóma Berenikes*, which Catullus translates as poem 66 and introduces with poem 65. If elegy retained any specific associations when taken up by Catullus, they were those of a didactic voice and prominent authorial presence. The garrulous door of Catullus 67 is a witty exploitation of this didactic element. The autobiographical content of poem 68 stands in the tradition of a prominent authorial presence, one that would in the next generation evolve into Roman amatory elegy.

The elegiac distich is also associated with another antecedent tradition. In archaic and classical Greece, distichs were commonly used for brief epigrams on actual objects, frequently memorials of the departed. This utilitarian and commemorative function was broadened in the Hellenistic period, when the epigram became a literary genre in its own right. Catullus' distich epigrams (69–116) are all literary, of course, though some (e.g., 87, 96, 101) evoke the meter's ancient funerary associations, and all in effect "label" the poems they constitute.

The most common meter in Catullus after elegiac distichs is the hendecasyllable or "Phalaecean." Said to have been used by Sappho, the hendecasyllable is very sparsely attested before the Hellenistic period and is infrequent even then (Gow 1965: 541). In origin it is a lyric meter – i.e., it was used in poetry set to music accompanied by the lyre. By the Hellenistic period the meter no longer had any musical identity, being purely a "book" lyric. Theocritus makes occasional use of hendecasyllables in his epigrams, and it is probably an association with epigram rather than lyric that lies behind Catullus' adoption of the meter. There are 42 hendecasyllabic poems in Catullus. Many of them are similar in content and tonal range (though not necessarily in style) to the distich epigrams. The hendecasyllables include lampoons, most of the obscene poems among the polymetrics, humorous anecdotes, and indeed actual "epigrams" in the original sense, like the dedicatory poem 1. But the hendecasyllables also include more "lyrical" compositions like poem 2 (*Passer deliciae meae puellae*), 5 (*Vivamus mea Lesbia*), and 46 (*Iam ver egelidos*). In short, the hendecasyllable seems to be the least thematically constrained verse-form in the corpus.

As a lyric meter, the hendecasyllable was built on the aeolic metrical colon known as the "glyconic." Other aeolic meters that Catullus uses generally have a more clearly lyric identity. Obviously poem 51, in Sapphic stanzas, evokes the famous Lesbian model that it loosely translates. Poem 11, in the same meter, has long been read as a kind of bookend to 51, though interestingly the reader encounters it earlier in the collection as we have it. The melancholy poem 30 is another lyric *melos*, well suited to its theme of disappointed friendship and longing. Poems 34 and 61 are both choral hymns in lyric stanzas of glyconics and pherecrateans. Since Sappho is known to have written hymns in lyric measures, the meter of these Catullan hymns is perhaps a bit of antiquarianism (see Fordyce 1961: 235–8 for a history of the genre). In any event, the idea was evidently approved of by Horace, who selected the Sapphic stanza as the meter for his *Carmen Saeculare*. The priapean meter of poem 17, although built of aeolic cola, is found in Greek old comedy but not in the Aeolic poets. Thematically it seems to have little in common with the other lyric compositions. It and the galliambics of poem 63 are best considered *sui generis*.

Finally we come to the iambic poems. Iambic metrical schemes in personal poetry (as opposed to drama and mime) were associated with a tradition of invective and mockery stretching back to Archilochus. Catullus himself refers to his *iambi* as instruments of attack (36.5, 40.2, 54.6, and fr. 3.1). One species of iambic verse was the "limping iambic" (choliambic), apparently first used by Hipponax in the sixth century BC. The choliambic is an iambic trimeter with a trochee or spondee in place of an iamb at verse-end. Of this "limping" cadence West (1982: 41) remarks: "This rough treatment of the cadence, normally the most strictly regulated part of any verse, may best be understood as a kind of deliberate metrical ribaldry, in keeping with these iambographers' studied vulgarity." The choliambic meter was revived in the Hellenistic period. It is the meter of Callimachus' *Iambi* 1–5 and 13, the only poems in that collection that involve the overt criticism or mockery of someone.[10] The same meter was used by Herodas (third century BC) in his pseudo-realistic *mimiamboi*, which are short dramatic compositions featuring dialogue between low characters, chiefly women, in ludicrous and often sexually charged situations. Catullus uses limping iambs in eight poems. It is the second most common meter in the polymetrics. Three of these poems (37 and 39 on Egnatius and his mouthwash, and 59 on Rufa's escapades in cemeteries) are withering lampoons delivered in a mocking tone that is seasoned with vivid scatological abuse. Two others also contain elements of lampoon, but are not nearly as mordant and in no way scatological. Poem 44 (*O funde noster*) is playfully addressed to the poet's Sabine farm (or is it Tiburtine?) in gratitude for the refuge it has provided from the pestilential oratory of Sestius. Yet Sestius, the butt of the joke, appears to be the poet's friend, someone who has invited him to dinner; and the criticism, assuming it is criticism of the oratory's style and not its content, is indirect and playful. Poem 22 (*Suffenus iste*) begins as an epigrammatic lampoon of a would-be poet, but ends with Catullus seeing everyone, including himself, as another Suffenus. The remaining three poems in choliambics seem to run even more directly against the generic conventions of the meter. Poem 31 (*Paene insularum, Sirmio*) is a light-hearted and unabashedly joyous celebration of the poet's Transpadane home. It bears no trace of lampoon or mockery, although the lightness of tone perhaps accounts for the choice of meter. Poem 8 (*Miser Catulle*) is addressed by the poet to himself. Possibly it begins as a lampoon (*desinas ineptire*), but it soon becomes an alternately reflective, consolatory, determined, and angry meditation on the end of a love affair. If the mocking associations of the choliambic still resonate in this poem, then there is an element of self-loathing that also runs through the composition. Finally, poem 60 is the most strikingly unconventional composition in the choliambics. The poem is a five-line rhetorical question that certainly implies strong criticism of its unnamed addressee, but the diction is high-style and tragic (*mente dura ac taetra, supplicis vocem in novissimo casu, a nimis fero corde*), and the allusions are highly literary (*leaena montibus Libystinis, Scylla*). There is a very strong tension between the formal style of the poem and its meter. The effect is like that of the *Pulcinèlla*, singing through his tears in Leoncavallo's *Pagliacci*. The pain is real, but the audience will see the costume and read it as farce.

Meter and rhythm

Quantitative metrical schemes are somewhat analogus to syntactic structures (West 1982: 4–6). A "foot" (e.g., iamb, dactyl, etc.) is like a word. A "metron" (iambic dipody, "ionic *a minore*," etc.) is like a phrase. A "colon" (e.g., glyconic, adonean, etc.) is like a clause, and a "period" (e.g., a line of dactylic hexameter, a Sapphic stanza, etc.) is like a sentence. Composing poetry in a particular meter requires the "mapping" of textual syntax onto metrical syntax. The synthesis of these two grammars is an important part of what constitutes rhythm.

Some meters are rhythmically slower than others, and some faster. The dactylic hexameter presents a relatively slow and stately rhythm; the iambic trimeter, a fast and bright one. This is because, first, the metrical word (dactyl or spondee) is longer in the former than in the latter;[11] second, the most common metrical phrases of the dactylic hexameter (e.g., the first part of the line to the penthemimeral caesura or to the trochaic caesura of the same foot, the remainder of the line after the caesura, or from the caesural break to the bucolic diaeresis, and the final adonic or double spondee) usually contain more syllables than iambic metrical phrases; and third, because the metrical period (the verse) usually contains more syllables overall than most iambic meters. The mapping of text onto these different metrical schemes can reinforce or undermine the inherent rhythmic potentialities of the meter in question. Enjambment, for example, obviously tends to mask the natural rhythmic pause at verse-end. A diaeresis, or syntactic pause coinciding with the end of a metrical word, will tend to interrupt the rhythmic continuity of the metrical period more forcefully than a caesural pause. That is because it literally pulls the verse apart at one of its seams. Critical to the constitution of rhythm, then, is the poet's manipulation of sense units in the textual syntax.

A notional but descriptively useful definition of "sense unit" is a group of contiguous words that make up a syntactic or rhetorical constituent of the sentence. The test of such a unit is whether the phrase can be omitted without altering the syntactic or rhetorical structure of the rest of the sentence. Since unitary words can presumably always be replaced by another word of the same function, they do not count as phrasal sense units by this definition. Sense units of this kind have been variously called "sentence constituents" (*Satzgliederungen*), or syntactic "*cola*," or "expressional phrases" (Sheets 2001: 11–14 with bibliography). "EP" is a convenient abbreviation for the latter term. An important aspect of the metrical technique of Catullus is how EPs are mapped onto metrical cola and periods. For example, poem 1.1–7 contains seven EPs of greatly differing length. They are reproduced in the numbered list below, with diagonal slashes marking the ends of metrical periods:

1   Cui dono lepidum novum *libellum/*
2   arida modo pumice *expolitum?/*

3 Corneli, tibi:
4 namque tu *solebas*/meas esse aliquid putare *nugas*/iam tum,
5 cum ausus es
6 unus Italorum/
7 omne aevum tribus explicare *cartis*/doctis, Iuppiter, et *laboriosis.*/

It will be seen that there is relatively little correspondence in this set of verses between the boundaries of EPs and the boundaries of metrical periods. Conversely, there is a high correspondence of rhyme (marked with italics) and the boundaries of metrical periods. These sound effects emphasize the metrical rhythm, while the phrasing of all but the first two verses undermines it. The effect is to map an essentially arrhythmic conversational style onto a meter that remains perceptible, but not dominant. The fluid length of the EPs creates other interesting effects. The very short third EP serves to enhance the rhythmic prominence of this dedicatory phrase and the decision it expresses. The sixth EP (*unus Italorum*) works in the same way, emphasizing the uniqueness of Cornelius' achievement. The final EP continues a single clause that takes up two full metrical periods. Its length and intricate syntax emphasize the contrast between Catullan *nugae* and Cornelian *cartae*.

Catullus is acutely aware of rhythmic effects. What makes it possible for him to calibrate his EPs so finely to the meter is the flexibility of Latin word order and the rhetorical device of hyperbaton. There is a relatively "natural" word order in any language, particularly in the vernacular register. It is "natural," for example, for noun phrases to be coherent and mutually separate from each other. This is another way of saying that it is natural for attributive modifiers to be adjacent to the nouns they modify. Variations from this standard emphasize anomalously positioned elements in prose, and help to structure the rhythm in verse. For example, the first five lines of poem 4 follow a quite natural word order. Three of the noun phrases consist of single words (*hospites…palmulis…linteo*). Of the three multi-word noun phrases, two have modifiers adjacent to the "head" (the modified element) of the phrase: *Phasellus ille…navium celerrimus*. Only one noun phrase involves a separation of the modifier from its head: *ullius natantis impetum trabis* (4.3), and that separation is but a single word in length (*impetum*). Rhythmically each multi-word noun phrase is an EP. This rhythm contrasts starkly with the noun phrase EPs in the first six lines of poem 76: *Siqua recordanti benefacta priora voluptas…sanctam violasse fidem…foedere nullo…divum ad fallendos numine abusum homines… multa parata manent in longa aetate, Catulle, / ex hoc ingrato gaudia amore tibi.* Hyperbaton, or "unnatural" word order, is what makes this difference possible. The hyperbaton takes two forms in the noun phrases of 76.1–6: (1) broad separations between the heads and their modifiers (*Siqua – voluptas, multa –gaudia*); and (2) the suppression of EP boundaries by the interlocking of noun phrases (*divum – numine* interlocked with *fallendos – homines*, *multa – gaudia* interlocked with *hoc – amore*). The contrast in rhythmic structure between poem 4 and poem 76 is a particularly good example of contrasts that exist throughout the corpus. Catullus tends to use briefer and more naturally ordered noun phrases in the iambic and hendecasyllabic poems, and longer and more artificially ordered noun phrases in his dactylic poems. The poems in aeolic meters occupy an intermediate position. It must be emphasized, however, that these are merely tendencies. Catullus can modulate the rhythm as suits the desired effect regardless of the metrical scheme. Poem 1, in hendecasyllabics, has long rhythmic phrases, as we have seen; poem 85, in elegiac distichs, has very short ones.

Rhythm and sound

As was seen in connection with rhyming effects in poem 1, sound is another important constituent of rhythm. The tropes of alliteration, assonance, homoioteleuton, and the like tend to reinforce EPs and their boundaries, or do just the opposite. A famous example of assonance to emphasize a rhythmic boundary is the collocation of *lux* and *nox* in 5.5–6:

> nobis cum semel occidit brevis <u>lux</u>,
> <u>nox</u> est perpetua una dormienda

Verse 5 is an EP as well as a metrical period concluding in a monosyllable (*lux*) following a disyllable (*brevis*) following a trisyllable (*occidit*). The rhythm grinds to an abrupt halt when life ends, then starts up again when death begins. The first word of the following verse – a monosyllabic noun in the same case and with the same sentence function as *lux*, a precise antonym in the same semantic field, and a word of very similar sound – rhythmically emphasizes the antithesis between the two adjacent words. The justly famous use of elision in *perpetua una* further emphasizes the chiastic rhythm as monosyllables give way to polysyllables.

Sound effects can also underline the rhythmic coherence of a phrase. A famous example is the EP, *sed . . . rumpens*, at 11.19–20:

> nullum amans vere, sed identidem omnium
> ilia rumpens.

The alliteration of /d/ and /m/ and the assonance and aural alternation of high, mid, and low vowels in *i-e-i-o-i-i-i-a* of the doubly elided phrase *identidem omnium ilia* tie the EP together in a lewd bouncing movement that in a sense promiscuously obliterates the proper boundaries of the words. The suitability of this rhythmic effect to the context is obvious.[12]

Another rhythmic strategy that Catullus exploits is repetition through the tropes of anaphora, polyptoton, epanaphora, paronomasia, chiasmus, etc. Anaphora, for example, is very common in Catullus: e.g., the repetition of *quae* at 36.12–15 and of *te* at 55.35. Sometimes the device is used to communicate an emotional intensity that verges on mania: e.g., *ego* and *mihi* at 63.63–72 (a total of 17 times in quick succession). Polyptoton is another form of anaphora, one that is also a learned mannerism, because of the considerable difficulty of using alternate case forms of the same word in structurally parallel positions, while not compromising either the realism or the meaning of the language. Catullus displays his virtuosity with numerous examples: e.g., 8.15–18:

> . . . <u>quae</u> tibi manet vita?
> <u>quis</u> nunc te adibit? <u>cui</u> videberis bella?
> <u>quem</u> nunc amabis? <u>cuius</u> esse diceris?
> <u>quem</u> basiabis? <u>cui</u> labella mordebis?

Multiple sound effects can of course be used in combination for rhythmic effect: e.g., 4.16–17, where the two lines are linked by beginning and end rhyme, by anaphora, by assonance between the two identically placed perfect infinitives, and by both being unitary EPs that are coterminous with the metrical periods:

> tuo stetisse dicit in cacumine,
> tuo imbuisse palmulas in aequore.

Finally, it should also be noted that not all forms of repetition are for rhythmic effect. Catullus often repeats words in quick succession to increase the emotional intensity of his poetry: e.g., *Caeli, Lesbia nostra, Lesbia illa, / illa Lesbia* (58.1–2); *eripuisti... eripuisti... eheu... eheu* (77.4–5); *prospicit... prospicit* (64.60–2); *invita... invita* (66.40ff.); *perfide... perfide* (64.132–3).

Pragmatic Issues

Style is not a matter of form alone. Of equal importance is the communicative function that style performs. The term "pragmatics" refers to a set of concepts and theories that relate to whatever fills the gap between the formal properties of a text (or utterance) – its syntax, lexical semantics, genre, etc. – and how the text is understood to mean something to someone in a particular social context.

Certain pragmatic phenomena are familiar under the traditional label of "figures of thought." These include metaphor and simile, metonymy and synecdoche, irony, puns, double meanings, and personification. All of these tropes are important features of Catullan style, and most are used in distinctive ways. The figure of simile, for example, is employed in a manner that evokes Homeric usage. A typical example is the famous flower simile at the end of poem 11. What makes the image so rich is not the comparison of dying love to a dying flower, particularly as that image may be freighted with a literary allusion to Sappho (*LGS* 225), but the contextual details and their connotations: the plow, its insentience, the location of the flower, the implication of contingency in the word *tactus*, etc. Another example, even more elaborate, is the simile at 65.19–24, where the poet speaks of his imagined failure to remember a request for a poem. He likens the request to a suitor's apple that slips from the lap of a young girl, when she jumps up on her mother's entrance, and blushes. Every detail in this vivid image is suggestive. Sometimes the poet develops his "Homeric" similes to the point of parody, or almost. A good example is the comparison he draws between the welcome aid given by a friend and a sparkling stream that drops from a mountaintop, cascading down mossy stones into a valley, where it flows across a road crowded with people, to succor the weary traveler midst his sweat, while the oppressive heat cracks the burnt-dry fields all around (68.57–62). As the text is punctuated by Mynors, the traveler of this simile is the poet, who in hot passion has been given a place by his friend to keep a tryst with a married lady. The simile seems too grand for the context, unless perhaps the poet is playing with the trope for humorous effect. Why, for example, is the traveler's road crowded with other people? Later in the same poem, in a particularly elaborate development of the multiple "Homeric" simile, the poet likens the love of Laodamia to a series of richly detailed vignettes that combine recherché Greek mythology and geography with the Roman law of succession, Roman testamentary practice, and the love-making of doves (68.107–23). In these and other examples Catullus displays his virtuosity with a traditional literary device, and thereby "says" something about the nature of his art. Space will not permit a detailed examination of other figures of thought, but it should be noted in passing that irony is an especially prominent trope in Catullus. Along with puns, vivid sexual metaphors, and double meanings, it is crucial to the poetic persona he creates.

Framing the discourse

Another important pragmatic phenomenon in Catullus is the poet's use of coded language. The term "code" in this connection is used with the technical meaning that it has acquired in semiotic theory. Semiotics is a discipline concerned with how meaning is constructed through the use of "signs," defined very broadly to mean anything that someone invests with meaning. For example, a text is a sign, and so are all of the constituent parts of it. How a text is presented is also a sign: e.g., if it is printed on paper or carved in stone. Systems of contrasting signs are called "paradigms." For example, all of the named individuals and personified entities who are addressed or referred to by Catullus in his poetry comprise one paradigm. Elements of the same or different paradigms can be combined to create "syntagms" that are themselves signs (e.g., the pair "Furius and Aurelius"), which can themselves be combined to create other syntagms (e.g., poem 11), etc. In order for a sign to have even approximately the same meaning for two individuals, the individuals must share the convention that assigns such a meaning to that sign. The sharing of interpretive conventions is called a "code" by semioticians. Readers who seek to "understand" a text "on its own terms" are "positioned" by the codes it makes use of. In a sense they accept, at least for the act of interpretation, the way the paradigms that underlie those codes "frame" reality.

The poetry of Catullus presents the reader with a number of different codes that are discussed in other chapters of this book. For example, terms like *lepidus, nuga, doctus,* and *venustus* fall within a code of "neoteric" aesthetics discussed by Johnson in chapter 10. The poet's learned intertextual references constitute another code, discussed by DeBrohun in chapter 16. Still other codes are the argot of social relations discussed by Krostenko in chapter 12, and the use of scurrility and obscenity as invective, discussed by Tatum in chapter 18. Many of the semiotic paradigms that underlie coded language in Catullus frame a reality of stark oppositions. For example, poem 5 imagines a world peopled by two groups of individuals: "us" and "them." This paradigm is aligned with other paradigms of semantic oppositions in the same poem: alive and dead, young and old, rumor and truth, valuable and worthless, day and night, now and hereafter. Many of these same paradigms are invoked in other poems that frame the poet's reality in terms of similar complementarities: e.g., the poet and his poetry (16), keeping and breaking faith (30), whore and respectable woman (42), *optimus* and *pessimus* (49), appearance and reality (67), truth and lies (70), friend and enemy (77), betrayer and betrayed (83), betrayal and loyalty (91), old poetry and new poetry (95), and others. In such a world there is no place for intermediate states of being, a condition that creates an illusion of passionate intensity in the poetry. The same condition accentuates the anomalous and untenable position of the poetic persona in, e.g., poems 85 (*Odi et amo*), 8 (*Miser Catulle*), 72 (*Dicebas quondam*), 75 (*Huc est mens*), 76 (*Siqua recordanti*), etc. All of these poems involve a persona who in a sense does not "fit" the dominant paradigms. A particularly good example of this tension is poem 22, where a large number of mutually reinforcing binary paradigms[13] are linked together, only to be called into question at the poem's conclusion. If we all might be Suffenus, then perhaps the poet's other realities too are problematic.

Although the meaning attached to any sign is arbitrary and conventional, some assignments of meaning will appear to be more "natural" than others in particular cultures. This happens when the arbitrary linkage between signifier and signified is so familiar as to be invisible by the norms of a given social ideology. For example, as Skinner (1991: 3) has argued in discussing the function of obscenity in Catullus, the alignment of masculinity with political and social power in Greek and Roman elite societies "made it natural...to categorize asymmetrical social relations in terms of gender and to use images of sexual intercourse to articulate messages of political and financial success or failure." Yet despite this appropriation of a conventional linkage, a characteristic quality of Catullan poetry is the problematizing of certain "natural" meanings in Roman social ideologies. As has often been noted, for example, the poet tends to blur the opposition of male vs. female and the associated paradigm of dominant vs. submissive. He does this explicitly in poem 63 and implicitly through-out the corpus by casting himself as the abandoned and helpless lover in his affair with Lesbia. This is a posture very different from the exaggerated masculinity of, e.g., poems 16 and 21.

Positioning the reader

The reader of Catullus' poetry is explicitly acknowledged in only a single poem: 14b, an elusive fragment that characterizes the *lectores* as likely to be shocked by the poet's inept compositions. Everywhere else the reader is, so to speak, left to find his or her own relationship to this highly prominent poetic persona. Although there might be disagreement on details, approximately 75 percent of the poems are explicitly addressed to someone other than the reader.[14] The effect is to position the reader as an outsider who overhears a conversation, perhaps surreptitiously. In six of these poems (8, 46, 51, 52, 76, 79) the addressee is Catullus himself, creating an even more illicit role for the reader, who is now in a position similar to that of a person glancing through someone else's private diary. In 24 poems (3, 4, 10, 34, 41, 42, 53, 61, 62, 67, 70, 73, 83, 85, 86, 87, 92, 94, 95, 95b, 97, 100, 104, 114) the reader is the implied addressee or implicitly among a group of addressees.[15] In these poems the reader is positioned as someone whom the poet knows, or is at any rate aware of. The remaining 14 poems (45, 57, 59, 63, 64, 66, 74, 78, 84, 89, 90, 105, 106, 115) are "public," in the sense of being addressed to everyone or to no one in particular. In these poems the poet refers neither to himself nor to an addressee, and the reader is in the position of someone viewing a work of publicly displayed art, or reading an inscription on a building or anonymous graffito on a wall. The reader's differing roles necessarily entail differences in how the poetry is engaged. In self-address, the poet's candor or sincerity will seem complete; in an anonymous screed, the reader's detached or amused skepticism will be at its greatest. Where the reader is put in the place of overhearing a private communication, she or he will be disposed to impute a context of "real" experiences and "actual" references to everything in the poem. Catullus is keenly aware of this pragmatic dimension to his poetry, and often exploits it within individual poems and groups of poems to shape their effects.

Conclusion

The extent to which style shapes and distinguishes the aesthetics of individual poems can be illustrated by comparing passages of similar content and dissimilar styles. A particularly good example is poem 4 and the opening 24 verses of poem 64. These two passages are of roughly equal length (138 words in poem 4 vs. 132 words in 64.1–24) and share numerous narrative motives, some structural similarity, and to a limited degree even some stylistic features. Both are about a boat that is Greek and that once stood on a mountain-top in the form of trees. Both boats took a long journey on rough and dangerous seas, carrying their respective master/heroes to exotic foreign lands. On both voyages a god assisted the journey by providing favorable winds. Structurally, both passages commence with an account in indirect speech and conclude with an apostrophe. At the stylistic level both boats are personi-fied: they have palms for oar-blades (*palmis/palmulas*), they fly on their way abroad (*volare, volitantem*), and they swim (*natantis, nasse*). They have drenched their oars or the boat itself in the water (*imbuisse, imbuit*). From so high a concentration of shared motives, images, and figures, one might expect the two passages to be more similar in aesthetic effect; yet, as anyone will readily perceive, they could hardly be more different. Poem 4 is playful, chatty, and familiar in tone. It is a fragment of a conversation that takes place right now and is situated in an ostensibly real place and social setting. The reader/listener is one of a group of "guests" with whom the speaking voice shares a bit of gossip about the boat that we are invited to look at for ourselves. By contrast, the first 24 verses of poem 64 are a stately procession, majestic and gorgeous in detail. The opening image of the poem is remote in time and place and delivered by an anonymous narrator to an anonymous audience. The subject is mythological and the story is situated in another time and a different reality. The language is highly artificial and densely allusive, esoteric qualities aimed to gratify a refined sensibility, or one that aspires to refinement, but that also intimidate the uninitiated. Both effects serve to distance the poem from its audience, much like a work of art on display in a museum. Even the connoisseur must stand behind the velvet rope, like any other patron. Metrically and rhythmically the poems sound a very different kind of music. The pure iambic trimeters of poem 4 smile and bounce, an effect that commentators often compare to the choppy waves over which the little boat skims. The stately hexameters of 64 rarely create any effect of speed or acceler-ation, but proceed *adagio*, with occasional rhythmic ornaments. The length of the clauses (though not of the sentences) is generally greater in poem 64, with a concomitantly greater complexity of syntax.

   Turning to diction, both passages include some vocabulary that is traditional in the Latin poetic register, but there is a much higher concentration of such words in 64: *liquidas* (as a stock epithet of the sea), *fines, optantes, vada salsa, puppi* (as metonymy for a ship), *pubis, ventosum, texta* (of the ribbing in a ship), *optato, gurges* (meaning "sea"), *deum* (genitive plural), *compellabo*, and *taedis* (as a metonymy for marriage). Additionally, the passage from poem 64 contains sacral and legal terms of a kind wholly absent from poem 4: *prognatae, monstrum, avertere* (*OLD* s.v. 9), *bona* (in the sense of "prosperous, blessed"), *felicibus, aucte*. Conversely, poem 4 contains a number of vernacular features that are alien to elevated poetry: e.g., emphatic superlatives (*cognitissima, novissimo*), redundancy (*iste <u>post</u> phasellus <u>antea</u> fuit; <u>ultima ex origine</u>; <u>fuisse et esse</u>*), the Greek word *phaselus* and Greek syntax of *fuisse celerrimus*, the playful diminutives *palmulis, gemelle*. Although both poems refer to exotic places with descriptive epithets, in poem 4 the toponym is typically the head noun of the phrase: *minacis Hadriatici, Rhodum nobilem, horridam Thraciam Propontida, Amastri Pontica, Cytore buxifer*.[16] These are, so to speak, real places that can be found on a map, and the modifiers indicate ostensibly real characteristics of those places. In poem 64.1–24 the toponyms never appear as the head nouns: *Peliaco vertice, Argivae robora pubis, liquidas Neptuni undas, Phasidos ad fluctus, fines Aeetaeos*. These periphrases have a less "indexical" toponymic function. These are not so much places as ideas of place that carry associations of more than mere location. There are numerous other differences of style between the two passages, but those already mentioned must suffice to demonstrate the poet's fine-grained control over his art. That control was possible because of his extraordinary sensitivity to diction, rhythm, and the pragmatic functions of language, as well as his strategic use of the same.

NOTES

1 Both terms are found in Cicero, who deliberately blurs the distinction in reference to his own epistolary style at *Fam.* 9.21.1.

2 This generalization is somewhat oversimplified. Social status is a function of multiple factors that vary from one community to another: e.g., age, gender, occupation, degree of social mobility, degree of urbanism, and others. Labov's (2001: 29–33, 500–2) more nuanced formulation of the "from below" principle argues that the leaders of language change are members of more "central" as opposed to "peripheral" status hierarchies. Both the highest and the lowest status groups are peripheral.

3 *oricilla* is Scaliger's emendation of *moricula* in V. If correct, *oricilla* shows the vulgar spelling of *o-* for *au-*. The diminutive *auricula* is used by Catullus at 67.44.

4 Perhaps also *unum...beatiorem* (10.17) "a guy with money," although commentators on this passage usually take *beatiorem* as a predicate adjective, not a substantive.

5 A similarly vulgar use of *de* is in the phrase *de meliore nota* "of the better sort" (68.28), occurring only once elsewhere in extant Latin literature, in a witty and breezy letter from Curius to Cicero, *Fam.* 7.29.1.8.

6 These would not include borrowings that had effectively become part of the lexical stock of Latin: e.g., *zona* (2b.13), *talento* (12.7), *poemata* and *poema* (22.15, 22.16), *pallium* (25.6), *nympha* (61.29).

7 The force of *notho* at 34.15 is less clear.

8 The relatively few diminutives in the epigrams are mostly confined to two poems: 80 and 99, where they complement the themes of pathic homosexuality.

9 The meaning of Greek *torón*, which I have translated "clear," is itself unclear in this context. Trypanis (1958: 246) translates *ou torón* as "inelegant." See Pfeiffer *ad loc*.

10 The very poorly preserved poem 9, primarily etiological in content, is perhaps an exception, but we do not know the tenor of Hermes' concluding words to the questioner.

11 Even a resolved iamb, which is a tribrach (⌣ ⌣ ⌣), is shorter in overall syllabic quantity than a dactyl.

12 In the oral reading that prevailed in antiquity, the enunciation of such a phrase requires multiple movements of lips and tongue, iconically enacting what the words seem to suggest. Another well-known example of the same kind of effect is the alliterative EP at 5.10 (*cum multa milia fecerimus*), which enacts the intense labiality of multiple kisses.

13 E.g., Suffenus vs. us; the beautiful, expensive, and polished outside of the book vs. the worthless and witless inside; the *urbanus* vs. the *caprimulgus* or *fossor*; self-contentment vs. repellent effect on others; self-delusion vs. critical acumen; etc.

14 This figure does not include the three hymns or any of the poems that contain apostrophes but are otherwise not addressed to the apostrophized individual.

15 Poems 41, 83, and 100 contain apostrophes to individuals who are mentioned in the poems.

16 Three counterexamples: *insulas Cycladas, Cytorio iugo, trucem Ponticum sinum.*

GUIDE TO FURTHER READING

A good introduction to the historical development of Latin literary idiom and of vernacular Latin can be found in Palmer (1961). The same author's companion study of the Greek language (1980) traces the origin and development of interconnections between genre, dialect, and meter in the Greek poetic tradition. For a detailed, formal analysis of Latin poetic diction, and the problems of defining it, see Coleman (1999). The introduction to the same collection of essays touches on many of the subjects covered in this chapter, and the composite bibliography at the end of the collection is rich and reasonably up to date. A persuasive and influential demonstration of stylistic differences between the "neoteric compositions" (1–68) and the distich epigrams (69–116) is Ross (1969). Jocelyn (1999) notes differences of style between the lyric and hendecasyllabic poems of Catullus. The technicalities of Latin meter are covered in D. S. Raven (1965). Cogent observations of figured language in numerous specific passages of Catullus can be found in J. Wills (1996) through his index. Loomis (1972) deals with rhythm and word-patterns in the polymetrics. A very readable introduction to semiotic theory is Chandler (2002). Recent important studies applying poststructuralist theory and concepts like "framing" and "positioning" to Catullus are Fitzgerald (1995) and Skinner (2003).

WORKS CITED

Adams, J. N. 1982. *The Latin Sexual Vocabulary.* Baltimore and London.

Adams, J. N. 1999. "Nominative Personal Pronouns and Some Patterns of Speech in Republican and Augustan Poetry." In Adams and Meyer (1999: 97–133).

Adams, J. N., and R. G. Mayer, eds. 1999. *Aspects of the Language of Latin Poetry* = Proceedings of the British Academy 93. Oxford.

Chandler, D. 2002. *Semiotics: The Basics.* New York.

Coleman, R. G. G. 1999. "Poetic Diction, Poetic Discourse, and the Poetic Register." In Adams and Meyer (1999: 21–93).

Conte, G. B. 1994. *Latin Literature: A History.* Trans. J. B. Solodow. Rev. D. Fowler and G. W. Most. Baltimore.

Ernout, A., and A. Meillet. 1967. *Dictionaire étymologique de la langue Latine.* 4th edn. Paris.

Fitzgerald, W. 1995. *Catullan Provocations: Lyric Poetry and the Drama of Position.* Berkeley, Los Angeles, and London.

Fordyce, C. J., ed. 1961. *Catullus: A Commentary.* Oxford.

Fraenkel, E. 1955. "*Vesper adest* (Catullus LXII)." *Journal of Roman Studies* 45: 1–8.

Gigante, V. 1978. "Motivi gnomici nella poesia di Catullo." *Vichiana* 7: 257–67.

Gow, A. S. F. 1965. *Theocritus Edited with a Translation and Commentary.* Vol. 2. Cambridge.

Heusch, H. 1954. *Das Archaische in der Sprache Catulls.* Bonn.

Hofmann, J. B. 1926. *Lateinische Umgangssprache.* Heidelberg.

Irvine, J. 2001. " 'Style' as Distinctiveness: The Culture and Ideology of Linguistic Differentiation." In P. Eckert and J. R. Rickford, eds., *Style and Sociolinguistic Variation.* Cambridge. 21–43.

Jocelyn, H. D. 1999. "The Arrangement and the Language of Catullus' So-Called *polymetra* with Special Reference to the Sequence 10–11–12." In Adams and Meyer (1999: 335–75).

Kroll, W. 1924. *Studien zum Verständnis der römischen Literatur.* Stuttgart.

Krostenko, B. 2001b. "*Arbitria urbanitatis:* Language, Style, and Characterization in Catullus cc. 39 and 37," *Classical Antiquity* 20.2: 239–72.

Kühner, R. K., and C. Stegmann. 1976. *Ausführliche Grammatik der Lateinischen Sprache.* Hanover.

Labov, W. 2001. *Principles of Linguistic Change: Social Factors.* Malden, MA.

Loefstedt, B. 1911. *Philologischer Kommentar zur Peregrinatio Aetheriae: Untersuchungen zur Geschichte der Lateinischen Sprache.* Uppsala and Leipzig.

Loomis, J. W. 1972. *Studies in Catullan Verse: An Analysis of Word Types and Patterns in the Polymetra. Mnemosyne* Supplement 24. Leiden.

Palmer, L. R. 1954. *The Latin Language.* London.

Palmer, L. R. 1980. *The Greek Language.* Atlantic Highlands, NJ.

Quinn, K., ed. 1973a. *Catullus: The Poems.* 2nd edn. London and Basingstoke.

Raven, D. S. 1965. *Latin Meter.* London.

Ross, D. O., Jr. 1969. *Style and Tradition in Catullus.* Cambridge, MA.

Sheets, G. A. 2001. "Rhythm in Catullus 34." *Memoirs of the American Academy in Rome* 46: 11–21.

Skinner, M. B. 1991. "The Dynamics of Catullan Obscenity: cc. 37, 58 and 11." *Syllecta Classica* 3: 1–11.

Skinner, M. B. 2003. *Catullus in Verona: A Reading of the Elegiac Libellus, Poems 65–116.* Columbus, OH.

Thomson, D. F. S., ed. 1997. *Catullus, Edited with a Textual and Interpretative Commentary.* Toronto.

Trypanis, C. A., trans. 1958. *Callimachus:* Aetia, Iambi, *Lyric Poems,* Hecale, *Minor Epic and Elegiac Poems, and Other Fragments.* Cambridge, MA.

West, M. L. 1982. *Greek Metre.* Oxford.

Wills, J. 1996. *Repetition in Latin Poetry: Figures of Allusion.* Oxford.

CHAPTER TWELVE

Catullus and Elite Republican Social Discourse

Brian A. Krostenko

Poets are, of course, indebted to the language and ideas of their times. The difficulty is in distinguishing adoption from adaptation. This chapter examines the relationship of Catullus' poetry, chiefly the polymetrics, to aspects of the ideas and language of the discourse of the late Republican social elite. That it does by examining some of the words the elite used to appraise the attractiveness of literary composition and social presentation. From that vocabulary Catullus drew keywords for the social and artistic vision of the polymetrics. But the words are not merely borrowed: in expressing his own vision, Catullus also comments pointedly on the habits of appraisal of elite culture and thus of political life, in which appraisal figured and in which struggles over evaluative language were regular.[1] Those habits are revealed in stark clarity by a poet who, if he was *in foro otiosus*, was perfectly alert in his leisure.

Some Catullan Keywords

A set of words common especially in Catullus' polymetrics has long been taken to reflect his poetic, social, and erotic standards. Most frequent in occurrence are *lepidus* "charming," *uenustus* "attractive," *bellus* "neat," and *facetus* "witty," with their derivatives. The programmatic value of these words is plain: *cui dono lepidum nouum libellum*, says Catullus, inaugurating his collection: "Whom do I give this nice little book to?" (1.1). Suffenus is a bad poet but a witty convivant, *uenustus et dicax et urbanus* "lovely and quick-witted and civilized" (22.2), *bellus...et urbanus* "stylish and civilized" (22.9). The age that would compare a provincial beauty to Lesbia is *insapiens et infacetum* "tasteless and witless" (43.8). In the patent programmatic force of these keywords the interpretive difficulty lies: their shades and nuances, and even definitions, will be formed by one's view of Catullus' tastes and sensibilities.

The difficulty is greater in that Catullus' *libellus* seems ineluctably to depict the passions and peccadilloes of a small, elegant, and highly self-conscious social circle – the very sort to fashion its own cant.

In the end there is no interpreting Catullus' polymetrics without imagining that group. But the act of imagination can be informed by looking to the force of Catullus' keywords outside of Catullus. This obvious philological measure, however, is not straightforward. The four words listed above, and like words, are slippery. Catullus' older contemporary Cicero uses the words both to praise and to blame. In speeches the latter use predominates. Catiline's dissolute supporters, "filthy adulterers" (*adulteri* and *impuri*), are also "fine pretty boys" (*pueri lepidi ac delicati, Cat.* 2.23), lovers and dancers and singers. The Pergamenes, alleges Cicero, meant an honorific citation to mock the honorand, Decianus: but he took them seriously, blind to their ironic "wit and humor" (*uenustatem et facetias, Flac.* 76). Cicero's defendant P. Quinctius, a paragon of duty, honesty, and diligence (*officium, fides, diligentia*), did not live the stylish high life of the plaintiff Naevius, among whose skills is "speaking nicely" (*belle dicere*) – flash and polish of the same order as throwing a good dinner party (*Quinct.* 93).

If our words thus express qualities of dubious value, as technical terms in late Republican rhetorical criticism they signal more respectable qualities. The inaugural catalogue of an orator's needful skills in *On the Orator* (1.17) includes humor: "The orator must also have a certain charming wit (*quidam lepos*) and sense of humor (*facetiae*); learning that befits a free man; and the ability to reply and attack quickly and curtly, with measured deftness (*subtilis uenustas*) and wittiness (*urbanitas*)." *Venustus* often thus describes rejoinders, *lepos* charm or wit broadly meant, and *facetiae* humor proper. *Bellus* appears, too, particularly for saucy or impish humor (*De or.* 2.277, 281–3). The *excursus de ridiculis* in *On the Orator* (2.216–90) has many such examples, devoted to defining the tasteful humor of civilized competition – a "wit that is not clownish" (*non scurrilis lepos*), in the phrase Cicero uses to describe Crassus' sense of humor in the *Brutus* (143).[2]

The words encompass more than humor. *Facetus* occasionally represents the charm of elegant speech. The *Rhetorica ad Herennium* describes the plain style of oratory as *illa facetissima uerborum attenuatio* "the very elegant reduced style" (4.16, cf. *Brut.* 63, 186; *Orat.* 20, 99). In Crassus' proem in *On the Orator*, he enthuses that, its practical uses aside, nothing is more pleasant or cultured than "witty speech without a trace of rudeness" (*sermo facetus ac nulla in re rudis*, 1.32). *Venustas* often describes graceful form, static or kinetic, and so frequently the charms of *actio*. The *Rhetorica ad Herennium* advises that speeches be delivered with "graceful moderation of voice, expression, and gesture" (*uocis uultus gestus moderatio cum uenustate*, 1.3). Graceful narration was *uenustus*: Cicero applies the word to Caesar's commentaries (*Brut.* 262) and to Lysias (*Orat.* 29). Details deftly crafted form another set: puns produced by a change of letter are *quaesitae uenustates* "contrived prettinesses" (*Orat.* 84), and anaphora is a figure that exhibits both elegance and serious intensity (*cum multum uenustatis… tum grauitatis et acrimoniae plurimum, Rhet. Her.* 4.19).

Lepidus may describe "attractive affectations": M. Antonius arranged his words into elegant rhythmic shape "less in the service of attractiveness than of impressiveness" (*neque… tam leporis causa quam ponderis, Brut.* 140). Cicero and the *Rhetorica ad Herennium* find *lepos* in figures of speech that feature repetition, *geminatio*

(*De or.* 3.206) and *gradatio* (*Rhet. Her.* 4.35). In letters Cicero uses *bellus* several times with technical terms from Greek rhetoric, registering the appreciation of a connoisseur: *parágramma bellum* "a nice little *jeu de mots*" (*Fam.* 7.32.2), *bellum akroteleútion* "a nice little *dénouement*" (*Att.* 5.21.3), *bellum hypómnema* "a nice *mémoire*" (*Att.* 16.14.4).

Catullus' Keywords and Political Aestheticism

Catullus' keywords could be assigned to either of these sets. The rhetorical uses connote charm and wit and polish, the very qualities of the polymetrics; the other uses have an undercurrent of rakishness, the very quality, it would appear, of Catullus' circle. But assigning the words merely to one category or the other misses something important. The positive and negative valences of the words are of a piece: they reflect precisely the ambivalence of the late Republican social elite toward aestheticism. On the one hand, elegance – of dress, of manner, of speech – was suspect, if that meant form and style had been favored over substance and character. Varro reflects the distinction – ironically – in describing what seems to be a swank *conuiuium*: *omnes uidemur nobis esse belli festiui, saperdae cum/simus saproí* "We're all chic and convivial, so we think – though in fact/We stink, like fetid fish" (*Men.* 312 Bücheler, 311 Cèbe). Cicero is less ironic in reproving Clodia's retinue: "They can be as witty (*faceti*) and clever (*dicaces*) as they wish at parties, and even fluent from time to time in their cups; but the forum is one thing and the couch quite another. The courtroom and the bedroom don't work the same way" (*Cael.* 67). On the other hand, elegance was a welcome mark of culture and status, particularly in a society where status was constantly symbolized. Cicero has such elegances in mind when – in the same speech in which he condescends to Clodia's retinue – he suggests that Herennius' attacks on Caelius' morals belied Herennius' participation *in hac suauitate humanitatis qua prope iam delectantur omnes* "in these cultured delights in which almost everyone takes pleasure" (*Cael.* 25). After the eastern wars of the second century, Greek culture – its art, its language and literature, its dress and habits – provided a deep well of such cultured delights that captured rustic Latium.[3]

How was the balance struck? In the gracious and old-fashioned world of *On the Orator*, style is kept carefully in its place, the handmaiden of high purpose: "I want to hear 'well done! splendid!' (*bene et praeclare*) as often as possible, 'nicely done! delightful!' (*belle et festiue*) not too often," avows Cicero's Crassus (*De or.* 3.101). The allure of *lepos* Cicero restricts largely to humor, and that of a careful and urbane sort. This subservience of *lepos* to *dignitas* is rather tidy. It thus provokes the suspicion that the late Republican elite could – or even had to? – give charm and style a larger role in fashioning their personae. Certainly suavity and even sauciness regularly appear in elite self-representation at this time. Caesar, who shaved his body (Suet. *Iul.* 45.2) and wore a suavely slack tunic (45.3), approached effeminacy – and, apparently, thereby signaled political potency (cf. 22.2). Perhaps M. Caelius, an aggressive prosecutor, imagined his elegant gleam the same way (*Cael.* 77). Cicero's gracious theory of humor belied his own practice: Cato called him a *geloîos hypatos* (Plut. *Cat. Mi.* 21; = *facetus consul*)[4] and contemporaries thought he went too far (Paetus *ap.* *Fam.* 9.20.1; Plut. *Cic.* 27.1; Quint. *Inst.* 12.10.12; Macrob. *Sat.* 2.1.12). If Cicero drove Verres from Rome under a crush of evidence, Hortensius, he of abundant graces, had doubtless planned to beguile by his art, which included gestures like a mime dancer's, or so a critic said (Gell. *NA* 1.5.3 = *ORF* 92.39; cf. Cic. *Quinct.* 77, *Brut.* 303).

Stylishness, then, was more than the vice it appears in Cicero's oratory or the subsidiary virtue it is in rhetorical theory; it was also practically a cardinal virtue – political aestheticism, we might call it.[5] Our keywords could describe stylishness in all these guises, and their slipperiness stems directly from the complexities of Roman views of stylishness. To be clear: this is a double claim on my part; first, that stylishness had multiple valences (a claim about culture); and, second, that our keywords reflect that multiplicity (a claim about semantics). There are two points to observe. First, the difference from English is noteworthy, where positive and negative assessments of style typically use different words altogether ("elegant" vs. "foppish," "funny" vs. "facetious," etc.). Second, the use of our keywords for praise and for blame gives them a certain (and, to my mind, delicious) instability. By assigning the Pergamenes *uenustas* and *facetiae*, for example, Cicero plainly intends to impugn their *fides*: their social gestures, like those of non-Romans generally, cannot be trusted. But Decianus is also a credulous fool, the victim of a prank – punk'd, if you like (or so Cicero would have it). The perpetrators of a successful prank, however cruel or puerile, do win a round on their terms. Cicero's disdain for the Pergamenes' cleverness thus shades into censure of Decianus' gamesmanship. Somehow *uenustas* and *facetiae* have their value even when contemptibly deployed.

I submit that it is this capacity of our keywords for ambiguity, effected by the Romans' ambivalence toward stylishness, that made them attractive to Catullus. On my view he uses the words not merely to represent one particular version of stylishness but to play against the complex ambiguities of its social construction. That is, Catullus does not merely describe the ethos of his own circle but describes it in a way that introduces, through its characteristic vocabulary, a cardinal concern of the larger society. Thereby Catullus both creates a distinctive erotic, social, and poetic ideal and raises challenging questions about the meaning of stylishness itself.

A New Erotics

Specific examples will clarify the point. *Venustas* appears in the well-known epigram praising Lesbia's beauty (c. 86):

> Quintia formosa est multis. mihi candida, longa,
>   recta est: haec ego sic singula confiteor.
> totum illud formosa nego: nam nulla uenustas,
>   nulla in tam magno est corpore mica salis.
> Lesbia formosa est, quae cum pulcerrima tota est,
>   tum omnibus una omnes surripuit Veneres.
>
> Quintia is beautiful, so they say:
>   I would say, fair-complected, tall, perfect posture,
> would grant the single points, deny
>   they all add up to beauty. So grand a body!

> But without attraction, without a single grain of salt.
>   Now Lesbia is beautiful: not only the fairest in every way,
> but also the one woman who's pinched from all the others
>   every gift that Venus gave them.

Venustas here might mean simply "erotic attractiveness," a frequent sense. So in a graffito from Pompeii: *diligo iuuenem uenustum* "I'm in love with a pretty young man" (*CIL* IV.5092.3, *CLE* 44.3). More usually *uenustas* is associated with women, corresponding to *dignitas* in men (Cic. *Off.* 1.130). But such a meaning suits the poem poorly. The poem describes the insufficiency of mere physical beauty, symbolized by Quintia, whose various pulchritudes – height and complexion and the rest – are all she has. She is, literally, statuesque: I translated *candida* "fair-complected" but *candida, longa, recta*, especially when Quintia's is a "grand," even "big," body (*magnum corpus* is not a very erotic expression), recall a sculpture. Lesbia's *uenustas* must transcend mere physical form.

Transcend how? Here the rhetorical use of *uenustas* is relevant. The conjunction of *uenustas* to *sal* "salt," a word which describes ironic, dissimulating or deadpan humor (Krostenko 2001a: 220 n. 59), recalls the *uenustas* that describes the humor of reply. The "salty" mind is alert and clever; so, too, the mind that can quickly toss off rejoinders with *uenustas*. Lesbia's *uenustas* has an active, performed quality – the sparkle of a *hetaira*, as it were, and not the gloss of a beautiful, but vacuous, trophy wife. The sentiment is that of an epigram of Petronius: *dicta sales lusus sermonis gratia risus/uincunt naturae candidioris opus* "Jests, wit, games, charming speech and laughter/overcome the handiwork of lovelier nature" (fr. 31 Bücheler). Hence, perhaps, Catullus' expression for Lesbia's excellence, *tum omnibus una omnes surripuit Veneres*: Lesbia is not merely "the fourth Grace," as in Greek amatory verse (e.g., Callim. *Epigr.* 51 Pf.; *Anth. Pal.* 5.70 [Rufinus], 5.148 [Meleager]), to be wondered at. Rather, Lesbia has "pinched" the Graces of others: she has consciously assembled her own superior repertoire. At any rate our keywords are elsewhere used for women who attract by their performative graces. Varus' girlfriend made a good first impression: she was a *scortillum / . . . non sane illepidum neque inuenustum* "a nice piece, no witless (*inuenustus*) or charmless (*illepidus*) one here" (10.3–4).[6] Flavius is ashamed to introduce a girlfriend who is *illepida* and *inelegans* (6.2). She was a good, or at least energetic, lover, but apparently not much else.

In short, Lesbia's "erotic attractiveness" is like the "cleverness" or "wit" of a quick-thinking orator or a wry prankster. The passive meaning of *uenustas* has, so to speak, been partly overwritten by the active meaning. That is itself a noteworthy piece of verbal art. But there is more here than a pun. The cultural associations, as well as the semantics, of active *uenustas* come into play. Active *uenustas*, of the kind Cicero's ideal orator needed, was a weapon of social competition – the usual arena for active wit and conscious self-presentation. Lesbia's erotic quality is thus likened to the stylishness that served competitors vying for power and influence. To put it another way, our words described an aestheticism that represented political identity; Catullus has used the characteristic descriptors of that aestheticism to represent a purely erotic identity.

Hence the points of comparison between political and erotic *uenustas* in the poem. Political aestheticism was competitive: likewise Lesbia is here a competitor, outdoing other women. Political aestheticism often had a Greek flavor: so, too, here, where Lesbia has Sappho's toponym, in distinction from the very plain name *Quintia*, and is praised by the refitted idioms of Greek amatory verse. An eye for wit – lacking (supposedly) in Decianus – was valued: in this poem Catullus' subtle taste shows that he is no mooning *iuuenis* out of comedy but a connoisseur, above the masses rejected in a priamel (*multis*). The capacity of active *uenustas* to describe both a valuable skill – an artifice of political life – and a dubious attainment – erotic grace – has eased Catullus' figuration of Lesbia.

Thus exploiting the meaning of aestheticism in contemporary political life, Catullus has vindicated an erotic type that existed in the Rome of his time – the modern Roman woman. The type is represented also by Sempronia, who "could compose poetry, raise a joke, give her conversation balance or delicacy or impudence; in short, hers was much wittiness (*facetiae*) and much charm (*lepos*)" (Sall. *Cat.* 25.5). Sallust, of course, whose Sempronia also "assayed many deeds as bold as a man's" (25.1), admired these attainments rather less than Catullus.[7] But the technique whereby Catullus has expressed his admiration raises troubling questions. For Sallust Sempronia's talents, pleasant though they are, mean nothing for political life: *lepos* is, at best, irrelevant to *grauitas*. Catullus, by contrast, defends the apolitical by adapting the patterns of political life and their characteristic idioms – an adaptation effected, it seems, rather easily. We have begun to see, as Selden (1992: 498) puts it, that "[b]y redirecting critical attention from questions of personal circumstance to the logic of self-presentation, the poet gets to the very heart of the politico-discursive system."

A New Social Order

Another poem illustrates Selden's point well. If c. 86 presents a novel vision of the erotic world, c. 12 presents a novel vision of the social world.[8] The poem, addressed to an Asinius Marrucinus, the alleged thief of a napkin from Catullus, features our keywords prominently. Of the actual pilfering Catullus says *manu sinistra/non belle uteris* "You're not using your left hand very neatly" (12.1–2). Marrucinus thinks his larceny is funny (*salsum*, 4) but in fact it is a "cheap and clumsy trick" (*sordida res et inuenusta*, 5). Marrucinus' brother Pollio understands the distinction and is ashamed of his brother's gaucherie: for he is a master of *lepores* and *facetiae* (8–9). The thief, Catullus concludes, risks poetic attack unless he returns the napkin, the value of which is not fiscal but sentimental: it was a gift from friends.

The meanings of our keywords are close to those of late Republican rhetorical criticism. *Inuenusta* describes bad *actio*: a clumsy gesture. *Bellus* signals the appreciation of astute critics, just as in Cicero's use of *bellus* for rhetorical artifices. *Lepores* and *facetiae* at the very least refer to "clever performances" and very likely also to verbal grace: if Pollio is C. Asinius Pollio, he was an orator, a fact whose relevance we will see presently. As in c. 86, not only are the semantics of our keywords apt, but their cultural associations come into play, recalling political aestheticism. The symposiastic aestheticism of c. 12 is, like the political, competitive: Marrucinus' action is turned into a performance for Catullus and Pollio to critique. Political aestheticism drew lines of exclusion and inclusion; as Caesar Strabo observes, "Not everything funny (*ridiculus*) is witty (*facetus*)" (Cic. *De or.* 2.251). Thus does Catullus exclude

Marrucinus, whose definition of *salsum* is faulty, and include (or shanghai) Pollio, who knows from wit. Political aestheticism, as we saw in c. 86, might also have a Greek cast. Here, the recompense which Marrucinus may expect – and which, indeed, c. 12 already examples – will be in a Greek meter named in Greek (*hendecasyllabos*, 10) and molded after Hellenistic "theft" poetry, like cc. 25 or 42. The sentimental value important to the poem is assigned to the napkin with a Greek word, *mnemosynum*.

Our keywords, in short, signal an aestheticism that, like its political counterpart, is competitive and exclusivist. But the group it demarcates is veritably anti-civic – or at least, beneath the easy finish of the poem, the ordinary order of things is perverted. The family is riven: the Asinii brothers are at odds (according to Catullus, anyway, who presumes Pollio will take his side). Generational roles are inverted: the master of this circle is no eminence but a *puer* (12.9) – the sort to spurn *senes seueriores* (cf. 5.3) and traffic with Catiline's *pueri lepidi ac delicati*. Roman law is controverted: sentimental significance did not affect *aestimatio* (12.12) or "market value" of possessions (Paul. *Dig.* 9.2.33), but such does Pollio esteem Catullus' affections that he would pay a talent to undo his brother's action. The Greek world does not complement the Roman: the Greek world provides tropes and language that supplant the Roman. The mannered discussion at Crassus' villa in *On the Orator* is high-minded and thoroughly political, *otium* serving *negotium*: but this group is all *otium*, jovial tipplers caught up *in ioco atque uino* (12.2); in a similar setting (*per iocum atque uinum*, 50.6) Catullus and Calvus exchanged, not rhetorical advice, but passionate poetry.

Like c. 86, c. 12 thus raises questions about the political aestheticism whose piquant vocabulary it has nimbly appropriated. Political aestheticism, like the rhetoric with which Plato wrestled, ran the risk of separating social standing from real substance – doubtless the very reason Cicero in his theoretical works strove so hard to subordinate *lepos* to *grauitas*. But what if *lepos* were cut utterly free of *grauitas*? Of law? Of family? What would happen to society? If that is one question of c. 12, one answer is that the like-minded would find each other and find in each other delight.

That is a thrilling proposition – how nice to be of a *salon*! But, as the poem is perfectly aware – and cold-bloodedly so, by my lights – the proposition is also dangerous. Marrucinus illustrates the danger. Stripped of a voice and inscribed with a failure, he becomes what Catullus wants him to be; the charming but, for Marrucinus, humiliating vignette of the poem – which threatens more of its like, or worse, to come – extinguishes any contrary voice. The crucial move of the poem is thus the depiction of Marrucinus thinking the theft is *salsum*: that move establishes the issue as taste and style, and in the world Catullus creates, where our keywords describe the central values, Marrucinus never had much of a chance. Even the urbane Suffenus, as we will see, requires a *deus ex machina*.

The issue of c. 12 is thus, as Fitzgerald (1995: 96) puts it, "not what the napkin signifies but who makes it signify and how." And that is the bite of the poem. What would happen to society if *lepos* were cut utterly free of *grauitas*? Perhaps not all that much: a small circle, bound by affections and tastes, would assign meanings based on those tastes and affections. "Influence, power, glory, wealth – all of it is either in their possession or located where they please," says Sallust's Catiline, speaking of the *nobiles* (*Cat.* 20.8): substitute *lepos* and *facetiae* for the subjects of the sentence and you have the situation as viewed by Marrucinus – sidelined by a verbal dexterity that manipulates, and even creates, reality (did Marrucinus *really* think the theft was *funny?*). Thus I prefer to think that the *lepores* and *facetiae* of which Pollio is master include verbal performance: a manipulator of language himself, he knows what the current poem and the threatened poems portend for his brother – *ut perueniat in ora uulgi*, to paraphrase c. 40.4. It is worth recalling here another poem which promises to create its own reality. As we have seen, in c. 6 Flavius is ashamed to introduce his girlfriend: she is apparently *illepida* and *inelegans* (6.2). Catullus cruelly infers that she is "some kind of malarial whore" (*nescioquid febriculosi/scorti*, 6.4–5). And yet Catullus wants to "send" or "voice" (*OLD* s.v. *uoco*, 8) Flavius and his lover to the heavens in charming verse (*uolo te ac tuos amores/ad caelum lepido uocare uersu*, 6.16–17). Catullus' *uox* can gift the carnal pair with a lovelier praise than their affair deserves. *Mutatis mutandis*, Hortensius was prepared to do no less for Verres (less ironically, one presumes). Catullus' little poem touches a nerve, and our keywords apply the sharpest pressure.

A New Poetics

Poetry, as we have seen, is important in the working of c. 12. Catullus also uses our keywords to represent his poetic ideals directly. *Lepidus, facetus,* and *uenustus* appear in connection with the kind of poetry important to Catullus: polished, learned, not bombastic. Polish is the hallmark of Catullus' *nouus lepidus libellus*: it is written on a scroll "just now buffed with dry pumice stone" (*arido modo pumice expolitum*, 1.2), plainly a metaphor for the *labor limae*. C. 1's dedicand Cornelius Nepos merits the dedication because he is a comparable artisan: by hard labor (*laboriosis*, 1.7) he compressed Italian history into three volumes. The *Annales* of Volusius, by contrast, ridiculed in c. 36, were *cacata charta* – egested without revision, like the two hundred verses that, in Horace's polemic, Lucilius could toss off while standing on one leg (*Sat.* 1.40). Lack of refinement is occasionally symbolized by the country. Suffenus' bad poetry makes him a "goatherd or a ditchdigger" (*caprimulgus aut fossor*, 22.10), with "less wit than a hick with no wit at all" (*infaceto ... infacetior rure*, 22.14). Volusius' *Annales* are "full of hickish witlessness" (*pleni ruris et infacetiarum*, 36.19).

Learning also mattered. Cornelius' three volumes were not only carefully crafted but also "learned" (*doctis*, 1.7). So was Caecilius' girlfriend, *Sapphica puella/musa doctior*, literally "a girl more learned than the Sapphic muse" (35.16–17), passionate about Caecilius not least because his poem about Cybele, *Magna Mater*, had "started off so attractively" (*uenuste/ ... incohata*, 35.17–18). There is perhaps some hint about Caecilius' style, and thus what qualified as *uenustus*, in c. 36. In that poem Catullus invokes Venus to accept payment of a vow with a hymn that is a neoteric *tour de force*, with Grecizing forms, learned epithets, and an etymological gloss.[9] *Venustus* occurs in that poem, too. Venus is only to accept the vow "if it's not unwitless or unlovely" (*si non illepidum neque inuenustum est*, 36.17). The adjectives describe not only the quality of the joke in the poem, discussed further below, but also the standards Venus is to use to judge the poetic quality of c. 36 itself.

The litotes of c. 36.17 examples another element of Catullan poetics: unpretentiousness. In 1.1 Catullus' *lepidus* book of poems is a *libellus*, not a *liber*, and by 1.8 it has become "this trifling booklet, such as it is" (*quidquid hoc libelli/qualecumque,*

8–9); the book is also *nugae* "trifles" (1.4). The impressive papyrus rolls of the pompous poet Suffenus stand in marked contrast (22.6–8). The "charm and wit" (*lepos, facetiae*) of Calvus that set Catullus aflame were manifest in "versicles" (*uersiculi*, 50.4, cf. 16.3, 6) produced as the poets "played" (*lusimus* 2, *ludebat* 5). That the Pollio of c. 12 is a "boy" I read above as agonistic; but it is an agonistic modesty: the boys play with trifles, while the old men grumble (5.3, 16.12).

These poetic ideals are plainly intended to recall those of Callimachus and like-minded Alexandrian poets. Those ideals are discussed in detail elsewhere in this volume (see Knox). Here I would address a different question: why did Catullus select our keywords to describe these ideals? One reason is that the established technical uses of the words in rhetoric were suitable. *Facetus*, as we have seen, described the easy charm of the plain style (*Rhet. Her.* 4.16) and educated conversation (*De or.* 1.32). *Venustas* characterized clever wit (*De or.* 1.17) and mannered elegances (*Rhet. Her.* 4.19, *Orat.* 84). *Lepos* took in metrical artifice (*Brut.* 140), artful repetition (*Rhet. Her.* 4.35, *De or.* 3.206), and the beautiful figures of speech of the most florid middle style (*Orat.* 96). In all of these there is something of Alexandrianism.

But seeing the metapoetic applications of our keywords simply as adaptations of the technical language of rhetoric misses something. In rhetorical texts, our keywords, repressed, as it were, by technical discourse, express ancillary, and not cardinal, virtues. For Catullus, *lepos* and the rest are, of course, guiding principles. Catullus has appropriated the technical language of rhetoric – but inflected it to capture the ambiguities of political aestheticism prevailing in the late Republic, when *lepos* was a slight and supplemental yet somehow central thing, when *uenustas* enhanced presentation and at the same time seemed to epitomize it, when *facetiae* marked the superior competitor. This conflation closely resembles the use of *uenustas* in c. 86: there "passive" *uenustas* was partly overwritten by its "active" counterpart, here the technical use of our keywords is partly overwritten by their freer and more exciting applications.

Catullus' programmatic use of our keywords thus challenges rhetorical discourse to confront the importance of the wit and attractiveness it carefully constrained; for rhetorical discourse claimed to inculcate, not attractiveness for its own sake, but respectability (cf. *Rhet. Her.* 4.69). Nor is Catullus' challenge merely contrarianism; rather the clashing tastes of Catullus' Rome give his preferences particular point. Cicero's ideal and practice was a virtuoso mastery of all three canonical rhetorical styles, the grand, the middle, and the plain (cf. *Orat.* 69). In response, it seems, a countermovement developed, perhaps as early as 60 BC, idealizing Lysias (*Orat.* 29) and scorning wit and humor (*Orat.* 99) – the "Atticist" movement to which Catullus' friend Calvus and Cicero's friend Brutus subscribed. That movement, of course, could do no other than privilege the plain style – which, as we have seen, could be described as *facetus* and *uenustus*. Catullus has thus appropriated technical terms that were probably coming to be associated with Atticism to valorize a flash and a humor quite unlike what Atticists evidently preferred. And hence a paradox: Cicero's highly flexible stylistic ideal made for a highly versatile speaker equal to any task; but Catullus' repertoire of elegances, narrow by Cicero's standards, makes him hardly less versatile: he, too, can plead a case irrespective of its real merits (c. 6), pillory an opponent (cc. 37, 39), and defend himself against insult (c. 16). One might say Catullus has pinched the graces of Latin rhetoric.

In these metapoetic applications, then, our keywords pass beyond the technical language of rhetoric to recall political aestheticism. Thus it is unsurprising to detect in them the now familiar agonism. In c. 50 Calvus and Catullus exchange poems, as equals it appears, but afterwards Calvus' charms leave Catullus overcome by a nearly erotic longing, enthralled by – and jealous of? – his friend's art, which calls forth from him his own art. Volusius' poetry is not ridiculed in c. 36 solely for literary critical reasons: Catullus is dragging Volusius into a fight between him and Lesbia. Catullus had been lampooning her, or worse, and she had vowed to burn "the very best works of a very bad poet" (*electissima pessimi poetae/scripta*, 36.6–7), meaning Catullus. Catullus deliberately misunderstands *pessimus poeta* to have meant, not "a trouble-some person who is a poet" – himself – but "a poet who is no good at poetry." Volusius is conscripted for the part and his works burnt accordingly. Onto Volusius' poetry and onto Lesbia's words Catullus has thus inscribed his own meaning, just as with the napkin of c. 12. Even the dedication of the book to Nepos in c. 1 repays compliments – not agonism, but reciprocity, its kinder cousin.

The apparent naturalness of our keywords in their programmatic contexts in Catullus is thus deceptive. It was not inevitable that Callimachean poetic ideals be expressed in Latin by those words in particular. The Augustan poets, after all, whose ideals are often comparable – they, too, valued polish and learning and modesty – eschewed the words almost entirely, preferring others like "slender" (*tenuis*) and "light" (*leuis*).[10] That throws into relief the different ways that they and Catullus read Alexandrian poetry. Flash and style, rhetorical or otherwise, involve a certain risk: the risk of failure for having tried too hard or gone too far or simply come up short. The same goes for humor and elegant tropes, to which Cicero and the *Rhetorica ad Herennium* largely restrict our keywords. Catullus, it would seem, enjoyed such risk. Not so the Atticists – or the Augustan poets, whose attitude to risk-taking is diffident: waging war and seeking wealth, two species of accumulating power, are kept at a distance in *recusationes*. The Augustans often configure as a retreat from the political world the same *conuiuium* that for Catullus in c. 12 is a venue of display and competition paralleling the political world, and not only paral-leling it, but revealing its principles with particular clarity. The centerpiece of the *conuiuium*, of course, is wine – which, if the polemics of Hellenistic poetry are relevant, aligns Catullus not with Callimachus, a "drinker from pure springs" (cf. *Aet.* 5.33), but with Dionysus and dithyrambic. That assumes these polemics of Hellenistic poetry really existed, which is by no means certain. Indeed Callimachus' alleged polemical stance against long poetry and the like may not have existed either. Callimachus, like Pollio, has been enlisted to defend Catullus on Catullus' terms. Alexandrianism is like Marrucinus' napkin: Catullus makes it mean what he wants, infusing it with an agonism and flash of a kind that in the first instance belonged to contemporary Roman society. One might say he has pinched Callimachus' graces.

A Total Ethos

For convenience I have thus far treated the erotic, social, and poetic worlds sepa-rately. Even so it has been plain that the ideals expressed by our keywords share terrain. Lesbia's *uenustas* is erotic but also poetic and rhetorical, if she is the like of

Sempronia, who wrote verse well and conversed wittily.[11] Caecilius' neoteric *Magna Mater* was poetically lovely and also won a girl's heart – a girl herself a keen critic of poetry. Calvus' *lepos* and *facetiae* are poetic but the passions they induce in Catullus are expressed in erotic language. Venus will judge Catullus' payment in c. 36 by the standards of *lepos* and *uenustas*: that implies poetic quality, as I have already suggested, but also wit – Catullus slyly misreads Lesbia – and, of course, erotic energy: this is a lovers' tiff being adjudicated by Venus.

The ethos expressed by our keywords is thus a complete package.[12] One of the best-known instances of *uenustus* depends on that totality. In c. 3, Catullus laments the death of his girlfriend's sparrow, bewailing its passage into the abyss and regretting that its death has reddened her eyes with crying. The poem begins thus (1–4):

> Lugete, o Veneres Cupidinesque,
> et quantum est hominum uenustiorum:
> passer mortuus est meae puellae,
> passer, deliciae meae puellae...
>
> Weep, ye gods of love and beauty,
> and all the beautiful people there are:
> my darling's sparrow has died,
> my darling's precious sparrow...

What, precisely, does *uenustiorum* mean here? Hard by *Veneres Cupidinesque*, the word has obvious erotic overtones: the *uenustiores* are "the beautiful people," the earthly counterparts of the gods of love and beauty. The erotic element goes deeper: in the vignette of the poem, the *uenustiores* are presumed to be sympathetic to Catullus' posture of sympathy with a grieving girlfriend: that is why they may be asked to join in his mourning. The eroticism may be deeper still, if *passer* is a double-entendre. Such a possibility might have occurred, in the first four lines anyway, to readers who knew Meleager.[13]

Thus we come to poetics: to be sympathetic to Catullus' posture, the *uenustiores* must have, not tender hearts, but knowledge of the conventions of light amatory verse. *Veneres Cupidinesque* is an unusual phrase: but it recalls the *Érotes* and *Khárites* of the *Carmina Anacreontea*.[14] Reflections on the death of a pet, familiar from the *Anthologia Graeca*,[15] explain and excuse the delicately exaggerated tone: for the poem is, *inter alia*, sententious (*qui nunc it per iter tenebricosum/illuc, unde negant redire quemquam*, "who goeth now down that glum path to the place whence they say no one returns," 11–12) and pathetic (*miselle passer* "poor little sparrow," 16; *turgiduli...ocelli* "sweet little eyes all puffed and swollen," 18). Grandiloquence and tenderness meld: the powers of hell, minions of an underworld god named with an old solemn name, are cursed with an antique-sounding polyptoton (*at uobis male sit, malae tenebrae/Orci*, "cursed be ye, cursed shades of Orcus," 13–14); but the wont of these fell shades is to "gobble everything pretty" (*omnia bella deuoratis*, 14), and thus they made off with "such a darling sparrow" (*tam bellum...passerem abstulistis*, 15).[16]

Reading the poem, in short, requires literary sophistication. To ask the *uenustiores* to mourn is to ask them to participate in the poem's premise. And therefore there is also a social element lurking in *uenustiorum*: a challenge, or rather a request to perform. The vocative is, so to speak, hortatory, or provisional, and the performance required of the reader is more than simply recognizing echoes and reworkings of Greek prettinesses. Appreciating artifice ultimately requires parsing the relationship between artifice and true character. That is, the poem raises a question: is there truth in the literary-critical principle so neatly formulated by the younger Seneca, "As the bent of the soul, so the style of the pen" (*non potest alius esse ingenio, alius animo color*, *Ep.* 114.3)?[17] Does literary bent really reflect moral inclination? If yes, then isn't Catullus a bit of a sap? If no, then isn't Catullus a bit of a player?

The comparative *uenustior* adds to the challenge. It might mean "*uenustus* as opposed to *inuenustus*," or it might mean "more *uenustus* than usual," "particularly *uenustus*," "really in the know, as far as *uenustas* goes." Either way, the expression *quantum est*, which implies a limit, sharpens the meaning; and either way the chasm of *inuenustas* opens up behind the adjective, threatening to engulf the tasteless as surely as hell engulfed the sparrow. An unsentimental reading of a pretty poem: but also the very mix of delicate artfulness and competitiveness, even aggression, that our keywords routinely express. As we will see, Catullus himself certainly responded to the imputation of delicacy by signal aggression, as if to repudiate the thought that they were incommensurate.

The totality of the ethos expressed by our keywords is confirmed especially well by another poem, c. 22, whose Suffenus we have seen several times already:

> Suffenus iste, Vare, quem probe nosti,
> homo est uenustus et dicax et urbanus,
> idemque longos plurimos facit uersus.
>   . . .
> haec cum legas tu, bellus ille et urbanus
> Suffenus unus caprimulgus aut fossor
> rursus uidetur; tantum abhorret ac mutat.
> hoc quid putemus esse? qui modo scurra
> aut si quid hac re scitius uidebatur,
> idem infaceto est infacetior rure,
> simul poemata attigit. neque idem umquam
> aequest beatus ac poema cum scribit:
> tam gaudet in se tamque se ipse miratur.

> The Suffenus whom you know so well, Varus,
> is a lovely, quick-witted, and civilized man –
> and also, without pause, writes very many verses.
>   . . .
> When you read them, that civilized stylish Suffenus
> turns into some goatherd or trencher
> just like that; that's how big the difference is.
> How can we make sense of it? Just a minute ago
> he was full of quips, the very summit of sharp.
> But as soon as he touches a poem –
> there goes his wit, he's left with less
> than a hick who has no wit at all. And yet:
> he's never happier than when writing a poem.
> He's so pleased with himself, so proud of himself.
>
> (1–3, 9–17)

Suffenus is a contradiction. Funny at dinner parties, he is a crashing bore as a poet.
He produces bloated affairs, if their excessively fancy manuscripts are any indication
(Catullus does not describe their content): fine papyrus, new rollers, tidy layout (6–8).
Worse yet, he loses that sense of self-conscious performance our keywords usually
imply. Suffenus thus merits the same skewering as Volusius. But instead Catullus spares
him, after a fashion:

> nimirum idem omnes fallimur, neque est quisquam
> quem non in aliqua re uidere Suffenum
> possis. suus cuique attributus est error;
> sed non uidemus manticae quod in tergo est.
>
> But that's how it is, though.
> We're all deceived in just that way, there's no one
> you can't see Suffenus in, in some respect.
> Everyone's been given a personal failing;
> we just can't see the part of the bag
> that's hanging on our back.
>
> (18–21)

In the bag on our backs, the fable has it, hang our faults, out of our view; our
neighbors' faults hang in a bag in front of us, perfectly visible (Babr. 66, Phaedr.
4.10). Catullus has used an old rhetorical trick, the *sententia* or *gnomé* (cf. *Rhet. Her.*
4.24) – a significant trick in this context. Proverbs belong to an entire community, the
distilled wisdom of its common life (Skinner 2003: 112–14). In that respect they
differ from the judgments our keywords deliver – sharp, elegant, witty, exclusionary.
It is as if, in order to redeem Suffenus, Catullus must appeal to an entirely different
value system. From a smart city boy he becomes, for the moment, a charitable old
man quoting an old saw. In that there is testimony to the totality of the ethos our
keywords encode.[18]

But the totality is attested in another respect: Catullus does not lose himself in
order to save Suffenus. He retains his stance as a Roman Alexandrian. The proverb is
not only the possession of the community: it is also an affect of the Hellenistic poetry
Catullus imitates (Gigante 1978). So is the literary-critical letter to a friend. Thus
even in saving Suffenus Catullus maintains his own poetic integrity. And though
Catullus certainly seems well disposed toward Suffenus, perhaps he has signaled that
Suffenus was destined to fail all along. Suffenus is not merely an urbane wit who
would fit right in with Pollio: he is exceptionally clever, the only person in Catullus to
be called *scurra* and *dicax*. The words express related ideas. *Dicacitas* describes the
"short" (*breuis*) and "sharp" (*peracutus*) quality of snappy comebacks and smart
remarks, as opposed to *cauillatio* "badinage," which is suffused through a whole
discourse (*De or.* 2.218). *Dicacitas* was the hallmark of the *scurra* (*De or.* 2.244). The
scurra was an urban type – the wag or jester or dandy, quick-tongued, apparently
often abusive.[19] The *scurra* had little respect for person or situation (cf. *De or.* 2.246)
and joked whenever possible (*Orat.* 88).

Of course the undertones of disapproval in the above examples reflect Cicero's
(professed) taste. The *scurra* was perhaps a more popular figure – some of them got
rich somehow (*Quinct.* 55, 62; *Har. resp.* 42; *Sest.* 39).[20] *Dicax* and *scurra* in c. 22

might thus reflect the cant of Catullus' circle: like *lepos* and *uenustas*, the words express what is attractive and yet of doubtful value. But *dicax* and *scurra* also connote more aggression and less grace than our keywords. If those connotations carry over to their sole appearances in the Catullan world, then Suffenus had more than one blind spot, which Catullus delicately signals even as he praises him. How to tell? The point, I think, is precisely that it is hard to tell.[21] Suffenus' words, after all, are not quoted – neither the sparkling *bons mots* nor the dull poetry. Here the fiction of the letter is relevant. Catullus is not addressing Suffenus or the reader: he is addressing Varus, registering a judgment with a man who knows the principal (*quem probe nosti*, 22.1) and is evidently a friend of Catullus (if the Varus of c. 10 is the same Varus). They share a set of standards (*quid hoc* putemus *esse*, not *putem*) and are communicating, in an almost technical language, about a member of their social scene who doesn't quite measure up ("You know the guy – he's hilarious, I'm telling you. But have you heard the music his band plays?"). This is their conversation and their aesthetic appraisal, and it excludes us as surely as it excludes Suffenus. That is not particularly consoling. At least Suffenus got Catullus to laugh – somehow.

The Difficulties of Reading Catullus (1)

Catullus, as we have seen, inscribed his own meanings onto Lesbia's words and Marrucinus' actions. But he was not immune to the same treatment. That, at any rate, seems to be the background of c. 16. Aurelius and Furius have impugned Catullus' manhood for writing light verse: *qui me ex uersiculis meis putastis/quod sunt molliculi, parum pudicum* "who take my little verses, soft as they are, to mean that I must be indecent" (3–4). They had apparently been reading the Lesbia or Juventius cycles: *uos, quod milia multa basiorum/legistis, male me marem putatis* "So you read my poems of thousands of kisses, and think that I'm no man?" (12–13).[22] These two readers, then, have done no more than apply the principle of reading we saw above: *non potest alius esse ingenio, alius animo color* (Sen. *Ep.* 114.3).

In response Catullus constructs a clever poem: its argument confutes such readers and its form entraps them. First the argument. Catullus asserts that author and text are distinct: *nam castum esse decet pium poetam/ipsum, uersiculos nihil necesse est* ("The dutiful poet must himself be clean, his verses – not at all," 16.5–6). The general claim, that persona is artifice, is predictable, given the way Furius and Aurelius interpret texts. But the particulars of the claim were not predictable. Catullus does not mount obvious defenses: that literary trifling is a harmless diversion, for example, or that literal readings betoken a dull mind.[23] Rather Catullus argues that unchaste verse is defensible because its charm is especially potent:

> qui tum denique habent salem ac leporem,
> si sunt molliculi ac parum pudici,
> et quod pruriat incitare possunt,
> non dico pueris, sed his pilosis
> qui duros nequeunt mouere lumbos.
>
> It's then, and only then, that [verses] have wit and charm
> if they're nice and soft and short of decent,

and if they're able to stir the part that itches –
and not in boys, either, but in these hairy men
who cannot move their stiffened loins.

(7–11)

This rhetorical maneuver was impossible without the *lepos* we have come to know: it is witty (*sal*), slight (*molliculi*), and erotic (*parum pudici*); and despite all that – or, because of all that – its power is considerable, enough to excite stiff older men. The parallel with political aestheticism is striking. Caesar's self-presentation provides an apt illustration. Like Catullus, Caesar affected delicacy, body depilated and tunic swashly loose. Like Catullus, Caesar was accused of unchastity, surely in part because of that style: he never shook the rumor that he had submitted to the Bithynian king Nicomedes (Suet. *Iul.* 2.49). And like Catullus, Caesar boasted of extravagant masculinity, even as he impishly flaunted the power of effeminacy:[24] having secured certain proconsular provinces despite resistance, Caesar abused his opponents in the senate, threatening to "jump on all their heads" (*insultaturum omnium capitibus*), an idiom for oral penetration. How could a woman do that? an opponent snidely remarked. The Amazons, Caesar replied, smirking (*adludens*), once ruled a great part of Asia (Suet. *Iul.* 22). There was more than one way to metaphorize power relations through gender.

Political aestheticism, then, gives real strength to the argument of the poem. The form of the poem makes Catullus' response all the keener. Catullus' defense of himself implies a principle: the meanings of words are not absolute but depend on the conceptual frame in which they are read. That possibility is exploited in the fabric of the poem itself in three places. First, the language of Catullus' accusers is taken from them. Furius and Aurelius had apparently called Catullus *parum pudicus* and his verses *molliculi*. The latter they meant sexually, with the diminutive signaling contempt; the former phrase sounds the equivalent of *impudicus*, with *parum* having privative value, like *male* in *male marem*.[25] But in the line *si sunt molliculi ac parum pudici*, *molliculi* sounds like a literary-critical term, virtually a term of the neoteric aesthetic proper,[26] and softens the imputation of insufficiency in *parum*, giving *parum pudici* the impish meaning "not quite decent," "just short of decent." Furius and Aurelius' criticisms are reappropriated as literary-critical language – exactly what Catullus did with Lesbia's *pessimus poeta* (36), overwriting the ethical with the aesthetic.

Catullus also reconfigures moral language. The imputation of *mollitia* and *impudicitia* leads him to claim that the *pius poeta* is *castus*. This defense plainly appeals to traditional Roman morality. But as the poem unfolds, morality is not the issue, or not quite. A poet's *pudicitia*, it would appear, is valuable not for its own sake but because it implies control – the very thing Catullus, through his poetry, exercises over the responses of the community. Comparably, *pius poeta* might at first suggest "a poet who is a *pius* person" but the poem will only support a meaning like "a poet who is true to his craft."[27] Certainly vaunting over older men is no act of conventional *pietas*. Laying claim to the positive resonances of the language of morality, the poem promptly reduces morality to power relations. That reduction is, at the first, mere frankness: in Roman ideology morality and power are regularly associated. Cicero had said of Pompey "no commander can control an army who cannot control himself" (*Leg. Man.* 38). But in our poem the *continentia* is aesthetic and, paradoxically, sexualized: the controlled artist controls his readers. There, again, is the like of political aestheticism. The choice of *decet* (and not *oportet* or *necesse est*) encapsulates the issue perfectly. The word sits at the intersection of moral force with taste and appearance: does it mean "morally obligatory," stressing reality, or "tasteful," stressing appearance?

These doublenesses of language, then, are traps: they lure in readers with one meaning and then spring on them another. So signally in the line that begins and ends the poem, a threat of demeaning sexual violence against Furius and Aurelius: *pedicabo ego uos et irrumabo.* The first time the line sounds simply like a curse in a heated quarrel; comparable is 37.7–8 (*non putatis ausurum/me una ducentos irrumare sessores*). The insults of the second line, *Aureli pathice et cinaede Furi,* also sound like mere curses; comparable is 57.1–2 (*pulchre conuenit improbis cinaedis,/ Mamurrae pathicoque Caesarique*). But the climate of the poem is different by the end: Catullus' alleged effeminacy betokened a titillating artfulness that gives him control over his readers – and control makes a real man. In that climate the opening line sounds quite different. The literal meaning of the curses is revivified. The effect is rather as if a poem began "Go to hell!" and then, having established the unrepentant sinfulness of the addressee, ended, "And on the last day you/Go to hell."

In short, the words of the first line mean something different when they reappear at the poem's end. That doubleness ensnares Furius and Aurelius. They misread Catullus' versicles; now they themselves have been forced to misread: Catullus' thousand kisses were not to be taken quite literally – but his sexual threats were. Confident in their hermeneutic, they declared Catullus *parum pudicus*: that same hermeneutic has robbed them of their own *pudicitia*, if not quite literally, then certainly as literally as the poem permits, making them sexually passive characters stigmatized in the very ideology of manliness from which their hermeneutic was derived. They took Catullus as a *puer lepidus ac delicatus,* as happy to be loved as to love; in Catullus' mind that was a theft of his words, and he responds to the theft like Priapus would: jumping on both their heads.

The Difficulties of Reading Catullus (2)

We have already seen an instance of one of our keywords that lacks the overtones produced by political aestheticism: the sparrow of c. 3 is *bellus*, but this is not Suffenus' *bellus*. There are several other instances – though rather less delicate than *tam... bellum passerem.* In c. 97 the repugnant Aemilius, whose apparently diseased gums make his mouth a fetid rictus, "fancies himself a ladies' man" (*se facit esse uenustum,* 9) merely because he is promiscuous. Physical repugnance also figures in c. 69: Rufus' unclean armpits make him "a nasty beast, not the kind a modern girl will sleep with" (*nam mala ualde est/bestia, nec quicum bella puella cubet,* 7–8). In other poems sexual transgression figures. In c. 89 Catullus alleges that a certain Gellius is skinny because he gets a lot of exercise: "his specialty is touching things that shouldn't be touched" (*qui ut nihil attingat, nisi quod fas tangere non est,* 5), including his good mother and his lovely sister (*cui tam bona mater/tamque ualens uiuat tamque uenusta soror,* 1–2). In c. 78 a certain Gallus has one brother with a "very pretty wife" (*lepidissima coniunx,* 1) and another with a "handsome son" (*lepidus filius,* 2). Indulgent man that he is (*bellus homo*, 3), he fixes them up, so the pretty boy and the pretty girl can sleep together (*cum puero ut bello bella puella cubet*, 4).

   Bellus, uenustus, and *lepidus* in these poems – all elegiacs – do not have quite the same edge as the instances we have surveyed thus far. These passages reflect not the idioms of political aestheticism but other, less subtle meanings. *Venustus* as simply "beautiful" is a sense we saw above. *Bellus* could apparently connote simply "sexually active."[28] *Lepidus* as simply "attractive" is an old Plautine use.[29] From these uses alone it is fair to say Catullus' tone of voice in these poems is different – commoner, more comic. The range of Catullus' tones of voice and its relation to generic distinctions between the elegiacs and polymetrics is a topic beyond the aims of this chapter. Here I would make another observation. C. 16 raises an important semantic point clear since the *Dissoi Logoi*: the meanings of words depend not only on the words themselves but on the conceptual frame in which they are lodged. Furius and Aurelius used the hostile construction of *mollitia* attested since Scipio Aemilianus asked whether someone who shaved his thighs was not guilty, too, of being a *cinaedus* (*ORF* 21.30). Catullus' own reinterpretations of *molliculus* and *parum pudicus*, and his use of our keywords, adapt the energies of political aestheticism to construct a far different vision of *mollitia*.

   Can the frame manifest in the elegiacs also be specified? In this place, no – not without interpreting the works in detail. But some elements are worth noticing. There is an element of self-presentation. Aemilius puts himself forward (*se facit*) as *uenustus*. Gellus is not really a *homo bellus*: he's a *homo stultus*, condoning cuckoldry when that might affect his own marriage (78.5–6). *Homo bellus* registers his own hopeful self-justification in arranging trysts. There is also an element of stylish modernity, mostly sexual: Rufus' hygiene excludes him from chic society; Gallus cheerfully embraces modern permissiveness, Gellius even more so.

   These elements recall the ethos of urbanity manifest in the polymetrics: aware of itself, stylish and modern, erotically sophisticated. But in the elegiacs that vision is much reduced: the *bellus* or *uenustus* person is chiefly a poseur and a sexual libertine – there is nothing here of humor or wit or poetic grace. Perhaps that was what our words connoted on the street, as it were. The echoes of comic language are also clear. But another possibility merits consideration: to someone outside of Catullus' circle and outside of the stylish life of the city, the fashionable slang those echelons used to describe themselves might well have seemed to connote little more than promiscuity and posing. It is as if Catullus could hear how his cant sounded to people outside his own covey. That is remarkable: having stolen his own language, Catullus could fiercely defend his vision – or look bemusedly upon its misunderstanding. Such a Protean persona is also a kind of commentary on elite discourse: Catullus adopts just the voice he needs to do whatever job he wants to do – perfect *decorum*.[30] Whoever it is exactly who lies behind these personae, his *Wille zur Macht* is always perfectly clear. There is no more pointed commentary on the meaning of *decorum* than that.

Conclusion

If I have depicted a Catullus who steals and reconfigures language, then looks bemusedly upon its misunderstanding, I might have given the impression of believing the Catullan project is a rhetorical game in which language has no real meaning. On the contrary, Catullus' keywords, at any rate, are supremely precise: they appeal irresistibly to that part of the heart and mind where your brilliant companions and exquisite lovers thrill to your clever remarks and elegant verses, while your feckless enemies, deftly skewered, wail and gnash their teeth outside. That is a very particular kind of passion. To express it, Catullus forms a rhetoric of small-group identity out of the rhetoric of political performances. There's the rub: that was a distinctly unsentimental choice. In politics there are winners and losers, and always self-interest. Likewise in Catullus, shared standards are, often as not, illustrated by exclusion and are even at their best rife with agonism. Your brilliant companions and exquisite lovers, to continue the image, share your ambition to be the cock of the walk. And sometimes they succeed.

The rhetoric of small-group identity thus reflects back on the political world from which it was borrowed, laying bare, through their own approbative language, the fervors of cliquishness and self-presentation in the late Republic. Deprived of respectable *prophaseis*, the *aitia* of style, and of politics, is clear: personal victory. In that there is a cutting critique of the nature of late Republican political life. Of course the critique falls short in one respect. Caesar might have liked the even style of Menander and affected a certain delicacy, but he also knew what Sulla and Sertorius knew and Octavian would presently illustrate: the direction of the Roman world was decided by men who had the brains to accumulate military power, the stomach to think out its implications, and the nerve to act accordingly. The Augustans saw that: but then they had reason to. Catullus' fascination with the joys and perils of social performance, a fascination that is of course a function of wealth, leisure, and intelligence, is also the privilege of a time without civil war. But that is not to say such fascination cannot be clear-eyed. Catullus' is, extraordinarily so. Thus he not only perceived, but also embodied in his poetry, a *lepos* that is as aggressive, even ruthless, as it is charming. If for that reason the polymetrics, in which our keywords are ever prominent, are not perfectly edifying to contemplate, nevertheless their harsh judgments, startling wit, and elegant style, their passions, peccadilloes, and personalities, attract contemplation irresistibly. So, too, the last generation of the Roman Republic. Such is the power of Catullus' *lepidus nouus libellus*.

ACKNOWLEDGMENT

This chapter, by the kind permission of the University of Chicago Press, presents a synopsis of the chief arguments of *Cicero, Catullus, and the Language of Social Performance* (å 2001 by The University of Chicago. All rights reserved.). Fuller philological detail may be found there. The treatments of individual poems differ somewhat, thus: c. 2, fuller reading; c. 16, lengthier treatment of doubleness of language; c. 22, different reading of the closing proverb; c. 86, statuesque quality of Quintia and comparison of Lesbia to Sempronia. This chapter takes more care than the book to integrate the individual readings to the "political aestheticism" herein defined. The text followed is that of Mynors' 1967 OCT. Martin Bloomer kindly offered suggestions on an earlier draft of this chapter.

NOTES

1   This study, then, belongs to those which see in Catullus an observer and critic of social relations, e.g., Nappa (2001); Fitzgerald (1995); Selden (1992).

2   *Lepos non scurrilis*: *Frasier*; *lepos scurrilis*: *South Park*.

3   For a fine appreciation of the ambiguities of Hellenism, see Feldherr (this volume).

4   Leeman (1963: I.61, II.398 n. 100) must be correct that Cato's original word was probably not *ridiculus* but *facetus*.

5   Like television presence in American politics: routinely regarded as insignificant or ancillary and routinely influential.

6   Quinn (1973a) *ad loc.* is, as far as I know, the first to see the adjectives as describing not appearance but urbanity. Skinner (1989) is the finest account of how that urbanity works.

7   Cato admired them still less: he savages an opponent who possessed the very same skills (*ORF* 8.115).

8   Probably not entirely novel: my guess is that the lost lines of Lucilius and Varro would provide convincing precedents.

9   Grecizing forms: *Ancona* 36.13 for *Anconam*, *Hadriae* 36.15 after Greek *Hadrias*; learned epithets: *caeruleo creata ponto* 36.11, *Cnidum … harundinosam* 36.13; etymological gloss: *Vriosque apertos* 36.12, "exposed Urii," where the name Urii recalls *ourios* "windy."

10 E.g., *carmen tenuastis*, Prop. 3.1.5; *tenui … auena*, Verg. *Ecl.* 1.2; *tenues grandia*, Hor. *Carm.* 1.6.9; *spiritum Graiae tenuem Camenae*, Hor. *Carm.* 2.16.38; *calamos inflare leuis*, Verg. *Ecl.* 5.2; *quaere modos leuiore plectro*, Hor. *Carm.* 2.1.40.

11 Indeed the whole poem can be read metapoetically, with Lesbia's beauty representing ideal poetic form: see Skinner (2003: 96–100) with references.

12 Like hippie and hip-hop cultures, in which tastes in clothing, music, language, and social attitude were or are prescribed.

13 R. F. Thomas (1993) summarizes the arguments for taking *passer* as code for the penis by reference to similar images in Meleager. Cf. Willie Dixon's "Little Red Rooster."

14 In the *Carmina Anacreontea*, *Érotes* "Loves" and *Khárites* "Graces" appear commonly (4.18, 25.19, 28.3, 38.5, 44.1, 55.7; 16.28, 44.11, 46.2, 55.6), sometimes together (5.15–16, cf. 55.6–7). Quinn (1973a: 97) notes *ad* 3.1, "The idea that there was more than one Aphrodite seems to have become a commonplace of Alexandrian mythology."

15 Cf. *Anth. Pal.* 7.189 (Aristodicus), 7.190 (Anyte or Leonidas), 7.197 (Phaennus), 7.204 (Agathias Scholasticus).

16 These are not instances of our keyword *bellus*. *Bella* is "pretty" or "dainty," as in *bello pede* (43.2, cf. Var. *Men.* 64). So, too, *bellum* of the sparrow, but with overtones of the use of *bellus* for family members held in affection, e.g., *Piliae et puellae Caeciliae bellissimae salutem dices* (Cicero, *Att.* 6.4.3, to Atticus of his daughter), cf. *Fam.* 14.7.3.

17 Nappa (2001: *passim*) persuasively depicts a Catullus who responds to this principle by creating ostensibly compromised personae that actually provide a platform for social critiques.

18 Catullus also turns to proverbial expressions in cc. 51 (if the transmitted last stanza belongs to the poem) and 70, with the comparable intent of creating perspective on an all-absorbing emotion; cf. G. Williams (1985: 584).

19 Jack of *Will & Grace*.

20 Karen of *Will & Grace*.

21 The text tradition makes the job harder: in *V* line 13, which glosses *scurra*, reads *aut si quid hac re tristius uidebatur*. "Sadder" or "more bitter" hardly seems the right sense. *Scitius* is L. Mueller's conjecture.

22 Thousands of kisses appear both in a poem to Lesbia (5.7) and in one to Juventius (48.3). The point of Selden (1992: 508 n. 139) is valuable: "Critics have often argued that the reference is to one set of poems or the other; the necessity to stake the claim is evidence enough that any knowledgeable reader is inevitably reminded of both."

23 Cicero makes the latter sort of argument against Antony, who had ridiculed the infamous line *cedant arma togae* (*Phil.* 2.20).

24 Thus the "hair bands" of the 1980s: extravagantly masculine, but moussed, eyeshadowed, Spandexed, and in flashy colors otherwise only allowed to sports teams – who, come to think of it, are also extravagantly masculine.

25 This is the privative value of *male* and *parum* familiar from Horace: *digito male pertinaci* (*Carm.* 1.9.24), *parum castis* (1.12.5), *parum comis sine te* (1.30.7).

26 The semantically comparable *tener* is certainly such a term (*poetae tenero, meo sodali*, 35.1); *mollis* occurs with *tener* in (the character) Quintus Cicero's literary-critical exclamation *o poema tenerum et moratum atque molle!* (*Div.* 1.66). Cf. *OLD* s.v. *mollis* 8b.

27 For this sense, cf. 14.7 *qui tantum tibi misit impiorum*, of bad poets.

28 So, at any rate, Pompeian graffiti suggest, e.g., *nemo est bellus nisi qui amauit mulierem adulescentulus* ("nobody's *bellus* unless he's loved a woman while he's young," *CIL* IV 1883 = *CLE* 233).

29 *Eu edepol specie lepida mulierem* (*Rud.* 415), cf. *Mil.* 782, 861, 967; *Per.* 130. Pyrgopolynices is also *lepidus* (*Mil.* 998, 1382), as is Menaechmus in a moment of vanity (*dic hominem lepidissimum esse me, Men.* 147). Catullus' line *cum puero ut bello bella puella cubet* closely resembles *Bacch.* 81, *ut lepidus cum lepida accubet*.

30 I have tried (2001b) to illustrate how Catullus creates two distinct voices to attack Egnatius from two different angles in cc. 37 and 39.

GUIDE TO FURTHER READING

Ramage's *Urbanitas* (1973) describes the chief phases of sophistication and urbanity in the Greco-Roman world. Urbanity as an instrument of inclusion and exclusion is one of Catullus' several dramatizations of the relations between poet, poem, and reader subtly explored in Fitzgerald (1995). Nappa (2001) is a penetrating treatment of Catullus' adoption and manipulation of compromised *personae* as a vehicle of social criticism. Selden (1992) illustrates Catullus' unmasking of the contradictions of professional rhetoric and thus of language as a tool for self-representation.

WORKS CITED

Fitzgerald, W. 1995. *Catullan Provocations: Lyric Poetry and the Drama of Position*. Berkeley, Los Angeles, and London.

Gigante, V. 1978. "Motivi gnomici nella poesia di Catullo." *Vichiana* 7: 257–67.

Krostenko, B. A. 2001a. *Cicero, Catullus, and the Language of Social Performance*. Chicago and London.

Krostenko, B. A. 2001b. "*Arbitria urbanitatis*: Language, Style, and Characterization in Catullus cc. 39 and 37." *Classical Antiquity* 20.2: 239–72.

Leeman, A. D. 1963. *Orationis ratio*. 2 vols. Amsterdam.

Nappa, C. 2001. *Aspects of Catullus' Social Fiction*. Frankfurt.

Quinn, K. 1973a. *Catullus: The Poems.* 2nd edn. London and Basingstoke.

Ramage, E. S. 1973. Urbanitas: *Ancient Sophistication and Refinement.* Norman, OK.

Selden, D. L. 1992. "*Ceveat lector*: Catullus and the Rhetoric of Performance." In R. Hexter and D. Selden, eds., *Innovations of Antiquity.* New York and London. 461–512.

Skinner, M. B. 1989. "*Ut decuit cinaediorem:* Power, Gender, and Urbanity in Catullus 10." *Helios* 16: 7–23.

Skinner, M. B. 2003. *Catullus in Verona: A Reading of the Elegiac* Libellus, *Poems 65–116.* Columbus, OH.

Thomas, R. F. 1993. "Sparrows, Hares, and Doves: A Catullan Metaphor and Its Tradition." *Helios* 20: 131–42.

Williams, G. 1985 [1968]. *Tradition and Originality in Roman Poetry.* 2nd edn. Oxford.

PART V

Poems and Groups of Poems

CHAPTER THIRTEEN

Catullus and the Programmatic Poem: The Origins, Scope, and Utility of a Concept

William W. Batstone

Definition and Examples

The identification and interpretation of "programmatic poetry" is an interpretive activity that is in many ways peculiar within the practice of classics in the wake of the old New Criticism. The term does not appear in *The Princeton Encyclopedia of Poetry and Poetics* (1993) or William Harmon's *A Handbook to Literature* (1996), and an internet search finds that in academic discourse and even in interviews with poets "programmatic poetry" usually refers either to poetry with a distinct political or ideological program or to poetry that is written for a specific occasion (like "programmatic music"). For most classicists, however, "programmatic poetry" refers to those poems or passages where poets, either directly or indirectly, speak of their poetry. They may outline the contents, themes, and subjects of a book of poetry or offer a general defense of a genre, like satire, or of an aesthetic, like neo-Callimacheanism. The program may take form as a positive assertion of values or as an attack on the aesthetics of those who do not share the poet's values and practice. Outside the program poems of satire, programmatic assertions are typically metaphorical or figurative, and even in satire the "figure of the satirist" is not to be equated with the poet, nor what he says with the purpose of the genre. Programmatic poetry is most interesting, illuminating, and controversial when it is concerned with poetic goals, literary approach, and stylistic preferences, but it is always taken to be a self-conscious authorial statement (which may still be ironic) about a poetic practice larger than the occasion of the particular poem or passage.

Catullus 1

Perhaps the most uncontroversial[1] example of a programmatic poem in the Catullan corpus is one that introduces the collection we have:

> To whom do I give my new pleasant little book,
> polished just now with the dry pumice?
> To you, Cornelius, because you used to
> think my stuff was worth something,
> long ago, when you alone of the Italians dared
> to unfold the whole of history in three rolls,
> learned, by Jupiter, and belabored.
> And so, have it yourself, whatever this little book
> is, whatever it's worth, and, O my patron Muse,
> let it remain through the years more than a lifetime.

Here, in the guise of a dedication poem, Catullus is understood to speak indirectly of the aesthetic values that his poetry will evince. His book, by being pleasant (*lepidus*), new (*novus*), and small (*libellus*), does not fit either the conservative tradition of moral *gravitas* or the tradition of historical epic. By referring to it as "stuff" (*nugae*) and by being self-effacing in his own evaluation ("whatever this little book is", "whatever it's worth"), he recalls its colloquial unpretentiousness. The papyrus roll is polished, which recalls the language of the neo-Callimachean tradition, one that values refined, careful attention to the minutiae of style, and this attention is illustrated by the reference to the "dry pumice," which recalls the language of style in the rhetorical tradition, and so specifies his stylistic proclivities in terms of precision, lack of excess, and elegance (Batstone 1998).

Even the dedicatee, Cornelius Nepos, plays a role in this program: as the recipient of the book, he both points to its value and represents the kind of person who will find value in this book: a man who appreciates the unpretentious, a man of intellectual daring and concision, a man of learning, and one who understands the need for hard work. Some of these characteristics Nepos shares with the Catullus of this poem: concision is found in the small book, daring in the publication of trifles, hard work in the polish. Other characteristics will be found to mark Catullus' own poetry: learning, as when Catullus complains that he cannot send Manlius a poetic gift because he did not bring his books from Rome (68.31–40); the lone figure standing amid history may recall Catullus wandering the reaches of the Roman Empire (c. 11).

On this reading of Catullus 1, the poet alludes to his style, his values, and his audience. One might say that it is an effort to introduce his readers to his poetic project by suggesting that they might adopt the values that he and Cornelius share. None of this means that the poem is not also a dedication poem to an older fellow Transpadane who could have, and may have, helped Catullus as a young writer in Rome. In fact, one may read this occasion as an introduction to the exchange value of poetry in Rome and in the Catullan corpus, to its role in friendship and gift-giving. Like many programmatic poems, Catullus 1 uses both its language of reference and its nominal occasion (see Feldherr, this volume) to make more general statements about Catullus' poetic practice.

Catullus 27

Another kind of programmatic poem addresses the contents of a specific book without elaborating a larger poetic practice. For instance, just before Catullus launches into satiric attacks upon Piso's staff and upon Caesar and Pompey, he inserts a poem, c. 27, that seems to be addressed to his attendant at a symposium, but may be read as an announcement of new concerns and the transition to a new stylistic register (Wiseman 1969: 7–8; cf. Thomson 1997: 200–1):

> Slave-boy, server of aged Falernian,
> fill for me more bitter cups
> as the law of Postumia requires, a mistress
> drunker than the drunken grape.
> But you, o waters, destroyers of wine,
> begone and away, and take up residence
> with the righteous: here is the undiluted Bacchic.

There is much that is disputed about this poem, but a programmatic reading will note that Catullus imagines his poetry in terms of a banquet, and, in fact, it is quite likely that the most common performance of his work would be as the entertainment at a banquet. The description of the cups as "bitter" is an apt description of satire in general and it is the dominant mood of Catullus' political satire. Consequently, the call for "more bitter" cups suggests that Catullus' poetry will become more savage. Postumia, whoever she is (perhaps the wife of Ser. Sulpicius Rufus, *cos.* 51), has the unusual and perhaps licentious (certainly drunken) role of presiding over the toasts – which may also be seen as a figure for Catullus' poems.

When the poet dismisses the water that is used to dilute wine, saying "pass over to the moralists," one may remember that he had earlier distinguished himself from these same moralists by rejecting their talk: "Let us live, my Lesbia, and let us love and value the talk of moralistic old men as worth a single penny!" (5.1–2). This suggests an alignment of poetry with its erotic and Bacchic concerns against both moralism and politics-as-usual, and a witty rewriting of the *lex Postumia* ("the Postumian law"), a law of Numa's time that regulated wine and libations. Thus, we seem to have an intersection of Falernian wine (an expensive aged wine from Naples, the favorite of poets and aristocrats) and poetic symposia, moral and political propriety, and the intensity of Catullan satire. Such an intersection of concerns would be a fitting introduction to the poems that follow. At the banquet of poetry, Catullus will now toast Memmius and Piso with "May the gods and goddesses bring many curses upon you, you disgraces to Romulus and Remus" (28.14–15) and attack the generals Caesar and Pompey with "Was it for this reason . . . that you have ruined the world?" (29.24–5).

Catullus 116

Just as the beginning of a collection serves to introduce the poems that follow, so the end is a convenient place to reflect on the completed collection or to look forward to what is to come. Poem 116 can be read as doing just this when Catullus refers again to the effectiveness of his poetry as a social and satiric weapon.

> Often before with eager heart I have wondered
>   how I could send you some Callimachean poems,
> to placate you toward us, and stop your efforts
>   to send hateful missiles against my head.
> Now I see that I have taken this labor in vain,
>   Gellius, and that our prayers have been ineffective.
> We will evade the missiles you have sent against us,
>   but you gonna be pierced by mine and you gonna pay.

This poem touches on common themes. Catullus characterizes himself as a Callimachean poet and Callimachean poetry as requiring zeal and labor. It is a poetry of connection (prayers) and part of its effect is to be soothing and peaceful. He compares this tradition with the hostile weapons of the satiric tradition. Just as Gellius is a bad (i.e., unmoved, unreconciled) reader of Callimachus, so he is a poor maker of satiric missiles. And so Catullus will reply. One may easily infer that Catullus' professed excellence as a satirist corresponds to an implied excellence as a Callimachean (certainly his preferred mode, according to this poem). Further, this poem recalls poem 1 (as well as poems 65 and 66) as a form of poetic exchange, recalling the social dimension of Catullus' poetry (W. J. Tatum 1997). It is also an inverted dedication (Macleod 1973), which replaces gift-giving with vengeance and closes the collection (Dettmer 1983, 1994). And so, the poem ends the collection insisting upon the role of Catullus' poetry in the exchanges of friendship or enmity, associating Catullus with the two kinds of poetry that have preceded, pointing to the potential vulnerability or ineffectiveness of merely Callimachean poetry, and promising to continue, perhaps with added satiric fire.

In all three of these examples, the interpretive "trick" is to read the particular circumstance (presentation of a book, ordering stronger wine, complaining about someone's attacks) as a general reference to poetic values. We construe some terms as affirming Callimachean values, others as recalling a satiric tradition that is in some sense opposed to Callimachean values. Since the Callimachean program itself is oppositional and aggressive, it is always possible to read opposition to or additions to the Callimachean program as the way in which a neo-Callimachean renews the aesthetic, that is, as itself a Callimachean move. For example, "dryness" in poem 1 can be a Roman way of talking about concision as well as a witty playfulness with the Callimachean program: Callimachus opposed the tiny clear stream to the epic river of refuse; Catullus takes it one step further and values the dry pumice. The strength of this kind of interpretation is that it finds coherence in the poetic corpus reflected in a metaphorical and allusive language.

Background

In Wheeler's classic study, *Catullus and the Traditions of Ancient Poetry* (1934), the term "programmatic poetry" is not found, although the function is clearly recognized. Of Catullus' first poem, Wheeler says, "The poem is intended as a dedication to Cornelius Nepos of a book (*libellus*) of the poet's trifles (*nugae*). The poet touches modestly on the character of the book not only by calling the poem 'trifles' but also in the phrases *quidquid hoc libelli*, 'this bit of a book,' and *qualecumque*, 'however poor it may be' " (1934: 221–2). Others will call these references programmatic, but Wheeler does not use the term or allegorize the occasion and the language. For him, the poem remains primarily a dedication poem that incidentally introduces poetic evaluations. Within the tradition of "programmatic poetry" the same poem is primarily a programmatic poem that poses as a dedication poem.

Here is the beginning of the first article that treats Catullus 1 openly and directly as a poem whose primary purpose is to talk, albeit obliquely, about the poet's aesthetic program:

> We should naturally expect the first poem in a collection which is extraordinarily varied in subject and form and which is often highly personal, to reveal something, obliquely or openly, about its author's general aesthetic attitude. Thus, in Catullus' opening poem we might reasonably look for something more than the literal fact that this slim new book is attractive – in itself this intelligence would seem almost coy – and for something more than a justified dedication and a final request of a nameless Muse that the collection may live for more than one generation. We should expect, in short, ... some sort of information about the whole collection's spirit and style. (Elder 1966: 143)

Although Elder reads poem 1 as programmatic, he still does not use the term.[2] In fact, the term which is so much in vogue these days first becomes current in classical scholarship in the 1960s. During this period, it is used primarily of those poems written by satirists in which they defend their literary, political, and moral purpose.[3]

During this same period, however, work on the relationship between the Roman poets and Callimachus was beginning to have a major impact.[4] By the mid-1970s, scholars had become attuned to the learned style of allusion that would shape Roman poetry from Catullus' generation on, and by 1980 Gordon Williams devotes seven pages to "programmatic poems" in *Figures of Thought in Roman Poetry* (1980: 34–40). It was found that the values and terms of Callimachean poetry (learned, refined, slowly wrought, daring, concise, discontinuous) along with the metaphors that recalled those values (slender, off the beaten track, clear streams, small springs) frequently appeared in this new Roman poetry. In Callimachus the pure, clear water from a holy and undefiled spring is opposed to the turbid, rushing, muddy river of epic; the slender muse to the fat victim (see Knox, this volume). Allusions to this language allowed Roman poets to claim affiliation as neo-Callimachean poets and to refine and contest various aspects of that affiliation.

The discovery of this poetic language and the way in which it transformed Roman poetry created a veritable industry in "programmatic poetry." One way to get a snapshot of this event, which continues even today, is to do a word search in a few journals. *L'Année philologique* records 4 instances of "programmatic" in our sense for the decade of the 1970s (none for the 1960s), a total that jumps to 14 in the 1980s and 22 in the 1990s; *Classical Philology* shows a similar pattern, with 7 for the 1960s, 12 for the 1970s, 17 for the 1980s, and 41 for the 1990s; likewise, *Classical Review* shows 2 for the 1960s, 21 for the 1970s, 27 for the 1980s, and 55 for the 1990s.

The reasons for this fascination with programmatic poetry are no doubt diverse. It is, however, useful to look at what the term has empowered. We have already mentioned its empowerment of the allegorical reading of minutiae. It may not be an accident that, just as the old New Criticism was gaining a foothold in the classics, classicists were provided with an interpretive tool that valued what was "in the poem itself'": "Why these seeming oppositions? What may they intend to say to us?" (Elder 1966: 144). At the same time, their interpretation required a learned, historical approach to literary discourse. In other words, the two objectifications most highly prized by classicists (the objectification of "the poem itself" and the historical bias of classical scholarship) were simultaneously satisfied and made to rest on the authority of the poet's self-understanding, which itself was a mirror image of the scholar's learning.

But the ascendancy of "close reading" in the classics coincided with the demise of the old New Criticism elsewhere in the humanities. The mid-1970s was a time of new directions in the human sciences. Many were exploring the slipperiness of language, intention, and meaning. Few believed that meaning was located in the poem. "Reader-response criticism" and "reception theory" appeared; deconstruction was already rattling the nerves of the old guard. And writers like Barthes (1977) and Foucault (1977) were proclaiming the "death of the author" and questioning the author-function. When set within this history, the classicist's interest in programmatic poetry was not just a late-coming concern with "the poem itself" but a reactionary impulse interested in limiting the inevitable slippage of language and in securing the authority of the author over his or her words. It was, in other words, itself a programmatic response to some of the most troubling (for some) and most liberating (for others) aspects of postmodernism. But it was also a new way of understanding what the poets of Rome were doing, and it was highly adaptable.

Defining the Poetry Book or Sequence

Perhaps the least controversial and the least interesting programmatic poems are those that refer only to the book the reader is reading. The first poem does more than that as it lays out a general aesthetic, but other poems, like poem 27 above, seem to introduce only a change in the contents of Catullus' book. Another example would be the fragment[5] attached to the end of poem 14:

> If there will happen to be any readers
> of my foolishness, and if you will not be horrified
> to touch us with your hands ...

Like poem 27, this poem can be read as introducing a new group of poems, the Furius, Aurelius, Juventius cycle (15, 16, 21,[6] 23, 24, 26), which indulge overtly sexual themes (Wiseman 1969: 7–10), or it may be read as marking the entire sequence from 15 to 26 as a series of *ineptiae*, "instances of foolishness," ironically meant, of course (Forsyth 1989: 81–5).

A more complex and elusive example would be poem 65. In this poem Catullus promises his friend a poem, a translation of Callimachus. In other words, it is a poem that introduces poetry and talks about poetry. The poem also comes at the point in the *libellus* where Catullus begins a sequence of long poems in elegiac couplets (65–8) followed by a sequence of epigrams, also in elegiac couplets (69–116). In other words, poem 65 seems to be the first poem in a sequence or book of elegiacs. Clues like this suggest that it can or should be read both in terms of the contents of the poems to follow and in terms of Catullus' general aesthetic. What can we discover if we do that?

Catullus mentions "Callimachean songs" in only two places in his corpus: poem 65 and poem 116. Since "ring-composition" is common in Catullus' poetry, this can be taken as further evidence that these poems mark the beginning and the ending of a sequence (Macleod 1973; Forsyth 1977b: 352–3). Furthermore, poems 1, 65, and 116 all use poetic gift-giving as a way of negotiating the social space in Rome, a task especially important if one is a noble at home in the provinces, as Catullus was, but a newcomer with few connections in Rome (Clausen 1976: 37; W. J. Tatum 1997). One critic notes that poem 65 marks a transition back to more personal poetry after the epyllion, poem 64 (King 1988). Others call attention to the claim: "I will always sing songs saddened by your death." Quinn comments: "Was the statement...retained by Catullus, as seeming to him the right light in which to view the whole body of his elegiac poetry? Not all of the elegiac pieces are sad in any simple sense of the word. It is true none the less that the gaiety of 1–60 is conspicuously absent and that a new sardonic note preponderates" (1972b: 265). Putting all this together, it becomes possible to read poem 65 as the first of a sequence of poems, one that announces a change in meter, subject matter, and tone, while declaring again the poet's Callimachean affiliations and emphasizing the social function of poetry.

All this seems plausible and interesting, but it depends upon major assumptions about the Catullan corpus. What if Catullus did not arrange his own poetry in the order in which we have it? Or, what if poem 65 begins a new book, instead of a new sequence, or if the sequence 65 introduces ends with the complex Callimachean elegy, 68b, on Laodamia and his brother's death? And, what if a reader refuses to accept the possibility that a poem like c. 85 is saddened by the death of Catullus' brother?

> I hate and I love. Why do I do it, perhaps you ask
> I don't know. It happens, I feel it, I'm tortured.

Or that a poem like c. 93 is in any meaningful way "sad"?

> I have no particular desire, Caesar, to want to please you
> nor to know if your skin is light or dark.

We will come back to these issues, but it seems useful to make one observation. At some point, "programmatic readings" depend upon assumptions that they can only support by circularity: e.g., poem 65 introduces an elegiac sequence because it is programmatic and, since it is programmatic, poem 93 must be read elegiacally. This is in the nature of a programmatic statement: it makes a general claim which requires (or compels) a complementary reading of other poems. Of course, if other poems contradict the claim, then either the programmatic reading is incorrect or it must be reread as ironic. This means that a "programmatic poem" does not tell you what you will find in the corpus or how to read it, but is the beginning of a relational activity: the "programmatic" language is adjusted to the reader's understanding of the corpus and vice versa.

Poems about Poets and Poetry

In addition to poems that articulate Catullus' poetic program by reference to his poems, there are those that can reveal the general poetic program by reference to Catullus' community of fellow poets. Here, the poet affirms his aesthetic preferences by allying himself with those poets who are like him, and distinguishing the poetic practices of his coterie from others. Perhaps most frequently cited in this regard (beginning with Wimmel 1960: 130–1 and Clausen 1964: 188–9) is poem 95:

> My friend Cinna's *Zmyrna*, finally after nine harvests
>   and nine winters since it was begun is published,
> while in the meantime Hortensius five hundred thousand . . .
>   in one. . . .
> *Zmyrna* will be sent to the hollow waves of Satrachus,
>   *Zmyrna* will be long read by the white haired generations.
> But the *Annales* of Volusius will die at Padua itself,
>   and become loose wrapping tunics for mackerel.

What marks this poem as programmatic is the references to Cinna and Volusius, the metaphorical language of style, and the combative tone. Cinna was a young poet of Catullus' generation, one who had adapted Callimachus' epigram on Aratus for his own purposes. In that epigram (27 Pf.), Callimachus had greeted Aratus' verses as "slender writings, the evidence of Aratus' sleeplessness" – particularly witty in reference to astronomical poetry. Cinna (fr. 11 Courtney) in his adaptation offers a book of Aratus' poetry to someone:

> These songs, the long night-watch by Aratean
>   lanterns, by which we know the aetherial fires,
> written in a little dry booklet of light mallow leaves,
>   I have brought you, my gift, on a little Bithynian boat.

The night-watch recalls Callimachus, but the diminutives, the light mallow and the dry little book, recall Catullus 1. Elsewhere (fr. 14 Courtney), Cinna celebrates a poem by Valerius Cato, *Dictynna*: "May our friend Cato's *Dictynna* last through the centuries." This is significant because Cinna's words again may seem to appear in Catullus 1. The last line of Catullus 1, *plus uno maneat perenne saeclo*, recalls, reverses, and even trumps Cinna's wish for Cato: *saecula per maneat nostri Dictynna Catonis*. In other words, these are poets who know each other's poetry and who share a common language and common aesthetic values.

Volusius, on the other hand, wrote the kind of poetry the neo-Callimachean neoterics had no patience for. "*The Annales* of Volusius, sheets of shit," begins one of Catullus' poems (c. 36), and the vehemence with which he rejects this poetry recalls the beginning of Callimachus' *Aetia*, as does his language: Cinna's *Zmyrna* (itself a recherché version of *Smyrna*) was slowly and carefully worked; it will live long and travel far. It will be read by the curling wave of the Satrachus River, which is the homeland of its own subject. Volusius' poem, on the other hand, is associated with excess, haste, and quantity (a line is missing in the Latin and so we can only guess at the content, although the contrast is clear). His poem will not travel beyond the Po, a wide, muddy river, presumably near Volusius' home. And his poem will not even be read, but serve to wrap mackerel in.

Poem 95 celebrates the poet Cinna and the shared values of this group of poets, just as it greets and predicts a long life for Cinna's newly finished poem. Poem 50, with more playfulness, again celebrates the shared aesthetic of Catullus' friends, but this time the poem takes the form of a challenge for more poetry. It begins:

> Yesterday, Licinius, when we had nothing to do
> we played around on my writing tablets,
> as we had agreed to be pleasure-seekers
> writing verselets, each taking his turn,
> playing now in one meter, now another,
> giving tit for tat amid laughter and wine.

Before 1970 (Segal 1970: 25), this poem was read as an occasional poem sent to Licinius after a night of drinking and versifying. But why would Licinius need to be told what they did? That they had nothing else to do? That they had agreed to be *delicati* (translated here as "pleasure-seekers")? And later in the poem Catullus even says, "I made this poem for you, sweet man." Today it is felt to be obvious that the language of poem 50 "contains the language of neoteric poetic preference (for example *otiosi, lusimus, delicatos, versiculos, lepore, facetiisque, iucunde*)" (R. F. Thomas 1979: 201). As this language weaves together passion and poetry, the language of love and the language of aesthetics, Catullus does so around the figure of "sleeplessness" – the delightful pleasure of Licinius and his wit keeps Catullus awake:

> And I went away from there enkindled
> by the pleasure of your wit, Licinius,
> so food did not help my misery
> nor did sleep close my eyes in peace
> but restless and fevered, all over the bed
> I tossed, eager to see the light
> that I might speak with you and be with you.

Like a lover he cannot eat or sleep, but his love is as much for Licinius as it is for the poetic game of making little verses. The result is now the sleeplessness of poetic composition, an explicit value as we saw in the poetry of Callimachus:

> But after my limbs exhausted with labor
> were lying half dead on the narrow bed
> I made this poem for you, sweet man,
> so you could see my pain.

Catullus ends his poem with a request that Licinius respond with another poem, that the poetic game of the prior night may continue to be played, but now, it would seem, in public, since Catullus' poem is a public production:

> Now, be careful, don't be proud, and, careful,
> I beg you, don't reject our prayers, dear one,

lest Nemesis demand her penalty,
she's a vehement goddess, careful, don't offend her.

The poem is programmatic to the extent that it celebrates the values of Catullus'
poetic community: love and passion, playfulness and sleeplessness as both the result of
poetry and the cause of more poetry. It locates these values within the Callimachean
tradition by emphasizing the small, refined composition (*versiculos*, cf. *lectulo*), technical experiments (*ludebat numero modo hoc modo illoc*), an interest in emotional
pathologies, but most of all by its playful reference to and expansion of Callimachean
"sleeplessness." As a challenge to Licinius, the poem serves both to recall aesthetic
values and to present them in its own performance of wit, threat, and friendship. The
fact that in many ways this poem recalls the language and ideas of both the introductory poem 1 (*lepor = lepidus, ludere = nugae*, diminutives, stylistic refinement,
the importance of friends and the exchange of poetry) and the opening pair of poems
on Lesbia's sparrow (Segal 1970: 26–7) makes it easy to read the poem as forming a
ring-composition with the opening poem. Such a structure suggests that poem 50
ends a collection that was published as poems 1–50 and was the *libellus* that Catullus
introduces in poem 1 (Clausen 1982: 193–7).

Our desire for historical and biographical information is pleased by such a theory,
but we cannot ignore its deep dependency on circular interpretation. Clausen, who
argued for this view, further speculated that poem 51 (Catullus' famous translation of
Sappho) had been left out of the original collection by Catullus because it was
unsatisfactory: "and no ingenuity of interpretation will make it seem otherwise"
(Clausen 1982: 196). It was added by an editor who connected the leisure of Catullus
and Licinius (the first line refers to them as *otiosi*) with the final stanza of poem 51 on
the destructive power of leisure. But what if we read the *otiosi* of the first line of 50
and the *otium* of the last stanzas of 51 themselves as ring-composition? For some
readers it becomes possible to find in the paired poems a programmatic statement
about poetry, passion, and society.

Poem 50, the argument goes, is not just a playful combination of passion and
poetry, but rather a challenge to the serious world of Roman business. The poem
"dwells upon the deliberately inconsequential activities, the frivolous – one might
almost say, defiantly frivolous – activities of a privileged class . . . The word [*otiosi*],
then, adumbrates both a mode of life and (indirectly) an aesthetic" and it does so
because *otium* is indispensable to both (Segal 1970: 25, 28; Pucci 1961: 249–56).
According to this interpretation, it is just this aesthetic, erotic life that poem 51 also
celebrates and judges: it celebrates *otium* first of all by translating Sappho into Latin
in the original Sapphic meter and it judges *otium* in the final added stanza:

Leisure, Catullus, is a dangerous thing.
Leisure delights and excites you too much.
Leisure has already destroyed both
    kings and their blessed cities.

Thus, the irony of poem 50 is that poetic pleasure produces pain, sleeplessness, and a
challenge that involves the vehement goddess Nemesis; the irony of poem 51 is that
leisure produces both a beautiful poetic translation and a troubling and dangerous

separation from the world of political and military accomplishment. "Taken together, 50 and 51 recreate and imaginatively affirm that mode of life – but without denying the pain and restlessness which may arise from its intensity and the self-doubt which may follow from its boldly asserted independence" (Segal 1970: 31). Once again we discover that the programmatic nature of a poem, like 50 or 51, depends upon both its interpretation and the interpretation of other poems. There is no way to choose between these alternatives, in part because they depend upon whether the reader judges 51 to be a failure or not and whether the reader thinks the book ended with poem 50.

But Segal's reading of 51 introduces something else into our discussion of programmatic poetry: performance as programmatic. Poem 51 addresses poetry and aesthetics in part by being itself a poetic artifact, and by its position in relationship to a poem more explicitly about poetry, poem 50. Previously in our discussion, we saw that what a poem does may support and illustrate the aesthetic that the poem professes. Poem 95 is an example, about which Clausen says: "a polemical poem in the Callimachean style was not merely a confutation; it was, simultaneously, a demonstration of how poetry ought to be written" (1982: 185). Here, it is the performance itself (both in its position and in its artistry) that makes possible the irony that a poem which criticizes leisure follows the delights of leisure and is itself the product of leisure.

The view that what a poem does can be as self-referential, and so as programmatic, as what it figuratively says opens new possibilities for interpretation. Poem 36 rejects the poetry of Volusius, "*Annales* of Volusius, sheets of shit," and consigns them to the fire. But this is a joke: Lesbia had said she would throw in the fire the select verse of the worst poet, meaning Catullus, if he stopped writing fierce iambs. When Catullus interprets "the worst poet" to be Volusius, it is both a joke on Lesbia and with Lesbia, because as they burn Volusius' *Annales* they reconstruct the bond that connects them as people who share erotic and aesthetic values: the joke is "not unpleasant" (*non illepidum*, cf. Catullus' book) and "not unlovely." Furthermore, it repays a vow to Venus, who is celebrated in terms of a personal and literary geography that requires learning and personal familiarity. The contrast between the joke with its playful learning and Volusius' poetry, "full of the farm and clumsiness," is an aesthetic contrast that the poem celebrates as it celebrates poetry's ability to win back Lesbia, to make the obscure and personal famous, to play with language, and to indulge life's lovely comedies.

Performing the Program

Irony and comedy are, of course, performances, and when Catullus in poem 36 seems intentionally to misunderstand Lesbia's vows, he presents himself, his world, and his aesthetic as elements that, like the clever slave of Roman comedy, escape the efforts of others to pin down or to make subject to their intentions and understandings. It is, therefore, not surprising to discover that many of the terms that we have been discussing as part of a sophisticated neo-Callimacheanism are also associated with the world of Roman comedy. Returning to poem 50, we find terms like *lusimus*, *ludebat* (comedy itself was called a game, *ludus*), *iocum atque vinum* ("jokes and wine"), and especially *lepidus* (the term for both the pleasant old man, a stock character in comedy, and the moment when the trick is successful), which also describes Catullus' book in poem 1 and his joke in poem 36.

This raises a programmatic issue: since Callimachus was himself ill-disposed to comedy (R. F. Thomas 1979: 180–7), how does Catullus see the relationship between his Callimachean aesthetic and his comic persona? Poem 7, although it is not in any literal sense about poetry, can be seen to allude to the neo-Callimachean aesthetic as well as to perform a revision of that aesthetic.

> You are asking how many kissings of yours
> are enough for me, Lesbia, and more.
> As great as the amount of Libyan sand
> that lies in Cyrene, rich in silphium,
> between the oracle of sultry Jove
> and the sacred tomb of old Battus,
> or as many as the stars in the still of the night
> that gaze on people's secret affairs,
> that you kiss me that many kisses
> is enough and more for your crazy Catullus,
> kisses that the curious cannot count up
> nor can the wicked tongue bewitch.

On the surface, this poem says little more than, "give me countless kisses." But it says it obliquely, as if one were supposed to figure out the difference between the amount of sand in Cyrene and that of sand somewhere else, and it says it twice. It is this disjunction between what the poem says and how it says it that calls attention to the manner of the poetry as some sort of marker in itself, and, if the poem is reflecting upon its own manner, it is in some sense programmatic.

In fact, the poem's mannerism is doubled. "Countless kisses" is first illustrated in highly allusive verse that names Cyrene, the home of Callimachus, with a mock-heroic epithet ("Cyrene, rich in Silphium," rather like "Ohio, rich in Hondas") and locates the sands of the desert by reference to the temple of Jupiter Ammon and the tomb of Battus, the name that Callimachus gives his father; then, again, in the old clichéd and sentimental image of countless stars. In other words, the first answer clearly parodies Callimachean allusiveness, the second seems to allude to the popular romance, and the secret nocturnal affairs of comic drama. And Callimachus himself is connected to both modes: in his epigrams, he both composed an epitaph for the tomb of his father (which would be a tomb of Battus) and rejected sentimental comic drama. If we choose to read this allusive performance programmatically, which is to say allegorically, we can arrive at something like the following.

Catullus asks what the limit to passion is. The answer, as everyone already knows, is that there is no limit. We can give the answer in the learned allusions of the neo-Callimachean style (with the appropriate degree of irony and playfulness – *lepide*) or we can repeat the sentimental images of popular comic drama (*lepide*). It makes no difference; the answer is the same and it is a cliché: desire is infinite, like the sands of the desert or the stars of the sky. This excess ("enough and more") is imitated by the poem's own form: two answers, both the same, overladen with poeticisms that make a clichéd answer seem obscure. The excess of kisses is, then, like the poem's own excesses: the poem illustrates with poetic superfluity the superfluity of desire. By this example, Catullan poetry joins (albeit self-consciously) the excesses of neo-Callimachean allusion with desire's own lack of limit to reveal, vivify, and play with what is common and already known by its readers. But there are two twists: to understand this you do not need to be a neo-Callimachean and the poem also goes beyond cliché: the idiom "enough and more" is commonly taken as the colloquial equivalent of "enough." But it is just here, in an idiom that begins and ends the poem, that we find a greater and literal truth: desire is never satisfied until it gets too much. "Enough!" means "Too much!" Thus, what everyone does know is hidden in complexities, but what we need to know is literally in front of our noses. But that's not all. If we pick up the Callimachean books to discover what is on the tomb of Callimachus' father we find: "I am the father and the son of Callimachus" (Callim. *Epigr.* 21.1–2). Thus it becomes possible to read poem 7 as a programmatic performance that claims affiliation and paternity as a neo-Callimachean: Catullus gives new birth to Callimachus by playing the program and paralleling its excesses with the excesses of erotic desire.

This Catullan mode, which seems more concerned to complicate than explain Catullan poetics, can be found at work in other poems that seem in their language and their references to offer opportunities for programmatic readings. We find a particularly drastic form of self-assertion in poem 16:

> I'm going to fuck you in the ass and in the mouth,
> Aurelius the cock-sucker and Furius the asshole.
> On the basis of my little verses, because they are
> a little dainty, you think I have no shame.
> A righteous poet ought to be clean and pure
> himself, but no need for his little verses.
> They only have salt and pleasure,
> if they are a little dainty and a little dirty
> and can incite the reader's itch,
> I don't mean boys, but hairy old men
> who find it hard to move their stiff limbs.
> But you, because you read of a thousand
> kisses, you think I'm not quite a man?
> I'm going to fuck you in the ass and in the mouth.

Clearly Catullus is talking about his poetry and how to read it. Efforts have been made to deny the programmatic nature of this poem by declaring that it is not about poetry in general, but about Catullus' "kissing poems." Such a claim is not a fact, but simply a decision: the decision not to read the poem programmatically. One might similarly say that Catullus' "pleasant new book polished with dry pumice" is not a statement about style and that it recalls neither the *lepidus* of comedy nor the polish and refinement of neo-Callimachean poetry. This only reveals the circular nature of all programmatic interpretations and the fact that they depend upon figurative readings.

Still, once we decide to read this poem programmatically, we have not solved the problem of interpreting the program. Some readers find here a poem concerned with power relations (see Manwell, this volume). By this interpretation, Furius and Aurelius have imputed effeminacy to Catullus on the basis of a poem (probably 48) asking for many thousands of kisses (if poem 48, then from the young man Juventius). Catullus, then, displays in this poem his fierce, competitive manliness. He stuffs the addressees with words and sexual threats. Their aggressive claim that Catullus and his poetry are effeminate is turned against them as they are made to assume the passive role. Catullus backs this up with the argumentative claim that good erotic poetry makes even stiff old men, who could not perform sexually if they wanted to, aroused or itchy. Poetry, then, is not about what excites Catullus, but about what excites the reader, and Furius and Aurelius have been bad readers both in their conclusions and in pathically accepting Catullus' words. Thus, the poem claims that readers need sophistication, while it turns the tables on its (unsophisticated) readers and reveals the social competitiveness that even poetry cannot escape (see, most recently, Fitzgerald 1995: 49–55).

It is, however, equally possible to find in this poem a claim about how the power of poetry is not in the poem or the poet at all but in the relationship between reader and poem. In other words, rather than saying that "my poetry does do this," Catullus says that poetry makes different claims depending on how you read it, and the successful poet deploys a rhetoric that turns the adversarial reading against the reader (see Tatum, this volume). Such a reading will emphasize the fact that, if it is unsophisticated to think that a request for kisses is a real request, then it is also unsophisticated to think that a threat of buggery is a real threat. In other words, as long as Furius and Aurelius continue their literal readings, they will be literally threatened by this poem. But the poem itself is telling them that all they need do is read these posturings as posturings. When they do, the threat goes away; it's just a figure of speech (Batstone 1993: 180–7).

But is it? Catullus' poem, when read in terms of its own logic, is trickier than it seems. If good, erotic poetry succeeds in making the incapable and stiff eager and itchy. But do they know that it's just a game? Or do they, for the purposes of the pleasure of that prurient itch, suspend their disbelief as well? And what is the status of the claim that is not literal when that claim is found in a poem? And notice that, to make sense of this very poem, we have to assume that Furius and Aurelius really did attack Catullus. But the poem keeps saying: don't be literal. The logical problem with the poem, and the feature that makes it a riddle when one treats the logic rigorously, is that one must make an assumption that contradicts the poem in order to get meaning out of the poem. Either one assumes that *this time* Catullus is really threatening in a poem where he says you must disaggregate poet and performance, or one assumes that Catullus is not threatening but joking and being ironic (male bonding, perhaps) in a poem where he says good poetry should produce the appropriate visceral effect.

As a programmatic performance, the poem refuses to make a univocal claim. It presents simultaneously two truths: poetic experience derives from real life, which it reflects; poetic experience is not to be equated with real life, which it only partially reflects, which it may reflect for rhetorical gain, for prurient pleasure, or as the kind of complex statement that creates a truth larger than truth claims can accommodate, namely that poetry (and every other performance of self) is a tricky act of revealing and hiding, of desire and feint. We are not who we seem, but we are not merely liars either. In presenting these truths the poet becomes, for those who want univocal reality, a trickster figure, teasing, threatening, laughing, slipping away.

Now part of the trick of reading programs into poetry is to find the program confirmed or repeated elsewhere. This, of course, is what makes the identification of neo-Callimachean values in Roman poetry so successful: there is an identifiable and repeated set of metaphors about style and aesthetics that continues to be used by generations of poets after Catullus. No one doubts that today, although there may disagreements about how far to extend the metaphorical language or in what circumstances it is self-consciously deployed.

Returning now to our elusive Catullus, we find him in poem 42 demanding the return of his notebooks from a nasty woman who, he says, thinks he's a joke. For several lines he calls her a "stinking fuck," but that does no good. So, at the end he calls her "modest and lovely." Programmatic for the illusions of poetic assertion? Again in poem 49 Catullus thanks Cicero in language that parodies Cicero's style and aspirations. Then he introduces a formula: Cicero is as much the "best patron" as Catullus is the "worst poet." But this does not create simple mockery. The parody of Cicero depends upon its recognizability. Catullus is, in fact, betting that Cicero's reputation, style, and self-importance will last as long as his own poetry – and, despite any irony or humor, that's a compliment. So, we have both compliment and parody/mockery. As a programmatic performance, Catullus' poetry engages the cultural antagonisms it thrives on. Catullan poetry, then, is the place where we exceed the limits of who we claim to be and where we spill over the boundaries of narrow logic.

Conclusion and Redefinition

It is time to return to our definition of "programmatic poetry." Programmatic poetry is any poem or passage that can be read as making a general or self-reflective comment on the poetry. Identification of a programmatic statement or poem entails an assignation of intention and a degree of self-understanding together with a generalizable claim about aesthetics and value. In Roman poetry, however, statements of this kind are figurative. They depend on metaphors, figures of speech, performative juxtapositions (that corroborate or ironize). Programs, then, must be read as allegories, which is always tricky, since you are asserting that some thing (some word or image or act) is "actually" a reference to some other thing (poetic values): the book, the girlfriend, the act of giving a poem stands for or instantiates the aesthetic values of the poet. On the other hand, since everything can be a figure for something else, there is no limit to what can be read as an allegory or a figure of speech. Identification of programmatic poetry is both allusive and illusive.

This means, of course, that different readers find different programs, even contradictory programs, in the same poem. Each reading depends upon interpretation and upon the interpretation of other poems that corroborate it. The programmatic poem allows one to imagine the poet and his corpus in terms of a particular self-understanding, and requires one to read one's own understanding of the corpus and the poet back into the programmatic poem itself. This is the familiar hermeneutic circle, and it means that you never know if you have actually figured out the program.

Consider poem 1 again. Above we found in it a figurative claim to certain Callimachean values and an implication that, just as Catullus' book was being offered to Nepos, so the contents were being entrusted to him as an ideal reader. As our discussion progressed we noticed that the programmatic term *lepidus* ("charming, pleasant") was also a term for the pleasures of comedy, and that Callimachus rejected the popular comic aesthetic, while Catullus enjoyed playing with it. This required a revision: while Catullus generally accepts the neo-Callimachean program, he also adds to it a Roman sensibility, one in which *lepidus* marks the fun and trickery of comedy (see further Newman 1990: 111–18).

But there is even more potential for revision. First of all, while Catullus describes the external appearance of his book with aesthetic and programmatic terms, when it comes to the evaluation of the internal contents he is particularly coy: you thought my "stuff, rubbish, trifles" (*nugae*) were "something" (*aliquid*); "whatever a book it is", "whatever sort." Second, within the corpus there is another poet with a lovely new book of verse, polished with pumice. It is Suffenus (c. 22), a man who is utterly deluded about the quality of his verse: "this guy's more clumsy than the clumsy farm" (14). And then there is Nepos himself: a friend of Cicero and Atticus, member of the older generation, writer of prose history and moralistic biography, who may have enjoyed Catullus but preferred Lucretius to Catullus' fellow neo-Callimacheans (Plin. *Ep.* 5.3.6). It's hard to imagine that this man had any idea what Catullus and Cinna and Calvus were doing to poetic style and aesthetic preferences. Would he have heard the echo of Cinna in the last line? Would he have fully understood what a "new, slender, charming little book polished with pumice" might mean?

Catullus' description does not allay doubts. To be sure Nepos is "daring" and his work is "learned," but he also writes of kings and heroes, and his work is "laborious" (a term equated with the farm by Calvus, fr. 2 Courtney). When Catullus asks for immortality, he turns to his "girlish muse and patron," while Nepos' work is associated with Jupiter: "learned books, by Jupiter." But Apollo is the Callimachean god: "Thundering is not my job, it's Jupiter's job" (*Aet.* 1.20). These features create a certain dissonance that is at odds with the claim that Nepos is an "ideal reader."

If the poem is making a programmatic statement by way of reference to Callimachean aesthetics, Roman comedy, obscure and dissonant evaluations, and an oddly inappropriate addressee, it seems to be a fairly contradictory statement. But there is a different allegory available: Catullan poetry adopts and adapts the neo-Callimachean aesthetics, but its appropriate evaluation will depend not upon what the cover of the book suggests (after all, no reader but Nepos gets the polished papyrus roll) but upon the reader of the stuff inside; and Nepos is as good a reader as one should expect. He shares some values (daring, learning, reduction) but not all (he writes history, by Jupiter, and it's laborious) or the wit (*lepidus*). Still, the life of poetry depends on readers who are daring, learned, reductive, and laborious just as much as it depends on readers who are new, and refined, and witty, and carefree. By this reading, the Catullan program is one that is open to many readers, each taking "whatever this is of a book" and discovering that it is "something." It turns out, then, that the modest, self-effacing language, which lets the reader "fill in the blank," is also programmatic.

This is a good place to end this chapter, since programmatic poetry can only turn over to the reader the task of connecting "this pleasant new little book . . . whatever it is" with the poems that follow. What this means is that the very task that programmatic poetry is being asked to do cannot be done. Catullus will not tell you how to read his poetry and he will not rigorously define his values. And, even if he did, you might still be just another Nepos or you might take him too literally, like Furius and Aurelius. This is, perhaps, why the modern languages are so little interested in "programmatic poetry": What the poet says he is doing or thinks he is doing is not relevant because it never determines anything, and the meaning of the poem, in which the poet tells us these things, is always "misread" anyway. Classical scholars, who turn to this designation in an effort to fix and determine the meaning and affiliations of a poetic corpus, ignore the fact that such readings always require an allegorical supplement which can only be confirmed by reference to the interpretation of other poems (also supplemented).

The programmatic poem, then, is not a thing that we discover in the corpus, a thing that tells us how to interpret a poet or other poems, but the product of an argument based on interpretation. It is a heuristic device that helps us think in new and interesting ways about poetics. It entails an assignation of self-consciousness and authority, but it does not thereby halt interpretation. Its validity or force always depends on argument and interpretation. But this is not bad news. We should read more poems programmatically, use this figure of speech to help us to figure out our poet. And if what we find is incoherent, then perhaps we are on the track of what eludes the poet's control or his self-awareness or the flexibility and capaciousness of his discourse – or, perhaps, the lack is in ourselves.

In fact, this is what scholarship does. One critic notices that poems 2, 2a, and 3 suggest a narrative of desire, marriage, and separation: the opening "triad" then becomes programmatic for the implied Lesbia narrative (M. Johnson 2003). In poem 85 the poet claims that he loves and he hates, but that he does not know why: the question and answer present a poet who will attempt to explain to his readers who he is and how he feels (Adler 1981: 3–8). Catullus is concerned with desire, and desire is a lack: let's read the gaps that the reader must fill programmatically as allegories of desire (see Janan 1994). In poem 12, Catullus demands that Marrucinus return a stolen napkin, a reminder of close friends: but the poem itself memorializes both the friendship and the napkin and so is programmatic for a poetry that replaces a literal "keepsake" with permanent poetic commemoration.

When used as a heuristic device, reading a poem programmatically can open new understandings of the figure of the poet, and the characteristics of his corpus. The only thing that is really at stake is the coherence of the narrative we develop, the persuasiveness of arguments we offer for the figures we see at work in the verse, and the pleasure we find in understanding (or in the illusion of understanding). So, go ahead! Accept the challenge! Read a different poem as programmatic; explore a strange figure of speech or an odd metaphor! Ask it to help you imagine relationships within the corpus that will help you understand the corpus or even yourself more convincingly. And do this with good hope. After all, if there is a poetic program, then every poem should be in some sense an instantiation of that program: if you find the way in which the poem does that, you've found a programmatic reading of the poem.

NOTES

1   Basic bibliography up until 1997 is in Thomson (1997: 200–1), a good resource; it will not be cited hereafter for every poem.
2   Later critics will refer to his essay as elucidating the programmatic nature of the poem. Already in 1961 Elder had used the term "programmatic" to refer to Callimachean affiliations in Vergil.

3 In *L'Année philologique*, the first references to "program" or "programmatic" in our sense appear in the early 1960s: Buchheit (1961b) speaks of Horace's program as an iambic poet and Anderson (1962) publishes "the programme of Juvenal's later books." A search of classical journals through JSTOR (Journal Storage: The Scholarly Journal Archive) finds nine references to programmatic satire in this period.
4 Despite the work of Wilamowitz (1924) and Kroll (1924), Quinn (1959) does not even list Callimachus in the "Index." In that study, "Alexandrianism" is still primarily a literary overlay. It was Clausen (1964), following Wimmel (1960), who focused on programmatic language.
5 Newman (1990: 307–8) reads 14a as part of 14.
6 Poems 18, 19, and 20 are priapic poems not thought to be by Catullus.

GUIDE TO FURTHER READING

There are no general works on programmatic poetry. Those interested in pursuing this topic need background knowledge of how Roman poets refer to other poets and the stylistic language and aesthetic debates of Catullus' generation. Much of that can be gained from this volume and the work of Wendell Clausen and Richard Thomas (see "Works cited"). However, the most useful exercise in further reading will be to note, in whatever you read, how the term "programmatic" is deployed by critics whenever they fall back on it, and to ask how it determines the reading of other poems and is itself already determined by the author's interpretation of those poems, to ask what metaphors and figures it depends upon, and whether that metaphorical language is consistent, ironic, playful, and so on. It will also be useful to notice how general works of interpretation privilege some poems as particularly indicative of the poetic project. Whether called programmatic or not, these poems are being treated as programmatic poetry.

WORKS CITED

Adler, E. 1981. *Catullan Self-Revelation*. New York.
Anderson, W. S. 1962. "The Programme of Juvenal's Later Books." *Classical Philology* 57: 145–60.
Barthes, R. 1977. "The Death of the Author." In *Image, Music, Text*. Trans. S. Heath. New York. 142–8.
Batstone, W. W. 1993. "Logic, Rhetoric, and Poesis." *Helios* 20: 143–72.
Batstone, W. W. 1998. "Dry Pumice and the Programmatic Language of Catullus 1." *Classical Philology* 93: 125–35.
Buchheit, V. 1961b. "Horazes programmatische Epode (VI)." *Gymnasium* 68: 520–6.
Clausen, W. V. 1964. "Callimachus and Latin Poetry." *Greek, Roman, and Byzantine Studies* 5: 181–96.
Clausen, W. V. 1976. "*Catulli Veronensis Liber*." *Classical Philology* 71: 37–43.
Clausen, W. V. 1982. "The New Direction in Poetry." In E. J. Kenney and W. V. Clausen, eds., *The Cambridge History of Classical Literature. Vol. II: Latin Literature*. Cambridge and New York. 178–206.
Courtney, E., ed. 1993. *The Fragmentary Latin Poets*. Oxford.
Dettmer, H. 1983. "A Note on Catullus 1 and 116." *Classical World* 77: 19.

Dettmer, H. 1994. "The First and Last of Catullus." *Syllecta Classica* 5: 29–33.

Elder, J. P. 1961. *"Non iniussa cano*: Virgil's Sixth Eclogue." *Harvard Studies in Classical Philology* 65: 109–25.

Elder, J. P. 1966. "Catullus I, His Poetic Creed and Nepos." *Harvard Studies in Classical Philology* 71: 143–9.

Fitzgerald, W. 1995. *Catullan Provocations: Lyric Poetry and the Drama of Position*. Berkeley, Los Angeles, and London.

Forsyth, P. Y. 1977b. "Comments on Catullus 116." *Classical Quarterly* n.s. 27: 352–3.

Forsyth, P. Y. 1989. "Catullus 14 B." *Classical World* 83: 81–5.

Foucault, M. 1977. "What is an Author?" In *Language, Counter-Memory, Practice*. Trans. D. F. Bouchard and S. Simon. Ithaca, NY. 124–7.

Janan, M. 1994. *"When the Lamp is Shattered"*: *Desire and Narrative in Catullus*. Carbondale and Edwardsville, IL.

Johnson, M. 2003. "Catullus 2b: The Development of a Relationship in the *'passer'* Trilogy." *Classical Journal* 99: 11–34.

King, J. K. 1988. "Catullus' Callimachean *carmina*, cc. 65–116." *Classical World* 81: 383–92.

Kroll, W. 1924. *Studien zum Verständnis der römischen Literatur*. Stuttgart.

Macleod, C. W. 1973. "Catullus 116." *Classical Quarterly* 23: 304–9.

Newman, J. K. 1990. *Roman Catullus and the Modification of the Alexandrian Sensibility.* Hildesheim.

Pucci, P. 1961. "Il carme 50 di Catullo." *Maia* 13: 249–56.

Quinn, K. 1959. *The Catullan Revolution*. Melbourne. Rpt. Cambridge 1969; Ann Arbor, MI, 1971. 2nd edn. London 1999.

Quinn, K. 1972b. *Catullus: An Interpretation*. London.

Segal, C. 1970. "Catullan *otiosi* – The Lover and the Poet." *Greece & Rome* 17: 25–31.

Tatum, W. J. 1997. "Friendship, Politics, and Literature in Catullus: Poems 1, 65 and 66, 116." *Classical Quarterly* n.s. 47: 482–500.

Thomas, R. F. 1979. "New Comedy, Callimachus and Roman Poetry." *Harvard Studies in Classical Philology* 83: 179–206.

Thomson, D. F. S., ed. 1997. *Catullus, Edited with a Textual and Interpretative Commentary.* Toronto.

Wheeler, A. L. 1934. *Catullus and the Traditions of Ancient Poetry.* Berkeley and Los Angeles.

Wilamowitz-Moellendorff, U. von. 1924. *Hellenistische Dichtung in der Zeit des Kallimachos.* 2 vols. Berlin.

Williams, G. 1980. *Figures of Thought in Roman Poetry.* New Haven, CT.

Wimmel, W. 1960. *Kallimachos im Rom. Hermes* Einzelschriften 16. Wiesbaden.

Wiseman, T. P. 1969. *Catullan Questions*. Leicester.

CHAPTER FOURTEEN

The Lesbia Poems

Julia T. Dyson Hejduk

To entitle a chapter "The Lesbia Poems" implies that Catullus' work includes a number of poems about Lesbia, which is true; that these poems form a cycle with a sort of plot or narrative structure, which is partially true; and that this cycle is detachable from the rest of Catullus' oeuvre, which is not true, despite the common practice of excerpting the Lesbia poems in anthologies. Much of the richness and strangeness of Catullus lies in his unsettling, brilliant decision to tell the "story" of his relationship with Lesbia all jumbled up, with poems about falling in love long after poems about breaking up, and poems on a variety of other topics interspersed. Whereas Propertius begins his collection with a resounding declaration of its dominant topic – "Cynthia first with those eyes of hers captured me in my misery" (Prop. 1.1.1) – Catullus neither begins nor ends his collection with Lesbia. Nevertheless, it is the poet's passionate affair with this woman that forms the book's dramatic core, giving meaning and coherence to the whole.

Before tackling the poems themselves, I should say a few words about who Lesbia was, a problem that has occupied scholars for many decades. It is nearly certain that Lesbia is a poetic pseudonym for Clodia, an aristocratic *femme fatale* of the late Roman Republic who was the sister of Cicero's arch-enemy, the demagogue P. Clodius Pulcher. Catullus encourages us to lift the flimsy veil of pseudonymity when he starts a poem with an unmistakable allusion, "Lesbius is beautiful (*pulcher*)" (79.1): Lesbia/Lesbius mirrors Clodia/Clodius, and *pulcher*, "beautiful," was Clodius' cognomen and nickname (Cicero's letters often refer to him as "Little Beauty"). The waters become murkier when we attempt to determine which of Clodius' three sisters Lesbia was, however, because all sisters in a noble family had the same name (the feminine form of the family name). As I have argued elsewhere (Dyson Hejduk forthcoming), it is most probable that the commonly accepted equation of Lesbia with Clodia Metelli (= "wife of Metellus") is correct. The strongest evidence for this equation comes, again, from clues Catullus plants in the poems themselves: around the time Catullus was writing (56 BC), Clodia Metelli was attacked by Cicero in a colorful and highly public court case involving her ex-lover Marcus Caelius Rufus, and Catullus addresses a "Caelius" and a "Rufus" (probably the same man) as a rival for Lesbia's love.

Yet the identity of the "real" woman behind the poetry and the "real" nature of her affair with the poet are in some ways irrelevant. Catullus chose to bound his poetic fiction by linking its characters with people personally known to most of his original readers. As I hope to demonstrate in this chapter, however, the impressionistic portraits of Lesbia that emerge from the different sections of the collection are so utterly different from one another – whatever the reality that inspired them – that this very difference must be essential to the meaning of the poems. With the exception of Homer, whose Penelope is a match for the cunning Odysseus in every way, Catullus is the first author to depict a romantic relationship between a man and a woman as true *amicitia*, "friendship," a meeting of minds presupposing both social and intellectual equality. So radical was this move that it was followed, as far as I can tell, by no other author before Jane Austen. Yet if we accept the division of Catullus' poems into three sections – the polymetrics (1–60), the longer poems (61–8), and the epigrams (69–116) – it is only in the third that the idea of Lesbia as the poet's "friend" emerges.

What makes Catullus so bewitching is the way he invites the reader to participate in this emotional journey, this transformation of himself and his love, even as he gives the appearance of revealing his most private thoughts. In this chapter, though necessarily highlighting certain passages to illustrate particular points, I shall give my own translations of the full text of the Lesbia poems in the order they appear, in hopes of recreating the experience of reading the story as it unfolds.

The Polymetric Lesbia

Sparrow, cherished delight of my girl,
she plays with you, she holds you in her bosom,
she gives your eagerness a fingertip
and often instigates your stinging bites,
whenever my gleaming object of desire   5
is pleased to trifle with some beloved toy –
a little solace also for her pain,
I think, that thus her burning heat may rest:
if only I could play with you as she does,
and lighten the sad cares that press my spirit!   10
    . . .
It is as pleasing to me as they say the little
golden apple was to the swift-footed girl,
which loosed the girdle that had long been tied.
                                        (poem 2)

When we first meet Lesbia, she is not named, nor is she the addressee of the poem: she is simply called "my girl," *mea puella*, a characterization that will cling to her throughout the polymetrics. Her pet sparrow is the divinity to whom the poem is ostensibly a hymn. Lesbia's play has manifestly amorous overtones – bosom-burying and "stinging bites" belonged to the Romans' sexual repertoire, and the poet specifies the mood his girl is in (burning with painful "heat") when she engages with her bird in this way. Whatever the relation between the last three lines of the poem and the beginning (some posit a lacuna, some see it as a logical continuation), the sexual implications of loosening Atalanta's long-tied girdle are obvious; it is significant that the poet casts not Lesbia but *himself* as the virgin on the threshold of sexual awakening, a gender-role reversal that will recur at key points in his poetry.

The vernal sweetness of this awakening love cannot last, however, for in the very next poem the sparrow is dead:

> Mourn, oh Venuses and Cupids, and all
> people there are of the more attractive sort:
> the sparrow of my girl has passed away,
> the sparrow, cherished delight of my girl,
> whom she used to love more than her own eyes.   5
> For honey-sweet he was, and knew his own
> mistress as well as a girl knows her mother.
> And he would not budge himself from out her lap,
> but frolicking about now hither, now thither,
> ever would twitter to his mistress alone: 10
> now he travels along the path of shadows,
> that path they say none travel in return.
> But you – curses on you! wicked shadows
> of Orcus, who devour all pretty things:
> such a pretty sparrow you've robbed from me.   15
> Oh, wickedly done! Oh, miserable little sparrow!
> Now, because of you, the darling eyes
> of my girl are red and swollen with her weeping.
>
> (poem 3)

As in the previous poem, the sparrow is a vehicle for telling us about the girl, the poet, and their relationship. The description of her eyes gives us an important piece of information: she is not only a "girl" but, implicitly, a young and tender-hearted girl. One of the hardest Latin mannerisms to convey gracefully in English is the common diminutive ending "-ulus" or "-ellus" (German "-lein" or "-chen" and French "-ette" do the job easily, but their English equivalents always sound humorous). English has no way to apply diminutives to adjectives and thus must transfer them to nouns, which is especially awkward when the noun is already diminutive. So the closing words of the poem, *flendo turgiduli rubent ocelli*, yield literally a spell-checker-stumping translation, "the swollen little little eyes of my girl are red with weeping." Although such diminutives in English can convey contemptuous sarcasm, the effect in Latin is one of tender affection, perhaps slightly humorous (since the poet clearly cares not for the bird whose eulogy he sings, only for the effect on his girl's pretty eyes), but not ridiculous or contemptuous. In any case, if we had only these two poems, our image of Catullus' "girl" would be of one very young, playful, passionate (she plays with the sparrow as a "little-solace" – another diminutive – for the pain of sexual desire), and sentimental enough to weep her little eyes out over the death of her pet.

And yet we have, along with the poems themselves, enough of their cultural and literary context to caution us against taking them at face value. The interpretive dilemma is this: is this sparrow only a sparrow, or is it also a double-entendre for the poet's penis? Some of the scholars included in the present volume would call the obscene interpretation "implausible," while others would call it "certain." Some arguments against the obscene reading: (1) the image of the sparrow twittering and jumping around hither and thither "brings us to the world of Benny Hill's Ernie the milkman rather than the urbanity of the neoterics" (Pomeroy 2003: 50); (2) the witty, mischievous Ovid, in his poem (*Am.* 2.6) about the death of his mistress's parrot, an obvious imitation of Catullus' sparrow-death poem, does not appear to have imitated the obscene aspect (though perhaps later readers will find that he has . . .); (3) why would Catullus wish to play with himself (how else can we interpret 2.9–10?) rather than reap the benefit of his girl's "burning heat"? Some arguments for the obscene reading (see R. F. Thomas 1993): (1) Martial, a first-century AD imitator of Catullus, embraced the obscenity (Martial's "sparrow" poems are collected in Dyson Hejduk forthcoming; for discussion, see Lorenz, this volume, pp. 425–6); (2) Greek epigrams – which Catullus knew well – provide several examples of impotence as the "death" of the phallus and the death of pets as a code for this phenomenon; (3) the exaggerated phallus of Roman mime was called a *strutheum*, from Greek *strouthos*, "sparrow" (Fest. 410 Lindsay *DVS*; quoted below in Gaisser, p. 447), and Roman comedy would appear to exploit the double-entendre potential of this proverbially salacious bird. In any case, it is appropriate that the introductory pair of love poems should leave us with an enormous question, an ambiguity of tone that characterizes, in fact, most of Roman erotic poetry: is the *puella* weeping tears of tender grief over her pet's death or tears of sexual frustration over her lover's impotence?

After a dedicatory epigram for the ship that carried Catullus home from Asia (poem 4), the sparrow and its attendant interpretive conundra are swept away by the first poem to tell us the *puella*'s name. One of Catullus' most loved and most imitated poems, it gives a snapshot of exuberant passion:

> Let us live, my Lesbia, and let us love,
> and let us calculate all the mutterings of
> curmudgeonly old coots to be worth one cent.
> Suns have the power to set and rise again;
> our brief light, when once it has set, leaves only   5
> one night we must sleep for all eternity.
> Give me kisses, a thousand, then a hundred;
> then another thousand, then a second hundred;
> then still another thousand, then a hundred.
> Then, when we will have made so many thousands,   10
> we'll garble them up, so that we may not know,
> nor any wicked man have power to give us
> the evil eye, knowing the quantity of kisses.
>
>   (poem 5)

Death is the shadow that gives poetry its brightness. Lines 5.4–6 are an exquisite expression of this theme – *the* theme of most love poetry, as of life. But amid the reflections on time and eternity, light and darkness, there is a slightly discordant insistence on what would at first seem an odd counterpoint: money. In addition to the obvious monetary metaphor in "calculating" the coots' mutterings "to be worth one cent," the word order in line 7, "Give me kisses, a thousand, then a hundred," recalls a request for goods at market, naming first the product and then the price (Quinn 1973a: 109). And yet, the juxtaposition of time, money, and love is perhaps not so strange after all. Our inability to stockpile time, its relentless shift from the black to the red despite all our attempts to save it, is one of the persistent frustrations of human existence. Love is caught uncomfortably between the other two: it increases with consumption yet cannot be stored. The avoidance of the "evil eye" from someone who knows the exact "quantity of kisses" alludes to the black-magical principle that possessing some piece of personal information about the victim is necessary to place a curse. But the first purpose clause, "so that *we* may not know," captures the lovers' longing to lose themselves in their own infinity, a desire made urgent by the desert of vast eternity lying before them.

In contrast to the joyous abandon of poem 5, so poignant under the threat of eternal darkness, poem 7 attempts to pinpoint precisely *how* infinite the lovers' embraces will be. It begins with an indirect question, the first we have "heard" from Lesbia herself:

> You ask how many of your kissations, Lesbia,
> would be enough for me and more than enough.
> How great the quantity of Libyan sands
> lying upon Cyrene, rich in silphium,
> between the oracle of steamy Jove   5
> and the sacred sepulcher of ancient Battus;
> or how many stars, when night is silent, gaze
> upon the furtive love affairs of men:
> for you to kiss so many kisses is
> enough and more than enough for crazed Catullus –   10
> too many for snoops to be able to reckon up
> completely, or an evil tongue to bewitch.
>
> (poem 7)

The conversation is full of playful erudition, a far cry from the girlish image conveyed by *turgiduli ocelli* ("swollen little little eyes"). Again, an ambiguity, this time about Lesbia's words, complicates interpretation: Did she actually say, "How many of my kissations are enough for you?" Or did the poet translate a simple question – "How many kisses are enough for you?" – into his own pseudo-intellectual jargon? (Teachers leading discussion groups are familiar with this phenomenon. "Aeneas is, like, such a nobody." "You mean Virgil has made his protagonist an unfilled signifier on whom other characters project their own personalities?") The reason it matters whether she has actually spoken the word "kissations" is that this neologism is the first indication that Lesbia has (to put it bluntly) anything upstairs. In fact, despite the common perception of Lesbia as an intellectual match for the poet, whose self-professed wit, charm, and polish are the trademarks of the "new poetry" he pioneers, this passage is one of only two in the polymetrics to suggest that wit plays any part in their relationship. (We may again compare Propertius' Cynthia, who is given long, colorful, witty speeches in her "own voice.") If *basiationes* is Lesbia's own coinage, then she displays her erudition; if it is Catullus' projection, then her level of intelligence is still an open question.

What poem 7 unquestionably does is mark the affair's loss of innocence, in a sense, by emphasizing its adulterous nature. Cyrene was the birthplace of Callimachus, the third-century BC Greek poet who was a paragon of the learned allusiveness and polish that characterize Catullus' "new" style of poetry; Callimachus is referred to as a "son of Battus" (an ancient king of Cyrene), and Catullus' allusion to Battus here alerts us to his own allusiveness. But the epithet "rich in silphium" signals adultery: silphium was a rare plant used as a highly effective contraceptive, facilitating the sterile promiscuity of the Roman upper classes. The allusion to the chief god's infamous philandering in "*steamy* Jove," followed by the stars' gazing upon the "*furtive* love affairs of men," leaves no doubt about the relationship's illicitness.

Whatever misgivings may have been engendered by poem 7 are confirmed by poem 8. Suddenly the playful passion of the first two pairs of Lesbia poems is overturned by the poet's announcement that the relationship is as dead as the sparrow:

> Miserable Catullus, please stop being idiotic
> and recognize that what you see has died is dead.
> Suns blazed for you radiantly once upon a time,
> when you would come and go wherever that girl led,
> loved by me as no other ever will be loved;   5
> at the time when all those fun-and-games were going on
> which you wanted, and the girl was not unwilling,
> suns blazed for you radiantly, without a doubt.
> Now she doesn't want them: don't you want them either,
> crazy fool – and don't chase her as she flees, and live in misery,   10
> but suffer it with obstinate mind, harden your heart.
> Girl, farewell! Now Catullus hardens his heart,
> and he won't seek you out, or ask you against your will.
> But you'll be sorry, when you aren't asked at all.
> Worse luck for you, damned bitch! What life remains for you?   15
> Who will go to you now? To whom will you seem pretty?
> Whom will you love now? Whose will you be said to be?
> Whom will you kiss? Whose little lips will you nibble?
> But you, Catullus, be resolved and harden your heart.
>
> (poem 8)

Poem 6, a nasty little gem that shines a cynical spotlight on the besotted "idiocy" of one Flavius, shows what an obsessive love affair looks like from the outside (see Wray 2001: 159); poem 8 shines a similar light on the "idiotic" Catullus. In contrast to the self-consciously learned, precious allusiveness of the previous poem, the phrasing of poem 8 is deliberately simple, as if Catullus has taken on the persona of a fool – or cast himself in the role of Lesbia's avian plaything. "You would come and go wherever that girl led" recalls how the sparrow, "frolicking about now hither, now thither, / ever would twitter to his mistress alone" (3.9–10). The poem's opening word, "miserable" (Latin *miser*), which becomes almost a technical term for love-sickness in all future Latin erotic poetry, is used first of the "miserable little sparrow" (3.16). The *puella* who "trifles with" (*iocari*, 2.6) her pet is echoed in the "fun-and-games" (*iocosa*) the girl and her lover enjoyed. The puerile whine of "you'll be sorry, when you aren't asked at all" contrasts comically with the allusive sophistication of "Cyrene rich in silphium."

The next Lesbia poem completes the initial "cycle": sparrow-pair, kiss-pair, renunciation-pair. If as a rule Catullus' poems are uniform in tone, with shifts *between* poems rather than within a single one, poem 11 breaks that rule not once but twice. The poet takes us first on a dizzying journey to the ends of the known world – a martial, masculine adventure with his "comrades," a word often used of fellow soldiers:

> Furius and Aurelius, Catullus' comrades,
> whether he penetrates to deepest India,
> where on the shore the eastern wave resounding
>   endlessly echoes,
>
> or to the Hyrcani, or the soft Arabs,   5
> or the Sagae, or Parthians skilled in archery,
> or to where the Nile of seven branches
>   colors the waters,
>
> or if he marches across the lofty Alps
> visiting great Caesar's monuments,   10
> the Gallic Rhine, the horrid sea, the Britons
>   furthest of all men,
>
> ready to undertake all these together
> with him, wherever the will of heaven will bear him –

... suddenly the key changes, he wrenches us out of the fantastic travelogue and back to the world of the heart:

> give a message to my girl, these words   15
>   few and not pretty:
>
> Let her live, and fare well, with her perverts,
> whom she clasps three hundred at a time,
> loving none truly, but grinding the groins of all of them
>   over and over;   20

It may seem, as some readers have objected, that the first half of the poem is disproportionate or irrelevant to the second. The poetic strategy, however, is the powerful rhetorical device known as a "priamel": a long list of "foils" is presented in apparent contrast to the subject to be praised (or, as here, blamed), and the reflected light from the foils ultimately illuminates the subject. (For a modern example of the priamel form, compare the Beach Boys song "California Girls.") So intense is the poet's love and hate that it encompasses the known world. His malediction, "Let her live, and fare well," reverses the passionate prayer of poem 5, "Let us live, my Lesbia, and let us love," with ironic bitterness; the gratingly crude phrasing of "grinding the groins," the absurd exaggeration of "three hundred" lovers, seem almost the stuff of satiric epigram.

Yet Catullus does not leave us there. The final stanza is astonishingly beautiful:

> and let her not, as before, look for my love,
> which through her wrong has fallen like a flower
> at the meadow's edge, once it is touched by the plow-blade
> heedlessly passing.
>
> (poem 11)

To appreciate the power of this stanza requires a short digression on Roman sexual mores in the late Republic and, in particular, the pervasive double standard that was taken for granted. Men had little to lose other than their own equanimity: to sleep with slaves, prostitutes, and adolescent males was perfectly acceptable, and even affairs with upper-class women were generally winked at as long as they produced no financial complications or illegitimate children. For a woman (or girl – upper-class females often married in their early teens) to be "deflowered," on the other hand, was seen as a kind of death, a spoiling beyond repair (see Dyson Hejduk 1999). Catullus shows the depth of his wound by assuming the role of one who actually has something to lose, a young female virgin. The flower is not deliberately cut or plucked, simply nicked by a plow "heedlessly passing" as it performs an unrelated task. If the Catullus of poem 8 feels the comic pathos of rejection, the Catullus of poem 11 feels the tragic agony of betrayal.

And then, after a poem about some idiot (the third we've seen so far) who thinks stealing napkins is clever (poem 12), the Lesbia landscape returns to harmless fun. The "Venuses and Cupids" of the sparrow-dirge are back, providing Catullus' girl with some very special scent:

> You will dine well at my place, my Fabullus,
> in a few days, if the gods are smiling on you –
> provided that you bring with you a fine, large
> dinner, not without a radiant girl
> and wine and salt and every sort of laughter.   5
> I say, if you'll bring these things, my attractive friend,
> you will dine well; for your own Catullus'
> wallet is overflowing with spider webs.
> But you'll receive in return pure essence of love,
> and something, if possible, smoother and more refined: 10
> for I'll provide a perfume that the Venuses
> and Cupids have bestowed upon my girl.
> Once you get a whiff of this, you'll beg
> the gods, Fabullus, to make you totally nose.
>
> (poem 13)

Whereas the sparrow poems (2 and 3) ended with "swollen little little eyes," the kiss-poems (5 and 7) with evil eye and wicked tongue, the renunciation poems (8 and 11) with bitten lips and broken groins, poem 13 concludes with that most primal of sense organs and comic of body parts: the nose. If we were encouraged by the tragic end of poem 11 to take the affair seriously, this return to comedy brings us up short. And that is the last we see of Lesbia for over twenty poems.

The next pair of Lesbia poems is a choice example of Catullus' ability to combine intense emotion, intellectual playfulness, and scatological crudity:

> "Annals" of Volusius, sheets of shit,
> be ye a votive offering for my girl.
> For she vowed to holy Venus and to Cupid
> that if I would be reconciled to her
> and cease to hurl my fierce poetic curses,   5
> then she would offer to the gimpy god
> the choicest writings of the worst of poets,
> to be scorched by an unhappy bonfire.
> And the girl saw that she was wittily vowing
> these, the very worst, to the merry gods.   10
> Now, oh goddess born of the blue-black sea,
> you who dwell upon holy Idalium,
> and open Urii, and Ancon, and sandy
> Cnidus, and Amathus, and Golgi, and
> Durrachium, the Inn of the Adriatic,   15
> let this vow be rendered and accepted,
> if it is neither uncharming nor unattractive.
> But you, meanwhile, proceed into the flames,
> ye paragons of boorish fatuosity,
> "Annals" of Volusius, sheets of shit.
>
> (poem 36)

As in poem 2, the real topic of this hymnic parody is of course Lesbia, whose threat to consign to the flames the "choicest writings of the worst of poets" Catullus willfully misinterprets, comically enlisting her vow in the battle between the slender elegance of his own "new poetry" and the bloated epic grandiloquence represented by Volusius' "Annals." Aside from "kissations" in poem 7, this is the only other polymetric passage that gives any echo of Lesbia's voice – and as in poem 7, the joke may be the poet's rather than her own. She is at least aware of the "fierce poetic curses" he hurls at her, but despite Catullus' declaration that her vow is "witty," the true wit appears to lie in his ability to deflect that vow away from his own verses and onto his poetic competitor's.

The shift from playful conversation to comic rejection that we saw in poems 7 and 8 is recapitulated in the shift from poem 36 to poem 37:

> Smutty tavern, and you all, its comrades-in-arms,
> nine columns down the street from the cap-wearing Brothers,
> you think that you're the only ones in possession of pricks?
> that you alone are free to fuck whatever girls
> there are, and to think the rest of us are rancid goats?   5
> Or, just because you clods all sit there in a row,
> a hundred or two hundred, you think I wouldn't dare
> to facefuck all two hundred sitting there at once?
> Well, you'd better think again: for it is my intention
> to scribble you dicks all over the front wall of this inn.   10
> For my girl, who has fled away out of my bosom,
> loved by me as no other ever will be loved,

on whose behalf great battles have been fought by me,
has pitched her tent there. All you fine and fortunate fellows
love her, and what's more – which is totally unfair –   15
all you beggars and buggers skulking around in alleys;
you above all, alone of all the long-haired dandies,
son of Celtiberia, that rabbity land,
Egnatius, whom a dark, shadowy beard makes fine,
and teeth shined to a sparkle by Iberian piss.

(poem 37)

Not only does this poem share the relatively rare meter ("limping iambs") of poem 8, but it contains a nearly direct quotation ($8.5 \approx 37.12$). Even more than poem 8, however, poem 37 plays like a scene from a comedy: as I have attempted to convey in my translation ("comrades-in-arms," "great battles," "pitched her tent"), Catullus is assuming here the comic role of the *miles gloriosus* or braggart soldier (Wray 2001: 85–6).

The "flight" of Lesbia in poem 37, like all the break-ups so far, turns out to be temporary, for she is back in the poet's good graces in the next Lesbia poem. If we can divine her personality only through indirect speech, we can divine her appearance only through a sort of indirect description, a catalogue of the defects of a competitor elsewhere identified as "Ameana":

Greetings, girl of not-the-smallest nose,
nor of pretty foot, nor of dark eyes,
nor of long fingers, nor of mouth undrooling,
nor, in fact, of tongue too elegant,
girlfriend of the depleted Formian.   5
The province is declaring *you* are pretty?
My Lesbia is being compared with *you*?
Oh fatuous and witless generation!

(poem 43)

Lesbia, presumably, is everything this woman is not. Once again, aside from the ambiguous "tongue" – whose inclusion in the list of body parts would seem to emphasize its corporeal rather than its linguistic aspect – the focus is entirely on isolated physical characteristics. The "generation" (*saeclum*) of judges is accused of lacking taste and wit, but the minds of Ameana and Lesbia play no explicit role in this beauty contest.

Yet Lesbia is not the only one portrayed in vividly physical terms. Poem 51, which is often considered the fictive "beginning" of the affair, captures the physiological effects of sexual obsession on the poet himself:

He seems to me the equal of a god,
he seems – if it is right – to surpass the gods,
who sits across from you and sees you and hears you
    over and over

sweetly laughing, which in my misery ravishes   5
all my senses: for when I have once laid eyes

> upon you, Lesbia, then of the voice in my mouth
>   nothing is left me,
>
> but my tongue grows numb, a slender flame
> oozes down within my limbs, my ears with   10
> their own sound are ringing, and my eyes are
>   buried in twin night.
>
> Leisure, Catullus, is troubling to you;
> leisure gets you too excited, too itchy.
> Leisure has been known to destroy both kings and   15
>   prosperous cities.
>
> (poem 51)

The poem is a translation of one by Sappho, the seventh-century BC Greek poetess from Lesbos whose songs to female lovers gave rise to the word "Lesbian" and Catullus' "Lesbia" (he chose the pseudonym for its association with Sappho's poetic genius, not her homoeroticism). Catullus elsewhere uses this "Sapphic meter" (three eleven-syllable lines capped by a five-syllable line) only for poem 11, with which poem 51 is often paired; the shared phrase "over and over" (Latin *identidem*) emphasizes both the obsessiveness and the timelessness of the affair, the impossibility of arranging it in a logical temporal sequence (see Janan 1994: 71). Another poem closely linked with poem 51, however, poses another crucial interpretive question: was the inspiration for this Sapphic tour de force Catullus' passion for Lesbia, or his passion for poetic tussling with a male friend (see Wray 2001: 95–100)? Poem 51 is preceded by a poem about male friendship and poetic creation, in which the aftereffects of a poetic sparring contest are portrayed in startlingly erotic terms; Catullus is "enflamed," "in misery," and unable to eat or sleep (50.7–10). He can find only one outlet:

> But after my limbs, exhausted by their labor,
> were lying half-dead upon the little bed,   15
> delightful friend, I wrote this poem for you,
> so from it you could clearly perceive my pain.
>
> (50.14–17)

It is tantalizingly unclear whether "this poem" in line 16 refers to the poem it is in (50) or the poem that follows (51). The idea that poem 50 is a sort of "cover letter" for poem 51 is supported by a strong parallel with poems 65 and 66: like poem 51, poem 66 is a translation from a Greek author, and Catullus' statement in poem 65, "I send you this poem" (*mitto haec . . . tibi carmina*, 65.15–16) – where "this poem" refers unambiguously to poem 66 – sounds suspiciously like the statement in poem 50, "I wrote this poem for you" (*hoc . . . tibi poëma feci*, 50.16). We can at least say with certainty that poems 50 and 51 are thematically linked: the ending of 51, decrying the troubling effects of leisure (*otium*), recalls the situation of decadent "leisure" with which 50 opens, and the depiction of erotic distress is common to both.

Whatever the genesis of poem 51, the ominous prophecy with which it closes melds into an even darker chord in our final view of the polymetric Lesbia. As in poem 11, the poet depicts Lesbia's betrayal as indiscriminate sexual rapacity, but this time with the added humiliation represented by what the Romans considered the most degrading of sexual acts:

> Caelius, our Lesbia, that Lesbia,
> that Lesbia whom alone Catullus loved
> more than himself and all his friends and family,
> now at every street-corner and back alley
> shucks great-hearted Remus's descendants.
>
> (poem 58)

The last polymetric, though not addressed specifically to Lesbia, borrows the language and imagery of epic to show the depth of the poet's despair:

> Did a lioness birth you in the mountains of Libya,
> or a Scylla, barking from the lowest depths of her loins –
> you, with your mind so hardened, so full of cruelty
> that you'd treat the final cry of a suppliant's despair
> with scorn, your heart as hard as that of a feral beast?
>
> (poem 60)

That the affair that began (poetically speaking) with such tenderness should end with such degradation and callousness, the pet sparrow replaced by wild beasts, is quintessentially Catullan.

Before we move on to the next chapter in the story, two points about the polymetric Lesbia should be emphasized. First, she is characterized by hyperbole, especially numeric hyperbole. The poet demands hundreds and thousands of kisses (poem 5); he discusses the precise dimensions of their infinity (poem 7); he invites his comrades to accompany him to the ends of the earth to tell his *puella* she can go to hell with her three hundred lovers (poem 11); he threatens to irrumate two hundred blockheads on barstools (poem 37). Yet Lesbia is not the only inspiration for these numeric fantasies. In addition to *basiationes*, two more "-ation" words designating very large numbers of physical embraces appear in the polymetrics. The first is with a woman named Ipsitilla whom earlier ages might describe as "no better than she should be," from whom Catullus is fishing for a post-prandial invitation:

> I will love you, my sweet Ipsitilla,
> my cherished delight, my captivating charm:
> bid me come to you to take a siesta!
> And if you bid me, help in this way too:
> don't let anyone put the bolt in the door,   5
> and don't be pleased to go away outside,
> but you remain at home, and prepare for me
> nine continuous, uninterrupted fuckations (*fututiones*).
>
> (32.1–8)

Like *basiatio*, *fututio* appears only in Catullus and his imitator Martial; also like *basiatio*, it refers to a number most would consider unreasonably large for the act in question. A third polymetric "-ation" word is used of an adolescent boy, Juventius, who in number of poems and depth of passion is Lesbia's chief rival for the poet's love, or lust – Latin *amor* covers both, and Juventius is twice called *meos amores*, "my love" (a term never used of Lesbia). This boy arouses in the poet an appetite for kisses not unlike that aroused by Lesbia in poems 5 and 7:

> Oh, Juventius, your honey-sweet eyes,
> if someone should allow me to keep kissing them,
> I would kiss three hundred thousand times,
> and I would never, ever be seen to be glutted,
> not even if thicker than a ripened cornfield   5
> were to grow the crop of our osculations (*osculationes*).
>
>   (poem 48)

The use of *basiatio*, *fututio*, and *osculatio* for hyperbolically large numbers of physical interactions with three different objects of *amor* can hardly be coincidental. One might note in passing the obvious double standard taken for granted in ancient Rome: multiple lovers for Lesbia meant betrayal, whereas multiple lovers for Catullus meant virility. Catullus sees (or professes to see) no contradiction between his love for Lesbia and his other sexual adventures. In fact, the intratextual connection forged by the three "-ations" invites the reader to "compare and contrast" them.

The second characteristic of the polymetric Lesbia is that she and the relationship are portrayed almost entirely in physical terms. With the exception of *basiationes* (poem 7) and her "witty vow" (poem 36), which are both likely to be the poet's own projections, the polymetrics contain not a single reference to Lesbia's mind. Her passion is represented by infinite kisses (poems 5, 7), her tenderness by swollen little eyes (poem 3), her allure by a perfume that would make one wish to be "totally nose" (poem 13), her betrayal by the grinding (poem 11) and shucking (poem 58) of her lovers' groins. The indirect description of her beauty is the negative of another woman's unappealing foot, nose, eyes, mouth, and tongue (poem 43). In short, there is little to suggest that she is more than a *puella*, a girl, whose physical attractiveness holds the poet in thrall. If her charms exceed those of a Juventius or an Ipsitilla, the difference is essentially one of quantity, not quality. Even when Catullus portrays himself in a female role, as in the stunning gender reversals of poems 2 and 11, the affair does not transcend the boundaries of physical sexuality.

But the story does not end there.

The Poem 68 Lesbia

With poem 68, considered by many "the most extraordinary poem in Latin" (Lyne 1980: 52; Feeney 1992: 33), Catullus completely changes the terms in which Lesbia is conceived. Poems 61–7 are all variations on the theme of marriage; in poem 68, Catullus and Lesbia enter into a pseudo-marriage that will set the tone for their relationship in the epigrams to follow.

The poem poses as a thank-offering to a friend of Catullus who provided his home as a trysting spot:

He with a broad path laid open a closed field,
   he, he gave his home to me and to my mistress,
a place for us to exercise our mutual love.
(68.67–9)

The word "mistress" hardly seems worth a second glance; centuries of adultery in literature and life have caused it to mean a "woman who has a continuing sexual relationship with a man to whom she is not married" (*American Heritage Dictionary*, "mistress" 6). Yet the Latin word *domina* had not – yet – acquired that meaning for the Romans: it refers solely to a woman in control of slaves. With this line, Catullus plants the seed for a theme to blossom fully only in his poetic successors, the *servitium amoris* or "slavery of love," which portrays the poet as the "slave" of a "mistress" in control of his heart. As he inverts gender relationships by casting himself as a deflowered maiden in poem 11, so here he inverts power relationships by casting himself as Lesbia's slave.

   A moment after introducing the slavery theme, Catullus endows his lover with two other provocative images absent from the polymetrics:

There with supple foot my radiant divinity   70
  entered, and resting her gleaming sole on the smooth-worn threshold
    she halted, with her sandal singing shrill,
  just as Laodamia once, burning with love,
    arrived at the home of Protesilaus, her husband,
a home commenced in vain. . . .
(68.70–5)

Lesbia's arrival is at once the epiphany of a goddess – another metaphor to bear its fruit only in later poets – and the ceremonial entrance of a bride into her husband's house. The tradition of carrying the bride over the threshold arose precisely to prevent such an ill-omened stumble or (as here) squeak of the shoe. With this image, Catullus recasts their relationship as a marriage – and an unlucky one, like that of Laodamia, the passionate bride of the first man to die in the Trojan War. After the most bizarre concatenation of similes to appear anywhere in Latin poetry (examined, fortunately, elsewhere in this volume by Theodorakopoulos, pp. 323–6), Catullus returns to the comparison of Lesbia with the unfortunate Laodamia:

My Light, then, who didn't fall short of her at all –
  or only a little – came into my lap;
Cupid flitting all around her, now here, now there,
  gleamed in his saffron tunic radiantly.
(68.131–4)

His "radiant divinity" has now become his "Light," and Cupid, wearing a tunic the color of wedding garments, appears to bless the "marriage." Yet the epiphany, the wedding, and the comparison with the mythically amorous heroine are subverted by another dissonant note, another squeak of the sandal. The understated phrase "or only a little" reminds us that Lesbia is really neither divinity nor bride nor heroine, nor is her passion for Catullus (it is implied) equal to his for her.

The next lines reveal her as a flesh-and-blood adulteress who does not remain faithful even to her lover:

> Even if she's not content with Catullus alone,   135
>   I'll bear the blushing lady's occasional cheating,
> so I won't be pestering her too much like some clown.
>   Often even Juno, greatest of goddesses,
> swallowed down her seething wrath at her husband's wrongs,
>   knowing all-lustful Jupiter's rampant cheating.
>   (68.135–40)

Lesbia is a "divinity," it seems, not in being all-powerful, but in being "all-lustful." Once again, the implicit equation of Lesbia with Jupiter and Catullus with the wronged Juno reinforces the inversion of power and gender relationships that characterizes the poem. After all the astonishing analogies, however, the poem sounds a note of realism bordering on cynicism:

> Still, she didn't come to me to a home perfumed
>   with Assyrian scent, led by her father's hand,
> but gave furtive little gifts in the amazing night,   145
>   stolen out of her very man's very lap.
> Therefore it is enough, if I alone am granted
>   the day she marks with a more radiant stone.
>   (68.143–8)

Catullus in these lines makes explicit two points that are absent from the polymetrics but defining for the epigrams: what he has with Lesbia is both like and unlike a marriage, and she is in fact married to someone else. The poem closes with a benediction on the friends who made the relationship possible:

> May both of you be happy, you and your Life together,   155
>   and the house where we had our game, my mistress and I,
> and he who introduced her to me in the beginning,
>   from whom all good things first came into being,
> and she who far before all is dearer to me than myself,
>   my Light: life is sweet to me while she's alive.
>   (68.155–60)

This ending encapsulates the paradox underlying Roman erotic poetry, whose inherently adulterous nature makes it an arena for intense emotions without real consequences. Though what Catullus and Lesbia have together is in a sense frivolous, a "game" (Latin *lusimus*, literally "we played"), this game and its player are dearer to the poet than life itself.

Poem 68, then, provides a crucial transition to the next movement in the Lesbia story. The polymetric *puella* – exclusively a sex object or subject – really had little to distinguish her from the polymetric *puer*, Juventius. The relationship between a man and an adolescent boy was characterized by its artificiality and temporariness: once body hair took over, the relationship would end (sex of any kind between adult men is the subject of disgust and ridicule in Roman poetry). With poem 68, however,

Catullus creates for Lesbia an entirely different role, one characterized by divinity, power, and adulthood.

The Epigrammatic Lesbia

In contrast to the polymetric Lesbia, with her schizophrenic variety of meters, generic experimentation (comedy, religious hymns, epistolography), and swings of tone, the epigrammatic Lesbia is quite simple. Catullus takes two dominant metaphors – marriage and political alliance – and spins them into a coherent narrative of betrayal, misery, and reconciliation, *in that order*. The turning point, as we have seen, is in poem 68, where amid evil omens, qualifications, and caveats, Catullus and Lesbia enter into a sort of marriage. Yet two other paths opened up by that extraordinary poem, Lesbia's "divinity" and the "slavery of love," turn out to be blind alleys, connoting as they do an inequality that would be symbolically incompatible with the mature relationship depicted in the epigrams. The wildly indulgent sensuality of the polymetrics is replaced by pure abstraction: though intertwined with overtly obscene material describing other people, the Lesbia epigrams contain not a single reference to any physical characteristic of or non-verbal action by Lesbia herself. Comic exaggeration has evaporated. The nameless hordes of lovers ground and shucked by the indefatigable polymetric *puella* are winnowed down in the epigrams to a handful of identifiable rivals, and buffoons like the urine-dentifriced coxcomb Egnatius (poem 37) are replaced by politically formidable opponents.

If the polymetric Lesbia cycle opened with the sweetness of awakening love (for all the ambiguity represented by the "sparrow"), the epigrams open (poem 69) with an outburst of acidic jealousy toward one "Rufus," probably the M. Caelius Rufus who was a lover of Clodia Metelli (see Noonan 1979; Dettmer 1997: 151–69; Dyson Hejduk forthcoming). This Rufus is ridiculed for the rancid goat that dwells in his armpits – just the sort of graphic physicality we have come to expect in the poly-metrics. Yet when Lesbia herself enters the scene in the next poem, we find that the *puella* ("girl") has become a *mulier* ("adult woman"), and indeed, one with whom the poet is talking about marriage:

> My woman [*mulier*] says that there is no man she would rather marry
>   than me, not even if Jove were to ask her himself.
> She says: but what a woman says to her longing lover
>   ought to be written on wind and rushing water.
>
> (poem 70)

We are confronted with yet another unanswerable interpretive question: Does this mean that Lesbia is in fact *available* – widowed, presumably, as we know the leading candidate for the "real" Lesbia to have been in 59 BC – or is it simply an exchange of sweet nothings, a contrafactual wish, "I would want to marry you if I weren't married"? Later epigrams will refer to Lesbia's husband, but given the scrambling of the affair's temporal sequence, she could conceivably be unattached at the narrative moment of this one. What is clear, in any case, is that the pseudo-marriage of poem 68 has ushered in a new movement in the relationship, the possibility of a permanence alien to the *carpe diem* theme of the polymetrics.

The idea of marriage, however, is tame compared with the theme introduced in the next Lesbia poem, which contains one of the most shocking couplets (lines 3–4) in all of Latin love poetry:

> Once you used to say that you knew Catullus alone,
>   Lesbia, and wouldn't want to hold Jove more than me.
> I loved you then not just as the crowd love their girlfriend, but
>   as a father loves his sons and sons-in-law.
> Now, I know you: so even if I burn more fiercely,   5
>   yet you are much cheaper and shallower to me.
> How can this be, you say? Because such injury forces
>   a lover to love more, but to wish well less.
>
> (poem 72)

Comparing romantic love to filial or parental love is striking and perhaps hyperbolic, but not exactly revolutionary; such emotions are primal, spontaneous, and fierce, qualities one can easily see a passionate lover seeking to convey. But love for *sons-in-law* is something else entirely, a cultivated affection arising from a contractual relationship with political repercussions. Fathers chose spouses for their daughters to cement political alliances, not because they felt any emotion toward the projected mate. With the astonishing word "sons-in-law," Catullus alerts us that the world of the sparrow has been left behind forever. Like the polymetric Lesbia, the epigrammatic Lesbia has power over the poet's heart, bringing him ecstasy through love and misery through betrayal – but the love and the betrayal have left the realm of pure sexuality and entered the realm of *amicitia*, "*male* friendship," between intellectual and social equals (see Ross 1969: 80–94).

The next two Lesbia poems are similarly cerebral, devoid of specifics, and infused with the language of political alliance:

> My mind has been dragged so far down, Lesbia, by your wrong,
>   and has so ruined itself by the favors it's done,
> that now it could neither wish you well, if you became perfect,
>   nor stop loving you, if you did – everything.
>
> (poem 75)

"Favor" (*officium*) and "wish well" (*bene velle*) are two key terms in the vocabulary governing the complex system of reciprocity that united the Roman aristocracy. Poem 76, by far the longest of the epigrams, spells out even more elaborately the sort of mutual responsibility that Catullus feels should characterize his relationship with Lesbia (italics mine):

> If there is any pleasure for a person remembering
>   *services* past, when he thinks how he is *righteous* [*pius*],
> and has not broken a sacred *trust* or abused the power
>   of the gods to deceive people in any *pact*,
> then many joys, Catullus, in a long life await you,   5
>   joys arising out of this *thankless* love.
> For all things people can *kindly do or say* to anyone,
>   these have been both done and said by you:

and all have gone sour, entrusted to a *thankless* heart.
    Therefore, why should you torture yourself any more?   10
Why not toughen your heart and bring yourself back from there
    and stop being miserable, since the gods are hostile?
It's hard to cast away a long love all of a sudden;
    it's hard – but do it any way you can.
This is your only salvation, this is the fight you must win;   15
    do this, whether it's possible or not.
Oh gods, if you have any heart, or if you have ever finally
    given aid to those on the verge of death,
look upon me in my misery, and if I've lived a pure life,
    snatch this plague and pestilence from me,   20
which creeps like numbing torpor into the depths of my limbs
    and utterly drives the happiness from my heart.
No more do I ask for this – that she love me in return,
    or (what is impossible) that she wish to be chaste:
I want to be healthy myself, and get rid of this foul sickness: 25
    oh gods, grant me this in return for my *righteousness* [*pietas*].
                               (poem 76)

In poem 51, Catullus describes his love and jealousy as a sort of illness; to see and hear Lesbia talking to another man ravishes his *senses*, causing his ears to ring, his eyes to go black, and flame to ooze down within his limbs. Poem 76 reads more like a catalogue of symptoms of the displeasing plague of reactive depression (Booth 1997): the agony of pondering Lesbia's infidelity, despite the poet's attempts to win her "favor" by his "righteous" display of "services," causes not excitement but "numbing torpor." There is of course a sharp irony in using *pietas*, "righteousness" or "dutiful responsibility," to describe an adulterous relationship, but those are the terms Catullus gives us.

    The polymetric Catullus and Lesbia exist in a sort of vacuum, a timeless, almost mythic world of thousands of kisses, hundreds of rivals. Their relationship with one another and with their friends and enemies and lovers is explored at length, but there is practically no mention of one of the primary realities of life, especially for the class-obsessed aristocratic Romans: family. The next Lesbia epigram, however, introduces this theme with a vengeance:

    Lesbius is beautiful [*pulcher*]. Of course he is! Lesbia would choose him
        over you, Catullus, with your whole family.
    But yet this beautiful man would sell Catullus, with family,
        if he could find three kisses from men who know him.
                                 (poem 79)

The rumor of an incestuous relationship between P. Clodius Pulcher and his sister (or all his sisters) runs throughout Cicero's oratory, and this poem, as noted above, provides the most compelling internal evidence for identifying Lesbia as Clodia. The *puella* could have been anyone; the *mulier*, by contrast, is defined by her role as an adult within a close-knit aristocratic community. Incest represents not merely moral depravity, but a particular kind of snobbery that Catullus associates with social corruption, one of his predominant themes in the "elegiac *libellus*," poems 65–116 (Skinner 1982a, 2003). This Lesbia is not a demimondaine, an object of mere physical desire, but a member of a clan so willfully exclusive as to choose incest rather than going outside the family.

Once Lesbia's relationship with her brother has been clarified, Catullus proceeds to tell us, for the first time, about her relationship with her husband:

> Lesbia hurls abuses at me in her husband's presence:
>   this is the summit of happiness for that dolt!
> You ass, don't you get it? If she kept quiet, oblivious of me,
>   she would be healed: but now, since she snarls and curses,
> not only does she remember, but – something fiercer by far –   5
>   she's furious! That is: she burns, and she speaks.
>
> (poem 83)

With the mention of the man who makes a true "marriage" between Catullus and Lesbia impossible, paradoxically, the dawn begins to break in Catullus' emotional world. Lesbia's verbal abuse, the poet now realizes (or professes to realize), is really a sign of her love. The depressive seriousness of the previous poems, the bitterness at her insincerity and infidelity, have given way to a sense of hope and humor. Catullus is not out of the woods yet, as the next epigram, the only Lesbia poem to comprise a single couplet, gives a taut summary of the lover's perpetual dilemma:

> I hate and I love. Why do I do this, you may well ask.
>   I don't know, but I feel it happen and it's torture.
>
> (poem 85)

But the "torture" will prove cathartic. After this poem, the bitterness disappears. Armed with the knowledge that Lesbia's "abuse" of him is actually a good sign, the poet from this point on invokes the language of political alliance only to show the restoration of their *amicitia*, not its breach.

The comparison between Lesbia and another woman considered "beautiful to many" is especially revealing of the difference between the polymetric and the epigrammatic Lesbia:

> Quintia is beautiful to many. In my eyes, she's radiant,
>   tall, good posture: I grant these single points.
> I deny that the whole is beautiful. For no attractiveness,
>   not a grain of salt resides in so great a body.
> Lesbia is beautiful; she is both entirely lovely,   5
>   and alone has robbed all the Venus from all other women.
>
> (poem 86)

In poem 43, Ameana was ridiculed for the inadequate beauty of her body parts, which the poet implied could not hold a candle to Lesbia's. In poem 86, the poet concedes that Quintia is physically beautiful, but – here is the crucial difference – he denies that physical beauty constitutes true "attractiveness" (*venustas*: see Krostenko 2001a: 40–51, and this volume). What Quintia lacks is "salt," that is, "wit": Lesbia, by implication, possesses this essential quality. Although this is Catullus' only explicit reference to Lesbia's mind, it highlights the metamorphosis in his depiction of their relationship. The epigrammatic Lesbia has something more distinctive to offer than the perfume of sexual allure.

The five remaining Lesbia poems tell a simple story, one perhaps best summarized in the trite but timeless formula, "They lived happily ever after."

> No woman is able to say that she's been loved so truly
>   as my own Lesbia has been loved by me.
> No faith so great was ever found in any pact
>   as has been found, from my side, in your love.
>
> (poem 87)

> Lesbia's always cursing me, and never keeps quiet
>   about me: damned if Lesbia doesn't love me!
> What proof? Because I'm exactly the same: I rail against her
>   constantly – but damned if I don't love her!
>
> (poem 92)

> You think that I could hurl abuses at my Life,
>   one who is dearer to me than both my eyes?
> I couldn't – nor, if I could, would I love so desperately:
>   but you, with Tappo, do all monstrous things.
>
> (poem 104)

> If ever anything comes to a man who is longing, wishing,
>   but hopeless – that is sweet to his spirit indeed!
> Therefore this is sweet to me, this is dearer than gold:
>   you restore yourself, Lesbia, to me in my longing,
> you restore to a longing and hopeless man, on your own you return   5
>   yourself to me. Oh day of more radiant note!
> What happier man lives than me only? Or who will be able
>   to name a thing more to be wished in life than this?
>
> (poem 107)

> You declare to me, my Life, that this our mutual love
>   will be pleasant and last for all eternity.
> Great gods, see to it that she be able to promise truly,
>   and that she say it sincerely and from the heart,
> so we may be allowed for our whole life to continue   5
>   this everlasting pact of holy friendship.
>
> (poem 109)

Our final glimpse of the polymetric Lesbia is utter degradation, shucking all comers in back alleys. Our final glimpse of the epigrammatic Lesbia is in an "everlasting pact of holy friendship," *amicitia*, a word denoting not only reconciliation but true equality. The *puella* has grown up.

Coda

Catullus' other "love," Juventius, also undergoes a transformation between the polymetrics and the epigrams. In the polymetrics, while the poet was careful to jumble up the thousands of kisses with Lesbia, he made the mistake of naming a round number for Juventius (three hundred thousand, to be exact, 48.3). It would seem that some snoop did reckon them up and place a nasty spell. Juventius, in his sole appearance in the epigrams, roundly punishes the poet's theft of a single little smooch (*suaviolum*, 99.2) by spending hours wiping the offending kiss from his lips, turning honey to gall. At the end, Catullus vows, "after this, I'll never steal kisses again" (99.16). Perhaps the *puer* has grown up as well. Has the poet?

GUIDE TO FURTHER READING

Wray (2001) offers a persuasive and theoretically sophisticated reading of Catullus' work as the "performance of Roman manhood," complementing the provocative analysis by Krostenko (2001a) of the "language of social performance" in Catullus and others. Skinner (2003) is an excellent treatment of the "elegiac *libellus*" (poems 65–116) as a coherent story. Dyson Hejduk (forthcoming) provides translations (with commentary and some analysis) of all the ancient sources on Clodia, along with selected later elegies showing her legacy in the poetic tradition. Quinn (1973a) is still valuable as a scholarly commentary, although Garrison (2004) is a better fit for modern Latin students. Dettmer (1997) provides a stimulating analysis of the elaborate structure of Catullus' book. Ross (1969) and Wiseman (1985) present important essays on Catullus' cultural context. Gaisser (1993, 2001, and this volume) gives an excellent view of Catullus' afterlife in the Renaissance and beyond. Lyne (1980) is a good read on Latin love poetry in general, as is Richlin (1992) on Roman sexuality and aggression. Of articles, I have found Noonan (1979), Richlin (1981), Skinner (1982a, 1983), R. F. Thomas (1993), and Clauss (1995) especially enlightening; Quinn (1972a) is a fine compendium of earlier articles by a variety of authors.

WORKS CITED

Booth, J. 1997. "All in the Mind: Sickness in Catullus 76." In S. M. Braund and C. Gill, eds., *The Passions in Roman Thought and Literature*. Cambridge. 150–68.

Clauss, J. J. 1995. "A Delicate Foot on the Well-Worn Threshold: Paradoxical Imagery in Catullus 68b." *American Journal of Philology* 116: 237–53.

Dettmer, H. 1997. *Love by the Numbers: Form and Meaning in the Poetry of Catullus*. New York.

Dyson Hejduk, J. T. 1999. "Lilies and Violence: Lavinia's Blush in the Song of Orpheus." *Classical Philology* 94: 281–8.

Dyson Hejduk, J. T. forthcoming. *Clodia: Readings in Roman Passion, Politics, and Poetry*. Norman, OK.

Feeney, D. C. 1992. " 'Shall I compare thee . . . ?': Catullus 68b and the Limits of Analogy." In A. J. Woodman and J. Powell, eds., *Author and Audience in Latin Literature*. Cambridge. 33–44.

Gaisser, J. H. 1993. *Catullus and His Renaissance Readers*. Oxford.

Gaisser, J. H. 2001. *Catullus in English*. London.

Garrison, D. H. 2004. *The Student's Catullus*. 3rd edn. Norman, OK.

Janan, M. 1994. *"When the Lamp Is Shattered": Desire and Narrative in Catullus*. Carbondale and Edwardsville, IL.

Krostenko, B. A. 2001a. *Cicero, Catullus, and the Language of Social Performance*. Chicago and London.

Lyne, R. O. A. M. 1980. *The Latin Love Poets from Catullus to Horace.* Oxford.

Noonan, J. D. 1979. "*Mala bestia* in Catullus 69.7–8." *Classical World* 73: 155–64.

Pomeroy, A. J. 2003. "Heavy Petting in Catullus." *Arethusa* 36: 49–60.

Quinn, K., ed. 1972a. *Approaches to Catullus.* Cambridge.

Quinn, K., ed. 1973a. *Catullus: The Poems.* 2nd edn. London and Basingstoke.

Richlin, A. 1981. "The Meaning of *irrumare* in Catullus and Martial." *Classical Philology* 76: 40–6.

Richlin, A. 1992 [1983]. *The Garden of Priapus: Sexuality and Aggression in Roman Humor.* Rev. edn. New York and Oxford.

Ross, D. O., Jr. 1969. *Style and Tradition in Catullus.* Cambridge, MA.

Skinner, M. B. 1982a. "Pretty Lesbius." *Transactions of the American Philological Association* 112: 197–208.

Skinner, M. B. 1983. "Clodia Metelli." *Transactions of the American Philological Association* 113: 273–87.

Skinner, M. B. 2003. *Catullus in Verona: A Reading of the Elegiac* Libellus, *Poems 65–116.* Columbus, OH.

Thomas, R. F. 1993. "Sparrows, Hares, and Doves: A Catullan Metaphor and its Tradition." *Helios* 20: 131–42.

Wiseman, T. P. 1985. *Catullus and His World: A Reappraisal.* Cambridge.

Wray, D. 2001. *Catullus and the Poetics of Roman Manhood.* Cambridge.

CHAPTER FIFTEEN

Sexuality and Ritual: Catullus' Wedding Poems

Vassiliki Panoussi

Though critics were slow to appreciate their beauty and poetic power, poems 61 and 62 always held a special place in the Catullan corpus. They are the first in a group of longer poems that occupy the central place in the collection as we have it, and both are customarily referred to as wedding hymns, although neither is a hymn in the technical sense of the term. Both poems celebrate marriage and its blessings for the couple, their families, and society in general. They also provide important information on aspects of Roman wedding ritual and illuminate the way gender roles were defined and understood within the framework of marriage, what part male and female sexuality played in the marital relationship, and the value placed on marriage from a personal, familial, social, and even political viewpoint. Lastly, these poems constitute a counterpoint to the disillusioned image of love expressed in the remainder of the corpus, the result of the poet's failed relationship with Lesbia. The wedding poems, concentrating on the festive, positive aspects of marriage, offer renewed faith in the institution and its ability to provide personal fulfillment and promote social stability.

Scholars have long debated the Greek or Roman pedigree of these poems, whether they were composed for an actual occasion, and how closely they represent Roman wedding ceremonies. Poem 61 in particular purports to commemorate the wedding of a member of the Torquati, a prominent family in Republican Rome, to an otherwise unknown Iunia (or Vinia).[1] For that reason primarily, the poem is thought to reflect Roman customs and beliefs. Poem 62 is a singing contest between choruses of maidens and youths. The antiphonal character of the poem led many to argue that it was performed after the nuptial dinner, and that it replicates Greek rather than Roman customs. Today scholarly consensus accepts that the poems were not performed at any particular wedding: even if we posit that 61 commemorates a real event and a real couple, the occasion rather serves as an opportunity for a more general celebration of marital love. Both poems omit important parts of the wedding ceremony, and the ritual acts that they represent do not fall within any distinct phase of Roman (or Greek) wedding ritual.

Yet the ritual context and content of the poems constitute an important lens through which we can gain a better understanding of their structure, themes, and problems. Ritual descriptions involve practices and customs recognized by all Romans, and thus furnish the poet with a shared "vocabulary" which is available for further manipulation and interpretation. Both poems are structured around specific moments of Roman wedding ritual: 61 begins as a hymn to Hymenaeus, the god of marriage; it continues as part of the *deductio* procession comprising the *fescennina iocatio*, and ends as an *epithalamium*, the song sung before the marital chamber. Although the specific ritual context of 62 is still the object of debate among scholars,[2] its format as a singing contest of choruses of young girls and boys, a custom consistent with (some) Greek weddings (Thomsen 1992: 166, 174), and allusions to the Roman archaic ritual practice of *raptio* provide a firm link with the wedding ceremony.

Before I go on to discuss how the ritual context of the poems informs their content, a few words on the ritual wedding practices they represent are in order. The *deductio* procession was one of the most prominent features of the ceremony, so that the term *uxorem ducere* came to mean "to marry." In the *deductio*, the couple's relatives and wedding guests take the bride to her new home, which is usually the husband's house. The procession was conducted by torchlight, and these torches (*taedae*) stand as a symbol for the wedding as a whole (Treggiari 1991: 166). There was musical accompaniment and the guests cried *hymen hymenaee*. The bridegroom does not take part in this event, as he has already gone to his house to welcome the bride. During the *deductio*, the *fescennina iocatio* took place. Although the precise origin of the name and the practice remain obscure (Fedeli 1983a: 86), it is certain that a group of young men sang obscene jokes at the expense of the groom. It seems that the groom himself was involved in the singing of the fescennine verses and that he threw nuts to the crowd (Treggiari 1991: 166). The ritual custom of *raptio*, no longer practiced at the time of Catullus, occurred at the beginning of the *deductio*. According to our sources (Fest. 364 Lindsay *DVS*; Macrob. *Sat.* 1.15.21), the members of the *deductio* pretend that they snatch the girl from her mother's arms. The rite is also thought to commemorate the first Roman marriage, the rape of the Sabine women (Fedeli 1983a: 53).

Close attention to the ritual context surrounding both poems, and of the *raptio* in particular, can shed light on the most troubling features of each: in the case of 61, the great emphasis placed on the violence of the sexual act; in that of 62, the maidens' negation of marriage. In the opening lines of 61 the marriage god Hymenaeus is said to promote the violent separation of mother and daughter (*qui rapis teneram ad uirum/uirginem*, "you who carry off the tender virgin to her husband," 3–4). Similarly, in 62, Hesperus, a figure equivalent to Hymenaeus (Thomsen 1992: 178–86), is described as having carried off the bride (*Hesperus e nobis, aequales, abstulit unam*, "Hesperus, friends, has taken one of us," 32). The fact that these themes would figure so prominently in poems celebrating marriage has caused great debate among scholars. If we look at the problem from an anthropological perspective, however, we can arrive at an explanation. The act of marriage entails a great change in the life of a Roman woman, who, at a very young age (Treggiari 1991: 400), is about to leave her natal family in order to live with her husband in her new, marital household. The prospect of permanent separation from the natal family is bound to generate feelings of great anxiety on the part of the bride. This anxiety is further compounded by concern over the sexual act and the act of defloration in particular. The bride's family, in turn, also experiences a loss, both emotional and physical, as one of their members is about to be permanently separated from the group. In ritual, these anxieties are often expressed with rites of capture or rape, as the Roman practice of *raptio* attests. Eventually, these feelings of anxiety will give way to joy over the positive aspects of the new life awaiting the bride and groom.

Ritual thus both celebrates social institutions and the roles that the individual is called to play therein and gives voice to anxieties surrounding these very institutions and roles. As a result, Catullus, by making ritual such an integral part of his poems, incorporates the doubts and anxieties at work during this important phase of transition in a young person's life. At the same time, however, ritual also helps assuage anxieties and celebrates the benefits of marriage for the individual and society at large, and therefore constitutes an excellent background against which the poet may explore the contours of these themes. Viewed in this light, the poems' inherent problems and contradictions can be readily related to the greater Catullan poetic corpus, where love's many forms and shapes are treated in as many different and often conflicting ways.

Although the poems overlap greatly in content and context, the following analysis will deal with them separately, focusing on what I believe are each poem's most prominent themes. Poem 61 centers on the theme of appropriate sexual activity within the framework of marriage and defines the roles of husband and wife accordingly. Poem 62, on the other hand, by dramatizing the bride's resistance to marriage, places emphasis on the competing nature of gender roles and the need for the individual to comply with society's demands. The chapter concludes with an examination of the ways in which both poems eventually assert the positive and beneficial aspects of marriage for the Roman family, society, and state.

Poem 61: Sexuality and Marriage

As we have seen, the poem is structured around three distinct ritual acts of the wedding ceremony: the hymn to Hymenaeus (1–75), the *deductio* and the *fescennina iocatio* (76–184), and the *epithalamium* (185–end). In all three sections of the poem, there is a great emphasis on love and more specifically on physical love. The poem moves from the different roles that Hymenaeus is called upon to play in the couple's union to the sexual obligations of man and woman in their new roles as husband and wife, and ends with an enumeration of the benefits of sexual concord for the couple and society.

Female sexuality

Physicality and violence as attributes of the god of marriage, Hymenaeus, emerge in the very first lines of the poem, where, as we have seen, he is said to "carry off the tender virgin to her husband" (*qui rapis teneram ad uirum/uirginem*, 3–4). The juxtaposition of *rapis* and *teneram* contrasts the violence of the god (and the groom) with the vulnerability of the maiden. By invoking the ritual background of *raptio*, the poem addresses both the problem of the bride's separation from her natal family and her fear over the prospect of defloration:

> te suis tremulus parens
> inuocat, tibi uirgines
> zonula soluunt sinus,
> te timens cupida nouos
>   captat aure maritus.
>
> tu fero iuueni in manus
> floridam ipse puellulam
> dedis a gremio suae
> matris, o Hymenaee Hymen,
>   o Hymen Hymenaee.
>   (51–60)

> you the trembling father calls
> for his children, for you the maidens
> loosen their dress from their girdle,
> for you the new husband listens
>   fearful with eager ear.
>
> you yourself gave into the hands
> of the fierce youth the blooming maiden
> from the embrace of her
> mother, o Hymenaeus Hymen,
>   o Hymen Hymenaeus.

Parental anxiety is expressed with the use of the words *suis tremulus* to describe the father;[3] the word order renders possible two readings: that the father is calling upon the god for the sake of his children and that the father is anxious for his children. The latter possibility is further strengthened by the subsequent reference to the potential violence of the sexual act. The image of the loosening of the maiden's girdle, an image symbolic of the consummation of marriage, is also commemorated in ritual, where the bride ties her girdle in anticipation of the groom's untying of it later on as they share their bed.[4] The violence of the sexual act is implicit in the subsequent description of the young man's eagerness (*cupida aure*) and fear (*tremens*) at the prospect; the use of the verb *captare* to indicate the husband's fervor for Hymen also bears intimations of violence: the verb is a frequentative of *capere* (*OLD* s.v. 1 "to try to touch or take hold of, grasp at;" see also 1b, as if in wrestling).

The themes of sexual violence and separation as well as references to their ritual and legal counterparts continue in the next stanza. The repetition of *tu* to refer to Hymenaeus is typical of the language of hymns and serves to underscore the solemn character of the prayer. Ritual underpinnings may also be detected in the use of the expression *a gremio suae/matris*. Festus' description of the *raptio* practiced in early Rome contains very similar language, leading scholars to believe he is replicating a ritual formula: *rapi simulatur uirgo ex gremio matris*, "they pretend to snatch the virgin from the embrace of her mother," 364 Lindsay *DVS* (Fedeli 1983a: 53). At the same time, legal language is also operative in these lines. The phrase *fero iuueni in manus* is thought to be referring to marriage *in manu*, whereby the bride passed from the *potestas* of her father to that of her husband. This practice was rare in Catullus' time but, like the *raptio*, it would be readily recognized by his audience. Through a combination of ritual and legal language symbolic of the bride's transition to her new family, Catullus draws attention to the problems of separation from the natal family and the act of defloration.

The bride's resistance to marriage is linked to her adherence to the female ideal of *pudor*, or modesty, which necessitates feelings of timidity toward her future husband but is also motivated by feelings of loyalty toward her own family. The bride's modesty and unwillingness to part with her loved ones are at work in the next section of the poem, where she is called to come out of her house so that the *deductio* may begin (*tardet ingenuus pudor./quem tamen magis audiens,/flet quod ire necesse est*, "Modest shame delays. Yet listening rather to it, she weeps because she must go," 79–81). The whole segment, the song before the bride's house (76–113), is structured around the delay that the bride's virtue and emotions necessitate and the chorus' efforts to overcome it so that the *deductio* may begin and the wedding be successfully completed.

The bride's physical desire for her husband is carefully associated with her eventual fulfillment of her new role as wife and mistress of a new household. The first address to the bride is as mistress of her new home (*domum dominam uoca*, "call the mistress to her house," 31). Her new social status is predicated upon the physical and emotional bond she feels for her spouse (*coniugis cupidam noui,/mentem amore reuinciens*, "desirous of her new husband, binding her mind with love," 32–3): this notion is reinforced by a simile from nature, where the bride is likened to ivy and the husband to a tree: *ut tenax hedera huc et huc/arborem implicat errans* ("as here and there the clinging ivy wandering enfolds the tree," 34–5). The connection of ivy and tree points to the physical and emotional connection of the couple, while the choice of the image of the clinging ivy enfolding the tree suggests both the wife's dependency on her husband and the strength of their bond. A similar image appears later on in the poem and renders even more explicit the physical aspect of marital love (*lenta sed uelut adsitas/uitis implicat arbores,/implicabitur in tuum/complexum*, "but as the soft vine enfolds the nearby trees, he will be enfolded in your embrace," 102–5): this time the wife is a vine that folds around the nearby trees and is equated with the bride's embrace (*complexum*). The physical connection of the spouses, emphasized in the two similes through the use of the same verb (*implicat*), also establishes the complementarity of their roles. Physical and emotional desire form the foundation on which the stability of the new *domus* will rest.

The poem associates female beauty and vulnerability with virginity through an array of floral images. In one such instance, the bride is likened to a hyacinth in the garden of a rich master (*talis in uario solet/diuitis domini hortulo/stare flos hyacinthinus*, "so the hyacinth flower is accustomed to stand in the colorful garden of a rich master," 87–8). The image of the garden flower within the context of wedding poetry is often employed to celebrate an ideal of female beauty that is free from the constraints of fertility and reproduction. Garden flowers do not participate in the cycle of cultivation and reproduction but exist apart, untouched by the world of agriculture and civilization.[5] As a result, the beauty of the flower alone justifies its existence. Catullus modifies this image common to *epithalamia* by qualifying the garden as belonging to a rich master. As part of the master's property, the beautiful flower thus enhances the owner's status and power. This appears to be one of the roles a wife may be expected to play in marriage later on in the poem, where the bride is invited to contemplate the fact that her husband's *domus*, to which she now belongs, is powerful (*potens*, 149) and prosperous (*beata*, 150). The wife's beauty and virtue as passive objects for display constitute assets for her husband and his household.

Virginity's desirability, however, may fall victim to violent male sexuality, as the image of the hyacinth makes clear elsewhere. The hyacinth of 61 is the object of admiration but does not appear to be threatened. Another flower, however, this time in poem 62, is in danger of losing its beauty in a violent manner:

> ut flos in saeptis secretus nascitur hortis,
> ignotus pecori, nullo conuolsus aratro,
> quem mulcent aurae, firmat sol, educat imber;
> multi illum pueri, multae optauere puellae:
> idem cum tenui carptus defloruit ungui,
> nulli illum pueri, nullae optauere puellae:
> sic uirgo, dum intacta manet, dum cara suis est;
> cum castum amisit polluto corpore florem,
> nec pueris iucunda manet, nec cara puellis.
>
> (39–47)

> As a flower is born hidden in a fenced garden,
> unknown to the herd, torn up by no plow,
> which the breezes caress, the sun strengthens, the rain raises;
> many boys, many girls desire it:
> when the same flower plucked by a sharp fingernail withers
> no boys, no girls desire it:
> so a virgin, while she remains untouched, is dear to her family;
> when she has lost her pure flower with body polluted,
> she remains neither sweet to the boys, nor dear to the girls.

The image of this flower has often been linked (Fraenkel 1955: 5; Stehle [Stigers] 1977: 90; M. J. Edwards 1992: 2) to a famous hyacinth in Sappho (L-P 105c):

> as the hyacinth in the mountains the shepherds
> trample with their feet, and its purple flower [falls] to the ground . . .

Female virginity is intensely sensual and thus precarious and fragile, subject to violence on the part of the male. By placing emphasis on these qualities of female sexuality, the chorus of the maidens in 62 does not recognize the possibility of defloration as a positive result of marriage, but rather prizes a perpetual existence in the sheltered world of virginity, exemplified by the image of the garden.

In 61, virginity as enhancing the power of female sexuality appears once again in the image of the bride waiting for her husband in the *thalamos*. She is described as glowing with a flowery face, like a white chamomile or a yellow poppy (*uxor in thalamo tibi est,/ore floridulo nitens,/alba parthenice uelut/luteumue papauer*, 185–8). The diminutive *floridulo*[6] conveys a sense of intimacy and tenderness towards the bride (Fedeli 1983a: 125) as well as a sense of vulnerability; the white *parthenice* draws attention to the bride's virginity, as the word evokes the Greek word for the virgin (*parthenos*); lastly, the color of the poppy, *luteum* (yellow/orange), is also firmly associated with the bride, as the slippers she wears during the wedding ceremony are of the same color (*lutei socci*, also mentioned earlier in 61.10; see too Treggiari 1991: 163).

Male sexuality

If poem 61 presents female sexuality as subtle, sensual, and ultimately passive, male sexuality emerges as rampant, violent, and not easily controlled. Catullus employs the wedding ritual practice of *fescennina iocatio* in order to focus on male sexual desire. The chorus' jokes involve a certain *concubinus*, or young male lover, who is now forced to end his affair with the groom. As the *deductio* marks in ritual terms the separation of the bride from her natal household, so the *fescennina iocatio* celebrates the man's abandonment of sexual affairs outside the framework of marriage (Fedeli 1983a: 98), his sexual aggression controlled and aimed toward the procreation of children.

The husband's attachment to the *concubinus* is the main theme of this portion of the poem;[7] he must give up his male partner in order to effect a successful transition to married life. The chorus also calls on the *concubinus* himself to accept this event, asking him to recognize the marriage god (*Talasius*) as his master (126–7). Like the husband, the *concubinus* needs to enter the world of adulthood, his transition ritually symbolized in the giving of the nuts to the chorus and the cutting of his hair.

Both the nuts and the cutting of the hair as markers of transition constitute integral parts of the Roman wedding ceremony: as we have seen, the groom threw nuts to the boys at the end of the *deductio*, when the procession arrived at his house. This gesture is generally thought to express his abandonment of childhood (Fedeli 1983a: 90). In the poem, Catullus transfers the groom's act to the *concubinus* to indicate that both need to relinquish former pleasures.[8] At the same time, there is also a hint that the *concubinus* may pose a threat to the union of the new couple. If he refuses to give the nuts to the boys, as the chorus implies (*nec nuces pueris neget*, 121; *da nuces pueris*, 124), the *deductio* cannot be completed, and the bride cannot assume her rightful place in her husband's home and *thalamos*. Indeed the chorus does not hesitate to remind the *concubinus* of who are appropriate sexual companions for him: the country wives (*uilicae*), whom he has so far despised (129–30). Presumably a slave, the *concubinus* will now have to forgo the society of elegant urban masters and settle for less refined female company.

The status of the *concubinus* as a potential threat to the couple is further emphasized through attributes he shares with the bride. One of these is the cutting of the hair (131–2). In Roman wedding ritual, the bride's hair was arranged with the aid of a spear that had shed blood.[9] The cutting of the *concubinus*' long hair on his master's wedding day mirrors the parting of the bride's hair with the spear. The chorus' *iocatio* uses irony to underscore the boy's effeminacy and laugh at his expense. They say that the cutting will be performed by the *cinerarius*, the person who normally warms the tongs used to curl the hair of matrons and of effeminate young men. The person who used to tend to the *concubinus*' long hair will now be cutting it (Fedeli 1983a: 94).

At the same time, the groom also shares with the *concubinus* traits which he is called on to give up as he is entering the state of marriage: the chorus refers to him as perfumed (*unguentate . . . marite*, 135). Romans believed that perfuming hair was a sign of effeminacy and that it was a practice wholly inappropriate for an adult male and a husband. The groom's perfumed hair thus corresponds to the *concubinus*' long hair, and their outward appearance reflects their status as adolescents in need of making the transition to adulthood. The groom's attachment to male partners (*glabris*, 135), young household slaves with whom he enjoyed sexual pleasures, may jeopardize the sexual role he must now play as husband.[10] As a result, the chorus calls on him to relinquish these pleasures (134–5), reminding him that they are no longer permitted to a married man (139–41).

The groom's effeminacy, depicting a reluctance to assume his full role as a male, contrasts sharply with the sexual aggression he exudes while he waits for his bride at their marital bed. The use of the word *immineat* (166) to describe the groom's state as he is lying on the bed not only intimates the physical aspect of male desire but also implies its aggressive and threatening nature: it is no coincidence that the same verb used in a military context describes a threat or menace (*OLD* s.v. 4b, 5, and 6). The potency of male desire is further confirmed in the next stanza, where the imagery of consuming fire, a *topos* in erotic poetry, here depicts the new husband. Once again, male desire is characterized as more intense than female, the man said to be "burning deeper inside" than the woman (*uritur . . . penite magis*, 170–1).

Effeminacy and liminality are also closely linked with sexual aggression in the description of the god of marriage himself, Hymenaeus. The poem opens by alluding to the god's feminine nature: he wears a garland of flowers and bridal accoutrements (6–10). Hymenaeus' feminine features are well established in literary and rhetorical descriptions of the god (Fedeli 1983a: 26–7). They also appear in the myths surrounding his person: he is said to have been a young man who disguised himself as a woman in order to be close to the woman he loved (Serv. *ad Aen.* 4.99). Hymenaeus' femininity reflects his status as a youth about to make the transition into manhood. His assumption of a female identity occurs before he is able to prove worthy of his future wife. Similarly, in another mythic version, Hymenaeus dies tragically on his wedding day (Pindar fr. 128c.7–8 S-M). In this case, his failure to enter male adulthood showcases the risks inherent in the stage of transition (treated at length in Catullus 63). Nevertheless, despite his femininity, the god's sexual aggression is unmistakable: as we have seen, Hymenaeus elicits the compliance of the bride for the sexual act and serves as a model for the groom (51–5). The portrait of the god thus resembles that of Manlius: the formerly effeminate groom is ready to perform his sexual role in the context of marriage.

Sex and the ideal marriage

Female and male sexuality are accordingly important elements in Catullus' conception of marriage. At the same time, however, the poem places great emphasis on the problems to the new couple's union that sexual desire may pose. The incredible power of sex necessitates that it be controlled through the laws of marriage. The goddess Venus as a metonymy for sexual power is redefined throughout the poem by a careful identification with Hymenaeus. Yet the power of Venus remains formidable and the question of whether it can be contained within the bounds of marriage is never fully resolved.

More specifically, the poem repeatedly asserts that Hymenaeus alone constitutes the repository of appropriate physical love. Venus is accompanied by the epithet *bona* to denote legitimate love (Fedeli 1983a: 44), (*dux bonae Veneris, boni/coniugator amoris*, "the herald of favorable Venus, the uniter of honest love," 44–5), as opposed to adultery (denoted by *malus* and *turpis*: *non tuus leuis in mala/deditus uir adultera,/probra turpia persequens,/a tuis teneris uolet/secubare papillis*, "your husband will not, devoted to a wicked adulteress, pursuing shameful disgrace, wish to lie far from your soft breast," 97–101). Hymenaeus is the deity with the ultimate power, as he alone is responsible for the love that brings *bona fama*, the only acceptable type of love. Venus' power is thus reconfigured to comprise physical love only within marriage (*nil potest sine te Venus,/fama quod bona comprobet,/commodi capere, at potest/ te uolente*, "without you [Hymenaeus] Venus can take no pleasure that honorable fame may approve: but she can, if you are willing," 61–4).

The final invocation to the groom also concludes with the theme of legitimate sexual pleasure. The chorus prays that *bona Venus* may help him as he seeks physical and emotional love in socially acceptable ways (*bona te Venus/iuuerit, quoniam palam/quod cupis cupis, et bonum/non abscondis amorem*, "may favorable Venus help you, because you desire what you desire openly and you do not hide your honorable love," 195–8; see also Fedeli 1983a: 127). The physical aspect of the groom's desire is meant here, as this portion of the song takes place before the *thalamos*, the marital chamber. The groom is in a hurry to meet his wife (194–5) and the chorus encourages him to give free rein to his desire after the delay of the ritual (Fedeli 1983a: 128).

Physical love as a primary concern for the felicity of the conjugal state is further conveyed through two images of counting, those of the sands of Africa and of the stars (199–203). Both images are used by Catullus in poem 7, in an explicitly physical context, as examples of the number of kisses the poet and Lesbia would share. Catullus' mobilization of the context of the earlier poem underscores the sexual aspect of the *ludi* the couple enjoys but also hints that this type of love may be as pleasurable in adultery, as in the case of our poet and his Lesbia. As a result, the images bring to the foreground the destabilizing, threatening nature of physical love.

The chorus's urging of the couple to enjoy the pleasures of marital sex (*ludite ut lubet*, 204) is followed by the reminder that its ultimate purpose is the procreation of legitimate children.[11] Having once again established appropriate parameters for sex, the chorus concludes by encouraging the newlyweds to enjoy physical love within the constraints of marriage (*at boni/coniuges, bene uiuite et/munere assiduo ualentem/ exercete iuuentam*, "but you happy spouses live happily and in constant pleasures engage your vigorous youth," 225–8). The vocabulary of marital felicity is repeated here to bring the poem's themes full circle: the couple will be virtuous and therefore happy in their marriage (*boni*) and will live in harmony (*bene*) (Thomson 1997: 363; Fedeli 1983a: 145). Yet the chorus's last exhortation is to the enjoyment of physical love (Fedeli 1983a: 146) and of the pleasures of youth, while they remain silent on the other important aspects of marital life. Thus the poem concludes with an emphasis on sexual pleasure. Whether it is possible to contain it within marriage alone is a question ultimately left open.

Poem 62: Resistance to Marriage

While poem 61 ends with the theme of marital harmony, poem 62 shifts gears and dramatizes the battle of the sexes and female resistance to marriage in particular. The poem belongs to the genre of the *carmen amoebaeum* or singing contest, developed by the Hellenistic poet Theocritus. In Roman literature, the most famous examples of such contests are Vergil's *Eclogues* 3 and 7. Like the other poems in this genre, Catullus 62 pays close attention to structural symmetry, whereby each stanza (*strophe*) is followed by a response (*antistrophe*) in the same number of lines. The poem begins with introductory lines spoken by a chorus of youths, followed by a response from a chorus of maidens (1–10). A statement on the part of the youths concludes this introductory section (11–19). Then follows the singing match proper, consisting of three pairs of stanzas (20–58). The poem ends with an epilogue (59–66). Throughout the poem, each stanza is followed by a refrain, which forms another important structural device. In the second pair of stanzas, however, the text is heavily damaged, which has resulted in lively scholarly controversy as to how many lines are spoken by the maidens and the youths (Thomson 1997: 365). Further debate has arisen over who speaks the final lines of the epilogue.[12]

As in 61, here too ritual elements underscore the poem's content. As a result, ritual once again constitutes a background against which the theme of female resistance to marriage is played out. The question of the precise ritual setting of the poem has given yet another occasion for debate among scholars. Fraenkel (1955), in a highly influential article, suggested that the poem reflects Roman rather than Greek wedding customs, while Tränkle (1981) and Courtney (1985) argued an opposing view.[13] More recently, Goud (1995: 31–2) has claimed that the contest takes place at the end of the banquet and before the *deductio* begins. This is the moment of the *raptio*, the ritual tearing away of the bride from her mother's embrace. Thomsen (1992: 166–73) believes that the contest is linked to the absence of the bride. He rightly points out that if the maidens are not defeated in the singing match and the bride does not return, the wedding cannot take place. As a result, the poem and its ritual context dramatize a moment of crisis. The resistance of the maidens and of the bride will, however, be eventually overcome with the return of the bride and the completion of the *deductio* procession. The bride's return symbolizes her willing integration into her marital household and her new role as a Roman wife. Thus the poem's ritual context serves to give voice to anxieties inherent in the events it celebrates, while at the same time it provides comfort and reassurance by stressing the benefits of marriage for all.

Let us now turn to the poem itself in order to observe how the contest between male and female is articulated; in what ways it provides a space where competing ideas about the role of men and women within marriage arise; and whether female resistance is eventually replaced by a joyful anticipation of married life.

The poem's opening stanzas state explicitly that the contest is about victory: the boys rise to sing (*surgere iam tempus*, 3), the girls rise in return (*consurgite contra*, 6) and express the wish to win the singing match (*canent quod uincere par est*, "they will sing something that it is right to surpass," 9). The boys further perceive that the girls are formidable competition (*non facilis nobis, aequales, palma parata est,* "no easy palm of victory is ready for us, friends," 11) and that their own lack of preparation will jeopardize their chances of winning (*iure igitur uincemur: amat uictoria curam*, "we will be defeated rightly: victory loves care," 16). The poem thus begins with the presumption that marriage provides resolution to an existing struggle between the sexes, whereby one will submit to the superiority of the other. In this light, the maidens' resistance is not wholly surprising. The vocabulary of victory (*uincere*, 9; *palma*, 11; *uincemur* and *uictoria*, 16) employed by both sides negates or at least undermines the professed complementarity and harmony in the roles of husband and wife and rather dwells on the necessity of a power differential between the sexes.

The context of competition and victory provides fruitful ground on which opposing attitudes to marriage on the part of the youths and the maidens are articulated. In each pair of stanzas, the girls call on Hesperus, the evening star, to complain of the violence of male sexuality and the dominance of male over female, while the boys cast the same god as a guarantor of progress and civilization. More specifically, in the first stanza of the contest proper, the reality of male violence is repeatedly asserted: Hesperus is called most cruel (*quis caelo fertur crudelior ignis?*, "what is a more cruel fire in the sky?" 20) and is twice said to tear the girl away from her mother (*qui natam possis complexu auellere matris,/complexu matris retinentem auellere natam*, "who can tear the daughter from her mother's embrace, tear away the clinging daughter from her mother's embrace," 21–2). Like Hesperus, the husband exhibits a burning desire for the girl (*iuueni ardenti*, 23) and his union with the bride is compared to the capture of a city by an enemy (*quid faciunt hostes capta crudelius urbe?*, "what more cruel thing do enemies do when they have captured a city?" 24). Marriage is thus presented as violent and destructive.

The boys, however, cast marriage as a social institution that guarantees unity not only between the sexes but also between families. The point is emphasized through the use of legal language to describe Hesperus/marriage as a mutual contract (*desponsa... conubia*, "the contracted nuptials," 27) which is enduring (*firmes*, "you confirm," 27) and binding for the spouses and their families (*quae pepigere uiri, pepigerunt ante parentes*, "which husbands and fathers have promised beforehand," 28).[14] Marriage also provides a most desirable unity among the parties involved, a unity not achieved by other means (*nec iunxere prius quam se tuus extulit ardor*, "united not before your fire has risen," 29). The chorus conclude their argument by attributing to divine authority the provenance of the institution of marriage (*quid datur a diuis felici optatius hora?*, "what more desirable thing do the gods give than the happy hour?" 30), thus establishing the superiority of the social aspects of marriage to the personal and familial ones invoked by the maidens. At the same time, the boys' version of the importance of marriage is confined to a male perspective: the contracts are made by husbands and fathers (*uiri, parentes*, 28), with the females thus relegated to the role of passive compliance. As a result, the boys' claim of unity and harmony is predicated upon female submission to male authority.

The theme of marriage as violent and lawless rape on the one hand and as an integral part of a lawful and civilized society on the other continues in the next pair of stanzas. Although the text of the strophe is badly damaged, most scholars agree that it contains an explicit reference to the *raptio* ritual. Thomsen (1992: 182) offers evidence that the verb *auferre* is also used in the context of Proserpina's rape in Ovid's *Fasti* (4.445, 4.448). The textual gap makes the context of the maidens' reproach to Hesperus particularly difficult to understand,[15] but the boys' response depicts him as a catcher of thieves and a guarantor of law and order in a manner very similar to that of their previous statement (*namque tuo aduentu uigilat custodia semper,/nocte latent fures, quos idem saepe reuertens,/Hespere, mutato comprendis nomine Eous*, "for when you come the guards are always awake, the thieves hide at night, whom you often catch when you return, Hesperus, the same but with changed name, Eous," 33–5; Thomsen 1992: 263). At the same time, the boys' claims once again undermine the validity of those of the girls: just as in the previous stanza female participation in the legal proceedings of the wedding was purely secondary, so in this instance the girls' reproaches to Hesperus are discredited as false (*ficto…questu*, "with false complaint," 36). As a result, the boys appropriate the function of Hesperus/marriage in order to validate their point of view, while they also affirm the superiority of their voice over that of the other sex.[16]

In the final pair of stanzas, the maidens and youths introduce images from nature to support their respective claims. As we have seen earlier, the girls advocate virginity in the image of a beautiful, untouched flower, whose purpose is a peaceful existence free from the constraints of marriage and fertility but which is subject to violent destruction on the part of the male. The boys manipulate the same concept and embed it in the realm of agriculture, which necessarily promotes fertility and reproduction, the indispensable consequences of marriage for society at large. Thus the flower now becomes a vine that needs to be united in marriage to the elm (*at si forte eadem est ulmo coniuncta marito*, "but if by chance the same one is joined to an elm as her husband," 54).[17] The image of marriage presented here initially appears as one that prescribes equal and complementary roles for husband and wife (*par conubium*, "equal marriage," 57),[18] and that promotes harmony between the sexes so that the important function of reproduction may take place. Yet the last statement of the boys' chorus returns to the theme of the antagonism between the sexes. The state of marriage emerges as most desirable for men (*cara uiro magis et minus est inuisa parenti*, "she [i.e., the bride] is more dear to her husband and less hateful to her father," 58), while there is no mention of the woman's sentiments. Thus the singing match concludes, as it started, with a privileging of the male perspective and an affirmation of the power differential between the sexes.

Ideal Marriage for Family and State

In both poems, female resistance to marriage eventually gives way to the joys of the new life awaiting the bride and groom. In the conclusion of poem 62, the bride is urged to comply with social demands that require that she enters the state of marriage willingly (60–5):

> non aequom est pugnare, pater cui tradidit ipse,
> ipse pater cum matre, quibus parere necesse est.
> uirginitas non tota tua est, ex parte parentum est,
> tertia pars patris, pars est data tertia matri,

> tertia sola tua est: noli pugnare duobus,
> qui genero sua iura simul cum dote dederunt.

> It is not right to vie with him to whom your father himself gave you,
> your father himself with your mother, whom it is necessary to obey.
> Your virginity is not all your own, part of it belongs to your parents,
> a third belongs to your father, a third was given to your mother,
> only a third is your own: do not vie with two,
> who have given to their son-in-law their rights along with the dowry.

Regardless of who speaks these final lines,[19] the arithmetic used to define the woman's identity[20] focuses on her obligations vis-à-vis her family and by extension on the reciprocity fundamental to the proper function of social relations. Personal attachments or other concerns, such as those voiced by the chorus of maidens in the course of the contest, must be abandoned. The language of arithmetic and ownership is accompanied by legal terminology (*sua iura*, *dote*),[21] thus validating the line of argument the boys have employed all along.

Marriage necessitates female submission to social constraints because its main purpose is socially determined. Through marriage the continuation of the family line, whose significance for society at large hardly needs mention, is ensured. Poem 61 takes special note of the importance of reproduction for the survival of the household while it also stresses the ideal of reciprocity governing the relationship between parents and children: just as the children depend on their parents in order to grow and reach adulthood, so the parents rely on their children in their old age: *nulla quit sine te domus/ liberos dare, nec parens/ stirpe nitier; at potest/ te uolente*, "no house can give children without you, nor a parent rely on his offspring; but it can if you are willing" (66–9).

Furthermore, marriage is the only framework within which familial felicity may be achieved, as the tender image of young Manlius on his mother's lap, reaching over to his father smiling (209–13), attests. Important reminders follow: legitimate children alone secure continuity within the family (214–23):

> sit suo similis patri
> Manlio et facile insciis
> noscitetur ab omnibus,
> et pudicitiam suae
>   matris indicet ore.

> talis illius a bona
> matre laus genus approbet,
> qualis unica ab optima
> matre Telemacho manet
>   fama Penelopeo.

> Let him look like his father
> Manlius and be recognized
> easily by all strangers,
> and by his face declare
>   the chastity of his mother.

> May such praise from a virtuous mother
> prove the worth of his family

> like the unparalleled fame
> that endures for Penelope's Telemachus
> from his honorable mother.

Continuity is particularly crucial in the case of the Torquati, a family famous for saving the Capitol from the Gauls and perhaps even more famous for putting a son to death, an action that appears to have rendered them in the eyes of their fellow Romans both heroic and inhuman.[22] The image of the young child reaching over to his father has therefore particular resonance. Without children this noble family, as well as any other family, is bound to face extinction (see also Newman 1990: 206–7).

Familial continuity, however, rests wholly upon female fidelity. The paradigm of Penelope is pivotal in making this point.[23] The magnitude of her contribution to her family's lasting fame may also be seen in the poet's naming of Telemachus. While one would expect a patronymic, Telemachus is instead defined as the son of Penelope (*Telemacho . . . Penelopeo*). Female fidelity is the sole means by which legitimate children may guarantee not only the family's survival but also its good standing in the community. It constitutes therefore an integral part of the greater network of social relations. The woman's willing participation in marriage is indispensable for the proper functioning of society as a whole.

Family in Roman thought often serves as a microcosm for the state, and poem 61 is no exception. In enumerating the blessings of marriage, the poet also makes a brief yet critical mention of the intimate relationship between procreation and the safety of the state: marriage produces soldiers who will defend the land (*quae tuis careat sacris,/non queat dare praesides/terra finibus: at queat/te uolente*, "the land which should lack your sacred rites could not give guardians for its borders: but it could if you are willing," 71–4). Rome's military and political power is therefore contingent upon this vital social institution.

Yet despite the positive view of marriage and its focus on social demands, hints of resistance persist. Poem 62 may assign two-thirds of the woman's identity to others but the final third belongs to herself. And though the boys' perspective may appear to prevail, many readers claim that the girls' arguments have greater resonance (Stehle [Stigers] 1977: 97; Thomsen 1992: 229) and fit neatly with the theme of the failure of marriage in the other long poems. Most importantly, the images of female resistance and vulnerability deployed in these poems find their starkest expression in the image of another flower touched by a plow in poem 11.22–4 (Stehle [Stigers] 1977: 98; M. J. Edwards 1993: 185–6; see Greene, this volume). The male narrator's self-identification with the delicate flower lends greater gravity and poignancy to the absence of a true integration of female anxieties and social constraints in 61 and 62.

Catullus' wedding poems have such a lasting impact on their readers precisely because they mobilize the emotive power of ritual in order to give expression to female anxiety over the violence connected with the act of defloration. Ritual context and poetic content validate female resistance to marriage as a powerful manifestation of the conflict between individual needs and societal demands. But unlike ritual ceremonies, where anxieties are expressed in order to be assuaged so that the new phase in the life of the couple can be duly celebrated, Catullus' poems are often most remembered for their haunting delineation of female fragility.

ACKNOWLEDGMENT

I would like to express my warm thanks to the editor for inviting me to participate in this volume and for her perceptive comments, which helped improve this chapter.

NOTES

1   On the debate on the bride's name, see Thomson (1997: 348); Ready (2004: 153 n. 1).
2   Some believe the poem to reflect Greek wedding customs (Tränkle 1981; Courtney 1985; Thomsen 1992), while others consider them Roman (Fraenkel 1955; G. Williams 1958).
3   The word has often been taken to mean "trembling with old age" on the basis of its use later on in the poem: *tremulum mouens/cana tempus anilitas*, "white-haired old age shaking its trembling head," 154–5. But, given the context, it is more likely that it is used here to convey parental distress (see Thomson 1997: 353–4).
4   It should be noted here that Catullus attributes to the bride a gesture that was performed by the groom. See Fest. 55 Lindsay *DVS*; Fedeli (1983a: 50). The active participation of the girl in the sexual act is incongruent with other images of her as a passive recipient of the groom's advances and anticipates her eventual sexual awakening – which, however, will be reserved for her husband alone.
5   Stehle [Stigers] (1977: 87) on the image of the flower in Sappho and Catullus.
6   On the use of this adjective, see also Ready (2004: 156–7).
7   Fedeli (1983a: 96–7) offers evidence that giving up illicit affairs was one of the standard themes of *epithalamia*.
8   On the debate on what the nuts may symbolize, see Fedeli (1983a: 88–90) and Thomsen (1992: 48–9).
9   Implications of violence are also inherent in this ritual act. The spear that has shed blood is also a symbol of the violence of the act of defloration, marked in humans by the shedding of blood. See Burkert (1983: 62).
10 On the groom as preferring homoeroticism to married life, see Thomsen (1992: 63–73). As a master, however, Manlius would have an active sexual role in his relationship with the young household slaves and there is nothing in the text to suggest otherwise. See Butrica (2005: 224); C. A. Williams (1999: 274 n. 97). On the role of the *glaber*, see C. A. Williams (1999: 73).
11 On the benefits of procreation, see discussion below.
12 See below, n. 19.
13 Thomsen (1992: 174–93) offers support for the importance of Greek wedding ritual for an understanding of poem 62, yet he admits that the references to the *raptio* point to Roman ritual customs. He concludes (p. 193) that the poem reflects mainly Greek customs but also contains Roman elements.
14 Thomson (1997: 367) notes that the lines refer to the ceremony of *sponsalia*, where the *sponsio*, the signing of the wedding contract between the bride's father and the fiancé, took place.
15 Thomsen (1992: 182) calls into question the scholarly consensus that the lacuna reproaches Hesperus as a thief. He rightly notes that after the previous stanza's references to Hesperus as a violent rapist a description of him as a thief would be rather anticlimactic.
16 On the importance of this statement for the poem as a whole, see Thomsen (1992: 227–30).
17 On the debate on the provenance of the image, see Fraenkel (1955: 8); Courtney (1985: 87).

18 *par* here also denotes an equal match with respect to social rank. See Quinn (1973a: 281).
19 Most commentators (e.g., Fraenkel 1955: 6; Quinn 1973a: 282) believe that the lines are spoken by the boys. Certainly the language the boys employ throughout the poem supports this argument. Others point out that the rules of the genre dictate that the contest concludes with the winner (see Thomsen 1992: 171). *Eclogue 7*, however, provides evidence that this is not always the case (M. J. Edwards 1993: 44). Goud (1995: 31–2) suggests that it is the leader of the girls' chorus, acting as a *pronuba*, who urges the bride to yield. Thomsen (1992: 223–30) argues that this is the poet's voice: he has the last word in the other long poems, while it is not surprising that the male point of view prevails, since the poet is a man after all. Earlier (pp. 212–14) Thomsen adduces yet another convincing argument for his case by drawing a parallel with Plautus' *Casina*: he interprets the passage as containing an exhortation to the bride to consummate the marriage, which in the play is uttered by the *pronuba* and in 61.204–5 by the poet.
20 On the pedigree of the division of identity into thirds, see Ellis (1889: 199) and Thomsen (1992: 217).
21 Thomsen (1992: 222) suggests that the use of these terms refers to marriage *in manu*.
22 Cic. *Fin.* 1.35. The speaker, a descendant of Torquatus, asserts that Manlius put his son to death for the sake of military discipline and the greater good. Livy's account (8.19) offers similar motives for Manlius' actions.
23 On the importance of Penelope at this juncture and its relationship to the poem's earlier reference to the myth of Paris, see Ready (2004: 155–6).

GUIDE TO FURTHER READING

There exist two monographs on the wedding poems, both indispensable for any in-depth study: Fedeli (1983a) on 61 and Thomsen (1992) on 61 and 62. Fedeli provides a thorough analysis of the ritual and stylistic elements of the poem; he extensively cites probable sources, and offers judicious discussion of all the evidence as well as valuable insights on problems of interpretation. Thomsen's book is not as easily readable. But the author rewards the reader patient enough to sift through his rather unusual expository method and provides subtle and interesting interpretations of the poems. He also offers a very thorough discussion of the existing bibliography. For those interested in the question of the Greek origins of these poems, Courtney (1985), Fraenkel (1955), Newman (1990), Tränkle (1981), and G. Williams (1958) will provide ample opportunity for further study. Additionally, on the relationship between Sappho and Catullus' wedding images, Stehle [Stigers] (1977) is an excellent place to start, while M. J. Edwards (1992) is also very useful. The existing commentaries on the poems offer little help: Thomson (1997) often falls short in answering the most vexing questions, but the bibliography appended to each poem is extremely helpful. Quinn (1973a) is perhaps more useful for the student beginning to tackle these poems, but unfortunately a lot of the information contained therein is out of date.

WORKS CITED

Burkert, W. 1983. *Homo Necans: The Anthropology of Ancient Greek Sacrificial Ritual and Myth.* Trans. P. Bing. Berkeley. First published as *Homo Necans*, Berlin 1972.
Butrica, J. L. 2005. "Some Myths and Anomalies in the Study of Roman Sexuality." *Journal of Homosexuality* 49: 209–69.

Courtney, E. 1985. "Three Poems of Catullus." *Bulletin of the Institute of Classical Studies of the University of London* 32: 85–100.

Edwards, M. J. 1992. "Apples, Blood and Flowers: Sapphic Bridal Imagery in Catullus." In C. Leroux, ed., *Studies in Latin Literature and Roman History VI.* Collection Latomus 217. Brussels. 181–203.

Edwards, M. J. 1993. "Catullus' Wedding Hymns." *Classical Review* 43: 43–4. [Review of Thomsen 1992].

Ellis, R. 1889. *A Commentary on Catullus.* 2nd edn. Oxford.

Fedeli, P. 1983a. *Catullus' Carmen 61.* Trans. M. Nardella. Amstersdam. First published as *Il carme 61 di Catullo*, Fribourg 1972.

Fraenkel, E. 1955. "*Vesper adest* (Catullus LXII)." *Journal of Roman Studies* 45: 1–8.

Goud, T. 1995. "Who Speaks the Final Lines? Catullus 62: Structure and Ritual." *Phoenix* 49: 23–32.

Newman, J. K. 1990. *Roman Catullus and the Modification of the Alexandrian Sensibility.* Hildesheim.

Quinn, K., ed. 1973a. *Catullus: The Poems.* 2nd edn. London and Basingstoke.

Ready, J. L. 2004. "A Binding Song: The Similes of Catullus 61." *Classical Philology* 99: 153–63.

Stehle [Stigers], E. 1977. "Retreat from the Male: Catullus 62 and Sappho's Erotic Flowers." *Ramus* 6: 83–102.

Thomsen, O. 1992. *Ritual and Desire: Catullus 61 and 62 and Other Ancient Documents on Wedding and Marriage.* Aarhus.

Thomson, D. F. S., ed. 1997. *Catullus, Edited with a Textual and Interpretative Commentary.* Toronto.

Tränkle, H. 1981. "Catullprobleme." *Museum Helveticum* 38: 245–58.

Treggiari, S. 1991. *Roman Marriage:* iusti coniuges *from the Time of Cicero to the Time of Ulpian.* Oxford.

Williams, C. A. 1999. *Roman Homosexuality: Ideologies of Masculinity in Classical Antiquity.* New York and Oxford.

Williams, G. 1958. "Some Aspects of Roman Marriage Ceremonies and Ideals." *Journal of Roman Studies* 48: 16–29.

CHAPTER SIXTEEN

Catullan Intertextuality: Apollonius and the Allusive Plot of Catullus 64

Jeri Blair DeBrohun

Catullus' neoteric masterpiece, his longest and most complex poem, belongs formally to the genre of epic, though its highly compressed quality has led modern critics to assign it to the category of epyllia ("mini-epics"). Insistent on its epic status, however, Catullus 64 demands to be read not only in relation to earlier epyllia (most prominently, Callimachus' *Hecale*) and to the similar productions of his neoteric contemporaries (such as Calvus' *Io* and Cinna's *Zmyrna*), but also as a representative of the epic tradition, with a particularly intimate relationship with his Hellenistic predecessor, Apollonius' *Argonautica*, and through Apollonius with the genre's fount, Homer. The central importance of the *Argonautica* for Catullus 64 has long been recognized, for Catullus at first appears to be intent upon a retelling of the *Argo* legend and the related myth of Jason and Medea, and allusions to both stories are prevalent throughout the poem (Perotta 1931; Braga 1950; Avallone 1953; Clare 1996; LeFèvre 2000a). What has not been fully appreciated is just how strongly Catullus marks Apollonius' epic as his primary model in his opening and how integral a role the earlier poem plays in the structural frame of Catullus 64, as well as in Catullus' representation of himself in relation to his poem's narrative. A deeper understanding of the relationship between these two poets will help to explain two aspects of Catullus' epyllion that have long troubled readers: why does a poem on the wedding of Peleus and Thetis start with the *Argo* (e.g., R. F. Thomas 1982: 163), and what, if any, Hellenistic precedent lies behind the poem's structure (e.g., Perotta 1931; LeFèvre 2000a)? The focus of these pages will be on the epyllion's opening and frame; our conclusions, however, will have implications for readings of the ecphrastic centerpiece as well.

What makes the narrative of Catullus 64 unusual is that the poet-narrator is alternately ostentatiously passive and insistently assertive. The narrative strategy of passivity serves, at one level, to signal the poem's alignment with the typically impersonal medium of epic, in which the poet's role is that of a conveyer of tradition rather than the creator of a new story. When, however, that passivity is prominently displayed (as we will see, for example, at the opening of the poem), this signal may carry more than one message. Because the narrator's (willfully) passive relationship to his poem is so clearly marked, his first-person entrances, most notably through apostrophe, but also through other means of authorial intervention, are highlighted all the more. Catullus further reinforces the assertive nature of these entrances through rhetorical devices such as exclamation (*o!* line 22; *heu!* line 94) or emphatic repetition (e.g., *neque tum ... neque tum ... /toto ... toto ... tota* in lines 68–70). The poet's first-person intrusions can also, however, like his passivity, convey more than one meaning, as his authorial *ego* itself may echo the words of earlier poets (Gaisser 1995; Wray 2000, on Apollonius).

All of this does not make the Catullan poet-narrator unreliable in any straightforward sense (on this aspect of 64, see Schmale 2004); for, as we will see, he has a direct precedent for the first instance of passive narration in the poem. It does, however, require an unusually high level of poetic engagement on the part of the reader. Neoteric readers are prepared for this, of course, aware as they are already that the effective power of intertextuality depends on their ability to read both what the poem before them says, on its surface, and what is said by additional voices, whether supportive or contradictory of the poem's surface meaning, that are simultaneously recalled and suppressed by the text (on allusion and necessary reader collusion, Goldhill 1991: 288–9; cf. Pasquali 1951; Conte 1986; Hinds 1998).

Catullus' alternately passive and assertive narrative self-positioning also serves another, larger purpose in the poem, as a vehicle through which the poet points to, and comments on, both his belatedness in the tradition he has entered and his own disruption of that tradition in order to make a place for himself (for other aspects of the problem of belatedness in 64, see Fitzgerald 1995: 140–68; Theodorakopoulos 2000: 139–41; Martindale 2005: 90–100). As Goldhill stated, "To write a Hellenistic epic, then, is to be inscribed in an especially intricate, overdetermined relationship with the literary past" (1991: 286; cf. Bing 1988: 73–5). The neoteric (and later, Augustan) poets have a heightened sense of their own epigonal status, since they are acutely aware that they have inherited even the problematic notion of belatedness itself from their Hellenistic predecessors. In addition, they now have their own Roman literary tradition before them. The Romans also inherited, from the Hellenistic poets especially, a recognition that establishing their own place within this continuing tradition required, at some level, a deliberate breach or rupture of it.

In adapting elements both of narrative structure and of content from Apollonius, Catullus establishes a continuity with the epic tradition as it is passed down from Homer, through Apollonius, to himself. Simultaneously, however, his drastic reworking of Apollonius' epic, which results in a complete suppression of the *Argonautica*'s principal story (and indeed, of the poem itself), signals a rupture of an extreme nature. Catullus' creative response to his late arrival in the tradition takes the form of first announcing his model in the poem's introduction, then eliminating that model's presence altogether from the surface of his poem. The tension between these two aspects of Catullus' poetic project is manifested throughout the poem, both narratively and thematically. The desire for continuity, on the one hand, is seen in Catullus' (and his poem's) expressed longing to reach a past that is no longer attainable (*o nimis optato saeclorum tempore nati/heroes*, "O heroes, born in a time of the ages too much hoped for!" 64.22). On the other hand, because Catullus has placed his model so thoroughly yet barely under erasure, his disruption of the tradition, also necessarily incomplete, is also strongly felt, most noticeably in the replacement of Jason and Medea with Theseus and Ariadne in the poem's ecphrastic centerpiece. Here, the tension between continuity and rupture is figured as a problem of murderous family relations, marked most strongly in the conflation, through allusion, of Ariadne's Minotaur brother, murdered by Theseus with her help, and Medea's brother Apsyrtus, murdered by Jason with Medea's support. The replacement of Medea's murder of her children with Ariadne's successful prayer for Aegeus' death may be seen, at one level, as a figure for the tradition at war with itself, since in Catullus' poem, the story's progenitor, rather than its progeny, is eliminated.

Problematic family relationships are also relevant to the story of Peleus and Thetis. In displacing the story of their courtship and marriage from its status as an event that had taken place prior to the time of the main story in Apollonius and Homer, and making it the beginning of his own poem, Catullus successfully inverts his relationship with both poets, eliminating his literary "father," Apollonius, and creating a space for himself before both the *Argonautica* and the Homeric poems. Catullus thus follows the same impulse that led Apollonius to make the *Argo* legend the subject of his epic. Even in his revised version of the Peleus and Thetis story, Catullus nonetheless manages to highlight elements in the tradition that point to the troublesome familial issues involved in the wedding. The relationships in the story serve, in a sense, as figures for the relationship between Catullus' poem and those of his predecessors.

The Opening of Catullus 64: An Apollonian Proem

Catullus establishes his poem as a creative rewriting of Apollonius' *Argonautica* in the first 30 lines of his epyllion, and those lines will be the initial focus of our attention. It will be useful to adumbrate my argument with an outline. In the structure of his opening, an elaborate *praeteritio*, or "passing over," Catullus not only allusively reworks his predecessor's proem but simultaneously responds to challenges implicit in Apollonius' text. Catullus presents in 1–24 a drastically compressed version of Apollonius' *Argonautica* (Gaisser 1995: 585). In this mini-*Argonautica*, Catullus marks the Peleus and Thetis story – told in a narrative digression in Book 4 of Apollonius' poem – as the particular aspect of his predecessor's epic with which he means to interfere. Lines 19–21, with their elaborate construction, introduce the element of disorder with characteristically neoteric flair. Immediately afterward, 22–4 serve simultaneously both to close the mini-*Argonautica* and to announce the true beginning of Catullus' narrative proper: the wedding of Peleus and Thetis. Catullus ensures that we recognize the new beginning through duplication and repetition, as he retells, in 25–30, the story already related once in 19–21, using language that both recalls and revises the earlier passage.

A Catullan praeteritio *begins as the mini-*Argonautica *opens*[1]

Peliaco quondam prognatae uertice pinus
<u>dicuntur</u> liquidas Neptuni nasse per undas
Phasidos ad fluctus et fines Aeeteos

Pines born on the Pelian peak once upon a time
<u>are said</u> to have swum through the clear waters of Neptune
to the waves of Phasis and the Aeetean borders.

The key word is *dicuntur*. Its employment here is an instance of the phenomenon rightly recognized as not only a general poetic appeal to authority (the Callimachean "I sing nothing unattested" [fr. 623 Pf.]) but, more specifically, a self-conscious marker of allusion, for which Ross coined the phrase "Alexandrian footnote" (1975: 78; Hinds 1998: 1–3). Gaisser raised a significant point, however, with her observation that *dicuntur* in line 2, which she called an "authority formula," also alerts the reader to the story's status as a fiction which has many authors (1995: 582). In this instance, the plural verb (strictly speaking, attached to its plural noun, *pinus*) is particularly apt, since, as R. F. Thomas (1982: 144–60) has shown, the poet pointedly alludes to a number of different literary texts in 1–18 (Zetzel 1983; Stoevesandt 1994/5).

Still, as Gaisser's observation reminds us, Alexandrian footnotes, even when they are footnotes, are not necessarily (or even usually) exhaustive, but more often serve, as *dicuntur* does here, as a signal to the reader that a certain selectivity has been employed by the poet in his handling of the tradition. This leads to two aspects of the opening of Catullus' epyllion that have not yet been fully explained. First, in his allusion to previous poetic versions of the *Argo* legend, the poet-narrator has been simultaneously selective and exhaustive. Selectively, in 1–18 (esp. 1–14), he has concentrated his (and his readers') attention on the ship, highlighting his predecessors' conflicting accounts of its material (pine versus fir), its maker (Argus or Athena), and the derivation of its name (from Argus, or from the nationality of the Argonauts themselves [*Argiuae robora pubis*, "strength of the Argive youth," 5], or from the adjective "swift" [Greek *argos*; Latin *citus*, in *cita decurrere puppi*, "to course along in a swift ship," 6]). Exhaustively, Catullus has recalled so many of the previous literary versions of the *Argo* story in his representation of the ship that the reader has the feeling the poet has surely included them all. A third quality of Catullus' intertextual practice might also be added: suppression. For the poet has done all of this without ever naming either the ship itself or its traditional creator (R. F. Thomas 1982: 162).

This raises certain questions: why has the poet selected the ship, in particular, as his focus, and why has he described it with such a display of learned detail yet omitted directly naming it or its (mortal) builder? The answer to these questions is found in Catullus' most important model, Apollonius' *Argonautica*, and is signaled by a second aspect of Catullus' initial verb that has not been fully appreciated: *dicuntur* is an unusual way for a poet-narrator to begin an epic. With his opening words, the poet first identifies his narrative role in relation to the story he will tell, and the reader expects either a request from the Muse (such as the *Iliad*'s "sing, Muse, the anger of Peleus' son Achilles") or a first-person beginning such as that which opened Hesiod's

Theogony ("From the Heliconian Muses let us begin to sing") and was later used by Aratus in the *Phaenomena* ("From Zeus let us begin") and by Apollonius in his *Argonautica* ("Beginning with you, Apollo, I will recall the famous deeds of men of ages past"). Vergil and Ovid both return to the first-person opening in their own highly allusive epic beginnings (Vergil's *Aristaeus* episode in *Georgics* 4 announces itself similarly [lines 285–6]); and the pseudo-Vergilian epyllion *Ciris* begins with the poet. As Bühler (1960: 47) noted, Catullus does follow Callimachus' precedent in the *Hecale* in "using an ornamental adjective with adverb to sum up the dateless past." Callimachus' first sentence, however, contains a finite verb ("once upon a time there lived an Attic woman in the hill country of Erechtheus" [Hollis 1990: 137]). While Callimachus' *Hecale* may well have been a source for the Theseus story in 64, Catullus is not following the earlier poet's lead with his *dicuntur*.

There is something unusually manneristic about Catullus' delegation of narrative authority as a means to open his poem. As has been suggested already, Catullus has taken his cue from Apollonius here, though not from his model's first line. The proem of Apollonius' *Argonautica* itself exhibits a complex structure, which alludes to both Homer's *Iliad* and *Odyssey* (Fantuzzi 1988: 22–3; Goldhill 1991: 288–91; Hunter 1993a: 119–23; Clauss 1993: 14–25; Clare 2002: 20–32, 261–2). Furthermore, Apollonius has adopted the structure of the *Iliad*'s beginning as the model for his own proem: "In both poems the opening verses foreshadow later major events – what the epic is *about* (*Argonautica* 1.1–4, *Iliad* 1.1–7) – and then a transitional passage fills in some of the background up to the point at which the narrative proper begins (*Arg.* 1.1–4, *Iliad* 1.12–42)." In doing this, the Hellenistic poet has drawn his readers' attention to Homer as the "touchstone against which to measure his epic" (Hunter 1993a: 119).

Apollonius is also concerned, of course, to differentiate himself from Homer and signal his own contribution to the epic tradition. He unveils his poem's true starting point with a second proem in 18–23:

> As for the ship, the singers who came before me still celebrate
> that Argus made it, under the guidance of Athena.
> But I now will tell the lineage and names   20
> of the heroes, and their long journeys over the sea,
> and the deeds they accomplished as they wandered.
> May the Muses be the inspirers of my song.

Apollonius uses a variant of the authority formula ("they celebrate") to locate himself within the tradition of poets who have also sung of the Argonaut legend. By opening his verse with "ship" (*nêa*), Apollonius emphasizes for the reader that poets of the past have made their subject the *Argo* itself. He, however, disposes of the vessel quickly, attributing its creation to Argus, with Athena's help (though as a learned poet himself, he was no doubt aware of competing versions). With his abbreviated yet prominent mention of the ship's treatment by earlier poets, Apollonius employs the strategy of *praeteritio* and simultaneously suggests that a detailed description of its creation is by now hackneyed, or that, in good Alexandrian fashion, he has selected one version, perhaps even alluding to a particular earlier treatment, and suppressed the others (Goldhill 1991: 290–1; Hunter 1993a: 122). The *praeteritio* also, of course, serves another, more significant function, which is that of staking the poet's claim for his own place in the tradition to which he has referred. His contribution, Apollonius announces in 20–2, will be the catalogue of heroes, which immediately follows these lines.

Apollonius' *praeteritio* in 18 provides the answer to our question(s) of why Catullus has chosen to begin with the *Argo* itself and why he has described it with such allusive precision. In 64.1–18, Catullus meets the implicit challenge he found in Apollonius' dismissal of a detailed description of the *Argo* as passé. In response, Catullus demonstrates ably what a talented neoteric poet can do with the long succession of predecessors available to him (including, now, Roman poets as well as Greek); and in this sense, his display of intertextual virtuosity in the opening of his epyllion exhibits a kind of literary polemic, though of a slightly different order than R. F. Thomas (1982) suggested. Catullus' suppression of the one fact directly included by Apollonius (Argus' manufacture of the ship) serves as a backhanded acknowledgment of his primary allusive model. It also puts us on the alert to the possibility that other aspects of Apollonius' epic might receive similar treatment.

Once we recognize that Catullus' *dicuntur* responds to a narrative strategy in Apollonius, we receive reassurance, on a metapoetic level, of what we have known all along, that our poet is in fact running the show from behind the curtain. But, as has been noted, in Apollonius' second proem (18–23), which follows his first-person opening, the Apollonian *ego* again appears, this time to announce the upcoming catalogue that is the genuine start of his narrative. Catullus, in contrast, has (thus far, at least) removed all personal identifying markers from his opening. His allusion to his predecessor's narrative strategy of *praeteritio* suggests that lines 1–18 of poem 64 similarly comprise a *praeteritio* (or part of one), albeit a more elaborate one. Furthermore, our confidence that Catullus recognized the Iliadic structure that lay behind Apollonius' start leads us to expect that he has similar plans to rework his own model's beginning. Catullus' decision to begin his poem with an allusion to the start of Apollonius' second proem is an example of the poet's determination simultaneously to continue and to disrupt the epic tradition as he received it. As Apollonius had imitated Homer's structure, then added a second proem, Catullus follows (and reworks) Apollonius, beginning at precisely the point where the earlier poet distinguished himself from his model.

Catullus' refusal to acknowledge his narrative control at the very start of his poem has a further effect. In the context of his own epyllion, we receive the impression that our poet, like the characters within the narrative, and like the reader, is reacting to the course of the poem rather than guiding it. The (unnamed) *Argo* itself seems to assert control over the narrative in 1–18. The first action narrated is that of the ship, in the form of personified pine trees, swimming through the sea (2), and it is the *Argo* as subject that "first initiated the inexperienced Amphitrite" (11) and that "plowed the sea with its beak" (12). Finally, it is the ship as *monstrum* ("marvel," 15) that draws the nymphs' admiring gaze and motivates them to emerge from the water and display themselves to the sailors (12–18).

A Catullan praeteritio *continues: the Apollonian* Argonautica *is interrupted*

In 19–21, Catullus introduces a startling twist to the *Argo*'s story. The surprise is accompanied by the second appearance of an authority formula, *fertur* (19).

tum Thetidis Peleus incensus <u>fertur</u> amore,
tum Thetis humanos non despexit hymenaeos,   20
tum Thetidi pater ipse iugandum Pelea sensit.

<u>Then</u> for Thetis Peleus <u>is said</u> to have been inflamed with love,
Then Thetis did not look down upon wedding a mortal,
Then to Thetis the father himself (sc. Jupiter) felt that Peleus should be joined.

In this instance, as Gaisser (1995: 585) noted, the formula does not appear to be fully reliable as an allusive marker. For here Catullus uses *fertur* when reporting an event whose timing, which the poet emphasizes with the first *tum* of an anaphoric trio, Catullus himself appears to have invented, in direct contradiction to traditional versions of the myth (see esp. Ellis 1889: 278–83). Most significantly, those earlier versions include Apollonius' *Argonautica*, in which Peleus and Thetis are married prior to the *Argo* sailing, and Chiron brings the child Achilles to see his father off (*Argon.* 1.558). Could it be that, as with *dicuntur*, Catullus is challenging the reader to seek a different kind of intertextual model, one that is again concerned not only with content but also, and more pointedly, with structure and narrative control?

With *fertur* following upon *dicuntur*, Catullus has allusively and authoritatively, if again obliquely, marked his disruptive contribution to the mythological (and literary) tradition as he received it, and directed his reader to the epic narrative (and narrator) that inspired his daring innovation and whose version of the story he has upset most dramatically. Our ability to recognize what this marker conveys depends upon our recognition of two additional aspects of Catullus' poem here that imitate Apollonius' narrative practice. First, we must recognize that Catullus is not simply producing a mini-*Argonautica* in his opening 24 lines; more specifically, the neoteric poet offers, within his condensed Apollonian epic, an extraordinarily compressed (and, as a result, heavily revised) version of the Peleus–Thetis episode as Apollonius himself had presented it (64.12–18). It is immediately after this, but before the (Apollonian) *Argonautica* ends, that Catullus inserts his chronological twist.

The reader must also recognize Apollonius as the model for the insertion of the twist itself. We may begin more readily with this second demand, since it has already long been suspected by Catullus' readers that Apollonius lies behind Catullus' audacious revision in line 19 (cf. Clausen 1982: 192: "Perhaps Catullus was emboldened by the example of Apollonius"). The grounds for this suspicion also provide the primary evidence in its support. For, in Catullus 64's second major reversal of traditional literary-mythological chronology, Catullus follows Apollonius' lead more directly (though no less obliquely: Weber 1983). A brief examination of this second reversal in Catullus 64, and of the Apollonian manipulation that inspired it, will be useful for our consideration of the epyllion's first switch.

As we have seen, the *Argo* is introduced by Catullus as the world's first ship ("that ship first initiated Amphitrite with its voyage," 64.11); but later, in the Theseus and Ariadne story embroidered on the wedding coverlet (*uestis*), Theseus is depicted sailing away in a ship, a chronological impossibility set up by the poem itself. For we are told that the coverlet depicts *priscis hominum...figuris* ("ancient figures of men," 64.50), which certainly suggests, if read straightforwardly, a time prior to that of the wedding for which the tapestry was woven. It has also been noted that Catullus, in reversing the chronology, has followed the precedent set by Apollonius, who similarly manipulated the relative timing of Theseus' legend and the Argonauts' journey in his own epic (Weber 1983: 269; Clare 1996: 66–8).

Catullus will have noticed that while Apollonius did not overtly signal the inconsistencies in his use of the Theseus tradition, he called attention to them nonetheless, and without taking full responsibility for the problems he had created. It is the poet-narrator who, in the catalogue of heroes, excuses Theseus from taking part in the expedition on the grounds that he was detained in the underworld (*Argon.* 1.101), not, as the later mentions of the hero in Books 3 and 4 would suggest, because he was chronologically unavailable. In Book 3, it is Jason, not the poet-narrator directly, who marks the remoteness of his story of Ariadne and Theseus with "once upon a time" (*dê pote, Argon.* 3.997), granting it an antiquity that contradicts the introduction of Theseus in Book 1. It is also Jason who emphasizes only the most positive aspects of Ariadne's story as he relates it to Medea, omitting the unpleasant elements and employing pointedly ambiguous language that is immediately noticed by every reader. Still later, in *Argonautica* 4, the robe sent by Jason and Medea among the gifts to lure Apsyrtus to his death is said to retain the divine fragrance from the time when Dionysus held Ariadne, whom "once upon a time (*pote*) Theseus had abandoned on the island of Dia, when she had followed him from Cnossus" (*Argon.* 4.430–4); and we learn in the same passage that Hypsipyle, the Lemnian queen who, as Jason's lover in Book 1, prefigures Medea's role in the epic, is the granddaughter of Dionysus and Ariadne (*Argon.* 4.424–7). In this instance, it is the poet-narrator who further complicates the poem's chronology of Theseus and Ariadne; and by mentioning Theseus' abandonment of Ariadne directly, he supplies the unpleasant aspect of Ariadne's story omitted from Jason's account to Medea in Book 3 (Weber 1983: 269; Fusillo 1985: 69–71; Hunter 1989 *ad* 997–1004; Goldhill 1991: 301–6).

Apollonius' treatment of Theseus (and no doubt of other aspects of his epic) sensitized Catullus to the idea that strict faithfulness to mythological-literary history was, or could be, a choice, and that violation of the tradition offered significant poetic possibilities. Also, as Catullus' expert manipulation of his allusive sources in 1–18 demonstrates, he was fully aware that the choice of which earlier versions, or even individual elements, of myths are selected and privileged as intertextual models also lies with the poet. In Catullus' rendition of the Peleus and Thetis story in 19–21, he takes his cues on narrative selection most strongly from Apollonius' Jason. Like the "once upon a time" of Jason in *Argonautica* 3.997, but with greater emphasis, Catullus marks his chronological revision with *tum* ("at that time") in 19. He then completes, in 20–1, his own highly selective and pointedly ambiguous – but not, apart from the timing, altogether false – description of the courtship of Peleus and Thetis. *Fertur* in 19 is not (again, apart from the chronology) employed by the poet in bad faith; for there are versions of the story (including that in *Argon.* 4.805–9) in which Thetis does not disdain the marriage itself (her anger comes later); and in Pindar (*Isthm.* 8.45–7), Zeus joins the other gods in favoring the union of Thetis with a mortal, once the prophecy that Thetis will bear a child greater than his father is known.

It is worth noting that apart from *fertur*, nothing about the poet's presentation of his mythological innovations in 19–21 is equivocal. The lines are presented with considerable fanfare, as a triplet, each beginning, as mentioned above, with anaphoric *tum*, the force of which is felt all the more strongly as it is followed in each instance with *Thetis* in polyptoton (*Thetidis … Thetis … Thetidi*).

Apollonius' Peleus and Thetis: Catullan compression and revision

The reader's recognition of Apollonius as the model for Catullus' chronological disruption in 19–21 is only one of the two aspects of his revision of the earlier poet's Peleus and Thetis story that Catullus expects his reader to notice. We turn now to the other: Catullus' allusive compression, in 11–18, of the Peleus and Thetis episode of Apollonius' epic.

In order to appreciate more fully what Catullus has done with his model, it will be useful to summarize the structure and character of the story as it is told in *Argonautica* 4, where it forms part of a digression from the main narrative: the escape of Jason and Medea, with the Argonauts, from the pursuit of Medea's family after the murder of her brother Apsyrtus. The account begins just after Circe's expulsion of the pair from her island with the warning that Medea's father will not give up his pursuit to avenge her brother's death. Hera, who has been monitoring events, sends Iris to summon Thetis, whose aid, together with that of her sister Nereids, Hera enlists to guide the *Argo* between the hazards of Scylla, Charybdis, and the Wandering Rocks. The episode is of considerable length (*Argon.* 4.757–968) and becomes itself part of a mini-*Odyssey*, which finally rejoins Medea's story at Alcinous' palace at Phaeacia, to which the Colchians have pursued the couple by an alternate route (Vian 1974–81: III. 46; V. Knight 1995: 207–16; Byre 2002: 134–9; Clare 2002: 139–44).

Within the digression, the story of Peleus' and Thetis' wedding, which (as it is told here) was followed shortly afterward by the goddess' angry departure when her attempts to insure immortality for Achilles were discovered by her husband, is related in a series of flashbacks and speeches, from the different viewpoints of Hera, Thetis, Peleus, and the narrator (Hunter 1993a: 96–100; V. Knight 1995: 297–303). As Hunter has shown, Apollonius has blended elements of two Homeric accounts (*Il.* 18.429–35, 24.59–63), as well as a number of additional sources, into his depiction of the pair's relationship. Thetis' anger, Hunter points out, has an intertextual referent, as it "is a characteristic of the Homeric Achilles which Apollonius has transferred to his mother in the previous generation" (1993a: 99). The couple have only a brief personal encounter ("she drew near and barely touched the hand of Peleus; for he was her husband," *Argon.* 4.852–3); and when she leaves after their short conversation, her anger unabated, Peleus remembers, painfully, her earlier angry departure (*Argon.* 4.865–8). Hunter describes the scene between them as "a powerful manifestation of the gulf between man and god" (1993a: 100).

With this in mind, let us return to Catullus 64 and examine the neoteric poet's revisionist compression of the episode in his introduction. For this, we need especially lines 11–18:

> illa rudem cursu prima imbuit Amphitriten;
> quae simul ac rostro uentosum proscidit aequor
> tortaque remigio spumis incanuit unda,
> emersere freti candenti e gurgite uultus
> aequoreae monstrum Nereides admirantes.   15
> illa, atque <haud> alia, uiderunt luce marinas
> mortales oculis nudato corpore Nymphas
> nutricum tenus exstantes e gurgite cano.

> That (ship) first initiated inexperienced Amphitrite in its course;
> as soon as it plowed the windy plain of the sea with its beak,
> and the wave, twisted by the oars, grew white with foam,
> from the churning surge of the sea the ocean's Nereids raised up
> their faces, marveling at the wonder.
> On that day, and no other, mortals saw with their eyes the sea Nymphs,
> their bodies bared as far as their breasts, rising forth from the gray-white surge.

While the allusions to Apollonius in this passage have long been recognized, R. F. Thomas (1982: 158–9; cf. Syndikus 1990: 120–3) demonstrated that, in fact, Catullus has conflated in these lines two different passages of the *Argonautica*. One is from the opening book, where the nymphs of Mount Pelion look down in wonder on the *Argo*, the world's first ship, as it embarks on its maiden voyage (*Argon.* 1.549b–52):

> On the topmost peaks the Pelian nymphs marveled
> as they looked upon the work of Itonian Athena, and at
> the heroes themselves, wielding the oars with their arms.

The other passage is from the episode just described, in the poem's final book. Despite the story's many unhappy elements, Catullus has selected a pleasant moment, near the end of the digression, when the Nereids are sporting about in the water, helping the ship along (*Argon.* 4.933–55). There is even a Catullan play with the Nereids' attire: Apollonius' nymphs are described as rolling up their garments to their waists (*Argon.* 4.948–50), while Catullus' Nereids are bare-breasted (64.17–18) (Cairns 1984: 100; Hunter 1991). This inversion of detail in Catullus' account draws the mortals' gaze to the nymphs and leads directly to the moment in which Catullus interrupts the *Argonautica* of his predecessor.

By selecting and recombining a moment from the *Argonautica*'s opening action with a (deceptively positive) moment from Apollonius' Peleus and Thetis episode, Catullus has successfully condensed the contents of Apollonius' *Argonautica* in a manner that serves his own aim of representing the Peleus–Thetis story as one of love at first sight, which occurred when the couple met, during the first sailing of the *Argo*. And in fact, Catullus' tendentious representation of actual events in his model's epic makes his chronological disruption, when read as it is presented on the surface of his own poem, appear to be the next logical phase in the *Argonautica*'s progress (Clare 1996: 62–5).

Once we recognize the purpose behind Catullus' conflation of the two Apollonian passages, we can see also that he has signaled his compression with *illa atque <haud> alia* (Bergk's correction of the corrupt manuscript is surely right) in 16. These words also find a correspondence in the passage from *Argonautica* 1: just before the Pelian nymphs are introduced, we learn that "on that day (*hēmati keínōi*) all the gods looked down from heaven upon the ship and the might of the heroes" (547–8). Catullus' addition of "and no other" points not only to his conflation of two different occasions in Apollonius' epic but also to two Homeric passages where Thetis and her sisters appear. One is from *Iliad* 18.35 ff., when the Nereids leave the sea to comfort Achilles after the death of Patroclus (first noted by Curran 1969: 187); the other appears in *Odyssey* 24.47–59, when Agamemnon reveals to Achilles in the underworld the details of the hero's funeral, including the fact that his mother came forth from the sea with her sisters upon hearing of her son's death. Here again, Catullus signals his continuity with the epic tradition even as he distinguishes himself from his immediate predecessor (and both of these passages, like the Peleus–Thetis episode in *Argonautica* 4, lend unhappy undertones to Catullus' happy love story: Curran 1969).

Catullus' praeteritio *(and mini-*Argonautica*) end, and his new poem begins*

We are beginning to gain a better understanding of Catullus' aims in these opening lines. In order to see the poet's plan more completely, it is necessary to examine closely not only 22–4 but those lines that follow (25–30) as well:

o nimis optato saeclorum tempore nati	22
heroes, saluete, deum genus! o bona matrum	
progenies, saluete iter<um ...	23b
uos ego saepe, meo uos carmine compellabo.	
teque adeo eximie taedis felicibus aucte,	25
Thessaliae columen Peleu, cui Iuppiter ipse,	
ipse suos diuum genitor concessit amores;	
tene Thetis tenuit pulcerrima Nereine?	
tene suam Tethys concessit ducere neptem,	
Oceanusque, mari totum qui amplectitur orbem?	30

O heroes, born in a time of the ages too much hoped for!	
Hail, offspring of the gods! O blessed sons of mothers,	
Hail again ...	23b
You (sc. heroes) often, you I will address in my song.	
And you especially, exceptionally blessed by happy wedding torches,	25
pillar of Thessaly, Peleus, to whom Jupiter himself,	
the father of the gods himself, gave up his own love.	
Was it you whom Thetis, the most beautiful daughter of Nereus, held?	
Was it you whom Tethys allowed to marry her own granddaughter,	
and Ocean, who embraces the whole world with his sea?	30

Lines 22–4, as both Zetzel (1983: 260–1) and Klingner (1964: 167–8) noticed, allude to the poet's words at the close of the *Argonautica* (4.1773–5; cf. also Gaisser 1995: 585):

> Be gracious, heroes, born of the blessed gods! And may these songs
> from year to year grow sweeter to sing among men.

But there is more going on here; for Catullus' apostrophe to the heroes is phrased not as a valediction but as a salutation (*saluete*, 23), which, as Fordyce (1961: *ad loc.*) notes, belongs to the style of hymns (Zetzel 1983; Gaisser 1995). Here, a recognition of the unusual character of Apollonius' closing (and opening) proves significant. As Goldhill (1991: 287) points out, performances of Greek epic were regularly preceded by a short hymn, and Apollonius' epic both begins (*Argon.* 1.1) and ends with language common to the closing formulas of hymns, "as if the complete *Argonautica* has become a (hymnic) prelude; as if the pretext to end is – playfully – an epic to come." Goldhill's words summarize well the strategy Catullus noticed in his epic model, and which he reworked, to new effect, in his epyllion.

For Catullus, lines 22–4 serve a dual role, both as an ending and as a new beginning; and we are meant to hear echoes of both the closing and opening (again *Argon.* 1.1 is meant) of Apollonius' epic. The transition in Catullus 64 is signaled by the repetition of *saluete* in 23 and 23b; and the hymnic resonance of these lines suits Catullus' intended subject, a wedding celebration. More significantly, we are also meant to hear an additional echo of Apollonius, signaled by the reduction of *uos* to *te* at the start of lines 24 and 25 and, more pointedly, by *teque adeo* in the latter. As both Fordyce (1961: *ad loc.*) and Quinn (1973a: *ad loc.*) note, *adeo* is used in line 25 to mark a climax. But what sort of climax? The opening passages of Vergil *Eclogues* 4 and *Georgics* 1, both adduced as parallels by Fordyce, serve as especially suggestive points of comparison. In *Eclogue* 4, a poem whose intertextual associations with Catullus 64 are well established, a series of expressions announcing a new age culminates in line 11, which begins *teque adeo* and singles out the consulship of Pollio as the contemporary moment that begins an age of renewal in Rome. (This is followed, anaphorically, by *te duce* at the start of line 13, a verse that echoes Catullus 64.295.) At the opening of Vergil's *Georgics*, the poet invokes, in hymn form, a long list of deities, culminating with Augustus, who is addressed with *tuque adeo* at the start of line 24. In Vergil's passages, therefore (which may, especially in *Ecl.* 4, find their models in Catullus 64), *teque adeo* and *tuque adeo* mark the climax of a series. This is the manner in which *teque adeo* is meant to be understood by Catullus in 64.25 as well. As he closes his mini-*Argonautica*, the poet-narrator invokes the poem's heroes, then immediately proceeds to single out Peleus among them. The repetition of *saluete*, further emphasized by *iterum* in 23b, drives home the point.

Catullus has, therefore, announced the true beginning of his poem with a multiple Apollonian allusion, pointing not only to the first and final lines of his model but also to the beginning that, as we saw earlier, was privileged by Apollonius as his own contribution to the Argonaut legend: the catalogue of heroes. Catullus, then, has closed his *praeteritio* with a reversal of his predecessor's use of the same rhetorical ploy, drastically reducing Apollonius' catalogue to a sole representative, just as Apollonius had reduced his depiction of the legendary ship to one line.

The fact that 25–30 constitute, for Catullus, a second and new beginning is further marked by the duplication, in this passage, of his first, brief narration of the Peleus and Thetis story in 19–21. As Quinn (1973a: *ad loc.*) notes, a second anaphora begins with *teque* in 25, continued by *tene . . . tene* to open 28 and 29; and this recalls the anaphoric *tum* in 19–21. While the polyptoton of *Thetis* in 19–21 is not repeated exactly, a similar effect is produced by *Thessaliae . . . Thetis . . . Tethys* in 26, 28, and 29. There is in the second version of the story, signaled by language repeated from the earlier lines, an emphasis on different details, to mark a transition from the courtship, related within the mini-*Argonautica*, to the wedding itself, the first event of Catullus' new poem.

The final element in the first story (21) is the report that Jupiter, expressed as *pater ipse*, "felt" (*sensit*) that Peleus and Thetis should be joined. In the new version, this event is relayed in a different manner, in a direct address to Peleus, and it receives two lines: in 26–7 Jupiter is introduced by name, and *ipse*, repeated in epanalepsis at the end of 26 and start of 27, recalls *pater ipse* from 21 and defines it more specifically, with *diuum genitor*, "father of the gods." With *concessit* (27) replacing *sensit* (21), emphasis is placed on the marriage to Thetis as a special favor granted to Peleus by Jupiter. There is also an allusion in both passages, more pronounced in the second, to the role that paternity played in Jupiter's decision. The question in 29, while it places proper emphasis, in a wedding context, on the extraordinary beauty of the bride, also recalls, and appears to query further, the lukewarm expression of Thetis' eagerness for the wedding in 20 (*non despexit*). There is also here an implicit reversal of the tradition, best known from Ovid (*Met.* 11.217–65), that Thetis herself was notoriously difficult to grasp. The description of Peleus as *incensus...amore* in 19 is replaced in 25 with a different kind of flame (*taedis felicibus aucte*, 25), and *amor* itself is transferred to Jupiter. Finally, 29–30 add details not present in the earlier story, as they trace Thetis' lineage back to her maternal grandparents, Oceanus and Tethys.

The emphasis in both passages on Jupiter's paternal role, and the mention of Thetis' father and grandparents in 28–30, evokes for the reader, both directly and allusively, the complicated familial relations involved in the couple's wedding story. Jupiter's description as *diuum genitor* (27) points to the prophecy that Thetis' son would be greater than his father, which would, in Jupiter's case, mean his potential displacement as supreme ruler of the gods. *Diuum genitor* also, however, recalls *deum genus* (and *matrum progenies*) in 23–4 and reminds us that Jupiter is well known as a progenitor of heroes as well as gods. Furthermore, Jupiter's surrender of his beloved to Peleus brings its own complications. When we learn the names of Thetis' father and (maternal) grandparents, we are encouraged to recall the groom's lineage as well, including not only his father, Aeacus, but also, and more significantly, his grandfather, who was, according to tradition, Jupiter himself (through a union with the daughter of a river god). The similar constructions of lines 27 and 29, including the repeated verb *concessit* with the same object expressed in different terms (*suos...amores* [27] becomes *suam...neptem* [29]), further highlights the awkward relations between the couple's families.

Juno/Hera is notably absent from either Catullan account; her presence is felt, however, since the choice of Peleus as Thetis' mortal husband is typically attributed to her (not Jupiter, as in 21). Apollonius' Hera in particular lies behind the description of Peleus as "raised up by the wedding torches" (25), which echoes Hera's recollection that she herself had raised the bridal torch in honor of Thetis' loyalty (*Argon.* 4.808–9). Hera's own relationship to the bride might also be suggested by the mention of Oceanus and Tethys in 29–30. Hunter, in his discussion of the scene between Hera and Thetis in *Argonautica* 4, pointed out that Hera's speech has, in addition to the Homeric intertexts in *Iliad* 18 and 24, "a further Homeric model which flickers over the Apollonian surface" (1993a: 98). He refers here to Hera's "Deception of Zeus" in *Iliad* 14 and, more specifically, to the speech of Hera to Aphrodite (*Il.* 14.200–10, later repeated in part to Zeus at 301–6), in which the goddess claims, falsely, that she is embarked on a mission to reunite her foster parents, Oceanus and Tethys, who have been separated for years after quarrelling. In *Argon.* 4.790–2, Hera represents herself as a foster mother to Thetis in words her Homeric counterpart used to describe the care she received from her adoptive parents (*Il.* 14.202–3). The similarities between the story in the *Iliad* and that of Peleus and Thetis in Apollonius' epic, as well as Hera's role as would-be conciliator in both, are clear. Catullus' *diuum genitor* in 19, and his allusive juxtaposition of the respective grandparents of the wedding couple, may provide a link with Hera's story in *Iliad* 14: in line 201, she refers to Oceanus as *theôn genesin*, "progenitor of the gods."

It is, of course, the lineage of Peleus that serves most readily as a figure for Catullus' relationship with his epic predecessors. This is not meant to be overly tidy. Even so, it is tempting to see in the figure of Jupiter the tradition's beginning in Homer; then, when Jupiter, fearful of the son who might overthrow him, surrenders the object of his affection to his grandson, the subject of Catullus' poem is created: the marriage of Peleus and Thetis. The elision of the link between grandfather and grandson, Peleus' father Aeacus (and perhaps also the suppression of the son Jupiter and Thetis might have produced), parallels the suppression in Catullus' poem of his immediate epic model.

Catullus' Epyllion Begins: The Wedding of Peleus and Thetis

We have reached what has always been recognized as the true starting point of Catullus' poem. As Apollonius did with Homer, now Catullus, by structuring his opening in response to Apollonius' *Argonautica*, has made the earlier poet's epic the touchstone for his epyllion. Apollonius' epic will serve as the primary intertext and structural model for the rest of his poem as well. While the brief space of this chapter does not allow for a full reading of the poem in this light, there is sufficient space to demonstrate, at least in broad outline, how Catullus has restructured elements from the *Argonautica* to new effect, as well as to suggest a few of the ways that a recognition of the particularly strong relationship between these two epics contributes to a fuller understanding of Catullus 64.

Once the poem begins anew at line 25, its structure, at its most basic, is twofold: the main story, the wedding of Peleus and Thetis, also serves as the frame for an inset narrative, the story of Ariadne and Theseus, related through an (extraordinarily) extensive ecphrastic digression. The story on the *uestis*, with its complex structure, juxtaposition of visual and verbal media, and representation through multiple viewpoints, occupies the narrative space of, and stands in for, the *Argonautica* itself. While there is not space to examine it in detail, we will return to consider its significance later. For now, however, our focus will be the frame.

It has long troubled Catullan readers that the wedding appears to have two separate parts (e.g., Klinger 1964: 29–31; Gaisser 1995: 590–1, 608; Lefèvre 2000a). The first begins at 31 with the arrival of the Thessalian guests and ends just after the ecphrastic digression, when we are explicitly informed that, having satisfied their desiring gaze by viewing the wedding coverlet, the mortal guests depart (267–8). Afterwards, the divine guests arrive and the second part of the wedding commences, leading to the song of the Fates. Once our attention has been directed by Catullus to Apollonius' *Argonautica*, and especially to Book 4, we can see that Catullus found his model for the wedding of Peleus and Thetis, with its inset digression, in the two-part wedding of Jason and Medea, the episode which, significantly, directly follows the Peleus and Thetis digression in Apollonius' poem. The strong intertextual resonances between the wedding in Catullus 64 and that in *Argonautica* 4 have, of course, been noticed (esp. Braga 1950: 160; Klingner 1964: 30; Konstan 1977: 69; Zetzel 1983: 260; Clare 1996: 65–6). What has not been fully appreciated, however, is that, as he did with other aspects of Apollonius' poem, Catullus has taken over his predecessor's narrative structure and created from it a new story that is, while obviously different, also closely related to its model, not only in structure but also in content and spirit.

An outline of Apollonius' narrative will again be useful for an understanding of what Catullus has done. Shortly after the Argonauts land on Phaeacia, they learn that the Colchians have also arrived by a different route, to demand Medea's surrender and return to her father (*Argon.* 4.1001–7). When King Alcinous promises his protection to the couple if they are already married, a quick wedding is arranged. The ceremony (*Argon.* 4.1128–60) is held in a sacred cave (and is well known to Vergil's readers as a model for Aeneas' marriage to Dido in *Aen.* 4, a story that draws from both Apollonius and Catullus 64). The wedding couch is covered with the golden fleece itself, "so that the marriage might be honored and made the theme of song" (1141–3), and this, as readers have long recognized, is the primary inspiration for Catullus 64's *uestis*. Nymphs (sent by Hera) and the Argonauts comprise the guest list, and Orpheus is reported to have sung the wedding-song (1159–60). After a brief interlude (to which we will return), a second phase of the wedding takes place the next morning when, after Hera has sent forth a "true report" of the news (1184), the entire city celebrates. Alcinous affirms the union and is faithful to his promise of protection for Medea (1170–1205). As Hunter (1993a: 73) notes, Apollonius' wedding of Jason and Medea has among its own models earlier poetic accounts of the wedding of Peleus and Thetis, the unhappy results of which, as noted above, Apollonius' readers have just encountered in the *Argonautica*'s preceding episode (cf. Vian 1974–81: III.49–50; Byre 2002: 134–9, 146).

Let us consider now the brief interlude that separates the two parts of the wedding of Jason and Medea (*Argon.* 4.1161–9):

> It was not in the land of Alcinous that the heroic son of Aeson had desired to complete his marriage, but in the halls of his father, after his return to Iolcos; this also, Medea had intended, but necessity forced them to join at that time. For never, in truth, do we tribes of suffering mortals tread joyfully with a full step, but there is always some bitter pain that accompanies our happiness. And so it was that they, too, although they were warmed by their sweet love, were fearful whether the judgment of Alcinous would be accomplished.

The emotional resonance of these lines with the spirit of Catullus 64 is obvious. More to the point, however, in the creation of his wedding poem Catullus has once again taken a number of cues from Apollonius' epic and recombined them for his own purposes. Most obviously, Catullus has taken over Apollonius' structure of a two-part ceremony with interlude and replaced Jason and Medea with Peleus and Thetis in his frame. This choice was motivated by the implicit comparison of the two pairs through their representation in successive episodes in *Argonautica* 4. Then, with the same audacity with which he drastically compressed his model's Peleus and Thetis episode for his opening *praeteritio*, here he expands – even more dramatically – Apollonius' very brief interlude, transforming it into a fully developed inset narrative introduced with the wedding couch and its coverlet, and replacing Jason and Medea with

Theseus and Ariadne. This decision was inspired especially by Apollonius' suggestive description of the purpose which lay behind the choice of the golden fleece as wedding coverlet for Jason and Medea ("so that the marriage might be honored and made the theme of song") and, as we saw earlier, by Apollonius' manipulation of the Theseus and Ariadne story as an example, as well as by the recognition, on the part of both poets, of the potential for creative juxtaposition inherent in the similarities and differences between the traditions surrounding the two couples.

The interlude in Apollonius played a role for Catullus as well. While the argument need not be pressed too far, in this short passage Apollonius casts a shadow over the wedding, and the future of Jason and Medea, in much the same way that he does with the Ariadne example. The expressed desires of the couple to marry after the *Argo*'s return, in Aeson's house, remind the reader of the exceptionally unhappy future that awaits them in their later literary-mythological tradition. The interjection of the poet-narrator's voice in reaction to the couple's fear, and his extension of their situation to all mortals, finds reflection in Catullus' poem in his division of the mortal and divine guests at the wedding of Peleus and Thetis immediately after the ecphrasis is completed. For, as the words of Apollonius' narrator remind us, it is mortals, not gods, for whom the images on the tapestry have meaning.

While Apollonius places the wedding of Jason and Medea in *Argonautica* 4 just after the digression which relates the unhappy result of Peleus' and Thetis' union, Catullus reverses this order in his poem: the first part of the wedding, which includes the arrival of the Thessalian guests, then the long ecphrastic digression and its exclusive viewing by the mortals, has as its primary correspondence the wedding of Jason and Medea in Apollonius' poem. (Even the juxtaposition of two peculiar versions of the Golden Age in 64.35–42 and 43–9, one evocative of Hesiod's "Myth of the Ages" in the *Works and Days*, the other characterized by the opulence of Peleus' palace, finds a parallel in Apollonius' description of the kingdom of Phaeacia, the site of his wedding. Phaeacia is first introduced with the story, most familiar from Hesiod's *Theogony*, of Cronos' mutilation of his father [*Argon*. 4.982–6; the story provides an etymology for the island's name Drepane, "sickle"], but is also the home, of course, of the Odyssean palace of Alcinous.)

What, then, of the second part of Catullus' wedding in poem 64? For this, the ceremonial banquet, Catullus has followed traditional versions of the Peleus and Thetis story (though of course, with his own revisions in the divine guest list), according to which all the gods attend the wedding, but no mortals apart from Peleus himself (Lefèvre 2000a: 187–9). The use of an elaborate Homeric simile to describe the departure of the mortal wedding guests is meant to signal to Catullus' readers that we have entered not only a new part of the wedding but also a new allusive world (64.269–77). For it is no longer Apollonius' *Argonautica* but now Homer's *Iliad* that serves as the primary intertext, especially for the telling of Achilles' future in the song of the Fates (Klingner 1964: 30–1; Stoevesandt 1994/5; *Od.* 24.35–97 is also a likely source, for Agamemnon concludes his description of Achilles' funeral with: "but what pleasure is this to me, that I have wound up the spool of war?").

Apollonius' epic does offer, in Hera's speech to Thetis, a prophecy concerning Achilles that is not included in the Fates' song (indeed, it cannot be, since it involves a character suppressed in Catullus' poem) but would naturally follow their vision of

Achilles' future and provide a direct link not only between Peleus, Thetis, and Medea but also, thematically, between all three pairs in both poems (*Argon.* 4.810–17):

> "But come, let me relate a tale (Greek: *mythos*) that is infallible. When your son comes someday to the Elysian plain,…it is fated that he will be the husband of Medea, daughter of Aeetes. Therefore help your daughter-in-law as a mother-in-law should, and help Peleus himself."

As Byre (2002: 136–7) noted, Hera's promise of a kind of immortality (combined with marriage) for Achilles and Medea suggests an alternative fate for both characters not dissimilar to that of Ariadne.

Conclusions (and Catullus' Epilogue)

Apollonius' *Argonautica* is not, of course, the single key to understanding Catullus 64. Versions of the Theseus tradition, for example (especially, one suspects, Callimachus' *Hecale*), are of great importance for the interactions between the two stories presented in the ecphrasis, one on the surface, the other barely beneath (see Knox, this volume). There is, however, much to be gained from a recognition that Apollonius' epic is not only a source of specific allusive references but also, and more importantly, a model for the complex structure of Catullus' poem and for the extraordinary character of its narrative. A recognition that 1–30 comprise an introduction constructed in direct response to Apollonius enables us to answer, once and for all, why a poem on the wedding of Peleus and Thetis starts with the *Argo*. And once we see that *dicuntur* in line 2 leads us specifically to the opening of Apollonius' second proem, we are primed to seek Apollonius (or, in some instances, another allusive source) behind every authority formula, even less clearly authorized ones such as the innocent-looking *locatur* in 47, when the coverlet is first "placed" in the middle of Catullus' poem (cf. *sedibus in mediis*, 48). We are now better assured that these lines mean to lead us, through allusion, to the placement of the couch over which the golden fleece is laid for Jason and Medea in *Argon.* 4.1141–3 (the responsibility for which is also not explicitly stated in Apollonius' poem).

Undoubtedly the most striking aspect of Catullus' restructuring of Apollonius' *Argonautica* is his complete suppression, in his own narrative, of Jason and Medea, and his notable abandonment, once his introduction is finished, of the *Argo* legend itself. It was suggested in the introduction to this chapter that this extreme combination of allusion and suppression is a means to convey the tension between the poet's desire for continuity with the literary tradition and his recognition that a break with it is necessary if he is to establish a place for himself. It was further suggested that this tension is figured by the poet as a problem of (murderous) family relations. One effect of Catullus' placement of the Peleus and Thetis story at the opening of his narrative proper is to straighten out chronology in his frame story, which now moves neatly from the wedding of Peleus and Thetis to its most important result, Achilles. In literary-historical terms, Catullus has placed himself early in the Homeric tradition, and his "Marriage of Peleus and Thetis" becomes, in a sense, "father" to its own "grandfather," Homer's *Iliad*, a family connection strengthened by the emphasis on

Achilles (with Homeric allusion) in the final section of the poem. To accomplish this effectively, the poet had to eliminate his own "father," Apollonius, as well as the *Argo* legend itself, in what might be viewed as a kind of literary-historical patricide.

Of course, Catullus also expects us to recognize that literary forefathers do not surrender easily to their sons. Catullus' attempt to replace Apollonius' *Argonautica* with Theseus and Ariadne, and to enclose it within the bounds of a narrative digression, has decidedly (and deliberately contrived) mixed results. At one level, the suppressed *Argonautica* still holds onto its proper position, between the wedding of Peleus and Thetis and the Trojan War; and the extraordinary length of the digression gives the impression that the (barely) hidden Apollonian epic is itself attempting to burst its confining frame. But of course, the *Argonautica* is also not there: Theseus and Ariadne are.

While the ecphrastic centerpiece has not been the focus of this chapter, it shares and exemplifies the concerns of the poem as a whole. Within the ecphrasis, the tension between continuity and rupture is figured, at an intertextual level, as a tension between the Theseus and Ariadne story and that of Jason and Medea. When Catullus' language (or that of his characters) directly evokes the contradictions between the two stories (as when Ariadne refers to the Minotaur as her brother), he means for his readers to notice not only his own disruption of the tradition, but his predecessor's similar behavior in using Theseus and Ariadne as an exemplum in his own epic; thus, of course, he establishes a continuity between himself and Apollonius.

It is time, at last, to introduce into the discussion the additional members of Catullus' (dysfunctional) literary-historical family. As Catullan readers know, it is through allusions not only to Apollonius and Homer, but to many other texts as well, that Catullus evokes the multiple additional poetic voices (including especially Euripides, Ennius, and his own lyric *ego*), along with the additional perversions of literary or mythological relationships those voices convey, all of which work together to produce his richly complex masterpiece. It is to this cacophony of voices, expressed and suppressed, and most notably to the suppressed voices of Apollonius and his main characters, Jason and Medea, that Catullus refers in his closing epilogue (64.397–408):

> But after the earth was initiated with unspeakable crime,
> and all mortals banished justice from their desiring minds,
> brothers soaked their hands in brothers' blood,
> the son stopped grieving for his dead parents,   400
> the father hoped for the death of his young son,
> so that he might be free to enjoy the flower of an unwed stepmother,
> and an impious mother, spreading herself under her unknowing son
> did not fear, impious as she was, the pollution of her family gods.
> All things, speakable, unspeakable, confounded by an evil madness,   405
> turned away the justice-wielding mind of the gods from us.
> Therefore they do not condescend to attend such gatherings,
> nor do they allow themselves to be touched in the clear light of day.

There could be no more apt expression of the juxtaposition, combination, and suppression of Catullus' allusive creation than *omnia fanda nefanda permixta* ("all things, speakable, unspeakable, confounded," 405). In their lament both for an irretrievable past and for the thorough degradation of familial relationships in the present, these lines express two of the chief concerns expressed by Catullus, both narratively and allusively, throughout his epyllion: the problem of belatedness, and the perversion of family relationships that has caused the rupture between the present and the past. In societal terms, Catullus was no doubt aware that his readers would find (as critics have done) in contemporary Roman society all too many possible reference points for the kinds of incestuous relationships his epilogue describes. In aesthetic terms, however, Catullus' lament is also a proclamation of his own poetic achievement. His fellow neoterics would have recognized it as such: Cinna and Calvus, whose epyllia Catullus may also mean to evoke here, had very likely thematized the tension between continuity and rupture similarly in their epics; and their subjects (the incestuous love of Myrrha; Jupiter's rape of Io) suggest that the perversion of relationships might well have been one of the strategies their poems shared with that of Catullus.

ACKNOWLEDGMENT

I am grateful to Michael Putnam, Stephen Hinds, and James Kennelly for their helpful comments and suggestions.

NOTE

1 Mynors's OCT text is quoted throughout, with my own translations.

GUIDE TO FURTHER READING

Catullus 64 has benefited in the past half-century from a great renewal of scholarly attention, beginning most notably with Michael Putnam's "The Art of Catullus 64" (1961) and Friedrich Klingner's "Catulls Peleus-Epos" (1964), two articles which revived scholarly appreciation of the poem and opened questions and controversies that continue to drive critical readings today. On Catullus' intricate reworking of his allusive sources, R. F. Thomas (1982) and Zetzel (1983) are exemplary. Gaisser (1995) offers a rich and detailed exploration of the poem's complex narrative, and Bramble (1970) is the best starting point for an exploration of the epyllion's thematic ambiguities and pessimistic undertones. Putnam (1961) and Wiseman (1985) provide insightful readings of the poem's interactions both with Catullus' lyrics and with the other long poems, including especially the shared themes of love, betrayal, and loss. There has been an increased recognition that Catullus' concern with the moral degradation of human society, expressed most pointedly in the poem's epilogue, has an aesthetic component as well (Konstan 1977; Theodorakopoulos 2000; Martindale 2005). Fowler (1991) on the relationship between ecphrasis and narrative, and Laird (1993) on the ecphrasis in Catullus 64, have contributed much to our understanding of Catullus' self-conscious juxtaposition of visual and verbal media in his poem's centerpiece, and Fitzgerald (1995: 140–68) explores the central role played by viewing throughout the epyllion.

A good starting point for those interested in Apollonius' *Argonautica*, apart from the studies already cited, is the collected essays in Papanghelis and Rengakos (2001). The standard text is the Budé edition of Vian (1974–81); and for Book 3, see also Hunter (1989). For the Greekless reader, Hunter's translation (1993b) is more approachable than the Loeb edition.

WORKS CITED

Avallone, R. 1953. "Catullo e Apollonio di Rodio." *Antiquitas* 8: 8–75.

Bing, P. 1988. *The Well-Read Muse: Present and Past in Callimachus and the Hellenistic Poets.* Göttingen.

Braga, D. 1950. *Catullo e i poeti Greci.* Messina and Florence.

Bramble, J. C. 1970. "Structure and Ambiguity in Catullus LXIV." *Proceedings of the Cambridge Philological Society* 16: 22–41.

Bühler, W. 1960. *Die Europa des Moschos.* Wiesbaden.

Byre, C. 2002. *A Reading of Apollonius Rhodius'* Argonautica: *The Poetics of Uncertainty.* Lewiston, NY.

Cairns, F. 1984. "The Nereids of Catullus 64.12–23b." *Grazer Beiträge* 11: 95–100.

Clare, R. J. 1996. "Catullus 64 and the *Argonautica* of Apollonius Rhodius: Allusion and Exemplarity." *Proceedings of the Cambridge Philological Society* 42: 60–88.

Clare, R. J. 2002. *The Path of the Argo.* Cambridge.

Clausen, W. 1982. "The New Direction in Poetry." In E. J. Kenney and W. V. Clausen, eds., *The Cambridge History of Classical Literature. Vol. II: Latin Literature.* Cambridge and New York. 178–206.

Clauss, J. J. 1993. *The Best of the Argonauts.* Berkeley and Los Angeles.

Conte, G. B. 1986. *The Rhetoric of Imitation: Genre and Poetic Memory in Vergil and Other Latin Poets.* Trans. C. Segal. Ithaca, NY.

Curran, L. C. 1969. "Catullus 64 and the Heroic Age." *Yale Classical Studies* 21: 169–92.

Ellis, R. 1889. *A Commentary on Catullus.* 2nd edn. Oxford.

Fantuzzi, M. 1988. *Richerche su Apollonio Rodio.* Rome.

Fitzgerald, W. 1995. *Catullan Provocations: Lyric Poetry and the Drama of Position.* Berkeley, Los Angeles, and London.

Fordyce, C. J., ed. 1961. *Catullus: A Commentary.* Oxford.

Fowler, D. 1991. "Narrate and Describe: The Problem of Ecphrasis." *Journal of Roman Studies* 81: 25–35.

Fusillo, M. 1985. *Il tempo delle* Argonautiche. Rome.

Gaisser, J. H. 1995. "Threads in the Labyrinth: Competing Views and Voices in Catullus 64." *American Journal of Philology* 116: 579–616.

Goldhill, S. 1991. *The Poet's Voice.* Cambridge.

Hinds, S. 1998. *Allusion and Intertext: Dynamics of Appropriation in Roman Poetry.* Cambridge.

Hollis, A. S. 1990. *Callimachus: Hecale.* Oxford.

Hunter, R. 1989. *Apollonius of Rhodes:* Argonautica *Book III.* Cambridge.

Hunter, R. 1991. "Breast Is Best: Catullus 64.18." *Classical Quarterly* n.s. 41: 254–5.

Hunter, R. 1993a. *The* Argonautica *of Apollonius: Literary Studies.* Cambridge.

Hunter, R, trans. 1993b. *Apollonius of Rhodes: Jason and the Golden Fleece.* Oxford.

Klingner, F. 1964. "Catulls Peleus-Epos." *Sitzungsberichte der Bayerischen Akademie der Wissenschaften. Philosophisch-Historische Klasse, Heft 6* (1956) = *Studien zur griechischen und römischen Literatur.* Zurich. 156–224.

Knight, V. 1995. *The Renewal of Epic: Responses to Homer in the* Argonautica *of Apollonius.* Leiden, New York, and Cologne.

Konstan, D. 1977. *Catullus' Indictment of Rome: The Meaning of Catullus 64.* Amsterdam.

Laird, A. 1993. "Sounding out Ecphrasis: Art and Text in Catullus 64." *Journal of Roman Studies* 83: 18–30.

Lefèvre, E. 2000a. "Alexandrinisches und catullisches im Peleus-Epos (64)." *Hermes* 128: 181–201.

Martindale, C. 2005. *Latin Poetry and the Judgement of Taste.* Oxford.

Papanghelis, T. D., and A. Rengakos, eds. 2001. *A Companion to Apollonius Rhodius.* Leiden.

Pasquali, G. 1951. "Arte allusiva." In *Stravaganze quarte e supreme.* 11–20. Venice. (Rpt. in *Pagnine stravaganti.* Florence, 1968. II.275–83.)

Perrotta, G. 1931. "Il carme 64 di Catullo e i suoi pretesi originali ellenistici." *Athenaeum* 9: 177–222, 371–409.

Putnam, M. C. J. 1961. "The Art of Catullus 64." *Harvard Studies in Classical Philology* 65: 165–205.

Quinn, K., ed. 1973a. *Catullus: The Poems.* 2nd edn. London and Basingstoke.

Ross, D. O., Jr. 1975. *Backgrounds to Augustan Poetry: Gallus, Elegy and Rome.* Cambridge.

Schmale, M. 2004. *Bilderreigen und Erzähllabyrinth: Catulls Carmen 64.* Munich and Leipzig.

Stoevesandt, M. 1994/5. "Catull 64 und die *Ilias.*" *Würzburger Jahrbücher für die Altertumswissenschaft* n.s. 20: 167–205.

Syndikus, W. P. 1990. *Catull: Eine Interpretation. Zweiter Teil: Die grossen Gedichte (61–68).* Darmstadt.

Theodorakopoulos, E. 2000. "Catullus, 64. Footprints in the Labyrinth." In A. Sharrock and H. Morales, eds., *Intratextuality.* Oxford. 115–41.

Thomas, R. F. 1982. "Catullus and the Polemics of Poetic Reference (Poem 64.1–18)." *American Journal of Philology* 103: 144–64.

Vian, F. 1974–81. *Apollonius de Rhodes* Argonautiques. 3 vols. Paris.

Weber, C. 1983. "Two Chronological Contradictions in Catullus 64." *Transactions of the American Philological Association* 113: 263–71.

Wiseman, T. P. 1985. *Catullus and His World: A Reappraisal.* Cambridge.

Wray, D. 2000. "Apollonius' Masterplot: Narrative Strategy in *Argonautica* 1." In *Hellenistica Groningana 4.* Leuven. 239–65.

Zetzel, J. 1983. "Catullus, Ennius, and the Poetics of Allusion." *Illinois Classical Studies* 8: 251–86.

CHAPTER SEVENTEEN

Poem 68: Love and Death, and the Gifts of Venus and the Muses

Elena Theodorakopoulos

In c. 68, "the most extraordinary poem in Latin" (Lyne 1980: 52), we find some of the most enticing expressions of what it means to love, and to lose. Its moments of exceptional emotional intensity and its inclusion of the two big Catullan themes, the loss of the brother and the great love affair, also make the poem subject to intense biographical speculation. Tantalizing fragments of a real life are here for the taking: correspondence between Verona and Rome, relationships with friends, the circum-stances of the affair with Lesbia, the poet's withdrawal after his bereavement. There are moments in this poem when the reader cannot help but be tempted to see the "real" Catullus and Lesbia – our own gleaming epiphany – within easy grasp. All it takes is a methodological leap or two and we are there: Allius' house with its worn threshold, Lesbia the shining goddess, Catullus the abject lover trying not to be a bore and demand faithfulness from his domineering mistress.

The poem is notoriously difficult, and has generated a substantial amount of scholarship over the last hundred years or so. Textual corruption disfigures it terribly in places, where it can become quite incomprehensible. So, for instance, we are still unable to determine whether we are looking at one poem, or two – or at two poems to be read as a pair. We also don't know the name or names of the addressee or addressees of the poems (or poem). We have no idea who, in lines 27–30, is warming their limbs in whose bed, and where. We do not know for certain who the person referred to as *domina*, and somehow linked with the *domus*, in lines 69 and 156 is – she may be a housekeeper, she may be Catullus' beloved, she may be Allius' (if that is his name) wife. We do not seem to know what the exact nature of the gifts requested by the correspondent in 68a is – what are *munera Veneris*, in particular? The lack of consensus regarding almost all these questions is remarkable – and results in a vast bibliography on the poem(s).

All this means that the classicist, when reading c. 68, is more than ever aware of the range of tools at her or his disposal, and of the many interpretive moves she or he makes, at every step, as the poem comes alive. Every philological or editorial intervention, every biographical guess or approximation, every assumption or speculation regarding publication and circulation, can make a difference to what the poem means. For instance, we assume that it is Lesbia who is the *candida diua* at the threshold – but the poet never names her as such – how would it be if it were not her, after all? What difference would it make if we could be certain that the Manlius possibly addressed in lines 1–40 were the Manlius Torquatus whose wedding hymn Catullus composed as c. 61? How would it affect our interpretation of the poem if we could be sure that Catullus had, or would have considered having, a homoerotic affair with the addressee of lines 1–40? What difference would it make to discover how and when, and if, Catullus edited and published his poems as three *libelli*, and what was in each?

In what follows, I propose to take a linear approach in working through the poem, addressing questions as they come up. That, it seems to me, is the task of the companion – to lend a hand in the endeavor of reading, and experiencing, it.

One Poem or Two?

The first question most readers have about poem 68 is: what is the relationship between lines 1–40, or "68a," and lines 41–160, or "68b"?[1] And how significant is it that the addressee of lines 1–40 (probably Manlius) does not appear to be the person lauded in lines 41–160 (possibly Allius)? Should we read lines 41–160 as the gift offered in response to Manlius' request? Or can lines 1–40 stand alone as a coherent poem?

Many of the arguments offered to explain the discrepancy in the names, and to interpret the poem as either a unit or two different poems, are based on editorial decisions that can look worryingly technical to the newcomer to the poem.[2] No scholarly agreement has been reached on the issue of unity despite good arguments on both sides. It is indicative of the state of affairs that in the mid-1990s one critic could claim that unity is the dominant view ("Like most of the recent students of this poem, I believe that c. 68 is to be thought of as a unit" [Fitzgerald 1995: 280 n. 1]), while another could claim the opposite ("modern scholarship is predominantly inclined toward separating 'poem 68' into two poems" [Thomson 1997: 472]). We will attempt here to untangle some of the evidence and to enable the reader to make a decision – or perhaps decide *not* to make a decision – on the question of unity.

This is the state of play in the main manuscripts, referred to as O, G, and R:[3] in G and R poems 68a and b are presented as one unit, under the heading *Ad Mallium*. This fact alone need not prove that they are one poem, because there are other instances of poems bunched together under headings which do not always make sense (Wiseman 1974: 89). The manuscripts seem to indicate two different addressees: all three agree on *Mali* in lines 11 and 30. O has *Alli* in line 50 and G and R have *Ali*. In line 66, O has *Allius* (and *vel Manllius* in the margin); G and R have *Manlius*.[4]

Editors who want to show that 68 is one poem, not two, frequently do so by arguing that Mallius and Allius are the same. This is mostly done by deciding to read *mi Alli* ("my Allius") in lines 11 and 30, instead of *Mali* – and so the entire poem is addressed to *Allius*.[5] It does seem strange that two such similar names, *Mallius* and *Allius*, should appear in these two consecutive poems. *mi Alli* is therefore a good solution for those who are looking for one poem. But *Mallius* occurs elsewhere in the collection as an error for *Manlius*: this would give us *Manlius* (probably the Manlius Torquatus of poem 61) as the addressee of lines 1–40, and *Allius* for the remainder – a satisfactory answer for those who want to read two poems.

The names are not the only problem. Many readers are troubled by the fact that lines 1–40 appear to show Catullus denying his friend the gift of poetry he seeks – only to follow it with the poem in praise of Allius. This need not be such a worry: poem 65 also is an assertion of the poet's inability to write, and is accompanied by the Callimachus translation, poem 66. And the *recusatio* (an apology for the inadequacy of the poetry provided, or a rejection of a demand for poetry from a friend or patron) becomes a common way of introducing some very substantial poems or collections of poems in the late Republican and Augustan ages. The fact that a group of lines constituting a lament for the poet's dead brother is repeated verbatim, as if in self-quotation, troubles many: does the repetition constitute an argument for or against unity? We will look at these lines in a later section – but the mere fact of their repetition is striking.

In all, I tend toward the line of least resistance (and least intervention). It seems to me that leaving the names alone, as far as possible, makes sense; if that means Mallius/Manlius and Allius, then we can live with that. The sensible conclusion to draw would be to view 68a and b as separate units, most likely I think as a letter and a poem that accompanies it, along the lines of the 65 and 66 pairing.[6] I can think of no real reason why Manlius' consolation should not be the praise of Allius; we do not know the circumstances and it is unlikely that we ever will. It may well turn out that this is the wrong approach, and that, after all, the whole poem is for Mallius, and in praise of Mallius – it is not clear to me that such a conclusion would alter much of the substance of our understanding and interpretation of the poem. We should still be looking at a work that begins with a form of *recusatio*, and then proceeds to celebrate the *officium* and the memory of a friend, and a love affair that turned out not to be a happy marriage.

Friendship and Reciprocity in 68: What *Are* the Gifts of Venus?

Let us see what happens if we read 68a and b as paired in the way that 65 and 66 are. Like 68.1–40, c. 65 purports to reply to, and initially to reject, a plea from a friend requiring poetry. Catullus takes care to establish his faithfulness to Hortalus: he must not think that his words were "written on the winds" (an image used by Catullus elsewhere for the empty promises of a treacherous friend, Alfenus, in c. 30).[7] The poem Hortalus will receive is a token of friendship, and a rejection of the very possibility of betrayal. Manlius asks for a similar token, and is keen to assert his status as Catullus' *amicus* – although some readers feel that he may not have as much claim on this as he thinks (Wiseman 1974: 102–3). In c. 38 poetry and *amicitia* are bound up together in a similar way.[8] Here, Catullus himself asks for poetry as consolation, and as proof of friendship. Unlike in 68, both correspondents' names are mentioned in the first line, and the connection between them is established: *malest, Cornifici, tuo Catullo*, "Your Catullus is in a bad way, Cornificius." Catullus feels neglected by Cornificius in his need for consolation, perhaps literally for a "talking to" (*allocutione*, 38.5). Their relationship must be closer than that between Manlius and Catullus, and it is subject to scrutiny in the poem: *irascor tibi. sic meos amores?* ("I am cross with you. So much for our love!" 38.6). The brunt of the poem rests on that last exclamation: it is the love and friendship between the two friends which makes the gift of poetry possible and likely.

In c. 50, composing poems seems to be the very fabric of friendship. And a poem is sent to the longed-for friend whose presence was such a pleasure: *hoc, iucunde, tibi poema feci* ("I made this poem for you, delightful one," 50.16). There has been much discussion over the erotic connotations of all these poems, and of c. 50 and 68 especially. In c. 50, Catullus famously describes himself longing to see Calvus, tossing and turning on his bed. It is easy to see how this looks like a declaration of love. In 68a, Manlius is suffering similar troubles at the hands of Venus – and the old poets are no help at all. Some suspect that Manlius is pining for Catullus, as Catullus pined for Calvus; others believe he is suffering from unrequited love for a third person, and wishes Catullus to console him. There are those who believe that Manlius wants Catullus to provide him with a girlfriend, and those who believe that Manlius wants Catullus himself to share his bed. Suspicion of Manlius' motives centers especially on his request for two things: the gifts of the Muses and of Venus: *muneraque et Musarum hinc petis et Veneris* ("and you seek from me the gifts of the Muses and of Venus," 68.10) The fact that there are two uses of *et* in the line, giving something like the sense of "the gifts of *both* the Muses and Venus," seems to imply that these are two separate things: the gift of love and the gift of poetry. In line 39 it does seem that *utriusque* refers to two distinct requests, and both are rejected. If they are two separate requests, then it seems reasonably clear that Manlius has asked for poems, *and* for love or sex.[9] The traditional alternatives to this envisage either a poem which is learned (gifts of the Muses) and has erotic subject matter (gifts of Venus), or two types of poetry – one learned, one erotic.

Looking back to the combination of erotic atmosphere with poetic innovation that governs c. 50, it seems to me that the convivial setting provides us with an important clue: *reddens mutua per iocum atque uinum* ("answering each other, laughing and drinking," 50.6). The majority of Catullus' poems are produced with a view to performance amongst friends, and with a view to delighting friends with their wit, their charm, their salaciousness at times (Wiseman 1985: 127; Newman 1990: 140–3; Skinner 1993a; Gamel 1998; Fredrick 1999; Wray 2001: 55–63; Skinner 2003: xxx–xxxi). And the atmosphere at such a convivial gathering, as we can see from c. 50, can come close to being erotically charged: *tuo lepore/incensus, Licini, facetiisque* ("set ablaze by your wit and fun, Licinius," 50.7–8). Licinius is *iucundus* – someone who is charming, delightful to be around, who makes good jokes, and creates a lovely atmosphere. As recollections of Crassus' entertaining in the *De oratore* demonstrate, such *iucunditas* is achieved by the ability to cast aside the serious business of the day: *tantam in Crasso humanitatem fuisse, cum lauti accubuissent, tolleretur omnis illa superioris tristitia sermonis; eaque esset in homine iucunditas, et tantus in loquendi lepos*, "such was Crassus' culture, that when they were bathed and settled down at the table, the grave tone of the previous discussion was lifted entirely, and such was the man's pleasantness and the charm of his speech" (*De or.* 1.27). It is credited to Crassus' personality that such gatherings are so successful. Like Calvus, Crassus is *iucundus*, he has charm (*lepos*), he makes good jokes. Catullus gives another example of such convivial talent in c. 12: Asinius Pollio has behaved unfortunately at the *convivium*. His lack of *uenustas* is disparaged (12.5), his brother is a nicer dinner guest: *est enim leporum/differtus puer et facetiarum* ("for he is a boy full of charm and wittiness," 12.8–9).[10] What is required of the ideal dinner companion, then, is the ability to charm and entertain, to contribute to an atmosphere of levity and cheerfulness that is also quite seductive. The quality of *uenustas* has been identified as vital to this achievement, expressive as it is of the overlap between erotic and aesthetic (or rhetorical) attraction.[11] So Lesbia, in c. 86, is truly and wholly beautiful because she, unlike her rival, has wit (*sal*) and charm (*uenustas*). And Catullus is explicit here that *uenustas* is given by Venus: *tum omnibus una omnis surripuit Veneres* ("she alone has robbed them all of every gift that Venus gave them," 86.6).[12]

In light of the established significance of convivial performance in Catullus' social circle, it is possible now to argue that "the gifts of the Muses and the gifts of Venus" are precisely Catullus' poetic talent and his *uenustas*: it is those two gifts which, combined, make him the most desirable of dinner companions, like his friend Caecilius, who has captivated his learned girlfriend, and Catullus himself, with poetry and with *uenustas* in c. 35.11–18. The compliment paid to Caecilius' appeal, through commiseration with the learned girl's suffering, demonstrates how aesthetic and erotic attractiveness come as part of a package. There is no need then to assume that Manlius' request for the gifts of Venus is a request for Catullus to act as a go-between, or to share his girlfriend, or indeed to share Manlius' bed himself. The Anacreon fragment (96 Diehl) that praises the good symposiast, who is able to bring together the gifts of the Muses and of Aphrodite in his performance, best captures the kind of thing that Manlius is looking for from Catullus:

> I do not like him who, drinking wine by the full mixing bowl, tells of strife and tearful war, but rather one who, mixing the splendid gifts of Aphrodite and the Muses, is mindful of lovely merriment.

The performer who creates this delightful atmosphere does *not* do so by offering sex as well as poetry to his companions. Instead, he chooses his subject matter (not war and battle) and his delivery with a mind to what is appropriate to the festivity and so creates the desired good cheer. The gifts of the Muses and Venus may be two distinct items in theory – but it is Catullus' special gift, as his friends and acquaintances know, to be able to combine the two, just like Anacreon's ideal sympotic poet.

Absent Friends

We have established that 68.1–40 could be part of a group of poems about friendship and the exchange of poetry between friends, and that presence and performance have to be part of the deal. That must be why the language of eroticism is so frequently used in these poems – it is the friend's presence, and the individual performance of the poem, that imbues them with the attractiveness and charm of a gift of Venus. Caecilius' girl may love the poem – but it is the poet's neck she clings to. And so Catullus' refusal of Manlius' request accompanies a rejection of his entire former way of life. He starts by making specific reference to his life as a Roman, assuming the *toga uirilis* (15). He then refers to the playfulness we know from c. 50, and to his love affairs (*multa satis lusi*, 17), as well as to his translations of Sappho: *non est Dea nescia nostri/quae dulcem curis miscet amaritiem* ("Not unknown am I to the goddess who blends sweet bitterness with cares," 17–18).

It was that life, and the poetry he wrote and performed as a part of it, which is now over because of the death of his brother. Bereavement means that he cannot partici-pate in the convivial delights of his circle of friends.[13] And whatever *lusi* means here, be it love or poetry, the point is that Catullus is no longer doing it. He must now absorb himself entirely in grieving, and so turns away, literally, from his addressee, to address the brother instead. Catullus' lament for his dead brother forms the center of 68.1–40. The loss of the brother is total and absolute, its consequences utterly devastating. Catullus' lines evoke the sense of a whole world in pieces – the house itself buried, all happiness dead. The final lines affirm the finality of death, the fact that only in life can we enjoy love: *omnia tecum una perierunt gaudia nostra/quae tuus in uita dulcis alebat amor* ("with you all our joys have perished, joys which, in life, your sweet love used to nourish," 23–4). One can think back here to c. 5 with its exhortations to love and live (*uiuamus, mea Lesbia, et amemus*) – and the threat of the long night of death hanging over it: *nobis, cum semel occidit breuis lux,/nox est una perpetua dormienda* ("for us, when our brief moment of daylight falls, there is just one long night to sleep through," 5.5–6). It seems that night has now arrived. As in c. 65, the grieving Catullus refuses to engage in the normal exchange of banter and/ or poetry. On both occasions, Catullus "breaks out" of the letter and addresses his dead brother instead of the letter's addressee. I think the apostrophes to the brother are also a way of not playing the game – of signaling the poet's complete absorption in his grief, and his withdrawal from other relationships. The insistent repetition of *tu/ tuus*, and *tecum*, and *frater* drives home that, really, there is only one addressee now. Manlius' attempt to lure Catullus from Verona seems singularly insensitive after Catullus' apostrophe to his brother. His intrusion into Catullus' grief and isolation, with a joke which we cannot quite reconstruct, gives rise to a correction from Catullus – and then to an assertion of his continuing to belong to Rome, in a way (though perhaps not in the way Manlius wants).

> quare, quod scribis Veronae turpe Catulle
>   esse, quod hic quisquis de meliore nota
> frigida deserto tepefactet membra cubili,
>   id, Manli, non est turpe, magis miserum est.

Wherefore, when you write "It is disgraceful, Catullus, for you to be in Verona, while here all the best people warm their cold limbs in a deserted bed" – that, Manlius, is more wretched than disgraceful.

It is difficult to work out what is going on in lines 27–30. I have reverted to the vocative *Catulle*, which the manuscripts show (so that line 27 at least seems to be

presented as a direct quotation from Manlius' letter), but which is often emended to
Catullo, to turn the quotation into indirect speech. The main problem, however, is
hic in line 28: does it mean Verona or Rome? Does it mean that the elite in Verona are
prudish and frigid, and lie tepidly in deserted beds? Or that everyone who is anyone in
Rome is piling into Catullus' deserted bed with his girlfriend?[14] What we *can* say is
that Catullus is reproached for being in Verona, and that Manlius has made some sort
of joke about Catullus' lack of sexual activity. This works with both versions: he is
accusing Catullus either of reverting to Transpadane provincial *mores*, or of neglect-
ing his usual Roman pursuits. In any case, it is Catullus' absence from Rome that is
being challenged. It seems that Catullus does not rise to the bait – whatever its exact
nature. Instead, he corrects Manlius' insensitivity: *turpe* is the wrong word, there is
no shame or disgrace in his leaving Rome, he is wretched and to be pitied, the right
word would have been *miserum*. With Manlius firmly in his place, Catullus returns to
the question of the gifts. His recent trauma and his removal from Rome mean that he
is no longer that ideal convivial partner who can bring joy to others by mixing the
gifts of the Muses and of Venus. Immediately after this final rejection, in what looks
like a curious *non sequitur*, there is the reference to the lack of books – given as one
last reason for not complying with the request. Are the books important because
Catullus wants to be thought of as not just a convivial poet of occasional verse, but
part of an intelligentsia of learned poets? I think so – and now especially, as his new
circumstances keep him away from social situations, and he has to rely on writing
rather than performance as a means of being heard (and remaining part of Roman
society). The *scriptores* he is missing have stayed behind because they belong – as he
himself claims to – in their real home, in Rome (34–6):

> hoc fit quod Romae uiuimus: illa domus,
>   illa mihi sedes, illic mea carpitur aetas;
> huc una ex multis capsula me sequitur.

that is because I live at Rome: that is my home, that is my residence, that is where my life
is spent. Only one book box out of many follows me here.

Catullus' striking and rhetorical insistence on belonging in Rome, and the present
tense verbs, must be telling us that Verona is temporary, and the poet does intend
eventually to return to Rome. When he does, however, he may wish to be known as a
different sort of poet: it will not be the bed but the library that will bring him back.

The Praise of Allius: Writing and Memory

So it is a written poem, rather than a piece for performance, which accompanies the
letter to Manlius.
   Lines 41–50 see a complete change of tone and approach – and new addressees –
the Muses (*deae*).This address to the Muses signals a new beginning, possibly a new
poem, and is a clear statement of intent: what follows is intended as a memorial to
Allius and to his friendship. In view of the demands clearly made for convivial
performance in lines 1–40, the most unusual aspect of this introduction is the
reference to the poem's status as memorial, and to a wide readership for it (41–6):

> ne fugiens saeclis obliuiscentibus aetas
>   illius hoc caeca nocte tegat studium;
> sed dicam uobis, uos porro dicite multis
>   milibus et facite haec carta loquatur anus.

lest the passage of time and the forgetful generations cover his concern for me with the darkness of night. But I will tell you, you in turn tell many thousands and make this paper speak in its old age.

It is rare for Catullus to refer to his own poetry as widely read or as long-lasting. The only examples of references to a readership beyond the small circle of addressees are the first poem and the fragmentary 14b. Poem 1, addressed to Cornelius Nepos, merely expresses the modest-sounding wish that it should "last for more than one generation" – there is no mention here of thousands of readers, or many generations. 14b appears to be a fragment of a similarly modest introductory or dedicatory poem: *si qui forte mearum ineptiarum/lectores eritis* ("if there will be any of you readers of my trifles," 14b.1–2). Indeed, wide circulation and permanence are not envisaged for any poetry in the Catullan collection. The exception is Cinna's poem *Zmyrna*, which will travel far as a book roll and last over several generations (95.6). In their assertion of both a long life and a readership of thousands, the opening lines of 68b are thus striking and unparalleled in the collection.[15] We are used to assertions of longevity, and to the linking of poetry with built memorials, from the Augustan poets – but Catullus' times are different, and the processes of circulation and "publication" not formalized in the way they became later (Kenney 1982; Starr 1987).[16] It is therefore worth stressing how the reference to an audience of thousands and to a lifetime of several generations is quite an ambitious claim, and should be seen as a measure of the value the poet himself attaches to this poem.

The proem differentiates the Allius poem from other Catullan poems as one that is meant to be read. The unusual emphasis on circulation, and the device of asking the Muses to breathe life into the paper and make it speak, are connected to the fact that Catullus is writing from Verona – and thus removed, physically, from his usual circle of recipients. It is worth considering, too, that the only other instance of speaking paper is in another letter from Verona, c. 35, in which Catullus asks his papyrus to speak to Caecilius (*uelim, Caecilio, papyre, dicas/Veronam ueniat*, "I would like you, papyrus, to tell Caecilius to come to Verona"). And so, in a way, these first lines of 68b lay the foundations for both the Augustans' preoccupation with the permanence and wide readership of their work, and the personified letters of Ovid's *Tristia*. They may also be the beginnings of the connection between writing and exile that dominates later Roman literature, and then reverberates through to modernity (Habinek 1998: 113). In writing away from Rome, and being unable to link his words to his person and his presence, Catullus becomes very aware of the difference between the spoken and the written word (Skinner 2003: xxxi). Writing in the wake of death, he may also want to remind us of the potential for poetry to overcome death – to stay perfect in the face of decay. When the poem returns to the praise of Allius at its close, it is offered as a gift which will ward off corrosion – the rust that will taint the name of Allius and his family without it: *ne uestrum scabra tangat robigine nomen* ("lest the roughness of rust should touch your name," 151). The passage of time, and the decay that comes with it, are relentless: *haec atque illa dies, atque alia et alia* ("this

day, and another, and another, and another," 152) (see Skinner 2003: 31–2). There
are more gifts for Allius, however: *quae Themis olim/antiquis solita est munera ferre
piis* ("those gifts which Themis once used to give to the faithful of old," 153–4).

In wishing for the gifts of Themis, what Catullus bestows on Allius is nothing less
than a return of the Golden Age – a reversal of that relentless passage of time, and a
return to an age of divine epiphany untouched by decay and corrosion.[17] Catullus will
provide poetic immortality for Allius; the gods, he hopes, will do the rest.

Allius' *officium*

Not everyone is convinced of Allius' good offices. Many critics think that what Allius
did in lending a home to the lovers was at worst immoral – and at best the shabby act
of a comic go-between (Skinner 2003: 43–4; Wiseman 1985: 160; Sarkissian 1983:
16). I cannot say that I am in sympathy with this view. This is what Catullus says
about what Allius did for him (67–9):

> is clausum lato patefecit limite campum
>   isque domum nobis isque dedit dominam
> ad quam communes exerceremus amores.

He opened a closed-off field with a wide path, he gave me a house and he gave a mistress.
There we could engage in our shared love.

Once more, a textual problem causes some difficulty, and we need to digress. The
accusative *dominam* in line 68 is what the manuscripts have, but most think that this
is a mistake (it would be an easy one for any scribe to make) and that what should be
there is the dative *dominae*. In this case the translation would say "he gave a house to
me and to the mistress" – and we might have a first precedent here for the Augustan
elegists' preference for the term *domina* to describe the mistress. In keeping
dominam we seem to be saying that Allius gave Catullus the house and provided
the girlfriend along with it – or that he provided a house with an amenable housekeeper. Both are awkward scenarios. I suggest a different solution to this problem: the
closeness of *domus* and *domina* is significant, as many say. But this does not need to
mean that the *domina* is already part of the household. What I think it could mean is
that for the short time that Catullus and his beloved are at Allius' house she becomes
its *domina* – just as the bride in c. 61 becomes a *domina* on being brought to her new
home: *ac domum dominam uoca/coniugis cupidam noui* ("summon the mistress to
her home, hungry for her new husband," 61.31–2).[18] This tallies with the way in
which Catullus plays throughout the poem with the idea of Lesbia as his bride – while
knowing that she is not. Allius then affords Catullus a brief glimpse of what it might
have been like to live with Lesbia as his *domina*, in their own *domus*. And this would
make Allius' *officium* a great one indeed: putting himself and his reputation at
considerable risk, to bring a moment of happiness to his friend in making the
impossible possible. This is not sordid, nor the stuff of comedy, but rather too sad
for words. When she arrives, as the *domina* to her *domus*, the beloved becomes a
goddess – and a bride (though a doomed one). The moment of epiphany is no simile;
there is no question that at the moment of her arrival Lesbia *is* a goddess: *quo mea se*

molli candida diua pede/intulit ("there my gleaming goddess came with soft step,"
70–1). But as she rests her foot (deliberately, it seems) on the threshold rather than
stepping over it as brides then and now are meant to, she crushes the hymeneal
illusion even before the ill-omened simile brings things to a head: *et trito fulgentem in
limine plantam/innixa arguta constituit solea* ("and paused, her shining foot on the
worn threshold, her sandal sounding as it stepped down," 71–2).[19] That creaking
sandal on the threshold echoes into the following two lines, which sound like a
wedding hymn with their reference to the new bride's burning love and to the new
home.[20] The whole thing comes crashing down when we realize that this *domus* will
never be complete (*inceptam frustra*) – just as Catullus' will not. For the next 55 lines
the poem will dwell on Laodamia's tragic love for Protesilaus. The goddess remains
on that threshold – until we return to her to find that things were not quite what
they seemed.

Laodamia and the Grave and the Pit

Let us look at the central section of the poem in outline: The Allius eulogy begins
with Catullus' suffering at the hands of Venus. The scorching she has inflicted on him
is compared to Mount Etna and the hot springs at Thermopylae. He is drenched in
tears. Then *something* is compared to a mountain stream offering relief to travelers
and to parched fields. Then Allius' help is compared to a favorable wind sent by
Castor and Pollux to relieve sailors cast about in a storm.[21] Allius lends a house and
makes a meeting possible. The beloved arrives at the house, a goddess. She is like
Laodamia when she came to Protesilaus as his bride. But their house was never
finished, because they did not perform the proper rites. Laodamia lost her husband
too soon because he went to Troy, where he was fated to die. Troy is also the grave of
Catullus' brother, with whose death Catullus' own *domus* is buried. Troy robbed
Laodamia of her marriage – the depth of her love plunged her into an abyss which was
like the pit Hercules dug near Pheneus. Her love was deeper even than that pit.
Protesilaus was dearer to her than a late-born only heir is to his ancient grandfather.
Her passion for him is greater than that of the most wanton dove for her mate. When
she came to Allius' house the beloved was almost like Laodamia.

The four similes which cluster around Catullus' symptoms and Allius' help with
them are excessive, and complicated in a way that can only be meant to signal the
"literariness" of this poem. There is nothing to parallel this in the shorter poems:
here Catullus is creating a literary artifact and he wants us to know it. My outline
shows how extravagant the piling up of similes is – and how strikingly it creates a kind
of visible, and audible, gulf at the very moment of Lesbia's epiphanic arrival at the
house. And it is true that both the grave and the pit visualize that gulf in a terrifying
way (Fitzgerald 1995: 209–10). When he needs to close that gulf, at the end of the
simile sequence, we find Catullus acknowledging, with the awkward formulation with
which he returns to the beloved's entry, how difficult the comparison in fact is: *aut
nihil aut paulo cui cum concedere digna* ("Worthy of yielding either nothing or very
little to her," 131).

What we have read on the way, of the depth of Laodamia's love and of her
devotion, clearly does not fit with what we know of Catullus' Lesbia. This asymmetry

is the focus of a number of recent studies of the poem – and may well be what c. 68 is, really, about. Many recent readers agree that a fundamental point of c. 68 is the chasm between experience and literature: between the fantasy (literary or mythological) of love, and its imperfect reality. And the abundance and *centrality* of the similes in the poem are one important way in which this chasm is highlighted.[22] For many readers the similes will appear labored or artificial and have an alienating effect (Lyne 1980: 52).[23] But the artificiality is a part of the poem's innovation: what Catullus is creating here is literature, that is, a poem meant to be read *at a distance* from its creator. So, yes, it is true that the poem is about the gap between poetry and real life – but it is so in more ways than one. Not only does the beauty of the poem point to the insufficiency of the real affair. The ostentatiously literary, and complex, quality of the language and the construction of the poem also point to the poet's labor and to his *absence* from that labor, in a way that other poems simply do not. And all this adds up to a poem that constructs itself for the purpose of speaking from a distance – first, from a quasi-exile in Verona; second, from an anticipated past (perhaps from the grave) to future generations.[24]

Troy plays a key role in all this, as a central image for the distant past of Rome, as *the* locus of great literature, and as the most prestigious of origins for those who wanted to matter at Rome (Fitzgerald 1995: 186). We should not forget that an "official" historical link between Troy and Rome is only on the cusp of being developed during Catullus' lifetime. As yet, Troy is still quite a long way from Rome – though attempts to access it as Rome's past are becoming prominent ideological moves (e.g., Julius Caesar's claim of descent from Venus via Aeneas). However, I suspect that for Catullus and his contemporaries, before Vergil and Augustus make it Roman, Troy belongs to Homer above all. The distance and the inaccessibility of Troy as Rome's ancestor, and its literary pedigree, are good ways for Catullus to highlight the written-ness, the distance from its author, of his poem. What strikes everyone about Catullus' use of Troy is the way in which he links personal tragedy with literary history and issues of cultural identity. I suspect that to his contemporaries this link would be more striking still. During this time, when exploiting Trojan genealogy is just coming into fashion with Roman patrician families, Catullus, who will never be a member of such a clan, is potentially very subversive: his family does not start at Troy, it is *buried* there.[25] His Troy is not the cradle of civilization, it is its grave (*commune sepulcrum*, 89). It is as a grave that Troy first comes into the poem, through the reference to the unfinished house of Protesilaus. The brief passage from the catalogue of ships in *Iliad* 2, the bare bones of Protesilaus' story, must be the main point of reference for Catullus' treatment of the myth. Here, we find first the swift and brutal contrast between life and death, and a Trojan grave: Protesilaus was the leader of the troops from Phylake while he was alive – now the black earth holds him (*Il.* 2.698–9). Then there is what is left behind: a wife (unnamed) who has torn both her cheeks, and an unfinished house (*dómos hēmitelḗs*, *Il.* 2.701) – complete devastation in other words, and the makings of tragedy (Macleod 1974; Lyne 1998: 200–9).

The immediate points of contact between Laodamia's story and Catullus' are two: arrival at a *domus*, and destruction of life at Troy. As we have noted already it is Lesbia's entry into the *domus*, as its *domina*, that precipitates the Laodamia simile. It is the loss of Protesilaus to Troy that precipitates the lament for the dead brother, in many ways the poem's center of gravity. In both parts of the story Troy, and death, destroy a *domus*. The stark contrast between death and life is I think what makes Troy such a powerful image in both contexts: one moment there is a house, and life and love – and the next death buries everything: *tecum una tota est nostra sepulta domus* ("with you our entire house is buried," 94). I have already pointed out how the Homeric lines Catullus was remembering express the starkness of that difference: Protesilaus was their leader – now the black earth holds him. Catullus has associated Troy with death before, in c. 64. As in 68.85 (*quod scibant Parcae*), the Parcae know all about it in 64. Their wedding-song for Peleus and Thetis shows the river choking with dead bodies and Achilles' tomb drenched in the blood of a slaughtered Polyxena as direct *outcomes* of the marriage. As in 68 the couple's *domus* receives attention, before the disastrous prophecy begins (*nulla domus tales umquam contexit amores*, "no house has ever sheltered such loves," 64.334). The houses of the mythological couples are both in a sense wrecked by Troy; and Catullus' *recollection* of his and Lesbia's short-lived *domus* is shattered by Troy, too. In both poems it is clear that Troy is an abomination, not the glory that contemporary Romans may have been seeking to gain from connection with it. Troy stands for the strangeness of death, for the remoteness of the world of the dead from that of the living. But Troy also draws men to it, in Homer as the place to seek and earn glory, in Rome as the place to seek literary and genealogical ancestry. But it remains, for all its pull, *terra aliena* (100). And the graves of those buried there are *not* the graves of relatives or ancestors: *non inter nota sepulcra/nec prope cognatos compositum cineres*, "not among familiar graves nor buried near kindred ashes" (97–8). Later, Augustan and imperial constructions make the Trojan graves familiar, but for Catullus' brother the black earth of Troy is as alien as it was for the Greek Protesilaus – and literature does not help to bridge that gap. The distance of Troy from Rome and from Verona is highlighted in the apostrophe to the dead brother, as the poem turns away from Laodamia and in on itself. Now it is Catullus' *domus* which is begun in vain; Catullus himself is left on the other side of the world, tearing his cheeks, while life and light have gone (92–6). This lament contains the lines which are repeated verbatim at 68a.20 and 22–4. I see no reason that the repetition should be seen as argument for or against unity of the poem. As a recurring theme, a kind of inset elegy for the dead brother, the repetition need not be criticized, either, as lacking in spontaneity or authenticity. Grief can be repetitive.

What is clear from these lines is that Laodamia's grief for the abrupt and premature end of her marriage *can* be compared with Catullus' grief at the loss of his brother: it is the irrevocable separation that is at issue here, rather than the *type* of love that was experienced before it: *omnia tecum una perierunt gaudia nostra,/quae tuus in uita dulcis alebat amor* ("with you all our joys have perished, which in life your sweet love nourished," 95–6).[26] Both erotic and familial love are sweet, and both are sustained by life, and sustain life. We have just seen the joy nurtured in Catullus' life by his brother's love (in uita dulcis *alebat amor*). There is also marriage, sweeter than life itself to Laodamia: *ereptum est* uita dulcius *atque anima/coniugium* (106–7). And the poem ends by invoking the sweetness of life itself, as long as the light of love is there: *lux mea*, qua uiua uiuere dulce *mihi est* (160; see also 65.10, and 64.215). The link between life and love, and the sweetness of life, runs through the poem, and is in keeping with its preoccupation with the possibility that the gift of poetry might survive beyond the grave.

Now the poem returns to Laodamia with a series of similes, removing us further and further from Troy and the grave. The first simile is the much discussed *barathrum*.[27] This is, as Denis Feeney says, "Catullus' most spectacular demonstration of the strange emotionally distancing effects of allusion" (1992: 44).[28] And it comes at the point when the poem seems to be trying to reach a sincere expression of what it is to love so deeply – and to lose so tragically. Laodamia is engulfed by the flood of love that sweeps her into the abyss. That abyss, the last, surprising, word in line 108, is called a *barathrum* – the Greek word for a kind of drainage hole in the ground. It is clear that the reader, or audience, is meant to see and hear the studied artificiality of the simile; the sentence structure alone, stacking up subclauses one after the other (*quale ferunt... quod... audit... tempore quo... perculit... ut... teretur... nec... foret*, 109–16) is a parody of simile and an excessive, and self-conscious, display of learnedness.[29] The simile ends up a very long way from the pit, with the loss of Hebe's virginity to the deified Heracles, again parodying the way in which similes can open up a whole world of their own within a poem. And Catullus tops all this by concluding that the comparison was not quite appropriate after all: *sed tuus altus amor barathro fuit altior illo* ("but your deep love was deeper than that *barathrum*," 117). All this does have the feel of the library: it smells of the lamp, as Quinn says (1973a: *ad* 108–10). Catullus cannot have been unaware of that smell, or of the ways in which it ruins a moment of wonderful emotional intensity; what he is doing is experimental and innovative, but it is not incompetent. We must be meant to feel the inappropriateness of that pit, and perhaps the insufficiency of literature in the face of experience.

The Grandfather and the Dove

The two subsequent similes might draw us back into the emotional world of the poem – although here, too, the juxtaposition of two very different images is baffling, as is the self-conscious "stacking up" of similes. The first image, in comparing Laodamia's love to that of a grandfather for his late-born grandson, is, to the modern reader, rather odd in assimilating two very different types of love. But as we have seen, that is part of the point of this poem: love, be it familial or erotic, is the stuff of *life*: *nam nec tam carum confecto aetate parenti/una caput seri nata nepotis alit* ("for not so dear to the parent worn out by age is the life of the late-born grandson, which his only daughter nurses," 121–2).

For the old man the *caput* (the head, or the life) of the new baby means the continuation of his family, and (as the shooing away of the metaphorical vulture, the hovering kinsman, shows, 124) a denial of his mortality.[30] When the child's name is inserted in the will (123), death is made harmless. But neither Catullus and Lesbia nor Laodamia and Protesilaus have children. Their absence, especially in the hymeneal context which Catullus has built up in this poem, is conspicuous and it is highlighted by the grandfather simile. While allowing for erotic playfulness (61.66–7 and 204–5), the wedding hymn for Manlius Torquatus is explicit about the connection between marriage and children: the image of the baby smiling at his father from his mother's lap, his legitimacy recognizable to all by the family features he bears, ends the hymn. It is introduced, however, by a reprise of a Lesbia poem, which is all about the endless pleasures of erotic love (61.199–203 recalls the counting of grains of sand and stars in c. 7). I suspect that in both contexts the contrast between issueless sexual love and reproductive sexual love, validated by a family and a *domus*, is close to Catullus' heart. Legitimacy is crucial, both in c. 61 and in the grandfather simile. And as in c. 61 the noticeable resemblance between father and child declares the mother's virtue and fidelity, so ultimately Catullus' lack of issue declares Lesbia's faithlessness.

The dove simile (125–8) may be closer to the mark. But many are confused by the strange dove, both faithful and sexually voracious – and by the comparison with a woman who clearly is promiscuous (*multiuola* occurs only here in classical Latin, but must mean "wanting many," just as Jupiter a little later is "wanting all," *omniuoli*, 140). But the *multiuola mulier* is only a point of comparison – all the extravagant kissing is represented as the dove's monogamous routine.[31] However, the dove's delight in her mate recalls that of the adulterous Paris (*gauisa*, 125; *gauisus*, 103) and her kissing recalls the equally adulterous Catullus' kisses for Lesbia (cc. 5, 7, 8.18). Judging from what we have seen of Laodamia, it seems that she (unlike Lesbia) could have lived up to the dove's faithful extravagance, given the chance: she was voracious, ablaze with love (73), needing the long nights to satisfy her hungry love (83).

Together the pair of similes illuminate the two aspects of Laodamia's love for Protesilaus, both equivalent to Catullus' for Lesbia – but not Lesbia's for Catullus. One thing is made clear by the end of the dove simile: that Laodamia has stood for Catullus all the time. *He* is the extravagant kisser, and *he* has expressed feelings of almost fatherly love toward Lesbia.

Catullus' Wondrous Night

On our return to the doorstep, a hymeneal atmosphere prevails still, the beloved's sheen untarnished. Cupid, as the bride's attendant, gleams (*fulgebat, candidus*, 134) as she had done before, in a saffron tunic. But immediately Catullus concedes that, unlike Laodamia (unlike a wife), *she* is not intent upon Catullus as her only love, *quae tamen etsi uno non est contenta Catullo* ("though she is not content with Catullus alone," 135). Having admitted the flaw, the poet makes one last attempt to elevate his mistress back to the divinity associated with the hymeneal atmosphere he strives for. She is to be Jupiter to his Juno – but the analogy does not hold up: *atqui nec divis homines componier aequum est*, "yet it is not right to compare men to gods" (141). But the whole poem so far has relied on comparing men to gods – as does the wedding hymn, and indeed other Lesbia poems (most notably the opening of c. 51). With the statement made in 141, the pile of similes at the center of the poem comes tumbling down – and with this, the fiction of a marriage between Catullus and Lesbia is also dismantled (142–6):

> nec tamen illa mihi dextra deducta paterna
>   fragrantem Assyrio uenit odore domum,
> sed furtiua dedit mira munuscula nocte,
>   ipsius ex ipso dempta uiri gremio.

For she did not come to me, led on her father's right arm, to a house fragrant with Assyrian perfume. But she gave me stolen gifts on that wondrous night, taken from the very lap of her husband.

At the moment of Catullus' admission, and his attempt at redemption, we meet another philological obstacle. The two principal scholarly editions of Catullus decide that *mira* in line 145 is a corruption – it can hardly be right for the poet to refer to this night as wondrous, in the same breath as he admits to the beloved's adultery. Fordyce (1961: *ad loc.*) has this: "romantic as the phrase sounds to modern ears, it can hardly be genuine: Heyse's *muta* is the most plausible correction." And Thomson (1997: *ad loc.*) suggests that the abbreviations for *mira* and *media* were confused in the manuscripts: "Though the notion behind *mira* may seem 'romantic' to modern eyes, it is quite unlike Catullus to cut across his meaning by introducing it." So that night – the pivotal moment, really, of the poem – the occasion of Catullus' profound epiphanic experience, exists under a cloud of editorial skepticism. It cannot be *mira* because in the lines immediately before and afterwards, the poet shows that he is aware of the imperfection of the occasion and of the relationship. The night must be silent (*muta*) – or it must be the middle of the night (*media*) when she comes, under cover of darkness.[32] What is striking about all this discussion regarding *mira* is that the manuscripts, in this case, do not seem to be problematic. Everyone agrees that *mira* is what is there – but editorial decisions and interpretive decisions can overlap in strange ways. And so, Catullus' night cannot be wondrous, because his editors will not allow him to contradict himself. For the poet who wrote *odi et amo*, this seems an odd criticism to make.[33]

There is more at stake here, of course, than textual corruption. We have already discussed the difficulty readers and critics have with the incompatibility between the beauty and sheen of the poetry and the "sordidness" of the situation described. Beginning with the poet's gratitude to his friend for the loan of the house, and focusing on the epiphany at the threshold, a common reaction among readers is that the gulf between the baseness of the situation (sleeping with another man's wife, in a borrowed "love-nest") and the height of the poetry must be deliberate. It is either ironic, or intended to mitigate the experience of "real life" with the power of art. While it is true that adultery was not accepted as "normal" in Roman society, and that Catullus appears disillusioned with Lesbia's morality in other poems, it seems none-theless obvious to me that the situation he evokes in 68 *can* be cause for celebration in its way. The poet who exhorted Lesbia to ignore the wagging tongues of society and live love to the full in the "kissing poems" was no less aware of the moral issues at stake than the poet who writes of his adulterous lover as a gleaming goddess. Euphoric love can and does at times make us blind to morality and to the views of others – and can account quite simply for contradictions like the ones that this poem, and indeed the entire collection, is full of (Lyne 1980: 19–20). And the poet should not, for the sake of editorial "coherence," be robbed of his wondrous night.

Moreover, Catullus clearly does not end on a bitter note toward the beloved – she is, for all her imperfections, still the light of his life – eclipsing perhaps even the death of his brother. The blessings with which the poem concludes culminate in these closing lines (159–60):

> et longe ante omnes mihi quae me carior ipso est
> lux mea qua uiua uiuere dulce mihi est.

And far above all she who is dearer to me than myself – she is my light and while she lives living is sweet for me.

In reaching this final point of reconciliation – a kind of return to the *uiuamus atque amemus* of c. 5 – c. 68 takes a position vis-à-vis the beloved which is unusually free from the anguish and division that characterizes other poems. While in the shorter elegies (70, 72, 75, 92) and in cc. 11 and 8, the gulf between what she was and what she is, or what she says and what she does, cannot be bridged and his love for her is a source of pain rather than sweetness, here the poem finds its natural resolution in affirming life and love over all else and at all costs.[34] How did we get to this point of untypical forgiveness and optimism?

Partly it is to do with the fact that this poem is written away from Rome to be read by others, and not as a convivial piece for performance by the poet. Comparison with some of the more ambivalent Lesbia poems throws up other clear markers of performativity. For instance, c. 70 draws attention to the woman's words (repeating *dicit* three times in the four-line poem) and then compares them to words *written* (*scribere*) on wind and water. In c. 72, as in c. 75, Lesbia is addressed directly, and her speech drawn attention to with the first word (*dicebas*). In the penultimate line she becomes an interlocutor within the poem (*qui potis est, inquis?*, " 'How can that be?' you ask," 72.7). In speaking to her directly, Catullus repeatedly draws attention to the impossibility of his situation, and to his mistrust of her. If we imagine such poems delivered *in ioco atque uino*, perhaps with some self-deprecation or irony, their point seems to be to play with the paradox of the bittersweetness of erotic love. Aggression and abuse are part of the game, with Lesbia as with everyone else. The point of c. 68 is different: viewed from a distance and worked into a densely allusive poem, the beloved's deficiencies are not insurmountable. Also, in the face of the loss of a brother the need to bridge differences and recover life and light is more important than the posturing required of the performer of masculinity at Rome. Indeed, there is something apotropaic in the insistence on life at the center of the last line (*uiua uiuere*) – as though the possibility of the beloved's own death, of the end of the light, must be warded off. It does seem that in the ambition to create something more permanent, a written work that does not need its author's presence, Catullus has found, after all, a way of defeating death and loss, and affirming the possibility of something like continuation and survival – immortality perhaps.

NOTES

1   Guy Lee's (1990) parallel text prints 68a and b. Quinn (1973a) and Fordyce (1961) print one continuous poem. Most recently, Thomson separates a and b.
2   The main literature on this question is: Most (1981: 116–17); Tuplin (1981: 113–14); Skinner (1972, 2003); Wiseman (1974).
3   See Butrica in this volume on the manuscript tradition.
4   Wiseman (1974: 88) has a useful discussion and a table which shows the readings of the names in the manuscripts. See also Godwin (1995: 203).
5   See Wiseman (1974: 88–9) or Godwin (1995: 209) for other ways of achieving one name.
6   See Feldherr in this volume (pp. 97–8) on the role of 66 as fulfilling social obligation. See Wiseman (1974: 102) on other pairs of poems.
7   Also of lovers' empty promises, e.g., 64.59.

8   On the "game" of exchanging poetry see Wray (2001: 103–4); Skinner (2003: 20, 41–2).
9   For suggestions on what is meant by the gifts of Venus see, e.g., Wiseman (1974: 94–5); Fear (1992); Forsyth (1987b).
10 See Krostenko (2001a: 241–5) on c. 12.
11 On the ramifications of the word *uenustas* as Catullus uses it to illustrate his combination of the erotic and the aesthetic, see Fitzgerald (1995: 34–6); Seager (1974).
12 I have appropriated Krostenko's translation of *ueneres*. See his discussion of the poem, and of *uenustas*, in Krostenko (2001a: 235–41, and in this volume).
13 See Feldherr (2000: 214) on how Catullus is ritually and socially barred from communication and exchange while mourning.
14 Skinner (2003: 147–51) discusses all this, with bibliography.
15 Only the song of the Fates in c. 64 is similarly long-lived (64.321).
16 See Habinek's discussion of writing as social performance (1998: 103–21).
17 See how Themis (*iustitia*) leaves humanity in 64.397, ending the Golden Age.
18 Lyne (1980: 56) understands the *domus–domina* connection in a similar vein – while keeping *dominae* (he translates: "he gave a house to me and to a (or *its* or *my*) mistress"). See also Miller in this volume (p. 412).
19 In 61.159–61 the bride is exhorted to lift her feet with good omen over the threshold.
20 See Feeney (1992: 33–4) on the hymeneal aspects of 68b. Compare, for instance, 61.149–50, and 61.31–2.
21 See Feeney (1992: 38–9) on the ambiguities of this pair of similes. Fordyce (1961) explains the textual problems at line 63.
22 See Feeney (1992), and in response Kennedy (1999).
23 Feeney (1992: 44) has a different interpretation.
24 Feldherr in this volume (pp. 103–4) discusses the significance of this kind of display of erudition as part of Catullus' negotiations of his social role.
25 For Troy as grave in Lucan and others, see Spencer (2005).
26 Catullus shows later (119–24) and in c. 72 that comparison between erotic and familial love can be fruitful.
27 Tuplin (1981: 119–36) is the most substantial discussion of the simile.
28 See also Fitzgerald (1995: 209); Skinner (2003: 163). But cf. Janan (1994: 132–4) for a more sympathetic reading of the *barathrum* simile, and of Hercules' role in the poem.
29 See Vandiver's discussion of the simile in this volume (pp. 535–7).
30 See Janan (1994: 135) on this simile as an image for the potential of poetry to transcend death.
31 For the dove see Feeney (1992: 41–2); Macleod (1974: 86).
32 Skinner (2003: 204 n. 60) goes with *media*. Feeney (1992: 43) has *muta*, but hedges his bets in referring to "Catullus' wondrous *nox*" just before.
33 In favour of *mira*: Sarkissian (1983: 54 n. 92); Quinn (1973a: 394). Wiseman (1974: 84–5) prints *mira* and translates "that miraculous night." Lee (1990: 120–1) translates *mira* as "wondrous night."
34 See Janan (1994: 140–1) for a persuasive reading of these lines.

GUIDE TO FURTHER READING

Mcleod (1974: 82–8) and Lyne (1980: 52–60) are engaging treatments of the poem, and a good place to start. Wiseman (1974: 77–103) is illuminating – again an excellent place to begin investigations. Every student of the poem should read Skinner (1972) and Tuplin (1981) on the poem's unity. On the similes, and the role of analogy in the poem, Feeney (1992) is essential. Within larger-scale treatments, there are prominent discussions of 68 in Janan (1994), Fitzgerald (1995), and most recently Skinner (2003), which places the poem in its context within the third part of Catullus' collection.

Fordyce (1961) is still an excellent guide to the poem. Thomson (1997) will be most useful to those interested in textual issues. Godwin (1995) has a parallel text and informative commentary.

WORKS CITED

Fear, T. 1992. "Catullus 68A: *Veronae turpe, Catulle, esse.*" *Illinois Classical Studies* 17: 245–63.

Feeney, D. C. 1992. "'Shall I compare thee...?': Catullus 68b and the Limits of Analogy." In A. J. Woodman and J. Powell, eds., *Author and Audience in Latin Literature*. Cambridge. 33–44.

Feldherr, A. 2000. "*Non inter nota sepulcra*: Catullus 101 and Roman Funerary Ritual." *Classical Antiquity* 19.2: 209–31.

Fitzgerald, W. 1995. *Catullan Provocations: Lyric Poetry and the Drama of Position*. Berkeley, Los Angeles, and London.

Fordyce, C. J., ed. 1961. *Catullus: A Commentary.* Oxford.

Forsyth, P. Y. 1987b. "*Munera et Musarum hinc petis et Veneris*: Catullus 68A.10." *Classical World* 80: 177–80.

Fredrick, D. 1999. "Haptic Poetics." *Arethusa* 32: 49–83.

Gamel, M.-K. 1998. "Reading as a Man: Performance and Gender in Roman Elegy." *Helios* 25: 79–95.

Godwin, J. 1995. *Catullus: Poems 61–68*. Warminster.

Habinek, T. N. 1998. *The Politics of Latin Literature: Writing, Identity, and Empire in Ancient Rome*. Princeton, NJ.

Janan, M. 1994. "*When the Lamp is Shattered*": *Desire and Narrative in Catullus*. Carbondale and Edwardsville, IL.

Kennedy, D. 1999. "'cf.': Analogies, Relationships and Catullus 68." In S. M. Braund and R. Mayer, eds., *Amor: Roma. Love and Latin Literature*. Cambridge. 30–43.

Kenney, E. J. 1982. "Books and Readers in the Roman World." In E. J. Kenney and W. V. Clausen, eds., *The Cambridge History of Classical Literature. Vol. II: Latin Literature*. Cambridge and New York. 3–32.

Krostenko, B. A. 2001a. *Cicero, Catullus, and the Language of Social Performance*. Chicago and London.

Lee, G., trans. 1990. *The Poems of Catullus*. Oxford and New York.

Lyne, R. O. A. M. 1980. *The Latin Love Poets from Catullus to Horace*. Oxford.

Lyne, R. O. A. M. 1998. "Love and Death: Laodamia and Protesilaus in Catullus, Propertius, and Others." *Classical Quarterly* n.s. 48: 200–12.

Macleod, C. W. 1974. "A Use of Myth in Ancient Poetry." *Classical Quarterly* n.s. 24: 82–93.

Most, G. 1981. "On the Arrangement of Catullus' *Carmina Maiora*." *Philologus* 125: 109–25.

Newman, J. K. 1990. *Roman Catullus and the Modification of the Alexandrian Sensibility.* Hildesheim.

Quinn, K., ed. 1973a. *Catullus: The Poems*. 2nd edn. London and Basingstoke.

Sarkissian, J. 1983. *Catullus 68: An Interpretation. Mnemosyne* Supplement 76. Leiden.

Seager, R. 1974. "*Venustus, lepidus, bellus, salsus*: Notes on the Language of Catullus." *Latomus* 33: 891–94.

Skinner, M. B. 1972. "The Unity of Catullus 68: The Structure of 68a." *Transactions of the American Philological Association* 103: 495–512.

Skinner, M. B. 1993a. "Catullus in Performance." *Classical Journal* 89: 61–8.

Skinner, M. B. 2003. *Catullus in Verona: A Reading of the Elegiac* Libellus, *Poems 65–116.* Columbus, OH.

Spencer, D. J. 2005. "Lucan's Follies: Memory and Ruin in a Civil-War Landscape." *Greece & Rome* 52: 46–69.

Starr, R. J. 1987. "The Circulation of Literary Texts in the Roman World." *Classical Quarterly* n.s. 37: 213–23.

Thomson, D. F. S., ed. 1997. *Catullus, Edited with a Textual and Interpretative Commentary.* Toronto.

Tuplin, C. J. 1981. "Catullus 68." *Classical Quarterly* n.s. 31: 113–39.

Wiseman, T. P. 1974. *Cinna the Poet and Other Roman Essays.* Leicester.

Wiseman, T. P. 1985. *Catullus and His World: A Reappraisal.* Cambridge.

Wray, D. 2001. *Catullus and the Poetics of Roman Manhood.* Cambridge.

CHAPTER EIGHTEEN

Social Commentary and Political Invective

W. Jeffrey Tatum

Kenneth Quinn once dismissed Catullus' "poetry of social comment" as little more than fascinating and vivid background material for the poet's demonstration of his affair with Lesbia, which, in his view, constituted the real subject of Catullus' poetic collection and his principal literary achievement (Quinn 1972b: 49–50). It was not that Quinn was uninterested in the atmosphere of the late Republic or in the historicist implications of the prosopography of the Catullan collection – far from it. But, for Quinn, these poems evinced lower "levels of intent," to the extent that most of Catullus' shorter poems could be described as "strictly personal poetry," exercises "in the process of working out how to record feelings in crisp, telling non-literary language" (Quinn 1972b: 277). Even in instances of invective directed against conspicuous political figures "his verse expresses no political ideas, no political attitude as such, except perhaps a general disgust with politics" (Quinn 1972b: 267; Quinn's work is put into context by Wray 2001: 30–5). Recent critical approaches, however, embrace a very different strategy. Current practices tend to break down distinctions between the poetics of eroticism and broader cultural concerns, a shift that has ended the strict segregation of the Lesbia poems from the remainder of the corpus (Kennedy 1993: 34–9; Skinner 2003: 60–95). Furthermore, it is now a regular habit of interpretation to detect in Catullan poetry, as in literary texts more generally, locations for the contesting and negotiation of societal dynamics (bibliography at Nappa 2001: 29; Skinner 2003: 22–3). No longer simply a backdrop for the narrative of Catullus' romance, then, the poems' social commentary has emerged as a persistent and even essential element of the Catullan poetic program, undeniable and unavoidable.

Understanding the degree to which Catullus' poems should be understood as social commentary – and what a reading along these lines meant and means – remains far from uncomplicated. One recent critic has gone so far as to describe Catullus' unifying poetic program as "sustained scrutiny and criticism of Roman society" (Nappa 2001: 23). If this is perhaps pressing the matter too hard, it is nonetheless the case that the importance and pervasiveness of social commentary in Catullus can hardly be missed. His opening poem invokes themes of friendship and the nature of Italian status in late Republican Rome; similar concerns, but from a darker perspective, arise in the final poem of the extant collection (W. J. Tatum 1997). And throughout the collection one finds an abundance of lyrics and epigrams censuring (or at the very least investigating) social exclusivity, treachery, and provincialism, as well as sexual misconduct, lapses of decorum (such as the thievery of napkins), luxuriousness, and the baleful influence of the nobility – sometimes lightly but often with a dark and biting humor and equally often in a tone of undiluted vituperation that finds its expression in enormities of obscenity.

Roman Invective

Critics tend to like Catullus, a reality that emerges in the history of his interpretation and that poses a potential impediment to any modern attempt to appreciate the nature of his social commentary: it is too easy to embrace what David Wray has called "the stratagem of making Catullus into our man in Rome, our secret periscopic eye viewing his world from our own ethical viewpoint" (Wray 2001: 129). Which is not to say that Catullus or his world are so alien from our own as to be incomprehensible, but instead to insist that ample attention be paid to the strong contrasts between the normal and normative expectations of our own society and the one that constitutes an essential context for Catullus' poems, not least when they are read as social commentary (Wiseman 1985: 1–14).

By their very nature Romans were censorious (Veyne 1983). Tradition was deemed irrefutably good, a habit of mind that entailed a strong belief in the value of conformity at every social level and in the importance of deference to established hierarchy. The Romans' commitment to consensus, at the everyday and elite levels alike (Oehler 1961), was essential both for ordinary instantiations of justice and to the comprehensive stability of the republic (Nippel 1995: 4–46). As a consequence, everything in Roman society was subject to intense and skeptical scrutiny. "No man can be a good judge," insists Cicero, "who is not affected by well-grounded suspicion" (Cic. *Verr.* 2.5.65). Even private life was open to view, not merely by way of gossip but also, for the aristocracy, in the very design and functionality of their homes (private life made public in politics: e.g., Q. Cic. *Comment. pet.* 17; cf. Richlin 1992: 83–6; houses: Wallace-Hadrill 1988). This moralizing examination went a long way in Rome: what to modern sensibilities seem nothing more than personal idiosyncrasies in physical appearance or dress or speech could be viewed, and were viewed, by the Romans as symptoms of a corrupt character and therefore a potential danger to the state (Richlin 1992; Gleason 1995; Corbeill 1996).

Consequently praise and blame were the essential tools of moral analysis. Horace (to cite a single yet illustrative example) represents his tradition-minded father as leaving moral arguments to the philosophers, instead dragging his son through the city pointing out living specimens of failure and vice, men whose immorality was demonstrated by public opprobrium (*Sat.* 1.4.124–6):

...an hoc inhonestum et inutile factu
necne sit addubites, flagret rumore malo cum
hic atque ille?

...do you doubt whether this is or isn't disgraceful or disadvantageous, when this man
as well as that man is blasted by evil repute?

Indeed, exemplarity remained basic to the Romans' investigation of virtue and its opposite (Roller 2004), and, as a result, negative examples served an obvious didactic purpose.

This mentality helps to explain the pervasiveness of invective in Roman society, the universal appeal of which is evidenced by its appearance in comic drama and scribbled graffiti. In political discourse, "the best of arguments was personal abuse. In the allegation of disgusting immorality, degrading pursuits and ignoble origin the Roman politician knew no compunction or limit" (Syme 1939: 149). Political opposition could be conveyed by means of straightforward abuse – cast in sexual and sometimes obscene terms. In forensic circumstances, vituperation advanced the case of prosecution and defense alike, so avid was each side to convince juries by means of *argumenta ex vita*, a staple of rhetorical education (Corbeill 2002; Craig 2004). In his defense of M. Caelius Rufus, Cicero impugned the testimony of Clodia Metelli on the grounds that she was lubricious, adulterous, and incestuous. L. Calpurnius Piso, the consul of 58, was, according to Cicero's hostile pamphlet *Against Piso*, derived from base origins, a glutton, a drunkard, greedy, and guilty of sexual immorality. Examples could be multiplied.

Imputations of personal immorality were relevant to political contests in Rome, where public life was conceptualized in terms of high calling and exemplary personal conduct (Earl 1967). At the same time, it was conceded that aristocratic service to the Republic was suffused with strife: competition for personal honor, even when properly subordinated to the best interests of the state, operated along personal lines. Rome lacked political parties. Instead, individuals joined with other individuals, in senatorial and forensic practices, on the basis of personal pledges of affection and obligation. Put differently, Roman political life was sustained by friendship and similar obligations. Seen in this light, the personal element of Roman politics is obvious: trustworthiness (*fides*) and duty (*officium*) were virtues crucial in leaders and followers alike. Hence the force of invective. An immoral statesman was an abomination: men might decently disagree (at least within certain limits) about matters of policy; but a man lacking satisfactory moral fiber, especially a powerful man suffering from this deficiency, was unacceptable as a (true) friend and represented a danger to the state. For this reason, Roman political discourse often appears personal to us. One's opponents were not merely mistaken: they were wicked. And because it was a Roman instinct that *any* moral lapse might well indicate *every* moral lapse (Cic. *Inv. rhet.* 2.33; *Rhet. Her.* 2.5), comprehensive invective frequently trumped narrower or more specific criticisms. The result is that political controversy in Rome regularly took place in more than one register: constitutional issues might rub shoulders with claims that this or that individual was insolent, immoral, or bestial (Hellegouarc'h 1971: 484–541; Achard 1981: 186–355), accusations that were simultaneously personal and of public significance.

So indispensable was invective that Cicero can attempt to deconstruct a prosecution's entire case with animadversions on its failure to adduce "any scandal, any crime, any shameful behavior arising from lust, effrontery, or reckless audacity. If there were not true grounds for suspicion, certainly some could have been fabricated" (*Font.* 37). Now by the late Republic defamation was actionable, though this reality seems to have imposed no limitations on invective, possibly owing to the traditional quality of legitimate public shaming in Rome, which ranged from public heckling to the infliction of ignominy in the census or in the courts (Crook 1967: 252–5). As the *Digest* puts it, "it is not just that anyone who defames a wicked person be condemned on that account, because it is fitting and beneficial that the wrong-doings of the wicked be known" (*Dig.* 47.10.18.pref.). Or, to turn to an actual specimen of (self-justificatory) invective, "the republic is made greater through private hostilities, when no citizen can disguise his nature" ([Cic.] *Sall.* 3).

Modern approaches to Roman invective either stress its conventionality by means of typological collections of its instantiations (Craig 2004, with further references) or attempt to explore its psychological and sociological premises and implications (Richlin 1992; Corbeill 1996). Romans resorted to invective in order to isolate and revile exceptionable divergences from reputable habits and practices, an aggressive exertion that was intended at once to humiliate the alleged miscreant and to help to fashion the speaker (or writer) as a champion of normative values – a representation which, in Roman terms, entailed a masculine and masterful pose. The Roman had at his disposal an array of hostile tropes (e.g., Cic. *Inv. rhet.* 1.34–6, 2.28–31, 2.177–8; *Rhet. Her.* 3.10–15). Invective commonplaces included slurs on an enemy's origins; reproaches for his failure to sustain his family's reputation; excoriation of his appearance, his appetites, and his sexual proclivities; denunciation of his pretensions; complaints about his treachery; and censure of his avidness for the property of others, his luxuriousness, and his financial failures. Cicero, repeating the doctrine of the rhetoricians, insists that a conviction is impossible if one cannot adduce faults of character that make an accusation plausible. Character assassination along these lines was equally vital in purely political denunciations of a rival position: Cicero's *Second Philippic* remains the classic (but scarcely the only) specimen.

But however compulsory invective was as a formal element of oratory, its claims could be rejected, not least by calling attention to its very conventionality. In his defense of Caelius Rufus, for example, Cicero reacts to the invective against Caelius delivered by the 17-year-old prosecutor, L. Sempronius Atratinus, by observing that his callowness inhibited the young man's ferocity and thereby reduced his abuse of Caelius to something ineffectual and strained, however obligatory in a case for the prosecution (Cic. *Cael.* 6–8; cf. Gotoff 1986). Atratinus simply failed to come across as authentic, and his attack could be reduced to a mere exercise. Invective, then, to be successful, had to be convincing, and the personality of the calumniator played an essential role. One always ran the risk, when abusing others, of revealing a flaw in one's own character (Cic. *Off.* 1.134), and while it remained the height of elegance (*urbanitas*) to point out the blemishes of others, it was nothing short of stupidity (*stultitia*) to allow blemishes to be observed in oneself (Quint. *Inst.* 6.3.8). Objective rhetorical constructions unfolding in authorial absence, however finely expressed, did not count as effective and affecting invective – in oratory.

Invective presented a moral lesson to its audience: behold an exceptionable man or woman. Furthermore, any resort to moralizing invective implied at least a belief that it was carried out in a robust moral environment in which said invective could reach a discriminating audience capable of appreciating and endorsing its criticisms (Corbeill 1996: 203–4). The audience is not merely flattered by this: Romans were invited to regard the prevalence of invective in their society not as an indication that all was lost but instead as a reassuring feature that proved Roman censoriousness persisted effectually and advantageously.

Catullan Invective

Catullan invective has much in common with the practices of oratory. The poems complain of pretensions (e.g., poems 22, 37.14, 49) and moral hypocrisy (e.g., poems 29, 51, 74), they register disgust when distinguished names fail to sustain their families' reputations for genuine excellence (e.g., poems 12, 28, 41, 58a), and they mock low and provincial origins (e.g., poems 37, 39, 41, 43, 57, 59, 84, 103). That a newcomer to the Roman scene like Catullus should adduce this reality as a fault in others is unremarkable: the new man Cicero, himself the object of senatorial abuse for that very cause, is perfectly capable of employing this commonplace in his invective oratory (Cic. *Pis.* 14, 24; cf. *Caecin.* 28; *Har. resp.* 5; *Phil.* 11.14). Lapses in speech and style (poems 14a, 22, 36, 44, 84, 95, 105) and objectionable physical attributes (e.g., poems 39, 41, 42, 43, 47, 52, 54, 57, 69, 71, 79, 81, 86, 97, 98) attract their share of obloquy. Catullus disapprobates theft, in registers varying from light-hearted (but not unserious) drollery over the removal of napkins (poem 12) to shocking obscenities (e.g., poems 25, 33) to vaporizing outrage over the wholesale plundering of the northern provinces by Caesar and his associates (poem 29). Prodigality and financial embarrassment – serious and unsentimental matters in Rome – are alleged, and, not unnaturally in Roman invective, they are connected to unrestrained physical appetites (e.g., poems 21, 23, 24, 26, 29, 33, 41, 43, 47, 59, 103, 114).

The bulk of Catullus' invective, by any method of quantification, is reserved for sexual misconduct: effeminate perversions, incest, and adultery are pervasive allegations (e.g., poems 15, 17, 21, 23, 25, 28, 29, 33, 37, 39, 40, 41, 42, 47, 54, 57, 58a, 59, 67, 74, 78a, 78b, 79, 80, 88, 89, 90, 91, 94, 97, 98, 106, 108, 111, 112, 113), all very interesting from the pen of a self-confessed adulterer (poem 83). Unfaithfulness in sexual matters looms large in Catullus' indictments. For instance, the poet openly detests the treachery of false and violated friendship (e.g., poems 12, 30, 72, 73, 76, 77, 91, 108), a transgression also regularly pilloried in oratory: in Catullus, however, false friendship is commonly (and remarkably) a means of configuring sexual betrayal. Catullus sometimes threatens his enemies with the perils of his shaming verses (e.g., poems 40, 54, 78b, 116), and in poem 42 he stages a *flagitatio*, an old-fashioned public heckling that employed disgrace in order to achieve justice, a literary gesture that underscores the poet's association with the traditional purposes and values inherent in Roman invective (though it is worth observing that Catullus' *flagitatio* is a failure which he abandons for flattery: 42.21–2).

It was not Roman instinct alone that led Catullus to social commentary in the shape of vituperation. He was also inspired by the traditions of Greek poetry. Catullan invective, though coarsest in his epigrams, iambics, and hendecasyllables – meters which, in Catullus' handling of them, display recognizable affinities in register, diction, and style (Jocelyn 1999) – finds a more restrained but nonetheless unmistakable manner in lyrics like poem 11 and poem 30. Abuse and obscenities were conventional in the "blame poetry" (*psogos*) of Greek lyric and elegiac, a fashion of poetry often referred to as *iambos* and prominently associated with Archilochus (West 1974: 22–39; Gentili 1988: 107–14). The fragments of Archilochus provide glimpses of a poet who, by adopting a range of literary postures (many of them disreputable), interrogated and exposed the pretensions and vices of his own society – not least by means of invective aimed at treachery and personal immorality. The vices they pillory were real enough, but their objects were often fictionalized, perhaps stock, characters, introduced in order to be reviled. Iambic poetry, though modified in important ways, continued popular in Hellenistic literature – Callimachus and Herodas are only two familiar practitioners – and Hellenistic epigram was adept at ridicule and abuse. Archilochus remained central to the reception of Greek iambic verse, and he was recommended reading for pupils in rhetoric (Men. Rhet. 2.393). His work appealed to Romans in the late Republic: even the strait-laced Cato, when once cheated of his betrothed by Metellus Scipio, resorted to composing invective verse along the lines of Archilochus (Plut. *Cat. Mi.* 7.2).

The voice of Catullan invective, like its Archilochean antecedent (Arist. *Rhet.* 3.1418b.23–33), is not evenly continuous throughout the collection: an adulterer decries adultery; the masterful moralizer is sometimes reduced to comic ineptitude (e.g., poem 8) or even to complete disgrace (e.g., poem 28), poses that seem to invite devaluation as *stultitia* from the viewpoint of practices of oratory (cf. Quint. *Inst.* 6.3.8, cited above; cf. Richlin 1992: 145; Skinner 1991: 2–3). In sum, the Catullan "I" can be very difficult to stabilize, which contrasts significantly with the expectations attending the auditor of invective delivered in forensic oratory or senatorial debate. The importance of Archilochus to Catullus' literary program – his style of abuse is more biting and personal than Callimachean iambic poetry (Fantuzzi and Hunter 2004: 8–13; cf. L. C. Watson 2003: 4–19, on the Roman reception of Greek iambic literature) – has rightly been stressed (Heyworth 2001; Wray 2001: 185). Even Catullus' elegiac poetry reflects the thematics and habits of archaic iambic (Heyworth 2001: 137–9). All of which offers a salutary reminder that the social commentary of "our man in Rome" comes refracted not only by the patterns of invective characteristic of late Republican public discourse but also by the literary conventions and traditions of Greek iambic poetry.

Caesar and the First Trimvirate

Caesar, in his early career, acquired a reputation for effeminacy and adultery (related vices from the Roman perspective, which is why C. Scribonius Curio could pillory Caesar as "every woman's man and every man's woman") along with broad popularity, owing to no small extent to his generosity in office (hence his enormous indebtedness), a disturbing mix from the conservative view made all the more worrisome (and conspicuous) by his repeated flashes of oratorical and military capacity. Caesar's elevation to the consulship of 59 coincided with the formation of his notorious friendship with Pompey the Great and P. Licinius Crassus, a political combination denominated by moderns as the First Triumvirate (and ridiculed in antiquity as the Three-Headed Monster; cf. App. *B Civ.* 2.9). Caesar's consulship advanced the interests of himself and his triumviral colleagues, but only by means of appalling violence that soon incurred hostility amongst Romans of all classes. Nevertheless, the dynasts, as they are often and misleadingly described in modern scholarship, were able to fortify themselves in the following year when partisans occupied the consulship and the formidable P. Clodius Pulcher was tribune of the people. Still, before that year was out, Clodius had turned on Pompey, and the clout of the triumvirs continued to diminish. For the remainder of the 50s Caesar was away from Rome waging war in Gaul, where he accrued glory and wealth (during which time he was also governor of Cisalpine Gaul, where Catullus' native Verona was located). By 56, a year in which each consulship was occupied by an enemy of the triumvirs, their association was itself nearly in tatters, but it was renewed by an expansion of their connections: Pompey's family formed a marriage alliance with the Claudii Pulchri, thereby adding Clodius to the number of his friends, and Cicero was deployed in the triumvirs' interests. Violence and constitutional chicanery got Pompey and Crassus the consulships of 55 (for each his second consulship). Even at this point, however, the might of the triumvirs is easy to overestimate. The real state of political affairs is obvious in the results of the elections for 54: one consul was Ap. Claudius Pulcher, friend and relation to the triumvirs; the other was L. Domitius Ahenobarbus, their bitterest enemy. And in the machinations for office for the next year, the importance of the triumvirs dissolved nearly entirely (contrast Konstan, this volume, p. 73). Notwithstanding the limitations of the triumvirate, indeed, to some degree because political antagonisms in Rome were so evenly matched in resources at this time, 55 and 54 and 53 were years of increasing political instability and public anxiety (Wiseman 1994; W. J. Tatum 2006). Catullus had his own views on whom to blame.

Catullus' attacks on Caesar – one of which (poem 29) is imitated in Horace's *Epodes* (poem 29.7; cf. *Epod.* 4.5, 17, 41, 5.69) and quoted both by the author of *Catalepton* 6.5 and by Quintilian (9.4.141) as an illustration of iambic malediction – made a deep and lasting impression. Even their target recognized their effect (Suet. *Iul.* 73):

> Valerium Catullum, a quo sibi versiculis de Mamurra perpetua stigmata imposita non dissimuleverat, satis facientem eadem die adhibuit cenae hospitioque patris eius, sicut consuerat, uti perseveravit.

> Caesar never disguised the fact that Catullus' poems about Mamurra inflicted a permanent stain on his reputation. But when Catullus apologized, Caesar invited him to dinner on the same day. And he continued without interruption his friendly relationship with Catullus' father.

In this instance, the actions of Catullus and of Caesar cut through the potential obscurities entailed by the varying literary personalities constructed by the authors of invective poetry: poems composed by Catullus constituted a personal persecution for which their author accepted responsibility. This bit of Catullan aggression, however Archilochean in sentiment or style, took aim at undisguised contemporaries in the hardy fashion of Roman oratory. Mamurra was not a Catullan invention but an equestrian from Formiae whose military service under Pompey and Caesar had proved profitable enough to elevate him to new standards of Roman luxuriousness (see Konstan, this volume, pp. 73–4). Catullus' hostility to the man and his morals, and by extension to the actions of his prominent associates, Caesar and Pompey, is unmistakable.

Quis hoc potest videre, quis potest pati,
nisi impudicus et vorax et aleo,
Mamurram habere quod Comata Gallia
habebat ante et ultima Britannia?
cinaede Romule, haec videbis et feres?   5
et ille nunc superbus et superfluens
perambulabit omnium cubilia
ut albulus columbus aut Adoneus?
cinaede Romule, haec videbis et feres?
es impudicus et vorax et aleo.   10
eone nomine, imperator unice,
fuisti in ultima occidentis insula,
ut ista vestra diffututa mentula
ducenties comesset aut trecenties?
quid est alid sinistra liberalitas?   15
parum expatravit an parum helluatus est?
paterna prima lancinata sunt bona:
seconda praeda Pontica: inde tertia
Hibera, quam scit amnis aurifer Tagus.
†hunc Galia timet et Britanniae†   20
quid hunc malum fovetis? aut quid hic potest
nisi uncta devorare patrimonia?
eone nomine, urbis o piissimi,
socer generque, perdistis omnia?

Who can look at this, who can bear it, except someone who is shameless, voracious and a gambler: the fact that Mamurra possesses what once belonged to Gallia Comata and remote Britain? Pervert Romulus, can you look at this and endure it? And will he, insolent and rich, stroll through everyone's bedroom like a white dove or Adonis? Pervert Romulus, can you look at this and endure it? You are shameless, voracious and a gambler. Was it for this, peerless victor, that you were on the most distant island of the West? Was it so that that fucked-out prick of yours could consume twenty or thirty million sesterces? If this isn't perverse generosity, what is? Hasn't he finished off enough and screwed enough? First his ancestral estates were ripped to bits, then his spoils from Pontus, then, third, his Spanish plunder – the gold-bearing river Tagus knows about that. Does he now get the best bits of Gaul and Britain? Why, damn it, do you favor this man? What can he do apart from devouring rich patrimonies? Was it for this, O paragons of Roman piety, father-in-law and son-in-law, that you have wasted everything? (c. 29)

Although it opens with a (possible) reference to Archilochean iambics (Fordyce 1961: 161), this poem is replete with commonplaces from Roman rhetorical invective. Mamurra's avid appropriation of Roman plunder (3–4), his prodigality, and his financial embarrassment, linked in the standard fashion to gluttony and sexual insatiability as well as adultery – failings that are themselves all staples of Roman vituperation – are deployed in order to shame and to disgrace Pompey and especially Caesar. The technique of abusing a leading political figure by means of insults aimed at a lesser associate was a regular oratorical strategy (Corbeill 1996: 112–24) and is employed more than once in Catullus' excoriations of Caesar (cf. poems 52, 54, 57, 105, 114, 115): Mamurra's wastefulness makes him an embarrassing connection, of course, but it also recollects Caesar's own notoriety for display and indebtedness, thereby forming an oblique slur on Caesar's prodigality.

Still, poem 29 does not eschew direct attack: Caesar is shamelessly immoral, greedy, and a gambler (a common term of reproach, recklessness being deemed un-Roman); he is also a pervert (*cinaedus*) whose actions travesty his family's claims to divine ancestry (29.8, which obliquely refers to Julian descent from the goddess Venus). Vituperation along these lines contradicts Caesar's pretensions to Roman virtue, a quality always best displayed in foreign conquests (the senate ordered thanksgivings in recognition of Caesar's victories in 56 and 55), thus rendering ridiculous (or at best disturbing) his claim to be Rome's peerless victor (29.11). Nor, in poem 29, can Pompey escape his connection with Mamurra or with Caesar: introduced as Caesar's son-in-law at line 24, his virtue is likewise challenged (20.23). The poem closes with an expression that has plausibly been identified as a political slogan of the opponents of Pompey and Caesar (Fordyce 1961: 164, with examples) but which here seems especially to emphasize the idea of financial waste and ruin that is central to Catullus' indictment of Mamurra (*TLL* 10.1: 1264–5). The effect of this poem is devastating and, in terms of the potentialities of Roman invective, very nearly total.

It is possible to date the composition of this poem within fairly narrow terms: Caesar's first landing in Britain took place in 55 and his daughter, Pompey's wife, died in 54. Catullus' attack on Caesar and Pompey, then, though expressed entirely in moral terms that make no reference to urban violence or to constitutional improprieties, seems nevertheless to be a reaction to the enormities perpetrated by the triumvirs in 55. Unlike invective in a political speech, however, which might be expected to offer, in addition to vituperation, substantive criticisms or positive recommendations for correcting an objectionable state of affairs, Catullus' poem decries the personal immorality of Caesar and of Pompey without offering hints of further political allegiances or associations. It will not be the case that Catullus objects to conquests or to monumentalizing military glory: the expanse of the Roman world is described by him, without obvious irony, by reference to campaigns in Gaul and Britain, the "monuments of great Caesar" (11.10), and in poem 55, a light-hearted piece, the portico of Pompey, dedicated in 55, is the natural setting for erotic adventure, a Roman fixture (contrast Konstan, this volume, pp. 77–8, 79–80). Catullus' attack, then, is personal, reflecting the emphasis on individual character and conduct that was crucial to traditional Roman conceptions of political excellence, an idea expressed by the word *virtus*, itself combining masculine superiority with devotion to the moral imperatives of the Republic (Earl 1967: 20–5). The leading classes in Rome and those loyal to them were deemed "good men" – *boni* – and many amongst the senate's elite regarded themselves as *optimates*, the "best men." The consulship – the greatest glory in Roman society (*summa laus*) – confirmed a man's noble quality and validated the reality of his *virtus*. Caesar's actions, by contrast, betray his fundamental unworthiness, his lack of any virtue, political or otherwise.

No value was dearer to Roman sensibilities than *fides* – trustworthiness – which was indispensable to all relationships, be they personal (*fides* was vital to friendship) or financial. Even in international dealings, Romans emphasized the *fides* of the Roman people. The moral mauling given Caesar in poem 29 denounces his performance as general (Romans believed their wars to be just, not simply excuses for plunder), provincial governor, and friend (Caesar's indulgence of Mamurra's appetites is not by Roman standards the action of a true friend, who is obliged to strive to improve his friends' character; cf. Cic. *Amic.* 88–91). This poem represents Caesar's familial tie to Pompey as entirely utilitarian and, in the worst sense, political – and with disastrous results for Rome's subjects and for the integrity of Roman families. In short, Caesar's connection with Mamurra instantiates a poisonous perversion of *fides*. Put differently, Caesar is a bad man – and the proof of it is Mamurra's reprehensible lifestyle.

Caesar's indulgence of unsavory types is also attacked in poem 54, though matters there are made unclear by the unsatisfactory condition of that poem's text; we can nevertheless see that Caesar, judged a "rustic" (54.2) despite his claim to be Rome's "peerless victor," remains vulnerable to Catullus' iambic onslaughts. The rise of P. Vatinius, another Caesarian crony, evokes shock in poem 52 (see Konstan, this volume, pp. 80–1). And Catullus composed a series of savage epigrams lampooning Mamurra – under the cryptonym Mentula ("prick," a reference to *ista vestra diffutata mentula* at 29.13) – for his adultery (poem 94), his literary failures (poem 105), and his extraordinary greed and luxuriousness (poems 114 and 115), each of which reflected poorly on Mamurra's masters (see Konstan, this volume, pp. 75–6). Again Caesar's baleful influence manifests itself in the repellent qualities of his friends: society, from any decent perspective, has gone topsy-turvy when figures of this quality dominate.

Poem 113 also inscribes the coincidence of sexual betrayal and the enormities of 55:

> Consule Pompeio primum duo, Cinna, solebant
>   Maeciliam: facto consule nunc iterum
> manserunt duo, sed creverunt milia in unum
>   singula. fecundum semen adulterio.

When Pompey was consul for the first time, Cinna, two men were accustomed to Maecilia. Now, when he is consul a second time, the two remain, but for each of them there has been a thousand-fold increase. Adultery's seed is fertile.

It is possible that this piece contributes to Catullus' persecution of Caesar. Although the name *Maecilia* is not unknown, and it can never surprise us when the specific identification of a woman in late Republican society eludes us, an emendation (not widely accepted) proposed by C. Pleitner, *Mucilla*, yields a reference to Mucia, who was Pompey's third wife and the mother of his sons. Upon his return from the East in 61, Pompey divorced Mucia – for no explicit reason (Plut. *Pomp.* 42) though it was alleged by Caesar's enemies that Caesar had seduced her in the great man's absence (Suet. *Iul.* 50.1). Poem 113, then, which in any case deploys Pompey's political career as the means by which to measure an explosion in Roman adultery, may also implicate Caesar's treachery – he was after all Pompey's friend and political ally in the 60s. The year 55, for Catullus, heralded a collapse in public and private morality.

Let us return to Mamurra. The equation of Caesar with his lieutenant is explicit in poem 57, where the two are twinned in their adultery, their perversion – Catullus goes so far as to denounce Caesar as a *pathicus* (57.2) – and their literary pretensions.

> Pulchre convenit improbis cinaedis,
> Mamurrae pathicoque Caesarique.
> nec mirum: maculae pares utrisque,
> urbana altera et ille Formiana,
> impressae resident nec eluentur: 5
> morbosi pariter, gemelli utrique,
> uno in lectulo eruditoli ambo,
> non hic quam ille magis vorax adulter,
> rivales socii puellularum.
> pulchre convenit improbis cinaedis.   10

The shameless perverts suit one another well, Mamurra and Caesar the faggot. No wonder: each of them carries the same stains, one from the city, the other from Formiae, deeply marked and never to be washed out. Equally diseased, perfect twins, together on a single couch, each a scholar, the one is not a more voracious adulterer than the other, at once rivals and allies for girls. The shameless perverts suit one another well.

Here the effeminization of Caesar is total: a *pathicus* was a man who relished the experience of sexual penetration by other men, and the poem's collocation of the two men on a single *lecticulum* at the very least suggests that it is Mamurra – the *mentula* of the epigrams – who is Caesar's defiler. The imputation of *os impurum*, a mouth befouled by oral sex, is made unmistakable by the phrase *vorax adulter*, and is, like *pathicus*, an extreme obscenity, deployed here not so much to shock as to underscore the degree to which the peerless victor has succumbed to his own minion: Caesar is a monster, at once warrior and sissy, proconsul and sex toy. His personal degeneracy vitiates, by way of transgression, his public estimation (see further Konstan, this volume, pp. 76–7).

Obscenity is a conspicuous and common feature of Catullan invective, and it has naturally attracted considerable critical scrutiny (Richlin 1992: 144–56; Skinner 1991; Fitzgerald 1995: 64–86). Amy Richlin has emphasized the super-masculine posture of aggressive obscenity in Rome: invective obscenity, when directed at men, regularly robs its targets both of their masculinity and their status as free men by threatening emasculation, often in terms of rape; these insults invite the reader or auditor to participate in the aggressor's stance, a move that further marginalizes the targets of obscene abuse. In his treatment of Caesar, Catullus contemptuously reduces the peerless victor to *pathicus* – a poetic expression of disgust that fashions the poet as comprehensively virtuous and confidently masculine. Marilyn Skinner rightly observes the intimate connection between Roman complaints of sexual dissipation and political or economic oppression: obscenity, in certain contexts, carries political overtones – and we have detected this link already. Caesar's reduction to Mamurra's catamite here unmistakably inscribes a complete failure of political probity. Caesar's leadership, and by association Pompey's leadership, is not merely disgraceful: it is destructive on an international scale, and even self-destructive. All of this is very far from Quinn's "general disgust" but is instead a strongly traditionalist judgment inviting the endorsement of the poet's audience. Invective, as we have seen, tends to imply a moral context in which wickedness can be blamed and potentially banished. Catullus' reaction to the appalling events of 55 and to the enormities of Caesar and his political associates need not place him in the company of Caesar's enemies in the senate, but it clearly appeals to the conventional public values of his readers.

Which brings us to the very odd poem 93:

> Nil nimium studeo, Caesar, tibi velle placere,
>   nec scire utrum sis albus an ater homo.

I'm far from keen to please you, Caesar, or even to know whether you are a white man or a black one.

It is obvious that this poem's posture of indifference is something of a contradiction (genuine indifference on an author's part would give us no poem at all), but that observation can be set aside. What is so striking about this poem is the complete absence of invective tropes. Still, the poem is hardly complimentary to Caesar. Nor does it represent his critic in the best light. However we take the speaker of this poem, he stands in violation of several Roman norms. If this is another instance of the historical Catullus who apologized to Caesar, it fits less neatly into the traditional moralism of the other poems attacking Caesar and Mamurra. After all, no landowner, and no son of a landowner, from Cisalpine Gaul could properly be indifferent to the proconsul who presided over his family's estates – if he respected the Republic and if he cared about his property and his household. And if Suetonius was correct when he stated that Catullus' father and Caesar were on consistently amicable terms, this poem hardly attests to Catullus' filial piety. It is no wonder, then, that Quintilian described this epigram as a specimen of insanity (*Inst.* 11.1.38). He goes on to say that, if the circumstances were reversed, so that it was Caesar and not Catullus who expressed such extreme indifference, the comment would become arrogant (political figures in Rome were obliged to stay accessible to lesser types and to express an interest in their well-being). But Catullus' posture in 93 cannot be arrogance: hence Quintilian's verdict (see also Konstan, this volume, p. 84).

But let us read less biographically. No one sharing the values of the poems discussed above could contemplate Caesar without outrage. An uninterested or even dismissive reaction to Caesar is entirely at odds with the moral urgency of poems 29, 57, and the rest. In other words, the speaker of poem 93, if he is not to be identified with the poet, must be an unsympathetic reader of the poet's work. In poem 93, then, there is something exceptionable about the speaker: his indifference to Caesar is plainly improper, a conclusion that tends against the poem's claim that Caesar is inconsequential even as the poem introduces a figure who is no admirer of him and should prefer to avoid his company. Here, then, instead of the authentic Catullus who ultimately offered his personal apology to the actual Caesar, we come up against the shifting personality of the iambic poet, whose presence here is perhaps signaled by this poem's recourse to proverbial language, a typical feature of iambic (Heyworth 2001).

Seek Noble Friends

The discontinuous nature of Catullan invective has been observed and is sometimes perceived as a problem (e.g., Skinner 1991: 1–3): the poem's speaking persona is often inept or disgraced, no longer a figure of thundering and morally intimidating moral outrage, like the speaker of poem 29, but instead a fallible or fallen figure evoking the iambic personalities of Archilochus or Hipponax. The contrast is made unmistakable more than once in the collection. The poem immediately preceding poem 29, for instance, is, like its successor, a hostile complaint about provincial governors and their relationships, again depicted in obscene and sexual language, with their equestrian subordinates.

> Pisonis comites, cohors inanis
> aptis sarcinulis et expeditis,
> Verani optime tuque mi Fabulle,
> quid rerum geritis? satisne cum isto
> vappa frigoraque et famem tulistis? 5
> ecquidnam in tabulis patet lucelli
> expensum, ut mihi, qui meum secutus
> praetorem refero datum lucello?
> o Memmi, bene me ac diu supinum
> tota ista trabe lentus irrumasti. 10
> sed, quantum video, pari fuistis
> casu: nam nihilo minore verpa
> farti estis. pete nobiles amicos!
> at vobis mala multa di deaeque
> dent, opprobria Romuli Remique. 15

Lieutenants of Piso, an empty-handed cadre, with baggage ready and unencumbered, excellent Veranius and you, my friend Fabullus, how are you? Have you endured enough cold and hunger with that stale fellow? Is there any expense counted as profit in your account books, as is the case with me, inasmuch as I, after serving my praetor, put my losses in the profit column? O Memmius, after you lowered me you made a fellator out of me – at considerable length and without hurry – cramming my mouth with that enormous beam of yours. Still, so far as I can see, you two are in the same condition, because you have been stuffed with no smaller a dick. Seek noble friends! Instead, may the gods and goddesses bring many curses on you, you blots on Romulus and Remus.

The thematic similarities between poems 28 and 29 can scarcely be missed. And the ostensible speaker of poem 28 is, once more, the historical Catullus, who served in Bithynia on the staff of C. Memmius (*pr.* 58 and, though wealthy and well-connected, not technically a noble; the advice to "seek noble friends" is clearly general and not specific to the poet's particular situation). Here the poet expresses his resentment at the unprofitable nature of his relationship with Memmius, misfortune he shares with his friends Veranius and Fabullus, who were in Macedonia with C. Calpurnius Piso (*cos.* 58 – father-in-law to Caesar and unquestionably noble). Here, unlike poem 29, the exploitation of provincials is itself unproblematic: the poet's objection is that neither he nor his friends were allowed even a taste of the spoils of empire. The poem is plainly intended to discredit Memmius and Piso. Memmius' mistreatment of Catullus is represented in terms of sexual penetration – he is an *irrumator* (a man who reduces another to the condition of a fellator) of exaggerated proportions, who subdues Catullus by way of oral rape – an action that was in fact a crime in Rome (the sexual violation of a free man was illegal). Memmius' masculine pose is not merely a threat of domination (itself a legitimately masculine gesture): instead we are shown an actualized violation of the law, which makes Memmius into a distorted parody of the manliness inherent in the Roman idea of *virtus*, the quality that defined the aristocracy and especially the nobility. Like poem 29, then, this poem exhibits a perversion of social relations between the senatorial and equestrian order configured in obscene terms.

But here the speaker is not an indignant observer: he is the emasculated victim, whose humiliation was total and extended (28.9–10). The poem's concentration on the duration and ease of Catullus' violation, it has been proposed, "causes the language of aggression to teeter over into the language of pleasure" (Fitzgerald 1995: 69; Nappa 2001: 95–6), a critical reaction that appreciates the fallen condition of the poem's speaker, who is no less polluted for having been unwilling and over-powered. Again we have Roman leaders who corrupt, but in this poem the speaker cries out from a far less lofty perspective than that of the speaker of poem 29. Indeed, in his avidity this Catullus resembles Mamurra, though he is far less successful: whereas the prodigal from Formiae was able to dominate his master, in poem 28 it is Catullus who is left supine (the entire experience is revisited, and again the Catullan persona displays blemishes, in poem 10, a piece of *vers de société*; cf. Nappa 2001: 85–93). There exists, then, a fracture between poems 28 and 29, a distinct discontinuity between the mishap and misery of the iambic protagonist in one poem and the righteous Roman of the other. This discrepancy is emphasized by the poems' common themes – each is an investigation into the morality of politicized Roman friendship established for the purpose of profit and power – and by their juxtaposition in the collection, an arrangement that urges the reader to confront the implications of Catullus' shifting invective voice.

Catullus insists that his poetic voice and its relationship to his historical identity remain an issue for the reader. In poem 16, perhaps Catullus' fiercest specimen of (non-political) invective, the poet deploys obscenities and super-masculine menaces in order to give a lesson on the perils of reading (text and translation in Manwell, this volume, p. 120). Here Catullus, reacting to the wrong readings of his work by Aurelius and Furius, explodes in threats of conventional masculinity, amidst which he makes the explicit point that readers err in attempting to grasp the poet's authentic identity by way of simple readings of his poems (16.5–6), a prescription expressed in a poem that once more gestures toward a reception of Archilochean poetics (Wray 2001: 185). The reader who accepts the interpretive principle of lines 5 and 6, a lesson the poet threatens to cram down his throat, seems obliged to draw no conclusions about the poet from the contents of his verses, all of which is fine for literariness of a familiar stripe but here entails the effect of problematizing certain aspects of poetic invective itself. For the orator who sought to dominate in vituperative exchanges in the senate or in the courtroom, an essential factor in his performance was self-fashioning, an activity that demanded convincing demonstrations of his own, unquestionably authentic, moral superiority: the practicing orator was a flesh-and-bone performer, known or at the very least knowable (one can compare Cicero's exploitation of Atratinus' youth in his *Defense of Caelius*, cited above). Poem 16 on the other hand draws attention to the invective poet's different circumstances: this author, indicted for being unmanly, retaliates with conventional aggression – the reality of which is put into question by the single literary-critical principle on which the poem insists. Catullus' inclination to repudiate authenticity, found in this poem and elsewhere (Selden 1992: 484), is – self-consciously and conspicuously – at odds with the requirements of invective in the performance of Roman oratory.

Throughout the collection, Catullus represents himself as an elite municipal who oscillates between the glamorous set in Rome and his hometown of Verona, self-fashioning that can be shown to be grounded in the realities of the rising fortunes of the Transpadane Valerii Catulli (Wiseman 1987: 311–70). The question of the degree to which Catullan fiction can be and must be mapped onto historical reality is confronted whenever a poem addresses a contemporary and public figure. An important instance is poem 79:

> Lesbius est pulcher: quid ni? quem Lesbia malit
> quam te cum tota gente, Catulle, tua.
> sed tamen hic pulcher vendat cum gente Catullum,
> si tria notorum savia reppererit.

Lesbius is handsome (also: is a Pulcher); why not? Lesbia prefers him to you and your entire family, Catullus. Nonetheless, let this handsome fellow (also: this Pulcher) sell Catullus and his entire family if he can get three acquaintances to kiss him.

Here the cryptonyms of Catullan erotic are dissolved in political invective. *Lesbius Pulcher* strips away the veil protecting the identity of Lesbia, who is here revealed as one of the sisters of P. Clodius Pulcher. Each is calumniated in poem 79, but the chief focus of Catullan hostility is clearly Clodius, who is vilified for incest and sexual perversion (his refusal to win the kisses of acquaintances is an unmistakable reference to *os impurum*). Furthermore, Clodius constitutes a potential threat to the freedom, the political identity, of Catullus and his family (W. J. Tatum 1993; Skinner 2003: 80–3).

Rumors of incest with his sisters dogged Clodius' public life, and this element in poem 79 both dishonors Lesbius and contributes to his proper identification. The charge of incest recurs in Catullus: another practitioner is Gellius (see below). Like Clodius, this Gellius was a formidable noble, L. Gellius Publicola (*cos.* 36), and also, like Clodius, derived from a family keen to maintain its traditional affinities and to exclude outsiders. Incest, then, while obviously reprehensible in itself, also points to elite Roman exclusivity that was certainly discouraging and potentially perilous to the municipal aristocracy whose admission to inner circles of power was not without resistance in the first century BC (W. J. Tatum 1997: 496–7, with further references). But in poem 79 it is the noble Clodius who is excluded from the greetings of his connections, owing to his degrading and effeminate personal qualities (because Clodius had once been tried for violating the rites of the Bona Dea while dressed in drag, he was especially liable to imputations along these lines despite his acquittal). Thus the poet is (only just) saved by public objections to Clodius' perversions. The suggestion that Clodius might put Catullus and his family up for sale – might strip them of their freedom – cannot fail to recall Clodius' legislation exiling Cicero (who as a senator enjoyed greater political resources than Catullus): this enactment also confiscated and auctioned off Cicero's property (W. J. Tatum 1999: 156–8).

Clodius was also a participant in the violence that thrust Pompey and Crassus into consulships in 55. Again sexual invective is the vehicle of political abuse, but here the link between depravity and oppression is explicit. The threat Lesbius poses to Catullus in this poem, though configured in invective language less graphic than that of poem 28, is in fact far more dangerous. Clodius, who was in Roman politics a champion of popular liberty (his law exiling Cicero was justified by the orator's violation of the basic Roman right to a trial), is here depicted as an enemy to the property and freedom of the prosperous classes, Clodian criticism common in Ciceronian invective (see especially Cicero's speech *On His Own House*). Catullus, then, once more comes very close to the voice of poem 29. Here he is vulnerable, but not obviously debased or suspect – until or unless he is viewed by readers as Lesbia's lover, a figure who elsewhere identifies himself as an adulterer and represents himself as unstable and inept. This Catullus, who once again locates his investigation of political probity in the issue of correct relations between the nobility and the equestrian order, blurs the distinction between the invective voices that contrasted so sharply through juxtaposition of poems 28 and 29, not least because the poet, in poem 16, has threatened the reader who attempts to make too much of his erotic persona.

Nevertheless, poem 79 shatters any attempt to segregate the Lesbia cycle from the poetry of social commentary, and it has not gone unobserved that the breakdown of the poet's relationship with his beloved is presented to the reader not only in terms of brutal (mostly sexual) abuse – Lesbia becomes every bit as repellent as Clodius or Gellius – but also and more importantly in terms of infidelity and ingratitude (Skinner 1991). Catullus' attacks on Lesbia, notably poems 11, 37, and 58, display the same complications in the speaker's fashioning that we have encountered already, with the added twist here that the poet's ineffectuality in confronting Lesbia's superior social status enacts an interrogation of "the notion of aggressive masculinity" (Skinner 1991: 10) that subtends the basic stance of Roman and Catullan invective in the first place. Put differently, the sheer efficacy of vituperation, when it is conveyed in terms of domineering machismo, is put into question (one can compare poem 42, where traditional *flagitatio* proves unsuccessful in the face of feminine resistance), all of which, at the very least, tends to interrogate the traditionalism to which conventional invective makes its appeal for validation. Still, as we shall see below, the poet by no means abandons the medium: in fact, he concludes his collection with invective threats.

The relationship between Catullus and Lesbia is regularly figured as a friendship entailing trustworthiness (*fides*), duty (*officium*), grateful reciprocity (*gratia*), and loyalty (*pietas*). Now this vocabulary once perplexed Catullan critics as an engaging intrusion of what was deemed technical political vocabulary into the realm of love poetry, a misunderstanding both of *amicitia* and of the role of personal morality in politics and political discourse (see above). The word "friend" could be used by the Romans in more than one register. On the one hand, friendship represented an ideal bond of mutual affection and goodwill, sustained by trust and common virtue. At the same time, the word "friend" could be applied, by way of a courtesy, to inferior acquaintances, even clients and supporters, and to others with whom one shared a relationship of more or less strict utility. Political life, and Roman society generally, relied on an application of the positive connotations of ideal friendship to its more practical counterpart (Brunt 1988: 351–81; Verboven 2002), a conflation that was indispensable to normal (*not* normative) political relationships. This is why it is a mistake to view the language of morally sound aristocratic relationships as something primarily political in connotation. Still, as Marilyn Skinner has rightly insisted, the vocabulary of friendship in the Lesbia poems, while not exclusively political, cannot be entirely excluded from the complaints of false friendship or any of the remaining moral failures that blight the reputations of the political figures whom Catullus attacks. Lesbia, like her brother, is depraved. And, like other nobles in the Catullan universe, she violates the principles of friendship and fidelity, not least because, when it concerns a municipal equestrian like Catullus, she can get away with it. While not everyone will go so far as to believe that Lesbia's vices "point to incurable defects in the system" (Skinner 1991: 10) of Roman society, her failure to enact the normative values of the aristocracy is unquestionably akin to the lapses of Caesar: treachery destroys everything, be it love or the Republic, and Catullus' Lesbia poems, in their engagement with the same issues of power and dishonesty that emerge in what is more straightforwardly political invective, underscore the degree to which public life in Rome was predicated on matters of personal integrity.

"Seek noble friends" was the unhelpful advice recollected by Catullus in poem 28, in which he recollects playing fellator to the violent sexual advances of Memmius. Not all of Catullus' contacts with Roman elites, however, were so disastrous, though each remains tinged by social anxiety. Lying outside the category of invective, but within the class of social commentary, are poems 65 and 66. In the former, Catullus responds to a literary request from Hortalus, presumably Hortensius Hortalus (*cos.* 69) though possibly his son, by protesting that his own grief for the loss of his brother renders poetic composition impossible. The poem configures a friendship, which constitutes the basis for Hortensius' request and the poet's desire to comply. But here the social gulf between Catullus and his addressee, who if not actually noble was nevertheless one of the leading senators of his day, is enormous. What Catullus ultimately offers Hortensius, poem 66, is a translation of Callimachus (the *Coma Berenices*), a literary gift the offering of which enacts their friendship. At the same time, however, by offering Hortensius a Latin translation of Alexandria's leading court poet, Catullus introduces the possibility that his composition might be read along the lines of the subordinate work of a court poet, a potentiality made more likely in Rome by the very real abundance of Greek poets-for-hire, whose second-class status was unmistakable, and by the very real tensions that existed in the late Republic between senators and municipal equestrians, who, because they often had to look to senators for protection, were seen and saw themselves as inferior friends to the mighty. That construction of Catullus' gift is never more than latent in the combination of poems 65 and 66, but their combination establishes a context for the two pieces in which it is the reception of these poems on the part of Hortalus that will ultimately put Catullus in his place, as friend or dependent, whatever the language of polite society (W. J. Tatum 1997: 488–97).

This relationship stands in contrast to Catullus' contest with Gellius. The two men, it is claimed in poem 91, had long been friends, though the poet, despite their acquaintance, had been unable to deter Gellius from his baser instincts (the poet's effort, however, displays the correct quality in his view of friendship). Still, it was a blow when Gellius violated *fides* (*sperabam te mihi fidum,* "I was hoping you would be loyal to me," 91.1) by seducing the poet's lover. Despite this break, Catullus endeavored to salvage their friendship, he reports in poem 116, by offering Gellius translations of Callimachus, the strategy of gift exchange operative in poems 65 and 66 – but to no avail. So instead Catullus turned to invective, and in poems 74, 88,

89, 90, and (even) 91 he depicts Gellius as the most abominable figure in his collection: Gellius seduced his uncle's wife and threatened the man with *irrumatio*; he himself is stained with *os impurum* (he is even imagined in self-fellation!); he extends the field of his incest to his mother and sister and ultimately to any woman related to him – in fact, this is what led to his seduction of Catullus' girlfriend: his friendship with the poet rendered her sufficiently forbidden fruit.

In the final poem of the collection, Catullus, by resorting to invective, turns the tables on the noble who proved his false friend:

> saepe tibi studioso animo venante requirens
> carmina uti possem mittere Battiadae,
> qui te lenirem nobis, neu conarere
> tela infesta meum mittere in usque caput,
> hunc video mihi nunc frustra sumptum esse laborem,   5
> Gelli, nec nostras hic valuisse preces.
> contra nos tela ista tua evitabimus acta:
> at fixus nostris tu dabi' supplicium.

Often, with a searching and serious mind, I have looked for some way to send you poems of Callimachus in order to soften you towards me, so that you would not try to cast hostile weapons at my head. Now I see that this effort on my part has been spent to no purpose, Gellius, and that my prayers have, in this instance, proved pointless. Those missiles of yours launched against me I shall evade, but you will be transfixed by mine and pay the penalty of death.

Here invective will triumph over compliment (unlike poem 42). Though patently the inferior man in contest with the noble Gellius – and hence the frustrated attempts to restore their friendship despite the extreme wrong Gellius has done him – Catullus closes this poem by echoing Romulus' fatal last words to Remus in Ennius' *Annales*, when the latter had leapt over the city's new wall (Enn. *Ann.* 1.95 Sk.). In this way, Catullus fashions himself as the very founder of Rome, a remarkable usurpation of status by the Transpadane, and transforms Gellius into the twin who made himself the ultimate outsider. The collection, then, closes with violent threats against a false and former friend from the ranks of the nobility. Although Gellius was not inactive in Roman politics, his quarrel with Catullus, admittedly implicated in the same moral topics – friendship, exclusivity, sexual probity – as the poet's disapprobation of Caesar, Memmius, or Clodius, nevertheless seems more an investigation of elite responsibilities in the matter of friendship and of the status of the Italian newcomer to the Roman cultural scene than a reaction to the triumvirate and its political violence (W. J. Tatum 1997: 497–500). But it is all of a piece. And it must surely matter that the collection closes, not in passive despair, but with violent and markedly Roman acerbity.

Conclusion

Not unexpectedly, Catullan invective is no simple matter. It draws on native and Greek literary traditions alike, a dual heritage that resists sorting out. Instead, the poems exhibit and exploit the contrast between the voice of righteous Roman moralizing and that of compromised iambic reviler, one effect of which is that

Catullus sometimes interrogates the very traditionalism toward which he gestures in his explosions of conventional censoriousness. Interrogates, but hardly rejects. The themes of Catullan social commentary are constructed around the values attending friendship and family: his invective concentrates on violations of trustworthiness – at every level of Roman society. The poet abominates the political enormities of the triumvirs in 55, but this reaction is expressed in the same terms as his repudiation of all those who transgress traditional values in social associations, including Lesbia, who, like Caesar or Gellius, becomes a locus for examining propriety in friendship and in elite authority. The poet often represents himself as vulnerable or marginalized, and although this is to some degree owed to the iambic background of his invective, it recurs frequently and underscores the weighty responsibilities of the nobility. Catullus is, unsurprisingly, a proponent of his own class and of its stake in Roman society: it matters that he configures himself as a municipal equestrian whose condition can be so easily and so severely affected by the personal immorality of the senatorial order. The nobility in fact ultimately failed the Republic, when Caesar and Pompey led the Romans into civil war. And the fullest integration of the Italian with the Roman aristocracy came only in the Republic's false restoration under Augustus, a regime whose moral anxieties and moral reforms are (perhaps unexpectedly) anticipated in the social commentary of Catullus.

GUIDE TO FURTHER READING

Syme (1939), though in many respects dated, emphasizes the emergence of the Italian aristocracy in Roman politics of the late Republic as well as the nobility's political failure during the same period; chapter 11, entitled "Political Catchwords," remains invaluable as an introduction to the Romans' deployment of invective in public life. Richlin (1992) is also a classic: its focus is not limited to humor, and its theoretical sophistication and its explication of the Romans' gendering of invective remain urgent. An important advance on Syme's venerable chapter is Corbeill (1996): he concentrates on Roman rhetoric (esp. Cicero). The context for Catullan invective and social commentary is clarified for modern readers in Wiseman (1985). Three excellent books examine, in admirable detail, various facets of Catullus' social commentary: Nappa (2001), Wray (2001), and Skinner (2003). Each is fundamentally literary in approach: Nappa emphasizes the centrality of social commentary in Catullan poetics, Wray combines anthropological theory with literary theory, and Skinner's reading of Catullus unites aesthetics with a sure grasp of the Roman social scene.

WORKS CITED

Achard, G. 1981. *Pratique rhétorique et idéologie politique dans les discours optimates de Cicéron.* Leiden.

Brunt, P. 1988. *The Fall of the Roman Republic and Related Essays.* Oxford.

Corbeill, A. 1996. *Controlling Laughter: Political Humor in the Late Roman Republic.* Princeton, NJ.

Corbeill, A. 2002. "Ciceronian Invective." In J. May, ed., *Brill's Companion to Cicero: Oratory and Rhetoric.* Leiden. 197–218.

Craig, C. 2004. "Audience Expectations, Invective, and Proof." In J. Powell and J. Patterson, eds., *Cicero the Advocate*. Oxford. 187–214.

Crook, J. 1967. *Law and Life of Rome*. Ithaca, NY.

Earl, D. 1967. *The Moral and Political Tradition of Rome*. London and Ithaca, NY.

Fantuzzi, M., and R. Hunter. 2004. *Tradition and Innovation in Hellenistic Poetry*. Cambridge.

Fitzgerald, W. 1995. *Catullan Provocations: Lyric Poetry and the Drama of Position*. Berkeley, Los Angeles, and London.

Fordyce, C. J., ed., 1961. *Catullus: A Commentary*. Oxford.

Gentili, B. 1988. *Poetry and its Public in Ancient Greece from Homer to the Fifth Century*. Trans. A. T. Cole. Baltimore.

Gleason, M. W. 1995. *Making Men: Sophists and Self-Presentation in Ancient Rome*. Princeton, NJ.

Gotoff, H. 1986. "Cicero's Analysis of the Prosecution Speeches in the *Pro Caelio*: An Exercise in Practical Criticism." *Classical Philology*. 122–32.

Hellegouarc'h, J. 1971 [1963]. *Le Vocabulaire latin des relations et des partis politiques sous la République*. 2nd edn. Paris.

Heyworth, S. J. 2001. "Catullian Iambics, Catullian *Iambi*." In A. Cavarzere, A. Aloni, and A. Barchiesi, eds., *Iambic Ideas: Essays on a Poetic Tradition from Archaic Greece to the Late Roman Empire*. Lanham, MD, Boulder, CT, New York, and Oxford. 117–40.

Jocelyn, H. D. 1999. "The Arrangement and the Language of Catullus' So-Called *polymetra* with Special Reference to the Sequence 10–11–12." In J. N. Adams and R. G. Mayer, eds., *Aspects of the Language of Latin Poetry* = Proceedings of the British Academy 93. Oxford. 335–75.

Kennedy, D. F. 1993. *The Arts of Love: Five Studies in the Discourse of Roman Love Elegy*. Cambridge.

Nappa, C. 2001. *Aspects of Catullus' Social Fiction*. Frankfurt.

Nippel, W. 1995. *Public Order in Ancient Rome*. Cambridge.

Oehler, K. 1961. "Der consensus omnium als Kriterium der Wahrheit in der antiken Philosophie und der Patristik." *Antike und Abendland* 10: 103–29.

Quinn, K. 1972b. *Catullus: An Interpretation*. London.

Richlin, A. 1992 [1983]. *The Garden of Priapus: Sexuality and Aggression in Roman Humor*. Rev. edn. New York and Oxford.

Roller, M. B. 2004. "Exemplarity in Roman Culture: The Cases of Horatius Cocles and Cloelia." *Classical Philology* 99: 1–56.

Selden, D. L. 1992. "*Ceveat lector*: Catullus and the Rhetoric of Performance." In R. Hexter and D. Selden, eds., *Innovations of Antiquity*. New York and London. 461–512.

Skinner, M. B. 1991. "The Dynamics of Catullan Obscenity: cc. 37, 58 and 11." *Syllecta Classica* 3: 1–11.

Skinner, M. B. 2003. *Catullus in Verona: A Reading of the Elegiac* Libellus, *Poems 65–116*. Columbus, OH.

Syme, R. 1939. *The Roman Revolution*. Oxford.

Tatum, W. J. 1993. "Catullus 79: Personal Invective or Political Discourse?" In F. Cairns and M. Heath, eds., *Papers of the Leeds International Latin Seminar* 7. Leeds. 31–45.

Tatum, W. J. 1997. "Friendship, Politics, and Literature in Catullus: Poems 1, 65 and 66, 116." *Classical Quarterly* n.s. 47: 482–500.

Tatum, W. J. 1999. *The Patrician Tribune: Publius Clodius Pulcher*. Chapel Hill, NC.

Tatum, W. J. 2006. "The Final Crisis, 69–49." In N. Rosenstein and R. Morstein-Marx, eds., *A Companion to the Roman Republic*. Oxford. 190–211.

Verboven, K. 2002. *The Economy of Friends: Economic Aspects of* Amicitia *and Patronage in the Late Republic*. Brussels.

Veyne, P. 1983. "La folklore à Rome et les droits de la conscience publique sur la conduite individuelle." *Latomus* 42: 3–30.

Wallace-Hadrill, A. 1988. "The Social Structure of the Roman House." *Papers of the British School at Rome* 56: 43–97.

Watson, L. C. 2003. *A Commentary on Horace's Epodes.* Oxford.

West, M. L. 1974. *Studies in Greek Elegy and Iambus.* Berlin.

Wiseman, T. P. 1985. *Catullus and His World: A Reappraisal.* Cambridge.

Wiseman, T. P. 1987. *Roman Studies Literary and Historical.* Liverpool.

Wiseman, T. P. 1994. "Caesar, Pompey and Rome, 59–50 B.C." In J. A. Crook, A. Lintott, and E. Rawson, eds., *The Cambridge Ancient History.* 2nd edn. Vol. IX. Cambridge. 368–423.

Wray, D. 2001. *Catullus and the Poetics of Roman Manhood.* Cambridge.

PART VI

<u>Reception</u>

CHAPTER NINETEEN

Catullus and Horace

Randall L. B. McNeill

Catullus and Horace are traditionally read together in sequence as the two major practitioners of Latin lyric poetry. For most first-time readers who encounter them in this fashion, it could be said that Catullus appeals primarily to the heart, while Horace appeals more to the mind. Catullus certainly feels more passionate, accessible, and immediate, speaking directly as he does to universal human emotions such as love, hatred, jealousy, and grief. Students frequently fall in love with Catullus for precisely this reason, although some will choose to resist what they regard as his overwrought representations of turbulent but essentially ephemeral bursts of feeling. Only later do both groups begin to appreciate the tightly controlled poetic craft that Catullus uses to produce these seemingly spontaneous expressions of his inner state of mind. Horace, by contrast, strikes his readers as more overtly literary from the start. After some initial struggles with his complicated stanzas and learned allusions, most will eventually become attuned to the sounds, images, and structures of his polished, smoothly flowing verse. Some grow to admire Horace for his subtlety, while others continue to view his poems as being rather too careful and cerebral to be particularly endearing (see, e.g., comments in Shorey 1960; cf. Fraenkel 1957). In either case, students of Horace tend to engage with him on a largely intellectual level, as they explore his skillful poetic treatments of topics in politics, society, moral philosophy, and the classical literary tradition.

As a result, it is not unheard of for beginning readers of Catullus and Horace to champion one or the other fiercely, as if they were being forced to choose between two diametric opposites: some will embrace Catullus for his passionate expression of raw human feeling; others will declare their preference for Horace's cool and elegantly composed lines. Needless to say, the vigilant instructor must stand ready to correct any such false dichotomy by reminding students that Catullus and Horace both deploy virtuosic craftsmanship in the service of intricate and self-conscious poetic expression, and that their many clear differences in style and tone should not be mistaken for some fundamental dissimilarity. Both men, of course, operated in a wide and disparate array of genres and forms (Catullus in lyric, iambic, epigram, love elegy, and the epyllion or "miniature epic," Horace in lyric, iambic, satire, and epistolary verse), so that to consider them solely in terms of their lyric output is to pass over some of their finest compositions and obscure their full artistic versatility and range. As such, it is helpful to approach Catullus and Horace in tandem with an eye to the totality of their poetic corpuses, as a way of discerning more clearly the underlying patterns of their literary interaction with each other. Indeed, many significant connections of genre, language, and theme can be traced between and across their works, underscoring the extent to which Horace should be recognized as having engaged with Catullan literary models throughout his career in a trans-generational poetic dialogue that is noteworthy for its exceptional complexity, richness, and depth.

Origins and Background

Wholly reliable biographical information about Catullus and Horace is somewhat difficult to come by. Nevertheless, a fairly clear picture of their lives can be constructed through an examination of references in their own writings, supplemented by evidence from later sources such as Suetonius (*Iul.* 73; *Vita Hor.*), Apuleius (*Apol.* 10), and Jerome (*Chron.* 150, 154). A fuller discussion of Catullus' life can be found in Marilyn Skinner's "Introduction" to this volume; only a few salient points need be repeated here. As a Roman citizen and provincial aristocrat from the Transpadane city of Verona, Catullus embarked upon at least the preliminary stages of a political career, coming to Rome and subsequently serving from 57 to 56 BC on the staff of C. Memmius, governor of Bithynia for that year. Nothing much came of this, however, and Catullus seems to have spent the remainder of his life as a man of leisure among the Roman elite, mixing socially with political leaders and high-ranking aristocrats including C. Julius Caesar, M. Tullius Cicero, and P. Clodius Pulcher (not to mention Clodia Metelli), as well as rising stars such as the orators M. Caelius Rufus and C. Asinius Pollio, and his friends and fellow poets of the neoteric circle (see, e.g., Hurley 2004; although for Catullus' later years cf. Wiseman 1985).

Horace, who lived from 65 to 8 BC, appears to have led a somewhat more colorful life. By his own account the child of a well-to-do auction agent and former slave from Venusia in Apulia (his father having perhaps been made prisoner in 88 BC at the end of the Social War), he was taken as a boy to receive an elite education in Rome, and later went on to further study in Athens. While there he accepted in 43 BC a commission as a military tribune under M. Brutus, who was then raising a pro-Republican army for the coming war with Octavian and Marc Antony. Following the defeat of Brutus at the battle of Philippi the following year, Horace returned to Rome under Octavian's general amnesty. By 39 BC he had become acquainted with the poets Vergil and Varius, and through them entered the social circle of C. Maecenas, Octavian's close friend and adviser. The friendship and support of Maecenas and Octavian (especially after the latter became the emperor Augustus) enabled Horace to devote the remainder of his life to writing poetry (see, e.g., Armstrong 1989).

While highly disparate, the lives of Catullus and Horace nevertheless generate some interesting connections in terms of their respective personal trajectories. Depending on when the young Horace arrived in Rome, he may have been in the city at the same time as Catullus, who would have died when Horace was around 11 years old. It is also important to note that Horace and Catullus were friends with many of the same people, notably Asinius Pollio, consul in 40 BC but barely out of his teens when Catullus knew him (see Catull. 12; Hor. *Carm.* 2.1), Catullus' fellow Transpadane Quintilius Varus, in his later years a noted legal scholar and literary critic (Catull. 10, 22; Hor. *Carm.* 1.24 and *Ars P.* 438–44), and Alfenus Varus, also a well-known jurist and a Transpadane, and suffect consul in 39 BC (Catull. 30; Hor. *Sat.* 1.3.130 and *Carm.* 1.18). (For those poems in which only the name "Varus" is given, scholars have variously identified the individual in question as Quintilius or Alfenus; in any event the available evidence supports the establishment of a link between both Varuses and our two poets, who would have known these men some fifteen years apart.) Lastly, Catullus and Horace both demonstrate a lingering awareness of their specifically Italian roots, as manifested for example in the expression of a certain self-conscious and almost defensive pride in their home districts (see, e.g., Catull. 39; Hor. *Carm.* 3.30). It could perhaps be argued that this regional consciousness was bolstered by the fact that both men hailed from distant corners of Italy but now were moving in the most exclusive circles of elite Roman society. Certainly Catullus and Horace appear at times to betray a certain ambivalence or sense of critical detachment regarding their lives among the powerful elite of the Roman metropolis, although their reasons for this ambivalence will have been very different (Wiseman 1985; Lyne 1995).

Connections of Meter

In the famous closing poem to *Odes* 1–3, Horace proudly predicts that he will receive undying acclaim as the first person to have adapted Greek lyric forms into Latin:

> crescam laude recens, dum Capitolium
> scandet cum tacita uirgine pontifex.
> dicar, qua uiolens obstrepit Aufidus
> et qua pauper aquae Daunus agrestium
> regnauit populorum, ex humili potens
> princeps Aeolium carmen ad Italos
> deduxisse modos.

I will flourish, ever fresh in my glory, for as long as the priest climbs the Roman Capitoline with the silent Vestal by his side. In Apulia, where the rushing Aufidus thunders and where Daunus, poor in water, once ruled over his peasant subjects, I will be spoken of: I, once a nobody, now a great man. I, the first one to have brought the Aeolian song into Italian strains. (Hor. *Carm.* 3.30.8–14; edition Wickham)

In delivering this ringing statement in his final lines, Horace effectively encompasses all the poems in the collection, rendering *Odes* 3.30 as the *sphragis* or signature poem to his *monumentum aere perennius* ("monument more lasting than bronze," 30.1). And indeed *Odes* 1–3 represented a stunning *tour de force* when it was published in 23 BC. Carefully arranged into three books, the work comprised 88 poems in 13 Greek lyric meters, the majority of them never attempted in Latin before. Such was the magnitude of Horace's achievement that most of these meters were never tried again, apart from the ones that appear in his own fourth book of *Odes* (ca. 12 BC) and a few scattered experiments by authors in later generations (notably Stat. *Silv.* 4.5 and 4.7).

However, Horace's outright claim to be "the first" is problematic. Catullus, after all, had written poems in a number of Greek lyric meters some thirty years before, and had adapted at least some of these into Latin for the first time. Horace, of course, knew this full well, as becomes clear when we examine the full range of meters used by the two poets across their complete range of works.

Table 19.1 reveals several intriguing elements of contrast and comparison. First, Horace worked in nearly twice as many meters as Catullus over the course of his career: 20 as compared with 12. Both Catullus and Horace seem to have tried out

Table 19. 1

Meter	Used by Catullus	Used by Horace	Used by both
Alcaic strophe		*Carm.* 1.9, 16, 17, 26, 29, 31, 34, 35, 37; 2.1, 3, 5, 7, 9, 11, 13, 14, 15, 17, 19, 20; 3.1–6, 17, 21, 23, 26, 29; 4.4, 9, 14, 15	
Alcmanic strophe		*Carm.* 1.7, 28; *Epod.* 12	
1st Archilochian		*Carm.* 4.7	
2nd Archilochian		*Epod.* 13	
3rd Archilochian		*Epod.* 11	
4th Archilochian		*Carm.* 1.4	
1st asclepiadean		*Carm.* 1.1; 3.30; 4.8	
2nd asclepiadean		*Carm.* 1.3, 13, 19, 36; 3.9, 15, 19, 24, 25, 28; 4.1, 3	
3rd asclepiadean		*Carm.* 1.6, 15, 24, 33; 2.12; 3.10, 16; 4.5, 12	
4th asclepiadean		*Carm.* 1.5, 14, 21, 23; 3.7, 13; 4.13	
Greater asclepiadean			Catull. 30; Hor. *Carm.* 1.11, 18; 4.10
Choliambic	8, 22, 31, 37, 39, 44, 59, 60		

(Continued)

Table 19. 1 (*Continued*)

Meter	Used by Catullus	Used by Horace	Used by both
Dactylic hexameter			Catull. 62, 64; Hor. *Satires, Epistles, Ars Poetica*
Elegiac couplets	65–116		
Galliambic	63		
Glyconic/Pherecratean	34, 61		
Hendecasyllabic	1–10, 12–16, 21, 23, 24, 26–8, 32, 33, 35, 36, 38, 40–3, 45–50, 53–8		
Iambic senarius	4, 29		
Iambic strophe		*Epod.* 1–10	
Iambic tetrameter catalectic	25		
Iambic trimeter			Catull. 52; Hor. *Epod.* 17
Ionic a minore		*Carm.* 3.12	
Priapean	17		
1st pythiambic		*Epod.* 14, 15	
2nd pythiambic		*Epod.* 16	
Sapphic strophe			Catull. 11, 51; Hor. *Carm.* 1.2, 10, 12, 20, 22, 25, 30, 32, 38; 2.2, 4, 6, 8, 10, 16; 3.8, 11, 14, 18, 20, 22, 27; 4.2, 6, 11; *Carm. Saec.*
2nd Sapphic strophe		*Carm.* 1.8	
Trochaic strophe		*Carm.* 2.18	

certain meters as one-time experiments, albeit in different proportions (9 of 20 for Horace, 5 of 12 for Catullus). Above all, it is striking that very little overlap occurs between the two poets. Horace never employs Catullus' most frequently used metrical forms (the hendecasyllabic and the elegiac couplet), while his own primary lyric meter (the Alcaic strophe) appears nowhere in the Catullan corpus.

Nevertheless, in three instances Horace returns to meters that Catullus had used before (leaving aside the dactylic hexameter in Catullus 62 and 64 and Horace's *Satires* and *Epistles*): the iambic trimeter, closely associated with Archilochus, in Catullus 52 and Horace *Epodes* 17; the greater asclepiadean, an Aeolic meter used by Sappho and Alcaeus, in Catullus 30 and Horace *Odes* 1.11, 1.18, and 4.10; and the Sapphic, famously used by Catullus in 11 and 51, and Horace's second favorite choice, appearing 25 times in the *Odes* as well as in the *Carmen Saeculare*. Out of the three, Horace's use of the Sapphic meter is the most intriguing, since his handling of it frequently suggests not only a full appreciation for the original Greek model, but also a careful assessment of Catullus' earlier innovations in adapting it. For example, in c. 51 Catullus uses the Sapphic's fourth line adonic as an evocative if sometimes ungrammatical distillation of the sentiment of each stanza (cf. Sappho 31, although a similar technique is perhaps identifiable in Sappho 1.4, 8, 20, and 28):

> Ille mi par esse deo uidetur,
> ille, si fas est, superare diuos,
> qui sedens aduersus identidem te
>   spectat et audit
>
> dulce ridentem, misero quod omnis
> eripit sensus mihi: nam simul te,
> Lesbia, aspexi, nihil est super mi
>   <uocis in ore>
>
> lingua sed torpet, tenuis sub artus
> flamma demanat, sonitu suopte
> tintinant aures, gemina teguntur
>   lumina nocte.

That man seems to me to be equal to a god. He seems (if I may say so) to surpass the gods, who sits across from you and again and again watches and hears you laughing sweetly – the very thing that tears all the senses from me in my suffering. For as soon as I have caught sight of you, Lesbia, there is nothing left of my voice on my lips, my tongue goes numb, a thin flame runs down under my limbs, my ears ring with their own sound, and covered with a double night are my eyes. (Catull. 51.1–12; edition Thomson)

Horace appears to follow Catullus' example in several of his Sapphic poems, as here in these individual stanzas from *Odes* 1.2:

> Iam satis terris niuis atque dirae
> grandinis misit Pater et rubente
> dextera sacras iaculatus arces
>   terruit urbem...
>
> audiet ciuis acuisse ferrum
> quo graues Persae melius perirent,
> audiet pugnas uitio parentum
>   rara iuuentus....
>
> ...siue mutata iuuenem figura
> ales in terris imitaris almae
> filius Maiae patiens uocari
>   Caesaris ultor.

The Father has already sent enough snow and awful hail down upon the earth, and striking the sacred citadels with his red hand has terrified the city...They will hear of battles, how citizens sharpened swords that should have been used against the harsh Persians. Because of their parents' crimes they will be a sparse generation....Or if perhaps with changed form you might assume the guise of a young man, winged son of kindly Maia, and allow yourself to be called avenger of Caesar. (Hor. *Carm.* 1.2.1–4, 21–4, and 41–4)

It would appear, then, that Horace was at least partly responding to Catullus' earlier recognition of the potential that lay within the Sapphic stanza for the creation of novel poetic expressions in Latin.

In any case, the overlap of Catullus and Horace in the use of specific Greek lyric forms is clear and undeniable. What, then, are we to make of Horace's claim in *Odes* 3.30 to be *princeps deduxisse Aeolium carmen*? "Aeolian song" refers to the poetry of Sappho as well as Alcaeus, and it cannot be the case that Horace is thinking here solely of his compositions in Alcaic strophes, especially since the influence of Sappho as well as Catullus can be detected throughout the *Odes* (Woodman 2002). It has been proposed that Horace may have felt justified in ignoring Catullus' earlier Sapphic poems because there were only two of them (Nisbet and Rudd 2004), or even that Catullus didn't think of himself as a lyric poet and therefore required no recognition (Mendell 1935), but these suggestions are in themselves troubling; the attendant implication is that 11 and 51 somehow "don't count," whereas they clearly stand forth as masterful poetic creations in their own right. At first glance, Horace's apparent refusal to point to Catullus openly as his generic and stylistic forerunner appears to confront us with something of a problem. The solution to this mystery will depend upon further examination of some of the deeper currents of their literary relationship.

Connections of Language and Phrasing

Although Horace never formally cites Catullus as a literary predecessor or source of poetic influence, direct and open echoes of Catullan language and poetic themes can be found throughout the Horatian corpus. As such, Horace is best understood not as glossing over the existence of his formal connections to Catullus, so much as indirectly alluding to these connections in tangential and self-conscious acknowledgment of the complicated bonds of influence and imitation that exist between them.

In *Epistles* 1.19 (published in 20 BC), Horace again declares that he was the first to render a number of Greek poetic forms into Latin:

> libera per uacuum posui uestigia princeps,
> non aliena meo pressi pede. qui sibi fidet
> dux reget examen. Parios ego primus iambos
> ostendi Latio, numeros animosque secutus
> Archilochi, non res et agentia uerba Lycamben....
> hunc ego, non alio dictum primus ore, Latinus
> uulgaui fidicen.

I was the first to lay down free tracks in an empty territory. I didn't walk in anyone else's footsteps. Whoever trusts in himself will be the boss and lead the crowd. I was the first to show the iambics of Paros to Latium. I copied the rhythms and style of Archilochus, not the subjects or the words that harassed Lycambes.... I, the Latin lyric poet, was the first to circulate Alcaeus, who had never been spoken by anyone else before. (Hor. *Ep.* 1.19.21–5, 32–3)

Here Horace reasserts his primacy as a virtual pioneer of literary exploration, while simultaneously offering a more nuanced picture of his poetic innovations.

He alludes to his groundbreaking achievements in both iambic and lyric, but is careful now to delineate more specifically the ways in which these genres can be regarded as "his." Thus, he emphasizes that he has adapted the iambic meter and overall tone of Archilochus but altered the subject matter and the phrasing; similarly, he declares himself the first to bring Alcaeus into Latin, but carefully avoids any extension of this statement to cover Sappho (making instead a pointedly respectful yet distancing reference to Sappho herself in *Ep.* 1.19.28). In this way, the passage comes across as something of a subtle revision of the sweeping claims he advanced in *Odes* 3.30: Horace now refocuses our attention onto Alcaeus, with whom he is able to establish a clear proprietary link; by the same token, he carefully hedges his discussion of Archilochus by limiting the discussion to matters of meter and tone.

Even so, the question of Catullan precedent remains. Catullus had of course written extensively in iambic as well as lyric, as we have seen. In addition, and more importantly, a careful examination of the Horatian corpus reveals a wide array of direct quotations of and allusions to individual poems of Catullus. Following are several representative instances where Horace quotes specific words and phrases of Catullus, often in markedly similar poetic contexts (in addition to these, we observe also the close interplay of Catull. 51 and Hor. *Carm.* 1.13, to which we will return below). In each case Horace demonstrates considerable sophistication and skill in his handling of the source material, managing on several occasions to compress Catullus' phrasing while retaining the essence of the poetic sentiment being expressed.

1   In *Epodes* 14, Horace alludes to Catullus 68 in a conscious evocation of the earlier poem's representation of an elegiac lover's complaint about his faithless mistress:

> ...me libertina neque uno
> contenta Phryne macerat.

> I am tortured by Phryne the freedwoman, nor is she satisfied with me alone.
> (Hor. *Epod.* 14.15–16)

> ...quae tamen etsi uno non est contenta Catullo

> Even though she is not satisfied with Catullus alone.
> (Catull. 68.135)

2   In *Epodes* 17, Horace quotes three different poems of Catullus within the span of five lines:

> ...siue mendaci lyra
> uoles sonari, tu pudica, tu proba,
> perambulabis astra sidus aureum.
> infamis Helenae Castor offensus uice
> fraterque magni Castoris

> ...Or if you want to be praised with a lying lyre, you are chaste, you are decent, you will stroll around the stars as a golden constellation. Angered by the fate of notorious Helen, Castor and great Castor's brother (Hor. *Epod.* 17.39–43)

pudica et proba, redde codicillos
Chaste and decent girl, give back the tablets
(Catull. 42.24)

perambulabit omnium cubilia
will he stroll around everyone's beds?
(Catull. 29.7)

gemelle Castor et gemelle Castoris
twin Castor and Castor's twin
(Catull. 4.27)

3   Catullus 11 clearly made a considerable impression on Horace, who quotes the poem in directly relevant contexts on three different occasions. In *Odes* 1.22, as part of a geographical catalogue, Horace's phrasing is highly reminiscent of Catullus' imagery and diction (for an earlier example of markedly similar phrasing, see Horace *Epodes* 1.1–10, with its further potential allusions to Catullus 51 and 16 in the use of the terms *otium* in line 7 and *molles viri* in line 10):

> siue per Syrtis iter aestuosas
> siue per facturus per inhospitalem
> Caucasum uel quae loca fabulosus
>   lambit Hydaspes

Whether preparing to travel through the sweltering Syrtes, or through the inhospitable Caucasus, or places washed by the fabled Hydaspes
(Hor. *Carm.* 1.22.5–8)

> siue in extremos penetrabit Indos . . .
> siue quae septemgeminus colorat
>   aequora Nilus

Whether he will venture into furthest India . . . or where the seven-mouthed Nile colors the sea (Catull. 11.2, 7–8)

In *Odes* 2.6, Horace includes echoes of Catullus' geographical expansiveness and exoticism, although here the tone is friendly rather than bitterly sardonic as in the Catullan original:

> Septimi, Gadis aditure mecum et
> Cantabrum indoctum iuga ferre nostra et
> barbaras Syrtis, ubi Maura semper
>   aestuat unda

Septimius, ready to go with me to visit Cadiz, and the Cantabrian who hasn't learned to bear our yoke, and the barbaric Syrtes, where the Moorish wave is always surging (Hor. *Carm.* 2.6.1–4)

> Furi et Aureli, comites Catulli,
> siue in extremos penetrabit Indos,
> litus ut longe resonante Eoa
>   tunditur unda

Furius and Aurelius, companions of Catullus, whether he will venture into furthest India, where the far-echoing shore is struck by the wave of Dawn (Catull. 11.1–4)

A large number of individual words and phrases in *Odes* 3.27 seem consciously designed to evoke Catullus 11's atmosphere of anguish and regret. Compare

> memor nostri, Galatea, uiuas
>
> may you live in memory of us, Galatea
> (Hor. *Carm.* 3.27.14)

with

> cum suis uiuat ualeatque moechis
>
> may she live and be happy with her lovers;
> (Catull. 11.17)

and

> rumpat et serpens iter institutum
>
> may a serpent break the journey begun
> (Hor. *Carm.* 3.27.5)

with

> ilia rumpens
>
> breaking their pelvises;
> (Catull. 11.20)

and again

> sentiant motus orientis Austri et
> aequoris nigri fremitum et trementis
> uerbere ripas
>
> may they feel the movement of rising Auster, and the roar of the black sea, and the shore trembling with the blow (Hor. *Carm.* 3.27.22–4)

with

> litus ut longe resonante Eoa
> tunditur unda
>
> where the far-echoing shore is struck by the wave of Dawn; (Catull. 11.3–4)

and, finally,

> nuper in pratis studiosa florum . . .
> carpere flores

recently in the meadows, absorbed in the flowers ... to pluck the flowers (Hor. *Carm.* 3.27.29 and 44)

with

> cecidit uelut prati
> ultimi flos

has fallen like a flower at the edge of the meadow. (Catull. 11.22–3)

4 In *Odes* 1.21, Horace establishes a close similarity of phrasing to Catullus 34 in a parallel invocation of the goddess Diana.

> Dianam tenerae dicite uirgines,
> intonsum, pueri, dicite Cynthium
> Latonamque supremo
> dilectam penitus Ioui

Sing of Diana, tender maidens, sing of unshorn Apollo, boys, and Latona who was loved deeply by all-powerful Jove. (Hor. *Carm.* 1.21.1–4)

These lines echo:

> Dianae sumus in fide
> puellae et pueri integri
> <Dianam pueri integri>
> puellaeque canamus.
>
> O Latonia, maximi
> magna progenies Iouis

We are under the protection of Diana, we girls and unmarried boys. Unmarried boys and girls, let us sing of Diana. O Latonia, great offspring of greatest Jove. (Catull. 34.1–6)

Horace establishes another such connection in *Odes* 3.22:

> Montium custos nemorumque, Virgo,
> quae laborantis utero puellas
> ter uolata audis adimisque leto,
> diua triformis

Oh guardian of the mountains and groves, Maiden, you who hear the young women in labor when they call upon you three times, and rescue them from death, the triple goddess (Hor. *Carm.* 3.22.1–4)

> montium domina ut fores
> siluarumque uirentium ...
>
> tu Lucina dolentibus
> Iuno dicta puerperis,
> tu potens Triuia et notho es
> dicta lumine Luna.

so that you might be the mistress of the mountains and the green woods, ... You are called Juno Lucina by women suffering in childbirth, you are called the powerful triple goddess, and Luna because of your false light. (Catull. 34.9–10, 13–16)

It should be noted that apart from a few instances of simple quotation, in most cases Catullus' original phrases and images have been adapted into notably similar contexts, such that they effectively reinforce and enrich the message of their Horatian analogues. The Catullan language of Horace's hymns places them firmly and explicitly within a tradition of Latin choral lyric, thereby enhancing their air of ritual solemnity. *Epodes* 17 takes on an extra dash of mordant wit by echoing Catullus' inversion of *moecha putida* to *pudica et proba* in c. 42, a poem that offers similar reflections on the mutability and unreliability of verse. The cloying sentiments of *Odes* 1.22 become more ambiguous and problematic (and therefore more intriguing) when one recalls that Catullus uses the exact same phrasing in c. 11 to introduce a portrait not of demure and virtuous love, but of bitterness and heartbreak. Ultimately, the array of references is too extensive, their parallels of construction and context too close, the effects of their placement too significant for this to be a matter of pure coincidence of poetic vocabulary. Rather, we can see that Horace consciously deploys Catullan references in his verse as a simultaneous act of homage and transformation of the older poet's work. He does so without explicitly citing Catullus as a model, counting instead on his readers to recognize and appreciate the sophistication of his literary allusions.

Connections of Subject and Theme

Other direct connections between individual poems of Catullus and Horace are based more generally upon the shared exploration of topics that are typical of iambic and lyric poetry. These include drinking songs and epigrams (e.g., Catull. 27; Hor. *Epod.* 13 and *Carm.* 1.9, 1.11, 1.18, 1.27, 1.38), expressions of love and erotic desire (e.g., Catull. 5, 7, 32, 86, 107; Hor. *Epod.* 15 and *Carm.* 1.19, 2.4), propemptica (e.g., Catull. 46; Hor. *Carm.* 1.3, 1.29, 3.27), return poems (e.g., Catull. 9, 31; Hor. *Carm.* 1.36, 2.7, 3.14), dialogues (Catull. 45; Hor. *Carm.* 3.9), poems of consolation (Catull. 96; e.g., Hor. *Carm.* 1.24), offerings (Catull. 101; Hor. *Carm.* 3.13), anecdotes (e.g., Catull. 10, 17, 56; Hor. *Epod.* 3, 5, and elements of *Carm.* 1.37, 3.5, 3.8), attacks (e.g., Catull. 16, 21, 25, 33, and the Gellius and Mamurra cycles, 74, 80, 88–91, 116, and 29, 41, 43, 57, 94, 105, 114, 115; cf. Hor. *Epod.* 8, 12, and *Carm.* 1.25, 4.13), and hymns (e.g., Catull. 34, 61, 62; Hor. *Carm.* 1.10, 1.21, 1.35, 2.19, 3.18, 3.22, 4.6, and *Carm. Saec.*).

Expanding the field of reference even farther, Horace frequently establishes wide-ranging connections to Catullus' poems across meters and genres alike; direct quotations and allusions are interlaced with subtle adaptations or overarching references to Catullan scenarios, sentiments, and themes. For example, Horace deftly works echoes of two very different Catullan poems into the lines of *Odes* 4.7, in such a way as to forge a striking juxtaposition between the eternal cycle of the natural seasons and the pathetic brevity of human life. Compare

frigora mitescunt Zephyris, ver proterit aestas

Frosts are softened by the west wind, Summer crushes the Spring (*Carm.* 4.7.9) with

> Iam ver egelidos refert tepores,
> iam caeli furor aequinoctialis
> iucundis Zephyri silescit aureis

Now the Spring brings back unchilled warmth, now the fury of the equinox sky grows quiet on the gentle breezes of the west wind (Catull. 46.1–3)

and

> cum semel occideris et de te splendida Minos
>   fecerit arbitria,
> non, Torquate, genus, non te facundia, non te
>   restituet pietas

Once you have died and Minos has rendered his distinguished judgment in your case, Torquatus, neither your lineage nor your eloquence nor your devotion to duty will bring you back (*Carm.* 4.7.21–4)

with

> nobis cum semel occidit breuis lux,
> nox est perpetua una dormienda.

Once our brief light has set, we must sleep through one long unending night. (Catull. 5.5–6)

Comparable manifestations of this transmetrical and transgeneric technique can be found at *Odes* 3.27 (with marked similarities in the lament of Europa to that of Ariadne in Catullus 64; see Lowrie 1997); *Satires* 1.3 and 1.4 (with their themes of universal but mostly harmless human failings and Callimachean literary criticism, both of which are explored together in Catullus 22); and *Satires* 1.9 (with widely noted connections to Catullus 10, especially in terms of the depiction of casual "street" encounters that serve as important mechanisms of social interaction and performance; see, e.g., Skinner 1989).

Finally, as the above examples from the *Satires* demonstrate, fertile points of contact abound between Horace and Catullus in terms of their respective depictions of themselves as characters in their poetry. Horace undertakes a highly conscious and sophisticated program of self-presentation across his literary compositions, deploying in his works a wide variety of self-images that are carefully tailored to specific social situations as well as to the rhetorical and thematic requirements of his verse (see, e.g., Oliensis 1998). Recent scholarship has shown that Catullus too engages in careful control and manipulation of his self-image, and that many of his poems serve as crucial venues for the portrayal and execution of meaningful acts of public social performance (see, e.g., Wray 2001; Krostenko 2001a).

As a result, despite significant differences in Catullus' and Horace's overall techniques of self-presentation, certain commonalities can be identified between them, further underscoring the extent to which Horace remains keenly aware of Catullus as a valuable thematic literary model in a variety of circumstances throughout his literary career. For instance, Horace follows Catullus (as Catullus follows

Sappho) in depicting the sensation of being in love as a series of physical symptoms, as he observes himself in the act of observing his beloved (Hor. *Carm.* 1.13.3–8; Catull. 51.7–12; cf. Sappho 31.5–14). Horace, like Catullus, experiments with lyrical adaptations of the conventions of love elegy in order to present himself in the guise of an unsuccessful lover – complaining miserably about his mistress' disdain (e.g., Catull. 60; Hor. *Carm.* 3.10.16–20), fretting over her faithlessness (e.g., Catull. 70; Hor. *Carm.* 2.8), or sadly contemplating the aftermath of a failed love affair (Catull. 8; Hor. *Carm.* 3.26). In a similar vein, each poet employs from time to time the tactic of artful self-deprecation as a means of winning over the sympathies of his audience or reinforcing its sense of affection for him. Thus Catullus presents himself at various points as being flustered and embarrassed when caught in a clumsy white lie (Catull. 10.24–34), comically poverty-stricken (Catull. 13.7–8), cheated and "screwed over" by a superior (Catull. 28.9–10), and ludicrously aroused after a good lunch (Catull. 32.10–11). Horace, meanwhile, offers self-portraits in which he imagines himself bleary-eyed and stood up by a prostitute (*Sat.* 1.5.30–1, 49, 81–5), beset by indigestion and practical jokes (*Epod.* 3.15–18), chasing hopelessly after a nymphet (*Carm.* 1.23), or farcically scampering out of a mistress' house when her husband comes home unexpectedly and the dogs start barking (*Sat.* 1.2.127–33).

As part of their self-representation within the context of established social relationships, Catullus and Horace alike place a special emphasis on the importance of reliability and friendship. It should be noted, however, that the two poets' depictions of their friendship differ in certain essential particulars. Catullus presents himself as moving within a wide circle of friends, acquaintances, and rivals, whose relationships and levels of intimacy with the poet are constantly shifting and must regularly be renegotiated (see Wray 2001; Nappa 2001). Horace, by contrast, focuses primarily on the careful depiction of a single relationship: his close yet highly complicated friendship with Maecenas, his patron and benefactor (see Bowditch 2001). Both Catullus and Horace address the issue of loyalty and trust in friendships, albeit in markedly different ways (Catullus dwells upon the emotional costs of betrayal, while Horace emphasizes the duties and obligations of *amici*; cf. Catull. 30, 73; Hor. *Sat.* 1.6 and *Ep.* 1.7). Teasing and practical jokes are acceptable among friends (e.g., Catull. 6, 14; Hor. *Epod.* 3), but can be greeted with disdain if attempted by outsiders or others who are for some reason deemed socially unacceptable (e.g., Catull. 12).

Nor indeed is friendship the only feature of social interaction to which Catullus and Horace turn their attention; the theme of social exclusion is nearly as frequent in the work of both poets. Catullus tends to mock the bumptious habits of upstarts and recent arrivals to Rome, while Horace focuses more upon social climbers eagerly trying to gain access to Maecenas and Octavian (see, e.g., Catull. 12, 22, 23, 25, 39, 84; Hor. *Sat.* 1.9, 2.8). Both poets tend to dwell with some satisfaction on the pleasant sensations of being on the inside of an exclusive social circle, Horace with somewhat more ambivalence (Catull. 12; Hor. *Sat.* 1.5, 2.6).

Points of Contrast

As this last observation suggests, there are of course many instances where Horace departs from the models provided by Catullus' work, or otherwise follows a slightly different path in his interpretation, execution, or emphasis of particular poetic themes. These points of divergence can be regarded as constituting further Horatian responses to the Catullan model, carefully tailored to the different social and political circumstances in which the later poet found himself.

In terms of their respective realizations of the lyric form, it could be said that Horace demonstrates a somewhat tighter control over its rhythms and sounds in the *Odes* than Catullus does in his poems. This is suggested, for instance, by the fact that Horace only rarely resorts to the elision or enjambment of individual words in order to fit them into each line, whereas Catullus frequently elides his words, and shows himself to be more willing to spread a single word across two lines of text (Horace *Odes* and Catullus *passim*; although cf., e.g., Hor. *Carm.* 1.2.19–20; Catull. 11.11–12). As a result, it is a commonplace to say that Horace's *Odes* exhibit an unmatched degree of polish and care, with not a single word out of place; many of Catullus' poems are traditionally regarded more as literary experiments, innovative but not always entirely successful. By the same token, however, it must be acknowledged that Horace's comparatively tidier construction of individual lines surely owes something to Catullus' earlier efforts in this regard.

Thematically, Horace manifests a greater interest in evocative descriptions of the natural world, combining sound and image to establish vivid pictures of the settings in which his poems take place. To take two famous examples, *Odes* 1.9 elicits in the reader an almost visceral appreciation for the silence and cold of a winter landscape:

> Vides ut alta stet niue candidum
> Soracte, nec iam sustineant onus
> siluae laborantes, geluque
> flumina constiterint acuto

You see how Mount Soracte stands gleaming in deep snow. The weighted woods no longer bear their burden, and the rivers stand still in the sharp frost (Hor. *Carm.* 1.9.1–4)

while *Odes* 3.13 conveys something of the music and movement of a bubbling forest spring:

> fies nobilium tu quoque fontium,
> me dicente cauis impositam ilicem
> saxis, unde loquaces
> lymphae desiliunt tuae.

You too will become one of the celebrated springs, when I sing of the oak tree above the hollow rocks from which your chattering waters leap down. (Hor. *Carm.* 3.13.13–16)

Catullus' natural settings, by contrast, tend to be delineated in more allusive and artificial terms, distancing the reader somewhat from the scene:

> ubi iste post phaselus antea fuit
> comata silua; nam Cytorio in iugo
> loquente saepe sibilum edidit coma.

Where that latter-day ship was formerly a long-haired forest; often, on the Cytorian ridge, it whispered with speaking hair. (Catull. 4.10–12)

On the other hand, in other respects it is Horace who contrives to leave his readers on the outside of things, restricting their role (as well as his own) to that of relatively detached observers, whereas Catullus more typically collapses the points of view of reader and poet into a single, intimate, and inwardly directed perspective that he presents as his (cf., e.g., *Carm.* 1.5; Catull. 8). This is reflected also in the way in which the two poets develop similar initial premises in very different directions: Catullus takes his personal experiences as a starting point for the exploration of peculiar yet wholly plausible psychological and emotional states (as in cc. 72 and 75, where Lesbia's unreliability has led Catullus to love her more, but like her less); Horace treats his experiences as pretexts for the expression of generalized philosophical or aesthetic sentiments (as in *Carm.* 2.13, where an accident involving a falling tree branch prompts reflections on the abiding power and appeal of poetry).

As a further reflection of this difference in emphasis, both poets provide ostensibly personal and autobiographical details in support of their broader poetic self-images. Catullus creates the impression of doing so almost spontaneously, as though poetry simply happened to be the medium through which he has chosen to express his true feelings and negotiate his actual personal relationships (see, e.g., c. 50 and especially c. 101, which is deeply moving precisely because it seems so naked and unguarded in its expression of grief). Horace, by contrast, engages in apparent autobiographical revelation as part of a more explicitly literary exercise, devoting entire poems to the artful, guarded, and self-consciously planned representation of his life, and purposely conjuring specific details in such a way as to call into question the basic veracity of the overall picture (e.g., in *Sat.* 1.4, 1.5, 1.6; see McNeill 2001).

Within these larger programs of seemingly personal revelation, the city of Rome itself fulfills slightly different functions in the works of the two poets. For Catullus, Rome plays an almost entirely negative role, suggestive perhaps of his alienation from the moral values of the city (Wiseman 1985). In his poems the capital becomes a place of low depravity, its streetscapes the setting for expressions of contempt and despair (e.g., c. 37 and especially c. 58), whereas his country estate at Sirmio is celebrated entirely on its own merits, with Rome wholly absent and Bithynia explicitly rejected (c. 31). While Horace seems on occasion to echo these sentiments (famously in *Carm.* 3.29.11–12: *omitte mirari beatae/fumum et opes strepitumque Romae*, "cease to marvel at the smoke and riches and noise of blessed Rome"), he also routinely frames his praise of the countryside and of his Sabine villa as constituting an indirect admission of the extent to which Rome represents the true focus of his attention, the source of his innermost anxieties as well as his greatest joys. In so doing, he openly acknowledges that he loves being closely associated with those in power in Rome; his avowed preference for the country imperfectly masks his real desire to be back in the city with them (*Sat.* 2.6.50–117; 2.7.28–35).

These different ways in which the two poets portray Rome, its atmosphere and preoccupations, are themselves suggestive of the very different social and political worlds in which they lived. In the late Republican Rome of Catullus' day, members of the elite could group themselves around a comparatively wide array of leading individuals as they competed for personal advancement – or, like Catullus, choose not to align themselves at all. By the mid-30s BC, however (and certainly by the Battle of Actium in 31 BC and the first constitutional settlement in 29 BC), one's chances for prominence in Rome were determined largely by one's closeness to Octavian/ Augustus and his associates, whose centralized network of patronage and control now sat atop the entire apparatus of Roman government. Men like Horace could enter the highest social and political circles by being invited or summoned inside (*Sat.* 1.6.52–62), only to serve subsequently as both adherents and gatekeepers of the new regime, a role that itself generated new personal anxieties. Horace's poetic gestures of friendship thus take on a political as well as a social resonance, in contrast to those of Catullus: a reference to his friend Pollio's literary compositions becomes a veiled warning of political danger; another friend's long-anticipated return prompts complicated reflections on the poet's past role in the civil wars (cf. Hor. *Carm.* 2.1 and Catull. 95; Hor. *Carm.* 2.7 and Catull. 9; cf. also Hor. *Epod.* 9 and Catull. 9). When Catullus dismisses Caesar in c. 93, he proclaims his freedom to adopt an attitude of indifference to the political affairs of his day; when Horace invites Maecenas to take a rest from all his cares in *Odes* 3.29.25–33, he obliquely celebrates his friend's indispensability as a key overseer of Rome's security. In these respective roles as urbane outsider and canny insider, both poets are very much representative of their times.

Horatian Silence and Horatian Response

These aforementioned points of dissimilarity represent a further point of contact between the poetry of Catullus and Horace. In light of the variegated array of links, allusions, and commonalities between their works, it seems indisputable that Catullus must be recognized as a hugely important model for Horace's poetic compositions, every bit as important for him as Lucilius in satire, Archilochus in iambic, or Pindar and Alcaeus in lyric. Even so, there remains a troubling discrepancy in Horace's declaration that he was "first" in Latin lyric; quite simply, the presence of Catullus throughout Horace's poetry makes this claim untenable. Later generations celebrated Catullus for his achievements in lyric, to the point that even Greek critics accepted him as being a match for Sappho and Anacreon (Gell. *NA* 19.9.7, although cf. Quint. *Inst.* 10.96). But Horace never openly acknowledges his relationship to his literary predecessor, much less his artistic debt to him. As a result, although Catullus clearly wields an influence upon many aspects of Horace's poetic composition, he remains virtually invisible as a figure in Horace's depicted world of poets and poetry.

Horace's refusal to give open recognition to Catullus as his predecessor in lyric and iambic has left many readers and scholars feeling somewhat uneasy (this despite the fact that Catullus himself does not mention any of his Greek models other than Callimachus). It is certainly true that the many connections that we have thus far identified between Catullus and Horace serve to cast this anomaly into sharper relief. Some may therefore be tempted to conclude that Horace is doing something almost underhanded in proclaiming himself "first to have brought the Aeolian song into Italian strains," thereby passing over Catullus in silence as though subjecting him to a kind of poetic *damnatio memoriae*. As we have seen, the most commonly suggested defense against this charge is that Horace somehow felt himself justified in ignoring Catullus (see above, also Ross 1969). Such a response, however, simply begs the question. Likewise, it is possible that Horace did not wish to draw all that much overt attention to his own artistic indebtedness to Catullus. Horace was a competitively minded artist, after all, and one who took enormous pride in his skill as a poet. As such, Catullus would have represented an awkward complication to his drive for poetic immortality as the "first in Latin lyric." Rather than embark upon an inter-generational literary rivalry (such as he had undertaken in his critique of Lucilius in *Sat.* 1.4, 1.10, 2.1), perhaps Horace simply decided not to raise the issue. Yet this still leaves the problem of *Odes* 3.30, *Epistles* 1.19, and the question of who was "first."

Instead, it could be argued that Horace's direct quotations, imitations, and other allusions to Catullus constituted in themselves a sufficient honor to the older poet, even in the absence of any formal words of acknowledgment. One important passage remains to be considered; indeed, it is here that the best solution to the silence of Horace can be found. Horace does in fact refer to Catullus by name once in his literary corpus, in *Satires* 1.10. While expressing his approval of the style of the playwrights of Greek Old Comedy, Horace makes an off-handed and contemptuous reference to some of the hack scribblers of his own day:

> hoc stabant, hoc sunt imitandi: quos neque pulcher
> Hermogenes umquam legit, neque simius iste
> nil praeter Caluum et doctus cantare Catullum.

That's how they did it – that's the way to do it. But pretty-boy Hermogenes has never read any of them, nor has that stupid ape who only knows how to recite Calvus and Catullus. (Hor. *Sat.* 1.10.17–19)

It is important to remember, of course, that Horace is not directing this crack at Calvus and Catullus themselves. His complaint is with their slavish imitators – low-grade poets who can only repeat and rehash the same tired old stuff. Even so, this hardly seems very complimentary to the two *neoteroi*. We detect an underlying note of scorn in these lines, a certain implicit expression of disdain for Calvus and Catullus as mass-market crowd-pleasers of the sort that vulgarians such as Hermogenes and his simian friend would be likely to admire. Just about the only positive thing that could be said for Catullus here is that he has apparently become a literary icon in Rome – an established literary model to which later poets necessarily have to respond, whether with adulation or contempt.

And yet, it is precisely at this point that a third interpretation of Horace's silence about Catullus finally becomes available, paradoxically at the very moment when Horace seems to dismiss Catullus as being unworthy of his attention. After all, he is expressing his loathing for so-called poets who have no wit or creativity, and cannot respond to the great poets of the past by generating new works of their own. Calvus and Catullus are merely a pretext for Horace's assertion of this literary-critical position. In other words, Horace can be seen here to be confirming the same artistic principle that guides his reception of Catullus throughout his career. For Horace, worthwhile poetic endeavor depends upon close engagement with those who came before: it manifests itself in careful study of their works, skillful adaptation of their materials, and creative transformation of their models into new literary creations. This in turn represents the true path to innovation and originality as a Roman poet, and is in effect the way in which one becomes "first" (G. Williams 1985; Oliensis 1998). Catullus doesn't want slavish imitators, Horace seems to be saying; later poets must engage with him not as blind worshippers but as participants in a great, ongoing conversation. Horace's silence can thus perhaps be interpreted in a positive light, provided that we recognize his Catullan allusions as acts of respectful literary adaptation and homage. In this sense, Horace's masterful reception of Catullus' poetry constitutes in itself the greatest form of recognition that it was in his power to give.

GUIDE TO FURTHER READING

Direct comparative analyses of Catullus and Horace have become somewhat infrequent in recent decades, but Putnam (2006), which appeared as this volume was going to press, renews our appreciation for their literary relationship by offering a sensitive investigation of Catullus' influence upon Horace's lyric poetry. Woodman (2002) also offers an excellent examination of the interplay of Catullus, Horace, and Sappho. Among the older book-length studies of the two poets taken together, Lyne (1980) is more literary, T. Frank (1928) heavily biographical. Hurley (2004) provides a very good general introduction to Catullus; Armstrong (1989) does the same for Horace. For the lyric and iambic meters see West (1982). For issues of originality and imitation, G. Williams (1985) is fundamental.

On the poetry of Catullus, Fitzgerald (1995) and Wray (2001) are useful for discussion of issues of self-presentation, social performance, and language; see also Selden (1992). Wiseman (1985) offers stimulating discussion of Catullus' life, background, and views. Among the commentaries in English, Thomson (1997) is popular, while Fordyce (1961) and Quinn (1973a) continue to be useful; for those who know German, Syndikus (1984, 1987, 1990) is excellent.

For Horace, Oliensis (1998) is important and influential; Fraenkel (1957) continues to be valuable. See also Davis (1991) and Lowrie (1997) for lyric; Rudd (1966) and Freudenburg (1993) for satire. Articles in Woodman and West (1984), Harrison (1995), and Woodman and Feeney (2002) together provide a good sense of the course of Horatian studies since the early 1980s. On Horace and his relationship with Maecenas, see Bowditch (2001). Lyne (1995) offers interesting ideas on Horace and the Augustan regime. For commentaries on the works discussed here: *Odes* 1–2, Nisbet and Hubbard (1970, 1978); *Odes* 3, Nisbet and Rudd (2004); *Odes* 4, Putnam (1986); *Epodes*, L. C. Watson (2003); *Satires* 1, Brown (1993); *Satires* 2, Muecke (1993); *Epistles* 1, Mayer (1994).

WORKS CITED

Armstrong, D. 1989. *Horace*. New Haven, CT.
Bowditch, P. L. 2001. *Horace and the Gift Economy of Patronage*. Berkeley.
Brown, P. M. 1993. *Horace: Satires I*. Warminster.
Davis, G. 1991. *Polyhymnia: The Rhetoric of Horatian Literary Discourse*. Berkeley.
Fitzgerald, W. 1995. *Catullan Provocations: Lyric Poetry and the Drama of Position*. Berkeley, Los Angeles, and London.
Fordyce, C. J., ed. 1961. *Catullus: A Commentary*. Oxford.
Fraenkel, E. 1957. *Horace*. Oxford.

Frank, T. 1928. *Catullus and Horace*. Oxford.

Freudenburg, K. 1993. *The Walking Muse*. Princeton, NJ.

Harrison, S. J., ed. 1995. *Homage to Horace*. Oxford.

Hurley, A. K. 2004. *Catullus*. London.

Krostenko, B. A. 2001a. *Cicero, Catullus, and the Language of Social Performance*. Chicago and London.

Lowrie, M. 1997. *Horace's Narrative Odes*. Oxford.

Lyne, R. O. A. M. 1980. *The Latin Love Poets from Catullus to Horace*. Oxford.

Lyne, R. O. A. M. 1995. *Horace: Behind the Public Poetry*. New Haven, CT.

Mayer, R. G. 1994. *Horace: Epistles, Book I*. Cambridge.

McNeill, R. L. B. 2001. *Horace: Image, Identity, and Audience*. Baltimore.

Mendell, C. W. 1935. "Catullan Echoes in the *Odes* of Horace." *Classical Philology* 30: 289–301.

Muecke, F., ed. 1993. *Horace* Satires II. Warminster.

Nappa, C. 2001. *Aspects of Catullus' Social Fiction*. Frankfurt.

Nisbet, R. G. M., and M. Hubbard. 1970. *A Commentary on Horace's Odes: Book I*. Oxford.

Nisbet, R. G. M., and M. Hubbard. 1978. *A Commentary on Horace's Odes: Book II*. Oxford.

Nisbet, R. G. M., and N. Rudd. 2004. *A Commentary on Horace's Odes: Book III*. Oxford.

Oliensis, E. 1998. *Horace and the Rhetoric of Authority*. Cambridge.

Putnam, M. C. J. 1986. *Artifices of Eternity*. Berkeley.

Putnam, M. C. J. 2006. *Poetic Interplay: Catullus and Horace*. Princeton, NJ.

Quinn, K., ed. 1973a. *Catullus: The Poems*. 2nd edn. London and Basingstoke.

Ross, D. O., Jr. 1969. *Style and Tradition in Catullus*. Cambridge, MA.

Rudd, N. 1982. *The Satires of Horace*. Berkeley.

Selden, D. L. 1992. "*Ceveat lector*: Catullus and the Rhetoric of Performance." In R. Hexter and D. Selden, eds., *Innovations of Antiquity*. New York and London. 461–512.

Shorey, P. 1960. *Horace: Odes and Epodes*. Chicago.

Skinner, M. B. 1989. "*Ut decuit cinaediorem*: Power, Gender, and Urbanity in Catullus 10." *Helios* 16: 7–23.

Syndikus, H. P. 1984. *Catull: Eine Interpretation. Erster Teil: Einleitung, Die kleinen Gedichte (1–60)*. Darmstadt.

Syndikus, H. P. 1987. *Catull: Eine Interpretation. Dritter Teil: Die Epigramme (69–116)*. Darmstadt.

Syndikus, H. P. 1990. *Catull: Eine Interpretation. Zweiter Teil: Die grossen Gedichte (61–68)*. Darmstadt.

Thomson, D. F. S., ed. 1997. *Catullus, Edited with a Textual and Interpretative Commentary*. Toronto.

Watson, L. C. 2003. *A Commentary on Horace's Epodes*. Oxford.

West, M. L. 1982. *Greek Metre*. Oxford.

Williams, G. 1985 [1968]. *Tradition and Originality in Roman Poetry*. 2nd edn. Oxford.

Wiseman, T. P. 1985. *Catullus and His World: A Reappraisal*. Cambridge.

Woodman, T. 2002. "*Biformis vates*: The *Odes*, Catullus and Greek Lyric." In Woodman and Feeney (2002: 54–64).

Woodman, T., and D. Feeney, eds. 2002. *Traditions and Contexts in the Poetry of Horace*. Cambridge.

Woodman, T., and D. West, eds. 1984. *Poetry and Politics in the Age of Augustus*. Cambridge.

Wray, D. 2001. *Catullus and the Poetics of Roman Manhood*. Cambridge.

CHAPTER TWENTY

Catullus and Vergil

Christopher Nappa

Readers since antiquity have recognized the frequent and extensive presence of Catullan intertexts in the works of Vergil. While many scholars have confined themselves to cataloguing and analyzing individual allusions, only a few have tried to articulate greater debts to Catullus' worldview or overarching themes.[1] Despite suggestions that Catullus does not play an especially great role in Vergil's works (e.g., Wigodsky 1972: 126–31, 139), it is clear that Vergil knew Catullus' poetry and knew it well. Vergil makes use of phrases, techniques, and themes found throughout Catullus' poems, but he seems to have focused on a small group of Catullan texts: poems 11, 61–8, and 101.[2] This group (especially 11, 64, and 101), however, is extremely influential. In what follows, I will survey each of Vergil's works with attention to these texts, pointing, when possible, to other Catullan texts that play a role in Vergilian poetry. Instead of trying to supply a complete and detailed catalogue of Vergilian references to Catullus, I will examine some of the more extensive and unambiguous points of contact while trying, in general terms, to describe "Vergil's Catullus."

Eclogues

One of the Vergilian texts in which an extensive Catullan presence is felt is the fourth, "Messianic," eclogue.[3] In vatic tones, this poem describes the new Golden Age to be inaugurated by the birth of an unnamed infant. It draws extensively on Catullus 64, both for its picture of a heroic age and for the song of the Fates that prophesies the dubious glories of the yet unborn Achilles. Since readings of *Eclogue* 4 often deal extensively with the role played by Catullus 64, I will not try to catalogue or summarize them all here; instead, I will focus on the larger picture that emerges from surveying the relationship between the two poems.[4]

Wilkinson (1969: 45) points out that the later poem shows a striking rhythm that is more characteristic of Catullus' hexameter than Vergil's. This switch in rhythm from

Eclogues 1–3 constitutes a musical echo that alerts the audience that Catullus' most famous hexameter work will be a presence in Vergil's poem.

Catullus' words can be heard as well as his rhythm:

> non rastros patietur humus, non uinea falcem,
> robustus quoque iam tauris iuga soluet arator.

The ground will endure no rakes, the vine-stands no sickle – now the strong plowman will even remove the yokes from the oxen. (*Ecl.* 4.40–1)

These lines recall and compress Catullus'

> rura colit nemo, mollescunt colla iuuencis,
> non humilis curuis purgatur uinea rastris,
> non glebam prono conuellit uomere taurus,
> non falx attenuat frondatorum arboris umbram,
> squalida desertis rubigo infertur aratris.

No one cultivates the fields – the bullocks' necks grow soft. The humble vine-stand is not pruned with curved rakes; the bull does not break up the clod of earth with downturned plowshare; the sickle does not thin the foliage of the leafy tree: rust makes its way onto abandoned plows. (Catull. 64.38–42)

Just as striking is Vergil's vatic

> "Talia saecla" suis dixerunt "currite" fusis
> concordes stabili fatorum numine Parcae

"Run on ages such as these!" said the Parcae to their shuttles, of one mind in the firm divinity of fate (*Ecl.* 4.46–7)

which recalls two separate parts of Catullus' song of the Parcae:

> haec tum clarisona uellentes uellera uoce
> talia diuino fuderunt carmine fata

Plucking at the fleeces, they then poured forth in clear voice such fates as these in their divine song

(Catull. 64.320–1)

and

> sed uos, quae fata sequuntur,
> currite ducentes subtegmina, currite, fusi.

"Run on, shuttles that draw the threads that the fates follow! Run on!" (Catull. 64.326–7)

Like Vergil's lines, Catullus 64.327 becomes a refrain; indeed, Vergil's song is virtually the same length (60 lines) as Catullus' song of the Parcae. But verbal parallels are not the only signs of direct influence. Catullus 64 famously depicts both a lost age of heroes and a corrupt present; *Eclogue* 4 announces the arrival of a new Golden Age. In Catullus' poem, the transition from the idealized past to the poet's present begins in the age of heroes, and the Fates' description of Achilles' exploits makes clear that the heroic age is closer to the present. Catullus 64 is set against a backdrop of heroic mythology: first Peleus and the Argonauts, then Theseus, and finally the Trojan War. Vergil's poem also makes use of the Argonaut myth and the Trojan War – and it does so precisely to define a transitional period, like Catullus' age of heroes, between the poet's present and the new Golden Age:

> pauca tamen suberunt priscae uestigia fraudis,
> quae temptare Thetim ratibus, quae cingere muris
> oppida, quae iubeant telluri infindere sulcos.
> alter erit tum Tiphys et altera quae uehat Argo
> delectos heroas; erunt etiam altera bella
> atque iterum ad Troiam magnus mittetur Achilles.

Nevertheless a few signs of the original deceit will surface, signs that bid us to try Thetis with boats, to gird our towns with walls, to cut furrows in the earth. Then there will be another Tiphys and another *Argo* to transport chosen heroes. There will be other wars, and again great Achilles will be sent to Troy. (*Ecl.* 4.31–6)

The last lines of *Eclogue* 4 suggest Catullus in two ways.

> incipe, parue puer, risu cognoscere matrem
> (matri longa decem tulerunt fastidia menses)
> incipe, parue puer: qui non risere parenti,
> nec deus hunc mensa, dea nec dignata cubili est.

Begin, little boy, to acknowledge your mother with a smile (for ten months brought your mother long discomfort). Begin, little boy. For neither has a god felt it worth sharing a table with those who have not smiled at their parent nor a goddess her bed. (*Ecl.* 4.60–3)

First, the passage evokes several lines of Catullus' wedding-song for Torquatus, in which the poet wishes that the couple's future son will smile at his mother:

> Torquatus uolo paruulus
> matris e gremio suae
> porrigens teneras manus
> dulce rideat ad patrem
> semihiante labello.

I wish for a dear little Torquatus, stretching his tender hands from his mother's lap, to smile sweetly at his father with his half-open mouth. (Catull. 61.209–13)

There is a sweetness in the image of a baby smiling at his parents, but context matters. In Catullus 61, these lines are followed by an explanation: the child is being watched for proof of paternity (Hubbard 1998: 84). Moreover, the passage also hearkens back to poem 64, with its heroic age in which gods and human beings intermingle. The references to a god's table or goddess's bed are not idle: one of the features of Catullus' fallen world is precisely that there is no longer mixing, social or sexual, between gods and mortals (64.407–8). The glorious child of *Eclogue* 4 is supposed to remedy that divide, yet the ending of the poem gives room for doubt. What if the child does not smile or is not found to be legitimate?

Most studies of the Vergilian poem suggest that it incorporates Catullus' vision in order to recast it in some more positive form (recently Van Sickle 1992: 37–64; Arnold 1994; Lefèvre 2000b; Marinčič 2001). Catullus' Achilles is the savage slayer of Trojans, his Golden Age a foil for the corrupt present. Vergil's Golden Age is in the future rather than in the past, his *Wunderkind* a savior rather than a destroyer. Yet Vergil's poem can be read as having a darker side of its own (e.g., Putnam 1970: 164–5; Petrini 1997: 111–21). Hubbard (1998: 83–6) sees a great deal of potential irony in *Eclogue* 4; in particular, he argues that the Catullan intertexts in the eclogue draw on the irony or negative associations present in their original contexts to call the later poem's optimism into doubt. One might also wonder whether line 5, in which the return of the Golden Age is seen to be part of a cycle, suggests that the miraculous child will end the cycle forever, leaving the world in eternal peace. May it not also hint that the prophesied Golden Age will once again yield to the darkness with which Catullus 64 ends?

Georgics

While less frequent than those in the *Eclogues* and *Aeneid*, there are several Catullan reminiscences in the *Georgics*; only a few indicative allusions will be treated here.[5]

At *Georgics* 1.203 a memorable simile describes a man who is swept downstream in his boat when he relaxes his arms for an instant:

> atque illum in praeceps prono rapit alueus amni.
>
> And the boat whisks him away headlong down the river.

This passage can be seen as a kind of leitmotif for a major theme of the *Georgics*: unstinting effort is necessary even to maintain the status quo, since life is in essence rowing against the current. The image resonates elsewhere in the poem, most famously when Orpheus glances behind him for an instant only to see his beloved Eurydice whisked back down into the underworld. Vergil takes his line from a particularly tender simile in Catullus 65. A young girl drops an apple, a secret love gift, which she has been hiding in the folds of her gown:

> atque illud prono praeceps agitur decursu
>
> and it rolls out headlong in a downward path
>
> (Catull. 65.23)

Catullus' image may seem an unusual model for Vergil's, but the two situations share at least one important feature. In Catullus' poem the girl has been hiding a gift from a lover. Her mother's arrival prompts an accidental revelation, and the apple that falls from the girl's gown comes to signify the girl's inevitable emergence into woman-hood. The revelation of the apple is thus also an inadvertent acknowledgement of a fact of life. In Vergil, the simile of the man in the boat reveals a no less inevitable fact of life, stripping the tenderness from the Catullan version and revealing the hard truth behind his gentle image.

More telling perhaps is *Georgics* 2.510, *gaudent perfusi sanguine fratrum* ("they rejoice, drenched in the blood of their brothers"). This clearly echoes Catullus 64.399, *perfudere manus fraterno sanguine fratres* ("brothers drenched their hands in a brother's blood"). Catullus is describing the corrupt men of his day in contrast with men of the distant past. Vergil is describing urbanites who lack the peace of mind he attributes to honest country folk, who recall the Golden Age and among whom (2.473–4) Justice dwelt longest before leaving the earth at the end of that age. This fact recalls the Catullan context: in the line preceding the one Vergil has closely imitated, we find *iustitiamque omnes cupida de mente fugarunt* (Catull. 64.398), "and they all routed justice from their greedy minds." Again Catullus 64's denunciation of the present becomes for Vergil a touchstone in his own attempt to understand the truth about the Golden Age and contemporary civilization.[6]

The most extensive example of Catullan influence on the *Georgics* is the story of Aristaeus with its inset narrative about Orpheus and Eurydice. Crabbe (1977) has demonstrated that this epyllion is closely connected to Catullus 64 both in specific verbal echoes and in structure, and others have also asserted a strong connection between Catullus 64 and the Vergilian epyllion (Wilkinson 1969: 115–16; Perutelli 1980; Jenkyns 1998: 304–7). Like Catullus 64, Vergil's epyllion consists of an outer frame and inner narrative, and Crabbe argues that verbal reminiscences link Vergil's outer frame (Aristaeus' quest for knowledge about his bees) with Catullus' frame (the wedding of Peleus and Thetis) while Vergil's inset (the story of Orpheus and Eurydice) contains echoes of Catullus' inner narrative (Theseus and Ariadne). Farrell (1991: 104–13) has discussed the ways in which Vergil's Aristaeus narrative adapts material from the *Iliad*; the Iliadic material in question is Achilles' appeal to his mother Thetis. Thus Crabbe's assertion that the Aristaeus narrative echoes the Peleus and Thetis sections of Catullus 64 gains support, since even when Aristaeus' speeches do not echo Catullus directly, they still draw on the major characters in Catullus 64's outer narrative.

Aeneid

Catullan intertexts are important throughout the *Aeneid* in ways both expected and surprising. Because Vergil's allusions to Catullus are often quite complex in the *Aeneid*, I will depart from my practice above of organizing discussion around the Vergilian text. Instead of trying to capture the complicated conflation of references in individual books of the epic, I will examine the role played by individual Catullan poems throughout the *Aeneid*.

Before looking at the principal Catullan poems (64, 66, 11, and 101) that play a role in Vergil's epic, I want to discuss an allusion to a different poem. At *Aeneid* 2.746, Aeneas asks *aut quid in euersa uidi crudelius urbe?* ("or what crueler thing have I seen in the overthrown city?"). His question recalls Catullus 62.24, *quid faciunt hostes capta crudelius urbe?* ("What crueler thing does the enemy do in a captured city?"). In Catullus' poem, a chorus of girls sings of their anxieties over marriage. Their captive city is purely hypothetical, its capture a metaphor for their view of marriage, whether we take them to be sincere in this view or simply pretending out of a kind of conventional decorum. The city Aeneas asks about was no metaphor and its destruction was very real. Catullus' hypothetical question has been turned into part of the *Aeneid*'s reality. Moreover, the specific context of Aeneas' remark, the referent of *quid crudelius*, is the loss of his wife Creusa during the escape from Troy – thus Vergil reverses the meaning of Catullus' passage (Wigodsky 1972: 127).[7]

Catullus 64

In what follows, I will focus on Vergil's use of Catullus 64 in the story of Aeneas and Dido, but Vergil draws on it elsewhere in the *Aeneid* too. Critics have, for example, often discussed the relationship between Catullus 64 and Vergil's descriptions of the *lusus Troiae* in Book 5 and the pictures on the temple doors at Cumae in Book 6, especially Vergil's adaptation of Catullus' *inobseruabilis error* (64.115) as *inremeabilis error* at 5.591 (Petrini 1997: 96–9) and *inextricabilis error* at 6.27 (Wigodsky 1972: 129–30; Putnam 1998: 13–15). Moreover, it has been suggested that the structure of Catullus' epyllion influenced Vergil's construction of episodes throughout the *Aeneid* (Mendell 1951).

To begin with, the wedding feast of Peleus and Thetis is set in a splendid palace:

> ipsius at sedes, quacumque opulenta recessit
> regia, fulgenti splendent <u>auro</u> atque <u>argento</u>.
> candet ebur soliis, collucent pocula mensae,
> tota <u>domus</u> gaudet <u>regali splendida gaza</u>.

But his [Peleus'] house, as far back as the luxurious palace extended, blazes with shining gold and silver. Ivory gleams on the chairs, cups glisten on the tables: the whole house rejoices, splendid with royal jewelry. (Catull. 64.43–6)

In *Aeneid* 1 Dido holds a feast for Aeneas, at which she hears of his adventures and falls in love. It recalls the wedding feast in Catullus:

> at <u>domus</u> interior <u>regali splendida luxu</u>
> instruitur, mediisque parant conuiuia tectis:
> arte laboratae uestes ostroque superbo,
> ingens <u>argentum</u> mensis, caelataque in <u>auro</u>
> fortia facta patrum, series longissima rerum
> per tot ducta uiros antiqua ab origine gentis.

But, within, the house is prepared, splendid with royal opulence, and they set up the banquet in the middle of the building, cloths worked with skill and proud purple, abundant silver on the tables, and, chased in gold, the brave deeds of ancestors, a very long array of accomplishments drawn down through so many generations of men from the ancient origin of the race. (*Aen.* 1.637–42)

The verbal reminiscences between *Aen.* 1.637 and Catullus 64.46 are especially notable, but both scenes also emphasize the gold and silver placed on the tables.

The gold and silver vessels on Dido's tables tell stories of her ancestors and the heroes of her people's past. There are also "cloths worked with skill and proud purple" that are described immediately before these silver and gold vessels. Catullus' passage goes on to describe another item at the wedding feast of Peleus and Thetis, a coverlet decorated with a story of its own:

> haec uestis priscis hominum uariata figuris
> heroum mira uirtutes indicat arte.
> 　　　　　　　　(Catull. 64.50–1)

> This cloth, elaborated with the ancient images of human beings, declares the excellent deeds of heroes with wondrous skill.

Thus Dido's feast is inaugurated not only by reminders of Peleus' and Thetis' wedding but specifically by a reference to Catullus' story of Ariadne and Theseus, to which the story of Dido and Aeneas will often hearken back.

Catullus' Ariadne is evoked at the very beginning of *Aeneid* 4, as Dido feels the effects of Cupid's spell:

> At regina graui iamdudum <u>saucia cura</u>
> uulnus alit uenis et caeco carpitur igni.
> <u>multa</u> uiri uirtus <u>animo multusque</u> recursat
> gentis honos.

> But the queen, long wounded by harsh cares, nurtures the wound in her veins and is seized by the hidden fire. The man's abundant courage and the abundant prestige of his lineage kept running through her mind. (*Aen.* 4.1–4)

The passion that has been nurtured in Dido still makes her concentrate on the *uirtus* of Aeneas himself and the status of his lineage. These lines recall the end of Ariadne's tragedy:

> quae tum prospectans cedentem maesta carinam
> <u>multiplices animo</u> uoluebat <u>saucia curas</u>.

> Then, sad, watching the ship grow distant, she turned over manifold cares in her mind, wounded. (Catull. 64.250–1)

Catullus' passage is more compressed. Ariadne is watching Theseus leave; she has already lamented her fate, reproached him, and cursed him.[8] The *multiplices curas* that she turns over in her mind are what is left of the more positive views she once held. Dido, by contrast, is still preoccupied by her rosy image of Aeneas. More importantly, Dido has not yet begun her affair with Aeneas, and, for her, the worst is yet to come, for the allusion to Catullus here suggests that Aeneas too will leave. In the lines immediately following in Catullus' poem, moreover, Bacchus comes on the scene and rescues Ariadne. The impossibility of such a savior, of course, is one of the defining aspects of Dido's story (*pace* Ferguson 1971–2: 31, who sees Sychaeus as the equivalent of Bacchus).

There is another recollection of Ariadne's lament at *Aeneid* 4.20–3:

> "Anna (fatebor enim) miseri post fata Sychaei
> coniugis et sparsos fraterna caede penatis
> solus hic inflexit sensus animumque labantem
> impulit."

"Anna (for I will confess it), after the death of poor Sychaeus, my husband, and after our house was spattered with bloodshed wrought by my brother, only he [Aeneas] has overcome my senses and overwhelmed my faltering mind."

These lines recall

> "an patris auxilium sperem? quemne ipsa reliqui
> respersum iuuenem fraterna caede secuta?
> coniugis an fido consoler memet amore?"

"Or am I to hope for my father's help, whom I myself abandoned when I followed this young man bespattered with my brother's blood? Or am I to comfort myself with the faithful love of a husband?" (Catull. 64.180–2)

For all the differences between the two passages and the two situations, they are linked in a number of ways. Both use a perfect participle of *spargo* in connection with *fraterna caede*, and both indicate the loss or absence of a husband: Dido indicates that her husband Sychaeus is already dead and Ariadne, with a certain sarcasm, admits to having none. Contrast is important too: Ariadne has lost the possibility of help from her family and of a normal married life because she has followed a young man, whereas Dido fled her homeland following no one.

Particularly striking are the similarities between Ariadne's speech to the departing Theseus and numerous phrases used by Dido in reproaching Aeneas.

> "dissimulare etiam sperasti, perfide, tantum
> posse nefas tacitusque mea decedere terra?
> nec te noster amor nec te data dextera quondam
> nec moritura tenet crudeli funere Dido?
> quin etiam hiberno moliri sidere classem
> et mediis properas Aquilonibus ire per altum,
> crudelis?"

"Did you even hope, traitor, that you could commit so great an outrage and leave my land in silence? And does our love not hold you, nor the pledge you once gave, nor Dido who will die a cruel death? No – are you even hurrying to ready your fleet under the winter sky and to cross the deep amid winter winds, cruel man?" (*Aen.* 4.305–11)

Her words here have long been felt to recall the beginning of Ariadne's great speech.

> "sicine me patriis auectam, perfide, ab aris,
> perfide, deserto liquisti in litore, Theseu?
> sicine discedens neglecto numine diuum,
> immemor a! deuota domum periuria portas?
> nullane res potuit crudelis flectere mentis

> consilium? tibi nulla fuit clementia praesto,
> immite ut nostri uellet miserescere pectus?
> at non haec quondam blanda promissa dedisti
> uoce mihi, non haec miserae sperare iubebas,
> sed conubia laeta, sed optatos hymenaeos.''

"Is this, traitor, how, after I sailed away from my ancestral altars, traitor!, you've abandoned me on an empty shore, Theseus? Is this how, in departing, the gods' power forgotten, you carry your accursed lies back home – ah! thoughtless man? Could nothing change the intention of your cruel mind? Have you no mercy that your hard heart might pity me? But these are not the things that you once promised me with your wheedling voice; you bid poor me to expect not this, but instead a happy marriage and longed-for wedding-songs." (Catull. 64.132–41)

The parallels here are obvious: the use of *perfide* in the opening of each woman's first speech to the departing lover, the similar concern with the fact that neither compassion nor promises made can turn the man in question away from his course, and finally the use of *crudelis* (Catull. 64.136; *Aen.* 4.311) to characterize each man.

Ariadne's words above also color Dido's speech a few lines later, for Dido's *per conubia nostra, per inceptos hymenaeos* (4.316) directly echoes Ariadne's *sed conubia laeta, sed optatos hymenaeos* (64.141). Ariadne uses the phrase to remind Theseus of what he promised as opposed to what he delivered; she knows now that she will not get these things after all. Dido, however, believes that she already has them; thus she swears by them. Here the change from Catullus' *optatos* ("desired") to Vergil's *inceptos* ("undertaken") is revealing. It is as though Dido has almost escaped the Catullan model, had almost been an Ariadne who was not abandoned by Theseus, only to realize that she also cannot count on *conubia* or *hymenaeos*.[9]

In Dido's next speech, she reproaches Aeneas for his coldness in terms that again recall Ariadne's denunciation of Theseus:

> "nec tibi diua parens generis nec Dardanus auctor,
> perfide, sed duris genuit te cautibus horrens
> Caucasus Hyrcanaeque admorunt ubera tigres.''

"And a goddess is not mother of your race nor Dardanus its father, traitor, but the bristling Caucasus bore you amid hard cliffs, and Hyrcanian tigers gave you their teats." (*Aen.* 4.365–7)

> "quaenam te genuit sola sub rupe leaena,
> quod mare conceptum spumantibus exspuit undis,
> quae Syrtis, quae Scylla rapax, quae uasta Charybdis?''

"What lioness bore you under a lonely cliff? What sea conceived you and spit you up from its frothy waves? What Syrtes, what rapacious Scylla, what vast Charybdis?" (Catull. 64.154–6)

The accusation that an unfeeling or cruel person was born of inhuman parents in a desolate wasteland goes back to Homer and occurs in Greek tragedy and Hellenistic poetry before Catullus, who uses it twice (cf. Catull. 60). While these passages may not seem to share many verbal echoes, the language of Catullus 64.154–6 shows up elsewhere in the *Aeneid*, especially Juno's chilling adaptation of 64.156 at *Aeneid* 7.302–3: *quid Syrtes aut Scylla mihi, quid uasta Charybdis/profuit?* ("What good have they done me, the Syrtes, or Scylla, or vast Charybdis?").

Ariadne plays a role in Dido's death scene too, where she echoes Ariadne's unfulfillable wish:

> "felix, heu nimium felix, si <u>litora</u> tantum
> numquam <u>Dardaniae tetigissent</u> nostra <u>carinae</u>."

"Happy, alas too happy, if only the Dardanian ships had never touched our shores." (*Aen.* 4.657–8)

> "utinam ne tempore primo
> Cnosia <u>Cecropiae tetigissent litora puppes</u>."

"If only in the beginning Cecropian ships had not touched Cretan shores." (Catull. 64.171–2)

Because both Ariadne and Dido see themselves as abandoned by cruel men, it makes sense for Vergil to use the words of the one in crafting the other. Contrast is just as important as similarity: Ariadne suffers at the hands of Theseus and curses him, but a god comes on the scene and saves her. By evoking Ariadne in the characterization and speech of Dido, Vergil points up the contrast that ultimately overwhelms any similarity between the two women: Ariadne has a savior; Dido does not.

Vergil also uses Catullus 64 to characterize Aeneas (Abel 1962; Zarker 1967; Putnam 1995–6: 85; J. Wills 1996: 28–30). Theseus' relationship with Ariadne is opportunistic and cruel. Yet, like Aeneas, he has a mission that cannot easily be dismissed as selfish or frivolous. Nor does Theseus return home to enjoy his victory, for Ariadne's curse has robbed him of his father, activating and turning against him his own *negligentia*, his tendency to forget what is important.[10] Dido's curse against Aeneas operates over a longer period of time, but when he arrives in his new homeland to refight the wars that he has been trying to escape, his own nature, perhaps, is one of the obstacles he faces. Finally, there is contrast here too, since Aeneas repeatedly protests his unwillingness in the face of his inevitable departure; he even requires divine intervention before he actually prepares to depart. Catullus' Theseus shows no reluctance in leaving either Crete or Ariadne. Some scholars (Abel 1962; Zarker 1967) have tried to show that Vergil uses Theseus as a kind of foil for Aeneas, who, they assert, is ultimately a positive figure whereas Catullus' Theseus is not. Yet, as Putnam (1995–6: 85) has seen, there are problems with these positive assessments. In particular, Zarker, looking at the Theseus references in Book 6, argues that Aeneas only resembles Theseus when the Athenian hero does truly heroic things and thus that Theseus' less creditable adventures show Aeneas' moral superiority. But Zarker does not consider Book 4, in which Aeneas clearly plays the role of Theseus during his least attractive exploit, the abandonment of the woman who sacrificed everything for him.

Catullus 66

Poem 66, Catullus' adaptation of Callimachus' *Lock of Berenice*, also plays an important role in the *Aeneid*. Like poem 64, it shows up in a number of different books and contexts, the most famous of which is also the most controversial: at *Aeneid* 6.460, Aeneas has come upon Dido in the underworld and tries one last time to explain himself.

> "inuitus, regina, tuo de litore cessi."

> "Unwilling, my queen, did I leave your shore."

This line is a clear, close echo of Catullus 66.39, spoken by a severed lock of hair:

> "inuita, o regina, tuo de uertice cessi."

> "Unwilling, my queen, did I leave your head."

A number of readings have been advanced to explain this apparently bizarre allusion: how could Vergil make Aeneas, during one of the most poignant moments of the *Aeneid*, speak words that evoke a *funny* poem of Catullus?[11] Some have suggested that the resemblance is either purely coincidental or a phrase that Vergil used without remembering the context (e.g., O'Sullivan 1993). In fact, the passage has become a kind of test case for the way intertextuality is now studied.[12] No interpretation is likely to satisfy everyone, but the alternative – to say that there is no meaning where we do not easily understand the meaning – is an obvious cop-out, especially in this case, since Vergil shows more than passing familiarity with Catullus 66 elsewhere in the Dido story.

Recent scholarship has found a great deal of relevance in the allusion and has done much to dispel the idea that the resemblance between *Aeneid* 6.460 must be either coincidental or absurd. More nuanced and less comic readings of Catullus 66 have allowed some of the dissonance seemingly created by Vergil's quotation to dissipate (J. Tatum 1984: 443; J. Wills 1998: 88–91); indeed, Catullus 66 has serious themes which are not irrelevant to the *Aeneid*. In particular, the separation from and reunion with husbands is central to both Catullus' poem and Vergil's story of Dido (Johnston 1987). Furthermore, Vergil's allusion to the *Coma* activates a system of correspondences and contrasts between Dido and three other relevant Hellenistic queens: Berenice, Arsinoë, and Cleopatra (Johnston 1987). Important too is the way the reference helps to characterize Aeneas (J. Tatum 1984: 440–4; R. A. Smith 1993). The *Coma Berenices* underwent catasterism just as Aeneas is prophesied to do. By citing the words of the lock among the stars, Aeneas reminds us, if not himself, that his fate is catasterism, apotheosis, and glory in the heavens, whereas Dido's is loss, shame, and resentment below the earth.

Moreover, several scholars have shown that the very obvious reference at *Aeneid* 6.460 to the nearly identical line at Catullus 66.39 is itself part of a larger, systematic pattern of allusions to Catullus 66 (J. Tatum 1984: 440–4; R. A. Smith 1993; J. Wills 1998: 292–302). Wills identifies this pattern as what he calls a "divided allusion," a practice he sees as particularly Vergilian: in essence, Vergil looks back to a model text or passage at multiple points in his poem, but the whole model is represented only by all of these allusive passages taken together. Vergil alludes to Catullus 66.39–41 in three different parts of the *Aeneid* (*Aen.* 4.491–2, 6.458–60, 12.807–18) and we can only really see the point of the allusion once we have had a chance to connect the three passages, along with a nexus of associations that connects them within the poem. Wills suggests, then, that as we read through the *Aeneid*, we reassemble the three lines of Catullus 66 (39–41). Thus, near the end of the poem, we finally have access to the whole network of associations that Vergil found in Catullus 66: the unwilling departures of Aeneas from Carthage and of Juno from the Italian battlefield spell, initially, the deaths of Dido and Turnus and, ultimately, both the catasterism of Aeneas and Juno's return to the gods.

Catullus 11

Allusions to Catullus 11 occur several times in the *Aeneid*, and Putnam (1995–6: 86–93) has traced an extensive pattern in Vergil's use of this text similar to that J. Wills (1998) discusses for other Catullan poems. Let us consider first the opening 12 verses of poem 11.

> Furi et Aureli, comites Catulli,
> siue in extremos penetrabit Indos,
> litus ut longe resonante Eoa
>   tunditur unda,
>
> siue in Hyrcanos Arabesue molles,
> seu Sagas sagittiferosue Parthos,
> siue quae septemgeminus colorat
>   aequora Nilus,
>
> siue trans altas gradietur Alpes,
> Caesaris uisens monimenta magni,
> Gallicum Rhenum horribile aequor ulti-
>   mosque Britannos

Furius and Aurelius, companions of Catullus, whether he will get all the way to the most remote Indians, where the shore is pounded by Dawn's far-echoing wave, or to the Hyrcanians and soft Arabs, or the Sagae or arrow-bearing Parthians, or to the seas that sevenfold Nile colors – whether he will cross the high Alps, looking upon the monuments of great Caesar, the Gallic Rhine, the bristling sea, and Britons at the world's end. (Catull. 11.1–12)

The catalogue of places and peoples located at the edges of Rome's expanding territory is more than a hyperbolic way of saying that Furius and Aurelius are willing to go to the ends of the earth for Catullus; it is also a way of linking the very personal mission that Catullus ultimately gives them with the idea of Rome's territorial expansion (Putnam 1989, 1995–6: 86–8; Konstan 2000/2: 224–8; see Konstan and Greene, this volume). Even if some of these places and peoples were never to fall under Rome's power, most would have had some kind of military or provincial associations for Catullus' audience, at least in a historical sense. But the catalogue is significant linguistically too, since it contains several words and formulations that seem to be Catullan innovations: for example, the adjectives *Eous, sagittiferus,* and

septemgeminus, and phrases like ultimos Britannos and in extremos penetrabit Indos all
seem to originate in this poem. Several passages in the Aeneid refer to these lines, the
first being Anchises' description of the territorial achievements of Augustus:

> "super et Garamantas et <u>Indos</u>
> proferet imperium; iacet extra sidera tellus,
> extra anni solisque uias, ubi caelifer Atlas
> axem umero torquet stellis ardentibus aptum.
> huius in aduentum iam nunc et <u>Caspia regna</u>
> responsis horrent diuum et Maeotia tellus,
> et <u>septemgemini</u> turbant trepida ostia <u>Nili</u>."

"He will extend his power beyond both the Garamantes and Indians; the land
lies beyond the constellations, outside of the paths of sun and year, where Atlas the
sky-holder turns upon his shoulders an axis fitted with blazing stars. Even now, in
anticipation of his arrival, both the Caspian kingdoms and the Maeotic land shudder at
the responses of the gods, and the trembling mouths of sevenfold Nile are in an uproar."
(Aen. 6.794–800)

It is worth noting here that Caesar (and the name Iulus, from which Iulius was
conventionally derived) is mentioned only a few lines before this passage. In addition
to the mention of the Indi and the septemgeminus Nilus, the context also evokes
Catullus in that here too we get a catalogue of places at the edges of the Roman
world. Moreover, Vergil's Caspia regna replace Catullus' Hyrcanos, who dwell near
the Caspian. Anchises' catalogue is not identical with Catullus' but is framed by the
Indi and the septemgeminus Nilus, which also frame the first two-thirds of Catullus'
list, and both catalogues move east to west.

Echoes of Catullus 11 occur again not much later. This time Julius Caesar and
Pompey are the subjects:

> "illae autem paribus quas fulgere cernis in armis,
> concordes animae nunc et dum nocte prementur,
> heu quantum inter se bellum, si lumina uitae
> attigerint, quantas acies stragemque ciebunt,
> <u>aggeribus</u> socer <u>Alpinis</u> atque arce Monoeci
> descendens, gener aduersis instructus <u>Eois</u>!"

"Moreover the ones whom you see blazing in equal arms – now like-minded souls so
long as they are enclosed by darkness – alas, how great a war between them, if they attain
the light of life! How great the battle-lines and slaughter they'll arouse! The father-in-law
coming down from the Alpine hills and the citadel of Monoecus, the son-in-law drawn
up with the East arrayed in opposition!" (Aen. 6.826–31)

Putnam (1995–6: 89) points especially to the last two lines here, with their reference
to the Alps and use of the substantive Eois, both of which he rightly takes to be
derived from Catullus 11. In fact the Catullan allusion in these lines is a conflation of
poem 11 and poem 29, in which Catullus famously skewers just this pair, Pompey and
Caesar, as socer generque, because at the time Pompey was married to Caesar's
daughter Julia. Given the obvious Catullan background to these lines (6.630–1)

we might also look at the preceding verses for signs of Catullus. Poem 29 castigates Pompey and Caesar for the unholy union which is destroying the world. Here Vergil describes them as *concordes animae* (6.827), a phrase which recalls their unity in poem 29 but also perhaps the unity of Furius and Aurelius in poem 11 and the loyalty they have apparently pledged to Catullus.

Next we turn to Book 7 and the custom of opening the gates of the temple of Janus when the state went to war:

> ...cum prima mouent in proelia Martem,
> siue Getis inferre manu lacrimabile bellum
> Hyrcanisue Arabisue parant, seu tendere ad Indos
> Auroramque sequi Parthosque reposcere signa.

As soon as they rouse Mars to battle, whether they prepare to wage with their own hands lamentable war against the Getae or Hyrcanians or Arabs, or to head for the Indians and to pursue the dawn and demand standards back from the Parthians. (*Aen.* 7.603–6)

Here we find Hyrcanians and Arabs, indicated with a phrase reminiscent of Catullus 11.5 (*in Hyrcanos Arabesue*); here again are the Indi, along with a word for the dawn to suggest the East, as at Catullus 11.3 (with the Latin *Aurora* replacing the Greek *Eos*, suggested by *Eoa*); finally come the Parthians.

Our next passage is 8.725–8, the shield of Aeneas, with another catalogue of places and peoples that bound Roman space, namely the peoples over whom Augustus will triumph.

> hic Lelegas Carasque sagittiferosque Gelonos
> finxerat; Euphrates ibat iam mollior undis,
> extremique hominum Morini, Rhenusque bicornis,
> indomitique Dahae, et pontem indignatus Araxes.

Here he had fashioned the Lelegae and the Carae and the arrow-bearing Geloni. Now the Euphrates went gentler in its waves; so too the Morini, most remote of human beings, and the two-horned Rhine, and the unconquered Dahae, and the Araxes that chafes at its bridge. (*Aen.* 8.725–8)

These lines show two obvious and two more subtle connections to Catullus 11. The more obvious are the use, again, of *sagittiferus* and the appearance of the Rhine (significantly, its only appearance in the *Aeneid*). More subtly, *Euphrates...mollior* recalls Catullus' *Arabesue molles* (11.5): Vergil's references to eastern peoples are notoriously inexact, so the change from the Arabs to a Mesopotamian river is unproblematic. Similarly, lines 727–8 are a complicated, but still intelligible, reference to Catullus 11.10–12. Except for the mention of the Rhine, the connections are not at first obvious, but when we consider that Aeneas' shield at this point describes the peoples over whom Augustus will have triumphed – at least in theory – it becomes clear that we have in these lines (as in those that precede) *monimenta Caesaris*. In fact, the name Caesar occurs not long before our passage, at 8.714. Vergil and Catullus mean different individuals by the word, but the fact that both men are Caesars is what allows Vergil to make such use of Catullus' poem. Catullus talks about the *ultimi Britanni*, "the Britons at the end of the world," and Aeneas' shield shows us the *extremi hominum Morini*, "the Morini, most remote of peoples." The Morini were not the *Britanni*, but Gauls who can easily stand in for the Britons here since they lived near the Channel (probably the *horribile aequor* of Catullus 11.11) and it was from their territory that Julius Caesar departed for Britain (*B Gall.* 4.22, 5.2). The same geographical inexactitude that allows Vergil to conflate the Euphrates with the Arabs also allows the Morini to stand in for the Britanni. Finally, we see here the same use of *extremus* as in Catullus 11.2.

The best-known reference to Catullus 11, however, in the *Aeneid* is not to the catalogue but to the famous simile at the end:

> nec meum respectet, ut ante, amorem,
> qui illius culpa cecidit uelut prati
> ultimi flos, praetereunte postquam
>   tactus aratro est.

and let her not look back, as in the past, on my love, which has perished through her fault like a flower at the meadow's edge, after it has been grazed by the passing plow. (Catull. 11.21–4)

This simile describes what has become of Catullus' love for Lesbia after her brutal mistreatment of him. In this poem Lesbia has a special relationship to the catalogue at the beginning in that her treatment of her lovers mirrors Rome's imperial spread (Konstan 2000/2: 227–8; Putnam 1995–6: 87–8). Catullus' *amor* has not survived her predatory and monstrous behavior. In the imagery of the flower and the plow we recognize not only that something beautiful and delicate has been callously destroyed but also that innocence has been lost, since the image suggests loss of virginity too. It is this latter idea that I think Vergil most evokes in the description of the death of the beautiful young Euryalus:[13]

> purpureus ueluti cum flos succisus aratro
> languescit moriens, lassoue papauera collo
> demisere caput pluuia cum forte grauantur.

just as when a purple flower, cut down by a plow, languishes in death, or when poppies with tired necks have laid down their heads when rains have chanced to be heavy. (*Aen.* 9.435–7)

These lines combine a reference to Catullus 11.22–4 with the description of a dying warrior at *Iliad* 8.306–8. The Homeric reference is appropriate to death in a fight, but the Catullan allusion reminds us that Euryalus does not die on the battlefield in the same way that Homeric warriors do; Vergil's worldview is not Homer's, and death has a different meaning in his lyrical epic (W. R. Johnson 1976: 59–66). Euryalus is still a boy, and his first fight is his last. Just as Catullus' innocence is lost as his love for Lesbia dies, so does Euryalus die as he loses his innocence. War is not the heroic adventure he and his friend Nisus thought they were signing up for, and we remember that *Aeneid* 9 features Ascanius playing the role of his absent father while Nisus and Euryalus play Homeric heroes. It is a book whose central figures are at the cusp of adulthood, and all three lose their innocence in different ways as Ascanius sends his young friends to their deaths.

The death of Euryalus reaches back through the other references to Catullus 11 and reassembles that text in a particularly poignant way. Catullus sends two companions (associated elsewhere in his poems as well) on a mission. They will go anywhere for him, and their imagined journey traces the boundaries of Rome's expanding dominion while making pointed reference to the achievements of Julius Caesar (and, to a lesser extent, those of Pompey). Finally they are dispatched on their actual mission to the less exotic but infinitely more dangerous Lesbia. At the end of the poem we see that Lesbia has stolen Catullus' innocence and destroyed his love. In *Aeneid* 9, Ascanius sends two companions, eager to prove their worth to their surrogate leader in any way they can, on a mission that ends by recalling the lost innocence and lost love of Catullus. Here Euryalus dies having botched the mission through childish greed, learning only at the end what he was really getting into.[14]

Putnam (1995–6: 92) captures the importance of poem 11 for the *Aeneid*:

> Catullus 11, in Virgil's adoptions, therefore proffers an important intellectual and spiritual map of the *Aeneid*, showing how the Augustan poet utilizes his great predecessor to make us turn from idealizing vistas of Roman glory to the lived horrors of human brutality. Or, to put the matter in terms of genres, by his linear survey of Catullus 11 Virgil in a special way personalizes the *Aeneid*, putting final stress, where Catullus does, on the immediacy and the problematics of human emotionality, not on the impersonal prowess of empire and its dreams of future glory. It is with stress on man's passional side, not on Rome's achievement, that the epic ends.

Catullus 101

Catullus' elegiac description of the journey to perform funeral rites for his brother is famous, especially for its opening evocation of the *Odyssey* (Fitzgerald 1995: 185–9):

> multas per gentes et multa per aequora uectus
> aduenio

Having sailed through many peoples and over many seas, I arrive. (Catull. 101.1–2)

Echoes of this opening occur at least 11 times in the *Aeneid* (Ferguson 1971–2: 32–3; Tracy 1977; Schmiel 1979; Conte 1986: 32–7; J. Wills 1998: 280–2). Cataloguing and analyzing these instances, Schmiel (1979) notes that the Catullan context is important in each case, for each reference to 101 combines themes of a journey with forms of *pietas* and usually with some notion of funeral rites or final meetings with the dead, especially in the first half of the poem. In the second half Schmiel finds a more encouraging use of Catullus' poem of grief: Catullus 101.1 shows up several times in Book 7 – the journey from Troy (a reversal of Catullus that leads us back to Odysseus) is no longer a journey to say goodbye to the dead; it is once again a journey home, and it has been successful.[15]

Since Vergil so often refers to Catullus 101, it is impossible to explore all the references here. Most are to the opening line of the poem, but a few are to other parts.[16] For example, Catullus' *more parentum* (101.7) is recalled at *Aeneid* 6.223.

Similarly, at *Aeneid* 11.97–8, there is a clear, and obviously appropriate, reference to 101.10, *atque in perpetuum, frater, aue atque uale*, as Aeneas says goodbye to Pallas.

In what remains, I will focus on the connections between the *Aeneid*, Catullus 101.1, and the *Odyssey*. Vergil's references constitute "window references" (or "double allusions"), through which Vergil accesses Homer's *Odyssey*, but in a way that has specifically Catullan associations (Conte 1986: 32–7; J. Wills 1998: 280–2). Vergil's poem is darker than the *Odyssey*; its hero's losses are more personal as he struggles to gain a metaphorical homecoming he doesn't especially want. By maintaining poem 101's association of Odysseus' journey with Catullus' odyssey of grief and loss, Vergil insures that the epic form and the obvious similarity between Odysseus and Aeneas do not lull us into a false sense of comfort. Odysseus suffers mightily but finally returns home to find a faithful wife well-suited to him in temperament and intellect; his son has grown to manhood and gives him reason for pride. Catullus' allusion to the *Odyssey*, however, reminds us that not all quests end in happy reunions. Catullus reverses Odysseus' path and reaches the Troad, where he has no reunion, only a traditional ritual that, as he well knows, is meaningless to the brother he has lost. Moreover, in acknowledging his brother's death, he also acknowledges that his family is gone (Skinner 2003: 8, 11–12, 19; see also Catull. 68.22, 94). Catullus 101 is a poem of grief, yet one which recognizes that the living need rituals and goodbyes, even if the dead do not. In the *Aeneid*, reference to Catullus 101 suggests that the epic journey is sometimes also a personal journey, that epic success is often personal grief. It is perhaps for this reason that Anchises, upon seeing Aeneas in the underworld, transforms him into Catullus with the words *et quanta per aequora uectus* (6.692). This passage too is an example of Vergil's tendency to conflate references to multiple sources; Putnam (1995–6: 93–9) has examined the way that the meeting between Aeneas and Anchises (6.687–94) combines references to four separate Catullan poems (9, 62.1–2, 64.165–6, 101.1–2). Thus Catullan poetry supplies a literary background to Aeneas' relationship with Anchises, but one that animates Vergil's description with notions of loss, grief, and the unbridgeable gap between living and dead. Anchises does not need Aeneas' visit – just as Catullus' brother is not really comforted by Catullus 101 – but, like Catullus, Aeneas does need it. He is the living man who seeks closure with the dead, an Odysseus whose Penelope is long gone.

Vergil's Catullus

Is there a consistent use of Catullus by Vergil? The answer to this question, incomplete though it must be, can tell us something not only about Vergilian poetry but also about Catullus: what features of Catullan poetry did the most distinguished poet of the next generation find significant? Who is Vergil's Catullus, and how does he differ from ours?

One important general feature of Vergil's engagement with Catullus has, as far as I know, gone unremarked. Nowhere does he signal interest in Catullus as a human being, whether as a historical person or as a type of the poet. Examples of Vergil's practice with another poet will make this clearer: near the beginning of the third *Georgic* (3.8–9), Vergil clearly refers to lines from Ennius (fr. 46 Courtney), but these lines are a first-person bit of self-assertion by Ennius; thus Vergil's allusion is both to Ennius' text and to Ennius' self-construction as a person. By using Ennius' first-person statements in his own first-person programmatic statement, Vergil lays claim to status as a new Ennius, writing himself into a tradition by "becoming" a famous predecessor (Hinds 1998: 52–98, esp. 52–5). Similarly, Vergil cites several authors not only as texts but as individual poets whom he uses in a program of self-definition. Catullus, however, is represented not by first-person statements but only by references to specific texts. Thus Vergil's Catullus is not the lover of Lesbia or even the neoteric poet; Vergil's Catullus is a body of poems. Even when he cites two of Catullus' most personal first- and second-person lyrics, poems 11 and 101, Vergil does not use the earlier poet's first-person words to define his own first-person voice. Thus while Vergil is a "modern" Homer, Hesiod, Apollonius, and Ennius, he is not a latter-day Catullus. Catullan poems are sources for his works but not models for his identity as a poet. Vergil's Catullus is largely a poet of loss (potential or actual), grief, abandonment, and even death. His Ariadne, as we have seen, recurs throughout Vergil's poems, epitomizing for him abandonment and the disillusioned outrage that grips us when we realize a promise has been broken. Catullus' Theseus represents for Vergil the pain that *negligentia* causes and the damage it does to personal relationships. Poem 101 is for Vergil the ultimate example of the personal side of epic, an odyssey that undoes the *Odyssey*, that ends in separation not reunion. Arkins (1986: 35) is worth quoting here: "In general Virgil draws on the highly individualistic poet Catullus when he wants to stress the pathos of what happens to individual persons." It used to be thought that the Augustan poets had turned their backs on the new poetry of Catullus and others of his generation, but, as the preceding examples have shown, Catullus plays a crucial role throughout Vergil's works.

NOTES

1   Three valuable thematic treatments are Arkins (1986: 35–9), Putnam (1995–6), and Petrini (1997). Jenkyns (1998: 73–127, esp. 100–5) examines the two authors as products of a common "Transpadane experience." Others have examined the importance of Catullus as a model for Vergilian composition: Otis (1964: 102–5) suggests that the quasi-narrative effects experienced in reading shorter poems of Catullus as a collection influenced Vergil's narrative technique and particularly the "subjective style." Petrini (1997: 13–14) likewise traces Vergilian subjectivity to Catullus; he also (1997: 84–6) sees Catullus as Vergil's model for the conflation of politics and *amor*. Newman (1990: 393–420) traces a number of connections between the modes of composition employed by the two poets.

2   While I do not emphasize them in this chapter, Catullus' wedding poems in general seem to have influenced Vergil greatly. See in particular Arkins (1986: 35–9); Jenkyns (1998: 143–5).

3   Catullus shows up elsewhere throughout the *Bucolics*, but nowhere as extensively as in *Ecl.* 4. See, for example, Otis (1964: 125–8) on *Ecl.* 6.45–60 and Hubbard (1998: 91–3, 102–3, 113–14).

4   For full bibliography see Hubbard (1998: 78 n. 65) and Marinčič (2001).

5   Other important ones are *G.* 1.31–4 and Catull. 64.29, 66.63–5; *G.* 2.103–6 and Catull. 7.3–6.

6   For allusions to Catullus 64 at the end of the first *Georgic*, when the poet describes the chaos that follows upon the death of Julius Caesar, see Buchheit (1966) and Wigodsky (1972: 131).

7   For a different view of this passage, see Petrini (1997: 44–5).

8   For a discussion of the use to which Vergil puts this passage of Catullus 64, as well as 64.241, see Putnam (1995–6: 84–5).

9   Ariadne and poem 64 are not the only Catullan intertexts in this speech; on Dido's famous wish for a *paruulus Aeneas* and Catullus 61.216, see Arkins (1986: 37–8) and Petrini (1997: 91–3).

10 It may be significant that the *Aeneid* has Aeneas return to celebrate funeral games for his father after he leaves Carthage: while he lost his father before he met Dido, Aeneas, like Theseus, abandons a woman and then goes on to deal immediately with the death of his father, Theseus because his has just died and Aeneas to celebrate funeral games for Anchises, who died before he reached Carthage.

11 Of the many treatments of the passage, I have found Johnston (1987), Lyne (1994), and J. Wills (1998) most useful. J. Wills (1998: 287–91) gives a useful summary of the thematic importance that scholars have given the allusion. For a summary and review of older works see Skulsky (1985) and Griffith (1995).

12 Most recently, the question is so used by Hubbard (1998: 15–16) and Heath (2002: 64–5, 100–1). See also the debate between O'Sullivan (1993) and Farrell (1993) in *Electronic Antiquity.*

13 Though his analysis is somewhat different from mine, Petrini (1997: 21–47) discusses Euryalus' story as one of coming of age or, in his terms, initiation.

14 On Catullus in Vergil's description of the dead Pallas (11.68–9) see Putnam (1995–6: 91–2) and Petrini (1997: 65–9).

15 Tracy (1977) identifies in *Aen.* 6.333–6 a combined allusion to Catullus 101.1 and 46.9–11. As he sees it, the echo of poem 46 establishes Aeneas' momentary joy at seeing his lost companions, but the echo of 101.1 at verse-end in 336 represents Aeneas' sense of grief as he realizes that these friends are now among the dead.

16 One might also connect the Catullan reference at *Aen.* 3.658, identified by Glenn (1974), with 101.6, *frater adempte mihi.*

GUIDE TO FURTHER READING

On Vergil's connections, stylistic and otherwise, to the neoterics, see Otis (1964: 31–40), Quinn (1968: 370–5), Wilkinson (1969: 39–48), Ross (1975: esp. 1–17), Clausen (1987: 1–14), and Jenkyns (1998: 133–9). See Farrell (1991: 276–8) for a critique of traditional views of the relationship between neoterics and Augustans.

For lists of Vergil's allusions to Catullus, with discussions of many passages and references to additional scholarship, the best starting points are Westendorp-Boerma (1958), Ferguson (1971–2), and Putnam (1995–6). The nineteenth-century commentary (later reprinted) on Catullus by Simpson (1879: xxxviii–xxxix) contains a handy list of parallel passages. Petrini (1997) is an extensive discussion of Vergil's debt to Catullus, focusing on childhood and coming of age but touching on much else too. In addition to these, see, for the *Eclogues*, Clausen's commentary (1994) and Hubbard (1998) *passim*; for the *Georgics*, R. F. Thomas's commentary (1988) gives much information. For Catullus 64 and the *Aeneid*, the best recent starting point is J. Wills (1996: 26–30). On Catullus 66, J. Wills (1998), Lyne (1994), and Griffith (1995) provide the best introduction to the topic; of other studies, J. Tatum (1984), Skulsky (1985), Johnston (1987), and R. A. Smith (1993) should be singled out.

On Catullan influence in the poems of the *Appendix Vergiliana*, not treated above, see, in
addition to commentaries on individual works, Rand (1906: 17–18), Westendorp-Boerma
(1958: 52–4), Gonnelli (1962: 227–35), Ferguson (1971–2: 38–40), and the more recent
remarks by Holzberg (2004).

Finally, a very helpful introduction to the topic of allusion is Farrell (1991: 3–25), which
traces the development of intertextual study of Latin poetry through the 1980s. Important
subsequent developments are represented by J. Wills (1996), Hinds (1998), Hubbard (1998),
and Edmunds (2001). R. F. Thomas (1982, 1986) are especially important for our subject;
these and other important articles are collected in R. F. Thomas (1999). Farrell (1997) is a
good introduction to particularly Vergilian modes of intertextuality.

WORKS CITED

Abel, D. H. 1962. "Ariadne and Dido." *Classical Bulletin* 38: 57–61.
Arkins, B. 1986. "New Approaches to Virgil." *Latomus* 45: 33–42.
Arnold, B. 1994. "The Literary Experience of Vergil's Fourth *Eclogue*." *Classical Journal* 90:
    143–60.
Buchheit, V. 1966. "Vergil in Sorge um Oktavian (zu georg. I, 498 ff.)." *Rheinisches Museum*
    109: 78–83.
Clausen, W. 1987. *Virgil's* Aeneid *and the Traditions of Hellenistic Poetry.* Berkeley and Los
    Angeles.
Clausen, W., ed. 1994. *Virgil:* Eclogues. Oxford.
Conte, G. B. 1986. *The Rhetoric of Imitation: Genre and Poetic Memory in Virgil and Other
    Latin Poets.* Trans. C. Segal. Ithaca, NY.
Crabbe, A. M. 1977. "*Ignoscenda quidem*: Catullus 64 and the Fourth *Georgic*." *Classical
    Quarterly* n. s. 27: 342–51.
Edmunds, L. 2001. *Intertextuality and the Reading of Roman Poetry.* Baltimore.
Farrell, J. 1991. *Vergil's* Georgics *and the Traditions of Ancient Epic: The Art of Allusion in
    Literary History.* Oxford.
Farrell, J. 1993. "Allusions, Delusions, and Confusions: A Reply." *Electronic Antiquity* 1.6.
    http://scholar.lib.vt.edu/ejournals/ElAnt/V1N6/farrell.html.
Farrell, J. 1997. "The Virgilian Intertext." In C. Martindale, ed., *The Cambridge Companion
    to Virgil.* Cambridge. 222–38.
Ferguson, J. 1971–2. "Catullus and Virgil." *Proceedings of the Virgil Society* 11: 25–47.
Fitzgerald, W. 1995. *Catullan Provocations: Lyric Poetry and the Drama of Position.* Berkeley,
    Los Angeles, and London.
Glenn, J. 1974. "The Blinded Cyclops: *lumen ademptum* (*Aen.* 3.658)." *Classical Philology*
    69: 37–8.
Gonnelli, G. 1962. "Presenza di Catullo in Virgilio." *Giornale italiano di filologia* 15: 225–53.
Griffith, R. D. 1995. "Catullus' *Coma Berenices* and Aeneas' Farewell to Dido." *Transactions
    of the American Philological Association* 125: 47–60.
Heath, M. 2002. *Interpreting Classical Texts.* London.
Hinds, S. 1998. *Allusion and Intertext: Dynamics of Appropriation in Latin Poetry.*
    Cambridge.
Holzberg, N. 2004. "Impersonating the Young Vergil: The Author of the *Catalepton* and His
    Libellus." *Materiali e discussioni* 52: 29–40.
Hubbard, T. K. 1998. *The Pipes of Pan: Intertextuality and Literary Filiation in the Pastoral
    Tradition.* Ann Arbor, MI.
Jenkyns, R. 1998. *Virgil's Experience: Nature and History: Times, Names, and Places.* Oxford.

Johnson, W. R. 1976. *Darkness Visible: A Study of Vergil's* Aeneid. Berkeley and Los Angeles.

Johnston, P. 1987. "Dido, Berenice, and Arsinoe: *Aeneid* 6.460." *American Journal of Philology* 108: 649–54.

Kilroy, G. 1969. "The Dido Episode and the Sixty-Fourth Poem of Catullus." *Symbolae Osloenses* 44: 48–60.

Knight, W. S. J. 1944. *Roman Vergil.* 2nd edn. London.

Konstan, D. 2000/2. "Self, Sex, and Empire in Catullus: The Construction of a Decentered Identity." In V. Bécares Botas, F. Pordomingo, R. Cortés Tovar, and C. Fernández Corte, eds., *La intertextualidad griega y latina.* Madrid. 213–31. (Also available online at http:// zeno.stoa.org/cgi- bin/ptext?doc=Stoa:text:2002.01.0005.)

Lefèvre, E. 2000b. "Catullus Parzenlied und Vergils vierte Ekloge." *Philologus* 144: 62–80.

Lyne, R. O. A. M. 1994. "Vergil's *Aeneid*: Subversion by Intertextuality, Catullus 66.39–40 and Other Examples." *Greece & Rome* 41: 187–204.

Marinčič, M. 2001. "Der Weltaltermythos in Catulls Peleus-Epos (*C.* 64), der kleine Herakles (Theokr. *ID.* 24) und der römische 'Messianismus' Vergils." *Hermes* 120: 484–504.

Mendell, C. W. 1951. "The Influence of the Epyllion on the *Aeneid.*" *Yale Classical Studies* 12: 205–26.

Mynors, R. A. B., ed. 1958 (rev. 1960). *C. Valerii Catulli Carmina recognovit brevique adnotatione critica instruxit.* Oxford.

Mynors, R. A. B., ed. 1969. *P. Vergili Maronis opera.* Oxford.

Newman, J. K. 1990. *Roman Catullus and the Modification of the Alexandrian Sensibility.* Hildesheim.

O'Sullivan, N. 1993. "Allusions of Grandeur? Thoughts on Allusion-Hunting in Latin Poetry." *Electronic Antiquity* 1.5. http://scholar.lib.vt.edu/ejournals/ElAnt/V1N5/osullivan.html.

Otis, B. 1964. *Virgil: A Study in Civilized Poetry.* Oxford.

Perutelli, A. 1980. "L'episodio di Aristeo nelle *Georgiche:* struttura e tecnica narrativa." *Materiali e discussioni* 4: 59–76.

Petrini, M. 1997. *The Child and the Hero: Coming of Age in Catullus and Vergil.* Ann Arbor, MI.

Putnam, M. C. J. 1970. *Virgil's Pastoral Art: Studies in the* Eclogues. Princeton, NJ.

Putnam, M. C. J. 1989. "Catullus 11 and Virgil *Aen.* 6.786–7." *Vergilius* 35: 28–30.

Putnam, M. C. J. 1995–6. "The Lyric Genius of the *Aeneid.*" *Arion* 3.2–3: 81–101.

Putnam, M. C. J. 1998. *Virgil's Epic Designs: Ekphrasis in the* Aeneid. New Haven, CT.

Quinn, K. 1968. *Virgil's* Aeneid: *A Critical Description.* Ann Arbor, MI.

Rand, E. K. 1906. "Catullus and the Augustans." *Harvard Studies in Classical Philology* 17: 15–30.

Ross, D. O., Jr. 1975. *Backgrounds to Augustan Poetry: Gallus, Elegy, and Rome.* Cambridge.

Schmiel, R. 1979. "A Virgilian Formula." *Vergilius* 25: 37–40.

Simpson, F. P., ed. 1879. *Select Poems of Catullus.* London.

Skinner, M. B. 2003. *Catullus in Verona: A Reading of the Elegiac* Libellus, *Poems 65–116.* Columbus, OH.

Skulsky, S. 1985. "'*Inuitus, regina* . . .': Aeneas and the Love of Rome." *American Journal of Philology* 106.4: 447–55.

Slater, D. A. 1912. "Was the Fourth *Eclogue* Written to Celebrate the Marriage of Octavia to Mark Antony? A Literary Parallel." *Classical Review* 26.4: 114–19.

Smith, R. A. 1993. "A Lock and a Promise: Myth and Allusion in Aeneas' Farewell to Dido in *Aeneid* 6." *Phoenix* 47: 305–12.

Tatum, J. 1984. "Allusion and Interpretation in *Aeneid* 6.440–76." *American Journal of Philology* 105.4: 434–52.

Thomas, R. F. 1982. "Catullus and the Polemics of Poetic Reference (Poem 64.1–18)." *American Journal of Philology* 103: 144–64.

Thomas, R. F. 1986. "Virgil's *Georgics* and the Art of Reference." *Harvard Studies in Classical Philology* 90: 171–98.

Thomas, R. F., ed. 1988. *Virgil:* Georgics. 2 vols. Cambridge.

Thomas, R. F. 1999. *Reading Virgil and His Texts: Studies in Intertextuality.* Ann Arbor, MI.

Tracy, S. V. 1977. "Catullan Echoes in *Aeneid* 6.333–36." *American Journal of Philology* 98: 20–3.

Van Sickle, J. 1992. *Virgil's Messianic Eclogue.* New York.

Westendorp-Boerma, R. E. H. 1958. "Vergil's Debt to Catullus." *Acta Classica* 1: 51–63.

Wigodsky, M. 1972. *Vergil and Early Latin Poetry.* Wiesbaden.

Wilkinson, L. P. 1969. *The* Georgics *of Virgil: A Critical Survey.* Cambridge.

Wills, J. 1996. *Repetition in Latin Poetry: Figures of Allusion.* Oxford.

Wills, J. 1998. "Divided Allusion: Virgil and the *Coma Berenices.*" *Harvard Studies in Classical Philology* 98: 277–305.

Zarker, J. W. 1967. "Aeneas and Theseus in *Aeneid* 6." *Classical Journal* 62.5: 220–6.

CHAPTER TWENTY-ONE

Catullus and Roman Love Elegy

Paul Allen Miller

There are two incontrovertible facts about Catullus' relation to the elegists. First, the elegists clearly recognized that they were writing in a genre of which he was among the most esteemed of pioneers. Second, the nature of that genre, and how it derives from the multifaceted corpus that is the Catullan collection (polymetrics, *carmina maiora*, epigrams; Lesbia poems, political poems, comedies of manners, translations, epyllia), is anything but clear. Indeed, while modern scholarship has widely, though not universally (Fantham 1996: 106; Veyne 1988: 12, 34–6), agreed with the Roman elegists' claim to be Catullus' heirs, there is no firm consensus on the nature of that kinship.[1] This chapter will examine under a variety of rubrics the forms of affiliation that unite them and will answer the following questions: what are the formal similarities between Catullus and the elegists; what are the thematic similarities; what are the generic similarities; and what is the relation between poem 68 and subsequent elegiac practice? Before turning to these questions, however, let us examine what the elegists themselves say.

Elegiac *Testimonia*

While Catullus is alluded to in both Tibullus' and Propertius' first books of elegiac poetry, the first fully explicit acknowledgment of their kinship is found in the final lines of Propertius 2.34. This is the last poem in Book 2 and a text with clear programmatic intent. In this poem, Propertius traces his poetic genealogy and contrasts his aesthetic project with that of Vergil, who was in the process of composing the *Aeneid*:

> Varro also when he had finished Jason, yes Varro,
>   played in verse the great passion of his Leucadia;
> the writings of wanton Catullus (*lasciui . . . Catulli*) sang (*cantarunt*) these matters too,

and thus Lesbia is better known than Helen herself;
    even the pages of learned Calvus confessed these things,
        when he sang of the death of poor Quintilia;
    on account of beautiful Lycoris how many things did Gallus sing just now,
        who dead washes his wounds in the infernal waters!
    Cynthia indeed shall live on praised, in the verse of Propertius –
        if Fame wishes to place me among the likes of these.

$$(2.34.85-94)^2$$

On the immediate thematic level, Propertius seems to say nothing more than that he, like Catullus and a number of other poets, chooses to sing of love rather than war, which is the matter of the epic poets like Vergil. A closer reading of the passage, however, tells a story of generic evolution that goes beyond the bounds of simple thematic resemblance.

The first poet mentioned, Varro of Atax, is known to have translated Apollonius' *Argonautica* before turning his hand to erotic verse. Nothing of the *Leucadia* survives, so we cannot judge for sure either its content or its meter, but the name Leucadia refers to an island sacred to Apollo on which Sappho was said to have thrown herself from a cliff for the love of Phaon. If we assume that Varro's beloved was given the name Leucadia in his collection of erotic verse, or that the name at least refers to her indirectly, then we have here an anticipation of Catullus' Lesbia, also named for an island associated with Sappho. Moreover, Varro's case is important because he effects a progression that is the opposite of Vergil's. Where the latter began with the erotic verse of the *Eclogues* and then moved through the didactic poetry of the *Georgics* to elegy's declared generic antagonist, epic, Varro moved from epic to erotic verse and hence to a prefiguration of Catullus' own beloved.

This same movement between opposed genres is continued in the next couplet, with the emphasis now firmly on the pre-eminence of Catullan proto-elegy. As lines 87–8 tell us, Lesbia became better known than Helen herself, and thus in Catullus we have the triumph of erotic verse over epic and hence the consummation of Varro's trajectory (Stahl 1985: 185). Calvus, who comes next in 2.34, was most famous for an elegy he wrote on the death of his beloved, Quintilia. Not only was he a good friend of Catullus (see Catullus 50, 53), but the elegy on Quintilia is specifically mentioned in Catullus' own elegiac epigrams in poem 96.[3]

If anything pleasant or acceptable is able to come
    from our grief to the speechless dead, Calvus,
through which longing we renew old loves and
    weep for friendships formerly abandoned,
then certainly her premature death will not cause Quintilia to grieve
    so much as she will rejoice in your love.

Not only, then, is Catullus a historical personage but his position in the poem also serves a clear structural function. He is the first poet on the list depicted as only writing erotic verse about a single beloved, Lesbia, and thus striking the pose typical of the Roman elegist (although in fact he practiced other types of poetry). He also is depicted as besting epic with his erotic verse and thereby establishing elegy's supremacy: "Lesbia is better known than Helen herself." Catullus in Propertius 2.34

introduces elegy both directly through the evocation of Lesbia and indirectly through the figure of Calvus' poem on Quintilia. We close with Gallus, who is considered the founder of erotic elegy proper, inasmuch as he wrote only elegy and was best known for his verses on Lycoris. He is the last poet to be named before Propertius. Catullus in the poetic genealogy Propertius uses to draw Book 2 to a close occupies a central position in the thematic and formal evolution of the genre. With him, the shift from epic to elegy becomes definitive and the list of erotic elegists begins.

Ovid in many ways echoes Propertius. In *Tristia* 2, the apology to Augustus, he explains from exile in Tomis why the *Ars Amatoria* was not "an incitement to adultery." In it, he includes a mocking literary history that aims to show that poets have always written about love. Elegy, therefore, which takes the erotic as its domain, is the true master genre and the *telos* of this genealogical narrative. After a survey of Greek poets from Anacreon to Sophocles, Ovid turns to the Roman tradition. There, Catullus, paired once more with Calvus, is cited as his first real predecessor in Roman literature:

> Thus often his woman, whose pseudonym was Lesbia,
>   was sung (*cantata est*) by wanton Catullus (*lasciuo . . . Catullo*);
> and not content with her, he publicized many loves
>   in which he confessed his adultery.
> Equal and similar was the license of slender Calvus,
>   who unraveled his infidelities in a variety of meters.
>
> (*Tr.* 2.427–32)

The pairing of the adjective *lasciuus* with the verb *canto* is clearly meant to recall Propertius 2.34.87. Ovid's catalogue is, as is his manner, longer and more inclusive than Propertius', but in it two predecessors hold pride of place as the only ones to receive more than a single couplet, Catullus and Tibullus. The latter, like Ovid a member of the poetic circle gathered around Messalla Corvinus, received a full nine couplets and clearly held a special place in Ovid's poetic imagination, but Gallus and Propertius only receive one apiece, whereas Catullus, who heads the list of Latin erotic poets, receives a pair.

Ovid and Propertius thus saw themselves as writing in a tradition of Latin poetry in large part founded by Catullus. Tibullus, who makes no significant explicit program-matic statements in his poetry, alludes to Catullus on several occasions (see 1.2.39–40, 1.4.21–4, 1.5.7–8, *inter alia*), while Ovid in his funeral poem on Tibullus pictures him being greeted in the underworld by Catullus, Calvus, and Gallus (*Am.* 3.9.61–4). Catullus is by universal account the undisputed ancestor of Roman love elegy.

Formal Similarities

Yet while the elegists were unanimous, the scholars did not agree. Why? The argu-ment centers on how the elegiac genre is defined. In the ancient world, poetic genres were in the first instance defined by meter. Archaic Greek lyric was written in meters sung to the lyre. Iambic invective was written in iambic meters. Elegy is written in elegiac couplets. By this criterion, Catullus, who wrote in a variety of meters, is not truly an elegist. And it is for this reason that Quintilian does not include Catullus in his canonical list of elegists (*Inst.* 10.1.93).

This is not of course to say that Catullus did not produce poetry in elegiac distiches. He most certainly did (65–116), but this is not the largest part of his work, which was written in a mixture of lyric and iambic meters as well as in the dactylic hexameters of epic (1–64). Moreover, there was a distinction recognized in the ancient world between two types of poems written in elegiac couplets. The first was the epigram. This is a short poem that eschews narrative and mythological elaboration in favor of compact rhetoric and a sting in the tail. Elegies by contrast are poems of some length that almost always contain narrative elements and frequently possess elaborate mythological exempla. The average elegy of Tibullus is 75 lines; the poems of Propertius in his first three books average 35 lines (86 in Book 4), and those of Ovid in the *Amores* 50 lines. Of Catullus' first-person erotic poetry written in elegiac couplets only one poem is of more than 35 lines, poem 68 (160 lines).[4] Poem 76, which is the next-longest erotic poem, consists of 26 lines, but it has neither the mythological nor the narrative elaboration characteristic of elegy.

The rest of the first-person erotic work in elegiac couplets is distinctly epigrammatic in nature. Catullus' most famous erotic epigram is poem 85, a marvel of concision whose conflicting emotions become the hallmark of erotic elegy as a whole: "I hate and I love. Perhaps you ask why I do it. I don't know, but I feel it happen and am torn apart." Yet, while a poem like this may feel like a miniature elegy, and that feeling is reinforced by the epigrammatic elegies of the only female elegist Sulpicia (average 7 lines),[5] the latter are more the exception than the rule. The epigram as a form is frequently a satirical poem with little amorous content and often an obscene directness.[6] This is as true in Catullus as in any other practitioner of the form. A too exclusive focus on the Lesbia poems has often given a distorted picture of the collection as a whole.[7] They are but one thread, although a brilliant one, in a larger tapestry. Thus the poem immediately preceding 85 is a lampoon on a certain Arrius' affected pronunciation, while poem 88 is one of a series of poems attacking Gellius for sexual perversity. The elegiac epigrams as a unit, then, can in no sense be seen as the predecessor of such thematically unified works as Propertius' *Monobiblos* or Ovid's *Amores*.

There is one sense, however, in which Catullus' poetry is the formal antecedent of the elegists. Catullus, like the elegists, wrote volumes of poetry that were meant to be read as books and that chronicled – nay, embodied and created – the experience of their first-person speaker. There has been disagreement on whether Catullus edited the collection we now have – and if so, whether he published it serially, as a unity, or first serially and then in an *opera omnia* edition (see Skinner, chapter 3 in this volume). Today the majority opinion has shifted firmly in the direction of Catullus as the editor of at least the major sections of the corpus (polymetrics, *carmina maiora*, elegiac poems),[8] although there is more disagreement about whether poems 65–8 belong with the longer poems or those in elegiac meter (Skinner 2003: xxvi, 1; King 1988; Quinn 1972b: 258–9; Wiseman 1969: 121), and whether Catullus edited his *opera omnia*. Yet even among those who remain agnostic or continue to hold out against the view that Catullus himself had a hand in the arrangement of the poems as we read them today, there is no doubt that these poems are meant be read in terms of one another and thus presume the existence of a collection in one form or another (Janan 1994: ix, 40, 43, 90).[9]

Catullus' poetry thus represents the first example of the composition of a self-conscious poetic collection in Latin, at least one that has come down to us.[10] This form of composition will become the norm in the Augustan period. It is one that allows for complex narrative relations between poems as well as sharp thematic juxtapositions. It demands not only reading, but also rereading (G. Williams 1980: ix–x; Skinner 1981: 106). Thus it is now well established that the opening of the polymetrics gives an encapsulated form of the narrative of the Lesbia affair as a whole: from the coy erotics of the sparrow poems (2 and 3); to the declaration of love and dawning awareness of mortality and infidelity in the kiss-poems (5 and 7); to the initial disillusionment and final break of poems 8 and 11 (Miller 1994: 63–72; Janan 1994: 78; Wiseman 1985: 147; Hubbard 1983: 230; Segal 1968: 311–16). A similar progression can be seen in the Lesbia poems at the beginning of the elegiac portion of the collection, although the movement there is less narrative than analytic (Skinner 2003: 85; Miller 2002: 115–19; Quinn 1972b: 40). Poem 68 presents an overview of the beginning of the affair, establishes it as adulterous, and depicts Catullus as struggling to adopt an attitude of sophisticated acceptance toward Lesbia's infidelities. Poems 70 and 72 present Lesbia's declaration of love to Catullus and the poet's subsequent disillusionment. Poem 72 also presents the first articulation of what will be the dominant theme in these poems: the poet's inability either to esteem his beloved or to stop loving her. The same antithesis is condensed and sharpened in 75 before receiving a much more expansive and analytic treatment in 76 (Ferguson 1988: 15; W. R. Johnson 1982: 122–3). Poem 79, then, reveals that Lesbia has a perfidious brother, Lesbius,[11] and 83 presents a flashback to an earlier, happier time, before the antithesis that defines the sequence as whole is distilled into the crystalline terms of 85's *odi et amo*.

In fact, the polymetric and the elegiac sequences are more complex than this schematic presentation allows, but for our purposes this should be sufficient to show the importance of the poetic book in establishing both relations between individual poems and the possibilities of narrative elaboration that will be central to the elegiac genre. Thus Propertius' *Monobiblos* will move from the moment when Cynthia first captured the poet with her eyes, through various quarrels, separations, and encounters with potential amorous and poetic rivals. The sequence is in no way a straightforward linear narrative but, on the analogy of Catullus, is replete with narrative potentiality. Similarly, Tibullus' books on Delia and Nemesis each present affairs that unfold simultaneously through time as the reader progresses through the scroll, as do Ovid's *Amores*.

Thematic Similarities

The thematic principle around which the elegiac collections were organized was the love affair. Each book of the canonical elegists was devoted to a single beloved of the opposite sex. Like all generic laws, this is more a rule of thumb than an unalterable decree of nature. Cornelius Gallus is the first true elegist, in that all four of his books were devoted to his beloved, Lycoris, and were written in elegiac couplets. Unfortunately, while Gallus looms large in the poetry of Vergil, Propertius, and Ovid, his poetry has all but disappeared. Tibullus wrote two books of poetry. The first is devoted to Delia, but also features three pederastic poems (1.4, 1.8, 1.9) dedicated to a certain Marathus. Tibullus here is following Hellenistic precedent in which erotic poetry written in elegiac meters was generally homoerotic in nature. Catullus did the same, writing erotic epigrams about his love for Juventius, as well as poetry on a variety of other subjects. Tibullus dedicates his second book exclusively to his travails with the ominously named Nemesis. Both books of Tibullus' poetry also feature poems dedicated to his patron, Messalla Corvinus. The first three books of Propertius are devoted to his love for Cynthia, yet they too are liberally sprinkled with poems addressed to Propertius' patron, Maecenas, with programmatic poetic statements, as well as with poems such as 2.7 and 3.4, which are at least as political as they are amatory. Ovid's *Amores* recount the course of his affair with Corinna. Thus, with certain exceptions, the works of the elegists are distinguished by their being thematically organized around the recounting of the events, if not the history, of a poet's all-consuming love affair with his mistress in what presents itself (however ironically) as a confessional mode.

Catullus' mistress, Lesbia, is the central focus of his most famous poetry too. Nonetheless, much of that poetry is not written in elegiac couplets, and much of what is written in them is on topics other than the poet's affair. Yet it is precisely the Lesbia poems that are adduced by Propertius and Ovid when Catullus is presented as the founder of love elegy. Moreover, where the polymetrics' influence on the elegists is widely conceded, the epigrams' condensed style, rough prosody, and eschewal of narrative, mythological elaboration, and other devices of Alexandrian learning were of more limited impact (Lyne 1980; 103; Ross 1975: 116; Quinn 1959 [1969 reprint]: 57).

The Problem of Genre

We are, then, faced with a paradox. Catullus is widely credited with being the founder, or at least a very significant predecessor, of Roman love elegy by ancient poets and modern critics alike. Yet the majority of his output in elegiac distichs bears only a passing resemblance to the elegies written by the canonical elegists; and, while the thematic resemblance between Catullus' poetry on Lesbia and that of Gallus, Propertius, Tibullus, and Ovid on their respective mistresses is undeniable, nonetheless many of the poems that had the most direct influence on the later elegists – both from a stylistic and a thematic perspective – are in the polymetrics. It is for this reason, as noted above, that Quintilian does not include Catullus in his list of canonical elegists and that Sharon James has denied any generic affiliation between Catullus' "lyric" poetry and the work of the elegists (2003: 255 n. 116, 319–20 n. 13).

One element of significant commonality, however, sticks out from our previous examination. Both Catullus and the elegists composed books, that is to say poetry meant to be read and reread. Individual poems relate to one another in a complex and multifaceted fashion that allows the emergence of a multi-temporal and self-reflexive poetic subjectivity that I have dubbed "lyric consciousness" (1994). Catullus, I contend, is the founder, or at least the first exemplar, of lyric consciousness in western poetry. The lyric of the poetic collection that we are familiar with from the work of Petrarch, Sidney, and Shakespeare finds its first example in the *liber Veronensis Catulli*. The poetry of the Alexandrian elegists, while featuring complex arrangements and subjective framings, as illustrated in Callimachus' *Aitia*, did not purport to present the complexity of the speaking subject's lived experience. Archaic lyric was, of course, more subjective in pose, but the poetry of Sappho, Alcaeus, and Anacreon was intended for public oral performance and symposiastic recreation. It was only later collected by the scholars of Alexandria and then preserved in books arranged largely according to meter. With Catullus, then, we see the emergence of a fundamentally new genre: collections of poetry that foreground the poet's dialogic relation with himself as exemplified in the complex, multi-temporal inter- and intra-textual relations that make up the collection.

If we take the example of the elegiac poems in the Catullan corpus (65–116), then, as we have just demonstrated, poems 68, 70, 72, 75, 76, and 85 form a coherent sequence. That sequence presents a narrative overview of the affair paired with a progressive analysis and condensation of the conflicting emotions that define it. Nonetheless, any notion of a straightforward narrative unfolding of events is complicated by at least four elements. First, the progression from 68 to 70, and from 72 to 75, 76, and 85, is not so much temporal as analytic. Only poems 70 and 72 bear clear temporal markers in relation to one another. Second, these poems are interlaced with other poems, which although often related on the level of diction or dramatic personae, bear no explicit narrative or analytic relation to the poems in question. Thus, poems 69 and 71 on Rufus and his perplexing combination of sexual conquest and body odor are clearly a pair of poems that parallel 70 and 72 in terms of form and temporal relation. Nevertheless, how 69 and 71 relate to their matching Lesbia poems is never spelled out. Still, the two pairs of poems, owing both to their formal symmetry and to their interlacing sequence, demand to be read in terms of one another, even as the reader strives to integrate them into the larger Lesbia sequence.

Third, the sequence itself disrupts its own quasi-temporal unfolding through the inclusion of poem 83, which clearly projects a dramatic date early in the affair when not only is Lesbia's husband[12] still a factor, but the poet can also still jokingly imagine her being infatuated with Catullus. This poem, in turn, makes us reread the earlier sequence from an alternative temporal and emotional perspective. Poem 83 functions, then, as both a narrative flashback and a return of the repressed: past pleasure reveals its trace in present misery.

> Lesbia always insults me with her husband present;
>   this is a great pleasure for that fool.
> Ass, do you feel nothing? If having forgotten us she were silent,
>   she'd be sane; because she growls and chides,
> not only does she remember, but what is more to the point,
>   she is aroused. That is, she burns (*uritur*) and stews.

This recollection of past erotic pleasure is present on the level of diction as much as it is on that of theme. The verb *uritur* thus clearly recalls and anticipates 72.5's *impensius uror* ("I burn more passionately"), which tells of Catullus' continued sexual passion even as he sees Lesbia "now" as "cheaper and more trivial"

(72.5–6). This verbal echo not only demands that 83 and 72 be read in terms of one another, but also provokes the questions: what is the artistic effect sought by this deliberate disruption of the temporal sequence immediately before 85's anguished *odi et amo*; and what is the poetic and aesthetic consciousness that lies behind this subtle manipulation of the narrative structure? The effect is to produce a depth that is simultaneously a *mise en abîme*.

Fourth, poem 79, "Lesbius est pulcer," as Marilyn Skinner has demonstrated, not only establishes that Lesbia has a brother, but that she is in fact Clodia Metelli the sister of Clodius Pulcher, the fiery tribune. The Rufus of poem 69, 71, and 77 can on this basis be identified as Caelius Rufus, the lover of Clodia Metelli and the object of Cicero's politically motivated defense in the *Pro Caelio* (Skinner 2003: 81–3, 92–3, 107; Wiseman 1985: 166–7, 1969: 28). Thus when Catullus refers to Rufus as a disease who is *intestina perurens* ("burning my guts," 77.3) and a *pestis* ("a plague," 77.6), we connect this imagery not only with his depiction of his love for Lesbia as a *pestis* from which he cannot free himself (76.20), but also with his own disillusioned but heightened sexual passion in 72.5 (*impensius uror*) and Lesbia's secret arousal in 83.6 (*uritur*). The fever of desire becomes the plague of betrayal. The sequence thus requires us to read not only forward and backward but also politically and personally. In the process, we uncover the image of a complex poetic subjectivity that both is profoundly self-reflexive and never exists except as the multiple possible recursive readings the collection engenders. Catullus' passion not only echoes (and anticipates) Lesbia's but is also subject to betrayal by Rufus, who is retrospectively identified – thanks to poem 79's Lesbius/Clodius – as Caelius Rufus. This identification, in turn, makes it possible to reread 69 and 71's invective against Rufus' sexual and hygienic sins in light of Clodius' political machinations as well as those poems' relation to 70 and 72. Each new determination thus requires a new reading as the reader unwinds and rewinds the scroll (Skinner 2003: 178–9).

This kind of complexity in the depiction of personal experience is unprecedented in the ancient world, and it was this phenomenon that I named "lyric consciousness" in 1994. The collections of the elegists embody these same complexities. We find in them the same internally dialogized subjectivity, but with a greater restriction of metrical and thematic materials. It is for this reason that I argued (1994: 49) that Roman love elegy was a subgenre of lyric, as defined by the Catullan collection, a definition consonant with both the explicit statements of the elegists and the perceived differences between elegy, as strictly described in terms of meter and theme, and the Catullan corpus. Nonetheless, it would be a mistake to see a wider gap separating the elegiac and Catullan enterprises than there actually is. Catullus may exhibit greater thematic variation than the elegists, but it should not be assumed that because the elegists pretend to write exclusively on love they do not engage other topics, including politics, poetics, and patronage.

If we examine the opening poems of Propertius' *Monobiblos* we see not only the same recursive structures of reading that we have just outlined in Catullus' epigrams and polymetrics, but also that the elegist, while ostensibly writing about love, uses those structures of reading to produce a similarly complex and multifaceted speaking subject, and does so in part by alluding to the works of his acknowledged predecessor.[13] We begin with 1.1.1–4 and its intertexts. Meleager 103, a pederastic epigram, is the recognized model for the opening of Propertius' first poem:

> Cynthia was the first to capture me with her eyes,
>   I who was stricken before by no desires.
> Then *Amor* cast down my face of unceasing pride
>   and pressed upon my head with his feet.

Fedeli notes that Catullus 1 had begun with a similar evocation of Meleager and argues that Propertius here is indicating his adherence to the principles of Alexandrian composition while tipping his hat to one of its earliest advocates in Rome, his acknowledged predecessor in erotic verse (1983b: 1865–6, 1980: 62). One of the most obvious ways in which Propertius' poem differs from Meleager's is that the gender of the beloveds has been switched. This inversion of genders, however, is part of a larger pattern of pederastic intertexts used to frame the relation of Propertius to Tullus, the representative of traditional Roman values in Book 1, Gallus, the elegist, and Bassus, an iambist. The density of inter- and intra-textual reference found here can be clearly seen by examining poems 1.1, 1.4, and 1.5.

To return to 1.1.1–4, then, the first thing that strikes the attentive reader is that the Meleager epigram has been recast in heteroerotic terms on only the most superficial level. The pederastic intertext remains clearly visible throughout. Cynthia ceases to be the subject of the finite verbs in lines 3 and 4 (Hodge and Buttimore 1977: 63–4), and *Amor*, who is male, replaces her. This metonymic evocation of a homoerotic context is made more explicit when it is recognized that in Meleager's poem no such substitution takes place. The *erômenos*, Mousikos, remains the subject throughout.

Within the first four lines, the boundaries between the masculine and the feminine, poetry and experience, the heteroerotic and the homosocial, have been called into question. The Propertian *coup de foudre* is an intertextual one. This process of decentering and inversion unfolds systematically throughout the poem. Indeed, as Duncan Kennedy notes, the very image of Love placing his feet upon the poet's head is a reprise of the gesture of triumph found in Roman depictions of single combat. The poet is portrayed within the poem as subjected and effeminized at the very moment in which the text effects a double gender substitution of Cynthia for the male beloved in Meleager and *Amor* for Cynthia (Kennedy 1993: 48). Subject and object, masculine and feminine, then, are in a very fluid relation to one another.

We must therefore constantly reread both the poem and its intertexts in terms of one another. We do so less in the hope of achieving a final resolution to these tensions than through the acceptance of a necessary practice of reading whereby we surrender ourselves to an ever expanding dialectic of mutual determination, as we continue to work on the poem and the poem continues to work on us. This process of dialectical interaction, *in fine*, produces the image of a multilayered and multi-temporal consciousness behind the *Monobiblos*, in much the same fashion as it produces the Catullan consciousness of the epigrams, the polymetrics, and, ultimately, the *opera omnia*.

Poems 1.4 and 1.5 follow the pattern outlined in 1.1. On the one hand, they articulate a relation between competing homosocial values and their associated poetic genres through the figure of Cynthia (Sharrock 2000: 270). On the other, they deploy this discourse within a complex weave of inter- and intra-textual homoerotic relations and inverted gender polarities. Poem 1.4 is addressed to Bassus, an iambic poet. Iambic, as exemplified in Catullus' polymetrics, was an invective genre that dealt with the seamier side of life. Thus, when Propertius presents Bassus trying to lure him away from Cynthia by praising the beauty of women of easy virtue, this is a recognizable iambic pose that can also be read as Bassus claiming the superiority of his own poetic genre to elegy/Cynthia (Hodge and Buttimore 1977: 100–1). Propertius responds by telling Bassus that he should cease and desist or Cynthia will so blacken his name that he will be welcome at no girl's door. Cynthia will be transformed into an iambist (the model of phallic aggression) whose invective will reduce Bassus to the archetypal position of the effeminized elegiac lover, the *exclusus amator*. Elegy will show that it can beat iambic at its own game (Fedeli 1983b: 1876; Hodge and Buttimore 1977: 103; Rothstein 1979: 1.88).

Poem 1.5, in turn, is widely recognized as the companion piece to 1.4 (Fedeli 1983b: 1878; Hodge and Buttimore 1977: 100; Richardson 1977: 158). Francis Cairns has demonstrated that the two poems correspond to one another in numerous ways (1983: 62–77). In fact, there seems to have been a deliberate conflation between the addressees. Poem 1.5's *topos* of erotic envy was a common theme of iambic poetry and would be appropriate for Bassus and for Propertius' warnings to him. Nor does Propertius give any indication that he has switched addressees. The name Gallus is deferred to the last line of poem 1.5 (Fedeli 1983b: 1878; Cairns 1983: 81, 96). Thus the poems as well as their addressees are cast as mirror images. As Cairns has argued, these parallels only make sense insofar as we see the Gallus of 1.5 as a rival poet like Bassus: but the Gallus of 1.5 (like Propertius) desires only Cynthia, where Bassus has urged Propertius to play the field. The symmetry of Gallus' desire with Propertius', and its contrast with Bassus', implies that Gallus is also an elegist. Where 1.4 presents the triumph of Cynthia over her rivals, 1.5 presents Propertius' competition for the possession of the crown of elegy with Gallus himself (Oliensis 1997: 159; King 1980: 219).

The most important parallel between 1.4 and 1.5 from our perspective, however, is their common set of Catullan intertexts. First, on a thematic level, Fedeli notes that both poems examine the topic of *fides* betrayed, in the context of failed *amicitia* and amorous betrayal. He cites specific parallels with epigrams 77 against Rufus and 91 against Gellius (1983b: 1876). However, the Catullan subtext goes much deeper and is more specific. The phrase *non impune feres* ("you will not get away with it") at 1.4.17 is a direct quotation from Catullus 78b.3 (Camps 1961: *ad loc.*; Rothstein 1979: *ad loc.*; Suits 1976: 88). The phrase is admittedly not uncommon, as Richardson observes (1977: *ad loc.*), but it is unexampled elsewhere in elegiac couplets, let alone in couplets written with clear iambic intent:

> But now I am pained at this, that your foul spit
>   has polluted the pure kisses of a pure girl.
> But you won't get away with it (*non impune feres*): for all the ages will know you
>   and old lady fame will say what you are.
>
>   (78b.1–4)

The Catullan and Propertian contexts here are identical. Propertius threatens Bassus the iambist with everlasting infamy from Cynthia's invective, while Catullus actually performs the invective and forecasts the same fate for the target of his abuse. Another interesting point for our argument, however, is the distinct possibility that Catullus' target is either named Gallus or metonymically associated with a Gallus.

Most modern editions print 78b as a separate fragment from poem 78 (Thomson 1997; Pöschl 1983; Quinn 1973a; Mynors 1958), but the relation between the two is uncertain. There may simply be a lacuna. Poem 78 is an invective elegy addressed to a Gallus accused of arranging a sexual liaison between the wife of one of his brothers and another brother's son. Poem 78b is also an invective on sexual impropriety and so it is entirely possible that we are dealing with a later part of the same poem. If 78b is also addressed to Gallus, the parallels between 1.4 and 1.5 already remarked upon are augmented by this intertextual resonance. But even if 78b is not addressed to Gallus, then it, like Propertius 1.4, is an iambicizing poem written in elegiac couplets and immediately succeeds a poem addressed to a Gallus. Propertius 1.5, in turn, is a poem addressed to Gallus immediately following an iambicizing poem written in elegiac couplets.

Verbal echoes match the structural mirroring between the two corpora: 1.5 ends with the phrase *non impune illa rogata uenit* ("that girl when asked does not come without you paying the price"). Cairns has noted the parallel with 1.4.17 (1983: 77). Camps and Rothstein, however, give another Catullan parallel as well, 99.3, *uerum id non impune tuli* ("but I did not get away with it"). Again the context is that of kisses and sexual misconduct, but this is a pederastic poem on Catullus stealing kisses from Juventius. Thus once more we have Propertius substituting a heteroerotic context for a homoerotic one, but with both contexts, each of which has a Catullan resonance, still visible.

Propertius 1.4 and 1.5 thus constitute a Catullan pair. Each makes use of a recognizably Catullan theme, the importance of *fides* in the context of *amor* and *amicitia*. The first is an elegiac poem on iambic themes and the second a poem that, while recalling iambic themes, addresses the question of elegiac rivalry with Gallus. Finally, poem 1.4 contains an allusion to a Catullus poem that is either about someone named Gallus or directly juxtaposed with a poem on someone named Gallus. The line containing this allusion is echoed in poem 1.5. This is the first time Gallus is named in the poem or the collection. The same passage to which poem 1.4 alludes and that 1.5 recalls has a further echo in the Catullan corpus at 99.3, where the kisses of the pure girl that the *spurca saliua* pollutes in 78b become those stolen by Catullus from Juventius, who in turn seeks to wash off the *spurca saliua* of the poet (99.10).

At the same time, each of these poems in Propertius' book opposes the life of poetry to the normative pursuit of the *cursus honorum* represented by Tullus, the dedicatee of poem 1.1 and the presumed patron of the collection. Tullus is also the addressee of poem 1.6, in which Propertius contrasts his *militia amoris* with Cynthia with the real-life hardship Tullus may endure accompanying his uncle, the proconsul, to his province. In the process, Propertius inverts normative Roman gender and political values by portraying Tullus as occupying the feminine position, since he is off to soft Ionia (1.6.31), while Propertius assumes the masculine, *durus*, position by staying home with his beloved, *tum tibi si qua mei ueniet non immemor hora/uiuere me duro sidere certus eris* ("then if ever an hour comes when you will not forget about me, you will be certain that I live under a hard star," 1.6.35–6). Poems 1.1, 1.4, 1.5, and 1.6 thus exhibit a systematic progression not dissimilar to that found at the beginning of the epigrams. In neither case is the progression so much narrative as analytical, and in both the progress of the affair is also used as a position from which to address a variety of personal, political, social, and aesthetic issues. The systematic responson of names, themes, and intertexts between the poems shows not only that Propertius is writing in a genre of composition directly cognate with Catullan lyric consciousness, but also that he recognizes that kinship through his use of systematic allusion. Propertius, however, is working on a larger scale, integrating a variety of topics and intertexts within a single poem and then juxtaposing them to one another, while Catullus in the epigrams is building his complex structures out of smaller poems.

Catullus 68

To this point, we have left aside a discussion of Catullus 68, the single poem in the Catullan corpus that most resembles a fully elaborated Roman love elegy. In it, we have a lengthy poem in elegiac couplets, devoted to the topic of the poet's relation to his beloved, one that features narrative and mythological elaboration as well as Hellenistic refinement. Thus a wide variety of scholars have claimed that Catullus virtually invented elegy with this one poem.[14] Nonetheless, as we have already seen, the situation is not quite so straightforward. Many of the borrowings made by the elegists derive from the polymetrics, and to a lesser extent the epigrams. Likewise, the complex and recursive narrative structures that animate the elegiac collection, from the Propertian *Monobiblos* to Tibullus' subtle interweaving of poems on Delia, Marathus, and Messalla, to Ovid's self-conscious three-volume elegiac *magnum opus*, derive necessarily more from relations between the poems of the Catullan corpus than from any single text.

Poem 68, moreover, is anomalous. Not only is it much longer than the average elegy, but its mythological exempla are also more complex than anything found in the elegiac works that come after it. In addition, those exempla are embedded in a complex interlocking set of epic similes that are unexampled either before or after in Greek and Roman poetry (Feeney 1992: 38; Whitaker 1983: 62; G. Williams 1980: 52; Luck 1960). Poem 68 is, thus, not the first Roman love elegy, if we mean by that the archetype from which all later instantiations can be said to derive. Rather it is a poem that in its relation to the rest of the Catullan corpus anticipates what will become some of the typical forms and themes of the elegiac subgenre.

In fact, as I have argued (2004: 32–3), the most significant relation tying Catullus 68 to the elegists is best described in terms of the speaking subject's self-constitution.[15] More specifically, I contend that Catullus bequeaths to the elegists the poetic precedent of a subject position constituted by a fundamental conflict between the speaker's imaginary self-identification and its recognition *as a subject* in the world of codified, signifying practices. The result of this conflict is a split subject whose own discourse is self-undermining and recognizably double, and whose position vis-à-vis communal, symbolic norms is therefore profoundly ambivalent.

To illustrate more precisely this split Catullan consciousness, let us examine selected passages from the poem. The last 120 lines of 68 (68b), as noted above, are written ostensibly to thank Allius for providing a *domus* in which Catullus and

Lesbia consummate their adulterous love. I want to look now at the theme of the house and show how the slippages embodied in its usage within the poem can be traced out into the larger corpus and its complex engagement with the norms of Roman ideology. *Domus* is not only a keyword in Roman ideology – Cicero terms it the *principium urbis et quasi seminarium rei publicae* ("the first principle of the city and the virtual seedbed of the republic," *De officiis* 1.17.54) – it is also one of the major structuring devices of the poem. The word *domus* simultaneously charts the poem's progression and establishes verbal links between its major portions: the initial similes describing Allius' aid; the mythological exemplum of Laodamia and Protesilaus; and the death of Catullus' brother (Whitaker 1983: 61).[16] The interpretive problem posed by this word stems from the fact that these contexts, which the poem invites us to compare to one another, are not commensurable. Not only are these different houses (Allius' in Rome, Laodamia's in Greece, Catullus' in Verona but buried with his brother at Troy), they mean different things. The *domus* Allius provides for Catullus and Lesbia is strictly a physical building. That of Laodamia and Protesilaus is both the household they would have established and the building that would never be completed due to Protesilaus' early death (*domum/inceptam frustra*, 68.74–5; Janan 1994: 121). Finally, the *domus* of the Valerii Catulli is the least substantial of all, since it refers not to Catullus' ancestral seat but to the ideal family unit for which the house stands as synecdoche, and which effectively perished with his brother (68.94). Thus there is a clear progression from the merely physical to the abstract and ideal, but that process of rarefaction is in turn associated with death, as each step beyond the initial threshold leads closer to the evocation of Catullus' brother's grave.

Indeed, the final *domus* of this series seems to defy any placement in space since it must be conceived as existing simultaneously in Verona, the actual home of the Valerii, and Asia Minor, the site of Catullus' brother's grave. This latter location is in turn assimilated within the poem to the mythical territory of Troy (68.89–92), a place outside of space and time that joins Catullus' loss of his brother to Laodamia's loss of her husband, the first Greek soldier to die in the Trojan War (68.83–8). The losses of Catullus and those of Laodamia in their common relation to Troy are then joined together, at the end of the poet's apostrophe to his brother's grave, by an evocation of the adultery of Paris with Helen, a violation of a lawfully constituted *domus*, which, as scholars note, echoes Catullus' adulterous affair with Lesbia (Janan 1994: 131; G. Williams 1980: 59). In this fashion, Catullus directly associates the death of his brother with his own adulterous behavior.

Moreover, the first and last usages of *domus* just examined are both accompanied by nostalgia for what could have been. In line 68, when Allius' *domus* is first introduced, Catullus writes *isque domum nobis isque dedit dominae* ("he gave the house both to me and to my mistress"). The word *domina* here is much debated. Many see it as the first example of the later elegiac usage in which the mistress is portrayed as the dominant partner in the relationship, as opposed to the poet's role as *seruus amoris*. This reading is strengthened by Catullus' use of the word *era* (slave-mistress) to describe Lesbia later in the poem (68.136). Such a reading is also consistent with the poet's anticipation of the elegist's inversion of normative sexual roles. Whether one accepts this reading or not, however, there is a definite etymological play on the relation between *domus* and *domina* that necessarily recalls the more normative use of the word *domina*, the mistress of a lawfully constituted household (Lyne 1980: 6–7), a household for which the poet can wish, but which he can never have.

This brings us to our fourth example of the *domus* motif, the ideal house of Catullan desire:

> She was not led to me by the hand of her father,
>   nor came to a *house* suffused with Syrian perfume.
> Yet one wondrous night she gave me her dear gifts,
>   stolen from the lap of her husband himself.
>
> (143–6)

This is how a Roman *domina* (as opposed to an elegiac one) comes to the lawfully constituted *domus* of her husband, the center of the Roman family and cultic life, the seat of the household gods. The *domus* is the site where individual desire is joined with the norms of law, property, and marriage, the institutions that constitute the foundation of political life. This is the ideal *domus*, which Catullus' brother's death has buried, and which the poet's adulterous desire can never realize.

The word *domus* then displays the slippages that constitute the Catullan subject position both in this poem and throughout the corpus: slippages between normative Roman sexual ideology (the *matrona* as *domina* or *era* of a lawfully constituted *domus*); Catullus' imaginary self-identification (the projection of such values onto his adulterous relationship with Lesbia); and a real world in which these two realms can never coincide. Moreover, as the complex and overdetermined use of the word *domus* – with its fusing of the themes of adultery, family, marriage, and death – indicates, poem 68 displays a profound disaggregation of the relation between the poet's constitution of his personal identity and the categories that Roman life offered to make sense of it.[17] The result is a gap or absence at the subject's center, a kind of death, that the poem identifies metonymically with his brother's tomb.

This gap, with its complex ideological articulations around traditional concepts of household, marriage, and their simultaneous sanctity and nullification, is evident throughout the poem. It posits a beyond that can only be imagined as absence or death. The sequence of thought is strikingly emblematic. We move from the *sepulta domus* of the *gens Valerii* (94) to the *domus* violated by the illicit love of Paris and his *moecha* (103), then to the passion of Laodamia's *domus incepta frustra* imagined as an abyss or tomb (107–8), and finally to Catullus' ideal *domus* unto which Lesbia's father never led her as a bride (143–6). At each stage in the progression, there is an evocation of the normative vision of the Roman household so dear to Catullus from the wedding hymns 61 and 62 (Feeney 1992: 33–4; G. Williams 1980: 56; Wiseman 1969: 20–3; see Panoussi, this volume).

In the end, the *domus* theme and its slippages reveal a longing for a lawful household with a lawful *domina* that Catullus cannot acquire. This slippage and the inversion of values it creates are parallel to the slippage and longing for lawfully constituted relationships in poem 76. Yet in that poem, as here, the invocation of traditional values such as *pietas*, *fides*, and reciprocal *benefacta* cannot manufacture a return to a vanished ideal of Roman normality, but instead produces images of transgression, splitting, and death.[18]

Catullus bequeaths this deeply divided subjectivity to the elegists, one in which the recognized structures of the Roman ideology are no longer adequate to contain the forces of the imaginary desire. Such a split subject can only be symptomatic of profound disturbances in the world beyond the text. It is the moment both obscene and sublime in which the subject cries out "neither is it possible to wish you well if you became the best of women,/nor to cease to love you, no matter what you would do" (75.3–4). It is a moment of crisis that constitutes and makes possible both Catullan lyric subjectivity and the elegiac poetry that deliberately and self-consciously follows in its wake.

Conclusion

Catullus then is explicitly recognized as the progenitor of Roman love elegy by Propertius and Ovid, and implicitly by Tibullus. In terms of metrical form, the Catullan corpus is atypical of elegiac production. Less than a third of it is written in the elegiac meter, and much of that is written in the form of epigrams rather than elegy proper. Thematically, the Lesbia poems clearly anticipate the later elegiac collections, which are united around the story (or stories) of the poet's affair with a single named beloved. Again, however, the Catullan corpus shows considerably greater variety than that found in its elegiac descendants.

Like Catullus, the elegists compose complex collections of first-person verse that present themselves as the recounting and ultimately the embodiment of the speaking subject's lived experience. The lyric consciousness projected by these collections is a complex, self-reflexive, and multi-temporal consciousness made possible by, and dependent on, the process of reading and rereading.

Poem 68, the one poem in the Catullan corpus that most resembles a fully elaborated Roman love elegy, not only serves as a formal antecedent to the genre but also, in its complex relation to the rest of the Catullan corpus, bequeaths to the elegists the model of a split consciousness. It is in this split, as exemplified in poem 68's use of the *domus* motif, that we see the emergence of that which ties the history of the elegiac subgenre to the world beyond either individual desire or symbolic institutions. Catullus, therefore, is not only the progenitor of the elegiac subgenre, he is also the symptom of a crisis in Roman political and cultural history that made that subgenre possible.

NOTES

1 Miller (2004: 31–59, 2002: 1–36; 1994: chs. 3 and 7); Lee-Stecum (1998: 16–18); Hinds (1998: 29); Albrecht (1997: 744); Benediktson (1989: 21); Elia (1981: 74–5); Boucher (1980: 34).
2 All translations are my own.
3 The two poets are frequently listed together. Compare Prop. 2.25.4. See also Prop. 2.32.45, where Lesbia is listed as a predecessor of Cynthia.

4   This poem is commonly divided into 68a and b. The first poem is a *recusatio*, while the
    second provides (or substitutes) for the verse requested by Allius in 68a (Skinner 2003:
    40–3; Lefèvre 1991: 312–14; Courtney 1985: 95). 68b is the poem that treats the poet's
    relation to Lesbia. It stretches to 120 lines. Some see 68 as one poem in two parts (Janan
    1994: 113; M. J. Edwards 1991: 80), although as Hubbard indicates the cash value of the
    distinction between these two positions is hard to determine (Hubbard 1984: 48 n. 44).
    My reference text for Catullus is Thomson (1997).

5   Sulpicia's work, however, is impossible to generalize from. Not only is she an anomaly in
    being the only female elegist, but her body of work is atypical in its shortness (six poems,
    the longest being ten lines long). She is not mentioned by the other elegists and does not
    appear in Quintilian's canonical list.

6   There are thus notable stylistic and prosodic differences in Catullus between the longer
    elegiac poems (65–8) and the epigrams (69–116). See Ross (1969: 115–37) and Skinner
    (2003: 98–9) on the traditions of Roman epigram. There was a rich tradition of Hellenistic
    pederastic epigrams.

7   The studies of David Wray (2001) and Christopher Nappa (2001) have drawn attention to
    the subtle poetics of the non-Lesbia poems through their exploration of the "poetics of
    Roman manhood" and of Catullus' "social fiction" respectively.

8   See Skinner (2003: xxvii; 1988: 337–8; 1981); Dettmer (1997); Minyard (1988); Fergu-
    son (1988: 12–15); Wiseman (1969: 30, 1985: 136–7, 147–51, 170–1).

9   None of this means that poems were not orally performed or composed for such perform-
    ance before being integrated into the structures of the poetic book.

10 The one exception may be the fragments of Lucilius, but the texts are so fragmentary that
    it is difficult to judge the degree of arrangement. They are also satires, rather than the
    more intimately self-reflexive genre practiced by Catullus.

11 On the importance of this poem for establishing Lesbia's identity as Clodia Metelli and
    making possible a political reading of this sequence, see Skinner (2003: 81–3, 107).

12 If we accept, as most do, the identification of Lesbia with Clodia Metelli, then this poem
    would have an early dramatic date, since Clodia's husband, Metellus Celer, died shortly
    after the affair began.

13 For a fuller reading of these poems, see Miller (2004: 60–94).

14 See Albrecht (1997: 744); Conte (1994: 150, 324); Fantham (1996: 105); Gold (1993:
    85); Benediktson (1989: 11); Grimal (1987: 253); Hubbard (1984: 41); Sarkissian (1983:
    1); Lyne (1980: 82); G. Williams (1980: 45); Luck (1960: 50).

15 As I make clear in *Subjecting Verses* (2004), this subject position is constituted in relation
    to the three fundamental realms of Lacanian thought: the Imaginary, the Symbolic, and
    the Real.

16 For a fuller reading of the poem from this perspective, see Miller (2004: 31–59).

17 On the centrality of the *domus* to the Catullan moral universe, see Nappa (2001: 31).

18 Using a different approach, Theodorakopoulos in this volume develops a similar reading
    of the *domus* theme: see above, pp. 322–3.

GUIDE TO FURTHER READING

I limit discussion here to books that deal with both Catullus and elegy and that have not been
discussed in the body of the chapter. The modern study of elegy begins with Luck's *The Latin
Love Elegy* (1960), which provides a useful synoptic view of the genre and of what the ancient
sources say about its authors. Lyne's *The Latin Love Poets from Catullus to Horace* (1980)

examines Catullus' role in legitimizing the "life of love" and sees him as establishing the thematics of the elegiac genre through a concept of "whole love," which goes beyond the traditional alternatives of sexual passion and marital duty. Paul Veyne's *Roman Erotic Elegy* (1988) insists on the self-conscious artificiality of the elegiac genre, which separates the elegists from Catullus, whose poetry, he asserts, was meant to be read as sincere. Veyne offers no real argument for this dichotomy, nor does he address the fact that the elegists themselves cite Catullus as their predecessor. His work does, however, provide a useful corrective to the once dominant biographical approach. Ellen Greene's *The Erotics of Domination* (1999b) is the first book-length study to apply feminist scholarship to Catullus in relation to Propertius and Ovid.

WORKS CITED

Albrecht, M. von. 1997. *A History of Roman Literature from Livius Andronicus to Boethius with Special Regard to its Influence on World Literature*. Vol. I. Rev. G. Schmeling and M. von Albrecht. Trans. M. von Albrecht and G. Schmeling with the assistance of F. and K. Newman. Leiden.

Barber, E. A. 1953. *Sexti Properti Carmina*. 2nd edn. Oxford.

Benediktson, D. T. 1989. *Propertius: Modernist Poet of Antiquity*. Carbondale.

Boucher, J.-P. 1980. *Études sur Properce: problèmes d'inspiration et d'art*. 2nd edn. Paris.

Cairns, F. 1983. "Propertius 1,4 and 1,5 and the 'Gallus' of the *Monobiblos*." *Papers of the Liverpool Latin Seminar* 4: 61–102.

Camps, W. A. 1961. *Propertius:* Elegies *Book I*. Cambridge.

Conte, G. B. 1994. *Latin Literature: A History*. Trans. J. B. Solodow. Rev. D. Fowler and G. W. Most. Baltimore.

Courtney, E. 1985. "Three Poems of Catullus." *Bulletin of the Institute for Classical Studies of the University of London* 32: 85–100.

Dettmer, H. 1997. *Love by the Numbers: Form and Meaning in the Poetry of Catullus*. New York.

Edwards, M. J. 1991. "The Theology of Catullus 68b." *Antike und Abendland* 37: 68–81.

Elia, S. d'. 1981. "I Presupposti sociologici dell' esperienza elegiaca Properziana." In F. Santucci and S. Vivona, eds., *Colloquium Propertianum (secundum): Atti*. Assisi. 59–80.

Fantham, E. 1996. *Roman Literary Culture: From Cicero to Apuleius*. Baltimore.

Fedeli, P. 1980. *Sesto Properzio: Il Primo libro delle elegie*. Florence.

Fedeli, P. 1983b. " 'Properti monobiblos': struttura e motivi." In W. Haase, ed., *Aufstieg und Niedergang der Römischen Welt*, II, 30.3. Berlin. 1858–1922.

Feeney, D. C. 1992. " 'Shall I compare thee…?': Catullus 68B and the Limits of Analogy." In A. J. Woodman and J. Powell, eds., *Author and Audience in Latin Literature*. Cambridge. 33–44.

Ferguson, J. 1988. *Catullus.* Greece & Rome New Surveys in the Classics No. 20. Oxford.

Gold, B. K. 1993. " 'But Ariadne Was Never There in the First Place': Finding the Female in Roman Poetry." In N. S. Rabinowitz and A. Richlin, eds., *Feminist Theory and the Classics*. New York. 75–101.

Greene, E. 1999b. *The Erotics of Domination: Male Desire and the Mistress in Latin Love Poetry*. Baltimore.

Grimal, P. 1987. "Catulle et les origines de l'élégie romaine." *Mélanges d'archéologie et de l'histoire de l'ecole française de Rome, antiquité* 99: 243–56.

Hinds, S. 1998. *Allusion and Intertext: Dynamics of Appropriation in Roman Poetry*. Cambridge.

Hodge, R. I. V., and R. A. Buttimore. 1977. *The "Monobiblos" of Propertius: An Account of the First Book of Propertius Consisting of a Text, Translation, and Critical Essay on Each Poem.* Cambridge.

Hubbard, T. K. 1983. "The Catullan *Libellus*." *Philologus* 127: 218–37.

Hubbard, T. K. 1984. "Catullus 68: The Text as Self-Demystification." *Arethusa* 17: 29–49.

James, S. 2003. *Learned Girls and Male Persuasion: Gender and Reading in Roman Love Elegy.* Berkeley.

Janan, M. 1994. *"When the Lamp is Shattered": Desire and Narrative in Catullus.* Carbondale and Edwardsville, IL.

Johnson, W. R. 1982. *The Idea of Lyric: Lyric Modes in Ancient and Modern Poetry.* Berkeley.

Kennedy, D. 1993. *The Arts of Love: Five Studies in the Discourse of Roman Love Elegy.* Cambridge.

King, J. K. 1980. "The Two Galluses of Propertius' *Monobiblos*." *Philologus* 124: 212–30.

King, J. K. 1988. "Catullus' Callimachean *carmina*, cc. 65–116." *Classical World* 81: 383–92.

Lee-Stecum, P. 1998. *Powerplay in Tibullus.* Cambridge.

Lefèvre, E. 1991. "Was hatte Catull in der Kapsel, die er von Rom nach Verona mitnahm? Zu Aufbau und Aussage der Allius-Elegie." *Rheinisches Museum für Philologie* 134: 311–26.

Luck, G. 1960. *The Latin Love Elegy.* New York.

Lyne, R. O. A. M. 1980. *The Latin Love Poets from Catullus to Horace.* Oxford.

Miller, P. A. 1994. *Lyric Texts and Lyric Consciousness: The Birth of a Genre from Archaic Greece to Augustan Rome.* London and New York.

Miller, P. A. 2002. *Latin Erotic Elegy: An Anthology and Reader.* London.

Miller, P. A. 2004. *Subjecting Verses: Latin Love Elegy and the Emergence of the Real.* Princeton, NJ.

Minyard, J. D. 1988. "The Source of the *Catulli Veronensis Liber*." *Classical World* 81: 343–53.

Mynors, R. A. B., ed. 1958 (rev. 1960). *C. Valerii Catulli Carmina recognovit brevique adnotatione critica instruxit.* Oxford.

Nappa, C. 2001. *Aspects of Catullus' Social Fiction.* Frankfurt.

Oliensis, E. 1997. "The Erotics of *amicitia*: Readings in Tibullus, Propertius, and Horace." In J. P. Hallett and M. B. Skinner, eds., *Roman Sexualities*. Princeton, NJ. 151–71.

Owen, S. G. 1915. *P. Ovidi Nasonis Tristium Libri Quinque Ibis Ex Ponto Libri Quattuor Halieutica Fragmenta.* Oxford.

Pöschl, V. 1983. *Catull.* Freiburg.

Quinn, K. 1959. *The Catullan Revolution.* Melbourne. Rpt. Cambridge 1969; Ann Arbor, MI, 1971. 2nd edn. London 1999.

Quinn, K. 1972b. *Catullus: An Interpretation.* London.

Quinn, K., ed. 1973a. *Catullus: The Poems.* 2nd edn. London and Basingstoke.

Richardson, L., Jr. 1977. *Propertius: Elegies I–IV.* Norman, OK.

Ross, D. O., Jr. 1969. *Style and Tradition in Catullus.* Cambridge, MA.

Ross, D. O., Jr. 1975. *Backgrounds to Augustan Poetry: Gallus, Elegy and Rome.* Cambridge.

Rothstein, M. 1979 [1920]. *Die Elegien des Sextus Propertius.* 2 vols. 2nd edn. New York.

Sarkissian, J. 1983. *Catullus 68: An Interpretation.* Mnemosyne Supplement 76. Leiden.

Segal, C. 1968. "The Order of Catullus, Poems 2–11." *Latomus* 27: 305–21.

Sharrock, A. R. 2000. "Constructing Characters in Propertius." *Arethusa* 33: 263–84.

Skinner, M. B. 1981. *Catullus' Passer: The Arrangement of the Book of Polymetric Poems.* New York.

Skinner, M. B. 1988. "Aesthetic Patterning in Catullus: Textual Structures, Systems of Imagery and Book Arrangements. Introduction." *Classical World* 81: 337–40.

Skinner, M. B. 2003. *Catullus in Verona: A Reading of the Elegiac Libellus, Poems 65–116.* Columbus, OH.

Stahl, H. P. 1985. *Propertius: "Love" and "War": Individual and State under Augustus.* Berkeley.

Suits, T. A. 1976. "The Iambic Character of Propertius 1.4." *Philologus* 120: 86–91.

Thomson, D. F. S., ed. 1997. *Catullus: Edited with a Textual and Interpretative Commentary.* Toronto.

Veyne, P. 1988. *Roman Erotic Elegy: Love Poetry and the West.* Trans. D. Pellauer. Chicago.

Whitaker, R. 1983. *Myth and Personal Experience in Roman Love-Elegy: A Study in Poetic Technique.* Göttingen.

Williams, G. 1980. *Figures of Thought in Roman Poetry.* New Haven, CT.

Wiseman, T. P. 1969. *Catullan Questions.* Leicester.

Wiseman, T. P. 1985. *Catullus and His World: A Reappraisal.* Cambridge.

Wray, D. 2001. *Catullus and the Poetics of Roman Manhood.* Cambridge.

CHAPTER TWENTY-TWO

Catullus and Martial

Sven Lorenz

One of the most famous pieces written by the first-century epigrammatist Martial is the thirty-second poem in his first book of epigrams, the model for the popular "I do not love thee, Doctor Fell" (cf. Howell 1980: 176–8):

> Non amo te, Sabidi, nec possum dicere quare:
> hoc tantum possum dicere, non amo te.

I don't like you, Sabidius, and I can't tell you why. All I can tell is: I don't like you.[1]

Below I discuss the question of why the speaker of this epigram does not like the Sabidius who is addressed in 1.32. For now it will suffice to point out that the epigram is probably indebted to another, even more popular poem: Catullus' c. 85:

> Odi et amo. quare id faciam, fortasse requiris?
> nescio, sed fieri sentio et excrucior.

I hate and I love. Perhaps you ask why I do this? I don't know, but I feel it happening and it tortures me.[2]

Martial repeats Catullus' verb *amo* ("like," "love"), the interrogative *quare* ("why"), and the idea that the reason why cannot be given. In addition, both poems consist of two lines in the meter of the elegiac distich. For these reasons, many scholars have concluded that Martial deliberately imitated Catullus (Paukstadt 1876: 19; Ferguson 1963: 10f.; Citroni 1975: 109). Furthermore, Howell (1980: 176; cf. Friedlaender 1886: I.185) has pointed out that "the repetition of the opening words at the end is Catullan."

In Martial's "books of epigrams" we come across numerous pieces which betray Catullan influence on Martial's choice of words or meter, on his themes or the structure of his poems. In addition, most of Catullus' *carmina* are, like Martial's epigrams, rather short and many of Martial's meters are also used by Catullus, so that their respective works bear a strong formal resemblance (Holzberg 2002b: 33–4). Furthermore, many poems show obvious structural parallels. Catullus may also have been an important forerunner of Martial's practice of assembling short poems on different topics and in different meters in books, instead of simply composing monothematic books of epigrams (Holzberg 2002b: 40–1, 47–8; Lorenz 2002: 64–5, 2004b: 255–6). And at least some parts of Catullus' and Martial's collections are similar in their compositional structures: some groups of poems are arranged in cycles and there are also extensive passages composed for linear reading (Barwick 1958; Scherf 2001; Claes 2002; Holzberg 2002b: 135–52; Lorenz 2004b). Finally, Martial mentions Catullus more often than any other poetic predecessor (cf. Swann 1994: 33–8). In an epigram from Book 10, Catullus is even granted a more prominent place in literary history than Martial himself (10.78.14–16):

> sic inter ueteres legar poetas,
> nec multos mihi praeferas priores,
> uno sed tibi sim minor Catullo.

Thus may I be read among the old poets, and may you not prefer many earlier poets to me, but for you may I be less than Catullus only.

There can be no doubt that Martial cherished Catullus' works and imitated his predecessor from Republican Rome in many of his own epigrams. This, however, is not the whole truth. In 1.32, for example, Martial turns Catullus' expression of unfulfilled love into an aggressive invective. Paukstadt (1876: 19) was the first to point out that Martial wanted the readers of 1.32 to remember Catullus' c. 85 – even though, as Paukstadt admitted, Martial's poem was "less weighty" ("quamquam non tam graue") than its Catullan model. But other scholars (Friedlaender 1886: I.185; Howell 1980: 175–6) denied that Martial 1.32 was a deliberate reminiscence of Catullus 85. Apparently, they would not accept that Martial could show so little respect for Catullus that he would turn c. 85 into a bad joke. Given the verbal and structural parallels between the two poems, however, Sullivan (1991: 96) is certainly right when he cites 1.32 in order to show that "Martial is quite capable of parodying Catullus and using some of his most elevated thoughts and phrases in banal or comic contexts."

Martial's usage of Catullan influences in his epigrams was obviously more complex than the mere imitation of a poetic idol. For this reason, there is no point in trying to find out who is the better poet – or, for that matter, whether Martial or Catullus is the better Catullus – as has been attempted, for example, by Offermann (1980; cf., on that doubtful practice, Swann 1994: 4 and Grewing 1996: 333). Neither do I want to offer exhaustive lists of passages from the two poets' works and analyze in what way Martial in each case made use of the Catullan model. Instead, I shall examine in what way Martial presents himself as Catullus' successor and to what extent he puts his own metapoetic statements – i.e., statements concerning his own poetry – into poetic practice: what aspects of Catullus' poetry are of primary importance for Martial's own poems?

The passage in Martial's works where his readers learn the most about this poet and his poetry is, of course, the beginning of his first book of epigrams (ca. AD 85), and this text will be the focus of my attention. A close look at the beginning of Book 1 will reveal that, in order to characterize himself and his epigrams, Martial explicitly states his debt to Catullus, and at the same time tries to turn his Catullan influence into something new. Let us start by looking at the prose epistle that serves as a preface to Book 1:

> Spero me secutum in libellis meis tale temperamentum ut de illis queri non possit quisquis de se bene senserit, cum salua infimarum quoque personarum reuerentia ludant; quae adeo antiquis auctoribus defuit ut nominibus non tantum ueris abusi sint sed et magnis, mihi fama uilius constet et probetur in me nouissimum ingenium. absit a iocorum nostrorum simplicitate malignus interpres nec epigrammata mea scribat:[3] im-probe facit qui in alieno libro ingeniosus est. lasciuam uerborum ueritatem, id est epigrammaton linguam, excusarem, si meum esset exemplum: sic scribit Catullus, sic Marsus, sic Pedo, sic Gaetulicus, sic quicumque perlegitur. si quis tamen tam ambitiose tristis est ut apud illum in nulla pagina latine loqui fas sit, potest epistula uel potius titulo contentus esse. epigrammata illis scribuntur qui solent spectare Florales. non intret Cato theatrum meum, aut si intrauerit, spectet. uideor mihi meo iure facturus si epistulam uersibus clusero:

> > Nosses iocosae dulce cum sacrum Florae
> > festosque lusus et licentiam uulgi,
> > cur in theatrum. Cato seuere, uenisti?
> > an ideo tantum ueneras, ut exires?

I hope to have achieved such a balance in my little books that nobody who thinks well of himself can complain about them, because they joke while preserving respect for persons, even of the lowest order. This respect was so lacking in older writers that they abused not only real names, but even great ones. Such a price I would not pay for fame and for that kind of cleverness I do not want to be praised. Let the malicious interpreter keep his distance from the harmlessness of my jokes and not rewrite my epigrams. It is not right to be clever with somebody else's book. I follow reality in using lascivious words – that is the language of epigram – and I would apologize for that if I were the first to do so: Catullus writes like that, and Marsus, and Pedo, and Gaetulicus, and everybody who is read all the way through. But, if somebody should be so keen on being prudish that one cannot speak plain Latin on any page in his presence, he can content himself with this letter, or better, with the title. Epigrams are written for those people who are accustomed to watch the games of Flora. Let Cato not enter my theater, or if he enters, let him watch. I consider myself acting within my rights if I finish this letter in verse:

> > Since you knew the sweet ritual of humorous Flora
> > and the jokes of that celebration and the people's license,
> > why, strict Cato, did you come to the theater?
> > Or did you just enter in order to leave?

No addressee is explicitly mentioned and that is why in some manuscripts the title *Ad lectorem* ("to the reader") has been added. Obviously this letter serves as an address to Martial's readership in general, but the first actual name that we read in Book 1 is *Catullus*. Martial mentions this predecessor as a precedent for a poet who wrote obscene poetry. But between the lines, Catullus is present much earlier than that. Some readers may note that the term *libellus* ("little book"), which both Martial (cf. Citroni 1975: 6–7) and Catullus (1.8, 14.12, 55.4) frequently use for their own works, is the fifth word in the text. It was also the fifth word in the first line of the first poem of Catullus' collection:

> Quoi dono lepidum nouum libellum

> To whom shall I give my elegant new little book?

At first we learn that Martial tends to criticize or, at least, make fun of others in his poems, but does not neglect the *reuerentia personarum* ("respect of persons"). In addition he points out that he does not attack anyone by using their real names (*nomina uera*), and he certainly does not attack any great names (*nomina magna*). Martial thus distances himself from poets who did not refrain from such personal attacks; i.e., he reflects on his role in comparison with the works of poetic predecessors and "consciously assumes a place within a tradition" (Newman 1990: 99). And many of Martial's contemporary readers will have thought of Catullus in particular. In fact, Catullus points out that his poems have the power to hurt his personal enemies (cf. below) and he does not refrain from attacking such powerful contemporaries as Caesar, Pompey, or Mamurra (Sullivan 1991: 97).

However, Martial does not say that he is not going to hurt anybody, but that only those who have a good opinion of themselves have nothing to fear from the epigrams – i.e., others may well have good reasons to fear this poetry. Especially when we have reached the end of the epistle and the appended epigram, it becomes obvious that the doubts concerning Martial's harmlessness have been justified. Here he uses a "real and great name": Cato, who is being ridiculed for his prudish comportment (Beck 2002: 197–8). Cato, of course, had died a long time ago, but it is worth noting that Martial (unlike Juvenal in his first satire: 1.170–1) does not emphasize that he refrains from attacking VIPs who are still alive.

Martial's next point is that he is going to talk about sexual matters and use an adequate language – i.e., we can deduce, obscene vocabulary. Martial gives three reasons why he writes obscene poetry.

First, he mentions *ueritas* ("truth," "realism") and the need to speak plain Latin (*latine loqui*). Martial claims that a realistic description of his world would not be possible without obscene terms (Banta 1998: 219). It is worth noting that Martial almost contradicts what he said before: having just distanced himself from using *nomina uera* ("real names"), he now presents *ueritas* as the ideal of his own poetry. Martial, in fact, contradicts himself so often that his contradictory manner is one of the key characteristics of his epigrams.

The second reason why obscene words must be used becomes clear when Martial mentions the *epigrammaton lingua* ("the language of epigram"). According to him, the rules of the epigrammatic genre dictate the use of obscenities. Here Martial also mentions Catullus and three other poets as epigrammatic predecessors.[4]

Having cited those precedents for obscene literature, Martial finally comes up with his third argument: those authors have a wide and eager readership. He thus tells us that literary fame is one of the goals he pursues with his poetry and implies that fame can only be obtained when one employs obscene language (Banta 1998: 220).

But Catullus is important not only because he wrote obscene poetry, for he also preceded Martial in justifying obscenities in his literary corpus. Many readers of Martial's prose epistle will have been reminded of Catullus' c. 16:

> Pedicabo ego uos et irrumabo,
> Aureli pathice et cinaede Furi,
> qui me ex uersiculis meis putastis,
> quod sunt molliculi, parum pudicum.
> nam castum esse decet pium poetam
> ipsum, uersiculos nihil necesse est;
> qui tum denique habent salem ac leporem,
> si sunt molliculi ac parum pudici,
> et quod pruriat incitare possunt,
> non dico pueris, sed his pilosis
> qui duros nequeunt mouere lumbos.
> uos, quod milia multa basiorum
> legistis, male me marem putatis?
> pedicabo ego uos et irrumabo.

I will fuck you in your ass and in your mouth, pathic Aurelius and Furius the sodomite, who think, because my verses are soft, that I am shameless. For a decent poet must be chaste himself, but for his verses that is not necessary. These, in a word, will have spice and wit, if they are soft and shameless, and if they can arouse something to itch – I don't say in boys – but in those bearded men who find it hard to move their hardened loins. Because you have read of many thousand kisses, do you therefore think that I am less a man? I will fuck you in your ass and in your mouth!

Unlike Martial, Catullus does not clearly refer to the language of his poetry, i.e., the usage of obscene words (*lasciuia uerborum*). He generally admits that his verses are "soft" (*molliculi*) and in particular alludes to the kiss-poems 5 and 7. But his claim that his poetry should arouse the readers sexually (9) is a clear indication that Catullus – like Martial – has the use of actual obscenities in mind. For obscene language was supposed to be titillating (cf. below on Martial 1.35). Considering that, it is quite naughty of Catullus to react to criticism of his obscene verses – be that criticism real or fictional – by justifying the use of obscenities in a poem which is itself obscene.

The epistle and the appended epigram finish with Martial's definition of his adequate readership – albeit an *ex negatiuo* definition. Prudish people – such as Cato Uticensis, who couldn't even bear to watch a public stage show that included nude dancing (Val. Max. 2.10.8) – should keep their distance from Martial's epigrams. Again, the description of an unsuitable recipient reminds us of Catullus – this time of his first kiss-poem, c. 5. There "old men who are too severe" (*senes seueriores*, 2) are presented as the opponents of joyful love and, we can deduce, love poetry. And Martial also uses Catullus' adjective *seuerus*. In addition, the verb *ludere* ("play"), from which Martial's noun *lusus* ("jests") is derived, frequently comes up in Catullus' poems (50.2, 61.126, 68.17, 68.156; cf. Swann 1994: 55–9). Furthermore, the readers of Martial's joke at Cato's expense may have thought of Catullus' c. 56, which begins as follows (1–4):

O rem ridiculam, Cato, et iocosam,
dignamque auribus et tuo cachinno!
ride quidquid amas, Cato, Catullum:
res est ridicula et nimis iocosa.

> Oh, what a ridiculous and funny thing, Cato, and worthy of your ears and your laughter. Laugh, Cato – your Catullus, whom you love, asks you to do so.[5] It is ridiculous and just too funny.

What follows is the description of a sexual encounter, and therefore many scholars have assumed that Catullus' poem cannot be addressed to the proverbially severe Cato Uticensis (Kroll 1968: 100; Thomson 1997: 339). However, some have also adduced convincing arguments in favor of the identification of the Cato in c. 56 with Cato of Utica (Buchheit 1961a: 353–6; Skinner 1982b). If this is correct, then Martial's prose preface with the epigram on Cato betrays another connection to Catullus' works: both poets address Cato in an erotic context even though – or, rather, because – this stern man does not fit erotic poetry at all (Beck 2002: 184). Even if Catullus and Martial did not refer to the same Cato, community of name nevertheless is a sufficient bridge from Martial's to Catullus' poem. Both Catullus and Martial adopt a deliberately provocative stance. Both are so bold that they only pretend to apologize for their obscene and aggressive poetry, but in fact make clear that they *want* to write obscene poems.[6]

Of course, in the epistle we do learn not only a lot about the kind of poetry that is going to follow in this book, but also about its author, or rather a certain representation of the poet. I have dealt with the characterization of Martial's literary *persona* ("mask") elsewhere (Lorenz 2002: 4–42; cf. Holzberg 2002b: 13–18), so I will not go into that in great detail here. But some of this speaker's character traits have already become obvious: the Martial whom we encounter in this epistle is very interested in erotic and obscene poetry (and in many poems that follow he will show too his enormous interest in sexual encounters). He also lacks respect for people of high rank or reputation and is presented as a rather naughty character. It is obvious that this fictional, or at least fictionalized, speaker is heavily indebted to the rules of the epigrammatic genre, e.g., that it is imperative for an epigrammatist to write obscene poetry. And in these traits he strongly resembles the personae of many other poets of the lower genres of erotic poetry (Lorenz 2004a: 119–21), especially the Catullan speaker, whose strong interest in sexual matters and often desperate attempts to fulfill his desires contribute to his presentation of an effeminate *uir mollis* ("soft man;" cf., e.g., Skinner 1993; Holzberg 2000, 2002a; Nappa 2001).[7]

Given all that, it comes as quite a surprise that the epigrams that immediately follow in Book 1 do not contain any obscene words whatsoever. Since Martial in Book 3 (and elsewhere) characterizes his readers as people who enjoy obscene poems and lose interest in a book that is not obscene (Lorenz 2002: 23–8), it seems as if the poet deliberately whets the readers' appetite for obscenities in order to disappoint them. But even though Martial does not indulge in Catullus' practice of using obscenities yet, other elements of the Catullan oeuvre are already present. This is obvious, for example, in epigram 1.1, which follows the epistle:

> Hic est quem legis ille, quem requiris,
> toto notus in orbe Martialis
> argutis epigrammaton libellis:
> cui, lector studiose, quod dedisti
> uiuenti decus atque sentienti,
> rari post cineres habent poetae.

Here he is whom you read and ask for: Martial, known all over the world for his funny little books of epigrams. The glory that you have given him while he is still alive and feels it comes to few poets after death.

Again we come across Catullus' term *libelli* ("little books"). It is interesting that Martial uses this diminutive in a claim to everlasting fame all over the world – and that in the first poem of his first book.[8] Catullus, in his first poem, discusses the same topic. But he seems to be much more careful than Martial: Catullus' only hope is that his book will last for a century, whereas Martial seems to take his immortal glory for granted. And while Martial addresses an anonymous readership from all over the world and claims that they enjoy his works, Catullus mentions only one specific addressee: he appeals to Cornelius Nepos' open mind. He even compares his own *libellus* to Nepos' massive literary oeuvre (cf. Skinner 1987; Feeney 1999: 13–14; Hutchinson 2003: 209). Catullus thus presents his little book as if it were a rather paltry piece of work – a stance which, of course, at the same time implies a clear statement in favor of the minor literary genres as opposed to really "great" literature (Summers 2001: 148).

The differences between Martial's epigram 1.1 and Catullus' introductory poem may result from the fact that Martial, who had more of a literary tradition to cling to, was in a more comfortable position than his predecessor, who made a strong point of presenting a "new" kind of book of poetry (*nouum libellum*, Catull. 1.1). However, Martial also tends to downgrade his own works in comparison with the greater genres. This aspect, in fact, is one of the key elements of Martial's metapoetic poems (Banta 1998). But in the case of epigram 1.1, it seems as if Martial wanted to surpass Catullus in his boldness to claim extensive fame for a book of mainly erotic poems of a low genre.

That Martial had Catullus in mind when he wrote the beginning of Book 1 is even more apparent in 1.4, where the emperor Domitian is mentioned for the first time. The poem ends with the line *lasciua est nobis pagina, uita proba* ("My page is immoral, my life is virtuous," 8), and this, of course, alludes to Catullus' c. 16. Unlike Catullus, however, Martial still has not used a single primary obscenity in his book.

Catullus is mentioned again in 1.7:

> Stellae delicium mei columba,
> Verona licet audiente dicam,
> uicit, Maxime, passerem Catulli.
> tanto Stella meus tuo Catullo
> quanto passere maior est columba.

My Stella's pet, his Dove (I may say it, even if Verona hears it), has surpassed Catullus' Sparrow, Maximus. My Stella is as much greater than your Catullus as a dove is greater than a sparrow.

Even though, for example, Ovid's works are also conspicuously present at the beginning of Martial's Book 1 (Lorenz 2002: 18–19), Catullus, whose name comes up again, is presented as Martial's primary model. And this is also true despite the fact that Martial's friend and patron Stella is praised for his poem *Columba* ("Dove"), which is said to be greater than Catullus' *Passer* ("Sparrow"). The first word from Catullus' second poem here denotes Catullus' poetry in general or is used as the title of the Catullan collection (Nauta 2002: 156–8 with n. 40).

But there is more to 1.7 than praise for a contemporary poet. It has been widely debated whether Catullus' poems 2 and 3 only lament the death of Lesbia's pet sparrow or whether this bird is a metaphor for the poet's often dysfunctional penis (see also Dyson Hejduk and Gaisser, this volume, pp. 257, 443–5). But Martial's poem with its rather ridiculous comparison between the size of Stella's dove and Catullus' sparrow is a clear hint that Martial did interpret his predecessor's verses in an obscene way:[9] not only does he use the comparative form *maior* ("bigger"), but also emphasizes the issue of size by addressing somebody named *Maximus* ("biggest").[10]

There are further epigrams in Martial's oeuvre where Catullus' "sparrow" is mentioned that also hint in the direction that Martial understood Catullus' sparrow as an image for the poet's penis. The most obvious case is epigram 7.14:

> Accidit infandum nostrae scelus, Aule, puellae;
>   amisit lusus deliciasque suas:
> non quales teneri plorauit amica Catulli
>   Lesbia, nequitiis passeris orba sui,
> uel Stellae cantata meo quas fleuit Ianthis,
>   cuius in Elysio nigra columba uolat:
> lux mea non capitur nugis neque amoribus istis
>   nec dominae pectus talia damna mouent:
> bis denos puerum numerantem perdidit annos,
>   mentula cui nondum sesquipedalis erat.

An unspeakable crime has happened to my girl, Aulus. She has lost her plaything and pleasure: not like the one that tender Catullus' girlfriend Lesbia wept for, when she had lost her sparrow's naughty tricks, and unlike the one that Ianthis, sung by my Stella, cried for, whose dove flies, now black, in Elysium. My darling is not impressed by trifles or by those loves, nor can such losses move my mistress' heart. She has lost a boy of twice ten years,[11] whose cock was not yet eighteen inches long.

The size of the dead boy's penis is grotesque and it may not be by accident that Catullus also used the numeral *sesquipedalis* in one of his poems (97.5). The punchline of Martial's poem creates the impression that the poet wanted to make clear what Catullus' lament (and also Stella's lament for his beloved Ianthis' pigeon) are *really* about.

The same is probably true of epigram 11.6 (cf. Obermayer 1998: 71–3). Following the description of a Saturnalian feast, Martial addresses a boy (14–16):

> da nunc basia, sed Catulliana:
> quae si tot fuerint quot ille dixit,
> donabo tibi Passerem Catulli.

Now, give me kisses, but Catullan kisses. If they shall be as many as he said, I will give you Catullus' Sparrow.

Of course, the primary meaning of *Passer Catulli* in this poem is that it is the title of Catullus' book, which contains two poems about counting kisses (5 and 7). In the erotic atmosphere depicted in this epigram, however, it makes sense that the speaker of the poem also offers the addressee some sexual favor rather than just the present of a book of poetry or even a pet bird (cf. Kay 1985: 75–6).

As Garthwaite (1978: 72) rightly puts it: "Whatever Catullus himself may have been suggesting in his sparrow poems is, of course, irrelevant here. Suffice it to note that Martial invariably uses *passer Catulli* in the sense of *membrum virile* [male member]." And this is, of course, also true of 1.7. Some will not find it easy to accept that Martial made a joke like this at the expense of his great predecessor Catullus and his powerful contemporary Stella. But we must not forget that boldness is an important characteristic of Martial's (and also Catullus') poetry in general. And again we must take into account that it is not the real Martial who speaks in the epigrams, but a fictional, typically epigrammatic persona that has to follow the rules of the genre. Stella, who himself seems to have been the author of erotic verse (P. Watson 1999), would certainly have understood that such jokes were an integral part of epigrammatic poetry.

However, people who read Martial's first book for the first time may still be surprised that so far no obscene term has been used, that there only have been obscenities hidden beneath the wording of the epigrams. They have to wait until they get to epigram 1.34, where we finally come across the kind of language that Martial justified in the epistle and poem 1.4. In 1.34 Martial addresses a woman (it may not be by accident that she bears the name of Catullus' beloved Lesbia) who enjoys having sex in the presence of people watching. He therefore offers the following piece of advice: *deprendi ueto te, Lesbia, non futui* ("I forbid you to get caught, Lesbia, not to get fucked," 10).[12] The last word of the poem is the first obscene term in the book.

But again Martial surprises his readers. For that initial obscene word is followed by yet another apologetic justification of obscene poetry in general. This is 1.35:

> Versus scribere me parum seueros
> nec quos praelegat in schola magister,
> Corneli, quereris: sed hi libelli,
> tamquam coniugibus suis mariti,
> non possunt sine mentula placere.
> quid si me iubeas thalassionem
> uerbis dicere non thalassionis?
> quis Floralia uestit et stolatum
> permittit meretricibus pudorem?
> lex haec carminibus data est iocosis,
> ne possint, nisi pruriant, iuuare.
> quare deposita seueritate
> parcas lusibus et iocis rogamus,
> nec castrare uelis meos libellos.
> Gallo turpius est nihil Priapo.

Cornelius, you complain that I write verses that are immoral and that a teacher cannot read out in class. But these little books – like husbands with their wives – can't please without a cock. Would you request me to sing a wedding-song with words that are not adequate for wedding-songs? Who clothes Flora's games or allows whores the modesty of the matron's stole? This law has been laid down for humorous poems: they cannot be enjoyable unless they arouse. That's why I ask you to put prudery aside and leave my jests and jokes alone, and not wish to castrate my little books. Nothing is uglier than a Priapus who is a eunuch.

Banta (1998: 230) points out that "Martial . . . employs obscenity here primarily as a vehicle for the continuation of his *apologia*, rather than the *apologia* as an *ex post facto* means of justifying his use of obscenity." It is indeed obvious that Martial has turned Catullus' topic "justification of obscene poetry" into a complex game he plays with his readers – a game that he started with the apologies expressed in the epistle and which he now continues. Again, Martial uses Catullan vocabulary, such as the term *seuerus* ("severe"), and it may not be by accident that 1.35, like Catullus 1, is addressed to a Cornelius (Beck 1996: 268–9; Summers 2001: 148). In addition, Martial alludes to Catullus 16 when his poem also expresses the idea that erotic poetry can serve as a sexual stimulant (Obermayer 1998: 260–1).

Whereas Catullus dedicated only one poem to the justification of obscene poetry, Martial deals with this issue in many poems and his first epistle. Thus he can play with the readers' expectations and make his collection as a whole much more intriguing. And the one primary source for all these metapoetic epigrams about the use of obscenity may well be Catullus' c. 16.

But Martial does surpass Catullus not only in the number and complexity of his apologetic pieces but also in the intensity of his obscenities. Catullus' boldness at justifying obscenities in the obscene poem 16 is just the starting point for Martial's moves – to make the readers wait for obscenities, then give them the verb *futuere* ("fuck"), then apologize for that again, but in a poem that contains the obscene word *mentula* ("cock"). Furthermore, Martial makes quite clear that using obscenities is a must for an epigrammatist and his derogatory remark about verses that "a schoolmaster would dictate in class" (1–2) leaves no doubt that he is quite happy to obey the "law of epigram" rather than compose verses fit for schoolchildren. Finally, it is worth noting that Martial illustrates his point with the highly provocative image of the married Roman lady who is pleased with her husband's penis. Holzberg (2006: 151–2) therefore concludes:

> [T]he later poet is already indicating in 1.34 that he wishes on the one hand to carry on in the tradition of the earlier poet, but that he plans, on the other, to outstrip him with the frankness of his obscenities. He then declares in the poetological epigram 1.35 – explicitly and much more emphatically than Catullus in c. 16 – that his verses are meant to be suggestive and arousing.

Martial thus presents himself as a new – and even naughtier – Catullus. It is remarkable how easily Martial makes use of his Republican predecessor and it has often been pointed out that Martial in his use of Catullus tends to blur the differences between the two poets' works and times. Swann (1994: 81) is surprised "that Martial so consistently attempted to transcend these differences in order to align himself with one whom he perceived chiefly to be another epigrammatist." For Martial, it is, in fact, crucial to emphasize the similarities between himself and Catullus. Martial's use of Catullus' poems works best when our attention is directed to the subtle differences between the two. We can only see what is typical of Martial when he slightly changes the Catullan pattern. Martial's more elaborated treatment of the topic "justification of obscene poetry" is a case in point.

It is therefore not surprising that Martial does not seem to be particularly interested in the Catullus who wrote the *carmina maiora* in the middle of the Catullan collection and that the "Alexandrian works of Catullus" are hardly mentioned at all (cf. Sullivan 1991: 96). In fact, Martial may even criticize Catullus' longer poems (2.86.4–5). However, in 1.35, Martial does mention *thalassiones* ("wedding-songs") and may thus allude to Catullus' long and learned wedding-songs, where the term *Talasius* is actually used (61.134; cf. Citroni 1975: 117; Thomson 1997: 349). Catullus' wedding-songs, however, do not contain any explicitly obscene vocabulary – no doubt unlike other ancient specimens of that genre. It is therefore possible that Martial actually wanted to indicate that he himself could only have written obscene *thalassiones*. So, again we get the impression that Martial presents himself as a poet who is more inclined to use obscene words than Catullus.

Banta (1998: 217 n. 81) is probably right to conclude that Martial's justifications of obscene poetry served the purpose of directing his readers' attention to it. As a result, Martial has obtained the reputation as the writer of obscene poetry, whereas Catullus, who apologized only once, has even been claimed to be a romantic poet (cf. Swann 1994: 5). This is even more surprising when we take into account that statistically Catullus' book contains a higher frequency of obscene terms than Martial's works.

In this context we must also take a further look at epigram 1.32, which I quoted at the beginning of this chapter. As I hope to have made clear, the fact that Martial admired Catullus does not exclude the possibility that he turned his model into the pretext for a joke. In fact, being too respectful of Catullus would have come close to violating the rules of their common genre. Furthermore, there are good reasons to believe that the poem expresses much more than "simply unanalysable dislike," as Howell (1980: 175) suggests. Jocelyn (1981: 278–9) points to epigram 3.17, where a Sabidius is criticized for his stinking breath – a vice that is usually associated with oral sexual practices, and not only in Martial (Obermayer 1998: 214–31; cf. Holzberg 2002b: 98–9). Another reader who believed that Martial in 1.32 was alluding to a predilection for oral sexual practices on Sabidius' part was Ben Jonson (Boehrer 1998: 373–4).

Of course, the first readers of Book 1 could not have known about Martial's criticism of Sabidius' stinking breath in Book 3. It is, in fact, the key feature of 1.32 that we are never explicitly told what is wrong with Sabidius. Martial thus makes his first-time readers wonder why he dislikes the man. And after those readers have come to 1.34 and 1.35 the suspicion of an obscene meaning may finally dawn – in retrospect. Considering that Martial has already apologized for obscene poetry, it is even more likely that he wants us to conclude that there is a hidden obscenity in 1.32. Martial not only parodies Catullus' famous poem on unhappy love, but also creates some space for obscene double-entendres between the lines of his epigram. Again, Martial implies his own preference for obscene jokes.

Furthermore, Sullivan (1991: 97) points out that Martial "could make a Catullan conceit prompted by an immediate situation into a universal witticism." This is certainly true of 1.32. The context of Catullus' c. 85 is quite clear because it fits perfectly with the other poems in the collection. As a result, most readers will assume that the person addressed by Catullus is his beloved Lesbia (on the absence of the name in c. 85, cf. Skinner 2003: 80), who features in many of his poems. Martial's Sabidius, on the other hand, is a rather flat character. There is nothing that we know about him for sure – we can only assume that he indulges in oral sexual practices.

The same is true of most of the characters that are presented in Martial's invectives – the other aspect of his oeuvre mentioned in the epistle at the beginning of Book 1. For example, a Postumus, who is addressed in many poems of Book 2, also seems to be depicted as an adherent of oral sexual practices (C. A. Williams 2004: 54–5). Likewise, a Zoilus is criticized for his sexual practices and as a nouveau riche with a tendency to show off his wealth (C. A. Williams 2004: 78–9). We do not learn much more about these characters, which are obviously not supposed to be more than the type of the sexual pervert or parvenu.

In many of his aggressive poems Catullus paints much more detailed pictures of his victims. When he attacked such VIPs as Caesar or Mamurra, his contemporaries were familiar with those people anyway. And other victims of Catullus' invectives, such as Furius and Aurelius, are described in greater detail than Martial's characters. Of course, there are exceptions, but even the Egnatius who is presented in a rather superficial way in cc. 37 and 39 is more than just a pervert who washes his mouth with urine – probably an allusion to fellatio (Nappa 2001: 69–70; Holzberg 2002a: 81). We also learn that he is a Spaniard and one of Lesbia's former lovers. All in all, in Catullus' oeuvre we read of fewer characters than in Martial, most of whom are in some way or another connected with Lesbia or Juventius. They are therefore integrated in some kind of ongoing plot and are thus characterized in a much more detailed manner than the many characters we encounter in Martial's epigrams.

Martial's frequently quoted statement that he wanted to "spare people and to speak of vices" (10.33.10: *parcere personis dicere de uitiis*) is obviously true to his poetic practice. In most of his poems, Martial does not even attempt to create full characters. Usually he limits himself to the depiction of a conspicuous vice. The more difficult it is to identify and describe the addressee of an invective, the less harmful is the attack (cf. Hickson-Hahn 1998: 29). Therefore, our first impression is that many of Martial's invectives are less aggressive than Catullus'. And the same impression is conveyed in Catullus' and Martial's metapoetic statements. For, as is the case with the obscene poems, Catullus not only writes invective poetry but also composes metapoetic poems about this poetic practice. One famous example is c. 40:

> Quaenam te mala mens, miselle Rauide,
> agit praecipitem in meos iambos?
> quis deus tibi non bene aduocatus
> uecordem parat excitare rixam?
> an ut peruenias in ora uulgi?
> quid uis? qualubet esse notus optas?
> eris, quandoquidem meos amores
> cum longa uoluisti amare poena.

> What insane mind, pathetic Ravidus, drives you headlong into my iambics? What god – not a good choice to ask for help – plans to arouse a mad quarrel for you? Is it your aim to be in the people's mouth? What do you want? Do you wish to be well known, no matter in what way? That you will be, since you wanted to love my lover – but with a long-lasting punishment.

As in many other *carmina* where Catullus talks about his poems' aggressive power, he uses the generic term *iambi* (40.2; cf. 36.5, 54.6, fr. 3). Heyworth (2001) points out that Catullus is rather flexible in his use of different generic influences (cf. Holzberg 2002a: 44–57), with the tradition of iambic poetry playing a prominent role in the invectives. Even though not all Catullus' poems in iambic meters are aggressive, the terms *iambi* and *hendecasyllabi* (the latter also explicitly refers to meter) usually denote aggressive poetry.

It is not easy to define clearly what is typical of the tradition(s) of iambic poetry and it is obvious that Catullus was influenced by many aspects of that tradition – not only the aggressive nature of the iambus. Furthermore, it is hard to differentiate to what extent the old iambic poetry of, among others, Archilochus and Hellenistic *iambi*, written for example by Callimachus, influenced Roman poets such as Catullus or Horace (cf. L. C. Watson 2003: 4–18). But one thing is certain: Catullus' way of using the generic terms *iambi* and *hendecasyllabi* makes clear that he viewed the aggressive element of iambic poetry as its key feature – a feature that he frequently took over into his own poems. A term that does not come up in Catullus is *epigramma*, even though Hellenistic epigrams certainly had an influence on the Catullan *carmina* (Holzberg 2000: 30–32, 2002a: 45; Hutchinson 2003).

Martial, however, never speaks of *iambi* or *hendecasyllabi*, even though Catullus' iambic poems had a strong influence on his use of meter (Ferguson 1963: 7–8). For him *epigrammata* is the primary generic term. When Martial's contemporary Pliny the Younger mentions that he has written a book of *hendecasyllabi* which could also be called *epigrammata* (*Ep.* 4.14.8–9), it is obvious that, at the time of the early Empire, those two terms were used to denote something very similar. Pliny wrote his verses in the tradition of both Catullus, whom he quotes (5), and Martial (Sherwin White 1966: 290). And Martial's term *epigrammata* seems to denote something very similar to Catullus' *hendecasyllabi*: it is worth remembering that in the epistle at the beginning of Book 1, Martial claims that obscene language and an aggressive stance are key features of the epigrammatic genre. One could say that Martial has replaced Catullus' terms *iambi* and *hendecasyllabi* with *epigrammata*, a more universal term that not only denotes aggressive poetry, but also encompasses other aspects of style and contents – as Martial's books of epigrams are more diverse in style and content than the Catullan collection.

But in the epistle Martial's invectives are presented as less harmful than the ones written by Catullus. The same notion is advanced in epigram 7.12, where Martial again asks for Domitian's favor and points out that his poems are completely harmless. As a starting point, he distances himself from an anonymous rival who is said to have written and published personal invectives under Martial's name:

> Sic me fronte legat dominus, Faustine, serena
> excipiatque meos qua solet aure iocos,
> ut mea nec iuste quos odit pagina laesit

et mihi de nullo fama rubore placet.
quid prodest, cupiant cum quidam nostra uideri,
   si qua Lycambeo sanguine tela madent,
uipereumque uomat nostro sub nomine uirus,
   qui Phoebi radios ferre diemque negat?
ludimus innocui: scis hoc bene: iuro potentis
   per genium Famae Castaliumque gregem
perque tuas aures, magni mihi numinis instar,
   lector inhumana liber ab inuidia.

So may our Lord read me with a content face, Faustinus, and listen to my jokes the way he usually does, as my page has not insulted even those that it justly hates, nor do I enjoy fame because somebody blushes. But what's the use, when certain people want that any weapons that drip with Lycambes' blood are thought to be mine, and someone who refuses to tolerate Phoebus' rays and the day vomits his snake venom under my name? I play harmlessly: you know that well. I swear it by the genius of mighty Fame and the Castalian group and by your ears, reader free from cruel jealousy – to me you are equal to a great divinity.

The terms that Martial uses to denote his poetry, *ioci* ("jokes," 2) and the verb *ludere* ("play," 9), are typical of the small poetic genres and are frequently employed by both Catullus and Martial. In this poem, they may also be used to underline the harmlessness of the epigrams. Furthermore, *pagina* ("page," 3) is a widely used neutral term for poetry in general (Galán Vioque 2002: 107). These words are contrasted with the images of "weapons that drip with Lycambes' blood" (6) and "snake venom" (7), phrases that hint at the iambic poetry of Archilochus, who was said to have driven Lycambes, his former betrothed's father, to death by composing aggressive verses. As a result, the name Lycambes became "an automatic reference to abusive poetry" (Galán Vioque 2002: 108; cf. Hor. *Ep.* 1.19.25). Martial makes clear that he wants to have nothing to do with that kind of poetry and he confirms this in epigram 7.72.

Here we detect a striking difference from Catullus' metapoetic statements. Catullus is ready to use his poetry as a weapon, for example in c. 40 and also in the final poem of his collection, c. 116, where he calls his poems *tela*, "weapons" (cf. Catull. fr. 3) – a word also used by Martial in 7.12.6. Martial, on the other hand, not only avoids addressing people by their real names – as he points out in the epistle – but also claims to refrain from excessively aggressive poetry in general.

Some readers of 7.12, however, may be surprised by this claim, if they remember epigram 6.64. That poem, a furious attack on a critic, bears the influence of not only iambic poetry but also the Roman *flagitatio*, the public denunciation of delinquents, which likewise influenced some of Catullus' invectives, most notably c. 42 (Fabbrini 2002: 551–2). In addition, in 6.64, Martial explicitly claims that his poem is able to stigmatize his victim (25–6) and in that respect, it is strongly reminiscent of Catullus' invectives, too (Grewing 1997: 422). So the two poets do not seem to be so different after all in their choice of weapons. Furthermore, one may guess that Martial's criticism of a woman's *poppysmata cunni* ("clamors of the cunt," i.e., noises audible during sexual intercourse), in epigram 7.18.11, which follows only shortly after 7.12, may have made some readers doubt that he is as harmless as he pretends to be.

And that is also the case with the beginning of Martial's tenth book. In 10.3, Martial distances himself from the *nigra fama* ("black fame," 9) of poems falsely published under his name. Poem 10.5 is then another attack on aggressive invectives. Probably both poems, like 7.12, are to be read as Martial's reactions to epigrams which were wrongly attributed to him (L. C. Watson 1991: 148; cf. Barwick 1958: 309–10). 10.5 reads as follows (cf. L. C. Watson and Watson 2003):

> Quisquis stolaeue purpuraeue contemptor
> quos colere debet laesit impio uersu,
> erret per urbem pontis exul et cliui,
> interque raucos ultimus rogatores
> oret caninas panis inprobi buccas.
> illi December longus et madens bruma
> clususque fornix triste frigus extendat:
> uocet beatos clamitetque felices
> Orciniana qui feruntur in sponda.
> at cum supremae fila uenerint horae
> diesque tardus, sentiat canum litem
> abigatque moto noxias aues panno.
> nec finiantur morte simplici poenae,
> sed modo seueri sectus Aeaci loris,
> nunc inquieti monte Sisyphi pressus,
> nunc inter undas garruli senis siccus
> delasset omnis fabulas poetarum:
> et cum fateri Furia iusserit uerum,
> prodente clamet conscientia 'scripsi.'

Anyone who, showing contempt for the stole or the purple,[13] has offended those whom he should respect with impious verses – let him walk through the city, an exile from the bridge and the slope. And let him, the last one among hoarse beggars, ask for mouthfuls of inferior bread fit for the dogs. For him let a long December, a wet winter and a closed archway make the miserable cold last longer. May he call them happy and proclaim that they are fortunate who are carried in a pauper's bier.[14] But when the threads of his final hour and the day of his death have come – but too late! – let him hear the fighting of dogs and use his rags to drive off harmful birds. And let his punishments not end with a simple death: now cut by the whip of strict Aeacus, now pressed by the mountain of restless Sisyphus, now thirsty in the waters of the garrulous old man [Tantalus], let him go through all the stories from the works of the poets. And when the Fury orders that he confesses the truth, let him, his conscience betraying him, shout: "I wrote it."

At first glance, in 10.5 – as in 7.12 – Martial distances himself from aggressive invective poetry. L. C. Watson (1991: 148) concludes that "10.5 can be read as a warning that [Martial] *could* write such poetry if sufficiently provoked." But Martial has already been "sufficiently provoked" and has already written such poetry. For 10.5 is an aggressive attack on aggressive invective poetry, or as Jenkins (1981: 5) puts it, "The fact that he himself does exactly the same thing to his own enemy is ironic" (cf. Banta 1998: 183–8; Lorenz 2002: 222). L. C. Watson (1991: 147–9) also shows that the epigram bears the influence of Hellenistic curse poetry. And that genre was influenced by early iambic poets such as Archilochus (L. C. Watson 1991:

56–62). It is therefore not true that Martial kept his distance from aggressive iambic poetry, as it was also written by Catullus. Again, it is obvious that Martial contradicts himself, i.e., his actual poetic practice does not fit his metapoetic statements.[15] The following example, 12.61, makes that even clearer:

> Versus et breue uiuidumque carmen
> in te ne faciam times, Ligurra,
> et dignus cupis hoc metu uideri.
> sed frustra metuis cupisque frustra.
> in tauros Libyci ruunt leones,
> non sunt papilionibus molesti.
> quaeras censeo, si legi laboras,
> nigri fornicis ebrium poetam,
> qui carbone rudi putrique creta
> scribit carmina quae legunt cacantes.
> frons haec stigmate non meo notanda est.

You fear, Ligurra, that I am going to write verses and a short, lively poem against you, and you wish to seem worthy of your own worries. But in vain you fear and you wish in vain. Libyan lions rush at bulls, they do not attack butterflies. I advise you, if you worry about being read of, to find a drunk poet from a dark archway who writes poems with rough charcoal or crumbling chalk which people read while they shit. This forehead is not to be marked with my brand.

It is obvious that this epigram alludes to Catullus' c. 40, which I quoted above. Both poets claim that their poetry has the power to dishonor people and both seem ready to make use of this power. And this is what both Catullus and Martial do at the end of their respective poems. A humorous twist in Martial's epigram, however, is that he claims to attack the victim of his invective by refusing to attack him (Németh 1974: 238), or as Bowie (1988: 294) puts it, "the main joke is that Ligurra is getting what he wants, although not in quite the way that he might have chosen."

It is worth noting that Martial, who more than once distances himself from aggressive iambic poetry, here seems to have no doubt that his epigrams, like Catullus' *iambi*, can hurt others. That Martial ridicules Ligurra by declaring him unworthy of a real invective does not change the fact that he takes the aggressive power of his epigrams for granted. If he did not think of his epigrams as invectives in the Catullan sense, the humorous variation of the invective theme in 12.61 would not work.

But again Martial does not use Catullus' term *iambi*, but refers to his poem as *uersus et breue uiuidumque carmen* ("verses and a short, lively poem," 2). Németh (1974: 239) points out that this is an apt description of Martial's diverse oeuvre, but could nevertheless also be used for Catullus' *carmina*. Again, Martial makes use of certain aspects of Catullus' poems, and employs those elements in a slightly altered fashion. He claims that what Catullus did also fits into his epigrams and he even uses Catullus' metapoetic statements as inspiration for his own poems about his poetry. Like Catullus, Martial writes obscene and aggressive poems. But Martial's justifications of this poetic practice are so complex that they are at least as important for his oeuvre as the obscene and aggressive poems themselves.

It is, of course, likely that some of the differences between the two poets' works result from the different times and political systems in which they lived (cf. Swann 1994: 10–9). In his life of Domitian, the biographer Suetonius (8.3; cf. Nauta 2002: 43–4) mentions that the emperor forbade the denunciation of leading citizens. We can thus assume that Martial was not allowed to write about his contemporaries as freely as Catullus did.

This may be one of the reasons why Martial's poems are more general and less linked to actual personages, or – as Gaisser (1993: 210) puts it – Martial substitutes "the abstract and impersonal for the emotional and subjective" (cf. Ferguson 1963: 4; Sullivan 1991: 97). I do not think that Offermann (1980: 115) is right to criticize Martial for being an imitator who misused Catullus' highly emotional poems merely to entertain his audience. But it is certainly true that Martial used Catullus in order to create something highly entertaining. This he achieved by not just imitating Catullus, but also explicitly comparing himself to Catullus and then intensifying and in a way surpassing his predecessor. In order to make this achievement clearly visible to his audience, Martial at first had to point out the similarities between himself and Catullus. Thus, he turned Catullus into an epigrammatist and himself into the new Catullus – albeit a new Catullus who was much more than a mere imitator.

ACKNOWLEDGMENT

I would like to thank Leofranc Holford-Strevens for his comments on this chapter.

NOTES

1 All passages from Martial's works are from Shackleton Bailey's (1990) edition.
2 All passages from Catullus' works are from Mynors's (1958) edition.
3 I retain the manuscript reading *scribat*, rather than printing Heinsius' conjecture *inscribat*.
4 From Domitius Marsus, Albinovanus Pedo, and Cornelius Lentulus Gaetulicus no obscene poetry has been preserved (Banta 1998: 219 n. 83; cf. Sullivan 1991: 97–100), but given the very low number of extant texts from those authors, this can hardly be surprising. Thus there is no reason for Newman (1990: 81) to wonder why Martial puts Catullus "in such professionally detached company." If from Catullus' works only the poem on Attis (c. 63) had survived, we should be quite surprised to find him here.
5 Cf. Kroll (1968: 100).
6 It is worth noting that Martial's Books 5 and 8 do not contain any obscene words – a move that Martial explains with his wish to please the emperor Domitian. In the context of Martial's complete works, however, these two books only emphasize his general attraction to using obscenity; cf. Lorenz (2002: 143–4).
7 As is common practice, I nevertheless use the names "Catullus" and "Martial" for the speakers of the poems.
8 The boldness of this statement has led many scholars to believe that the poem had been a later addition to a revised edition of the book. However, the introductory passage from Book 1 is a coherent piece of work, where Martial – as in many other passages in his oeuvre – tends to contradict himself; cf. Lorenz (2002: 18–19 with n. 62).

9   Cf., for a summary of the discussions on this topic, Gaisser (1993: 236–43); Obermayer (1998: 71–2 with n. 239, older literature there); furthermore Jones (1998); Holzberg (2002a: 61–7).
10 It does not make a big difference whether this Maximus is a real person or a fictional character; cf. Citroni (1975: 40–1); Nauta (2002: 66 n. 92).
11 In line 9, I prefer the manuscript reading *denos* over *senos*, which has been adopted by Shackleton Bailey; cf. the arguments put forward by Howell (1993: 277, 1996: 37) and Galán Vioque's (2002: 127–8) summary of the discussion on this line.
12 In addition, the poem also alludes to Ovid; cf. Giordano (1996).
13 Cf. Shackleton Bailey's note (1993: II.329), "I.e. of married ladies or magistrates or senators."
14 Cf. Shackleton Bailey's note (1993: II.329) and Jenkins (1981: *ad loc.*).
15 Cf. Lorenz (2002: 222–3) on other poems at the beginning of Book 10, where the contradictory nature of the epigrams is especially conspicuous.

GUIDE TO FURTHER READING

The first extensive treatment of Catullus' influence on Martial is Paukstadt's (1876) dissertation. Paukstadt provides a wealth of relevant passages and offers some very useful interpretations. His findings had a strong influence on the annotations in Friedlaender's (1886) commentary, and also on all subsequent commentaries on Martial's books of epigrams. A list of further passages from Martial (and others) which betray Catullan influence has been provided by Schulze (1887). Barwick (1958; cf. Beck 1996) offers a contrastive analysis of Catullus' and Martial's book structure. Ferguson (1970) concentrates on the two poets' respective use of meter.

Most modern publications on Catullus and Martial mainly present passages from the two poets in order to point out similarities and differences. Nowadays, Ferguson's (1963) and Offermann's (1980) approach of analyzing the two poets' characters and motivations to write poetry feels rather outdated. Swann (1994; cf. his short article from 1998) examines Martial's reception of Catullus within the wider spectrum of the two poets' *Nachleben*. When Swann analyzes the poems with regard to the times Catullus and Martial lived in, his interpretations often add up to little more than cataloguing parallels. On the two poets' fate in the Renaissance, Gaisser (1993) offers much deeper analyses. Some ideas on the history of epigram in general are also offered in Summers's (2001) short article.

There is some interesting work on single instances of Catullan influences on Martial. Németh's (1974) contrastive analyses of Catullus 40 and Martial 12.61 discusses many aspects of the two pieces. Grewing (1996) compares Catullus' Lesbia poems with Martial's epigrams on his beloved boy Diadumenos (cf. Obermayer 1998: 66–9). Offermann (1986) discusses how Martial's adaptations of Catullus' poems could be used in the classroom.

A list of further publications referring to parallels between the two poets is provided by Lorenz (2003: 253–5). In order to point out Martial's debt to Catullus as well as his originality, Fedeli (2004) examines various epigrams that betray Catullan influence.

WORKS CITED

Banta, D. S. 1998. "Literary Apology and Literary Genre in Martial." Dissertation. Duke University.

Barwick, K. 1958. "Zyklen bei Martial und in den kleinen Gedichten des Catull." *Philologus* 102: 284–318.

Beck, J.-W. 1996. *"Lesbia" und "Juventius": Zwei* libelli *im Corpus Catullianum. Untersuchungen zur Publikationsform und Authentizität der überlieferten Gedichtfolge.* Göttingen.

Beck, J.-W. 2002. Quid nobis cum epistula? *Zum Anfang von Martials erstem Epigrammbuch.* Göttingen.

Boehrer, B. T. 1998. "Renaissance Classicism and Roman Sexuality: Ben Jonson's Marginalia and the Trope of *os impurum*." *International Journal of the Classical Tradition* 4: 364–80.

Bowie, M. N. R. 1988. "Martial Book XII: A Commentary." Dissertation. Oxford University.

Buchheit, V. 1961a. "Catull and Cato von Utica (c. 56)." *Hermes* 89: 345–56.

Citroni, M. 1975. *M. Valerii Martialis Epigrammaton Liber Primus.* Florence.

Claes, P. 2002. *Concatenatio Catulliana: A New Reading of the* Carmina. Amsterdam.

Fabbrini, D. 2002. "Mart. VI 64, 25 *toto orbe* o *tota urbe*? Considerazioni sull'ambito di destinatzione della poesia diffamatoria." *Maia* 54: 543–56.

Fedeli, P. 2004. "Marziale Catulliano." *Humanitas* 56: 161–89.

Feeney, D. 1999. "*Mea tempora*: Patterning of Time in the *Metamorphoses*." In P. Hardie, A. Barchiesi, and S. Hinds, eds., *Ovidian Transformations: Essays on Ovid's Metamorphoses and its Reception.* Cambridge. 13–30.

Ferguson, J. 1963. "Catullus and Martial." *Proceedings of the African Classical Associations* 6: 3–15.

Ferguson, J. 1970. "A Note on Catullus' Hendecasyllabics." *Classical Philology* 65: 173–5.

Friedlaender, L. 1886. *M. Valerii Martialis Epigrammaton Libri mit erklärenden Anmerkungen versehen.* 2 vols. Leipzig. Rpt. Amsterdam 1961.

Gaisser, J. H. 1993. *Catullus and His Renaissance Readers.* Oxford.

Galán Vioque, G. 2002. *Martial, Book VII: A Commentary.* Trans. J. J. Zoltowski. Leiden, Boston, and Cologne.

Garthwaite, J. 1978. "Domitian and the Court Poets Martial and Statius." Dissertation. Cornell University.

Giordano, F. 1996. "Ricontestualizzazioni ovidiane in Mart. I 34." In G. Germano, ed., *Classicità, medioevo e umanesimo: studi in onore di Salvatore Monti.* Naples. 203–14.

Grewing, F. 1996. "Möglichkeit und Grenzen des Vergleichs: Martials *Diadumenos* und Catulls *Lesbia*." *Hermes* 124: 333–54.

Grewing, F. 1997. *Martial, Buch VI: Ein Kommentar.* Göttingen.

Heyworth, S. J. 2001. "Catullian Iambics, Catullian *iambi*." In A. Cavarzere, A. Aloni, and A. Barchiesi, eds., *Iambic Ideas: Essays on a Poetic Tradition from Archaic Greece to the Late Roman Empire.* Lanham, MD, Boulder, New York, and Oxford. 117–40.

Hickson-Hahn, F. 1998. "What's so Funny? Laughter and Incest in Invective Humor." *Syllecta Classica* 9: 1–36.

Holzberg, N. 2000. "Lesbia, the Poet, and the Two Faces of Sappho: 'Womanufacture' and Gender Discourse in Catullus." *Proceedings of the Cambridge Philological Society* n.s. 46: 28–44.

Holzberg, N. 2002a. *Catull: Der Dichter und sein erotisches Werk.* Munich.

Holzberg, N. 2002b. *Martial und das antike Epigramm.* Darmstadt.

Holzberg, N. 2006. "Onomato-Poetics: A Linear Reading of 7.67–70." In J. Booth and R. Maltby, eds., *What's in a Name? The Significance of Proper Names in Classical Latin Literature.* Swansea. 145–58.

Howell, P. 1980. *A Commentary on Book One of the Epigrams of Martial.* London.

Howell, P. 1993. Review of Sullivan 1991. *Classical Review* 43: 275–8.

Howell, P. 1996. Review of Shackleton Bailey 1993. *Classical Review* 46: 36–8.

Hutchinson, G. O. 2003. "The Catullan Corpus, Greek Epigram, and the Poetry of Objects." *Classical Quarterly* n.s. 53.1: 206–21.

Jenkins, J. 1981. "A Commentary on Selected Epigrams from Martial Book 10." Dissertation. Cambridge University.

Jocelyn, H. D. 1981. "Difficulties in Martial, Book 1." *Papers of the Liverpool Latin Seminar* 3: 277–84.

Jones, J. W. 1998. "Catullus' *passer* as *passer.*" *Greece & Rome* 45: 188–94.

Kay, N. M. 1985. *Martial Book XI: A Commentary.* London.

Kroll, W. 1968 [1923]. *C. Valerius Catullus, herausgegeben und erklärt.* 5th edn. Stuttgart. (1st edn. Leipzig.)

Lorenz, S. 2002. *Erotik und Panegyrik: Martials epigrammatische Kaiser.* Tübingen.

Lorenz, S. 2003. "Martial: 1970–2003. 1. Teil." *Lustrum* 45: 167–277.

Lorenz, S. 2004a. "*Nulla virtus dulcior esse potest*: 'Mannestum' und 'Männlichkeit' in der erotischen Kleindichtung." In G. Partoens, G. Roskam, and T. Van Houdt, eds., *Virtutis imago: Studies on the Conceptualisation and Transformation of an Ancient Ideal.* Louvain. 117–43.

Lorenz, S. 2004b. "Waterscape with Black and White: Epigrams, Cycles, and Webs in Martial's *Epigrammaton liber quartus.*" *American Journal of Philology* 125: 255–78.

Mynors, R. A. B., ed. 1958 (rev. 1960). *C. Valerii Catulli Carmina recognovit brevique adnotatione critica instruxit.* Oxford.

Nappa, C. 2001. *Aspects of Catullus' Social Fiction.* Frankfurt.

Nauta, R. R. 2002. *Poetry for Patrons: Literary Communication in the Age of Domitian.* Leiden, Boston, and Cologne.

Németh, B. 1974. "Zur Analyse von Catull, c. 40." *Wissenschaftliche Zeitschrift der Universität Rostock* 23.3: 237–43.

Newman, J. K. 1990. *Roman Catullus and the Modification of the Alexandrian Sensibility.* Hildesheim.

Obermayer, H. P. 1998. *Martial und der Diskurs über männliche "Homosexualität" in der Literatur der frühen Kaiserzeit.* Tübingen.

Offermann, H. 1980. "*Uno sim tibi minor Catullo.*" *Quaderni urbinati della cultura classica* 5: 107–39.

Offermann, H. 1986. "Catull-Martial: Dichtung im Vergleich." *Anregung* 32: 226–35, 316–25.

Paukstadt, R. 1876. "De Martiale Catulli imitatore." Dissertation. Halle.

Scherf. J. 2001. *Untersuchungen zur Buchgestaltung Martials.* Munich.

Schulze, K. P. 1887. "Martials Catullstudien." *Jahrbücher für Classische Philologie* 33: 637–40.

Shackleton Bailey, D. R. 1990. *M. Valerii Martialis Epigrammata.* Post W. Heraeum edidit D. R. S. B. Stuttgart.

Shackleton Bailey, D. R. 1993. *Martial: Epigrams. Edited and Translated.* 3 vols. Cambridge, MA, and London.

Sherwin White, A. N. 1966. *The Letters of Pliny: A Historical and Social Commentary.* Oxford.

Skinner, M. B. 1982b. "Supplementary Note on the Latin Sexual Language: Catullus 56.5–6." *Liverpool Classical Monthly* 7: 140.

Skinner, M. B. 1987. "Cornelius Nepos and Xenomedes of Ceos: A Callimachean Allusion in Catullus 1." *Liverpool Classical Monthly* 12: 22.

Skinner, M. B. 1993b. "*Ego mulier*: The Construction of Male Sexuality in Catullus." *Helios* 20: 107–30 (= J. P. Hallett and M. B. Skinner, eds., *Roman Sexualities.* Princeton, NJ, 1997: 129–50).

Skinner, M. B. 2003. *Catullus in Verona: A Reading of the Elegiac Libellus, Poems 65–116.* Columbus, OH.

Sullivan, J. P. 1991. *Martial: The Unexpected Classic. A Literary and Historical Study.* Cambridge.

Summers, K. 2001. "Catullus' Program in the Imagination of Later Epigrammatists." *Classical Bulletin* 77: 147–60.

Swann, B. W. 1994. *Martial's Catullus: The Reception of an Epigrammatic Rival.* Hildesheim.

Swann, B. W. 1998. "*Sic scribit Catullus:* The Importance of Catullus for Martial's Epigrams." In F. Grewing, ed., Toto notus in orbe: *Perspektiven der Martial-Interpretation.* Stuttgart. 48–58.

Thomson, D. F. S. 1997. *Catullus, Edited with a Textual and Interpretative Commentary.* Toronto.

Watson, L. C. 1991. Arae: *The Curse Poetry of Antiquity.* Leeds.

Watson, L. C. 2003. *A Commentary on Horace's Epodes.* Oxford.

Watson, L. C, and P. Watson. 2003. *Martial: Select Epigrams.* Cambridge.

Watson, P. 1999. "Martial on the Wedding of Stella and Violentilla." *Latomus* 58: 348–56.

Williams, C. A., ed. 2004. *Martial, Epigrams: Book 2.* Oxford.

CHAPTER TWENTY-THREE

Catullus in the Renaissance

Julia Haig Gaisser

The Renaissance history of Catullus begins with a riddle, the mysterious epigram written in the first years of the fourteenth century by Benvenuto Campesani commemorating the discovery of a manuscript of the poet after his works had been lost for a thousand years (for a text and translation, see Butrica, this volume, p. 27). The manuscript celebrated by Benvenuto (called *V* for Verona) was soon lost, but not before it was copied at least once. All of our extant manuscripts of the complete text – four from the fourteenth century (*O*, *G*, *R*, and *m* [Venice, Biblioteca Marciana lat. 12.80 (4167)]) and roughly 125 from the fifteenth – are descended from this single lost manuscript. A ninth-century florilegium or anthology preserves one poem, 62, whose text is descended from the same archetype as *V* (Thomson 1997: 24–38, 72–93).

The fact that Catullus survived the Middle Ages only in a single manuscript may surprise the modern reader, for Catullus (perhaps after Vergil) is the most popular Roman poet of our time, and in Antiquity he exercised a profound influence on both the Augustan poets and those of the Silver Age. Catullus is not the only ancient author to come to us in a single manuscript – Apuleius' *Golden Ass* and the surviving parts of Tacitus' *Histories* and *Annals* had the same narrow escape (Reynolds 1983: 15–16, 406–7) – but his history is still a little disquieting. How could it happen that such a poet was reduced to such a slender lifeline?

The answer – at least part of it – seems to be Martial, for it is one of the ironies of literary history that the admiration and imitation of Martial, along with that of Pliny and other lesser poets of the Silver Age, probably contributed to Catullus' virtual eclipse from the second century on (Gaisser 1993: 7–15). Martial and his contemporaries had no interest in the qualities that our time admires in Catullus – his elegant urbanity, his learned Alexandrianism, his passionate emotion. Instead, they promoted him as a poet of light verse and epigram (see Lorenz, this volume). As a consequence he was soon supplanted by his chief imitator. Why read an old-fashioned and sometimes difficult poet like Catullus, when one could so easily enjoy Martial's smooth and racy epigrams? In the second century Aulus Gellius and Apuleius knew some of

Catullus' poems; the poet of the *Ciris* and the author of an *epicedion* on a pet dog knew others (Goold 1969; Walters 1976). But even then texts were no doubt already becoming scarce, and we can be sure that fewer still were preserved when scribes transferred the works of ancient authors from roll to codex around the fourth century AD. There are echoes of tags and single verses in authors from the fourth to the seventh century (Schwabe 1886: xi–xiii; Wiseman 1985: 246–61; Ullman 1960); but after that Catullus goes underground. The only people we can identify with certainty as readers of his poetry in the Middle Ages are the anonymous scribes of *V* or its archetype and the florilegium containing poem 62.

Martial's Legacy

The humanists greeted the rediscovery of Catullus with enthusiasm but did little with his poetry for nearly a hundred and fifty years. They tried to correct the text, collected quotable verses for their anthologies, and included Catullus in lists of obscene poets excusing or condemning scandalous verse. For the most part, however, they did not imitate or try to interpret his poetry – largely because they could not read it. Catullus' text was notoriously corrupt. Meters were confused. Poems were run together. The point, and often even the subject, of many poems was lost. Furthermore, although the humanists admired the learning of Catullus' poetry – or rather, admired the *idea* that it was learned – they were vague about the details. They knew that he was called *doctus Catullus* ("learned Catullus") by other ancient writers, but they did not know what his learning entailed. Greek studies were in their merest infancy, and much that we take for granted about Alexandrian literature was unknown. (In fact, two of the texts most important for understanding Catullus' learned Alexandrianism were discovered only in the twentieth century. Both are from the *Aetia* of Callimachus: the prologue setting out Callimachus' poetic program, and the *Lock of Berenice*, which Catullus translated as poem 66.)

Real engagement with Catullus began in the fifteenth century, and the first steps were taken by two Florentine poets, Leonardo Bruni (1370?–1444) and Cristoforo Landino (1424–1504). Between 1405 and 1415 Bruni wrote an obscene hendeca-syllabic pastiche of poems 41–3 (transmitted in a single block in *V*), probably using either *R* or *m* – the one owned by his mentor, Coluccio Salutati, and the other probably transcribed by his friend and colleague Poggio Bracciolini (Hankins 1990; Gaisser 1993: 211–15). A generation later, Landino completed a collection of poems he called the *Xandra* (Landino 1939). The work opened with a dedication in hendecasyllables in imitation of Martial; but the use of hendecasyllables seems also to have been a programmatic hint of Landino's affinity with Catullus (Ludwig 1990: 188–9). But Landino did not imitate Catullus' hendecasyllabic poems. Instead, he wrote an imitation of poem 11 (*Xandra* 50) and a set of three variations on poem 8 (*Xandra* 6, 34, 35), keeping the Sapphics of the one and transposing the limping iambs of the other into elegiac couplets. Neither Bruni nor Landino, however, had any influence on later Catullan poetry. Bruni's ugly pastiche sank with hardly a trace, and Landino's imitations, metrically and thematically more like Roman elegy than Catullan lyric, were left behind in what would turn out to be the main focus of Renaissance imitation, the hendecasyllabic poems.

It was Giovanni Gioviano Pontano (1429–1503) who set Catullan poetry on the course it was to follow throughout the Renaissance. Pontano, one of the greatest Renaissance Latin poets, had come to Naples as a young man and become a friend and disciple of the poet Antonio Beccadelli, known as Panormita, who had written a collection of obscene poetry called *Hermaphroditus* in imitation of Martial and the *Priapeia*. Pontano's association with Panormita and his poetry would be decisive, for it showed him that he could use Martial as a way to approach Catullus. The idea is not so strange as it might seem to a modern reader. Catullus had landed in the Renaissance virtually out of nowhere, in only the corrupt text he stood up in, and with no baggage of late antique or medieval imitation, interpretation, or scholarship. But Martial could supply the lack. Reversing what might seem to us the obvious order, most people in the Renaissance read Martial before they read Catullus. Many manuscripts of Martial were available; he had been studied by Boccaccio in the 1370s, and by nearly every humanist afterwards; and his epigrams were widely imitated (Hausmann 1980: 249–54; Sullivan 1991: 253–70; Swann 1994: 89–91). Best of all, his accessible epigrams both imitated and interpreted Catullus. Reading Catullus through Martial, Pontano saw a light and racy epigrammatist, witty and often obscene, without emotional complexity, political animus, or Alexandrian intricacy. It was this Catullus who would dominate fifteenth-century interpretation.

With Martial as his guide, Pontano produced a collection of Catullan poetry within a year of his arrival in Naples (*Pruritus*, 1449). Two other collections followed: *Parthenopaeus sive Amores* (1457) and *Hendecasyllabi sive Baiae*, written throughout the 1490s and completed around 1500 or so (Ludwig 1990). The three collections differed in tone and subject. *Pruritus* was more explicitly obscene than the others and closer to Panormita and the *Priapeia*. *Parthenopaeus* (which incorporates some of the less obscene poems from the *Pruritus*) embarks on a sophisticated literary program. The *Hendecasyllabi*, erotic poems of Pontano's old age, have moved farthest from explicit imitation of Catullus subjects to an almost elegiac celebration of the enfeebled and fragile, but enduring, *Eros* of old men. (For the texts of *Pruritus* and *Parthenopaeus* see Pontano 1902; for *Hendecasyllabi* see Pontano 1978, 2006.)

In spite of their differences, however, the collections had two points in common that would become distinguishing features of later Catullan poetry: their models and their meter. Pontano focused on a small number of Catullus' poems, above all the kiss-poems, especially 5 and 7, the sparrow-poems 2 and 3 (transmitted in *V* as a single block and printed as a single poem until the first Aldine edition of 1502), and 16, which he treated as a poetic manifesto. Pontano used the idea from 16 that light verses should arouse and titillate the reader:

> qui tum denique habent salem ac leporem,
> si sunt molliculi ac parum pudici,
> et quod pruriat incitare possunt,
> non dico pueris, sed his pilosis
> qui duros nequeunt movere lumbos.
>
> They only have wit and charm
> if they're a little soft and not quite modest,

and can stir up what feels sexual excitement –
I don't mean for boys, but for these hairy old men
unable to move their stiffened loins.
                                              (Catull. 16.7–11)

His successors, however, would prefer the other part of Catullus' statement in poem
16, the denial of a connection between the character of the poet and the nature of his
verses:

> nam castum esse decet pium poetam
> ipsum, versiculos nihil necesse est.

> For it is right for the true poet to be chaste
> himself, but not necessary for his verses to be so.
>   (Catull. 16.5–6)

Pontano wrote most of his imitations in hendecasyllables (other meters predominate
only in *Parthenopaeus*), creating the particular version of the hendecasyllable that was
to predominate in subsequent Catullan poetry. Pontano's meter is recognizably
Catullan, for it reproduces Catullan tricks of style and achieves a lightness and delicacy
generally absent in earlier imitators like Martial and the poets of the *Priapeia*; but it
also exaggerates Catullan features (particularly assonance, diminutives, and the use of
internal repetitions or refrains) to create an effect that is unmistakably new – sensu-
ous, lyrical, and sometimes almost hypnotic. The first verses of his poem "To Fannia"
from *Parthenopaeus* exemplify his treatment:

> Amabo, mea cara Fanniella,
> Ocellus Veneris decusque Amoris,
> Iube, istaec tibi basiem labella
> Succiplena, tenella, mollicella;
> Amabo, mea vita suaviumque,
> Face istam mihi gratiam petenti.

> Please, my dear Fanniella,
> Apple of Venus' eye, and ornament of Amor,
> Tell me to kiss these lips of yours
> Juicy, delicate, so very soft;
> Please, my life, my kiss,
> Do me this favor, since I ask.
>   (*Parthenopaeus* 1.11.1–6)

Pontano's sensual erotic poetry was often more explicit than anything in Catullus
himself, as in *Parthenopaeus* 1.5, "Ad pueros de columba" ("To the boys, concerning
the dove"), which evokes both the kiss-poems and Lesbia's sparrow. In it Pontano
asks who should be the proper recipient for his "snow-white dove." Rejecting the
boys of his title as *mali cinaedi* ("wretched catamites"), he decides that the dove
wishes to go to his girl (*puella*) instead:

> Huius tu in gremio beata ludes,
> Et circumsiliens manus sinumque
> Interdum aureolas petes papillas.

> You will play happily in her lap,
> and hopping about, you will peck her hands and bosom
> and sometimes her pretty golden breasts.
>> (*Parthenopaeus* 1.5.17–19)

He continues:

> Impune hoc facies, volente diva,
> Ut, cum te roseo ore suaviatur
> Rostrum purpureis premens labellis,
> Mellitam rapias iocosa linguam,
> Et tot basia totque basiabis,
> Donec nectarei fluant liquores.

> You will do this without fear, if the goddess wishes:
> so that when she kisses you with her rosy mouth,
> pressing your beak with purple lips,
> you may playfully snatch her honey-sweet tongue
> and you will give kisses and kisses again,
> until the streams of nectar flow.
>> (*Parthenopaeus* 1.5.26–31)

There could hardly be a better example of the Renaissance tendency to read Catullus through Martial. Pontano's poem is a *contaminatio* or blending of Catullus 2–3 and Martial 11.6, which interprets Catullus' sparrow not as a bird but a penis (Ludwig 1989: 175 n. 58; Hooper 1985).

Pontano's poem (originally in the *Pruritus* of 1449 and subsequently brought into *Parthenopaeus*) was the first obscene reading of Catullus' sparrow in the Renaissance. But the one that everyone would remember was published 40 years later by Angelo Poliziano in his *Miscellanea* (1489):

> *Quo intellectu Catullianus passer accipiendus, locusque etiam apud Martialem indicatus.*
> Passer ille Catullianus allegoricôs, ut arbitror, obscoeniorem quempiam celat intellectum, quam salva verecundia, nequimus enunciare. Quod ut credam, Martialis epigrammate illo persuadet, cuius hi sunt extremi versiculi:

>> Da mihi basia, sed Catulliana:
>> Quae si tot fuerint, quot ille dixit,
>> Donabo tibi passerem Catulli. [Mart. 11.6.14–17]

> Nimis enim foret insubidus poeta (quod nefas credere) si Catulli passerem denique ac non aliud quidpiam, quod suspicor, magis donaturum se puero post oscula diceret. Hoc quid sit, equidem pro styli pudore suae cuiusque coniecturae, de passeris nativa salacitate relinquo.

> *In what sense the sparrow of Catullus is to be understood and a passage pointed out in Martial.*
> That sparrow of Catullus in my opinion allegorically conceals a certain more obscene meaning which I cannot explain with my modesty intact. Martial persuades me to believe this in that epigram of which these are the last verses:

>> Give me kisses, but Catullan style.
>> And if they be as many as he said,
>> I will give you the sparrow of Catullus.

For he would be too inept as a poet (which it is wrong to believe) if he said he would give the sparrow of Catullus, and not the other thing I suspect, to the boy after the kisses. What this is, for the modesty of my pen, I leave to each reader to conjecture from the native salaciousness of the sparrow. (Poliziano, *Miscellanea* 1.6, in Poliziano 1971: 1.230–1)

After Pontano Renaissance poets wrote scores of poems on sparrows and doves and literally hundreds on kisses, often combining the sparrow and kissing themes to speak more or less openly of both homosexual and heterosexual intercourse. As time went on many poets also added the idea of the "soul kiss" from pseudo-Plato (Gell. *NA* 19.11.11–17) – that the lover's spirit (breath of life) departs with the kiss, entering into and animating the beloved (Perella 1969). The most important poems in this vein are the work of the major Neo-Latin poet Johannes Secundus (1511–36), especially in his elaborate sequence *Basia* (Godman 1988, 1990; Gaisser 1993: 249–54). But not everyone enjoyed obscene, or even erotic, poetry. Around 1490 the Carmelite poet Mantuan (Battista Spagnoli) published a long attack on all light poetry: *Contra poetas impudice scribentes carmen* ("A poem against poets writing unchastely"). Mantuan completely rejected the excuse for racy poetry that his contemporaries had found in Catullus 16.5–6:

> Vita decet sacros et pagina casta poetas:
> > Castus enim vatum spiritus atque sacer.
> Si proba vita tibi lascivaque pagina, multos
> > Efficis incestos in veneremque trahis.

> A chaste life *and* a chaste page befit holy poets,
> > for chaste and holy is the inspiration of bards.
> If your life is upright and your page lascivious,
> > you make many unchaste and draw them into venery.
> (Mantuan, *Contra poetas* 19–22, in Mantuan ca. 1490)

Not only monks objected to lascivious verse: one of Pontano's friends and protégés, the young Marco Marullo, although embracing love poetry and rejecting Mantuan's strictures, disdained the "Catullan excuse" (Gaisser 1993: 231–30):

> Sic iuvat in tenui legem servare pudore
> > Et quae non facimus dicere facta pudet.

> Thus, we are pleased to keep the law in delicate modesty
> > and ashamed to speak of things we do not do.
> > (Marullo, *Epigram* 1.62.17–22, in Marullo 1951)

Poliziano's interpretation of the sparrow was also criticized, but less by moralists than by his fellow humanists. He was a polemical man with many enemies, and many considered his interpretation an attack on Catullus himself. The sparrow-poems (or rather *poem*, as it was generally thought to be) seemed straightforward and affecting, and readers who had shed a tear with Catullus over the death of Lesbia's sparrow were chagrined to be told (even indirectly) that they had really been feeling sentimental over the poet's impotence. Feeling was still running high some thirty years later, when Pierio Valeriano broached the matter in his lectures on Catullus at the University of Rome in 1522:

Bone Deus, an non satis in corpus saevitum erat, nisi animum ipsum etiam extinguere cogitassent? . . . At scimus quidem nos passeres adeo salaces esse, ut vel septies una hora saliant. Scimus ex medicorum dictatis passeribus in cibo datis, vel eorum ovis, venerem concitari. Scimus quid turpitudinis in mimis significet *tôn strouthôn* hoc est passerum nomen . . . Scimus ex sacerdotum Aegyptiorum commentationibus per passeris picturam prolificam hominis salacitatem significari. . . . Haec inquam scimus, sed quod apud Catullum, forte etiam apud Martialem, pudenda pace vestrarum aurium dixerim, virilia sub nomine passeris intelligi debeant, neque scimus, neque scire volumus. (Gaisser 1993: 350 n. 114)

Good god! Had Catullus' body not been treated cruelly enough without their planning to quench his spirit? . . . We know that sparrows are so salacious that they mate seven times an hour; we know from medical writings that eating sparrows (or even their eggs) has an aphrodisiac effect. We know what filth the term *strouthoi* (that is, "sparrows") signifies in mimes; . . . we know from the writings of the Egyptian priests that human lust is symbolized by the picture of a sparrow. . . . We know these things, I say, but we neither know nor wish to know that in Catullus or perhaps even in Martial the male genitals (if you'll pardon the expression) ought to be understood under the word "sparrow."

The First Interpreters

When the first edition of Catullus was printed in Venice in 1472, Catullus instantly became more available than he had been at any time in his history. But that does not mean that his poems appeared in a form that his readers found comprehensible or that he himself would have recognized. When Renaissance readers opened the edition, they saw and handled something quite different from Catullus' "charming new little book, just polished with dry pumice" (Catull. 1.1–2). They held a large quarto volume that contained not only Catullus, but also Tibullus, Propertius, and Statius' *Silvae* – all, like Catullus, making their first appearance (or, in the case of Propertius, first important appearance) in print (Butrica 1984: 160). The page that met their eyes was large and luxuriously arranged, with good-sized initial letters alternately colored red and blue to mark the beginning of each poem, and wide margins that presented an irresistible space for annotation – or in some cases, illumination, since wealthy readers liked having their printed books adorned as expensively as their manuscripts.

The text printed in this handsome volume had been corrected and tinkered with by various humanists since the fourteenth century, but major corruptions remained on every page; long blocks of poems were run together in defiance of sense or meter; additional metrical problems marred even correctly separated poems. All of the poems had titles, many of which were as misleading as that of poem 1: *Val. Catulli Veronensis Poetę Cl. Liber Ad Cornelium Gallum* ("The book of the famous Veronese poet Valerius Catullus of Verona to Cornelius Gallus"). The block containing poems 2 and 3 was entitled *Fletus passeris lesbię* ("Lament for Lesbia's sparrow").

Within a year two men of very different abilities and methods set themselves to the task of correcting the first edition – Francesco dal Pozzo, called Puteolano, a hard-working and entrepreneurial humanist, and the very young Angelo Poliziano, who would become the greatest philologist of the age. Puteolano's corrections made their way into an influential edition (Parma 1473) and became an important element in the base text of Catullus. Poliziano's corrections for the most part lay unpublished in the margins of his book (a handful later made their way into his *Miscellanea*). The book that contains them, now preserved in the Biblioteca Corsiniana in Rome (Corsiniana 50. F. 37), presents a valuable record not only of contemporary Catullan emendation and interpretation but also of Poliziano's own method and scholarly development (Gaisser 1993: 42–7, 403–7).

Poliziano began to correct the first edition almost as soon as it appeared and continued to add to his notes at least until the mid-1480s, entering his own corrections and the readings he had found in manuscripts or other sources, and collating his text with each new edition as it appeared. Two dated subscriptions in his book give his own evaluations of his work. The first is dated August 12, 1473 – not quite three weeks before the publication of Puteolano's edition. In it Poliziano, then just 18 years old, proudly announces:

> Catullus Veronensis, si minus emendatus, at saltem maxima ex parte incorruptus mea opera meoque labore et industria in manibus habeatur!

> Here is Catullus of Verona, if not completely corrected, at least sound for the most part through my effort and toil and industry. (Rome, Bibl. Corsiniana 50. F. 37, fol. 37r)

In his second subscription, dated 1485, he is less optimistic, excusing his errors to future readers of his book. He had been very young when he began his corrections, he says, and now he no longer approves of many of them himself (*Quo fit ut multa ex eis ne ipse quidem satis [ut nunc est] probem*, Rome, Bibl. Corsiniana 50. F. 37, fol. 127v).

No doubt Poliziano was more realistic about his accomplishments at 30 than he had been at 18. But his second subscription also reflects a changed state of affairs in Catullan studies. In mid-August 1473 a young man could dream of making his reputation with Catullus simply by correcting the single corrupt edition before him, but within a dozen years at least five more editions were published, and his corrections seemed less impressive. Nonetheless, Poliziano's book is an important document. Its margins are filled with explanations of hard words and grammatical points, metrical comments, and parallel passages from other authors, both Latin and Greek. Although the ink in many places has faded almost to the vanishing point, one can still discern the horizontal lines he has drawn to separate poems and the dozens of tiny corrections he has written, very neatly, above the lines of every poem. His corrections include readings found in various manuscripts and in editions that would have been available to him before 1485, including the important editions of Francesco Puteolano and Giovanni Calfurnio (1481), and perhaps that of Antonio Partenio (1485). But they also include good readings not found before 1485, or even before Poliziano's death in 1494, as well as two emendations with which he is credited in modern editions (66.48 *Chalybum* or *Chalybon*; 84.2 *hinsidias*). If Poliziano had published an edition with the corrections in his book (including his separation of poems) it would have surpassed all the editions available before the first Aldine (1502).

The young Poliziano probably intended to produce an edition, perhaps even a commentary. But by the time of his second subscription the moment for such a project had passed. Rejecting the plodding work of editing and commentary, he sought a different medium for displaying his philological genius. He wrote short essays setting out his solutions to particular problems and collected them in a work he called *Miscellanea* (1489). Poliziano devoted seven of the 100 chapters of the *Miscellanea* to Catullus (Gaisser 1993: 67–78). In five of the seven he develops ideas that appear in his marginalia. Two of these interpretations had been already been published by others: the identification of poem 84 as the one mentioned in Quintilian's discussion of aspirates (*Inst.* 1.5.20) and the explanation of the hair-raising poem 74, in which Catullus tells how Laelius made his uncle a silent Harpocrates. Poliziano vehemently claims priority in both cases, and his marginalia tend to bear him out, for they not only contain these ideas, but contain them in less developed forms than those in which they appear either in other sources or in the *Miscellanea* itself. The marginalia on poem 84 are particularly interesting (Rome, Bibl. Corsiniana 50. F. 37, fol. 34r; Gaisser 1993: plate 4). There we find: the *h*'s that make sense of the epigram (in tiny letters above the appropriate words), the relevant passage from Quintilian (in the margin), and a horizontal line separating the poem from 83, with which it had been printed in a single block entitled *Ad Mullum*.

The two chapters without precedent in the marginalia suggest (although they cannot prove) that Poliziano did not add to his notes after he wrote the subscription of 1485, for both are apparently inspired by the famous Codex Farnesianus of Festus, which he saw in the spring of 1485 (Poliziano 1971: 1.284; Maïer 1966: 426). In *Misc.* 1.73 Poliziano tells how he had found the rare word *suppernati* ("hamstrung") in Festus and realized that he could use it to correct poem 17.19, where *separata* was read by *V* and the editions. The second chapter without precedent in the marginalia is *Misc.* 1.6 (on the sparrow). Poliziano certainly knew the relevant verses from Martial (11.6.14–17) when he was writing his marginalia (he quotes them in his notes on poem 5), and he probably knew Pontano's poem on the "snow-white dove"; but his notes on poem (s) 2–3 show no sign of Martial or that he suspected an obscene innuendo. In Festus he could have seen another hint of the sparrow's obscene identity:

> Strutheum in mimis praecipue vocant obscenam partem virilem, <a> salacitate videlicet passeris, qui Graece στρουθός dicitur.

> In mimes especially they call the obscene male member "the sparrow" [*strutheum*], evidently from the salaciousness of the sparrow, which is called στρουθός in Greek. (Fest. 410 Lindsay *DVS*)

Poliziano does not mention Festus in *Misc.* 1.6, but he might well have used him either to arrive at or to confirm his interpretation. A portion of Poliziano's transcription of the Festus manuscript is preserved (Biblioteca Apostolica Vaticana, Vat. lat. 3368; Lindsay 1913: xii–xiv). It contains not only *suppernati* (fol. 11r) but also *strutheum* (fol. 11v) – the latter with the marginal gloss *passer Catulli* ("the sparrow of Catullus") probably in the hand of Poliziano himself (Gaisser 1993: 314 n. 38).

Poliziano's chapters in the *Miscellanea* were brilliant, but they treated only a few passages in the Catullan *corpus*. The task of editing and explaining nearly every line of every poem had been performed four years earlier by Catullus' fellow Veronese, Antonio Partenio (1456–1506), who was nearly Poliziano's exact contemporary, but (like most people) nothing like his intellectual equal. The need for a commentary was clear. Perhaps the very learned could enjoy Catullus' poetry without assistance even when much remained obscure or problematic, but most readers were unprepared to decipher Catullus by themselves. They were confused and discouraged not only by real difficulties with the text and its interpretation but also by the unfamiliar characters, place names, and mythological allusions they met on every page.

In the long preface to his commentary Partenio makes two key points (Partenio 1491: fol. 1r–v). First, he wants to make Catullus accessible, not merely to mature scholars and university students, but also to schoolboys and their teachers. His aspiration is an interesting comment both on his ambition (making an author of Catullus' difficulty comprehensible to schoolboys was no small undertaking) and on the moral climate of his period in contrast to that of the recent past and not so distant future. Partenio had been teaching Catullus in his school for years, and his commentary displays no inhibitions. In the previous generation, however, Catullus had been deemed unsuitable for schools (Sabbadini 1914: 2.201); in the next, as we shall see, his obscenity would be an obstacle at the University of Rome. Second, Partenio has a clear conception of the progress of scholarship and of his own place in it. Standing at the beginning of the process, he does not expect to have the last word. "Under my auspices," he says, "little by little our poet will be assisted, and through the agency of many writers inspired by equal zeal he will recover his glory" (*auspiciis meis paulatim adiuvabitur poeta noster atque per multos scriptores pari studio motos decus suum reparabit*, Partenio 1491: fol. 1r). Alone among Catullan interpreters of his century, Partenio makes it clear that he understands what it means for an ancient author to lack a critical tradition and that one man cannot remedy the deficiency.

Partenio had undertaken a formidable task: to explain every separate point of difficulty in a corrupt and diverse corpus as long as three books of the *Aeneid* – all without the benefit of any of the lexica, concordances, encyclopedias, or onomastica that later classicists would take for granted. The results were imperfect, for Partenio, as he freely admits, was a man of only moderate learning, and his ideas about Catullus are not sophisticated either as philology or as literary criticism. Like most Renaissance school commentators, he deals largely in the elementary and obvious, paraphrasing poems, spelling out details of grammar and usage, and explaining historical and mythological references. Often his basic information is wrong.

Nonetheless, he had his share of successes. One of his greatest triumphs appears in his summary of poem 1: "the poet dedicates this book to his friend Cornelius Nepos and publishes the work in his name" (*poeta Cornelio Nepoti amico suo libellum hunc dicat atque in eius nomine opus edit*, Partenio 1491: fol. 2r). The comment seems obvious until we remember that every previous edition had followed the lead of the first in identifying Catullus' friend with Cornelius Gallus. Partenio had discovered from the dating in Jerome's Eusebius that the identification with Gallus was anachronistic. Besides, Gallus was known to be an elegist (*Cornelium autem Gallum elegiarum poetam fuisse constat*, Partenio 1491: fol. 2r), and Catullus' allusion to his friend's literary endeavors points to a work of history. The relevant verses are *cum ausus es unus Italorum/omne aevum tribus explicare cartis*, 1.5–6 ("since you alone of the Italians have ventured to unfold all time in three rolls"). Partenio caps his discussion by producing the identity of the author and his book from Aulus Gellius, glossing 1.6 as follows:

Omne aevum: omne saeculum praeteritum. Quum autem dicit omne aevum plane indicat Cornelii Nepotis chronica quorum meminit Gellius in noctibus atticis.

omne aevum: Each past age. Moreover, when he says, "each age," he clearly indicates the *Chronica* of Cornelius Nepos, which Gellius mentions in the *Attic Nights* [Gell. *NA* 17.21.3]. (Partenio 1491: fol. 2r)

When he saw that Catullus' friend was a historian Partenio managed for once to surpass the young Poliziano, who had identified him with the poet Cornelius Cinna, thinking that the verse *doctis Iuppiter, et laboriosis* ("learned, by Jupiter, and full of hard work," 1.7) referred to Cinna's notoriously learned poetry (Rome, Biblioteca Corsiniana 50. F.37, fol. 4r).

Partenio's method, to the extent that he had one, was similar to that followed by Poliziano in his interpretation of poem 84: to seek out clues to meanings and identifications in other ancient authors. Unfortunately, such information was often confusing, mistaken, or incomplete. Sometimes it was simply extraneous, lending his comments a touch of strange, unconscious humor. On poem 15.19, for example, he explains that adulterers were punished by having radishes thrust up their anuses, and then adds irrelevantly: "In Germany radishes grow as large as babies. They thrive on cold, but dislike manure. Read more in Pliny" (*Raphani in Germania ad infantum magnitudinem excrescunt. Frigore gaudent, fimum oderunt. Apud Plinium plura legito* [Plin. *HN* 19.26.83]. Partenio 1491: fol. 6r.)

Partenio's commentary, with all its deficiencies, fulfilled his hopes for it. It made Catullus accessible to a wide audience, proving so popular that it was reprinted five times in the 15 years after its first publication. It also laid a foundation for improvement by his successors. The commentaries that followed his, however, made only moderate headway with either interpretation or textual improvement (Gaisser 1993: 97–108). Palladio Fosco published a commentary in 1496, Alessandro Guarino in 1521. Neither had a particular interest in Catullus. Palladio, like Partenio, was a schoolmaster. He made a few contributions of his own (he made sense of poem 35, for example, by realizing that its hero Caecilius had composed a poem on the *Magna Mater*); but many of his ideas are taken without acknowledgment from other sources. The best that we can say for him is that his wide if unscrupulous research allowed him to correct Partenio in more than a few places and to present his readers with helpful information from various and sometimes unlikely sources. Guarino was a courtier at the court of Ferrara; his commentary is largely based on the work of his father, Battista Guarino (d. 1513), whose work was made redundant when Partenio managed to get into print first. Guarino likes to charge Partenio with ignorance, but corrects no major errors himself.

The most important successor of Partenio in the fifteenth century, however, was not a commentator, but a text critic: the Veronese humanist Girolami Avanzi. Avanzi, a generation younger than Partenio, Palladio, and Battista Guarini, produced several major works on Catullus over the course of a long career: *Emendationes* (1495 and 1500), the first and second Aldine editions (1502 and 1515), and the Trincavelli edition of ca. 1535. In each he revisited the text, thought about its problems again, and revised some of his earlier ideas. His most interesting work from a historical point of view is the earliest, the *Emendationes* of 1495. In it we can see Avanzi consulting not just the text of Partenio, but the whole printed tradition, scanning every verse, and indulging in numerous interesting (if often misguided) attacks on Poliziano (Gaisser 1993: 52–65). (He did so, it seems, largely for reasons of local patriotism: Poliziano had not only impugned the honor of Catullus' sparrow, but attacked an important Veronese humanist, Domizio Calderini.) Avanzi was a better scholar than any of his predecessors (with the obvious exception of Poliziano), and his work provided the basis for a text that far surpassed those of the fifteenth century: the edition published in Venice by Aldo Manuzio in 1502. The novelty of the edition consists not only in its text, but also in its physical aspects: Aldo's handy octavo, with its almost unprecedented press run of 3,000 copies, made Catullus far more widely – and more conveniently – available than he had been in the unwieldy tomes of the fifteenth century (Lowry 1979: 174 n. 96; 257; Fletcher 1988: 100–2).

Catullus at the University of Rome

In November 1521 a humanist named Pierio Valeriano began a series of lectures on Catullus at the University of Rome (Gaisser 1993: 109–45, 1999: 1–39). The moment was right, for Valeriano was at the height of his success, and Roman poetry and humanism were enjoying a golden age under the patronage of the Medici pope Leo X. Valeriano was well suited to his task: he was a poet as well as a philologist, he had an interpretive method, and he was an entertaining and lively lecturer. His lectures were taken down as he spoke, with the intention that they would be published as a commentary. Valeriano's lectures were never published, but they are preserved in a manuscript (or rather manuscript fragment) in the Vatican Library (Biblioteca Apostolica Vaticana, Vat. lat. 5215). The fragment is substantial. There are 249 folios, which contain two introductory lectures and detailed discussions of poems 1–22. The manuscript contains no breaks except that the discussions of the obscene poems 15, 16, and 21 are missing – an important point that we will consider presently.

Valeriano was not the first humanist to lecture on Catullus. Puteolano probably promoted the sales of his edition with lectures at the University of Bologna; Calfurnio, editor of the 1481 edition, regularly lectured on Catullus in Padua at least up to 1493; and Partenio lectured at his school in Verona in the 1480s. (Palladio may also have lectured on Catullus in the 1490s.) But the lectures of Puteolano and Calfurnio are lost, and those of Partenio were revised to make his published commentary. Valeriano's lectures have come down to us nearly as he delivered them, if we can believe their title:

> Pierii Valeriani Bellunensis Ro. Gymnasii Professoris Praelectiones in Catullum Auditorum Quorumdam Diligentia Dum Profiteretur Ad Verbum Exceptae.

> The Lectures on Catullus of Pierio Valeriano of Belluno, Professor of the University of Rome, Taken Down Word for Word as He Spoke, through the Care of Some of his Listeners. (Biblioteca Apostolica Vaticana, Vat. lat. 5215, fol. 1r)

There is also another difference. Partenio and Palladio were schoolmasters; Puteolano and Calfurnio, their university positions notwithstanding, were comparative small-fry. But Valeriano was a major figure, and his professorial debut was an important literary event. His lectures were learned and instructive, to be sure, but also personal, literary, and witty. Thanks to the faithful amanuensis, who has recorded interruptions, asides, and digressions along with the central material of the lectures, we are able to catch some of the flavor of his performance.

Valeriano also approached Catullus in a different spirit from that of his fifteenth-century predecessors. He was a better scholar than Partenio, Palladio, and either Guarino; and he had the advantages not only of Avanzi's two Aldines (1502 and 1515), but also of access to Catullus manuscripts owned by the Medici or housed in the Vatican Library. (He was a Medici client and secretary of the pope's cousin, Giulio de' Medici, the future Pope Clement VII.) But two other points of difference are of greater importance. First, Valeriano was a Neo-Latin poet with a professional interest in poetic style and meter, and one of the purposes of his lectures was to encourage his students to write their own Neo-Latin poetry. Many were already doing so, for he had fellow humanists as well as university students in his audience. Second, both by temperament and because of his period and his location in papal Rome, Valeriano had a different attitude to obscenity from that of his predecessors. He was not a stiff-necked puritan like Mantuan, but he did not flaunt or revel in the obscene like Pontano and the three fifteenth-century commentators (by whom Catullan obscenity was explained more enthusiastically and knowledgeably than it would be again for nearly five hundred years).

Valeriano saw Catullus above all as a poetic model. He ends his second lecture with this exhortation:

> age esto Catullus primus, qui profecturis in poetice discipulis proponatur, ut quum unusquisque in eum ex numeris inciderit, qui genio suo sit accomodatior, quo scilicet se non aliter moveri atque attrahi sentiat quam ferrum a magnete, paleam a succino, se ad eius imitationem accingat, eoque carminis genere sese exercere incipiat, quod magis ideae suae proprium esse animadverterit.

> come, let it be Catullus first who is set before students about to make their way into poetry, so that when each has fallen upon that rhythm which is well suited to his spirit, by which he feels himself moved and attracted as iron by a magnet or chaff by amber, he will gird himself up to imitate it and begin to practice with that type of poetry which he sees is proper to his ideal. (Vat. lat. 5215, fol. 25r)

Rhythm was of professional concern to Valeriano, and his facility with metrics (like that of Pontano in the previous century) far exceeded that of humanists who merely scanned Catullus' verse, but did not write their own. Much of his approach is the result of his study of the metrical treatise *De metris* by the second-century grammarian Terentianus Maurus, apparently unknown to his predecessors.

Terentianus' treatise was discovered in 1493. The first edition appeared in 1497, followed by several others in the period 1500–10 (Keil 1874: 6.245, 315–17). The work was interesting because of its antiquity and the metrical lore it contained, but especially because it was written in verse. Terentianus founded his treatise on the fact that the verse may be divided at different points, and that different meters can be achieved simply by omitting, adding, and transposing segments. He applied his principle to most of the main metrical types, but especially to the hendecasyllable, which he divided in seven different ways, rearranging and adding segments to form everything from hexameters to galliambics (Ter. Maur. 2539–912 in *GLK* 6.401–11).

The demonstration provided Valeriano with the perfect opening for his lecture on poem 1 (in hendecasyllables). It had the added benefit of being appropriate to the diverse needs of his audience, which included both young students who required fairly elementary instruction and those who expected entertainment and virtuoso display. Best of all, however, Terentianus' approach was active: he showed not how to scan, but how to create the various meters.

Valeriano turns Terentianus' discussion into a treatment of the meter of poem 1. The first four verses are the basis of his discussion:

> Cui dono lepidum novum libellum
> arida modo pumice expolitum?
> Corneli, tibi: namque tu solebas
> meas esse aliquid putare nugas.
> (Catull. 1.1–4)

He begins with the basic components of the hendecasyllable:

Id vero potissimum dignitatis habet carmen hoc, quod constat ex tomis eorum versuum, qui antiquissimi omnium ac celeberrimi censentur. Ex heroica quippe tome, atque ex iambea. Est autem tome ut iuniores intelligant, pars alicuius carminis [the following words are crossed out: uno plus pede numerosa] quae ab reliquo dissecatur, ita ut vel ipsa per se genus aliquod carminis adstruat vel sectioni alteri copulata diversam efficiat speciem.

This meter has the particular distinction of being formed from the segments [*tomis*] of those verses considered the most ancient and celebrated, that is, from an epic *tome* and from an iambic one. Moreover, (so that the younger students may understand), a *tome* is a portion of a verse that is cut off from the rest in such a way that it either makes some type of verse by itself or creates a different form when joined to another segment. (Vat. lat. 5215, fol. 28v)

Thus, we may regard the first line of poem 1 as containing an epic segment, *Cui dono lepidum*, which is the first half of a hexameter verse, and an iambic segment, *novum libellum*, the first colon of an iambic trimeter. We may turn the line into a hexameter by trimming the second segment and inserting words drawn from elsewhere in the poem. Thus: *Cui dono lepidum | Corneli docte | libellum*. Valeriano creates an iambic verse by completing the iambic segment with a phrase borrowed from poem 4.1. Thus: *novum libellum | quem videtis hospites*. The argument that follows is technical but entertaining, as Valeriano turns the verses of the first poem into alcaics, priapeans, asclepiadeans, and galliambics (Gaisser 1993: 412). "If we have a thorough understanding of this rhythm," he concludes, "we can exercise our talent through many kinds of verses." ([*ut*] *hoc uno recte percepto numero facile possemus per multa versuum genera ingenium exercere*, Vat. lat. 5215, fol. 36r.)

Valeriano's attitude toward obscenity was highly personal, and it was closely related to his idea of an affinity between the poet and himself as the poet's interpreter; or it might be better to say that – like all of Catullus' interpreters, from Martial to the present – he created a Catullus in his own image (Gaisser 2002). If Pontano's Catullus was a sensualist, Valeriano's is a teacher who both delights and instructs. Catullus pleases by the charm of his poetry, Valeriano tells his students, but he is also instructive and useful:

Prodest utique quum virtutes celebrat...dum vitia carpit, malos mores exsecratur, et mortales omnes a sceleratorum quos carminibus proscindit imitatione conatur avertere.

He is useful particularly when he celebrates virtues [and]...chastises vice, criticizes evil ways, and attempts to deter mankind from imitating the wicked men he chastises in his poetry. (Vat. lat. 5215, fol. 18r)

This surprising description of Catullus is close enough to Valeriano's conception of his own role to make him reject a reading like Poliziano's interpretation of Catullus' sparrow, which he found unnecessary and prurient. But Valeriano's picture of Catullus the teacher is not always serious. Here is how he makes the sparrow useful and instructive to his students in the conclusion of his discussion of poem 3:

Nunc unum addam pro corollario, quod ad has extincti passeris inferias conferamus. Nam et vos delectare possunt audiendo et exemplo plurimum iuvare. Passeribus vitae brevitas angustissima. Eorum enim mares anno diutius durare non posse tradunt, qui rerum huiusmodi historias conscripsere; cuius rei causam esse aiunt, incontinentissimam salacitatem; quae tot hominum etiam ante diem effoetos tradit senectuti. Contra vero corvinum genus, quia rarissime coit vivacissimum. Quare si vos vitae dulcedo capit adolescentes nihil vobis magis praestiterit quam venerem et caeci stimulos avertere amoris.

Now I will add one thing as a corollary, which we can apply to these rites of a dead sparrow. For they can both amuse you in the listening and benefit you greatly by their example. The life of a sparrow is very short. For, as those who write of these matters tell us, the males can live no more than a year, and they say that the reason is unrestrained lust – which also wears out so many men before their time and hands them over to old age. The crow, on the other hand, is very long-lived, since it copulates most seldom. Wherefore, young men, if the sweetness of life delights you, nothing will be more useful to you than to reject Venus and the goads of blind passion. (Vat. lat. 5215, fol. 63r)

Valeriano rejected Poliziano's interpretation of the sparrow, but he was willing to give frank (not prurient) explanations of Catullus' sexual language and obscenities. At poem 6.13, for example, he glosses *latera ecfututa* as "loins spent and exhausted by sexual intercourse" (*latera coitu frequenti tam exhausta et debilitata*, Vat. lat. 5215, fol. 95 v). In poem 11 he explains the penultimate stanza and the force of *omnium/ ilia rumpens*: "by such constant activity let her continue to render so many men impotent" (*tali assiduitate pergat viros tot elumbes reddere*, Vat. lat. 5215, fol. 164v).

Real events outside the lecture room, however, prevent us from knowing how Valeriano treated Catullus' most obscene poetry. Valeriano began his lectures under his Medici patron, Pope Leo X, who died unexpectedly very soon afterwards. The pope's death, Valeriano's grief, and the election of the new pope, Adrian VI, are all reported at the beginning of the third lecture. The lectures continued, but broke off for the summer of 1522. They resumed in the late autumn, by which time Adrian VI, a pious and puritanical Dutchman, had at last arrived in Rome – "together with the plague," as Valeriano was to say some years later (Valeriano, *De litteratorum infelicitate* 1.16, in Gaisser 1999). As luck would have it, Valeriano came to the first truly obscene poem (15) after the new pope's arrival. At the beginning of his lecture he debates about whether he should omit it, claiming that his students are outraged at the very idea:

> Alii recidisse nos iterum in Gottica et Vandalica tempora lamentantur, quod videatur, veluti statuis omnibus illi virilia decutiebant, nunc quoque e libris, siquid pruriat, tolli.

> Some lament that we have fallen back into the times of the Goths and the Vandals because it seems that just as they used to cut off the genitals of all the statues, so now anything titillating is taken out of books, too. (Vat. lat. 5215, fol. 194v)

Valeriano apparently gave his lecture, but we will never be sure, since he (or someone else) has cut out all the pages that would have contained it. The manuscript resumes with lectures on poems 17 and 22 (poem 21 is omitted). (For the numbering of the poems see the next section.) It is not clear how long the lectures continued. Conditions in Rome in autumn 1522 and spring 1523 were bad for humanists and poetry: the pope was hostile to secular intellectual activities; finances were so tight that university salaries often went unpaid; and the plague continued to ravage the city. A final catastrophe makes it impossible to know the extent of the lectures. In 1527 Rome was sacked by the troops of Charles V, and the manuscript with Valeriano's lectures was among the casualties. A comment on the last folio contains the poignant note: "the rest was lost in the Sack of Rome" (*Reliquum in direptione Romae desideratum*, Vat. lat. 5215, fol. 249v). The lectures lay in obscurity until the twentieth century (Alpago-Novello 1926).

The French Connection

For over two hundred years after his discovery Catullus was studied primarily in Italy and by Italians. But in the middle of the sixteenth century Catullan studies moved farther afield, and within around twenty years three non-Italians produced important commentaries: Marc-Antoine de Muret (1554), Aquiles Estaço (better known as Statius, 1566), and Joseph Scaliger (1577).

Marc-Antoine de Muret, like Valeriano, was a successful and charismatic university lecturer with a deep interest in poetry. He arrived in Paris in 1551 at the age of 25, already a famous professor, and was soon taken up by the new school of French poets who called themselves the Brigade – especially Joachim Du Bellay, Jean-Antoine de Baïf, and Pierre Ronsard. Muret spent two years in Paris lecturing to enthusiastic crowds of students, working on a Catullan commentary, and in literary collaboration with the poets of the Brigade, who aspired to create a new French poetry integrating the French literary tradition with classical learning on the one hand and with Neo-Latin and Italian poetry on the other (Morrison 1956; Silver 1966).

One of the most important products of this collaboration was Ronsard's *Livret de folastries*, published anonymously in 1553. The *Folastries* ("Little Follies") were conceived as French counterparts of the Catullan hendecasyllable; their title recalls Catullus' names for his own verses: *nugae, ineptiae, lusus* ("trifles," "foolishness," "play"). Ronsard used Catullus' poem 16.5–6 as the epigraph for his collection, and his dedication is a *contaminatio* of poem 1 and a dedication by the Neo-Latin poet Marcantonio Flaminio (Laumonier 1923: 93–8). The flavor is Catullan:

> A qui donnai-je ces sornettes,
> Et ces mignardes chansonnettes?
> A toy mon Janot, . . .

> ...
> Pren le donc, Janot, tel qu'il est,
> ...
> Afin que toy, moy, et mon livre,
> Plus d'un siècle puissions revivre.
>
> To whom do I give these trifles
> and these dainty little verses?
> To you, my friend Janot...
> ...
> Take it then, Janot, such as it is
> ...
> so that you and I and my book
> may live more than a single age.
> (Ronsard, *A Janot Parisien*, 1–3, 23, 29–30; Ronsard 1928: vv. 3–5)

Others in Paris also wrote Catullan poetry, imitating Catullus in both Latin and French and drawing on Italian Neo-Latin poetry as well. Soon the influence went both ways, so that we find French and Latin poetry borrowing from each other (Morrison 1955, 1956, 1963; Ginsberg 1986).

Near the end of 1553 Muret was forced out of Paris by charges of heresy and sexual immorality. He fled to Venice and another fruitful collaboration, this time with the printer Paolo Manuzio, who published Muret's commentary on Catullus in 1554. The commentary shows its mixed Italian and French parentage. It contains a measure of contemporary Italian philological polemic, for Muret makes sure to attack the Catullan ideas of Manuzio's arch-enemy, Pier Vettori (Grafton 1983: 88–96; Gaisser 1993: 151–3). But it is also steeped in the poetic interests and theory of Paris, and it is here that it is most innovative.

Fifteenth-century readers had interpreted Catullus through Martial, and like Martial himself, they largely ignored both Catullus' emotional depth and his learned Alexandrianism. (Only Poliziano took a real interest in tracing Catullus' Alexandrian models.) Muret and the French poets had a different approach. They separated Catullus from Martial, especially in the matter of epigram, admiring the one as much as they disdained the other (Hutton 1946: 51–3). Muret is of the same opinion, remarking:

> inter Martialis autem et Catulli scripta tantum interesse arbitrer, quantum inter dicta scurrae alicuius de trivio, et inter liberales ingenui hominis iocos, multo urbanitatis aspersos sale.

> I think there is as much difference between the writings of Martial and Catullus as between the words of some wag on the street-corner and the well-bred jests of a gentleman, seasoned with sophisticated wit. (Muret 1554: iii)

Like his French colleagues, Muret studied both archaic and Alexandrian Greek poetry. He regrets the loss of Callimachus' *Lock of Berenice* (translated by Catullus in poem 66) and admires Catullus' Alexandrian poems for their learning and emotion. His particular favorite is poem 68, but he also pays attention to poem 63, prefacing his commentary on it with a poem of his own in galliambics. (Here Muret was doing nothing new, for Catullus' galliambics had inspired imitation since the fifteenth century; see Campbell 1960.) More important, however, is the fact that Muret was the first to identify Sappho 31 as the model for poem 51, publishing the two poems side by side (Muret 1554: 56v–58r). The first detailed comparison of Sappho and Catullus would appear much later, in the 1592 discussion of Janus Dousa the younger (Gaisser 1993: 165).

Muret was not a distinguished editor. He based his edition largely on the base text, unsystematically consulting various editions and an occasional manuscript. His principal contribution to the text is an error that would confuse later readers: the insertion after poem 17 of three *priapeia* that later editors numbered 18, 19, and 20. The *priapeia* were banished by Lachmann in the nineteenth century, but by then the numbering was canonical – hence the anomalous gap between poems 17 and 21 in modern texts.

Muret's commentary was followed by those of Statius and Scaliger. Statius was Portuguese, Scaliger French. Both were better text critics than Muret and less interesting commentators (Gaisser 1993: 168–92). Statius, like Muret, published his commentary with Paolo Manuzio in Venice in 1566. He studied the text more thoroughly than anyone since Avanzi, consulting and collating (though not systematically) at least seven manuscripts including *R* (Ullman 1908) and controlling the whole printed tradition. He discussed his readings in his commentary, but did not produce a new edition. Like Muret, Statius began his career in Paris and took an early interest in poetry. By 1555 he had published a book of his own poems, written a commentary on Horace's *Ars Poetica*, and (a sign of French influence?) translated two hymns of Callimachus. By 1566, however, he was a papal secretary in Rome and his interests had changed from pagan poetry to Christian theology. Statius is the first Catullan scholar not to express great enthusiasm for his subject, and the influence of the Council of Trent (1564) on his commentary is clear. Noting that Catullus was famed for elegance of style, he claims to have studied ancient poetry in order to master Latin meters for his own translations of the Psalms. And he excuses Catullus' indecency by pointing out the general licentiousness of paganism (the same grounds that the Council of Trent had used to exclude ancient authors from its ban on obscene literature):

> Nam, quod idem lascivius, ac mollius scripsit, id vero temporum illorum sive mos, sive licentia potius, ac vitium fuit, quamquam de se ipse tamquam suppudens dicit, "Nam castum esse decet pium poetam/ipsum, versiculos nihil necesse est" [16.5–6].

> For, as to the fact that he wrote somewhat racily and effeminately, this was the habit of those times, or rather the license and defect, although he says of himself as if in embarrassment: "For it is right for the true poet to be chaste/himself, but not necessary for his verses to be so." (Statius 1566: A2v–A3r)

Scaliger's commentary (the first published outside Italy) was printed in Paris in 1577. The work also includes Tibullus and Propertius. (Scaliger called the three poets *tresviri amoris*: "the triumvirate of love.") Scaliger's *Catullus* enjoys an exalted position in the history of textual criticism, for its method has been seen to anticipate that of the great nineteenth-century philologists (Kenney 1974: 55–7; Grafton 1977, 1983: 160–79). Scaliger was the first to understand that all the manuscripts of

Catullus were descended from a single exemplar, which he reconstructed (to his own satisfaction, at least) down to its place of origin and the peculiarities of its script – creating a model that explained the genesis of errors in Catullus' text and showed the way to their correction. But his method is more important to the history of philology than to the correction of Catullus (Gaisser 1993: 178–92, 414–15). He was a greater editor than any of his predecessors, but not because of his method, which produced far more wrong answers than right ones. Instead, his successes result from a combination of great natural ability, judicious use of his predecessors, and the knowledge of the manuscripts that he had gained from his own collations and those of Statius. Scaliger was more interested in Catullus' text than in his poetry, and, like Statius, he felt he needed to justify studying it. His excuse is that he worked on Catullus when he was recovering from a debilitating illness and too weak to study more edifying authors (Scaliger 1577: a2r–v). Like Statius, he disliked obscenity. He avoided it as much as possible, skirting it easily, he claims, as experienced sailors avoid reefs in the sea (Scaliger 1577: a4v–5r).

Conclusion

Scaliger's commentary was the last major Catullan event of the sixteenth century. Poets continued to write Catullan poetry in both Latin and the vernacular, and there were some textual discussions or partial commentaries, the most important being the works of the Dutch scholars Janus Dousa *pater* and *filius* published in 1581 and 1592 (Gaisser 1992: 271–5; Heesakkers 1976). The most interesting treatment, however, was a collection of parodies of poem 4 printed in 1579. This work, entitled *Phaselus Catulli*, was edited under the pseudonym Sixtus Octavianus by the Belgian humanists Victor Giselinus and Janus Lernutius and dedicated to their friend Janus Dousa the Elder (van Crombruggen 1959: 3–11; Gaisser 1993: 255–71). It contained both *Catalepton* 10 and a number of sixteenth-century parodies (convivial, invective, religious, obscene, and "literary"), together with a discussion of parody by Julius Caesar Scaliger.

But the times were not favorable to Catullan studies. Catullus' obscenity was part of the problem (it had worried both the papal secretary Statius and the Protestant Scaliger), but all of his work was uncongenial to the general spirit of the age, which was increasingly concerned with serious moral, philosophical, and theological questions. Catullus' highest values, by contrast, are personal and aesthetic: the bonds of trust and obligation between individuals, and a poetic credo founded on learning, craftsmanship, and – above all – charm and wit. There is no room in his poetic landscape for large moral or national themes, no reference to ideals or claims beyond those of the individual. Such a poet cannot be recruited to the cause of moral utility and can be taken seriously only by those who put a premium on poetry and poetics and the bonds of personal affection. It is no accident that those who enjoyed and profited from him most in the second half of the sixteenth century were Muret and the French poets of the Brigade, and the Dutch and Belgian parodists who studied his techniques and saw Catullus and his friends as the model for their own sodality.

GUIDE TO FURTHER READING

Note: much of the important bibliography is in languages other than English. For additional references on specific points see the bibliography in Gaisser (1993).

For the medieval and early Renaissance transmission of Catullus, see Ullman (1960) and Thomson (1997: 22–43); both discuss the important role played by the Florentine humanist Coluccio Salutati (1331–1406), who commissioned and annotated *R*. In an important unpublished dissertation McKie (1977) discusses the relation of *V* and its descendants, postulating a lost intermediary (called *A* by Thomson) between *V* and *O* and *X* (the lost parent of *G* and *R*). The place of *V*'s discovery is disputed. Guido Billanovich (1958: 155–70, 191–9) called Benvenuto's epigram a "fairy tale," arguing that *V* was discovered in Verona in the thirteenth century and read by the Paduan poets Lovato Lovati (d. 1309) and Alberto Mussato (d. 1329). As Butrica (this volume, pp. 24–5) remarks, Ullman (1960) was skeptical about the idea and Ludwig convincingly refuted it (Ludwig 1986), but it still occasionally surfaces. Citations of Catullus by Geremia da Montangone (ca. 1315?) are discussed by Ullman (1955); McKie uses them to demonstrate the existence of *A* (McKie 1977: 80–93). Citations by Benzo of Alessandria (ca. 1320) are discussed by Hale (1910). Petrarch's use of Catullus is treated by Ellis (1905) and Ullman (1960). Bosco (1942) lists Petrarch's quotations.

Important theoretical discussions relevant to imitation both by Martial and by the Renaissance poets include Conte (1986), Pigman (1980) and especially Pasquali 1951) and T. M. Greene (1980: 4–80). Ludwig's treatment of Pontano's imitations (Ludwig 1989: 162–94) was the starting point of the subsequent discussions. Recently the topic has been treated more fully in a collection of essays (Baier 2003). The anthologies of Nichols (1979) and Perosa and Sparrow (1979) provide excellent starting points for texts and biographies of the Neo-Latin poets.

Several recent studies have treated the Catullan lectures of Pierio Valeriano. See especially Di Stephano (2001) and Campanelli and Pincelli (2000).

WORKS CITED

Alpago-Novello, L. 1926. "Spigolature vaticane di argomento bellunese. I. Un'opera inedita ed ignorata di Pierio Valeriano." *Archivio Veneto Tridentino* 9: 69–96.

Baier, T., ed. 2003. *Pontano und Catull*. Tübingen.

Billanovich, Guido. 1958. "*Vestigia veterum vatum* nei carmi de preumanisti Padovani." *Italia medioevale e umanistica* 1: 155–243.

Bosco, U. 1942. "Il Petrarca e l'umanesimo filologico." *Giornale storico della letteratura italiana* 120: 108–16.

Butrica, J. L. 1984. *The Manuscript Tradition of Propertius*. Toronto.

Campanelli, M., and M. A. Pincelli. 2000. "La lettura dei classici nello *studium urbis* tra umanesimo e rinascimento." In L. Capo and M. R. Di Simone, eds., *Storia della Facoltà di Lettere e Filosofia de "La Sapienza."* Rome. 93–195.

Campbell, D. 1960. "Galliambic Poems of the 15th and 16th Centuries: Sources of the Bacchic Odes of the Pléiade School." *Bibliothèque d'humanism et renaissance* 22: 490–510.

Conte, G. B. 1986. *The Rhetoric of Imitation: Genre and Poetic Memory in Virgil and Other Latin Poets*. Ithaca, NY.

Crombruggen, H. van. 1959. *Lernutiana*. Mededelingen van de koninklijke vlaamse Academie voor Wetenschappen, Letteren en schone Kunsten van Belgie, Klasse der Letteren 21. Brussels.

Di Stephano, A. 2001. "Pierio Valeriano e la nascita della critica catulliana nel secolo XVI." In P. Pellegrini, ed., *Umanisti bellunesi fra quattro e cinquecento*. Atti del Convegno di Belluno November 5, 1999. Florence. 137–76.

Ellis, R. 1905. *Catullus in the XIVth Century*. Oxford.

Fletcher, H. G., III. 1988. *New Aldine Studies*. San Francisco.

Gaisser, J. H. 1992. "Catullus." In V. Brown, ed., *Catalogus Translationum et Commentariorum* 7. Washington, DC. 197–292.

Gaisser, J. H. 1993. *Catullus and His Renaissance Readers*. Oxford.

Gaisser, J. H. 1999. *Pierio Valeriano on the Ill Fortune of Learned Men: A Renaissance Humanist and His World*. Ann Arbor, MI.

Gaisser, J. H. 2002. "Picturing Catullus." *Classical World* 95: 372–85.

Ginsberg, E. S. 1986. "Peregrinations of the Kiss: Thematic Relationships between Neo-Latin and French Poetry in the Sixteenth Century." *Acta Conventus Neo-Latini Sanctandreani*. Binghamton, NY. 331–42.

Godman, P. 1988. "Johannes Secundus and Renaissance Latin Poetry." *Review of English Studies* 39: 258–72.

Godman, P. 1990. "Literary Classicism and Latin Erotic Poetry of the Twelfth Century and the Renaissance." In Godman and Murray (1990: 149–92).

Godman, P., and O. Murray, eds. 1990. *Latin Poetry and the Classical Tradition*. Oxford.

Goold, G. P. 1969. "Catullus 3.16." *Phoenix* 23: 186–203.

Grafton, A. 1977. "Joseph Scaliger's Edition of Catullus (1577) and the Traditions of Textual Criticism in the Renaissance." *Journal of the Warburg and Courtauld Institute* 40: 150–88.

Grafton, A. 1983. *Joseph Scaliger: A Study in the History of Classical Scholarship*. Vol. I. Oxford.

Greene, T. M. 1980. *The Light in Troy: Imitation and Discovery in Renaissance Poetry*. New Haven, CT.

Hale, W. G. 1910. "Benzo of Alexandria and Catullus." *Classical Philology* 5: 56–65.

Hankins, J. 1990. "The Latin Poetry of Leonardo Bruni." *Humanistica lovaniensia* 39: 1–39.

Hausmann, F.-R. 1980. "Martialis." *Catalogus Translationum et Commentariorum* 4. Washington, DC. 249–96.

Heesakkers, C. L. 1976. *Praecidanea Dousana*. Amsterdam.

Hooper, R. W. 1985. "In Defence of Catullus' Dirty Sparrow." *Greece & Rome* 32: 162–78.

Hutton, J. 1946. *The Greek Anthology in France*. Ithaca, NY.

Keil, H. 1874. *Grammatici latini VI*. Leipzig.

Kenney, E. J. 1974. *The Classical Text: Aspects of Editing in the Age of the Printed Book*. Berkeley.

Landino, C. 1939. *Christophori Landini Carmina Omnia*. Ed. A. Perosa. Florence.

Laumonier, P. 1923. *Ronsard, poète lyrique*. 2nd edn. Paris.

Lindsay, W. M., ed. 1913. *Festus: De verborum significatione*. Leipzig.

Lowry, M. 1979. *The World of Aldus Manutius*. Cambridge.

Ludwig, W. 1986. "Kannte Lovato Catull?" *Rheinisches Museum* 129: 329–57.

Ludwig, W. 1989. "*Catullus renatus*: Anfänge und frühe Entwicklung des catullischen Stils in der neulateinischen Dichtung." In L. Braun, W. W. Ehlers, P. G. Schmidt, and B. Seidensticker, eds., *Litterae Neolatinae: Schriften zur neulateinischen Literatur*. Munich. 162–94.

Ludwig, W. 1990. "The Origin and Development of the Catullan Style in Neo-Latin Poetry." In Godman and Murray (1990: 183–98).

Maïer, I. 1966. *Ange Politien: la formation d'un poète humaniste*. Geneva.

Mantuan (B. Spagnoli). ca. 1490. *Contra poetas impudice scribentes carmen*. Paris.

Marullo, M. 1951. *Michaelis Marulli Carmina*. Ed. A. Perosa. Zurich.

McKie, D. S. 1977. "The Manuscripts of Catullus: Recension in a Closed Tradition." Dissertation. Cambridge University.

Morrison, M. 1955. "Catullus in the Neo-Latin Poetry of France before 1550." *Bibliothèque d'humanism et renaissance* 17: 365–94.

Morrison, M. 1956. "Ronsard and Catullus: The Influence of the Teaching of Marc-Antoine de Muret." *Bibliothèque d'humanism et renaissance* 18: 240–74.

Morrison, M. 1963. "Catullus and the Poetry of the Renaissance in France." *Bibliothèque d'humanism et renaissance* 25: 25–56.

Muret, M.-A. de. 1554. *Catullus et in eum Commentarius*. Venice.

Nichols, F. J. 1979. *An Anthology of Neo-Latin Poetry*. New Haven, CT, and London.

Partenio, A. 1491. *Antonii Parthenii Lacisii Veronensis in Catullum Commentationes*. Venice.

Pasquali, G. 1951. "Arte allusiva." In *Stravaganze quarte e supreme*. 11–20. Venice. (Rpt. in *Pagine stravaganti*. Florence, 1968. II.275–83.)

Perella, N. J. 1969. *The Kiss, Sacred and Profane*. Berkeley.

Perosa, A., and J. Sparrow. 1979. *Renaissance Latin Verse: An Anthology*. London.

Pigman, G. W., III. 1980. "Versions of Imitation in the Renaissance." *Renaissance Quarterly* 33: 1–32.

Poliziano, A. 1971. *Opera Omnia*. Ed. I. Maïer. 3 vols. Turin.

Pontano, G. G. 1902. *Ioannis Ioviani Pontani Carmina*. Ed. B. Soldati. 2 vols. Florence.

Pontano, G. G. 1978. *Ioannis Ioviani Pontani, Hendecasyllaborum Libri*. Naples.

Pontano, G. G. 2006. *Giovanni Gioviano Pontano: Baiae*. Trans. R. G. Dennis. I Tatti Renaissance Library 22. Cambridge, MA, and London.

Reynolds, L. D., ed. 1983. *Texts and Transmission: A Survey of the Latin Classics*. Oxford.

Ronsard, P. de. 1928. *Oeuvres completes*. Ed. P. Laumonier. Paris.

Sabbadini, R. 1914. *Le scoperte dei codici latini e greci ne' secoli xiv e xv*. 2 vols. Florence.

Scaliger, J. 1577. *Castigationes in Valerii Catulli librum*. Paris.

Schwabe, L., ed. 1886. *Catulli veronensis liber*. 2nd edn. Berlin.

Silver, I. 1966. "Marc-Antoine de Muret et Ronsard." In R. Antonioli, R. Aulotte, M.-E. Balmas, et al., eds., *Lumières de la Pléiade*. Paris. 33–48.

Skutsch, O. 1970. "The Book under the Bushel." *Bulletin of the Institute of Classical Studies of the University of London* 17: 148.

Statius, A. 1566. *Catullus cum commentario*. Venice.

Sullivan, J. P. 1991. *Martial: The Unexpected Classic. A Literary and Historical Study*. Cambridge.

Swann, B. W. 1994. *Martial's Catullus: The Reception of an Epigrammatic Rival*. Hildesheim.

Thomson, D. F. S., ed. 1997. *Catullus, Edited with a Textual and Interpretative Commentary*. Toronto.

Ullman, B. L. 1908. *The Identification of the Manuscripts of Catullus Cited in Statius' Edition of 1566*. Chicago.

Ullman, B. L. 1955. "Hieremias de Montagnone and his Citations from Catullus." In *Studies in the Italian Renaissance*. Rome. 181–200.

Ullman, B. L. 1960. "The Transmission of the Text of Catullus." In *Studi in onore di Luigi Castiglioni*. 2 vols. Florence. II.1027–57.

Walters, K. R. 1976. "Catullan Echoes in the Second Century A. D." *Classical World* 69: 353–60.

Wiseman, T. P. 1985. *Catullus and His World: A Reappraisal*. Cambridge.

CHAPTER TWENTY-FOUR

The Modern Reception of Catullus

Brian Arkins

It is increasingly accepted within the field of classics that the area of reception studies – previously known as the classical tradition, or as *Nachleben* – is not something peripheral that can readily be dispensed with, nor something of concern only to specialists in later eras. Rather, the reception of Greek and Latin authors is a vital part of what we know about them (Hardwick 2003). Here there is a complex interaction between past and present that involves not just the obvious phenomenon of a later writer appropriating Greek or Latin material, but also the more subtle phenomenon of that later writer altering the way we perceive the writer of the past. Hence T. S. Eliot wrote that it is possible "that the past should be altered by the present as much as the present is directed by the past" (1958: 24). Indeed Gadamer held not only that the past conditions the present, but that the mediation of the present is required to grasp the past, a process brought about through "a fusion of horizons" (Perkins 1981: 243). A major example of how a contemporary work of art can alter the way we view a Latin poet is provided by Ezra Pound's *Homage to Sextus Propertius* (1919). This version of Propertius captures not just the poet's stress on sexual love and on art, but also a vein of humor, a refined use of the meter of elegiac couplets, and a special use of language (*logopoeia*) that pushes it to the very edge of possibility – all these well before professional classicists observed them (Arkins 1988).

This chapter deals with selected aspects of the reception of Catullus in the Romantic and Victorian eras and in the twentieth century. Since in general the Romantic and Victorian eras were much more preoccupied with Greece than with Rome, the stress will be on the appropriation of Catullus by figures writing mainly or wholly in the twentieth century such as Pound, Yeats, Frost, Wilder, and Graves (but for the Victorian period see Vance 1997).

It is therefore fitting to begin with the concept that Catullus is a modern poet, one who appeals to contemporary poets and, as the large number of recent translations attests, to the Common Reader of Dr Johnson. Catullus appears to be modern because he is an advocate of sexual love (despite its pain), because his approach to everything is highly individualistic, because he was devoted to the art of poetry, and because he employs a brief, lucid, hard style (Arkins 1999: 7–17).

Hence the complex assignment of modern characteristics to Catullus by figures of his own era in the historical novel *The Ides of March* (1948) by the writer Thornton Wilder (1897–1975). Referring to this work as "a fantasia on certain events and persons of the last days of the Roman republic" (1961: 7) and believing that the historical novel does not work when presented in narrative form, Wilder presents a collection of documents (mostly letters) that purport to be authentic. In *The Ides of March*, these documents have much to say about Catullus, quote a number of his poems (5, 8, 51, 76), and deal with his relationship with Lesbia (presumed to be Clodia Metelli).

There is a pervasive sense in *The Ides of March* that the characters are well aware of what Quinn famously called "the Catullan revolution," that Catullus "invented the love poem" (Quinn 1959; Stoppard 1997: 13). Writing to Atticus, Wilder's Cicero holds of Catullus' verse that "[t]hese poems are in Latin but they are not Roman," partly because, as his character Caesar writes of Catullus, they elevate love (*amor*) to a central position in life: "he is certain that love is the only manifestation of the divine, and that it is from love, even when it is traduced and insulted, that we can learn the nature of our existence." In the novel Catullus himself states: "Love is its own eternity. Love is in every moment of its being: all time. It is the only glimpse we are permitted of what eternity is." But Clodia Metelli, who has been reading the fourth book of Lucretius, denounces Catullus' idealization of her: "I have as high an opinion of myself as the next woman, but I never pretended to be all the goddesses rolled in one, nor Penelope, to boot" (Wilder 1961: 65, 152, 100, 32).

Another aspect of Catullus' modernity is found in Louis MacNeice, who sees in Catullus' life and work an analogue for modern poets (Dodds 1966: 210):

> The Individual has died before; Catullus
> Went down young, gave place to those who were born old
> And more adaptable and were not even jealous
> Of his wild life and lyrics. Though our songs
> Were not so warm as his, our fate is no less cold.

A present-day critic, G. S. Fraser, can also find modernity in Catullus: "We find something 'modern' in Catullus, but not in Virgil," and he cites "a feeling of harsh, unresolved complexity" that he locates in poem 85, *Odi et amo* (1964: 12, 31). Juxtaposition of Catullus and Vergil is indeed a constant in the modern reception of Catullus: Pound and Graves elevate Catullus, while they denigrate Vergil; Eliot reverses this process by lauding Vergil and denouncing Catullus; Banville notes that Catullus can be a model for contemporary writers, but that Vergil cannot; Swinburne, professing ignorance of Vergil, praises Catullus.

It is by the slenderest of threads that we possess the poems of Catullus, but for the novelist John Fowles they are irreplaceable:

> I think of two poets whose poetry I have a special love for: Catullus and Emily Dickinson.
> If their poetry were not to exist, no amount of historical and biographical information

about them, no amount of music or painting they might have made, no quantity even (were such a thing possible) of interviewing and meeting them, could compensate me for the loss and precise knowledge of their deepest reality, their most real reality, that their poems give. I wish there was a head of Catullus, I wish there was more than one miserable daguerrotype of Emily Dickinson, and a recording of her voice: but these are trivial lacks beside the irreplaceability the absence of their poetries would represent. (Fowles 1981: 197)

A very striking feature of Catullus' poetry is the wide variety of mood and tone: he can be passionate in love or in friendship, violent in hate and enmity, serious, comic, happy, sad, witty, sarcastic. Boring he is not, despite the assertion of Basil Bunting (1900–85) that follows his translation of the magnificent opening lines (1–28) of poem 64 (Arkins 1982b): " – *and why Catullus bothered to write pages and pages of this drivel mystifies me*" (Bunting 1978: 131). This chameleon-like quality in Catullus might seem to provide ammunition for those who reject the concept of a unitary self. But we should reckon with the concept that the self is *unitary, but complex*, as in Whitman's famous dictum ("Leaves of Grass" 1321–3):

> Do I contradict myself?
> Very well, then, I contradict myself;
> (I am large – I contain multitudes).

So labels for Catullus tend to be reductive and must be used with care. Tennyson called Catullus "Tenderest of Roman poets nineteen hundred years ago" (Tennyson 1899: 574), a view supported by, for example, the famous vignette of baby Torquatus in poem 61 (209–13), the even more famous elegy for his dead brother (poem 101), and poems about friends such as Veranius (poem 9), Calvus (poem 50), and Cinna (poem 95). But a contrary view can certainly be held, as Harold Nicolson, stressing Catullus' capacity for hate, makes clear: "It passes my comprehension why Tennyson could have called him 'tender.' He is vindictive, venomous, and full of obscene malice. He is only tender about his brother and Lesbia and in the end she gets it hot as well" (Nicolson 1968: 305). The point here is that neither man is wholly right (or wrong).

The obscenity of Catullus to which Nicolson refers was not, by the last decades of the twentieth century, an issue to be passed over in silence. Though Byron's assertion that "Catullus scarcely has a decent poem" (*Don Juan* I.xlii.3) is exaggerated, there is plenty of obscenity in his work that is now being evaluated. This obscenity, which expands the use of obscene language in iambic verse, may involve a desire to see sex exposed, to get to the core of a human person, to express aggression.

In earlier times, indeed up to the 1960s, editors and translators of Catullus turned themselves into moralists who objected to plain speaking about sex (a practice of the Stoics). This kind of censorship, which prevented people having access to the totality of Catullus' poetry, is a form of intellectual dishonesty; Yeats rightly held that all censorship is an attack on the intellect. In so far as this censorship of Catullus is imposed on moral grounds as opposed to questions of taste, it is sufficiently rebutted by Cardinal Newman's dictum that "it is a contradiction in terms to attempt a sinless Literature of sinful man" ("Duties of the Church towards Knowledge," in *The Idea of a University*, quoted by Whitehouse 1997: 127).

As late as 1961, Fordyce's commentary on Catullus omitted 32 poems – about one quarter of the total – on the grounds that they "do not lend themselves to comment in English" (p. v); as Edward Gibbon said: "My English text is chaste" (quoted in Kemp 1999: 77). Hence a student of Fordyce wrote, in referring to novels by Henry Miller and by D. H. Lawrence, "*Tropic of Cancer* has been published in vain. Lady Chatterley has tiptoed naked through the bluebells to no avail" ("Asinius Pollio", reviewing Fordyce, quoted in Ferguson 1998: 3). For in 1960 Penguin Books had been acquitted at the Old Bailey in London of publishing, in Lawrence's *Lady Chatterley's Lover*, an obscene book, and more was to come: in 1965, a major taboo was broken when the drama critic Kenneth Tynan became the first person to say "fuck" on British television; in 1967, Tynan was largely responsible for bringing the stage censorship of the Lord Chamberlain to an end. With this sort of change in mores, recent scholarship (such as that of Skinner 1991) and recent translations (such as that of Lee 1990) face up to the issue of obscenity in Catullus. But the issue had already been put in its place by Walter Savage Landor (1775–1864) in "On Catullus":

> Tell me not what too well I know
> About the bard of Sirmio –
>   Yes, in Thalia's son
> Such stains there are – as when a Grace
> Sprinkles another's laughing face
>   With nectar, and runs on.
>   (1853: 366)

Landor is indeed the Romantic poet who engages most with Catullus, as Swinburne is the equivalent Victorian poet. Landor's most sustained treatment of Catullus is to be found in his long essay "The Poems of Catullus," which, though rambling and contentious in places, often champions with éclat "the vigorous and impassioned Veronese" (1853: 238). For Landor indulges freely in hyperbole in his judgments on the poems of Catullus: of poem 31 about Sirmione: "Never was a return to home expressed so sensitively and beautifully as here"; of the translation of Sappho (poem 51): "Nothing can surpass the graces of this"; of the epithalamium for Manlius and Aurunculeia (poem 61): "Never was there, and never will there be probably, a nuptial song of equal beauty"; of the Attis (poem 63): "Nothing breathes such an air of antiquity as his galliambic" (1853: 261, 264, 265, 244). It is indeed the extraordinary Attis and the worship of Cybele with which Landor concludes his essay: "They who have listened, patiently and supinely, to the catarrhal songsters of goose-grazed commons, will be loth and ill-fitted to mount up with Catullus to the highest steeps in the forests of Ida, and will shudder at the music of the Corybantes in the temple of the Great Mother of the Gods" (1853: 281). But Landor also recognized the *urbanitas* of Catullus, which he regards as superior to that of Lucretius: "there is more of what Cicero calls *urbane* in the two provincials, Virgil and Catullus, than in the authoritative and stately man who leads Memmius from the Camp into the gardens of Epicurus" (1853: 238).

A final piece of hyperbole from Landor about Catullus 64.269–75, together with his translation of that passage: "In Catullus we see morning in another aspect; not personified: and a more beautiful description, a sentence on the whole more harmonious, or one in which every verse is better adapted to its peculiar office, is neither to be found nor conceived."

> As, by the Zephyr wakened, underneath
> The sun's expansive gaze the waves move on
> Slowly and placidly, with gentle plash
> Against each other, and light laugh; but soon,
> The breezes freshening, rough and huge they swell,
> Afar refulgent in the crimson east.
>
> (Landor 1853: 249–50)

Swinburne (1837–1909) is the Victorian poet who is most obviously devoted to Catullus. In a letter of August 18, 1894, Swinburne, professing ignorance of Vergil, pays an eloquent tribute to Catullus and cites poems 4, 31, 64, 101, and 63 (Meyers 2004: 72):

> The first if not the only Latin poet I ever thoroughly loved is Catullus: I remember the delight & wonder with which it dawned on me as a schoolboy, when I had got into the division in which he was read, that here at last was a poet – a Latin writer – who was man & not a ^school^book - & a very lovable man too. Of course we read him in select poems ^(&<ed> some of them'edited, with omissions')^, but of course these contained almost every line worth reading, bar a dozen or less scattered here & there: I could almost find it in my heart to wish there were no more left of him. Do you not agree with me that it is a great traditional mistake to inflict such elaborate & literary poetry as Virgil's or Horace's on boys at an age when such straightforward ^& imaginative^ poetry, so 'simple, sensuous, & passionate' as 'Phaselus iste,' Sirmio, Peleus & Thetis, ^the poem in which he bewails his brother's death,^ Julia & Manlius (duly edited, of course), & Atys (minus a line or so) above all, must & would appeal to all youngsters with spirit & sense enough to appreciate anything?

We might now feel that Catullus is not as "simple" as might at first appear, but the notion that he would appeal to adolescents more than his Augustan successors Vergil and Horace seems valid.

Swinburne lauded Catullus in verse as well as in prose. His poem "To Catullus" is a variation on the French rondel, just two rhymes, with opening words used as a refrain (Swinburne 1912: V.185):

> My brother, my Valerius, dearest head
> Of all whose crowning bay-leaves crown their mother
> Rome, in the notes first heard of thine I read
>   My brother.
>
> No dust that death or time can strew may smother
> Love and the sense of kinship inly bred
> From loves and hates at one with one another.
>
> To thee was Caesar's self nor dear nor dread,
> Song and the sea were sweeter each than other:
> How should I living fear to call thee dead,
>   My brother?

Viewed as the pre-eminent Roman poet, Catullus is noted for devotion to the art of poetry ("song"), for the depiction of the sea in poems 63 and 64, for confronting Caesar with *sprezzatura*. But these qualities are adduced in order to stress Swinburne's affinity with Catullus, his view that Catullus is his "brother," especially in a capacity to express love and hate. So Swinburne transposes the distance between Catullus and his brother in poems 68a, 68b, and 101 into a closeness between ancient and modern poet. But in another poem, "Dolores," Swinburne feels that Catullus is superior to contemporary poets (1912: I.54):

> Old poets outsing and outlove us,
> > And Catullus makes mouths at our speech.

A number of modern poets have taken Catullus as a model and the novelist John Banville explains why: Catullus is one of those "artists whom one can use, from whom one can learn one's trade," because "one can see, or at least glimpse here and there on the surface, the processes by which the work was produced.... This generative and transfiguring process is a large part of the greatness of the *Carmina Catulli*." Contrast Vergil, one of "the artists who are of no use to the tyro, from whom one learns nothing," because "the methods of production are well-nigh invisible, buried so deeply inside the work that we cannot get at them without dismantling the parts"; works like those of Vergil are "in an essential way, *closed ... mysterious at their core*," and "utterly impenetrable" (Banville 1990: 74).

The most important figure in the reception of Catullus in the twentieth century is Ezra Pound (1885–1972). Pound was a very important poet who, after a conventional start, sought to write a new sort of poetry not only in shorter sequences such as *Cathay* and *Hugh Selwyn Mauberley*, but also in the vast epic *The Cantos*, whose method relies on the accumulation of significant detail. Pound was also an indefatigable supporter of other writers who aimed to make it new, including Eliot, Frost, Williams, Joyce, Hemingway, and Wyndham Lewis. More: Pound was a significant critic who had a largely unerring eye for the best in world literature. Pound's aesthetic sense here can rarely be faulted, but it must be remembered that a vicious distortion of that aesthetic led him to disastrous support for Italian Fascism; as Benjamin (1999: 235) points out, "*Fiat ars – pereat mundus*, says Fascism" ("so long as there is art, let the world perish").

Catullus ranks very high in Pound's personal canon, and is constantly invoked as a touchstone of excellence in poetry. So, as Pound anticipates contemporary views about the originality of Latin literature, Catullus is one of the authors prized: "It is my firm belief that no study of Greek authors offers a fully satisfactory alternative to reading of Tacitus, Catullus, Ovid, Propertius" (Pound 1973: 286).

Pound constantly cites Catullus in discussions about what the best poetry is. Catullus is at least the equal of the Greeks: "the Greeks might be hard put to it to find a better poet among themselves than is their disciple Catullus" (1960: 240). Indeed in Latin literature Catullus is essential: "Catullus, Propertius, Horace and Ovid are the people who matter. Catullus most. Martial somewhat ... Catullus has the intensity" (1982: 87). For Catullus is, with Propertius and Ovid, part of "the minimum basis for a sound and liberal education in letters" (1960: 38). Because Catullus possesses a special intense quality or *virtù* that makes him unique: "It is by reason of this *virtù* that a given work of art persists. It is by reason of this *virtù* that we have one Catullus, one Villon" (1973: 28).

Crucial to Pound are Catullus' language and his meter. For Pound, the direct, hard language of Catullus anticipates that of modern poets like Rimbaud and the Imagists, who believed in "Direct treatment of the 'thing' whether subjective or objective" (1960: 3). He continues: "In Rimbaud the image stands clean, unencumbered by non-functioning words; to get anything like this directness of presentation one must go back to Catullus, perhaps to the poem [i.e., poem 39] which contains *dentos habet*" (1960: 33). In that poem, Catullus derides a Spaniard named Egnatius, who is one of Lesbia's lovers (poem 37), for wearing a perpetual grin:

> Egnatius, because he has teeth gleaming white,
> grins on every possible occasion. If people come to
> the defendant's bench,
> when his advocate makes them cry,
> he grins, if people mourn at a pious boy's
> tomb, when a bereaved mother cries for her only son,
> he grins. Whatever happens, wherever he is,
> whatever he does, he grins: he has this disease,
> neither elegant, in my view, nor urbane.
> So I must give you some advice, "good" Egnatius.
> If you were Roman or Sabine or Tiburtine
> or a well-fed Umbrian or a fat Etruscan
> or a swarthy Lanuvian with fine teeth
> or, to mention my own people too, a Transpadane
> or anybody who washes his teeth with clean water,
> then I wouldn't want you to grin on every possible occasion;
> for nothing is more foolish than a foolish laugh.
> In fact you are Spanish: in the land of Spain
> what each man has pissed he uses every morning
> to rub hard his tooth and red gum,
> so that, the more polished that tooth of yours is,
> the more piss it declares you have drunk.
>
> (trans. Brian Arkins)

Pound's advice to the prospective poet about metrical technique is: "If you want the gist of the matter go to Sappho, Catullus, Villon, Heine when he is in the vein, Gautier when he is not too frigid" (1960: 7). Central to the use of meter in Latin poetry is the ability to harness various Greek meters to the demands of the Latin language. The classic affirmation in Latin poetry of a poet's achievement in this area is found in Horace, *Odes* 3.30.13–14: *princeps Aeolium carmen ad Italos/deduxisse modos*, "first to have brought the song of the Aeolians to Italian measures." "First" might seem a shade excessive to Catullus, who composed poems 11 and 51 in Sapphic meter, and wrote poem 61 in Aeolic stanzas of four glyconics and a pherecratean. It is indeed the meter of Catullus 61 (together with the rhythms of Sappho and Propertius) that Pound singles out for praise: "There is the *Poikilothron*, and then Catullus, *Collis O Heliconii*, and some Propertius, that one could do worse than know by heart for the sake of knowing what rhythm really is" (1970: 65). Impressive here is the *speed* of poem 61, in which Catullus begins the vast majority of lines with a trochee rather than a spondee.

It is not surprising, then, that Catullus 61 makes an appearance in *Cantos* IV and V. Amid themes of sexual violence in *Canto* IV, the references to Aurunculeia, the name of the bride in poem 61, to her bridal shoe, and to the marriage god Hymenaeus suggest her beauty and the legitimate sex of marriage (*bonus amor*): "Saffron sandal so petals the narrow foot: Hymenaeus Io!/Hymen, Io Hymenaee! Aurunculeia!" (1987a: 15).

Similar references to poem 61 are found in *Canto* V: Pound quotes or refers to the bridal shoe of Aurunculeia, the practice of scattering walnuts among the crowd during the singing of ribald, apotropaic lines, and the marriage god's bringing of the bride to her husband (1987b [1971]: 17):

> Gold-yellow, saffron ... The roman shoe, Aurunculeia's
> And come shuffling feet, and cries "Da nuces!"
> "Nuces!" praise, and Hymenaus "brings the girl to her man."

Pound's stress on Catullus' achievements in meter is echoed in various ways by the Victorian poets Hopkins, Tennyson, and Swinburne. Having written poems in Latin early in his career, Hopkins then stopped – "my Latin muse having been wholly mum for years" – but in Dublin in 1866, when he was professor of Greek at University College Dublin, he translated three songs of Shakespeare into Latin (*The Tempest* 2.1; *The Merchant of Venice* 3.2; *King Henry VIII* 3.1). The meter of the second two of these poems is the phalacean hendecasyllabic meter, in which about two-thirds of Catullus' poems in the group 1–60 are written; this meter can be analyzed as a glyconic followed by a bacchiac. Hopkins held that in his rhythms he uses "Catullus for my warrant only, not my standard," since his almost invariably spondaic opening and his limited use of elision bring his practice closer to Martial's use of this meter (Abbott 1955: 224–5, 339).

Poets might also make use of Catullus' hendecasyllabics for poems written in English. Indeed Pound stated that "I think progress lies ... in an attempt to approximate classical meters in English" (1970: 349). So Tennyson wrote a poem, "Hendecasyllabics," that is "All composed in a meter of Catullus" (Tennyson 1899: 243). Swinburne followed suit in the poem "Hendacasyllabics," but went one better in his poem "Ad Catullum" by writing it in Latin in the difficult meter of pure iambics (as in Catullus 4 and 29). Swinburne provided a further demonstration of metrical virtuosity by writing two poems in the greater asclepiad meter of Catullus 30: one is in Latin, an elegy for Gautier called "In Obitum Theophili Poetae"; one is in English, entitled "Choriambs."

Further involvement of Pound with Catullus is found in his own short poems and in some translations. Catullus' highly personal approach to poetry is adopted by Pound in his volume *Lustra* (1916). The reviewer of this volume in the *Times Literary Supplement* is critical, but notes that Pound appropriates Catullus: "In matter he seems to have taken Catullus for his model. He expresses any chance whim of his own, any liking, or more often dislike, that he happens to have experienced" (Stock 1985: 245). As Davie says, "the one of his ancient masters who served Pound best was Catullus, in these of his epigrams which were at the furthest remove from the sardonic harshness of Martial" (1975: 41).

Writing in 1942, Pound claimed that "No one has succeeded in translating Catullus into English" (1973: 324) and also asserted that "I have failed forty times myself so I do know the matter" (1982: 69). But in recent times there have been successful translations of Catullus into English by Peter Whigham (1966), James Michie (1969), Guy Lee (1990), and, most recently, Peter Green (2005) – the last three with facing Latin text, and Green's with accompanying commentary. Pound's three translations from Catullus that appear in his volume *Translations* are all in the epigrammatic mode he often favors, two dealing with Lesbia (poems 43 and 85), and one about money (poem 26), which became an obsession with Pound.

In poem 43, Catullus attacks a woman from his own province of Cisalpine Gaul, where she is praised, by denigrating her physical characteristics (which contrast with those favored by the Roman elegists, small feet, dark eyes, long fingers). Here is Pound's adaptation (1987b [1971]: 113):

> TO FORMIANUS' YOUNG LADY
>   FRIEND
> After Valerius Catullus
>
> All hail! young lady with a nose
>   by no means too small,
> With a foot unbeautiful,
>   and with eyes that are not black,
> With fingers that are not long, and with a mouth
>   undry,
> And with a tongue by no means too elegant.
> You are the friend of Formianus, the vendor of
>   cosmetics,
> And they call you beautiful in the province,
> And you are even compared to Lesbia.
>
> O most unfortunate age!

Pound captures well the physical detail about the woman, but changes her identity from being the mistress of Mamurra, Caesar's chief engineer in Gaul, to being the "lady friend" of Formianus, who sells cosmetics (a touch of Martial). A signal defect in Pound's translation is the feeble punch-line that seeks to render *o saeclum insipiens et infacetum* as "O most unfortunate age!"; try instead "O coarse and tasteless era."

Pound's translation of Catullus 85 is:

> I hate and love. Why? You may ask but
> It beats me. I feel it done to me, and ache.

Pound here falls into a trap which hardly any translator has avoided by rendering the Latin *odi et amo* as "I hate and love." But, as is clear from poems 72 and 75, this is *not* what Catullus means: because of Lesbia's perceived infidelity, Catullus no longer likes her, but wants her physically all the more, so that the translation we need is "I loathe her, I lust for her" (Arkins 1987).

Pound's poem "Catullus: xxvi" is a version rather than a translation. Omitting the name of the owner of the mortgaged villa (Furius), and the names of three of the four winds, Pound stresses the issue of overdraft by drastically increasing the sum of money owed from 15,200 to 200,000 sesterces (in poem 23, Furius seeks a loan of 100,000 sesterces). That this is a significant amount is shown by the fact that Marcus Caelius Rufus could rent an apartment in the fashionable Palatine area of Rome for 10,000 sesterces a year (Cic. *Cael.* 17):

> This villa is raked of winds fore and aft,
> All Boreas' sons in bluster and yet more
> Against it is this TWO HUNDRED THOUSAND sesterces,
> All out against it, oh my God
>   some draft.

In poem 31, Pound was concerned with not just the achievement and texture of Catullus' poetry, but also with his sense of place – with Sirmione on Lake Garda (Latin Benacus), where the family had an elaborate villa (Wiseman 1987: 307–70). Indeed Catullus' home at Sirmione became one of Pound's "sacred places," and he waxes very eloquent about "the same old Sirmio that Catullus raved over a few years back" (Stock 1985: 107). And Sirmione has achieved legendary status in the history of Modernism, because Pound met Joyce there in 1920, and persuaded him to go to Paris: "a small rain storm . . . /recalling the arrival of Joyce et fils at the haunt of Catullus" (Pound 1987a: 456).

In his poem "The Flame," Pound locates reality in the concrete fact of the transparent blue of Lake Garda (1987b: 50):

> Sapphire Benacus, in thy mists and thee
> Nature herself's turned metaphysical
> Who can look on that blue and not believe?

Pound elaborates on the worship of this earthly paradise in the poem "Blandula, Tenella, Vagula," finding at Sirmione three types of blue – transparent blue ("sapphire"), darker greenish blue ("cobalt"), and deep royal blue ("cyanine") – and locating there both Pound's soul and "She," the Muse of poetry (1987b: 39).

Sirmione has attracted other poets too, Catullus 31 being a favorite poem of the nineteenth century. Leigh Hunt (1784–1859) produced a reasonably close translation of poem 31 in his poem "Catullus' Return Home to the Peninsula of Sirmio," whose ending well captures the joy and laughter experienced by Catullus and by Lake Garda (the learned reference to "Lydian," i.e., Etruscan, settlements in the area is omitted):

> Hail, lovely Sirmio! Hail, paternal soil!
> Joy, my bright waters, joy: your master's come!
> Laugh every dimple on the cheek of home!
>   (Hunt 1849: 197–8).

Having read Catullus in his youth, Thomas Hardy (1840–1928) wrote a poem called "Catullus xxxi (After passing Sirmione, April 1887)," whose ending (unlike Hunt's) omits the joy of Lake Garda to focus entirely on that of the poet: "then hail, sweet Sirmio; thou that wast,/And art, mine own unrivalled Fair" (1902: 244–5).

But Hardy's poem is marred by a mass of archaic diction – "thou," "mine," "doth," "wast," "art," "stretchest," "moils" – and confirms, in a very striking way, the view of Hopkins, the linguistic innovator, that "This Victorian English is a bad business" (Abbott 1955: 89).

Tennyson's pleasing poem "Frater Ave atque Vale," which combines references to poem 31 and to poem 101 on the death of Catullus' brother, was written on a visit to Sirmione in 1880, a few months after the death of his brother Charles (1899: 574):

> Row us out from Desenzano, to your Sirmione row!
> So they row'd, and there we landed – "O venusta Sirmio!"
> There to me thro' all the groves of olive in the summer glow,
> There beneath the Roman ruin where the purple flowers grow,
> Came that "Ave atque Vale" of the Poet's hopeless woe,
> Tenderest of Roman poets nineteen-hundred years ago,
> "Frater Ave atque Vale" – as we wander'd to and fro
> Gazing at the Lydian laughter of the Garda Lake below
> Sweet Catullus's all-but-island olive-silvery Sirmio!

Tennyson preserves part of Catullus' poem: the Latin quotations *O venusta Sirmio*, "O lovely Sirmio," from poem 31, and *Frater, ave atque vale*, "brother, hail and farewell," from poem 101, together with the phrase "all-but-island" (*paene insularum*) and the learned Lydian reference. But Tennyson's poem is primarily that of the modern observer, who notes present-day olives, purple flowers, and the ruins of Catullus' villa which, as picturesque, appeal powerfully to the Romantic imagination. That Romantic imagination is famously found in Yeats's poem "The Lake Isle of Innisfree," which was written in 1890 and possibly echoes Catullus 31. Just as Catullus leaves Bithynia and arrives home to Sirmio, so Yeats imagines leaving London and coming to a small island on Lough Gill in Sligo, where he will lead a solitary life (as in Thoreau's *Walden*).

The twentieth century might be expected to strike a more astringent note, and so it proves with the poem "Dear Little Sirmio: Catullus Recollected" by Stevie Smith (1902–71). She injects a note of irony that mocks Catullus' reference to the two tribes of Thyni and Bithyni by means of a nonchalant question: "No sooner had I left Bithynia – and what was the name of the/other place?" Yet it is Smith's punch-line that establishes a radical difference between her poem and Catullus 31. It notes that the modern person, unlike the local aristocrat Catullus, must work very hard to pay for the comforts of home: "Even if one wears oneself out paying for them" (Smith 1972: 348).

Pound was not the only Modernist poet to have a high regard for Catullus: the part-time Modernist Yeats wrote about the Latin poet in prose and in verse, and acknowledged the impact of Catullus' poetry on his own. In London in the 1890s, Yeats belonged to a loose group of poets called the Rhymers, who valued Catullus as a writer of pure poetry like that of Callimachus and Asclepiades in the *Greek Anthology*, and like seventeenth-century English poets such as Thomas Campion, Donne, Jonson, and, in particular, Herrick: "We tried to write like the poets of the Greek Anthology, or like Catullus, or like the Jacobean lyrists, men who wrote while poetry was still pure" (Yeats 1961: 495).

Yeats himself is explicit about the debt he owed to the fine translations of Catullus by Arthur Symons (1865–1945), about which Pound affirmed that "we can but wonder if any man, in English, has better succeeded in finding the tone and idiom to render him or his poetry" (Pound 1979–80: 57). Yeats wrote of Symons that "my thoughts gained in richness and in clearness from his sympathy, nor shall I ever know how much my practice and my theory owe to the passages that he read me from Catullus and from Verlaine and Mallarmé" (1953: 192).[1] Here the French symbolist poets, whom Symons was to explicate in his book *The Symbolist Movement in Literature* (1894), join the roll-call of pure poetry.

What Pound and Yeats saw in Symons's translations of Catullus can be grasped from his rendering of poem 8, in which the poet experiences a conflict between his intellectual realization that Lesbia is lost to him and his emotional inability to act on that knowledge. Here is the translation by Symons (1973: III.164):

> Miserable Catullus, put an end to this folly:
> Let all things dead be over and ended wholly.
> Once the sun was bright and the light was fair,
> And there was a woman to love, and she waited there,
> And never a woman was better loved than she.
> Surely the sun was bright and fair to see,
> And merrily then the hours of love went by
> When nothing that you desired would she deny.
> Now the woman, desiring no more, denies:
> You too, deny, nor follow her as she flies.
> Be miserable no more, for all is vain:
> Set your soul steadfast and harden your heart again.
> Farewell: Catullus has hardened his heart again,
> He will not follow nor cry to you now in vain.
> No, it is you that shall weep, as you lie alone,
> And no man cries at your gate, and the night goes on.
> What shall remain to you then? who shall come to your call?
> Who shall call you fair? nay, whom shall you love at all?
> Who shall have you for his? whose lips shall you bite and kiss?
> But you, Catullus, harden your heart at this.

In such a guise, then, Catullus offered Yeats a means of escaping the excessive vagueness of his early verse, and the ability to write of heroes, of daily life, and of love in a concrete way that combined metaphysical wit with a romantic sensibility. Again, the practice of Catullus may have influenced Yeats's idiosyncratic choice of poems for the *Oxford Book of Modern Verse* (1937), his preference for poets such as Edith Sitwell and Oliver St John Gogarty.

Yeats's famous poem about Catullus, "The Scholars," demonstrates his close association with Pound not only because it was first published by the American poet in the *Catholic Anthology* in 1915, but also because it mirrors the sort of attack on the arid scholarship of classicists that is typical of Pound, and that he will have passed on to Yeats when they lived together at Stone Cottage in Sussex in the period 1913–16. Pound felt that classicists were concerned almost entirely with the textual criticism and linguistic niceties of Greek and Latin authors at the expense of the literary qualities of those works, a charge echoed time after time in the nineteenth and early twentieth centuries. The curious case of A. E. Housman, a poet and professor of Latin at Cambridge, will serve to illustrate the issue: Housman posited a radical dichotomy between his own poetry on the one hand and his scholarship about Latin poetry on the other, so that he refused to treat Latin poetry as literature. As the character AEH (Housman at 77) asserts in Tom Stoppard's play *The Invention of Love*, "Poetical feelings are a peril to scholarship" (1997: 36).

"The Scholars" establishes a radical binary apposition between elderly, tepid, bourgeois scholars who have forgotten the sins of their youth and young, warm-hearted, bohemian love poets who write about the pain of love (as did Catullus). When those scholars write about the work of poets, they lack all energy and mouth *idées recues* (ironically, Housman makes the same complaint about textual critics). Yeats ends his poem with a terminal question (a favorite device): "Lord, what would they say/Did their Catullus walk that way?" Unlike most of Yeats's terminal questions, this one is not rhetorical, but open: we do not know what the scholars would say if a poet like Catullus turned out to be like them.[2]

Robert Graves (1895–1985) is another important poet who owes a debt to Catullus. Graves had a considerable involvement with the Roman world, producing translations of Lucan's *Pharsalia* (1956), Suetonius' *The Twelve Caesars* (1959), and Apuleius' *The Golden Ass* (1950), and writing the historical novels *I, Claudius* and *Claudius the God and his Wife Messalina* (both 1934), eventually to be made into a highly successful television series by the BBC. After Graves was seriously wounded at the battle of the Somme in 1916, he returned to France in January 1917 with the Latin texts of Lucretius and of Catullus. Graves's biographer asserts that Catullus is "one of the poets who helped form [Graves's] mature style" (Seymour-Smith 1983: 52–3), a style which, like that of Catullus, is concise, lucid, and elegant, manifesting itself most obviously in Graves's many excellent love poems. A good example is the poem called "The Thieves" (2000: 388), written to Graves's second wife Beryl in 1939 and dealing with what he calls "the intractability of love" (1961: 139):

> Lovers in the act dispense
> With such meum-tuum sense
> As might warningly reveal
> What they must not pick or steal,
> And their nostrum is to say:
> "I and you are both away."
>
> After, when they disentwine
> You from me and yours from mine,
> Neither can be certain who
> Was that I whose mine was you.
> To the act again they go
> More completely not to know.
>
> Theft is theft and raid is raid
> Though reciprocally made.
> Lovers, the conclusion is
> Doubled sight and jealousies
> In a single heart that grieves
> For lost honour among thieves.

Robert Frost (1874–1963) is yet another important modern poet involved with Catullus (Putnam 1983). Frost often kept a copy of Catullus by his bed, and, in his last years, frequently referred to the Latin poet. So in glossing the star in his poem "Take Something Like a Star," Frost is reported to have said: "And I often think it's Catullus. I get out Catullus when I'm too bothered about my having been wrong in politics" (quoted in Putnam 1983: 262). Two phrases of Catullus made a particular impact on Frost, *mens animi* (poem 65.4), and *aliquid* (poem 1.4).

The Catullan phrase *mens animi* is used by Frost on several occasions to illustrate his view that a poem first comes from the heart (*animus*) before being fixed in thought (*mens*): "Poetry is the thoughts of the heart. I'm sure that's what Catullus means by *mens animi*. Poetry is hyphenated, like so many British names. It's a thought-felt thing" (1995: 446). Frost returns to this theme in his poem "Kitty Hawk" (1969: 428–43). That same poem also quotes the Catullan phrase *aliquid* in the context of man's ability, literally, to fly: "we're/What Catullus called/Somewhat (*aliquid*)" (lines 197–9). *Aliquid* is equally crucial in Frost's poem "For Once, Then, Something," where the speaker experiences some kind of epiphany. Though he cannot denote what it was, he knows it was *something*: "For once, then, something" (1969: 225). That the "something" must be Catullus' *aliquid* is confirmed by the fact that Frost's poem is written in the Phalaecian hendecasyllabic meter of Catullus 1.

Less satisfactory is the involvement with Catullus of a key figure in Modernism, T. S. Eliot. In a letter to his mother in June 1918, Eliot stated that "I have also read this week most of Catullus" (V. Eliot 1988: 235). But this reading of Catullus did not lead Eliot to any kind of useful or sympathetic view of the Roman writer's poetry. In the extraordinary claims that Eliot makes for Vergil in his 1945 essay "What is a Classic?" – "Our classic, the classic of all Europe, is Virgil" – he finds it necessary to denigrate Catullus (as well as Propertius and Horace): "I think that we are conscious, in Virgil more than in any other Latin poet – for Catullus and Propertius seem ruffians, and Horace somewhat plebeian by comparison – of a refinement of manners springing from a delicate sensibility, and particularly in that test of manners, private and public conduct between the sexes" (1969: 62).

This attack on Catullus as a "ruffian" – defined by the *Oxford English Dictionary* as "a man of a low and brutal character" – is the etiolated snobbery of a London clubman with Anglo-Catholic and royalist leanings (one who conveniently forgot his own writing of obscene verse). But the attack is also part of Eliot's campaign to establish Vergil as a man who, unlike Catullus, is "uniquely close to Christianity." That Catullus is not a proto-Christian we may readily allow, but neither was Vergil, whose philosophical leanings were, in the main, Epicurean (as Pound sardonically remarked, "We all know Propertius went to mid-week prayer meeting" [1970: 89]). What Catullus does exhibit, *pace* Eliot, is precisely "a delicate sensibility" that is applied to a wide variety of human situations, together with – in the Lesbia poems – an original and refined mode of dealing with "conduct between the sexes."

Then, in writing of Vergil, Eliot contrives to pay Catullus a back-handed compliment: "Even for intensity of physical passion, Virgil is more tepid than some other Latin poets, and far below the rank of Catullus" (1969: 131). We may grant Catullus' passion, without downgrading that of Vergil: his depiction of *amor*, sexual passion, is very powerful in, for example, *Eclogue* 10 and Book 4 of the *Aeneid*.

The remainder of this chapter analyzes the engagement of various writers with three of Catullus' poems that have proved specially influential: the Lesbia kiss-poems, 5 and 7, and poem 101 on the death of his brother.

In 1798, at the time that Samuel Taylor Coleridge (1772–1834) was writing "The Rime of the Ancient Mariner" and "Kubla Khan," he produced a poem described as "Lines imitated from Catullus" that is a version of poem 5 (Coleridge 1912: 60–1):

> My Lesbia, let us love and live,
> And to the winds, my Lesbia, give
> Each cold restraint, each boding fear
> Of age and all her saws severe.
> Yon sun now posting to the main
> Will set, - but 'tis to rise again; -
> But we, when once our mortal light
> Is set, must sleep in endless night!
> Then come, with whom alone I'll live,
> A thousand kisses take and give!
> Another thousand! to the store
> Add hundreds – then a thousand more!
> And when they do a million mount,
> Let confusion take the account, –
> That you, the number never knowing,
> May continue still bestowing –
> That I for joys may never pine,
> Which never can again be mine!

Coleridge's opening weakens Catullus' injunction to enjoy life and love (like most translations), but he then adds the vivid image of hurling the restraint and fear of old age to the winds. Coleridge deftly catches the famous lines about the sun's ability to renew itself constantly, contrasted with human inability to do so. The following command to Lesbia to provide hundreds and thousands of kisses is amplified by the reference to a total of "a million." But Coleridge alters the end of Catullus 5, so that the jumbling of the account is designed not to avoid the evil eye of the man who can count the number of kisses, but to permit Lesbia to continue the roll-call of kisses (although these may not in fact be available in the future).

One of the most impressive and metaphysical of the Lesbia poems, Catullus 7 (Arkins 1979), is translated in Flann O'Brien's novel *At Swim-Two-Birds* by the character Brinsley, who is based on O'Brien's friend Niall Sheridan (1967: 38–9):

Ah, Lesbia, said Brinsley. The finest thing I ever wrote. How many kisses, Lesbia you ask would serve to sate this hungry love of mine? – As many as the Libyan sands that bask along Cyrene's shore where pine-trees wave, where burning Jupiter's untended shrine lies near to old King Battus' sacred grave:
Three stouts, called Kelly.
Let them be endless as the stars at night, that stare upon the Lovers in a ditch – so often would love-crazed Catullus bite your burning lips, that prying eyes should not have the power to count, nor evil tongues bewitch, the frenzied kisses that you gave and got.

Though Brinsley sticks quite closely to Catullus, he and his drinking companions Kelly and Trellis move the poem into the Irish present. Brinsley has the Roman lovers function in an Irish "ditch," where Trellis imagines them "at their hedge-pleasure in the pale starlight, no sound from them, his fierce mouth burying into hers"; and when the barman is slow to provide "*three more stouts,*" Kelly imagines that Catullus' African desert has been transported to Dublin: "God, he said to me, it's in the desert you'd think we were."

Catullus' individual reaction to the death of his much-loved brother at Troy in poem 101 ends with the famous line *atque in perpetuum, frater, aue atque uale*, "and forever, my brother, hail and farewell." George Moore finds this poem incomparable: "a poem which none can read today, even in a prose translation, without weeping. . . . No poet has found a more perfect expression for the resigned grief we feel – which we must feel – for those who have just gone" (Frazier 2000: 353). Moore used Catullus' line to provide the title of his autobiographical trilogy *Hail and Farewell*. Indeed when Moore was finally leaving Ireland in 1911, after a tempestuous relationship with his native land, he altered Catullus' kinship term *frater* (brother) into *mater* (mother):

> On a grey windless morning in February the train took me to Kingstown, and I had always looked forward to leaving Ireland in May, seeking the words of a last farewell or murmuring the words of Catullus when he journeyed over land and sea to burn the body of his brother, fitting them to my circumstance by the change of a single word:
>
> ATQUE IN PERPETUUM, MATER, AVE ATQUE VALE...
>
> (Moore 1985: 684)

NOTES

1 Reprinted with the permission of Scribner, an imprint of Simon & Schuster Adult Publishing Group, from AUTOBIOGRAPHY OF W. B. YEATS by William Butler Yeats. Copyright ©1916, ©1936, by The Macmillan Company; copyright renewed ©1944, ©1964 by Bertha Georgie Yeats. All rights reserved.

2 Reprinted with the permission of Scribner, an imprint of Simon & Schuster Adult Publishing Group, from THE COLLECTED WORKS OF W. B. YEATS, VOLUME I: THE POEMS, revised and edited by Richard J. Finneran. Copyright ©1919 by The Macmillan Company; copyright renewed ©1947 by Bertha Georgie Yeats. All rights reserved.

GUIDE TO FURTHER READING

For overviews of Catullus see Wiseman (1985); Arkins (1999). Very valuable for translations and versions of Catullus is Gaisser (2001). For biographies of the crucial figure of Ezra Pound see Stock (1985); Carpenter (1988); for Pound and Latin poetry, including Catullus, see Thomas (1983). For Catullus and the Victorians see Vance (1999: 112–32). For Tennyson and Catullus see Ferguson (1961). For Swinburne and Catullus see Ridenour (1988). For Frost and Catullus see Putnam (1983). For Eliot and Latin literature see Arkins (2001). For the minimal impact of Catullus on Joyce see Schork (1997: 187–94).

WORKS CITED

Abbott, C. C., ed. 1955. *Letters of Gerard Manley Hopkins to Robert Bridges*. London and New York.

Arkins, B. 1979. "Catullus 7." *L'Antiquité classique* 48: 630–5.

Arkins, B. 1982b. "Tradition Reshaped: Language and Style in Euripides *Medea* 1–19, Ennius *Medea Exul* 1–9 and Catullus 64. 1–30." *Ramus* 11: 116–33.

Arkins, B. 1987. "A New Translation of Catullus 85." *Liverpool Classical Monthly* 12: 12.

Arkins, B. 1988. "Pound's Propertius: What Kind of Homage?" *Paideuma* 17: 29–44.

Arkins, B. 1990. *Builders of My Soul: Greek and Roman Themes in Yeats*. Gerrards Cross.

Arkins, B. 1999. *An Interpretation of the Poems of Catullus*. Lewiston, NY.

Arkins, B. 2001. "Eliot as Critic: The Case of Latin Literature." *Yeats-Eliot Review* 17.3: 10–17.

Banville, J. 1990. "Survivors of Joyce." In A. Martin, ed., *James Joyce – The Artist and the Labyrinth*. London. 73–81.

Benjamin, W. 1999. *Illuminations*. London.

Bunting, B. 1978. *Collected Poems*. Oxford.

Carpenter, H. 1988. *A Serious Character – The Life of Ezra Pound*. London.

Coleridge, E. H., ed., 1912. *The Complete Poetical Works of Samuel Coleridge*. Oxford.

Davie, D. 1975. *Pound*. London.

Dodds, E. R., ed. 1966. *The Collected Poems of Louis MacNeice*. London.

Eliot, T. S. 1958. *Selected Prose*. Harmondsworth.

Eliot, T. S. 1969. *On Poetry and Poets*. London.

Eliot, V., ed. 1988. *The Letters of T. S. Eliot. Vol. 1: 1898–1922*. London.

Ferguson, J. 1961. "Catullus and Tennyson." *English Studies in Africa* 12: 41–58.

Ferguson, J. 1988. *Catullus. Greece & Rome* New Surveys in the Classics No. 20. Oxford.

Fordyce, C. J., ed. 1961. *Catullus: A Commentary*. Oxford.

Fowles, J. 1981. *The Aristos*. London.

Fraser, G. S. 1964. *The Modern Writer and His World*. Baltimore.

Frazier, A. 2000. *George Moore, 1852–1933*. New Haven, CT.

Frost, R. 1969. *The Poetry of Robert Frost*. Ed. E. C. Latham. New York.

Frost, R. 1995. *Collected Poems, Prose and Plays*. New York.

Gaisser, J. H. 2001. *Catullus in English*. London.

Graves, R. 1961. *Poems Selected by Himself*. Harmondsworth.

Graves, R. 2000. *Robert Graves: The Complete Poems in One Volume*. Eds. B. Graves and D. Ward. Manchester.

Green, P., trans. 2005. *The Poems of Catullus*. Berkeley, Los Angeles, and London.

Hardwick, L. 2003. *Reception Studies*. Oxford and New York.

Hardy, T. 1902. *Poems of the Past and the Present*. London and New York.

Hunt, L. 1849. *The Poetical Works of Leigh Hunt*. London.

Kemp, P., ed. 1999. *The Oxford Dictionary of Literary Quotations*. Oxford.

Landor, W. S. 1853. *The Last Fruit off an Old Tree*. London.

Lee, G., trans. 1990. *The Poems of Catullus*. Oxford and New York.

Meyers, T. L., ed. 2004. *The Uncollected Letters of Algernon Charles Swinburne. Vol. 3: 1890–1909*. London and Brookfield, VT.

Michie, J., trans. 1969. *The Poems of Catullus*. London.

Moore, G. 1985. *Hail and Farewell*. Ed. R. A. Cave. Gerrards Cross.

Nicolson, H. 1968. *Diaries and Letters 1945–1962*. London.

O'Brien, F. 1967. *At Swim-Two-Birds*. Harmondsworth.

Perkins, J. 1981. "Literary History: H.-G. Gadamar, T. S. Eliot and Virgil." *Arethusa* 14: 241–9.

Pound, E. 1960 [1935]. *The Literary Essays of Ezra Pound*. New York and London.

Pound, E. 1970. *Ezra Pound*. Ed. J. P. Sullivan. Harmondsworth.

Pound, E. 1973. *Selected Prose of Ezra Pound 1909–1965*. New York and London.

Pound, E. 1979–80. "Arthur Symons." *Agenda* 17–18: 54–57.

Pound, E. 1982 [1950]. *Selected Letters of Ezra Pound*. Ed. D. D. Paige. New York and London.

Pound, E. 1984 [1963]. *The Translations of Ezra Pound*. New York and London.

Pound, E. 1987a [1970]. *The Cantos of Ezra Pound*. New York and London.

Pound, E. 1987b [1971]. Personae: *The Shorter Collected Poems of Ezra Pound*. New York and London.

Putnam, M. C. J. 1983. "The Future of Catullus." *Transactions of the American Philological Association* 113: 243–62.

Quinn, K. 1959. *The Catullan Revolution*. Melbourne. Rpt. Cambridge 1969; Ann Arbor, MI, 1971. 2nd edn. London 1999.

Ridenour, G. M. 1988. "Swinburne's Imitations of Catullus." *Victorian Newsletter* (Fall): 51–7.

Schork, R. J. 1997. *Latin and Roman Culture in Joyce*. Gainesville, FL.

Seymour-Smith, M. 1983. *Robert Graves: His Life and Work*. London.

Skinner, M. B. 1991. "The Dynamics of Catullan Obscenity: cc. 37, 58 and 11." *Syllecta Classica* 3: 1–11.

Smith, S. 1972. *Collected Poems of Stevie Smith*. London.

Stock, N. 1985. *The Life of Ezra Pound*. Harmondsworth.

Stoppard, T. 1997. *The Invention of Love*. London.

Swinburne, A. C. 1912. *Poems and Ballads*. 6 vols. London.

Symons, A. 1973. *The Collected Works of Arthur Symons*. 9 vols. Rpt. of 1924 edn. New York.

Tennyson, A., Lord. 1899. *Poetical Works of Alfred Lord Tennyson*. London.

Thomas, R. 1983. *The Latin Masks of Ezra Pound*. Ann Arbor, MI.

Vance, N. 1997. *The Victorians and Ancient Rome*. Oxford and Cambridge, MA.

Whigham, P., trans. 1966. *The Poems of Catullus*. Harmondsworth.

Whitehouse, J. C., ed. 1997. *Catholics on Literature*. Dublin.

Wilder, T. 1961 [1948]. *The Ides of March*. Harmondsworth.

Wiseman, T. P. 1985. *Catullus and His World: A Reappraisal*. Cambridge.

Wiseman, T. P. 1987. *Roman Studies Literary and Historical*. Liverpool.

Yeats, W. B. 1953. *The Autobiography of W. B. Yeats*. New York.

Yeats, W. B. 1961. *Essays and Introductions*. New York.

PART VII

Pedagogy

CHAPTER TWENTY-FIVE

Catullus in the Secondary School Curriculum*

Ronnie Ancona and Judith P. Hallett

Mantua Vergilio gaudet, Verona Catullo;
Paelignae dicar gloria gentis ego.

Mantua rejoices in its Vergil, Verona in its Catullus:
I will be called the glory of the Pelignian people.
Ovid, *Amores* 3.15.7–8

From the perspective of the College Entrance Examination Board (CEEB), Catullus is the second most popular classical Latin author currently being studied in the United States at the secondary school level. Its evidence is the number of students taking each of the CEEB Latin Advanced Placement (AP) examinations.[1] In the spring of 2004, 3,973 students took an examination on Vergil while 3,001 took one of three versions of an examination on Latin literature.[2] All three versions of the Latin literature syllabus include the same 42 Catullan poems. One version features these poems in combination with 20 of Horace's *Odes* and *Satire* 1.9. Another combines them with selections from Cicero's works: previously, selections from a single oration (*Pro Caelio*), but, starting in 2006–7, both an entire oration (*Pro Archia*) and passages from *De amicitia*. A third joins the Catullan poems with five stories from Ovid's *Metamorphoses* and six of his *Amores*. This last version, introduced only in 1993–4, has become by far the most popular, attracting 1,953 students, or 65 percent of those who took the 2004 Latin literature examination. It is noteworthy, if not necessarily significant, that this ranking of Roman poets in terms of their popularity – first Vergil, next Catullus, and then Ovid – calls to mind the couplet quoted as our epigraph. There Ovid lists himself third, after Vergil and Catullus, in the roster of Roman bards who confer glory on their native regions.

Latin textbooks published in the United Kingdom and aimed at a secondary school audience also testify to Catullus' popularity at this level, not only in Great Britain and Ireland but in other Commonwealth countries as well. For example, the *Oxford Latin Reader* (*OLR*) edited by Balme and Morwood (1997a; first published 1988) includes 26 Catullan poems along with selections from Cicero, Caesar, Vergil, Livy, and Ovid.[3]

---

* This chapter reflects the circumstances of teaching Catullus in the US Secondary Curriculum in 2007. That information is now outdated, because in 2009 the Advanced Placement Committee removed Catullus from the AP syllabus.

Twenty-three of these poems also appear on the current AP Latin Literature syllabus; three that do not (9, 53, and 62) appeared on the preceding version. Among the celebrated Catullan poems included (at least in part) on the AP syllabus but omitted by the *OLR* are 7, the second of the kiss-poems, and 45, the "love duet" of Acme and Septimius; 64 and 68, two of Catullus' longer and more learned efforts; and various poems articulating his literary concerns, among them 35, 36, 65, and 116. The absence of Horace from the roster of *OLR* authors is striking, since his life and work provide the central focus of the introductory Latin materials in the Oxford Latin Course (OLC).

Catullus also figures among the authors in the advanced Latin literature curriculum designed by the International Baccalaureate (IB) Diploma Programme. A pre-university course of study created in 1968 by educators in several countries, it prepares "internationally mobile" students aged 16–19 for universities all over the world. Fifteen of Catullus' poems – 2, 5, 7, 8, 45, 51, 62, 70, 72, 83, 85, 86, 87, 92, and 109 – are presented, along with 11 of Horace's *Odes*, in their units on "Love Poetry," one for "Standard Level" and one for "Higher Level." Teachers must choose two out of five such units to read along with a "prescribed" author at each level, such as Ovid or Livy.[4] Three of these 15 poems (62, 83, and 92) are not currently on the AP syllabus; five (7, 45, 62, 83, 92) are not in the *OLR*.

The differences between various "canonical" lists of representative Catullan poems merit further attention and explanation. So, for that matter, does another major dissimilarity between the study of Catullus at the secondary school level in the United States and in the United Kingdom. Although there is a long tradition of introducing some of Catullus' poems to British secondary school Latin students, and although his poetry has appeared on the AP syllabus from its earliest days, in the United States Catullus' prominence, and in many instances presence, on the secondary school Latin scene is a fairly recent development.

Simon Raven's novel *Fielding Gray* (1967), set in 1945, testifies to the mid-twentieth-century British curricular importance of Catullus. Raven's eponymous hero is a 17-year-old sixth former at what is known in Britain as a public school (and in the US as a private school), clearly based on Charterhouse, Raven's own *alma mater*. Early in the narrative, after presenting an accomplished verse translation of Catullus 5, Gray proceeds to champion the author's "pagan position" on sexual morality to a disapproving Latin master. This classroom encounter with Catullus, moreover, is apparently not the first experienced by boys of Gray's age at this particular school. In trying to seduce a younger, less academically talented fellow student, Gray pointedly asks, "Christopher...When you still did Latin, did you get as far as Catullus?" (S. Raven 1967: 37–9).[5]

While attending what in the US are called public (and in the UK called state) secondary schools in Pennsylvania from 1957 through 1962, one of us followed a very different curriculum. During her five years of studying Latin, which culminated in the AP Vergil exam, Judith P. Hallett never read any of Catullus' poems.[6] It was not until her first semester of Latin at Wellesley College, an all-female institution in Massachusetts, that she encountered his poetry in a Latin classroom, as the first of the three authors read in a year-long introductory Latin literature course.[7] The textbook employed was E. T. Merrill's *Catullus*, originally published in 1893. In a foreword to the second printing, Elder (1951a: viii) justifies Harvard University Press's decision to reprint by claiming that "when [Merrill] was allowed to go out of print, classical studies suffered a severe blow. For this was the only brief, sufficiently annotated edition available in English of the complete works of one of antiquity's most attractive poets." The choice of the complete Merrill text for a class of young women at Wellesley in 1962 warrants notice in view of Gilbert Highet's serious reservations about teaching Catullus' poetry:

> Even in ancient times, he was not universally studied and revered as a "classic"...[He] was not exactly suitable to be taught in colleges and schools. He is still unsuitable. It is extraordinarily difficult to read and discuss one of Catullus' poems of passionate love in any classroom; and still more difficult if, two or three pages away, the readers can see another poem which begins and ends with a revolting obscenity. (1957: 3)[8]

Hallett's experience is evidently not unusual: in the United States during the 1960s and early 1970s, students who studied Latin for four or more years in secondary schools normally postponed their encounter with Catullus until the first year of college. That experience has pedagogical consequences for those presently teaching Latin at the college and university level. In presenting Vergil's *Aeneid*, instructors can often look back at their own secondary school teachers as memorable role models. Hallett uses the same textbook with which she herself was taught: Clyde Pharr's *Vergil's Aeneid Books I–VI*, first published in 1930. As she plans her Vergil classes, she can even hear the voice of her teacher, Marie Hildebrand Bintner, illuminating difficult passages, providing instruction on scansion and figures of speech. Yet she cannot draw on the inspiration of similar models who introduced her to Catullus in the secondary school classroom. When preparing contemporary teachers for that challenge, improvisation and faith in the pedagogical power of the Catullan text are all that she has.

Why has this curricular change occurred in the United States since the 1960s? During an era when secondary school Latin enrollments first declined precipitously and now are gradually increasing (though by no means to the levels that they reached in the 1960s), why have we witnessed not merely the inclusion of Catullan texts but their prominence within the curriculum?[9] Our discussion will explore some reasons for that major shift in the syllabus at this educational level and reflect upon its impact. We will survey how Catullus has been presented in secondary school Latin classrooms, and which poems have been judged worthy of teaching, and hence "canonized," over the past several decades; in so doing, we will accord special attention to present curricular practice in both the United States and Britain, and to how approaches to Catullus in the US and UK in turn differ from one another.

Central to this survey is an investigation of the role played by the College Board AP Examination in bringing about curricular changes in the United States. In the context of this investigation, we will consider special features of Catullus' poems that make them so successful in the secondary school Latin classroom. First and foremost is the "adolescent personality" that many of the poems project, especially those that treat love and its complications. We do, however, recognize that demographic, social, and cultural developments since the 1960s, in various other Anglophone countries as well as in the United States, may have also contributed to Catullus' ever-increasing appeal.

Such a study would be remiss if it did not contemplate some of the challenges posed by teaching Catullus to students at this level. Chief among them is, of course, the sexual context and explicit, often obscene language that so disconcerted the urbane and literarily sophisticated Gilbert Highet. But other pedagogical issues not dealt with in our study demand attention as well, i.e., how to teach the "long poem" 64, a substantial section of which was recently added to the Catullan selections on the AP syllabus.[10] Finally, our chapter discusses some classroom strategies for tackling these and other challenges that Catullus poses for secondary school students and their teachers.

Catullus in the United States Secondary Curriculum

At all levels of instruction Catullus is a major resource for teachers of Latin attempting to expose their students to "real" Latin from classical antiquity as soon as possible. Prompted in part, perhaps, by increased recognition of the potential value afforded by a reading approach to Latin language learning, they turn to Catullus for unadapted Latin, used either as a supplement to a traditional grammar/translation-based textbook or as additional support for a reading-based textbook.[11] Lines and passages such as *uiuamus, mea Lesbia, atque amemus* (5.1), or *cenabis bene, mi Fabulle, apud me/paucis, si tibi di fauent, diebus,/si tecum attuleris bonam atque magnam/cenam non sine candida puella* (13.1–4), provide relatively easy Latin to translate. Memorable illustrations of the subjunctive mood, conditionals, vocatives, and ablatives, as well as opportunities for discussing love, Sappho, meters, friendship, rhetorical devices (e.g., litotes), and word order are found in the corpus. In addition, secondary school teachers eager to increase or maintain enrollments at higher levels of Latin may use such Catullan snippets to give their students a taste of what material awaits them further down the path of their Latin education.

Here in the United States, the days of a regimented Latin secondary school sequence – one year of beginning Latin, followed by Caesar in level 2, Cicero in level 3, and Vergil in level 4 – are over. During the 1960s, when that traditional curriculum still prevailed, study of Catullus typically *followed* those authors. For that reason, students like Hallett never encountered Catullus when studying Latin in secondary school. Today, secondary school teachers and many college teachers tend to spread the beginning stages of Latin study over a longer period of time. It is not unusual to spend two years covering the basics, a task that would have been allotted only one year in the past. What is more, the Latin authors studied after those initial stages now vary widely.

When secondary school students in the United States will first encounter *extended* reading of Catullus (if they ever do) is far less predictable than it once might have been. Depending on what elementary Latin textbook a student has used, he or she may or may not encounter some Catullus along the way, while teachers will differ as to whether they introduce Catullus to their lower level classes. Some teachers use Catullus, for example, in the third year of high school. Others do not have students read his poetry until they reach more advanced levels, as part of the AP Latin curriculum or the IB curriculum, or in advanced courses of their own design in situations where they are completely free to choose which poems to cover.

Certainly the most easily accessible and thoroughly documented study of Catullus at the secondary school level in the United States is that of the College Board AP Latin program.[12] This program has now been in existence for half a century. The following short account is largely derived from the AP Latin page on the College Board website (http//:apcentral.collegeboard.com). It recaps the highlights of the program's history and shows how it has evolved since its inception.

- 1956: The first time that AP Latin exams were administered there were two, named "IV" (for fourth year Vergil) and "V" (for fifth year prose, comedy, and lyric).
- 1969: The Latin IV and Latin V exams were divided into four discrete exams: Latin Vergil, Latin lyric, Latin prose, and Latin comedy. Students could take one or two of these four exams.
- 1973: The exams were renamed "classics," and only the Vergil and lyric options remained, with a common multiple-choice section.
- 1978: The exams' title reverted to "Latin," and the two exams became known as "Latin: Catullus and Horace" and "Latin: Vergil."
- 1994: The current form of the exams was introduced, with the options being "Latin: Vergil" and "Latin literature." This latter exam is based on works of Catullus, Ovid, Cicero, and Horace.

From this brief history and from the materials Ronnie Ancona was able to study at the archives of the Educational Testing Service (ETS) in Princeton, New Jersey, we can trace the changing role of Catullus in the AP curriculum. What follows incorporates information from past Latin AP course description booklets – known as the "acorn books" from the symbol used on their covers – which are located in the ETS archives. ETS produces the AP exams in conjunction with the College Board and its AP program.

The names given to the original exams from 1956 indicate what Latin authors were being read and when they were being read in secondary school classrooms. At that time Vergil's *Aeneid* was studied in the fourth year and the "other" authors in the fifth. While Catullus' poetry was included from the start, it *followed* Vergil in the curriculum and shared a place on the level V syllabus with other authors and even other literary genres. The fact that students who scored a passing grade on the Latin IV Vergil exam initially earned only one semester of college placement credit, whereas a passing score on the Latin V exam covering Catullus' poetry earned two semesters of credit, warrants emphasis. It indicates the canonical position formerly accorded to Vergil in the fourth year high school Latin classroom as well as the "higher" level of Latin achievement once associated with the study of Catullus.

The acorn booklet for 1966–8 still refers to the Latin exam that includes Catullus as "Latin V," and requires students who take it to have already completed a course on Vergil. By 1969, though, each exam is described as "equated with approximately one semester's college work." So, too, students are allowed to take one or two of the Latin AP exams. The acorn booklet for 1969–70 no longer employs the titles "Latin IV" and "Latin V," nor does it list a course on Vergil as a prerequisite for taking any other Latin AP exam. By 1969 "Latin Lyric" became a separate exam, featuring Catullus and Horace. Shortly thereafter, in 1973, "Vergil" and "Latin Lyric" became the only two AP options, leaving prose and comedy behind.

In 1994 prose returned, in the form of Cicero, and Catullus became the core of the "non-Vergil" AP exam, that is, the Latin literature examination, comprising the required half of the syllabus. Horace was switched to a Latin literature "option," joining Cicero and the newly introduced Ovid as the author with whom teachers would pair Catullus. Today, secondary schools choose to offer either the Vergil or the Latin literature AP courses, or both. Their reasons for offering these courses are not based upon the students' level of Latin proficiency, but on other factors: the preparation and interests of teachers themselves; curricular preferences of individual schools or school systems; perceptions about the relative ease or difficulty of specific courses. Some schools administer two different Latin AP exams in alternating years. Others give two different exams every year. Some always give one or the other. There is great variety.

The current AP Catullus syllabus consists of the following 42 poems or parts of poems: 1, 2, 3, 4, 5, 7, 8, 10, 11, 12, 13, 14a, 22, 30, 31, 35, 36, 40, 43, 44, 45, 46, 49, 50, 51, 60, 64 (lines 50–253), 65, 68 (lines 1–40), 69, 70, 72, 76, 77, 84, 85, 86, 87, 96, 101, 109, and 116. As one can see, they include polymetrics, selections from the long poems, and elegiacs. Particular poems on the syllabus are changed every few years, but the changes are usually minimal. Some teachers present the poems in the order listed above; some choose to group them by theme or other elements. Others choose to intersperse the reading of Catullus with the other AP Latin author option, e.g., reading some Horace one day and some Catullus the next. The poems chosen for the Catullus syllabus range fairly widely, including many of the best-known poems as well as some that are less popular. The themes of love, friendship, wit, poetics, politics, etc., that one would expect to see represented are all there.

Although the most obscene Catullan poems do not appear on the syllabus, the syllabus is by no means "tame." Words denoting sexual behavior and bodily parts appear from time to time; sexual infidelity, of course, makes an appearance through the Lesbia poems; homoerotic desire is portrayed, as well, if one reads either poem 30 or 50 or both with attention to the language of love and desire. Whether intentionally or not, the syllabus does admittedly downplay the depiction of male–male amatory relationships in the Catullan corpus, but it cannot be said to avoid them completely.

Possibly the Test Development Committee has decided to steer clear of including poems which would prompt objections and might lead to a school's decision to stop offering this AP Latin exam. Inasmuch as there are some schools in the United States where teachers are not even supposed to mention homosexuality, such a motivation would not be surprising. Other school environments, though, do not interfere at all with what material is taught, and how it is taught, in Latin classrooms. There, teachers are free to present Catullus in whatever ways they judge appropriate. When explicit sexual language does appear in poems on the syllabus – e.g., *scortillum*, *irrumator*, and *cinaediorem* in 10, *ilia rumpens* in 11 – teachers, textbooks, and students choose to handle, understand, and translate these terms with differing degrees of literalness and euphemism.

Many of us in the United States who have influenced current teaching of Catullus at the secondary level, either directly (by training teachers or writing high school textbooks) or indirectly (through scholarship), never studied him in high school. Hallett, who belongs in both categories, has already been mentioned. Ronnie Ancona, who has also trained teachers, written a textbook, and contributed to the scholarly literature, first encountered the poet in an advanced level Latin lyric poetry course at the University of Washington. Ancona, moreover, did not begin her study of Latin until after secondary school. Prior to taking the advanced course, she had, as an undergraduate at Grinnell College, read a few lines of Catullus in her introductory Latin textbook: Frederic Wheelock's *Latin: An Introductory Course Based on Ancient Authors* (New York, 1956). Later she attended graduate level Catullus courses at both the University of Washington and Ohio State University. She recalls being enchanted by both Catullus and Horace when she met them in the Latin lyric course. The text used was *Roman Lyric Poetry: Catullus and Horace*, by A. G. McKay and D. M. Shepherd (New York, 1969), which arranges the poems thematically and puts the authors side by side. Periodically, Paul Pascal, professor of classics at the University of Washington, gave a much-needed mini-lecture on Latin sexual vocabulary, without which much of both Catullus and Martial would have been incomprehensible. This was in the days before the *OLD* (1982) was published and other resources, both print and internet, had made such information easily accessible (e.g., Adams 1982; Richlin 1992 [1st edn. 1983]).

Michael C. J. Putnam of Brown University, a path-breaking and influential Catullan scholar, recalls in a private communication:

> I didn't read any Catullus or Horace in school, and went to Harvard prepared to major in mathematics. Luckily, in the fall of 1950, I was steered into Latin 2a (Catullus and Horace) with Peter Elder – and the rest is history. Kenneth Reckford was in the class and I'm sure that Steele [Commager] was also. Peter was deeply involved with Catullus at the time (his splendid article on "Some Conscious and Subconscious Elements in the Poetry of Catullus" was published in 1951). I don't think that, during those early months of my freshman year, it was the quality of the poets per se that got to me so much as the fact that I was at last learning how to "read" – discovering what figuration was, the meaning of metaphor, starting (very vaguely) to think about theory, etc. etc. Only later in the semester, and in the coming years, did I begin to appreciate the genius of the poets I was being taught. It was Peter's doing as well as Cedric Whitman's, as I have often said in public and in print. [Eric] Havelock was at Harvard, too, but he was doing more Greek than Latin. My dissertation was an attempt to bring the long poems, especially 64, into the conversation.[13]

While the backgrounds of Hallett, Ancona, and Putnam may or may not be the norm, it is clear that the way Catullus is taught today in the United States at the secondary school level is shaped, at least in part, by teachers and scholars whose own first approaches to Catullus postdate their high school years.[14] There are positive and negative sides to this phenomenon. One negative aspect would be ignorance of how an adolescent might experience reading Catullus. But the positive side might involve raised expectations for a first encounter with the poems.

In the United States, today's secondary school teachers bring much to their classrooms in addition to their familiarity with Catullus' poetry. They have many teaching techniques and strategies at their disposal for making the learning process enjoyable and effective. Their theoretical and practical knowledge of adolescents affords them insight into the different kinds of responses that Catullus' writing might elicit. They know their own particular students – and successful teaching, especially at the secondary school level, requires knowing how to reach a particular student population.

The following brief quotations illustrate the points just made. They come from a diverse group of secondary and college teachers: many of them responded to a questionnaire we circulated in spring 2005 on various electronic lists and in the *British Classical Association Newsletter* requesting information about their experiences with Catullus; others responded to requests from the authors in private correspondence. To judge from this correspondence as well as that informal survey, Latin teachers in secondary schools across the United States are introducing the poems of Catullus, or at least *selections* from *particular* poems, to secondary school students with apparent success. The same phenomenon obtains at the college level (see Garrison, this volume).

While Judith de Luce, a professor of classics at Miami University, has never taught at the secondary school level, her work as former chief reader for the AP Latin exam brought her into frequent contact with Latin teachers. She sums up adolescent students' experience of studying Catullus, as reported by many high school teachers:

> Teachers have commented on how appealing many of the Catullan poems are to their secondary school students who are themselves trying to understand relationships, how to form them, how to maintain them, what happens when they turn out to be less satisfying than they expected. The immediacy and vibrancy of the poetry certainly seem to appeal to these readers, as does the variety of the poems. And a longer poem like 64 is exciting reading in part because the narrative so pointedly asks them to consider this representation of the hero Theseus and the abandoned Ariadne.

John Sarkissian of Youngstown State University had also read AP Latin exams for many years before serving as chief reader. He observes that Catullus' appeal is not merely to the "best" Latin students:

> It is always satisfying in the grading process to encounter essays in which students display both sophistication in their analysis and facility in dealing with the Latin text.... Even students who have difficulty organizing effective essays or whose control of the Latin texts is limited often give evidence of having been affected by their exposure to Catullus.
>
> Of course, it is the affair with Lesbia to which students most often respond.... [Students] often set a poem or passage into the context of the entire Lesbia cycle and inject some remarks which go beyond the analysis of the specific passage in front of them. There is no consensus on the relationship with Lesbia and the degree of sympathy students feel for Catullus ranges from excessive to non-existent. Some students recognize the validity, or at least the plausibility, of his conflicting emotions – love, lust, jealousy, self-pity, etc. – while others are dismissive of him (the word "wimp" sometimes is used). What I want to emphasize here is that many of the students have read the Latin poems thoughtfully and open-mindedly.... Of course, some level of competence in Latin is necessary for students to enjoy the poems and to make sense out of them. But it is by no means only the students who record the highest scores who give evidence of having given serious thought to the content of the poems.

In furnishing her own pedagogical perspective on why she teaches Catullus, and why she thinks her students like to read him, Nancy Wilson, a teacher at Decatur Central High School in Indiana who studied with Frank O. Copley at the University of Michigan, also emphasizes the emotional appeal of the poems as well as the aesthetic achievement:

I teach Catullus because his poetry is beautiful and extremely well structured ... [T]eenagers relate more to him than to Caesar and his war battles and descriptions of terrain they've never seen.... [H]is poetry is so emotional and it allows us to see that these ancient Roman people we study were just like those of us today. They possessed jealousies, fear, hurt, and love. It makes them more real to the students. By reading Catullus we also get a chance to examine ourselves, our motives, our pains and sorrows – in other words, to examine our humanity.[15]

Irving Kizner, Latin teacher at the Spence School in New York City, specifies which Catullan poems his students have liked more than others. Adopting a long view shaped by his five decades in the Latin classroom, he reserves his reactions for the poems on the earlier AP Latin syllabus:

My thoughts about teaching Catullus to high school students, and most recently only to female students, are probably in line with most high school teachers.... Generally speaking, the love poems (male and female) are looked forward to and the critical poems are accepted as being necessary. I find Catullus a pleasure to teach and I am no longer inhibited by discussions about erotic (within bounds) topics.[16]

Barbara Ellis, who teaches Latin and Greek at the Fieldston School in New York City, introduces Catullus to her secondary school students during the year immediately following the completion of elementary-level Latin, rather than as part of an AP curriculum. In approaching Catullus' poetry with them, she looks to her own experiences as a graduate student, and also contemplates changes in her selection of poems in view of evolving social attitudes:

I did study Catullus in graduate school [at Columbia University]. We used the Merrill text. We read most of the short poems and long poems. Catullus was characterized as a witty, serious, somewhat iconoclastic poet ... We teach the course in the 10th grade after the students have covered basic syntax. We do one semester of prose and one semester of Catullus' poetry. I try to model my approach on Professor Commager's [her instructor at Columbia], but I try to gear it, of course, to a secondary school level. I don't have the students read any of the poems which involve homoerotic themes, but I'm beginning to think that I should include a few.

Marianthe Colakis, a teacher at the Covenant School in Charlottesville, Virginia, points out that students in an AP class who learned Latin from the popular *Ecce Romani* series, published by Prentice Hall, can build on a prior reading of Catullus. In choosing secondary scholarship on Catullus to share with students, she observes, teachers give careful consideration to how these readings might improve performances on the AP examination:

Ecce Romani II has a few selections ... the dinner invitation to Fabullus [13], the poem at his brother's grave [101], an excerpt from Poem 61 ... My approach to the poems is pretty similar to that of Steele Commager [her undergraduate professor]. He always gave you the impression that he was reading the Latin as a Roman would have – catching all the nuances of the language, but never over-interpreting. I have read other articles dealing with specific poems and I use them in accordance with how they fit with what AP examiners are likely to ask.

At Westlake High School in Austin, Texas, Jo Green teaches AP Catullus to students who would have met him already in another popular introductory Latin textbook:

> I have always taught Catullus as part of the AP syllabus ... I have taught *vivamus, mea Lesbia* and *lugete* in my third year class the last two years, We use the Cambridge Latin Course – and these poems appear in Stage 45 of the Unit 4 book.

Also using the Cambridge Latin Course (CLC), Karen Zeller of Homesource, a publicly funded private alternative school catering to the needs of home-schooling families in Eugene, Oregon, presents Catullus to classes at several levels:

> In first and second year, I give kids exposure mainly to the "Vivamus, mea Lesbia" and to poem 46. Of course, there is a chapter and a half of Catullus in CLC Unit 4.

Amy Spagna, Latin teacher at Langley High School, McLean, Virginia, discusses how the ways in which she teaches Catullus change, depending on the level and type of class involved.

> I have taught Catullus four times, either as part of a Latin III course designed to introduce students to poetry, or as part of the International Baccalaureate curriculum ... With IB, I was limited to doing the Lesbia cycle as part of a topic titled "Love Poetry". ... My approach is a hybrid of those used by my teachers and professors [at Patrick Henry High School in Ashland, Virginia, and Randolph Macon College] ... IB forced me to use an approach that encourages the students to think about what the words themselves really mean. I will *not* be happy to have to change that when I teach AP (anticipated in fall of 2006) – the students seem to get more out of it than having to spend the entire time translating and finding rhetorical devices. ... Students are usually assigned a poem for homework, and spend some time the next class meeting correcting their translations of it, followed by more in-depth "thinking" and analytical questions, posed usually as the beginning of a writing task. With a Latin III class, I focus more on the mechanics of the Latin itself, as well as the students' general comprehension of an authentic text, though the general approach is the same.

Thomas Hayes, Latin teacher at Ward Melville Senior High School in Long Island, New York, describes several ways in which he "pre-teaches" the AP Catullus curriculum in his lower-level classes.

> Usually I teach the Catullus-Ovid selections ... I start introducing the poems in first and second year so that by the time the kids get to the AP level they have already read (generally speaking) 1, 2, 3, 5 (memorized), 11 maybe, 12, 13, 22 maybe, 43, 49, 50, 51 maybe, 84 and a sprinkling of the 2- and 4-line epigrams. They also memorize at least two poems a year. ... We thus have had the opportunity to discuss poetic devices, etc. This "strung out" reading gives us some space in the AP year to look a bit more leisurely at the poems qua poems, rather than as lines that must be trudged through.

Virginia Latin teacher Lori Kissell discusses some of the differences she sees between male and female student reactions to Catullus. Her recollection of her own undergraduate days suggests that gender would appear to have affected her treatment of explicit sexual material in her classroom.

When I have an all female class (as I did last term) they seemed to be more sympathetic to his lovelorn poems, and when I have a mixed group or a predominantly male group, they seem to see him as a fool for putting up with Lesbia.... I don't think that I talk more or less frankly about love or passion or sex with a single sex group than I do with a mixed group, but I remember (often being the only woman in my Latin classes) that some of my college classes either tried to shock me with discussion of an "obscene/explicit" passage, or would try to tone the discussion so far down as to exclude all sex or passion, as "there was a lady present."

Lauri Dabbieri, Amy Spagna's colleague at Langley High School, captures perfectly how issues of obscenity and sexual explicitness in Catullus' poetry are shaped by the pedagogical context in which they are encountered. The Catullus poem read in high school becomes a "different" poem in college once the euphemistic translation of the obscenity is abandoned.

I remember reading the Ameana poem in high school and translating the word "defututa" as "exhausted." I never thought twice about it. It seemed innocuous enough and the "racy" elements of Catullus were thoroughly played down. When I got to [the all-female] Sweet Briar College, and we had the same poem and I translated the poem as I had remembered, with the same, tame definition, [my professor] Judith Evans-Grubbs responded, "Lauri, I never thought of you as a prude!" I didn't understand what she was talking about. It was only after she explained what sort of exhaustion was implied in the words that I understood that I had read a very different Catullus in high school.

There are many Catulluses out there in secondary school classrooms. The Catullus that the authors of the present chapter would want others to see might be different from the choice of other teachers and scholars. Indeed, it is likely that there is not even one Catullus we would agree upon in all particulars. However, we would like to turn to some of the challenges in the areas of language and culture that teaching Catullus in the secondary classroom presents, whatever Catullus one presents.

As we have already seen, one reason that Catullus "works" so well at the secondary level is that students today can easily identify with him and his circumstances. But, as T. P. Wiseman emphasizes in his initial chapter "A World Not Ours" (Wiseman 1985: 1–14), Catullus' world was not our world in many significant ways. In workshops and courses designed for teachers offering the AP Latin syllabus, Ancona and Hallett both recommend Wiseman's discussion to counter the perception that Catullus is so "modern," so "like" us and our students. Wiseman also provides a brief summary of Roman sexual mores, as well as the relevant ideas and vocabulary associated with Roman notions of "hetero/homosexuality." Enthusiastic but careful and conscientious teachers will ride the wave that their students' identification with Catullus can create, and at the same time call attention to other aspects of Catullus' poetry that make study of his work more historically accurate and literarily comprehensive.

In writing her own Catullus AP textbook, Ancona decided that she could not in good conscience give students the impression that the only love affair represented in the Catullan corpus had a woman as its object. On the other hand, from discussions with Latin teachers in what we call public schools (British "state" schools), she was aware that some school districts in more conservative parts of the United States might look askance at adopting a textbook that is in any way sexually explicit or refers to love between men. Yet her sense is that many AP Latin teachers welcome an approach to Catullus that allows high school students to view his poetry with the same sophisticated attitudes generally adopted by college students.

Admittedly, secondary school students are not college students. But a very persuasive argument to use with school boards, administrations, or parents who may find some of the Latin AP syllabus reading "objectionable" is that the AP *requires college-level work*. This appeal to the academically practical value of reading Catullus in an intellectually mature fashion – one that will enable students to obtain college credit or place out of lower level college courses – can work wonders!

The absence of, e.g., the Juventius poems from the AP curriculum makes it easy to avoid discussing male homoerotic relationships in the secondary school classroom, a situation which some might view as unfortunate, others as fortunate, still others as pragmatic. But a poem like 30, addressed to Alfenus, and added to the syllabus in 2004–5, allows for a discussion of this sort without necessitating it in the way that the Juventius poems would.[17] In her textbook Ancona uses the presence of this poem in the revised AP curriculum to educate students further about the range of themes in Catullus' work. Her paragraph introducing the poem points out some of its similarities to poem 76, where the love object is a woman. She then states: "Seeing these issues in the context of a male lover and beloved should remind the reader that Catullus wrote poems about men desiring men as well as men desiring women" (2004: 55). While some Catullan scholars regard poem 30 as more, some as less, erotic than other poems, its inclusion in the AP syllabus furnishes an ideal teaching opportunity.

The authors of this chapter would be quite surprised if Catullus' important, programmatic poem 16 ever were to appear on the AP Latin syllabus. As we shall see, efforts to include it on a comparable list of required Catullan texts for British secondary school students in the 1980s met with significant resistance. Still, the central issues that poem 16 raises, about sexual and literary power, can be incorporated into the study of other Catullan poems by astute and creative teachers in whatever fashion they find appropriate.

As for Catullus' use of sexually explicit and at times obscene language, it is present even on the AP syllabus. The days of being able to keep high school Latin students at the level of euphemism in their Catullan translations are over. Books, articles, and internet access make literal translations all too easy. While textbooks do vary in terms of how they handle explicit language, ultimately teachers and students, together or apart, will decide which kinds of translations are true to Catullus' Latin and which are not. Why not engage in that translation enterprise together? After all, students will in this way learn not only about Latin and about Catullus, but, more generally, about the power of words.

Catullus in the British Secondary Curriculum

To appreciate what is distinctive and challenging about the Catullan poems selected for the current AP Latin literature syllabus, it is profitable to compare them, as a group, to those presented in the *OLR*. As we have noted, the *OLR* differs from the AP syllabus by including fewer poems. Unlike many of the textbooks designed for students preparing to take the AP Latin literature examination, the *OLR* does not present the poems in the sequence found in our surviving manuscripts of Catullus: polymetrics (1–60), then longer poems (61–8), then elegiacs (69–116). The 26 poems instead appear out of order, without regard to their meter.

After an introductory discussion incorporating Catullus 1, the *OLR* organizes the other 25 poems into three thematic sections, entitled "Catullus and his Friends," "Catullus in Love," and "The Sequel." The first of these sections consists of seven poems, in the order 50, 53, 49, 93, 14, 9, and 13, a sequence that surrounds an elegiac couplet, 93, with three hendecasyllabic poems on either side. The second consists of 12 poems said to be about a woman whom the *OLR* identifies as Clodia: 51, 2, 3, 5, 43, 109, 70, 72, 85, 8, 76, and 77. Some of these poems refer to her as Lesbia, others as Catullus' *puella*, or *mulier mea*, or *mea uita*; some do not mention her at all. This section begins with one of his two poems in the Sapphic meter, followed by four in hendecasyllabics, then four in elegiac couplets, one in limping iambics, and two more in elegiacs.

The third section treats some of Catullus' poems about imagined and actual travels as endeavors "to try to forget Clodia." It consists of 11, 46, 101, 31, 4, and 10. Again, a poem in Sapphic meter heads the list, followed by a metrical assortment of poems in hendecasyllabics, elegiacs, limping iambics, and iambic trimeter.

The reasons for this thematic mode of presentation merit attention. Like the decision to limit the selection in the *OLR* to 26 poems, these particular poems are evidently determined by the context in which Catullus has been studied in the UK. In the United States, Catullus has since 1969 been paired on the AP Latin literature syllabus with only one other Latin author – first Horace, then Cicero or Ovid – on the assumption that his poetry will be the object of study for approximately half the academic year. But the British GSCE examination for which the *OLR* was originally designed covers a larger number of authors. The *OLR* features six: three poets and three prose writers; three authors from the late Republic and three from the Augustan period. Accommodating several more authors means less space for Catullus; it also means constructing a Catullus who resembles those other authors.

Consequently, the unit on Catullus adopts an explicitly historicist focus, and an emphasis not found in the AP curriculum: on not only the larger socio-cultural context in which he wrote but also the "real people" in his milieu. Such a focus parallels the historically grounded approach of the OLC, centered, as we noted earlier, on the figure of Horace. It also appears to explain why the *OLR* highlights Catullus' poems about his contemporaries in the first and third sections, and why it claims that the 12 amatory poems in the second part chronicle an actual affair with Clodia. In so doing, it simplifies, and tends to distort, the Catullan text and its context, particularly in attempting to reconstruct the love affair with "Clodia" along the lines of earlier scholarship now fallen from fashion.[18] However, it acknowledges doing so and furnishes a rationale for this decision in the teacher's handbook.[19] And this thematic mode of presentation apparently has enjoyed considerable success in engaging the interest of its intended secondary school audience.

While by no means representative of the entire Catullan corpus, the *OLR* roster of 26 poems also seems to incorporate those traditionally favored, whether unofficially or officially, in a variety of British secondary schools – to judge by the reminiscences of former British secondary school Latin students, offered in response to our informal survey described above and in personal correspondence. Reflecting on his classical education in the 1940s, the distinguished author and translator Frederic Raphael – who attended Charterhouse from 1945 to 1950, overlapping briefly with Simon Raven – remarks:

> Catullus was the non-curricular, not quite forbidden poet. Yet his qualities could not be denied, nor his place in the Golden Age. [A]nthology pieces – such as *paene insula Sirmionis* [31]; Lesbia's sparrow (or golden finch) cutenesses [2 and 3]; the imitation of Sappho [51]; the lament for his brother [101] – must have figured in some forgotten chrestomathy. The attraction was clearly the passion and sincerity. . . . Catullus was the sexy young man par excellence, and aggressive and wounded as well.[20]

Barry Baldwin, emeritus professor of classics at the University of Calgary, attended Lincoln School from 1948 to 1956, where he did "Latin and Greek from scratch to O[rdinary], A[dvanced] and S[pecial] levels," the first two linked with standardized subject examinations for 16-year-olds and 18-year-olds respectively, the third a higher special paper. He acknowledges that "Catullus made very few appearances in our classical lives," but recalls "the Sirmio poem (31) . . . mainly as background to the obvious Tennyson [who evokes Catullus in his *Frater Ave Atque Vale*], occasional small pieces, e.g. *sentio et excrucior* (85)." At the grammar school attended from 1957 through 1963 by Leofranc Holford-Strevens, now a scholar and editor with Oxford University Press:

> Catullus was not on the official syllabus. However, the senior English master, who also took some Latin classes, did include him. I wasn't in any of those classes, but from what I knew of him I think he must have treated him [and his Lesbia poems] much as he would have done an English Romantic poet of the nineteenth century . . . with sensitivity to language, and as the account of a love-affair that went wrong. I don't mean as pure biography . . . rather as how relations between a man and a woman might go.

Jan Williams was introduced to Catullus in 1962 at Howell's School, Llandaff, a girls' school in Cardiff, during her third year of learning Latin. She still remembers the 10 poems that her class read, noting:

> We started with *Lugete, O Veneres* (3) and also read *Vivamus* (5). When we read *Multas per gentes* (101), I was completely hooked – and I still am. Other poems studied were *Furi et Aureli* (11), *Cenabis bene* (13), *Paene insularum* (31), *Egnatius quod* (39), *Nulli se dicit* (70), *Chommoda dicit* (84) and *Odi et amo* (85). . . . For me these poems were a revelation . . . the discovery that Latin could be used to express such emotion was wonderful and may have been the reason I became a classicist.

While 39 and 84, which might be characterized as depicting "Catullus and individuals he deemed unworthy of his friendship," are not among the poems in the *OLR*, the other eight are. Together this octet creates and sustains a sentimental impression of Catullus as emotionally powerful and romantic, aggressive and wounded, yet morally palatable to mid-twentieth-century tastes. It is an impression reinforced by Highet's portrait of Catullus, proffered along with his assertion that the poet is still unsuitable to be taught in schools and colleges:

There were three important events in his life. The first was the death of his elder brother. The second was his tour of duty as a government official in Asia Minor. The third was his love affair with a beautiful and conscienceless woman called Clodia. All three meant failure and heartbreak for him. He was a man doomed to suffer.[21]

Three years after Williams's encounter with these 10 poems, five of them (3, 5, 11, 13, and 85) joined seven others (8, 45, 46, 51, 72, 75, and 104) in *Aestimanda*, by M. Balme and M. S. Warman. Published by Oxford University Press, it was, as Morwood notes in private correspondence, the first textbook in the English-speaking world to invite and give guidelines for practical criticism of Latin and Greek poets. Several of the 10 poems – 3, 5, 11, 13, 31, 70, and 85 – read by Williams in 1962 and presented again by *Aestimanda* in 1965 are featured again in an experimental 1970 volume, designed to accompany the O-level selections of Catullus for 1971–2 and train "the young to read ancient poetry as poetry." Entitled *Nine Essays on Catullus for Teachers*, it was edited by Clary Greig, production director of Cambridge School Classics. The authors include Greig himself (on 70 and 85); Balme, a Latin master at Harrow (on 3); and a variety of Latinists teaching at university level. Some were affiliated with Cambridge: E. J. Kenney (on 4), J. C. Bramble (on 5), R. O. A. M. Lyne (on 11). Others – L. A. Moritz (on 13), C. Witke (on 31), N. Rudd and J. Foster (on 51) – were not. According to the introduction by C. O. Brink, these essays, each no more than 1,000 words in length, were commissioned to "show the diversity of competent critical approaches" and "to stimulate and provoke the teacher to work out his own approach." Now that Catullus had been welcomed into the official, required Latin curriculum, he needed to be taken seriously.

Only one of these essays, Witke on 31, mentions what Wiseman would later call "Catullus' world": the socio-cultural context in which he lived and wrote. By limiting the selections to a few, traditionally beloved, Catullan poems concerned with Lesbia and the emotions that she arouses, and by emphasizing Catullus' emotionally charged language, these essays for the most part continue to construct Catullus in a sentimentalizing way, as a romantic. Clodia and her brother are not mentioned in these essays, but English Romantic poets such as Wordsworth, Scott, and Tennyson are.

Yet these essays also hint at approaches to Catullan literary interpretation that were gaining currency at the time *Nine Essays* was published. Balme, for instance, takes cognizance of New Critical concerns by underscoring "the recurrent note of irony" in 3, and labeling it "highly ambivalent" because "it is both a lament and a love poem" (Balme 1970: 12). So, too, in accounting for the changes that Catullus 51 makes to the poem by Sappho that it "imitates," Rudd and Foster point out that "Callimachus and his age (the third century BC) had intervened between Sappho and Catullus" (Rudd and Foster 1970: 47). They thereby allude to the emerging body of scholarship on Catullus' Hellenistic, Alexandrian dimensions, foregrounded by Fordyce in his 1961 commentary.[22]

Still, their narrow range of approaches to reading Catullus as poetry contrasts with what we find in the *OLR*, which not only expands the number and scope of Catullan selections deemed worthy of study but also widens the perspectives afforded by these strategies. While the *OLR* primarily presents the poems from a historicist vantage point, its notes and study questions also situate Catullus' poetry in Callimachus' Alexandrian traditions, focus on patterns of imagery as well as ironic modes of expression, and encourage the student to ponder the kind of questions associated with reader-response criticism. It asks too for comparisons between different modern English translations of poems 13 and 5.

Another recent attempt in the United Kingdom to expand the number of perspectives on Catullus did not fare very well. As Cathy Mercer recalls in responding to our questionnaire:

> I taught Classics for 16 years in state schools in the UK, and was also chief examiner for Latin and Greek A level with the London Examinations Board. The students always loved Catullus above all other Latin poets.... The poems they responded to most enthusiastically were of course the Lesbia poems, as befits hormonally challenged adolescents. Candidates could write pages on *Odi et amo*.... In the late 1980s, before I was examiner, the London board very courageously prescribed some of the fruitier erotic poems, including some with homoerotic interpretations.... There was quite a fuss from some teachers and the story hit the national press.

A letter to the *Guardian* on March 15, 1989, by Michael Bulley, a Latin teacher from Ashford, Kent, provides more information about that "fuss," what Mercer also calls "the homoerotic furore." It notes that the University of London Schools Examination Board had just written, late in the academic year, to announce that three poems by Catullus "prescribed as part of the Latin A-level system, will not now appear on the examination paper in the summer, because objections ... have been made about the sexual nature of this subject matter of these poems, nos. 15, 16 and 25 in the Catullan catalogue." It lists the details that apparently prompted these objections: the hope, expressed in 15, "that a certain boy will not be corrupted by you and your dangerous penis"; the witty exploitation in 16 of the linguistic tension between the literal and expletive senses of expressions like "bugger you"; the description in 25 of someone as "softer than the floppy, cobweb-covered penis of an old man." And it defends these poems as "just the thing that intelligent sixth-formers should be reading" and praises Catullus as "one of the greatest poets of all time in combining wit, sophistication and verbal felicity with a sometimes surprising depth of feeling and seriousness."

Mercer emphasizes that Bulley's letter to the press, along with a letter supporting the board's choice from Mark Vermees, her predecessor as head of classics in her Catholic girls' school in Upminster, had some impact. "In the end," Mercer relates, "the board decided to stick to the prescription." But teachers were informed that, in Mercer's words, "no questions would be set specifically on the offending literature. In other words, stick to the Lesbia poems."

While sticking to, indeed privileging the Lesbia poems, the *OLR*, as we have observed, also neglects Catullus' longer poems, many of his important poems about the creation of poetry, and the bitter expressions of abuse and invective that reveal a vicious side to this poet "of many friends." Such poems, of course, include various homoerotic pieces, among them poem 16 and those featuring Juventius.

Final Thoughts

This observation brings us back to the issues raised in our discussion of how Catullus is presented to contemporary secondary school students in the United States. Clearly he appears in varying guises, depending on the particular poems selected to represent his body of work: there is no standard Catullus canon. Not only does the Catullus of the British *OLR* differ from that of the American AP syllabus, but the image of Catullus projected by the AP has been modified in certain respects over the past several decades.

But which Catullus is presented? Is it legitimate to short-change the richness and diversity of this corpus by reducing Catullus to "the Lesbia poet," or by failing to disclose the sexually suggestive connotations of Catullus' erotic language in such canonical Lesbia poems as 2 and 3?[23] Might a brief study, by mature secondary schoolers, of Catullus as "the Juventius poet" enrich their appreciation of his Lesbia poems? In view of the difficulties encountered by the London Examinations Board, how might such a study be conducted without giving offense to students and teachers, parents and administrators? Questions of this kind suggest that additional, more subtle instructional strategies may be needed if more of Catullus' sexually explicit poems, especially those about homoerotic desire and activity, are to be read and appreciated by secondary school students in the United States and elsewhere.

Catullus' undisputed popularity, in these different guises, in secondary school classrooms throughout the Anglophone world thus raises another, abiding question: about literary proprietorship. Whose Catullus? From our survey and correspondence, and the experiences that prompted us to conduct this survey and engage in this correspondence, it is clear that the answer to this question is being determined on a daily basis and in constantly changing fashion: by students and teachers, administrators and textbook writers, and Catullan scholars alike.

ACKNOWLEDGMENTS

The authors would like to extend their deep appreciation to Michael Bulley, Judith DeLuce, Sheila K. Dickison, Daniel Garrison, Jenny Marsh, Gavin McDuffie, James Morwood, Lee T. Pearcy, Michael C. J. Putnam, Frederic Raphael, John Sarkissian, Christopher Stray, and above all the editor of this volume, Marilyn Skinner, for their help on this chapter. They would also like to thank the following for responding to our Catullus survey, and for sharing their experiences and insights about Catullus in their training and teaching: Barry Baldwin, Henry Bender, Ruth Breindel, Alan Brown, Stephen Ciraolo, Marianthe Colakis, Donald Connor, Lauri Dabbieri, John McCallie Devine, Barbara Ellis, Rubén García Fernández, Julia Haig Gaisser, Jo Heim Green, Thomas Hayes, Leofranc Holford-Strevens, Paula James, Diana Jensen, Pat Jones, Caroline Switzer Kelly, Lori Kissell, Pamela Lackie, Keely Lake, Brennus Legranus, Jeanne Listermann, JoAnn Luhrs, Carol Stern McMichael, Cathy Mercer, Diann Nickelsburg, Rick Norton, Emil Penarubia, Leslie Perkins, Steven Perkins, Kevin Perry, Father William Pitt, Steven Prince, Deborah Roberts, Carl Sesar, Leonor Silvestri, Niall Slater, James Sharpe, Amy Spagna, John Warman, Caitlin Watt, Robert White, Jan Williams, Rose Williams, Nancy Wilson, Bob Young, Karen Zeller.

For information about IB Latin, the authors would like to thank Mary Catherine Moshos, who taught the IB curriculum in Fairfax County, Virginia, until the spring of 2005; Charles Myers, Latin teacher, and Thomas O'Brien, IB coordinator, both of

Lower Merion School District, Pennsylvania; and Kathleen Earles, Jeanne Friedman, Laura Giles, Joan Lewis, and Andrew Miles, who responded with additional information solicited through a posting to Latin Teach, the electronic discussion list for Latin pedagogy.

Ronnie Ancona is grateful to Kate Rabiteau, Educational Testing Service consultant for Latin, for letting her know of the Educational Testing Service archives' existence and to Julie Duminiak, Educational Testing Service archivist, and her staff for facilitating her use of the materials there.

NOTES

1   The Advanced Placement program, a mainstay of advanced education at the high-school level in many fields, allows students not only to do college-level academic work while still attending high school but also to apply for college course credit and/or placement (advanced standing) from the institution they will eventually enter. Thus the study of Catullus' poetry that occupies one half of the AP Latin Literature program is college-level reading done in high school.

2   For statistics on the number of students taking the 2004 AP Latin exams, see Sarkissian (2004), who provides figures for both 2003 and 2004. While the number of students taking both examinations rose from 6,319 in 2003 to 6,974 in 2004, an increase of 10.4 percent, the rise in the number taking the Latin literature exam – from 2,569 to 3,001, an increase of 432 students (16.8 percent) – was substantially higher than the increase for the Vergil exam, which grew from 3,750 to 3,973, only 223 students (5.9 percent). Sarkissian also notes the 27 percent increase in students choosing the Ovid option on the Latin literature examination, concluding "[Catullus]-Ovid has clearly become the most popular option, as 65% of the students taking the Latin literature exam took the Ovid option, as compared with just under 26% for Horace and a bit over 9% for Cicero" (2004: 1).

3   Balme and Morwood's acknowledgments, thanking "the many consultants in the United Kingdom and the United States for comments and suggestions that have contributed towards this second edition" (1997a: 4), indicate that they have a United States constituency as well. While several of the six consultants thanked – e.g., John Gruber-Miller of Cornell College – teach at the college level, others are secondary school teachers, such as Dennis Herer of Tabor Academy and James Lowe of the John Burroughs School. As Christopher Stray observes (private communication), Cookesley (1845), a Catullus textbook for secondary students written by a classics master at Eton, and revised by the American Charles Bristed, offers a precedent for the involvement of American Latin teachers in revising the first edition of the *OLR*. In 1849 the book was reissued from the New York publishing house of Stanford and Swords as *Selections from Catullus, rev. Bristed*. Bristed became acquainted with William Cookesley when he attended Trinity, Cambridge. Morwood notes (private communication) that the *OLR* is in fact a revision of the original Oxford Latin Course (OLC) Part III. The absence of Horace's poetry from the *OLR* may therefore be explained by the substantial number of unadapted passages from his work in the earlier parts of the OLC.

4   The International Baccalaureate (IB) Diploma Programme does not make the information about specific course content for its courses of study readily available to those who are not fee-paying subscribers. For further information on the IB Latin curriculum, see Murphy, Thiem, and Moore (2005).

The 15 Catullus poems are presented along with 11 of Horace's *Odes* at both levels: "Standard" level students also read Book I of Ovid's *Amores* in translation; "Higher" level students also read six of Ovid's *Amores* in Latin, and Propertius, Books 1, 2, and 3 in translation. Topics of the other optional units include epic (with readings from Vergil's *Aeneid*); Roman satire (with readings from Juvenal, and at the "Higher" level readings in translation from Petronius' *Satyricon*); Cicero's political speeches; and Tacitus' presentation of imperial policy (with readings in the later books of the *Annales*). These alternatives differ significantly from those offered on the Latin AP exams, which feature only one prose option and no post-Augustan texts.

5 For Raven's own experience at Charterhouse, see his obituary by Michael Barber in the *Guardian*, May 16, 2001.

6 The first two years of Latin, which she took in the eighth and ninth grades at Elkins Park Junior High School, together covered what was then the beginning Latin curriculum; the third, in the tenth grade at Cheltenham High School, was called Latin 2 and was devoted mostly to Julius Caesar's *Gallic Wars*; the fourth, Latin 3, focused largely on Cicero's writings; and the fifth, Latin 4, covered the AP Vergil syllabus.

7 A selection of Catullus' poems shared the first semester with Plautus' *Mostellaria*; Horace's *Odes* occupied the entire second semester. As we shall see, the prominent presence of Plautus on this first-semester college syllabus in 1962 was reflected in the Latin AP curricular options at the time, which paired comedy with lyric poetry.

8 For the life and career of Highet (1906–78) and other distinguished teachers and scholars mentioned in this chapter (W. L. Carr, H. S. Commager, Jr., F. O. Copley, J. P. Elder, Eric Havelock, E. T. Merrill, Clyde Pharr, Cedric Whitman) see the biographical entries in Briggs (1994).

9 For US Latin enrollments, see LaFleur (1997).

10 On the challenges of teaching these selections from Catullus 64 cf. the remarks of Judith DeLuce below, and Garrison, this volume.

11 For grammar/translation and reading-based approaches to Latin language learning at the secondary level, see Singh (1998) and Perry (1998).

12 There are also a small number of students taking the AP Latin exams outside of the United States.

13 Elsewhere Putnam (1994) remarks that Elder's (1951b) essay "sets a new standard for probing the relationship of form, content and feeling in Catullus' lyric genius." Commager too wrote a pioneering article on Catullus (1965); among the poems discussed are 7, 8, 76, and 85. While primarily a Hellenist, Eric Havelock is also remembered for *The Lyric Genius of Catullus* (1967). Whitman's publications include the posthumously published *Fifteen Odes of Horace* (1980), a translation.

14 Lee T. Pearcy of Episcopal Academy in Merion, Pennsylvania, recalls reading some Catullus as a junior at Little Rock Central High School in Arkansas during the mid-1960s after finishing *Aeneid* 1, 2, 4, and 6 in the spring. His textbook (Carr and Wedeck 1940) contained three-and-a-half of Catullus' poems – 34, 13, the first six lines of 5, and 101.

15 Frank Copley's publications on Catullus include a translation, *Catullus: The Complete Poetry* (1957), as well as articles on such Catullan poems as 1, 4, 11, 35, 38, 51, 55, and 67.

16 Kizner's comments merit particular attention, for he was a reader/grader of the AP Latin Exams and for many years a College Board consultant presenting AP workshops for teachers.

17 Poem 30 was on the AP syllabus in the past. It appears in the 1970–2 acorn book, but then disappeared.

18 For Ludwig Schwabe's 1862 chronological reconstruction of the love affair with Lesbia from Catullus' poems as a *Catullroman*, which "underlay Catullan criticism for generations," and how it has been "displaced from its supporting position" by contemporary scholarship, see Skinner (2003: xix–xx) and Wiseman (1985: 217).

19 See Balme and Morwood (1997b: 29): "The identification of Catullus' Lesbia with Clodia, the sister of Publius Clodius [previously introduced in the section on Cicero], is made by Apuleius . . . as if it were uncontroversial and it has been accepted by most scholars since. Clodius had two sisters and we assume that Lesbia is the notorious Clodia, wife of Metellus Celer; but some modern scholars, e.g., Wiseman, consider that she was more probably the other sister. It is common practice to treat the Lesbia poems as if they were autobiographical but this is by no means certain. Our arrangement of the poems in a biographical sequence seems to us at least a plausible reconstruction and it would be a very austere teacher who would reject such a gambit in introducing Catullus' poetry to young pupils."

20 Raphael, personal correspondence. For his classical training, see especially Raphael (2003: 55), where he says that the first-form prize he received in 1939, a child's edition of Hawthorne's *Tanglewood Tales*, "introduced me to the Graeco-Roman world in which I was to be immersed for the next decade and in which I have never ceased to continue to take regular holidays," and (2003: 71) on the "labyrinthine grammar" of Latin.

21 Highet (1957: 7). For the reception of Catullus during the first half of the twentieth century by what he terms other sentimentalizing "moralizers," see Wiseman (1985: 218–29).

22 Fordyce leaves out 32 poems "which do not lend themselves to comment in English" (1961: v).

23 Here, again, the *OLR* teaching materials prepared in the United Kingdom deserve recognition for forthrightness and frankness about Catullus' sexually charged vocabulary, what Morwood characterizes in personal correspondence as an "important moment in the journey of Catullus into the secondary classroom." See the remarks (Balme and Morwood 1997b: 29) about poem 2: "Why a sparrow, not the most obvious of pets? Sappho (1.9–10) represents Aphrodite, the goddess of love, as riding in a chariot drawn by sparrows, and sparrows were emblematic of lechery and salaciousness in the ancient world. There is also the theory, which goes back at least as far as the Renaissance . . . that the Latin word for sparrow, *passer*, refers to the poet's phallus."

GUIDE TO FURTHER READING

Teachers of Catullus at the secondary school level in the United States use a variety of textbooks. Those written specifically with AP Catullus students in mind are Ancona (2004); Arnold et al. (2000); Bender and Forsyth (2005). The Latin Literature Workbook Series published by Bolchazy-Carducci includes Dettmer and Osburn (2006, 2007). Garrison (2004) is also used in many AP Catullus classrooms. Ancona (2004) and Bender and Forsyth (2005) contain all of the poems on the syllabus in effect since 2004–5. Although Arnold et al. (2000) contains the former AP syllabus, it can be used in conjunction with Lawall and Baer (2004) to cover the whole syllabus. Many teachers also use the editions of Merrill (1893, rpt. 1951) and Quinn (1973a), Wiseman's critical examination (1985), and the articles by Elder (1951b) and Commager (1965) for their own added preparation. Quinn has also published several influential critical studies (e.g. 1959 [2nd edn. 1999], 1972b). The "Paedagogus" section of *Classical World* (2002) is devoted to methods of teaching Catullus. Greenberger (2001) provides sample syllabi, bibliography, and teaching suggestions for Catullus and the other AP authors, while the "Teachers' Resources" section of the College Board website (see p. 485 above) contains reviews of books and online resources as well as teaching strategies. Both the "AP" and the "non-AP" Catullus teacher may consult these College Board resources with profit.

In the United Kingdom, the selections from Catullus presented in Balme and Morwood (1997a: 102–39) are often supplemented by those in Godwin (1995, 1999). In addition to the critical studies also consulted in the United States, teachers often use Bramble (1970), Lyne (1980), Jenkyns (1982), and Fitzgerald (1995).

WORKS CITED

Adams, J. N. 1982. *The Latin Sexual Vocabulary.* Baltimore and London.

Ancona, R. 2004. *Writing Passion: A Catullus Reader.* Wauconda, IL.

Arnold, B., A. Aronson, and G. Lawall. 2000. *Love and Betrayal: A Catullus Reader.* Upper Saddle River, NJ.

Balme, M. 1970. "Poem III." In Greig (1970: 6–12).

Balme, M., and J. Morwood, eds. 1997a. *Oxford Latin Reader.* 2nd rev. edn. Oxford.

Balme, M., and J. Morwood, eds. 1997b. *Oxford Latin Reader: Teacher's Book.* Oxford.

Balme, M., and M. S. Warman. 1965. *Aestimanda. Practical Criticism: Latin and Greek Poetry and Prose.* Oxford.

Bender, H., and P. Y. Forsyth. 2005. *Catullus: Expanded Edition.* Wauconda, IL.

Bramble, J. C. 1970. "Structure and Ambiguity in Catullus LXIV." *Proceedings of the Cambridge Philological Society* 16: 22–41.

Briggs, W. W., Jr., ed. 1994. *Biographical Dictionary of North American Classicists.* Westport, CT, and London.

Bulley, M. 1989. "Please, Not in Front of the Latin A-Level Students." Letter to the *Guardian*, March 15: 18.

Carr, W. L., and H. E. Wedeck. 1940. *Latin Poetry.* Boston.

Commager, H. S., Jr. 1965. "Notes on Some Poems of Catullus." *Harvard Studies in Classical Philology* 70: 83–110.

Cookesley, W. G. 1845. *Selecta e Catullo: In Usum Iuventutis./Notas Quasdam Anglice Scriptas Adjecit Gulielmus Gifford Cookesley.* Eton.

Copley, F.O., trans. 1957. *Catullus: The Complete Poetry.* Ann Arbor, MI. Rpt. 1964.

Dettmer, H., and L. A. Osburn. 2006. *A Catullus Workbook.* Wauconda, IL.

Dettmer, H., and L. A. Osburn. 2007. *A Catullus Workbook: Teacher's Guide.* Wauconda, IL.

Elder, J. P. 1951a. "Foreword." In Merrill (1893: viii).

Elder, J. P. 1951b. "Notes on Some Conscious and Subconscious Elements in Catullus' Poetry." *Harvard Studies in Classical Philology* 60: 101–36.

Fitzgerald, W. 1995. *Catullan Provocations: Lyric Poetry and the Drama of Position.* Berkeley, Los Angeles, and London.

Fordyce, C. J., ed. 1961. *Catullus: A Commentary.* Oxford.

Garrison, D. H. 2004. *The Student's Catullus.* 3rd edn. Norman, OK.

Godwin, J. 1995. *Catullus: Poems 61–68.* Warminster.

Godwin, J. 1999. *Catullus: The Shorter Poems.* Warminster.

Greenberger, J., ed. 2001. *Teacher's Guide: AP Latin.* New York.

Greig, C., ed. 1970. *Experiments: Nine Essays on Catullus for Teachers.* Cambridge.

Havelock, E. 1967 [1939]. *The Lyric Genius of Catullus.* New York.

Highet, G. 1957. *Poets in a Landscape.* New York.

Jenkyns, R. 1982. *Three Classical Poets: Sappho, Catullus and Juvenal.* London.

LaFleur, R. A. 1997. "*Latina resurgens*: Classical Language Enrollments in American Schools and Colleges." *Classical Outlook* 74: 125–30.

LaFleur, R. A., ed. 1998. *Latin for the 21st Century: From Concept to Classroom*. Glenview, IL.

Lawall, G. and E. Baer. 2004. *Catullus Supplement: The New Selections of the Advanced Placement Syllabus*. Amherst, MA.

Lyne, R. O. A. M. 1980. *The Latin Love Poets from Catullus to Horace*. Oxford.

Merrill, E. T., ed. 1893. *Catullus*. Rpt. 1951. Cambridge, MA.

Murphy, C. A., D. Thiem, and R. T. Moore. 2005. *Embers of the Ancient Flame*. 2nd edn. Wauconda, IL.

"Paedagogus." 2002. Contributions by H. Bender, J. P. Hallett, P. A. Miller, L. Pearcy, M. Skinner. *Classical World* 95.4: 413–38.

Perry, D. J. 1998. "Using the Reading Approach in Secondary Schools." In LaFleur (1998: 105–16).

Putnam, M. C. J. 1994. "Elder, John Petersen." In Briggs (1994: 159–60).

Quinn, K. 1959. *The Catullan Revolution*. Melbourne. Rpt. Cambridge 1969; Ann Arbor, MI, 1971. 2nd edn. London 1999.

Quinn, K. 1972b. *Catullus: An Interpretation*. London.

Quinn, K., ed. 1973a. *Catullus: The Poems*. 2nd edn. London and Basingstoke.

Raphael, F. 2003. *A Spoilt Boy: A Memoir of Childhood*. London.

Raven, S. 1967. *Fielding Gray: A Novel*. New York.

Richlin, A. 1992 [1983]. *The Garden of Priapus: Sexuality and Aggression in Roman Humor*. Rev. edn. New York and Oxford.

Rudd, N., and J. Foster. 1970. "Poem LI." In Greig (1970: 42–8).

Sarkissian, J. 2004. "The Grading of the 2004 Advanced Placement Examinations in Latin: Vergil." *Classical Outlook* 82.1: 1–18.

Singh, K. L. 1998. "Grammar-Translation and High-School Latin." In LaFleur (1998: 90–104).

Skinner, M. B. 2003. *Catullus in Verona: A Reading of the Elegiac* Libellus, *Poems 65–116*. Columbus, OH.

Whitman, C. H., trans. 1980. *Fifteen Odes of Horace*. Lunenburg, VT.

Wiseman, T. P. 1985. *Catullus and His World: A Reappraisal*. Cambridge.

Witke, C. 1970. "Poem XXXI." In Greig (1970: 36–41).

CHAPTER TWENTY-SIX

Catullus in the College Classroom

Daniel H. Garrison

If there were ever a Latin author perfectly suited for the college curriculum, Catullus is the gift from heaven. Though a wholesome selection is offered to high school students via Advanced Placement (AP; see Ancona and Hallett, this volume) and similar prescriptions, Catullus is on the whole a more adult author than can easily fit within the confines of the adolescent imagination. Teenagers are fascinated by his turbulent obsessions, but he wrote for adults, and his diversity is better suited to adult readers. Young readers can be misled, even disturbed, by Catullus' well-planned coarseness of language and subject. Or they may be bored by what is neither outrageous nor pretty. Worse yet, they can be too inclined to view his poems as the unfiltered outpouring of an adolescent personality. They have been encouraged to understand that poets write about what they know and feel, and it will therefore seem obvious to them that the poems of Catullus are strictly autobiographical, impulsive, and unspoiled by literary convention. The average teenager will be impatient of the meticulous construction of lyrics that seem so natural, and will as a rule be bored by the literary construction of the *libellus* and its lyrics. Adolescent students will focus narrowly on the basic sentimental content of a Catullan lyric without having much interest in nuance. The few that do will, of course, be readier as mature readers to return to Catullus for a more articulated approach, and they will contribute much to college level discussions of whatever they have read before.

By college age, readers of Catullus will have a somewhat greater aptitude for the complexity of the *Carmina*, but as before they are pulled in two directions. On the one hand they are readier than ever to appreciate literary craft on a great variety of subjects, while on the other a great many will be interested chiefly in getting through a language requirement and maintaining the best possible grade point average in an academic term that is full of distractions.

The realistic teacher of college level introductions to Catullus will have to navigate these extremes. The more perfunctory members of a class will expect to replicate the high grades they were given in high school for memorizing translations, repeating what they have heard about poetic artistry, and expressing their opinions about Catullus and his friends. Such students want to get Latin (and with it the need ever to deal with a foreign language) out of their way. Those who have not started Latin in a well-executed program will need to unlearn some bad habits acquired earlier. The cardinal bad habit is the thought that memorizing English translations is the main objective of any Latin course. Correlated to this are such pernicious assumptions as *Latin is easy, Latin is a silent language, Latin is like English with a different vocabulary*, etc. Some may be initially (or permanently) uncomfortable in a course that is not dumbed down to keep enrollments high and parents happy. These will miss the beloved teacher who had a proper respect for their self-esteem and the sanctity of their personal opinions.

The hardest part of every college Latin teacher's task is to unteach the bad habits and crippling misconceptions acquired in earlier stages of Latin study. Not every student will be burdened with these handicaps. But the majority will, and the first things learned are always the hardest to unlearn. For many, the study of Catullus will entail a certain amount of wrecking and rebuilding.

These apparently cynical warnings grow out of nearly four decades of teaching Latin at a highly selective Midwestern university and paying attention to the remarks of my colleagues about the work of introducing students to college level study. Though AP is all about college level study, its good influence does not usually last into college.

Any college classroom, if it is to succeed with Catullus, needs to blend the mechanical bones and sinews of his Latin with the artistry in such a way that the relation will appear seamless. There is nothing that is merely mechanical and nothing that is pure artistry because the two are inseparable in great writing. The purpose of classroom work is to work toward that understanding.

It is a much-neglected truism that the object in any language course is to *think in the target language*. Though the objective with an ancient language is chiefly to read rather than speak, that does not nullify the general rule. Too many instructors, forgetting this, slide into the frame of mind where the objective is to *translate*. Though translation may be a good test of basic understanding, it can also interfere with the primary goal of familiarity and is likely, if misapplied, to retard the development of reading skill and understanding of the writer's craft.

It is also well to keep in mind the commonplace of instruction in any language, living or dead, that *memorization in the original language promotes familiarity* on every level. This is particularly true when learning poetry, because meter is more an instinctual than an intellectual skill. In the hands of a real artist, meter reinforces the natural cadences of the language. The sound, rhythms, and tonality of Catullus can scarcely be learned without memorization. Undergraduates determined to pass their foreign language requirement with as little effort as possible will resent this. Though they will be willing to memorize "correct" translations of assigned poems before a test, other memorization tasks will not amuse them.

A few home truths about instruction in the college classroom follow. They began to evolve in my first job teaching Latin under close watch at Phillips Exeter Academy in 1959–60 and developed over the next 46 years. It is gratifying that so much of what I learned while teaching at the secondary level proved to be no less useful in the college classroom – certainly no less formative than college experience has been for the best high school teachers.

- Class time for students at any level can best be treated as a workshop whose main business is the exchange of questions and answers. If possible, members of the class should provide the answers as well as the questions, starting with matters of syntax, idiom, meter, and other mechanics and over time working into rhetoric and other features of literary craft. With a few exceptions, students who are most involved with questions and answers will do best; those who don't participate are the most likely to be in trouble early and often. College level education assumes that students are mature enough to be self-starting, but this does not come without prodding because of the habit of passivity. Every class needs frequent reminders that this is *their* class, not yours.

- Assure your students that there are no bad questions: only bad answers. If one of them has a question that needs an answer, chances are there will be others who need an answer to the same question. Part of the classroom skill of any good instructor is to turn all questions into good questions leading to a useful and interesting answer.

- Slack time, when all the questions seem to have been answered, is your time to ask questions. If you are sure the language is well understood, this is the time to introduce new points of poetic rhetoric, artistry, and whatever is available to enrich your classroom conversations with literary analysis. But meaning always comes first: *never leave syntax out of the picture.* Many of your students will have entered college with the delusion that syntactic structure is just for beginners and can be forgotten as soon as they move on to higher ground. You will soon become aware that a large number have, in fact, forgotten important parts of syntax and can't read the Latin.

- Once you have begun to get some of the mechanics under control, pay attention to the formal structure of each poem studied. Catullus deploys his sentences into the cola or "limbs" of a poem, the section breaks on which his lyric is hinged. Considering what happens at the midpoint of a poem is one way to start. After you have taken your class through a few poems, they will be aware of the classic points of emphasis in lyric poetry, such as the first word and the last word, and the usual points of division. I have found it is useful at the beginning of every class to hand out a well-spaced printed copy of each poem to be discussed (if this requires more than one side of one sheet, you are probably assigning too much). Each student will then have a scratch sheet on which to draw lines of demarcation showing the main sections of a poem, make additional notes, and mark keywords. They will be surprised to see how orderly the layout turns out to be, even in what seem to be Catullus' wildest effusions. Marking out the units of composition will drive home the point that Catullus reflected before he composed his lyrics and paid close attention to the formal aspects of his composition.

- Handing out a printed copy of each poem at the beginning of every class will be your way of driving home the point that good workshops involve active learning and will produce notes, diagrams, and other graphical aide-mémoires that can be used in review.

- Some of your students will need to unlearn certain Romantic preconceptions, such as the notion that poetry is the sudden eruption of powerful emotions that seize control of the imagination and sometimes the pen itself. Your questions and answers should suggest that feeling may be the *subject* of a poem; it has on some level driven the poet, but emotion did not write the poem.

- Assignments should be short and intensive. Nobody is counting how many poems or lines you assign. It should become clear that unlike most courses, the assignment here is not to be read just once, but many times, to the point of memorization because the object is familiarity. Point out that your course has the shortest reading list on campus.
- Far from being a silent art form, lyric poetry has a performative, heard value that requires it be heard and spoken out loud as part of its reception. Whenever possible, Catullus' lines should be sounded out as a necessary part of their understanding. The music of the words is part of their meaning. Classroom discussion of a poem is enriched when the teacher repeats the words and phrases in Catullus' own language, remembering that the object of study is not a translation.

What follows will illustrate how attention to the basics can illuminate aspects of Catullus that may not come through in a published translation. Rather than a descent into the mere mechanics of meter, grammar, vocabulary, and discursive structure, attention to particulars is the only way to raise the poetry of Catullus above the banality of mere translation.

Diction and Color

When first learning a language, students are in no position to judge the quality of a new word: we just try to learn a bare meaning, which in Latin will mean its English equivalent (if there is one). When there is no equivalent, translation fails and you begin to miss the point of what is being said. Diminutives are one example of such words because English uses them so seldom. Some languages use them all the time, especially in the vernacular. When Catullus uses diminutives, they impart a colloquial, vernacular color which he and the other *noui poetae* liked, but in addition to that there is usually another layer of meaning when a diminutive is employed, a rhetorical color ranging from pathos (e.g., *frigidulos singultus* in 64.131) to affectionate intimacy (*Veraniolum* in 12.17) to contempt (e.g., in 57.7 *erudituli*). There are some thirty diminutives in the first 28 poems of Catullus, most of them difficult or impossible to render into English. These are not petty details. Classroom discussion should try to elicit the *force*, point, or rhetorical color of a diminutive; students of Catullus should be prepared to explain the "force" of a word, not just its approximate meaning in English. Students who have memorized an English translation will be clueless because they haven't read the Latin poem.

Translation: The "Kid Brother" Test

For all its limitations, translation is not a useless test of understanding and should be a significant fraction of what is tested so long as it remains clear that translation is not the end product of study and cannot by itself guarantee a passing grade. Anyone can benefit from translating poems into English as a part of preparation for classroom discussion. No one will benefit from copying out a translation made by someone else.

Some will continue to harbor the notion that if they look up all the words in a Latin sentence and make up a plausible story about them, they will squeak through. The problem is that most of the translations so generated are short on plausibility. It may therefore help you to suggest a simple, self-administered test: if your kid brother would not understand your translation, you probably don't either. This is a corollary of the simple test General Eisenhower applied to letters received from his staff during World War II: if they can't explain their idea in a one-page letter, it's probably not a very good idea.

Alliteration, Assonance, and Other Sound Effects

Though it is no longer as true as it once was that college Latin students believe they have read all of the *Aeneid* in high school, veterans of AP courses on Vergil will have learned about his famous word music and will expect to eke out *some* credit for remarks about the sound effect of words that sound alike or unalike in a sentence and are full of g's and f's or some other phonemes. Some such discussion, however implausible, will be thought a good way to play the poetic artistry card. Though Catullus also works with the sound of his language, he is usually uninterested in the kind of sonority heard in the *Aeneid* (especially as the works of Vergil had not yet been written). Sound analysis is likely to be taken as a free fire zone, and creative remarks on your tests, especially when not specifically asked for, should be taken with caution.

Reading Catullus Out Loud

Though you may already have learned that asking students to read parts of a Latin poem out loud is a prodigal use of class time, you should insist that they pronounce his words correctly as classical Latin (not in ecclesiastical or Anglo-Latin ways). It is also a very good use of class time if you read a poem or a stanza out loud in class to convey a feeling for the sound of his language. It doesn't hurt if it sounds a little like modern Italian, for example when you sound both letters of a double consonant separately (*libel-lus*) as they were in fact pronounced in antiquity. Such reading is especially important to convey the sense of the most often-used meters, such as the hendecasyllabic, hexameter, choliambic, and elegiac couplet. Even the galliambic, which was hideously hard to write in Latin, is easy to read out loud; its power is impossible to comprehend until it is read in this way. Latin meter is intimidating until it is heard. It then becomes instinctual.

Doing Verbs

One of the first things learned about Latin is that verbs drive the sentence, extending their influence to adjacent nouns, pronouns, and adverbs and showing tense, mood, and subject by their inflection. Though you are presumably teaching a literary subject, class time must be spent relentlessly on the syntax of subjunctives and participles even though your students are supposed to know these basics. For example, do a reality check with one of the kiss-poems that every freshman who "did" AP Latin literature probably read, c. 5: *Vivamus, mea Lesbia*. If you assign the poem (which you should), ask your class to write down the form, English meaning, and syntax of the verbs in the last line of the following verb-intensive sentence:

> Soles occidere et redire possunt;
> nobis cum semel occidit breuis lux,
> nox est perpetua una dormienda.

Unless you have already performed this experiment, you will be amazed how few have anything more than the most fleeting impression about the form and meaning of *est . . . dormienda*, or for that matter about the syntax of *nobis* in the preceding line. It will be protested that college level Latin should be about literary value, not syntax. But you can't do the literature without doing the verbs, and students will miss the literary *topos* in these lines if they don't see how the verbs work.

A similar experiment may be tried with the ending of the second kiss-poem, c. 7, another standard AP Catullus lyric:

> tam te basia multa basiare
> uesano satis et super Catullo est;
> quae nec pernumerare curiosi
> possint nec mala fascinare lingua.

If your students have ever heard about the relative clause of purpose, it is a good guess their eyes glazed over at the time and they will have trouble explaining this instance of it. In such a case, the point of the poem's ending will be lost. The point of the experiment is to demonstrate that the basics don't lose their importance after they have been forgotten: if you don't go after verbal constructions with the persistence of a hammerhead shark, your students will not be reading Catullus as literature – or as anything else.

Commentaries

Experience will show (if it has not already) that if the notes at the end of the book or the bottom of the page do not provide your students the English translation they are looking for, they will be dismissed as merely ornamental, intended only for geeks and graduate students. That may be true of some bulky commentaries written by geeks (you will think of examples), but it is also true that *no serious student of an ancient text reads the original without constant recourse to a commentary*. An adequate school commentary will tell the reader the minimum that should be known to appreciate the meaning, syntax, and literary content of the words commented upon when these are not self-evident. Aspects of literary artistry and historical explanation are also the stuff of school commentaries because the audience for whom Catullus' poems were written is long dead and our brains are packed with other matter. The more you are reading Catullus as the literary record of a time and way of life instead of as a set of grammatical exercises, the more important the school commentary will be to the student of Catullus.

Trots or Ponies

To make the job of construing the Latin easier, students will be tempted to rely upon an English translation (referred to as a "trot" or "pony," or, in British parlance, a "crib"). The best way to meet this issue is to assign one and explain how it should be used. Because the Latin text of Catullus is so often subject to emendations and alternative readings, the translator will probably be using a slightly different text. This is good. Your students need to learn as soon as possible that a translation is useful only as a kind of thumbnail representation, indicating the general drift of the poem for a first-time reader needing to know what to expect. The trot will show that there is no such thing as a "correct" English translation, and it is thereafter up to us to discover what the poem is really saying. Translations are realities constructed after the fact when the actual meaning is in the Latin.

Reality Checks

Perhaps no other field in academia is as prone to self-delusion as Latin, with teachers at every level tempted to swell enrollments by making it a feel-good course. My favorite example comes from a recent student who had come to Northwestern from a public school in Michigan: "I loved my Latin teacher. He was the best teacher I had in four years, but I didn't learn a darn thing from him." Pressures for mediocrity in college Latin teaching are not as murderous as in high school, though it is still true that serving up lashings of good feeling in return for driblets of actual learning is a proven technique for becoming the Beloved Professor. If, on the other hand, you are willing to endure some hard looks and whiny course evaluations consequent upon your hard work and tough grading, you will bring high quality students into your program. They will develop a lasting determination to prove themselves, as well as high literacy and other mental powers. Good quality instruction attracts more and better classics majors than flabby courses with low standards.

In the initial years of language instruction, it is axiomatic that reality checks should be frequent, at least weekly. Without spending too much class time in testing, it should be possible to devote 15–20 minutes a week to quizzes, the fewer surprises the better, along the following lines:

- a few syntax questions, always with a standard, unvarying protocol for answers;
- a translation or two of short sentences or clauses;
- questions that ask the student to place a few words from a recently studied lyric in their context, or ask who is being addressed, etc.; such questions reward familiarity with the poems assigned;
- a few lines of scansion.

- a question or two about a specific rhetorical or literary device; these may be more or less technical, or they may ask what makes some lines funny, ironic, or typically Catullan.

Such tests should reward students for knowing terms of art such as adversative asyndeton, hyperbaton, syncope, rhetorical color, and the like that apply to literary techniques often seen in the *Carmina*. Scoring should be as objective, consistent, and transparent as you can make it and should be described in terms of rewards instead of penalties, e.g., "You had 45 opportunities to earn a top score of 40 points on this quiz." Of course, this is double talk but it creates a flexibility and assures the class we do not expect perfection. Do not be offended if a mercenary student asks how many points a certain question was worth, or if somebody makes a wild guess. In fact, you should encourage such enterprise as a creative alternative to leaving an answer blank. You will learn more from wrong answers in some cases than you will from right ones. Wrong answers will tell you what you can be teaching better.

To maintain morale and a positive attitude to redemption, consider basing your quiz average in the course on the best 80 percent or so of all grades received, including tests not taken. This provides leeway for illness, family emergencies, bad hair days, oversleeping, and hangovers. If a student in your class asks to be excused from a quiz for any reason, you can then answer "Of course! You are automatically excused from any two quizzes in this course whether or not you actually take them." My experience with this policy over the last 39 years is that it all but eliminates absences from quizzes, just as frequent testing all but eliminates cutting of other class meetings.

Obscenity

The chapter by Ancona and Hallett in this volume on teaching Catullus in the secondary school curriculum says most of what should be considered at the college level, except that parents, administrators, and the outside community need not be feared as a source of possible interference. There was a time when the use of rude vernacular language by Catullus was thought unsuitable for any classroom discussion. E. T. Merrill's 1893 commentary, which was widely used in colleges until very recently and is still kept in print by no less a publisher than Harvard, condemned c. 97 as "exceedingly coarse." Like c. 16, which is actually about poetry, the offending poem received even less than the skimpy annotation that Merrill was willing to expend on any poem of Catullus. Today, obscenity is good for business in the entertainment industry and is something like a mark of authenticity in the representation of talk. For example, we know from the release of all sorts of White House transcripts that formerly offensive language has for at least a generation been commonly used by presidents and their associates in the Oval Office. In academia, students with access to a good lexicon and modern annotation will not need to have the dirty parts explained in a way that could possibly embarrass or require the repetition of words that could offend delicate ears. What does bear classroom discussion is why such language is good or bad rhetoric.

It is worth noting that *futuo*, which with its compounds appears seven times in Catullus, can be correctly translated by only one English verb, which has no synonyms that are not slang and is one of the oldest and most frequently employed verbs in English. When the publisher of *The Student's Catullus* (Garrison 2004) asked politely whether it was absolutely necessary to use the f-word (they are in the middle of the Bible Belt and had never printed the word before), they gracefully agreed when told there is only one transitive verb in English with the same meaning. They had just published a book about the experience of American soldiers in Vietnam without once (they told me) using the offending expression – a remarkable accomplishment.

Good and Bad Memorization

In the student lexicon, "memorization" connotes unpleasant learning. Latin vocabulary must in student dialect be "memorized" instead of learned. This is delusional, because learning implies active use where memorization is the kind of passive rote learning we like to avoid because it tends to drive out real learning. As already noted, good Latin teachers discourage their students from memorizing English translations of language we want them to learn. That kind of memorization is part of the guerrilla action conducted by students against teachers willing to accept it as evidence of language skill. It is a form of cramming, instantly forgotten after the test. Good memorization is a powerful learning tool. Memorizing poems of Catullus in Latin for oral recitation promotes correct pronunciation, a feeling for the meter in which it is composed, an enriched understanding of vocabulary, and an appreciation for the natural cadences of Latin.

Besides being the mother of the Muses, memory is an intellectual muscle. In the Greek world of Euripides and Socrates, the Latin world of Cicero and Catullus, and once again in the Renaissance, it was a science as well as an art. People memorized for pleasure, not as an odious task (so perceived by undergraduates not involved in the arts). Plutarch records that the Syracusans were so fond of memorizing passages from Euripides that they freed Athenian captives who could recite what they remembered from his plays (*Nic.* 29.4).

In a college Catullus course, it will greatly advance familiarity with meter if you assign memorization of c. 1 *Cui dono* (hendecasyllabic) at the beginning and later c. 85 *Odi et amo* (elegiac couplet). Anyone can do this easily, and will benefit greatly from doing so, if only because these two poems tell so much of what Catullus is about and because they showcase two of his most-used meters. It will be a trophy achievement, a final proof to skeptics that they really know some Latin. As an option for much-needed extra credit, a needy student should be offered the opportunity to memorize and recite Ariadne's lament, 64.132–201 (hexameters), a passage never surpassed in Latin and superbly fit for performance. Weak students will never learn more than a few lines of this masterpiece; those who succeed in this undertaking rarely need the extra credit, and they usually become Latin majors thereafter. This is further proof, if proof were needed, that it is hard work that produces classics majors, not easy grades.

Language, Persona, and Personality

Although the text of Catullus has been damaged in transmission and has required some guesswork to make readable, it provides a remarkably direct window into the world from which it came. But for all its vividness, we cannot tell how accurately the *libellus* reflects its author. That is the Catullan question. If all reality is to some extent constructed, we are forced to admit that even if Catullus set out to be objectively autobiographical in his *Carmina*, the personality he reveals must be a literary artifact. Poets are not necessarily the best witnesses, especially concerning themselves. Even when they admit to some faults, there is a strong tendency to self-justification.

The Catullus of the *Carmina* holds our attention, but he does not justify himself so much as he exhibits behavior that fits a discernible profile. In a culture where self-possession was the highest virtue, the Catullus published in the poems that bear his name (he mentions himself by name 25 times in his lyrics) is signally lacking in this. That is one reason why it has been almost irresistible to read the *Carmina* as self-revelation rather than fiction. In this way Catullus is the opposite of a Homer, who tantalizes because he so completely hides himself. After generations of fussing over the Homeric question, scholars grew tired of the subject and agreed to think about more interesting subjects. The Catullan question has come to a similar end. Whether the Catullus of the poems is a literary artifact or a biographical fact, he is a character worth knowing. We read for personality.

That personality is revealed (*inter alia*) in the syntax of the *libellus*. To return to the kiss-poems, it is significant that Catullus is the one who wants to be kissed: *Da mi basia mille* (5.7). This sets the grammatical context for c. 7:

> Quaeris quot mihi basiationes
> tuae, Lesbia, sint satis superque.

The force of the possessive adjective *tuae*, emphasized by enjambment, is subjective: Lesbia is doing the kissing. This is again implicit in lines 9–10:

> tam te basia multa basiare
> uesano satis et super Catullo est

where it is the context rather than a rule of grammar that makes *te* the subject rather than the object of *basiare*. That same female-active role returns near the end of the poem that follows, *Miser Catulle*:

> Quem basiabis? Cui labella mordebis?

It is also prominent in the sexually passionate character given to Queen Berenice in c. 66, whose newly wedded spouse goes off to war bearing the marks of their erotic scuffle:

> dulcia nocturnae portans uestigia rixae,
> quam de uirgineis gesserat exuuiis.
> (13–14)

In the continual conversation that goes on between the poems of the *libellus*, c. 48 to the boyfriend Juventius is in pointed contrast to 5 and 7 to Lesbia:

> Mellitos oculos tuos, Iuuenti,
> si quis me sinat usque basiare,
> usque ad milia basiem trecenta.

Here it is Catullus who wants to do the kissing, as he does again in 99 where he steals a kiss from Juventius (*surripui* and *surripiam*, the first and last words of the poem). Such are the significant particulars that illuminate the different modes of Catullus' bisexuality.

Catullus North and South

In making a representative selection of the *libellus* for class study, it should be remembered that Catullus was not a Roman poet in every sense. None of the great "Roman" writers in poetry or prose actually came from Rome, and not all were even Italian. Like Vergil and Livy, Catullus and his family were not, strictly speaking, Italian. As he reminds us in c. 39, he was a *Transpadanus*, from a long-civilized part of subalpine Europe north of the Po River known at the time as Gallia Transpadana. His native Verona became a Latin colony only about the time of Catullus' birth, and it did not become fully united with Italy until 42 BC, after the assumed date of Catullus' death.

Catullus came from a prominent family in Verona that also owned a villa on a peninsula named Sirmio that runs out into the Lago di Garda about twenty miles west of Verona. His father was a friend of Caesar, and though Catullus had some extremely rude things to say about his father's friend, Caesar is said to have admired Catullus' poetry. We know little about the family beyond Catullus' strong love for his brother, but the poet expressed a deep affection for his northern homes, both Sirmio and Verona, and appears to have returned frequently for visits. More importantly, Catullus had a sober, conservative side which emerges in several of his lyrics as an alternative to his more obsessive character. This alternative has been convincingly linked to the poet's roots in Transpadane Gaul. The view of a husband's duty to control a young wife expressed in c. 17 and the wedding hymns c. 61 and 62 speak in this traditional northern voice. More interesting for classroom discussion are the poems in which the soberer, saner Catullus tries to reason with the obsessive lover. Poem 8, *Miser Catulle*, can be paired in this way with poem 76, *Siqua recordanti*. Both show that more self-possessed Catullus remonstrating with the heartbroken discarded lover of Lesbia who cannot take control of himself. Similarly, the non-Sapphic coda attached to the end of c. 51, *Otium, Catulle, tibi molestum est*, pulls the reader out of the enchanted world of erotic seizure and returns to the hardworking, sensible ethos of Transpadane Gaul.

Arranging the Poems

For more than forty years, we have seen the emergence of a substantial bibliography about the Hellenistic poetry-book (e.g., Lawall 1967; van Sickle 1980, 1989) and its influence on arrangements of their own poems made by Vergil, Tibullus, Propertius, and Horace.[1] It is now clear that the Augustan poets were preceded in Latin by Catullus, with publications by Marilyn Skinner (1981, 2003) and Helena Dettmer (1997) arguing that the poems of Catullus were arranged by the poet and were meant to be read in relation to each other (see Skinner, this volume, pp. 35–53). The order in which these poems were transmitted is therefore not only canonical but arguably purposeful, in contrast to the thematic rearrangements preferred by school editions such as the *Oxford Latin Reader*. Collections specifically prepared for AP classes may reasonably be allowed more latitude in the presentation of Catullan lyrics; college classes, even when there is no time to read the entire *libellus*, should have all the poems in order. While it is important to consider each lyric as a free-standing artifact, each gains meaning by its intertextuality within the collection as well as with works by earlier authors. At this level of study the importance of a commentary, discussed earlier, should be self-evident. The selection of poems for class preparation and study will be affected by this relation between poems, and it should be emphasized that the book as a whole is as much a literary artifact as each poem within it.

Like *The Sopranos* and similarly multi-threaded dramas, the *libellus* mingles the threads of Lesbia, politics, literature, the demi-monde, Juventius, and other topics. We are not meant to construct a time line, and those who have tried have labored in vain.

The Poetry of Scandal

Not just because they were too hot for the AP selection but also because they are good reading, college level assignments should include some poems about what may be called *ineptiae* or hanky-panky. A good example is c. 6, *Flaui delicias tuas*, which is rich in the language of style, elegance, and social performance that became so important in the age of Cicero.[2] It is also of interest because it brings out a voyeuristic aspect of the poet's character or persona that some have missed. This comes out also in cc. 10, 13, 35, and 55. The cheerfully coarse Ipsitilla ode, c. 32, dispels the notion that sexuality was all pain and ecstasy for Catullus; c. 37, *Salax taberna*, is important not only for the vignette it provides of sleazy Rome but also for the Lesbia theme and the aggression rather than self-pity it provokes. Poem 42, *Adeste, hendecasyllabi*, shows another side of the demi-monde with a literary twist, reminding us, as does poem 55 and a score of others, that the *libellus* is a portrait of Rome as Catullus found it and as no one else of the time described it. Nor is the ribaldry confined to Rome: close to the surface of c. 17, *O Colonia*, set somewhere near Verona, it comes to the surface in c. 67, where a house door tells about the scandalous liaisons of its mistress.

The AP list understandably constructs a simplified world around Catullus, one free of sleaze, ugliness, and politics if not of sexual ambiguity. The college reading list should redress that imbalance, adding enough about the public world Catullus described to do justice to the diversity of his collection. Catullus did not hate politics; he was well enough connected to see that public life had been surrendered to depraved personalities about whom he loved to tell what he felt was the truth.[3]

Poetry of Friendship

More has been written on this topic with regard to Horace than Catullus.[4] But where for Horace friendship is sometimes involved with patronage, Catullus needed no patron and his personal ties were therefore more intimately personal. Cicero was not to write his essay *Laelius de Amicitia* until 44 BC, but Plato's *Lysis*, Aristotle's *Nichomachean Ethics*, and three lost volumes of Theophrastus had laid the foundations of what became an important theme in Hellenistic ethics, perhaps more important on the whole than the archaic and classical virtues of self-sufficiency. Though Catullus' friendships with men were intense and demanding, sometimes employing language suggestive of erotic involvement, they were not necessarily homoerotic and there is no reason to construe them in that way. Unlike the poetry of sleaze and scandal, the poetry of friendship is well represented in the AP prescription (e.g., 1 [but not 6], 10, 13, 14, 30, 35, 50, and 96). Licinius Calvus, Veranius and Fabullus, Camerius, Hortalus, and C. Cinna are warmly rewarded in the *libellus* as friends of the poet, who was anything but a loner. Catullus did much to establish the poetry of friendship for later development by Horace. This side of his achievement should be kept prominent, especially for students who will later be reading Horace.

High and Low Diction

The typical style of the polymetrics is short and vernacular, inspired in part by the language of the Roman stage but also reflecting the tendency of the *noui poetae* to give Latin poetry a native idiom and liberate it from the tyranny of high Greek literature. The other side of Catullus is the one that could not rest until he had proven that Latin poetry could achieve the same effects as Greek. The college classroom is the appropriate place to cultivate a sense of the difference between the vernacular and the high literary modes. This is why the longer masterpieces of the middle section, such as the poem about Attis in galliambic meter, c. 63, should not be excluded. Not only does Catullus essay the high poetic diction of Greek poetry, but he projects his enslavement to Lesbia into an ancient myth about a religious fanatic who unmans himself to serve a cruel goddess. He also begins the long process of dismantling the sentimental *locus amoenus* tradition which had already produced some dull Greek poetry and would soon produce some even duller Latin. The dark forests of Bithynia, seen at first hand by Catullus during his colonial service in 57–56 BC (and the European forests seen by countless Roman soldiers during Caesar's conquests in Transalpine Gaul), are the sinister backdrop of this unique poem, which opened paths into the many gruesome groves of later Latin poetry (Garrison 1992).

The other long poem that should be considered required reading at the college level is c. 64, of which a portion (50–253) is in the AP prescription. This homage to the Hellenistic epic is easier to fit into a semester's work than a quarter's, but at least a portion such as Ariadne's lament (132–201, mentioned earlier) should be accommodated. Taken as a whole, this epyllion displays a Hellenistic temper in oblique approaches to a story and the skeptical view of traditional epic heroes. Ariadne's lament is more performative than narrative. As Attis in 63 resonates with the Catullus of the Lesbia cycle, Ariadne is a transsexual projection of Catullus; tags from earlier lyrics support this reading, one again illustrating the use of myth as a vehicle for present-day experience. The poetic justice that overtakes Theseus is like the justice that Catullus invokes upon Alfenus in c. 30.11–12:

> Si tu oblitus es, at di meminerunt, meminit Fides,
> quae te ut paeniteat postmodo facti faciet tui.

and on his own behalf in c. 76.17–19:

> O di, si uestrum est misereri, aut si quibus umquam
> extremam iam ipsa in morte tulistis opem,
> me miserum aspicite.

Compared to the polymetrics, Catullus' hexameters in c. 64 have a ceremonial aspect, felt in the several golden lines (59, 129, 163, 172, 235, 351) and near-golden lines found here as well as frequent hyperbaton, epanalepsis (61–2, *prospicit, eheu,/prospicit*), polyptoton (19–21, *tum Thetidis…tum Thetis…tum Thetidi*), anaphora (255, *euhoe bacchantes, euhoe capita inflectentes*) and other techniques of the high poetic style. There are also the compounds avoided by the neoterics – *fluentisono* (52), *Nysigenis* (252), *unigenam* (300), *ueridicos* (305) – and learned circumlocutions such as the metonymic *Amphitriten* for the sea (11) and *Amarunthia uirgo* for Artemis (395). Yet we seldom feel that the poet is contriving to push all the buttons of high poetry. Moreover, this elevated rhetoric is important because it is sometimes folded into other poems that are not in the epic mold and must be recognized as a change of tone when used in a non-epic context (see further Sheets, this volume).

Conclusion

We can hope that college classes reading Catullus will benefit from the preparation received in AP courses, but for several reasons we cannot expect perfect continuity. Many students will not have read Catullus before college. They will feel at a disadvantage because they have been thrown in with others who have already read this author. The fraction who feel they have already "done" Catullus in AP Latin will feel they should not be expected to repeat high school work. But experience shows it is sometimes the novice readers who do better because they know their education is not yet complete. The veterans who "did" Catullus studied a thoughtfully chosen subset of his work that was tailored to their youth rather than the complexity of Catullus' actual oeuvre. Depending on the instruction they received, they will have expectations the college instructor can scarcely hope to satisfy (or may prefer not to satisfy), and they may have forgotten all but fleeting impressions of the Catullus they must meet anew in the college classroom. There is a steep gradient between the best high school instruction and the average, which further limits what the college instructor can expect of students matriculating from AP Catullus.

As argued at the beginning of this chapter, the greatest challenge at the college level may be to unteach attitudes learned early in Latin study which violate the fundamental, universally acknowledged tenets of all foreign language instruction. The cardinal error of mediocre Latin instruction is that the object is to *translate*, when the only reasonable object in the study of language and literature is to *think in the target language*. The teacher caught in the grip of this delusion thinks "I am teaching my class to *translate* Catullus" rather than "I am teaching my class to *read* Catullus." If this distinction seems a quibble, substitute another author. Would you take a course from an instructor who proposed to teach you how to translate Goethe or Mallarmé?

The proper study of Latin revives the dying art of reading slowly. The best goals of the college classroom – reading rather than translating, memorization of key lyrics, close analysis of the Latin text – are also goals of the best high school teachers. Though the range and depth of reading increase in college, well-prepared students at every level have more fun with Catullus, find more in his language, and have a stronger appetite for more.

ACKNOWLEDGMENT

I am grateful to Ronnie Ancona for her salubrious comments about an earlier draft of this chapter.

NOTES

1 For a summary of work up to 1986, see Santirocco (1986: 179 n. 13). More recently, and with particular reference to Catullus, see Hutchinson (2003).
2 Krostenko (2001a) places this subject in its full cultural context. Words like *lepidus* (used programmatically in c. 1, *lepidum nouum libellum*), *elegans*, and *uenustus* and their compounds, which appear 27 times in Catullus, have a social meaning peculiar to Catullus' Roman setting. See also Krostenko, this volume.
3 For a vivid account of warfare and politics in Catullus' lifetime and immediately afterward, see Holland (2004). Though written by a novelist, this is non-fiction and more readable than the standard histories of the period. Highly recommended for undergraduate reading.
4 I know only of Foster (1994).

GUIDE TO FURTHER READING

Readings cited by Ancona and Hallett (this volume) that are not aimed at AP will also be of interest to undergraduate students and their instructors, particularly the complete annotated editions of Forsyth (1986), Garrison (2004), and Quinn (1973a). These are written primarily for adults reading Catullus for the first or second time. Commentaries for more advanced students will also be useful. Though flawed by its omission of 32 poems thought to be indecent, C. J. Fordyce's commentary (1961) still carries authority. A more recent edition with commentary is D. F. S. Thomson's (1997). Three important books about the arrangement of Catullus' poems and the relations between them are Marilyn Skinner's *Catullus' Passer* (1981) and *Catullus in Verona* (2003) and Helena Dettmer's *Love by the Numbers* (1997). A standard Latin grammar is essential to settle arguments about how Latin works. Though anything but new, J. H. Allen and Greenough's *New Latin Grammar* (1888, with numerous subsequent revisions, editors, and publishers, most recently Dover Publications, 2006) is the classic reference for readers of Latin at any level.

Catullus is the earliest of many writers stimulated by the tumultuous, gruesome, and depraved goings-on of the Roman Republic in its final years. Several modern authors have also written about the age of Catullus, Cicero, and Caesar. Written with the imaginative grasp and pace of a novelist, Tom Holland's nonfiction *Rubicon: The Last Years of the Roman Republic* (2004) describes the political events surrounding the life of Catullus. At least three recent novelists have built entire series around this period that undergraduate readers will find interesting: Benita Kane Jaro (1988, 2002a, 2002b); Coleen McCullough – Masters of Rome series (1990, 1991, 1993, 1996, 1997, 2002); Steven Saylor – Roma sub Rosa series on the investigations of Gordianus the Finder (1991, 1992, 1993, 1995, 1996, 1997, 1999, 2000, 2002, 2005). The classic in this genre is Thornton Wilder (1961).

WORKS CITED

Allen, J. H., and J. B. Greenough. 1888. *New Latin Grammar for Schools and Colleges, Founded on Comparative Grammar.* Boston.
Dettmer, H. 1997. *Love by the Numbers: Form and Meaning in the Poetry of Catullus.* New York.
Foster, J. 1994. "Poetry and Friendship: Catullus 35." *Liverpool Classical Monthly* 19.7–8: 114–21.
Fordyce, C. J., ed. 1961. *Catullus: A Commentary.* Oxford.
Forsyth, P. Y. 1986. *The Poems of Catullus: A Teaching Text.* Lanham, MD.
Garrison, D. H. 1992. "The *locus inamoenus*: Another Part of the Forest." *Arion*³ 2.1: 98–114.
Garrison, D. H. 2004. *The Student's Catullus.* 3rd edn. Norman, OK.
Holland, T. 2004. *Rubicon: The Last Years of the Roman Republic.* New York.
Hutchinson, G. O. 2003. "The Catullan Corpus, Greek Epigram, and the Poetry of Objects." *Classical Quarterly* n.s. 53.1: 206–21.
Jaro, B. K. 1988. *The Key.* New York.
Jaro, B. K. 2002a. *The Lock.* Wauconda, IL.
Jaro, B. K. 2002b. *The Door in the Wall.* Wauconda, IL.
Krostenko, B. A. 2001a. *Cicero, Catullus, and the Language of Social Performance.* Chicago and London.
Lawall, G. 1967. *Theocritus' Coan Pastorals: A Poetry Book.* Washington, DC.
McCullough, C. 1990. *The First Man in Rome.* New York.
McCullough, C. 1991. *The Grass Crown.* New York.
McCullough, C. 1993. *Fortune's Favorites.* New York.
McCullough, C. 1996. *Caesar's Women.* New York.
McCullough, C. 1997. *Caesar: A Novel.* New York.
McCullough, C. 2002. *The October Horse.* New York.
Quinn, K., ed. 1973a. *Catullus: The Poems.* 2nd edn. London and Basingstoke.

Santirocco, M. S. 1986. *Unity and Design in Horace's Odes.* Chapel Hill, NC.

Saylor, S. 1991. *Roman Blood.* New York.

Saylor, S. 1992. *Arms of Nemesis.* New York.

Saylor, S. 1993. *Catalina's Riddle.* New York.

Saylor, S. 1995. *The Venus Throw.* New York.

Saylor, S. 1996. *A Murder on the Appian Way.* New York.

Saylor, S. 1997. *The House of the Vestals.* New York.

Saylor, S. 1999. *Rubicon.* New York.

Saylor, S. 2000. *Last Seen in Massilia.* New York.

Saylor, S. 2002. *A Mist of Prophecies.* New York.

Saylor, S. 2004. *The Judgment of Caesar.* New York.

Saylor, S. 2005. *A Gladiator Dies Only Once.* New York.

Skinner, M. B. 1981. *Catullus' Passer: The Arrangement of the Book of Polymetric Poems.* New York.

Skinner, M. B. 2003. *Catullus in Verona: A Reading of the Elegiac* Libellus, *Poems 65–116.* Columbus, OH.

Thomson, D. F. S., ed. 1997. *Catullus, Edited with a Textual and Interpretative Commentary.* Toronto.

Van Sickle, J. 1980. "The Book-Roll and Some Conventions of the Poetic Book." *Arethusa* 13: 5–42.

Van Sickle. 1989. "The Hellenistic Background." *Augustan Age* 9: 42–8.

Wilder, T. 1961 [1948]. *The Ides of March.* Harmondsworth.

PART VIII

Translation

CHAPTER TWENTY-SEVEN

Translating Catullus

Elizabeth Vandiver

Compared to other Roman poets, Catullus came late to English translation.[1] Although the Voss edition of 1684 made the Catullan corpus easily available in England, the first complete English translation appeared only in 1795 (Gaisser 2001: xxviii–xxxii).[2] Various poets had produced translations of individual poems even before Voss's edition; for instance, Sidney, Campion, Jonson, and Crashaw all translated at least one or two poems, and Lovelace translated 13 (Gaisser 2001: 4–17, 26). However, many of these early versions were free adaptations rather than actual translations.

The tendency to adaptation was undoubtedly caused, in part, by the fact that the first English poets who turned their attention to Catullus were not coming to him fresh, so to speak; their reception of Catullus was deeply influenced by continental imitations and adaptations. Catullus "arrived in England surrounded by generations of European . . . literary and scholarly interpretation and there was no possibility for English readers and poets to have an unmediated encounter with him" (Gaisser 2001: xxix). The familiarity of some of the short poems' themes made those poems (particularly ones about Lesbia) seem easily available for adaptation; however, the idea of translating the entire corpus was another matter. The sheer variety of Catullus' poems, both in form and in content, his unabashed use of obscenity, and the Alexandrianism of the long poems apparently discouraged translation (see Gaisser 2001: xxxii–xxxiv).

These aspects of Catullus remained problematic for translators throughout the nineteenth and twentieth centuries and are no less so today, although the last several decades have seen a steady stream of new translations of Catullus.[3] The precise focus of the difficulties changes – so, for instance, Catullus' obscenity poses a different challenge for the translator in the twenty-first century than it did in the nineteenth century. The modern-day translator has to grapple with rendering the precise register of the obscenity, while her nineteenth-century predecessor was far more likely to omit or to bowdlerize beyond recognition. But the complexity of rendering Catullus' many tones into English remains unchanged.

Some of these problems are inherent in translation itself, some are caused by the nature of the Latin language and its differences from English, and some are specific to this particular poet. This chapter discusses these difficulties and different translators' strategies for meeting them. I will begin with a brief discussion of the project of translation in general and the pitfalls of poetic translation in particular. I will then discuss problems of translating Latin into English and specific difficulties that Catullus' own poetics pose for translators.

"Poetry is What is Lost in Translation"

Robert Frost's often-quoted statement occurs as part of a discussion of "Stopping by Woods on a Snowy Evening." Frost says: "You've often heard me say – perhaps too often – that poetry is what is lost in translation. It is also what is lost in interpretation. That little poem means just what it says and it says what it means, nothing less but nothing more" (Untermeyer 1964: 18). Yet despite Frost's assertion that meaning is straightforward, it is never a simple matter to determine "what a poem means." Frost may claim that "Stopping By Woods on a Snowy Evening" in fact "means just what it says and . . . [says] what it means," but this leaves unaddressed the question of *how* it means, of what might be the relationship between the poem's form, sound, and vocabulary and its meaning. Surely Frost would agree that the poem's formal elements are crucial, since "poetry is what is lost in translation"; and yet even for native speakers of a poem's language, the exact relationship between form and content is deeply problematic. The critics whose work Frost was deprecating were native speakers of his own language, reading a poem in that shared common language, within a few years of the poem's creation. How much more impenetrable is the exact relationship between sound and sense when we are grappling with a poem written in another language, another era, and a radically different culture?

As Holmes says, poetic translations "differ from all other interpretative forms in that they also have the aim of being acts of poetry"; he suggests the term *metapoem* "for this specific literary form, with its double purpose as metaliterature and as primary literature" (Holmes 1988: 24, building on Barthes's terminology of "metalanguage"). Concerning the question of what form a metapoem should take, Holmes says that "no other problem of translation . . . has generated so much heat, and so little light, among the normative critics" (1988: 25). Different critics argue passionately for using equivalent verse-forms, for translating into native meters, and for translating into prose, and each of these options has arguments both for and against it.

Every translator of poetry must decide which of two goals is most important for the metapoem: to write poetry that succeeds *as poetry* in the target language, or to convey the tone, structure, and overall "feel" of the source text for those who cannot read the original language. Ideally, the translator would bridge this gap and perform both types of translation simultaneously; but while it is a rare translator who aims for one of these goals to the exclusion of the other, in practice it is seldom if ever possible to give equal prominence to both.

The question of which to privilege, the poetry of the target language or of the source text, affects every decision about vocabulary or form that the translator makes. Not only word choice but word placement, patterns, and sound are crucial in poetry, so much so that one could say that poetry *consists in* the deliberate arranging of words in certain patterns; the sound to a large extent makes the poetry. Since the sound of a poem depends not only on its words but also on its meter and structure, the translator has to decide from the outset whether and to what extent the original's form is crucial. Should the translator attempt to reproduce the meters of the original? Should she attempt to mimic the source text's sound, the interplay of alliteration, assonance, the use of particularly evocative words? Does a version that addresses only the lexical content of the original and gives no hint of its sound in fact *translate* the original at all? Consider, for example, Shakespeare's line "O, she doth teach the torches to burn bright" (*Romeo and Juliet* I.v). If we paraphrase "O, she shows the lights how to glow brightly," does the poetry remain? Or is it precisely the sound of the line that makes it beautiful, memorable, and moving – in short, that makes it poetry: the repetition of the sounds *t, ch, b,* and *r* in the words teach/torches/burn/bright, and in those same words the chiastic arrangement of long and short vowels with the short vowels followed by an r (teach, torch, burn, bright), the preponderance of monosyl-lables, the regular iambic pentameter? In this line, is the sound not far more impor-tant than the content; at the very least, is not the sound a primary means by which the sense is enhanced, and made to seem profound, to an extent that mere paraphrase of content cannot convey?

If sound trumps content, then we can understand the extreme view which claims that the only method for conveying poetry in translation is to "hear the sounds of the original while reading literal renditions" of the content (Baker 1998: 173, discussing Burnshaw 1960). On this view, the translation of poetry is impossible, and all that can honestly be offered a reader who does not know the source language is a paraphrase of the poem's basic content into prose that aims for the nearest possible lexical fidelity, while the rest of the poem – sound, meter, word placement, and so on – should be left to "speak for itself." Most translators would not agree with this assessment, which seems close to an argument of despair (and which, in fact, leaves unanswered many questions, not least among them what is meant by "lexical fidel-ity"), but different translators and translation-study theorists disagree about the degree to which any other approach to translating poetry can be successful.[4]

All of these issues confront the translator of any poetry, even when the source is one modern language and the target another, closely related modern language. But these difficulties become even more formidable when the translator is working not only across languages but across many centuries as well; in Hardwick's formulation, "translating words also involves translating or transplanting into the receiving culture the cultural framework within which an ancient text is embedded" (Hardwick 2000: 22). For the "cultural translation" of Catullus or of any Latin verse, issues of meter and of vocabulary are particularly important.

The Problem of Meter

The translator of any metrical poetry faces the question of what to do about meter; however, several factors exacerbate the difficulty for the would-be translator of Latin verse into modern English. Modern English poetry tends to shy away from formal metrical patterns, "effectively leaving only free verse to the translator, and leaving that in such a deadened form it often lacks even the ghost of some regular meter lurking behind the arras" (Willett 2001: 221). It is therefore difficult for a modern translator to use intricate or regular meters without giving the resulting poem an aura of archaism.

But even if a translator chooses to use strict meter, exact equivalency with Latin meters is not a simple matter; English meter is stress-based, but Latin meter was quantitative. Latin meter, that is, was built around the alternation of long and short syllables, not of stressed and unstressed ones (though stress accent, and its counterplay against the rhythm of syllabic length, was also an important element of Latin verse).[5] In addition, Latin meter was very regular; while substitution (i.e., replacing a long syllable by two short ones) was allowed in some metrical situations, Latin poetry had nothing corresponding to modern "free verse." Modern English speakers, therefore, are faced with a doubly foreign system in Latin (and for that matter Greek) poetry; both the quantitative basis of Latin meter and its extreme regularity are unfamiliar.

Catullus uses 11 different meters: Phalaecean hendecasyllabics, choliambics, Sapphic stanzas, glyconic stanzas, priapeans, the greater asclepiad, iambic trimeter, iambic tetrameter catalectic, galliambics, dactylic hexameter, and elegiac couplets. All of these meters were originally Greek and some of them probably had never been used in Latin before Catullus; the hendecasyllable, which Gaisser calls "the Catullan meter *par excellence*," apparently had formerly been quite rare even in Greek (Gaisser 1993: 4). By choosing to use Greek meters, Catullus marks his debt to the Alexandrians and lays out an important aspect of his poetic program (see Gaisser 2001: xvii; Thomson 1997: 19–20); to ignore his metrics, therefore, is to ignore a central part of his achievement.

A translator who hopes to convey some sense of Catullus' metrics has two choices: to use native English meters, which are fundamentally different from Latin meters, on the assumption that there is some sort of equivalency of "feel" or "mood" between the two systems; or to try to replicate Catullan metrical patterns in English. Catullus' earliest translators favored the first of these approaches; it does not seem to have occurred to poets such as Raleigh or Campion to try to translate Catullus into anything *but* "natural" English meters, which usually meant iambics. So, for instance, Campion turns the hendecasyllables of poem 5 into iambic pentameter:

> My sweetest Lesbia, let us live and love;
> And though the sager sort our deeds reprove,
> Let us not weigh them: heaven's great lamps do dive
> Into their west, and straight again revive;
> But, soon as once set is our little light,
> Then must we sleep one ever-during night.
>   (Campion n.d.: 8)

But however pleasant this is to the English-speaker's ear, it in no way replicates or even suggests the hendecasyllables of the original; furthermore, the use of rhymed couplets implies a connection between pairs of lines that is entirely absent in Catullus' poem.

The other possible approach is to try to replicate the metrical patterns of Latin in English. However, this, too, runs the risk of fundamental distortion. It is certainly possible to create stress-accent patterns in English that correspond to the quantitative patterns of Latin, but such meters do not come easily or naturally to English, and English readers are not trained to "hear" them. It is a very rare translator who can write English equivalents of Catullan meter that do not sound forced, and in which the meter emerges from the natural pronunciation of the lines.[6] Tennyson did about as well as can be done with his *jeu d'esprit* "Hendecasyllables":

> O you chorus of indolent reviewers,
> Irresponsible, indolent reviewers,
> Look, I come to the test, a tiny poem
> All composed in a metre of Catullus.
> (Ricks 1989: 616)

For those who can "hear" Catullus' Latin hendecasyllables in their mind's ear, Tennyson's feat is impressive; but for a reader who did not already know the Latin meter, I question the extent to which even Tennyson's poem would convey it.

Considering the profound differences between Latin and English metrics, it is not surprising that the metrical strategies adopted by recent translators of Catullus have varied widely and radically. In the mid-twentieth century, the fashion seemed to be to ignore meter, despite its importance in Catullus' poetic practice; so Copley's translation (1957 [1964 rpt.]) makes no attempt at any metrical patterns at all, either Latin-based or native, and as recently as 1974, Sesar followed the same method. Neither Copley nor Sesar mentions his choice to eschew meter in his introduction; apparently they both assume that this choice needs no justification, and that for twentieth-century readers, personal lyric automatically implies a completely free style. A corollary of this choice, of course, is that it foregrounds content to the complete diminution of form; at the very least, this choice implies that the form of Catullus' poems is incidental rather than essential.

More recently, however, the pendulum has swung back in the direction of translations that, if they do not actually attempt to reproduce Latin quantitative meters in English stress-meters, at the very least try to suggest the original meters. Two of Catullus' most recent translators, Mulroy and Green, both include careful and thoughtful descriptions and justifications of their own metrical practices (Mulroy 2002: xxxiii–xxxix; Green 2005: 27–32). Green aims for, and comes very close to achieving, a true recapitulation of Catullan meters in English, while Mulroy says that he has "attempted to capture the general effect of such rhythm in a way that is perceptible to English speakers" (Mulroy 2002: xxxiv). Which system is more effective is, of course, largely a matter of the reader's taste.[7]

Vocabulary and Lexical Fidelity

The translator's decision about meter dictates the form of the metapoem; decisions about word choice dictate its content. With each choice of word, the translator must negotiate a balance between reflecting the basic lexical meaning of the source text's words and conveying a sense of the poetic tone of that text. How much a translation should strive for "fidelity" to its original's meaning is, like everything else in translation, a hotly debated point.

At this point, we must consider what exactly is meant, or can be meant, by the idea of "lexical fidelity." On the very most basic level, obviously, the "same" meaning can be conveyed in two different languages; "the dog is black" and "canis niger est" convey the same basic information. But when we move beyond that level, the question of how or if the vocabulary of the source language can be represented by the vocabulary of the target language becomes far from simple. The exact resonance or semantic field of a word (even that of "dog" or "canis") is never the same from one language to another; any word a translator chooses will leave some meanings out and import others. In the case of Latin-to-English translation, this problem is exacerbated by the fact that the vocabulary of classical Latin is far smaller than the vocabulary of modern English.[8] The translator must choose precisely which resonance is at play in every word; but the choice of any one particular term in the target language ("dog" rather than "hound," "cur," "pooch," or "canine") already demolishes any kind of one-to-one correspondence of vocabulary between source and target texts, already chooses one semantic field and register, and already imposes one interpretation on the reader of the translation, without in any way signaling that such interpretation has happened.

Furthermore, Latin and English construct meaning very differently. For one thing, Latin is an inflected language, which uses the form of the words themselves rather than the order in which they appear in a sentence to construct meaning. While there are certainly situations in which Latin word order is fixed, overall it is far more flexible than English word order and poets exploited this aspect of the Latin language to great effect. Inflection also means that Latin is much more concise than English; an English translation almost invariably inflates the Latin original, because English simply takes more words to express an idea than Latin does. The translator Rolfe Humphries comments (1959: 61): "Latin does not have to use all those miserable little space-taking pronouns, articles, prepositions – he, she, it, the, an, a, of, to – words that, before you know it, creep in, like the termites they are, to eat away the whole fiber of a line." This difference in the verbal economy of the two languages causes particular difficulties for translators who strive for line-by-line correspondence between a Latin original and their own English versions. Such line-by-line correspondence is, of course, made even more difficult if the translator is also attempting metrical equivalence.

Thus far, I have been discussing difficulties of word choice in Latin-to-English translation in general; however, Catullus' specific vocabulary brings troubles of its own to the translator. The basic problems of word choice become even more complicated when we consider words that form part of the neoterics' key vocabulary. The first two lines of Catullus' introductory poem illustrate the problems neatly:

> Cui dono lepidum nouum libellum,
> arida modo pumice expolitum?[9]

To whom do I give this charming new little book, polished just now with dry pumice?

Lepidum, which means "charming" or "elegant," is one of the most important neoteric catch-words, and directly reflects the Callimachean *leptos* and *leptaleos*; by using it Catullus is announcing in his opening words that his book will be

Alexandrian, that his poems will be "slender" as were Callimachus'. Together with the diminutive *libellum*, "little book," and the adjective *nouum*, "new," this word sets out Catullus' poetic program, situates his work in a particular poetic tradition, and states his view about the type of poetry he is writing.

The book is new; it is small; and it is polished. *Arida modo pumice expolitum* refers, on one level, to actual production practices of ancient book-making; the scroll would quite literally be polished with pumice (see Quinn 1973a: 89). But *expolitum* here also has the metaphorical sense that "polished" carries in English; this is, perhaps, the only easy lexical choice in these two crucial first lines. The exact resonance of *lepidum* presents formidable problems for the translator; so, perhaps more surprisingly, does *libellum* (which literally means "little book"). Recent translations include: "new witty booklet" (Green 2005: 45); "debonair, new...booklet" (Mulroy 2002: 3); "this little book, polished, new" (Balmer 2004: 29); "a neat new booklet" (Lee 1990: 3). Witty, debonair, polished, neat – each of these choices foregrounds one aspect of *lepidum*, but none gives its full flavor. Three of these four sample translators agree on "booklet" for *libellum*; at first glance, this would seem to be the obvious choice, one which maintains lexical fidelity remarkably well – it is a diminutive, just as *libellum* is. But paradoxically, this apparently obvious choice severely distorts the implications of Catullus' word choice. "Booklet" in modern English carries connotations that are entirely wrong for Catullus' *nouum libellum*. Modern booklets are often results of cheap production, items that did not merit full book status. In addition, booklets are almost never literary; they are ephemeral, cheap, and perhaps a bit shoddy. They are, in short, the opposite of the *libellum ... arida modo pumice expolitum* of Catullus' poem, where he stresses the elegance and careful production of both the physical volume and its contents. Modern English, so far as I can ascertain, has no precisely equivalent term; although rather dated, the phrase "slim volume of verse" is the best candidate, and indeed Raphael and McLeish use it ("my brand-new slim volume," 1979: 25).

Lexical difficulties easily merge into cultural difficulties; at times, a word's meaning may be clear, but the associated resonances of that word with overall concepts can distort the reader's understanding of the poet's meaning. In Catullus' work, these problems are particularly obvious in three areas: issues of gender and sexuality (including Catullus' use of obscenities); issues of word-play and topical references; and issues of learned, Alexandrian obscurity. To clarify the problems the translator faces in each of these areas, I will now turn to discussion of three specific poems: 16, 84, and 68.107–14.

Sexual Invective and Obscenity

The assumptions of Catullus' society about gender and sexuality are not the assumptions of our own society; the problems this raises for the translator are illustrated forcefully by poem 16:

> Pedicabo ego uos et irrumabo,
> Aureli pathice et cinaede Furi,
> qui me ex uersiculis meis putastis,
> quod sunt molliculi, parum pudicum.

> nam castum esse decet pium poetam
> ipsum, uersiculos nihil necesse est;
> qui tum denique habent salem ac leporem,
> si sunt molliculi ac parum pudici,
> et quod pruriat incitare possunt,
> non dico pueris, sed his pilosis
> qui duros nequeunt mouere lumbos.
> uos, quod milia multa basiorum
> legistis, male me marem putatis?
> pedicabo ego uos et irrumabo.

This poem, which gives us Catullus' most significant statement about the relation-ship between the author and his work, is a veritable minefield for the translator. The most obvious difficulty is with rendering the obscenities of lines 1, 2, and 14; however, even leaving these lines aside for the moment, the rest of this poem is filled with key words, some of them drawing on Roman morality in general, some on Roman assumptions about sexuality, and some on the Catullan (and neoteric) poetic program. The terms *mollis, pudicus, pius, castus, sal, lepor, mas* are all problematic in translation:

> [You] think, based on my verses – which are rather soft (*mollis*) – that I am insufficiently decent (*pudicus*). For it is proper that the dutiful (*pius*) poet be chaste (*castus*), but there's no need at all that his little verses be so, which, after all, have salt (*sal*) and charm (*lepor*) if they are rather *mollis* and scarcely *pudicus*, and are able to incite what itches – I don't mean in boys, but in those hairy men who can't move their hard groins.[10] You, because you've read about many thousand kisses, think that I am a bad male (*male marem*)? *Pedicabo ego uos et irrumabo.*

"A translation aims to produce a new text that matters to one community the way another text matters to another" (Appiah 1993: 425); to make poem 16 thus "matter" in translation, every one of the Latin words I have quoted above would require a whole discourse, a whole apparatus of editorial notes. Such a discussion is beyond my scope here; let us focus in on the most obvious problem of this poem, the obscene threats with which it opens and closes.

What do these lines mean? Martin offers what he calls "a prose paraphrase, far from adequate in its brio, but sufficiently explicit: 'I will rape the pair of you as each of you prefers it: you rectally, anal-receptive Furius, and you orally, oral-receptive Aurelius' " (Martin 1992: 60). This does, indeed, convey some sense of the lexical meaning of the words *pedicare, irrumare, pathicus,* and *cinaedus,* though as we shall see Martin's treatment of *pathicus* and *cinaedus* are not quite accurate, and he also elides the fact that Catullus threatens both men with both forms of assault. What this prose paraphrase does not do is to convey any sense of poetry; nor, for that matter, does it convey the cultural assumptions behind Catullus' insults. As Williams has said:

> Here we run into the basic difficulty confronting both the translator and the ethnog-rapher: how to describe one culture in another's language. On the one hand, it has often been noted that Latin has no words identical in meaning to "homosexual" or "hetero-sexual" . . . On the other hand, many of the terms that Romans did use are untranslat-able: *stuprum* and *pudicitia* are far more specific than "debauchery" and "chastity," and *cinaedus* is not the same as "faggot" (C. A. Williams 1999: 6).

Martin's prose paraphrase does not translate Catullus' *culture* into terms that are comprehensible to the modern English-speaking reader. All four of the terms used in the first two lines of poem 16 – *pedicare, irrumare, cinaedus,* and *pathicus* – align themselves quite strictly with Roman views of masculinity and its proper constitution; the translator's difficulty lies in the fact that these words do not "map" onto the assumptions about sexuality, sexual invective, and gender roles that inform modern British and American culture, and thus modern English language.

Since English does not have precise equivalents for these four words, the translator must either give an excruciatingly literal rendition (as Martin does), which is in effect more a commentary upon the poem than a translation of it, or must try to find some modern register of obscene insult that parallels, or is the "equivalent of," the Catullan insult. Here, however, the difference between Roman and modern views of what masculinity *is* becomes crucial. As Williams fully demonstrates, for the Roman male the act of penetrating another male was an assertion of masculinity; the act of being penetrated was an admission of non-masculine status (C. A. Williams 1999). But modern English slang terms that use references to male homosexuality as insults by no means correspond exactly to the Latin terms. *Pathicus* is, at least, easy to define; it "denotes a male who is anally penetrated" (C. A. Williams 1999: 175).[11] *Cinaedus* is far more difficult to define precisely, since it refers to a whole category of non- or anti-masculine behaviors; the *cinaedus* was "a man who failed to be fully masculine, whose effeminacy showed itself in such symptoms as feminine clothing and mannerisms and a lascivious and oversexed demeanor" (C. A. Williams 1999: 178). The *cinaedus'* effeminacy could manifest itself in a desire to be penetrated, but was by no means limited to such activities; indeed, a *cinaedus* could engage in sex with women (C. A. Williams 1999: 177–8). Clearly, "queen," "faggot," and so on are by no means exact equivalents of *pathicus* and *cinaedus*; still less do we have any terms with which one male can, by threatening another male with oral penetration, assert his own hypermasculinity. But this is the sense of *irrumare*, the term in these lines that seems to cause translators the most trouble.

English lacks a single word meaning "to penetrate orally."[12] *Irrumabo* thus defies exact lexical transference into English, since we are dealing not just with a missing term but with an entirely different way of conceptualizing the act in question; English speakers tend to assume that in an act of oral sex, the owner of the mouth is the agent and the owner of the genitals the passive recipient. As Fitzgerald says, "In English the action, even when degrading to the person who performs it, is all on the side of the fellator" (1995: 65). This difference in the way the act of oral penetration is viewed seems to exercise an astonishing limiting force on the imagination of some translators, so much so that at times they even mistake who is the penetrating party in *irrumabo* – for instance, Sisson renders *irrumabo* as "I'll . . . suck your pricks" (1967: 35) – or omit the second threat entirely (Myers and Ormsby 1970: 23). Green uses the noun "sucks," as do Raphael and McLeish, but here again the English slang term seems to imply that the speaker will fellate, not orally rape, the recipient of the insult (Green 2005: 63; Raphael and McLeish 1979: 37).[13] Lee's "stuff your gobs" is probably very effective for British readers, but it is meaningless to Americans (1990:19); Balmer's "get stuffed" does not specify that the mouth is the target and also elides the first-person singular of Catullus' threat (2004: 57). Mulroy's "rape you front and back" makes sense to readers who know the term *irrumabo*, but I am uncertain whether a reader encountering this poem for the first time in Mulroy's translation would understand that the "front" in question was the mouth (2002: 15).

This may seem like overanalysis of a few obscene terms, but the obscenity here is not incidental or unimportant. By threatening Furius and Aurelius with direct and vivid displays of his masculinity, Catullus is making a statement about the nature of poetry and its relationship to its author; and by intertwining these obscene threats with concepts of traditional Roman morality such as *pudicitia* and *pietas*, he is situating both his poetry and his own masculinity in a much larger (and more complex) context. Indeed, he is stressing the deeply paradoxical nature of this connection; he claims the virtues of *pietas* and *castitudo* for himself at the same time that, as Selden says, he threatens those who have questioned his *pietas* with *stuprum*, a "forcible violation...[which] was by no stretch of the imagination compatible with either *pietas* or *castitudo*" (Selden 1992: 478; on *stuprum*, see J. N. Adams 1982: 200–1; C. A. Williams 1999: 96–124).

We cannot, therefore, simply elide the obscenity out of this poem or render it as a generalized, non-specific threat, as Copley notoriously does with his translation "Nuts to you, boys, nuts and go to hell" (1957 [1964 rpt.]: 19); here I must disagree with Green's statement that "the first and last lines...are surely no more than a baroque extension of the kind of threat typified in English by the phrase, 'Fuck you,' without any suggestion of actual sexual intercourse" (Green 2005: 218). Certainly, Catullus is not anticipating a genuine physical encounter with Furius and Aurelius; and certainly, obscene threats in any language do not usually carry any assumption of actual sexual assault. But poem 16 – whose main point is the exact relationship between the erotic encounters described in poetry and the actual masculinity of the poet – works directly against the "normal" assumption that sexual terms are mere generalized threats by drawing direct and specific attention to the precise sexual and physical content of those terms. (See Wray 2001: 185; Selden 1992: 477–89.) Catullus asks us – forces us? – to pay attention not only to the tenor of these threats but also to their vehicle; the basic physical meaning, if I may put it this way, thrusts itself upon us. We are not to take Catullus "literally" – there was no need for Furius and Aurelius to lock their doors at night. And yet we are to take him "literally" – the acts described prove his masculine status, especially in comparison with the feminized status of the addressees Furius and Aurelius, and by implication of every reader: "The pair of slurs that the lyric levels against its addressees...are not simply gratuitous insults, but accurately describe the reader's submission – not to the poet's person, but – to the personified pressure of his text" (Selden 1992: 488). Catullus here uses words as acts with which to prove his masculinity; those words are both descriptive and performative, in that the words now perform the same assertion of masculinity that their literal meaning describes.[14]

From this brief discussion, it is very clear the translator is faced with a formidable difficulty; the exact register of the obscene insults is crucial to the entire sense of poem 16, and yet there is no direct way to render these terms in English. One can use technical terms that are unlikely to be familiar to most readers (so Goold gives "catamite" for *pathicus*, 1983: 52); or one can use generalized insults such as Mulroy's "queer" for *pathicus* and "nymphomaniac" for *cinaedus* (2002: 15), or Green's "queen" and "faggot" (2005: 63). Either way, the Roman cultural assumptions fail to come through and thus the point of the poem, Catullus' forceful assertion of his own penetrative masculinity, is lost.

In this instance, specificity that does not provide lexical fidelity is perhaps the best choice. Balmer renders *pathicus* as "prick-sucker" and *cinaedus* as "dick-lover" (2004: 57); while the first of these changes the practice in question[15] and the second is completely non-specific, still they perhaps come closer than other English possibilities to conveying the contemptuous tone and register of Catullus' insults against Aurelius and Furius. But these choices reinforce the same shift between active and passive that we observed with translators' attempts at *irrumabo*; Catullus is not, in fact, casting Aurelius as a *fellator*. We are left, then, with the uncomfortable conclusion that English translation simply cannot render one of Catullus' most important statements of his own poetic credo; here, more than the poetry is lost in translation.[16]

When the Sound *Is* the Sense

Poem 16 illustrates the difficulty of "cultural translation"; no less vexing for the translator are poems in which the point of the piece rides mainly (if not entirely) on its sounds and word-play. Among these, the most intractable is poem 84. Skinner remarks that "if there is one piece in the collection that displays the wit and technical brilliance . . . essential to the neoteric epigram, . . . it is certainly poem 84, the splendid lampoon – justly famous even in antiquity – on Arrius' mistreatment of the aspirate" (2003: 104). Splendid though this poem is in Latin, however, the modern reader confronting it *in translation* is almost inevitably left with the feeling that something must have been funny about this poem, but that whatever it was eludes us.

> Chommoda dicebat, si quando commoda uellet
> dicere, et insidias Arrius hinsidias,
> et tum mirifice sperabat se esse locutum,
> cum quantum poterat dixerat hinsidias.
> credo, sic mater, sic liber auunculus eius,
> sic maternus auus dixerat atque auia.
> hoc misso in Syriam requierant omnibus aures:
> audibant eadem haec leniter et leuiter,
> nec sibi postilla metuebant talia uerba,
> cum subito affertur nuntius horribilis,
> Ionios fluctus, postquam illus Arrius isset,
> iam non Ionios esse sed Hionios.

The problems this presents to the translator are formidable indeed. The most obvious question is what precisely is the *point*: why are Arrius' misaspirations funny, or at least worth satirizing? Kelley's absolutely literal prose translation (1891: 91–2) demonstrates that the answer is not transparently obvious from the poem's content:

Whenever Arrius had occasion to say the word *commodious* he would say *chommodious*, and *hinsidious* when he meant *insidious*, and he hoped that he had spoken marvellously well when he had aspirated *hinsidious* as much as he could. I believe his mother, his uncle Liber, and his maternal grandfather and grandmother spoke thus. When he was sent into

Syria, our ears all had a respite, for they heard the same words pronounced smoothly and lightly. Thenceforth they had no dread of them, when suddenly the horrible news arrives, that the Ionian waves, after Arrius had gone thither, were no longer *Ionian* but *Hionian*.

This translation is lexically precise and a complete failure at conveying the slightest hint of the original poem's *sal* and *lepor*; in particular, it gives no indication of the word-play that forms the poem's punch-line. The last four words are almost certainly a bilingual pun, where the Latin *Hionios* represents the Greek *chioneous*, "snowy." As Quinn says, Arrius' aspirates have "inflicted a chill upon the Ionian" (Quinn 1973a: 421; cf. E. Harrison 1915: 198, Green 2005: 261).

I have argued elsewhere that this poem's point lies in the actual sounds that Catullus uses to create the poem; the placement not only of the aspirates but also of the sibilants mimics the mistakes of Arrius' over-breathy pronunciation (Vandiver 1990). In short, the interplay of sound and sense is not an ornament to this poem, but *is* the poem. In translation, when these elements are lost, the poem falls very flat. If sounds are what matter in this poem, then might this be the place where the Zukofsky version comes into its own? To my mind, the answer must be no. The Zukofsky does achieve some remarkable parallel sounds spelled as English words; for instance, the end of line 11, *postquam illuc Arrius isset*, is rendered as "post qualm ill look Arrius' is it?" (1969: n.p.). Apart from omitting the elision of *postquam* and *illuc* (which would be pronounced, more or less, *postquilluc*), the correspondence of sound is striking; but the sense of the translation does not resemble, let alone reproduce, the sense of the original. This is sound devoid of any coherent sense, sound overprivileged to the exclusion of meaning. This fails in the opposite direction from Kelley's literal prose paraphrase, but is no less a failure.

Most translators are interested in conveying the poem's meaning, however; and the fact that this poem deals with the aspirate presents translators, particularly British translators, with a great temptation. Do we not have a ready-made strategy for translation, a perfect fit, if we simply turn Arrius into a Cockney, whom we can easily call 'Arry? The 1876 version by Hummel and Brodribb demonstrates how this particular act of cultural translation could work:

> Whenever 'Arry tried to sound
>   An H, his care was unavailing;
> He always spoke of 'orse and 'ound,
>   And all his kinsfolk had that failing.
> Peace to our ears. He went from home;
>   But tidings came that grieved us bitterly –
> That 'Arry, while he stayed at Rome,
>   Enjoyed his 'oliday in Hitaly.
>   (Hummel and Brodribb 1876: 15)

This is an example of "domesticating" translation with a vengeance. Not a clue remains to tell us that this was ever a Latin poem; not a trace of strangeness, of cultural "otherness," is left behind. This version also highlights the conceptual pitfalls involved in translating the Roman social system into the nineteenth-century British one. The picture of "'Arry" as a *parvenu* trying to pass himself off as upper-class, discussing hunting ("'orse and 'ound") and taking a holiday in Italy, is at least a partial cultural fit for the picture of Arrius as a provincial trying to sound urbane. But the fit is only partial, and perhaps deceptive. Probably Catullus is indeed satirizing a social upstart, the bombastic orator Q. Arrius, who Cicero tells us rose well beyond the level of his abilities (*Brut.* 242–3; for a discussion of the identification, see Skinner 2003: 105–7). More generally, Catullus may be mocking any speaker who tries to sound sophisticated and fails miserably. But the situation is far from simple, especially when we remember that Catullus himself was a provincial. The lens of the British class system is not, perhaps, the most helpful one through which to view this poem. However, the temptation to Anglicize not just the language of poem 84 but its entire social situation is a powerful and long-lasting one. For Raphael and McLeish, for instance, Arrius becomes "Alf" instead of 'Arry (1979: 105). Their version too, like Hummel and Brodribb's, makes assumptions of class in such phrases as "That's our Alf"; not only the nickname but the use of "our" almost as an honorific before a family member's name are class-linked.

A middle ground between painful literacy and over-domestication would seem desirable, and in fact many modern translators have attempted such a version. Most modern translators let the subject's name remain "Arrius," not 'Arry or Alf (e.g., Whigham 1966; Sesar 1974; Goold 1983; Martin 1990; Lee 1990; Mulroy 2002; Green 2005).[17] However, almost all these translators avoid the problem of an aspirated *consonant* (which is meaningless to most English speakers) and choose a word beginning with a vowel to translate *commoda*; so, Arrius says such things as "hadvantages" (Goold 1983: 201), "hemoluments" (Lee 1990: 131) or, in Martin's version, threatens his listeners with "hawful hinsidious hach-shuns" (1989: 121); Green stays closer to the Latin sounds by rendering *chommoda* as "chommodore." In almost all modern versions, the Ionian Sea of the last line still becomes Hionian – and fails to be funny. Sesar sends Arrius to Asia rather than the Ionian Sea, and translates *Hionios* as "Hasiatic" (1974: n.p.). However, this shift does not significantly improve the humor of the English version, and so the overall problem still remains, in Sesar as in other modern translators – why is the poem funny?

Carmina Battiadae: The Alexandrian Catullus

Poem 16 presented us with problems of vocabulary choice, especially connected with cultural concepts; poem 84 foregrounded issues of sound and its interactions with sense. The final translation crux that we shall consider is how to handle Catullus' learned allusions and mythological references, which are especially prominent in the long poems. Should such references be made self-explanatory or at least recognizable, or should they be left obscure? For instance, how should a translator render *falsiparens Amphitryoniades* (68.112)? Literally, this means "the false-parented son of Amphitryon." To understand this term, the reader must recognize a reference to Heracles, and to the story of Heracles' parentage; Zeus seduced Alcmena by disguising himself as her husband Amphitryon, and their union resulted in the birth of Heracles. Very few modern readers, however, are likely immediately to recognize this back story; very few will have any sense at all of who the false-parented son of Amphitryon might be. Should the translator, then, simply change those words to "Heracles" (or Hercules), which is, after all, what they "mean"? But if the translator simply says "Heracles," then the whole Catullan *flavor*, the tone of poem 68 that does so much to make it what it is, is lost. Such a translation not only removes the allusivity, but also masks the fact that *audit falsiparens Amphitryoniades* is a three-word pentameter, a dazzling metrical achievement and one that displays Catullus' Alexandrianism at its most accomplished. Fordyce's comment bears repeating: "The circumlocution, the compound . . . , the patronymic form, and the rhythm make this one of the most Greek-sounding lines in Latin" (1961: 356).

So much for the line itself; the difficulties of translating this phrase are increased by the context in which it is located. Catullus here is using the story of Laodamia and Protesilaus as a comparandum for his own affair with his unnamed *domina*;[18] within that comparison, the pit (*barathrum*) that Heracles once dug is cited as a comparandum for the depth of Laodamia's passion. Allusions are nested inside one another here to an extent that makes the passage all but incomprehensible to any but the most mythologically sophisticated reader. The passage refers to the *barathrum*

> quale ferunt Grai Pheneum prope Cyllenaeum
>   siccare emulsa pingue palude solum,
> quod quondam caesis montis fodisse medullis
>   audit falsiparens Amphitryoniades,
> tempore quo certa Stymphalia monstra sagitta
>   perculit imperio deterioris eri,
> pluribus ut caeli tereretur ianua diuis,
>   Hebe nec longa uirginitate foret.

Such as the Greeks say, near Cyllenaean Pheneus, dries the rich soil as the marsh is drained, which once the false-parented son of Amphitryon is said to have dug through the cut marrow of the mountain, at the time when with a sure arrow he killed the Stymphalian monsters at the order of a lesser master, so that the door of the sky might be trodden by more gods and that Hebe might not be in long virginity. (68.109–16)

Not only Heracles' birth story, but his famous labors, his *parerga*, his service to his cousin Eurystheus (the unworthy master of line 14), and his eventual apotheosis and marriage to Hebe are all referenced here, in terms as elusive and as allusive as possible. Indeed, this passage is so convoluted that some critics think it is meant as a spoof of neoteric poetic practice; so, for instance, Skinner says that these references are "heaped up paratactically, almost as a travesty of the mannerisms of Alexandrian narrative" and calls the Heracles exemplum "the most precious and contrived passage in poem 68" (2003: 162–3). Clearly, the words *falsiparens Amphitryoniades* carry a great deal of Alexandrian weight; what can the translator do with them?

As with the other passages we have examined, translators' approaches run the full gamut of possibilities, from Myers and Ormsby's simple "Hercules" to Green's "Amphitryon's falsely ascribed offspring" (Myers and Ormsby 1970: 139; Green 2005: 175–6). Mulroy refers to "Amphitryon's pseudo-son" (2002: 86), while Raphael and Macleish have a foot in both camps with "Hercules, Greek-named 'son of Amphitryon'" (Raphael and McLeish 1979: 97). Lee chooses the completely literal (and to most readers incomprehensible) "false-fathered Amphitryóniades" (1990: 119). Lee includes an endnote explaining the sense of this phrase; others, including Green and Mulroy, also provide explanatory notes (Lee 1990: 174–5;

Mulroy 2002: 88; Green 2005: 253–4). Is this the best possibility for dealing with Catullan allusivity, to follow, in effect, Burnshaw's recommendation of letting the original speak its own sounds and then providing a literal paraphrase (or explanation)? Of the three problems we have discussed, this is in some ways the most intractable, for it involves the Alexandrianism of the neoterics, which is even more resistant to cultural translation than is the sexual invective of poem 16 or the word-play of poem 84.

There are no clear paths out of these labyrinths; rather than offering answers, I want to end this chapter by looking at Catullus' own practice of translation.

Catullus Translates

We are fortunate to have two poems (51 and 66) in which Catullus himself undertook the translator's task. The first of these translates a poem by Sappho; the second, a poem by Callimachus. As Hooley says, "Twenty centuries ago Catullus was translating Sappho and Callimachus and in so doing was allowing us a glimpse into the operations of his own creative intellect, and, consequently, into the heart of his poetry as a whole" (Hooley 1988: 15). Only fragments of the Callimachean original remain, which makes sustained comparison difficult;[19] however, poem 51 reproduces the three surviving stanzas of Sappho 31, thus allowing us to compare the two poems (see E. Greene 1999a and this volume; Janan 1994: 72–6; Miller 1994: 101–7; Wormell 1966: 187–94; Wray 2001: 88–93).

Greene translates both poems and discusses the relationship of the Catullan version to the Sapphic original elsewhere in this volume; therefore I will not reproduce the poems here, but will confine my remarks to a few points of interest for our contemplation of Catullan translation. First, Catullus reproduces the Greek meter with great fidelity.[20] Given the degree to which the entire Catullan corpus is a metrical tour de force, it perhaps should not come as a surprise that he considers form of the utmost importance, but the implications are worth considering; those English-language translators who try to convey Catullus' own meters in English are following Catullan practice more closely than translators who use "native" English metrics and verseforms. But it is equally important to notice that Catullus departs quite noticeably from his original's content in several instances. Even if we sidestep the question of the *otium* stanza's relationship to the rest of the poem, it is still notable that Catullus adds several striking images and leaves out others; there is no "double night" in Sappho and no "greener than grass" in Catullus. The unnamed "he" of Sappho's poem equals the gods but does not surpass them; Catullus' beloved only laughs, but does not speak. And, as Janan notes, where Sappho uses the first-person singular, in Catullus the verbs describing the effect of Lesbia upon him are all third-person: "no 'I' remains within the words of the strophe" (Janan 1994: 74).

Perhaps most strikingly, Catullus includes the name of his *puella* at least once[21] (*nam simul te,/ Lesbia, aspexi, nihil est super mi . . .*), where the addressee of Sappho's poem remains anonymous. Catullus thus domesticates his translation by bringing it specifically into his own time and his own imaginative world; in this regard, Ben Jonson's adaptation of poem 5 follows in the translative path Catullus has laid out, as Jonson makes the poem applicable to the situation in his play *Volpone* by substituting the name of Mosca's beloved Celia in the place of Catullus' Lesbia:

> Come, my Celia, let us prove,
> While we can, the sports of love.
> Time will not be ours for ever;
> He, at length, our good will sever.
> Spend not then his gifts in vain.
> Suns that set may rise again;
> But if once we lose this light,
> 'Tis with us perpetual night.
>   (III.vii; Jonson 1983: 133–4)

In short, Catullus' rendering of Sappho goes beyond what most modern theorists would consider strict translation, and moves instead into the realm of adaptation.

If we take Catullus' own translation practice as normative, then we can surmise that he would disdain the metrical adaptiveness of Raleigh and Campion, preferring the strict metrical equivalency of Green; but he would also eschew the line-for-line equivalency of content of Green or Mulroy, and might approve more of the free adaptiveness of Jonson. His own translations foreground "cultural translation" of the sort that adapts the original to its target culture; they make no attempt to preserve the sense of the original's different culture and different context.

In his story "Pierre Menard, Autor del Quijote," Borges presents the paradox that a word-for-word recreation of Cervantes' language, written in the twentieth century, is an entirely different text from the seventeenth-century original; the sameness between the texts is a mark not of their identity but of their difference (Borges 1954: 45–57). Are translators who try to convey a sense of Catullus' culture to modern readers falling victim to this same Borgesian paradox, and giving their readers not similarity but increased difference? As with any other question about translation and metapoetics, there are no simple answers; all translators can do is "celebrate their Catullus"[22] and trust to the power of his *libellus* to endure, for future readers to re-create, in English as well as in Latin.

NOTES

1 I will limit my discussion here to English-language translations, but *mutatis mutandis* the problems, questions, and strategies I describe in this chapter could apply to translations of Catullus into other languages as well.

2 The 1795 translation is anonymous but "is generally acknowledged to be the work of a physician and scholar named John Nott" (Gaisser 2001: xxxii).

3 These include, most recently, Peter Green's magnificent 2005 translation, which appeared just in time to be considered in this chapter.

4 The (in)famous Zukofsky translation of Catullus (1969) agrees that sound is foremost in poetry but, instead of following Burnshaw's recommendation of giving a lexically precise prose paraphrase of the original and leaving the reader to encounter the sounds of the source text in the original language, the Zukofsky version transposes the sounds of Catullus' Latin into English that is, often, nonsense (at least at first reading). For sympathetic discussions of the Zukofsky translation, see Hooley (1988: 55–69); Wray (2001: 40–2).

5 For a thorough and very helpful discussion of the difference in Latin and English metrics, see Green (2005: 27–32).

6 Peter Green comes as close to achieving this as anyone ever has, but even he at times has to resort to accent marks to indicate where the stress should fall in a particular line; see, for instance, his translation of poem 68.67: "He opened up énclosed land with a spacious driveway" (2005: 173), and his discussion of his use of accent marks: "I count it as a kind of failure when I need to nudge the reader, as is sometimes unavoidable, with diacritical signs" (2005: 31).

7 Interestingly, Goold includes an extremely thorough description of Catullan meters, with examples of English equivalents, but does not use these equivalent meters in his own translation (Goold 1983: 19–27). He comments that "Catullus should be read in Latin and aloud" (p. 19).

8 On this point, see Wilson's useful discussion of *puella* (2005: 33).

9 I use Thomson's (1997) text throughout.

10 On this ambiguous phrase and its probable reference to the movements of the penetrated partner in anal intercourse (described by the verb *ceuere*), see Selden (1992: 485). On *ceuere*, see also C. A. Williams (1999: 161–2); however, Williams understands *duros… mouere lumbos* as "stir up their toughened groins" (p. 164), which would seem to imply achieving an erection rather than moving during anal penetration.

11 Martin obviously disagrees, since he takes *pathicus* as referring to a man who prefers to be penetrated orally (1992: 59–60); in this he follows Quinn's note on 16.2: "*pathicus = is qui irrumatur, cinaedus = is qui pedicatur*" (1973a: 144). However, C. A. Williams comments that such a meaning for *pathicus* "is nowhere suggested in the sources" (1999: 335 n. 78), and his overall discussion of *pathicus* is persuasive (pp. 174–5).

12 This lack is most noticeable in news reports of sexual assault that resort to such phrases as "the attacker forced the victim to perform oral sex on him," thus making the victim the *active* party in her or his own oral rape.

13 I admit that I am uncertain about the exact sense of the slang "sucks" or "sucks to you." The *Oxford English Dictionary* gives "an act of fellatio" as one meaning for the noun "suck" (suck n [1] 1c); concerning the plural "sucks," it says "Used as an expression of contempt, chiefly by children" (suck n [1] 11); in either case, the register seems wrong for *irrumabo* (http://dictionary.oed.com/cgi/entry/50241462 accessed December 17, 2005).

14 On the distinction between descriptive and performative language and the implications for poem 16, see Selden (1992: 480–9). He defines performative language as "utterances whose function is not to inform or to describe, but to carry out an operation, to accomplish something through the very process of their enunciation" (p. 480). On Catullus' poetry and the performativity of Roman manhood, see Wray (2001: 57–63 and *passim*).

15 See above, on Martin's and Williams's interpretations of *pathicus*.

16 Cf. Fitzgerald's statement about *irrumare*: "Although we know the meaning and etymology of this word, it is quite literally untranslatable" (1995: 64).

17 Goold does, however, give the poem the title "A Roman Cockney" (1983: 201)

18 I have no doubt that the *candida diua* of 68 is in fact Lesbia, but it is worth noting that she is not so named in this poem.

19 But see Wormell (1966: 194–9).

20 For a discussion of Catullus' meter in comparison to Sappho's, see Wormell (1966: 190–1, 199–201).

21 The missing fourth line of stanza 2 has been reconstructed as "Lesbia, uocis," a supposition which would explain (by haplography) why that line dropped out; see Quinn (1973a: 244), attributing the suggestion to Friedrich.

22 The phrase is taken from line 5 of Benvenuto Campesani's epigram on the discovery of Catullus: *quo licet ingenio uestrum celebrate Catullum*. See Gaisser (1993: 18); Butrica, this volume.

GUIDE TO FURTHER READING

The field of translation studies has a vast and growing bibliography; the interested student may begin by browsing through the *Routledge Encyclopedia of Translation Studies*, ed. Mona Baker (1998). The article on "Poetry translation" is a useful starting point; see also "Adaptation" and "Imitation." Holmes (1988) and Venuti (2000) contain several essays on translating poetry; Venuti (1998: ch. 5) includes cogent remarks about the use of translated literature in the monoglot college classroom. Brower (1959) remains a very useful collection; for the student interested in classical poetry, the essays by Humphries and Lattimore are of particular interest.

Hardwick (2000) gives a valuable discussion of the issues involved in translating ancient Greek and Latin poetry; she discusses epic and dramatic poetry as well as lyric. McPeek (1939) remains a useful discussion of Catullan translation in particular; see also Lefevere (1975). The English versions of Catullus by Campion, Tennyson, and Jonson discussed here, along with those of numerous other poets, are now collected in Gaisser (2001); see her introduction for a brief survey of the practice of Catullan translation in English. Both Mulroy (2002) and Green (2005) provide illuminating discussion of their own choices and approaches in their introductions. Finally, to get a thorough sense of the difficulties, different approaches, and interpretive strategies of English-language translations of Catullus, the student can do no better than to read as many translations as possible, from all periods.

WORKS CITED

Adams, J. N. 1982. *The Latin Sexual Vocabulary*. Baltimore and London.
Appiah, K. A. 1993. "Thick Translation," *Callaloo* 16.4: 808–19. Rpt. in Venuti (2000: 417–29).
Baker, M., ed. 1998. *Routledge Encyclopedia of Translation Studies*. London and New York.
Balmer, J. 2004. *Catullus: Poems of Love and Hate*. Tarset.
Borges, J. L. 1954. *Obras completas*. Vol. 2. Buenos Aires.
Brower, R. A., ed. 1959. *On Translation*. New York. Rpt. 1966.
Burnshaw, S., ed. 1960. *The Poem Itself: 45 Modern Poets in a New Presentation*. New York.
Campion, T. n.d. *Poetical Works*. Ed. P. Vivian. London and New York.
Copley, F. O., trans. 1957. *Catullus: The Complete Poetry*. Ann Arbor, MI. Rpt. 1964.
Fitzgerald, W. 1995. *Catullan Provocations: Lyric Poetry and the Drama of Position*. Berkeley, Los Angeles, and London.
Fordyce, C. J., ed. 1961. *Catullus: A Commentary*. Oxford.
Gaisser, J. H. 1993. *Catullus and His Renaissance Readers*. Oxford.
Gaisser, J. H. 2001. *Catullus in English*. London.
Goold, G. P., ed. and trans. 1983. *Catullus*. London.
Green, P., trans. 2005. *The Poems of Catullus*. Berkeley, Los Angeles, and London.
Greene, E. 1999a. "Re-Figuring the Feminine Voice: Catullus Translating Sappho." *Arethusa* 32: 1–18.
Hardwick, L. 2000. *Translating Words, Translating Cultures*. London.
Harrison, E. 1915. "Catullus, LXXXIV." *Classical Review* 29: 198–9.
Holmes, J. S. 1988. *Translated! Papers on Literary Translation and Translation Studies*. Amsterdam.
Hooley, D. M. 1988. *The Classics in Paraphrase: Ezra Pound and Modern Translators of Latin Poetry*. Selinsgrove, London, and Toronto.
Hummel, F. H., and A. A. Brodribb, trans. 1876. *Lays from Latin Lyrics*. London.

Humphries, R. 1959. "Latin and English Verse: Some Practical Considerations." In Brower (1959: 57–66).

Janan, M. 1994. *"When the Lamp is Shattered": Desire and Narrative in Catullus*. Carbondale and Edwardsville, IL.

Jonson, B. 1983. *Volpone*. Eds. B. Parker and D. Bevington. Manchester and New York.

Kelley, W. K. 1891. *The Poems of Catullus and Tibullus . . . A Literal Prose Translation*. London.

Lee, G., trans. 1990. *The Poems of Catullus*. Oxford and New York.

Lefevere, A. 1975. *Translating Poetry: Seven Strategies and a Blueprint*. Amsterdam.

Martin, C., trans. 1990. *The Poems of Catullus*. Baltimore and London.

Martin, C. 1992. *Catullus*. New Haven, CT, and London.

McPeek, J. A. S. 1939. *Catullus in Strange and Distant Britain*. Harvard Studies in Comparative Literature 15. Cambridge, MA. Rpt. 1972.

Miller, P. A. 1994. *Lyric Texts and Lyric Consciousness: The Birth of a Genre from Archaic Greece to Augustan Rome*. London and New York.

Mulroy, D., trans. 2002. *The Complete Poetry of Catullus*. Madison, WI.

Myers, R., and R. J. Ormsby, trans. 1970. *Catullus: The Complete Poems for American Readers*. New York.

Quinn, K., ed. 1973a. *Catullus: The Poems*. 2nd edn. London and Basingstoke.

Raphael, F., and K. McLeish, trans. 1979. *The Poems of Catullus*. Boston.

Ricks, C. B. 1989. *Tennyson: A Selected Edition Incorporating the Trinity College Manuscripts*. Berkeley and Los Angeles.

Selden, D. L. 1992. "*Ceveat lector*: Catullus and the Rhetoric of Performance." In R. Hexter and D. Selden, eds., *Innovations of Antiquity*. New York and London. 461–512.

Sesar, C., trans. 1974. *Selected Poems of Catullus*. New York.

Sisson, C. H., trans. 1967. *The Poetry of Catullus*. New York.

Skinner, M. B. 2003. *Catullus in Verona: A Reading of the Elegiac* Libellus, *Poems 65–116*. Columbus, OH.

Thomson, D. F. S., ed. 1997. *Catullus, Edited with a Textual and Interpretative Commentary*. Toronto.

Untermeyer, L. 1964. *Robert Frost: A Backward Look*. Washington, DC.

Vandiver, E. 1990. "Sound Patterns in Catullus 84." *Classical Journal* 85: 337–40.

Venuti, L. 1998. *The Scandals of Translation: Towards an Ethics of Difference*. London and New York.

Venuti, L, ed. 2000. *The Translation Studies Reader*. London and New York.

Whigham, P., trans. 1966. *The Poems of Catullus*. Harmondsworth.

Willett, S. J. 2001. "Recent Trends in Classical Verse Translation." *Syllecta Classica* 12: 221–63.

Williams, C. A. 1999. *Roman Homosexuality: Ideologies of Manhood in Classical Antiquity*. New York and Oxford.

Wilson, E. 2005. "Sparrows and Scrubbers" (review of Green 2005). *New Republic* November 14: 30–3.

Wormell, D. E. 1966. "Catullus as Translator (C. 51)." In L. Wallach, ed., *The Classical Tradition: Literary and Historical Studies in Honor of Harry Caplan*. Ithaca, NY. 187–201.

Wray, D. L. 2001. *Catullus and the Poetics of Roman Manhood*. Cambridge.

Zukofsky, L. and C. Zukofsky, trans. 1969. *Catullus* (Gai Valerii Catulli Veronensis liber). London.

Consolidated Bibliography

Abbott, C. C., ed. 1955. *Letters of Gerard Manley Hopkins to Robert Bridges.* London and New York.

Abel, D. H. 1962. "Ariadne and Dido." *Classical Bulletin* 38: 57–61.

Achard, G. 1981. *Pratique rhétorique et idéologie politique dans les discours optimates de Cicéron.* Leiden.

Acosta-Hughes, B. 2002. *Polyeideia: The* Iambi *of Callimachus and the Archaic Iambic Tradition.* Berkeley.

Adams, J. N. 1982. *The Latin Sexual Vocabulary.* Baltimore and London.

Adams, J. N. 1999. "Nominative Personal Pronouns and Some Patterns of Speech in Republican and Augustan Poetry." In Adams and Meyer (1999: 97–133).

Adams, J. N., and R. G. Mayer, eds. 1999. *Aspects of the Language of Latin Poetry* = Proceedings of the British Academy 93. Oxford.

Adams, R., and D. Savran, eds. 2002. *The Masculinity Studies Reader.* Malden, MA.

Adler, E. 1981. *Catullan Self-Revelation.* New York.

Albrecht, M. von. 1997. *A History of Roman Literature from Livius Andronicus to Boethius with Special Regard to its Influence on World Literature.* Vol. I. Rev. G. Schmeling and M. von Albrecht. Trans. M. von Albrecht and G. Schmeling with the assistance of F. and K. Newman. Leiden.

Allen, J. H., and J. B. Greenough. 1888. *New Latin Grammar for Schools and Colleges, Founded on Comparative Grammar.* Boston.

Allen, W. 1940. "The Epyllion: A Chapter in the History of Literary Criticism." *Transactions of the American Philological Association* 71: 1–26.

Alpago-Novello, L. 1926. "Spigolature vaticane di argomento bellunese. I. Un'opera inedita ed ignorata di Pierio Valeriano." *Archivio Veneto Tridentino* 9: 69–96.

Ancona, R. 2002. "The Untouched Self: Sapphic and Catullan Muses in Horace, *Odes* I.22." In E. Spentzou and D. Fowler, eds., *Cultivating the Muse.* Oxford. 161–86.

Ancona, R. 2004. *Writing Passion: A Catullus Reader.* Wauconda, IL.

Anderson, W. S. 1962. "The Programme of Juvenal's Later Books." *Classical Philology* 57: 145–60.

André, J. M. 1966. *L'otium dans la vie morale et intellectuelle romaine.* Paris.

Appiah, K. A. 1993. "Thick Translation." *Callaloo* 16.4: 808–19. Rpt. in Venuti (2000: 417–29).

Arkins, B. 1979. "Catullus 7." *L'Antiquité classique* 48: 630–5.

Arkins, B. 1982a. *Sexuality in Catullus.* Altertumswissenschaftliche Texte und Studien 8. Hildesheim.

Arkins, B. 1982b. "Tradition Reshaped: Language and Style in Euripides *Medea* 1–19, Ennius *Medea Exul* 1–9 and Catullus 64. 1–30." *Ramus* 11: 116–33.

Arkins, B. 1986. "New Approaches to Virgil." *Latomus* 45: 33–42.

Arkins, B. 1987. "A New Translation of Catullus 85." *Liverpool Classical Monthly* 12: 12.

Arkins, B. 1988. "Pound's Propertius: What Kind of Homage?" *Paideuma* 17: 29–44.

Arkins, B. 1990. *Builders of My Soul: Greek and Roman Themes in Yeats.* Gerrards Cross.

Arkins, B. 1999. *An Interpretation of the Poems of Catullus.* Lewiston, NY.

Arkins, B. 2001. "Eliot as Critic: The Case of Latin Literature." *Yeats-Eliot Review* 17.3: 10–17.

Arnold, B. 1994. "The Literary Experience of Vergil's Fourth *Eclogue.*" *Classical Journal* 90: 143–60.

Arnold, B., A. Aronson, and G. Lawall. 2000. *Love and Betrayal: A Catullus Reader.* Upper Saddle River, NJ.

Armstrong, D. 1989. *Horace.* New Haven, CT.

Asper, M. 1997. "Catull, Mamurra und Caesar: Eine öffentliche Auseinandersetzung?" In T. Baier and F. Schimann, eds., *Fabrica: Studien zur antiken Literatur und ihrer Rezeption.* Stuttgart and Leipzig. 65–78.

Austin, R. G. 1977. *P. Vergili Maronis Aeneidos Liber Sextus.* Oxford.

Avallone, R. 1953. "Catullo e Apollonio di Rodio." *Antiquitas* 8: 8–75.

Badian, E. 1977. "Mamurra's Fourth Fortune." *Classical Philology* 72: 320–2.

Baier, T., ed. 2003. *Pontano und Catull.* Tübingen.

Baker, M., ed. 1998. *Routledge Encyclopedia of Translation Studies.* London and New York.

Balme, M. 1970. "Poem III." In Greig (1970: 6–12).

Balme, M., and J. Morwood, eds. 1997a. *Oxford Latin Reader.* 2nd rev. edn. Oxford.

Balme, M., and J. Morwood. 1997b. *Oxford Latin Reader: Teacher's Book.* Oxford.

Balme, M., and M. S. Warman. 1965. *Aestimanda. Practical Criticism: Latin and Greek Poetry and Prose.* Oxford.

Balmer, J. 2004. *Catullus: Poems of Love and Hate.* Tarset.

Banta, D. S. 1998. "Literary Apology and Literary Genre in Martial." Dissertation. Duke University.

Banville, J. 1990. "Survivors of Joyce." In A. Martin, ed., *James Joyce – The Artist and the Labyrinth.* London. 73–81.

Barber, E. A. 1953. *Sexti Properti Carmina.* 2nd edn. Oxford.

Barchiesi, A. 2005. "The Search for the Perfect Book: A PS to the New Posidippus." In K. Gutzwiller, ed., *The New Posidippus: A Hellenistic Poetry Book.* Oxford. 320–42.

Barthes, R. 1977. "The Death of the Author." In *Image, Music, Text.* Trans. S. Heath. New York. 142–8.

Barton, C. 1992. *The Sorrows of the Ancient Romans: The Gladiator and the Monster.* Princeton, NJ.

Barwick, K. 1958. "Zyklen bei Martial und in den kleinen Gedichten des Catull." *Philologus* 102: 284–318.

Batstone, W. W. 1993. "Logic, Rhetoric, and Poesis." *Helios* 20: 143–72.

Batstone, W. W. 1998. "Dry Pumice and the Programmatic Language of Catullus 1." *Classical Philology* 93: 125–35.

Beck, J.-W. 1996. *"Lesbia" und "Juventius": Zwei* libelli *im Corpus Catullianum. Untersuchungen zur Publikationsform und Authentizität der überlieferten Gedichtfolge.* Göttingen.

Beck, J.-W. 2002. Quid nobis cum epistula? *Zum Anfang von Martials erstem Epigrammbuch.* Göttingen.

Bender, H., and P. Y. Forsyth. 2005. *Catullus: Expanded Edition.* Wauconda, IL.

Benediktson, D. T. 1989. *Propertius: Modernist Poet of Antiquity.* Carbondale.

Benjamin, W. 1999. *Illuminations.* London.

Billanovich, Giuseppe. 1959. "Dal Livio di Raterio al Livio di Petrarca." *Italia medioevale e umanistica* 2: 103–78.

Billanovich, Giuseppe. 1974. "Terenzio, Ildemaro, Petrarca." *Italia medioevale e umanistica* 17: 1–60.

Billanovich, Giuseppe. 1981. *La tradizione del testo di Livio e le origini dell'umanesimo.* Padua.

Billanovich, Giuseppe. 1988. "Il Catullo della cattedrale di Verona." In *Scire litteras = Bayerische Akademie der Wissenschaften, Philosophisch.-historische Klasse, Abhandlungen* 99. Munich. 37–52.

Billanovich, Guido. 1958. "*Veterum vestigia vatum* nei carmi dei preumanisti padovani." *Italia medioevale e umanistica* 1: 155–243.

Bing, P. 1988. *The Well-Read Muse: Present and Past in Callimachus and the Hellenistic Poets.* Göttingen.

Bing, P. 1997. "Reconstructing Berenike's Lock." In G. W. Most, ed., *Collecting Fragments: Fragmente sammeln.* Göttingen. 78–94.

Birt, T. 1882. *Das antike Buchwesen in seinem Verhältnis zur Litteratur.* Berlin. 2nd impression Aalen 1959.

Boehrer, B. T. 1998. "Renaissance Classicism and Roman Sexuality: Ben Jonson's Marginalia and the Trope of *os impurum*." *International Journal of the Classical Tradition* 4: 364–80.

Boës, J. 1986. "Le mythe d'Achille vu par Catulle: importance de l'amour pour une morale de la gloire." *Revue des études latines* 64: 104–15.

Booth, J. 1997. "All in the Mind: Sickness in Catullus 76." In S. M. Braund and C. Gill, eds., *The Passions in Roman Thought and Literature.* Cambridge. 150–68.

Borges, J. L. 1954. *Obras completas.* Vol. 2. Buenos Aires.

Bosco, U. 1942. "Il Petrarca e l'umanesimo filologico." *Giornale storico della letteratura italiana* 120: 108–16.

Boucher, J.-P. 1980. *Études sur Properce: problèmes d'inspiration et d'art.* 2nd edn. Paris.

Bowditch, P. L. 2001. *Horace and the Gift Economy of Patronage.* Berkeley.

Bowie, M. N. R. 1988. "Martial Book XII: A Commentary." Dissertation. Oxford University.

Braga, D. 1950. *Catullo e i poeti Greci.* Messina and Florence.

Bramble, J. C. 1970. "Structure and Ambiguity in Catullus LXIV." *Proceedings of the Cambridge Philological Society* 16: 22–41.

Braund, D. C. 1996. "The Politics of Catullus 10: Memmius, Caesar and the Bithynians." *Hermathena* 160: 45–57.

Briggs, W. W., Jr., ed. 1994. *Biographical Dictionary of North American Classicists.* Westport, CT, and London.

Brower, R. A., ed. 1959. *On Translation.* New York. Rpt. 1966.

Brown, P. M. 1993. *Horace: Satires I.* Warminster.

Brunér, E. a. 1863. "De ordine et temporibus carminum Valerii Catulli." *Acta Societatis Scientiarum Fennicae* 7: 599–657.

Brunt, P. 1971. *Social Conflicts in the Roman Republic.* New York.

Brunt, P. 1988. *The Fall of the Roman Republic and Related Essays.* Oxford.

Buchheit, V. 1961a. "Catull und Cato von Utica (c. 56)." *Hermes* 89: 345–56.

Buchheit, V. 1961b. "Horazes programmatische Epode (VI)." *Gymnasium* 68: 520–6.

Buchheit, V. 1966. "Vergil in Sorge um Oktavian (zu georg. I, 498 ff.)." *Rheinisches Museum* 109: 78–83.

Bühler, W. 1960. *Die Europa des Moschos.* Wiesbaden.

Bulley, M. 1989. "Please, Not in Front of the Latin A-Level Students." Letter to the *Guardian*, March 15: 18.

Bunting, B. 1978. *Collected Poems*. Oxford.

Burkert, W. 1983. *Homo Necans: The Anthropology of Ancient Greek Sacrificial Ritual and Myth*. Trans. P. Bing. Berkeley. First published as *Homo Necans*, Berlin 1972.

Burnett, A. 1983. "Desire and Memory (Sappho Frag. 94)." *Classical Philology* 74: 16–27.

Burnshaw, S., ed. 1960. *The Poem Itself: 45 Modern Poets in a New Presentation*. New York.

Burrus, V. 2000. *Begotten, Not Made: Conceiving Manhood in Late Antiquity*. Stanford, CA.

Butler, J. 1990. *Gender Trouble: Feminism and the Subversion of Identity*. New York.

Butler, J. 1993. *Bodies That Matter: On the Discursive Limits of "Sex."* New York.

Butrica, J. L. 1984. *The Manuscript Tradition of Propertius*. Toronto.

Butrica, J. L. 2002. "Clodius the 'pulcher' in Catullus and Cicero." *Classical Quarterly* n.s. 52: 507–16.

Butrica, J. L. 2005. "Some Myths and Anomalies in the Study of Roman Sexuality." *Journal of Homosexuality* 49: 209–69.

Byre, C. 2002. *A Reading of Apollonius Rhodius'* Argonautica: *The Poetics of Uncertainty*. Lewiston, NY.

Cahoon, L. 1988. "Bed as Battlefield: Erotic Conquest and Military Metaphor in Ovid's *Amores*." *Transactions of the American Philological Association* 118: 293–307.

Cairns, F. 1983. "Propertius 1,4 and 1,5 and the 'Gallus' of the *Monobiblos*." *Papers of the Liverpool Latin Seminar* 4: 61–102.

Cairns, F. 1984. "The Nereids of Catullus 64.12–23b." *Grazer Beiträge* 11: 95–100.

Calame, C. 1994. *Choruses of Young Women in Ancient Greece*. Trans. J. Orion and D. Collins. Lanham, MD.

Cameron, A. 1995. *Callimachus and His Critics*. Princeton, NJ.

Campanelli, M., and M. A. Pincelli. 2000. "La lettura dei classici nello *studium urbis* tra umanesimo e rinascimento." In L. Capo and M. R. Di Simone, eds., *Storia della Facoltà di Lettere e Filosofia de "La Sapienza."* Rome. 93–195.

Campbell, D. 1960. "Galliambic Poems of the 15th and 16th Centuries: Sources of the Bacchic Odes of the Pléiade School." *Bibliothèque d'humanism et renaissance* 22: 490–510.

Campion, T. n.d. *Poetical Works*. Ed. P. Vivian. London and New York.

Camps, W. A. 1961. *Propertius:* Elegies *Book I*. Cambridge.

Carpenter, H. 1988. *A Serious Character – The Life of Ezra Pound*. London.

Carr, W. L., and H. E. Wedeck. 1940. *Latin Poetry*. Boston.

Carson, A. 1986. *Eros the Bittersweet*. Princeton, NJ.

Chandler, D. 2002. *Semiotics: The Basics*. New York.

Cioran, E. M. 1998. *The Temptation to Exist*. Trans. R. Howard. Chicago.

Citroni, M. 1975. *M. Valerii Martialis Epigrammaton Liber Primus*. Florence.

Claes, P. 2002. *Concatenatio Catulliana: A New Reading of the* Carmina. Amsterdam.

Clare, R. J. 1996. "Catullus 64 and the *Argonautica* of Apollonius Rhodius: Allusion and Exemplarity." *Proceedings of the Cambridge Philological Society* 42: 60–88.

Clare, R. J. 2002. *The Path of the Argo*. Cambridge.

Clausen, W. V. 1964. "Callimachus and Latin Poetry." *Greek, Roman, and Byzantine Studies* 5: 181–96.

Clausen, W. V. 1970. "Catullus and Callimachus." *Harvard Studies in Classical Philology* 74: 85–94.

Clausen, W. V. 1976. "*Catulli Veronensis Liber*." *Classical Philology* 71: 37–43.

Clausen, W. V. 1982. "The New Direction in Poetry." In Kenney and Clausen (1982: 178–206).

Clausen, W. V. 1987. *Virgil's* Aeneid *and the Traditions of Hellenistic Poetry*. Berkeley and Los Angeles.

Clausen, W. V. 1988. "Catulliana." In N. Horsfall, ed., Vir Bonus Discendi Peritus: *Studies in Celebration of Otto Skutsch's Eightieth Birthday. British Institute of Classical Studies* Supp. 51: 13–17.

Clausen, W. V., ed. 1994. *Virgil:* Eclogues. Oxford.

Clauss, J. J. 1993. *The Best of the Argonauts.* Berkeley and Los Angeles.

Clauss, J. J. 1995. "A Delicate Foot on the Well-Worn Threshold: Paradoxical Imagery in Catullus 68b." *American Journal of Philology* 116: 237–53.

Coleman, R. G. G. 1999. "Poetic Diction, Poetic Discourse, and the Poetic Register." In Adams and Meyer (1999: 21–93).

Coleridge, E. H., ed. 1912. *The Complete Poetical Works of Samuel Coleridge.* Oxford.

Commager, H. S., Jr. 1965. "Notes on Some Poems of Catullus." *Harvard Studies in Classical Philology* 70: 83–110.

Conte, G. B. 1986. *The Rhetoric of Imitation: Genre and Poetic Memory in Virgil and Other Latin Poets.* Trans. C. Segal. Ithaca, NY.

Conte, G. B. 1992. "Proems in the Middle." In F. M. Dunn and T. Cole, eds., *Beginnings in Classical Literature.* Yale Classical Studies vol. 29. Cambridge, MA. 147–59.

Conte, G. B. 1994. *Latin Literature: A History.* Trans. J. B. Solodow. Rev. D. Fowler and G. W. Most. Baltimore.

Cookesley, W. G. 1845. *Selecta e Catullo: In Usum Iuventutis./ Notas Quasdam Anglice Scriptas Adjecit Gulielmus Gifford Cookesley.* Eton.

Copley, F. O., trans. 1957. *Catullus: The Complete Poetry.* Ann Arbor, MI. Rpt. 1964.

Copley, F. O. 1974. "The Structure of Catullus C. 51 and the Problem of the *otium* Strophe." *Grazer Beiträge* 2: 25–37.

Coppel, B. 1973. *Das Alliusgedicht: Zur Redaktion des Catullcorpus.* Heidelberg.

Corbeill, A. 1996. *Controlling Laughter: Political Humor in the Late Roman Republic.* Princeton, NJ.

Corbeill, A. 2001. "Education in the Roman Republic: Creating Traditions." In Y. L. Too, ed., *Education in Greek and Roman Antiquity.* Leiden. 261–87.

Corbeill, A. 2002. "Ciceronian Invective." In J. May, ed., *Brill's Companion to Cicero: Oratory and Rhetoric.* Leiden. 197–218.

Courtney, E. 1975. "The Interpolations in Juvenal." *Bulletin of the Institute of Classical Studies of the University of London* 22: 147–62.

Courtney, E. 1985. "Three Poems of Catullus." *Bulletin of the Institute of Classical Studies of the University of London* 32: 85–100.

Courtney, E., ed. 1993. *The Fragmentary Latin Poets.* Oxford.

Crabbe, A. M. 1977. "*Ignoscenda quidem*: Catullus 64 and the Fourth *Georgic.*" *Classical Quarterly* n. s. 27: 342–51.

Craig, C. 2004. "Audience Expectations, Invective, and Proof." In J. Powell and J. Patterson, eds., *Cicero the Advocate.* Oxford. 187–214.

Crawford, M. 1993. *The Roman Republic.* 2nd edn. Cambridge, MA.

Crombruggen, H. van. 1959. *Lernutiana.* Mededelingen van de koninklijke vlaamse Academie voor Wetenschappen, Letteren en schone Kunsten van Belgie, Klasse der Letteren 21. Brussels.

Crook, J. 1967. *Law and Life of Rome.* Ithaca, NY.

Crowther, N. B. 1970. "OI ΝΕωΤΕΡΟΙ, Poetae Novi, and Cantores Euphorionis." *Classical Quarterly* 20: 322–7.

Crump, M. M. 1931. *The Epyllion from Theocritus to Ovid.* Oxford.

Curran, L. C. 1969. "Catullus 64 and the Heroic Age." *Yale Classical Studies* 21: 169–92.

Davie, D. 1975. *Pound.* London.

Davis, G. 1991. *Polyhymnia: The Rhetoric of Horatian Literary Discourse.* Berkeley.

DeJean, J. 1989. *Fictions of Sappho, 1546–1937.* Chicago.

Dench, E. 2005. *Romulus' Asylum: Roman Identities from the Age of Alexander to the Age of Hadrian*. Oxford.

Detienne, M. 1994. *The Gardens of Adonis*. Trans. J. Lloyd. Princeton, NJ.

Dettmer, H. 1983. "A Note on Catullus 1 and 116." *Classical World* 77: 19.

Dettmer, H. 1994. "The First and Last of Catullus." *Syllecta Classica* 5: 29–33.

Dettmer, H. 1997. *Love by the Numbers: Form and Meaning in the Poetry of Catullus*. New York.

Dettmer, H., and L. A. Osburn. 2006. *A Catullus Workbook*. Wauconda, IL.

Dettmer, H., and L. A. Osburn. 2007. *A Catullus Workbook: Teacher's Guide*. Wauconda, IL.

Deuling, J. K. 1999. "Catullus and Mamurra." *Mnemosyne* ser. 4, 52: 188–94.

Dion, J. 1993. "La composition des 'carmina' de Catulle." *Bulletin de l'Association Guillaume Budé* 2: 136–57.

Di Stephano, A. 2001. "Pierio Valeriano e la nascita della critica catulliana nel secolo XVI." In P. Pellegrini, ed., *Umanisti bellunesi fra quattro e cinquecento*. Atti del Convegno di Belluno November 5, 1999. Florence. 137–76.

Dixon, S. 2001. *Reading Roman Women: Sources, Genres, and Real Life*. London.

Dodds, E. R., ed. 1966. *The Collected Poems of Louis MacNeice*. London.

Dover, K. J. 1978. *Greek Homosexuality*. London and Cambridge, MA.

DuBois, P. 1995. *Sappho is Burning*. Chicago.

Duhigg, J. 1971. "The Elegiac Metre of Catullus." *Antichthon* 5: 57–67.

Dupont, F. 1998. *The Invention of Literature: From Greek Intoxication to the Latin Book*. Trans. J. Lloyd. Baltimore.

Dyson Hejduk, J. T. 1999. "Lilies and Violence: Lavinia's Blush in the Song of Orpheus." *Classical Philology* 94: 281–8.

Dyson Hejduk, J. T., forthcoming. *Clodia: Readings in Roman Passion, Politics, and Poetry*. Norman, OK.

Earl, D. C. 1961. *The Political Thought of Sallust*. Cambridge.

Earl, D. C. 1967. *The Moral and Political Tradition of Rome*. London and Ithaca, NY.

Edmunds, L. 2001. *Intertextuality and the Reading of Roman Poetry*. Baltimore.

Edwards, C. 1993. *The Politics of Immorality in Ancient Rome*. Cambridge.

Edwards, M. J. 1991. "The Theology of Catullus 68b." *Antike und Abendland* 37: 68–81.

Edwards, M. J. 1992. "Apples, Blood and Flowers: Sapphic Bridal Imagery in Catullus." In C. Leroux, ed., *Studies in Latin Literature and Roman History VI*. Collection Latomus 217. Brussels. 181–203.

Edwards, M. J. 1993. "Catullus' Wedding Hymns." *Classical Review* 43: 43–4. [Review of Thomsen 1992].

Elder, J. P. 1951a. "Foreword." In Merrill (1893: viii).

Elder, J. P. 1951b. "Notes on Some Conscious and Subconscious Elements in Catullus' Poetry." *Harvard Studies in Classical Philology* 60: 101–36.

Elder, J. P. 1961. "*Non iniussa cano*: Virgil's Sixth Eclogue." *Harvard Studies in Classical Philology* 65: 109–25.

Elder, J. P. 1966. "Catullus I, His Poetic Creed and Nepos." *Harvard Studies in Classical Philology* 71: 143–9.

Elia, S. d'. 1981. "I Presupposti sociologici dell' esperienza elegiaca Properziana." In F. Santucci and S. Vivona, eds., *Colloquium Propertianum (secundum): Atti*. Assisi. 59–80.

Eliot, T. S. 1958. *Selected Prose*. Harmondsworth.

Eliot, T. S. 1969. *On Poetry and Poets*. London.

Eliot, V., ed. 1988. *The Letters of T. S. Eliot. Vol. 1: 1898–1922*. London.

Ellis, R. 1878. *Catulli Veronensis Liber*. Oxford.

Ellis, R. 1889. *A Commentary on Catullus*. 2nd edn. Oxford.

Ellis, R. 1905. *Catullus in the XIVth Century*. Oxford.

Ernout, A., and A. Meillet. 1967. *Dictionnaire étymologique de la langue Latine*. 4th edn. Paris.

Ewbank, W. W. 1933. *The Poems of Cicero*. London.

Fabbrini, D. 2002. "Mart. VI 64, 25 *toto orbe* o *tota urbe*? Considerazioni sull'ambito di destinazione della poesia diffamatoria." *Maia* 54: 543–56.

Fantham, E. 1996. *Roman Literary Culture: From Cicero to Apuleius*. Baltimore.

Fantuzzi, M. 1988. *Richerche su Apollonio Rodio*. Rome.

Fantuzzi, M., and R. Hunter. 2004. *Tradition and Innovation in Hellenistic Poetry*. Cambridge.

Farrell, J. 1991. *Vergil's* Georgics *and the Traditions of Ancient Epic: The Art of Allusion in Literary History*. Oxford.

Farrell, J. 1993. "Allusions, Delusions, and Confusions: A Reply." *Electronic Antiquity* 1.6. http://scholar.lib.vt.edu/ejournals/ElAnt/V1N6/farrell.html.

Farrell, J. 1997. "The Virgilian Intertext." In C. Martindale, ed., *The Cambridge Companion to Virgil*. Cambridge. 222–38.

Fasteau, M. 1975. *The Male Machine*. New York.

Fear, T. 1992. "Catullus 68A: *Veronae turpe, Catulle, esse*." *Illinois Classical Studies* 17: 245–63.

Fedeli, P. 1980. *Sesto Properzio: Il Primo libro delle elegie*. Florence.

Fedeli, P. 1983a. *Catullus' Carmen 61*. Trans. M. Nardella. Amsterdam. First published as *Il carme 61 di Catullo*, Fribourg 1972.

Fedeli, P. 1983b. " 'Properti monobiblos': struttura e motivi." In W. Haase, ed., *Aufstieg und Niedergang der Römischen Welt*, II.30.3. Berlin. 1858–1922.

Fedeli, P. 2004. "Marziale Catulliano." *Humanitas* 56: 161–89.

Feeney, D. C. 1992. " 'Shall I compare thee . . . ?': Catullus 68b and the Limits of Analogy." In A. J. Woodman and J. Powell, eds., *Author and Audience in Latin Literature*. Cambridge. 33–44.

Feeney, D. C. 1999. "*Mea tempora*: Patterning of Time in the *Metamorphoses*." In P. Hardie, A. Barchiesi, and S. Hinds, eds., *Ovidian Transformations: Essays on Ovid's Metamorphoses and its Reception*. Cambridge. 13–30.

Feeney, D. C. 2005. "The Beginnings of Latin Literature." *Journal of Roman Studies* 95: 226–40.

Feldherr, A. 2000. "*Non inter nota sepulcra*: Catullus 101 and Roman Funerary Ritual." *Classical Antiquity* 19.2: 209–31.

Ferguson, J. 1961. "Catullus and Tennyson." *English Studies in Africa* 12: 41–58.

Ferguson, J. 1963. "Catullus and Martial." *Proceedings of the African Classical Associations* 6: 3–15.

Ferguson, J. 1970. "A Note on Catullus' Hendecasyllabics." *Classical Philology* 65: 173–5.

Ferguson, J. 1971–2. "Catullus and Virgil." *Proceedings of the Virgil Society* 11: 25–47.

Ferguson, J. 1986a. "The Arrangement of Catullus' Poems." *Liverpool Classical Monthly* 11.1: 2–6.

Ferguson, J. 1986b. "The Arrangement of Catullus' Poems." *Liverpool Classical Monthly* 11.2: 18–20.

Ferguson, J. 1988. *Catullus*. Greece & Rome New Surveys in the Classics No. 20. Oxford.

Fernández Corte, J. C. 1995. "Parodia, *renuntiatio amicitiae* y *renuntiatio amoris* en Catulo XI." *Emérita* 63: 81–101.

Finamore, J. 1984. "Catullus 50 and 51: Friendship, Love and *otium*." *Classical World* 78: 11–19.

Fitzgerald, W. 1995. *Catullan Provocations: Lyric Poetry and the Drama of Position*. Berkeley, Los Angeles, and London.

Fletcher, H. G., III. 1988. *New Aldine Studies*. San Francisco.

Fordyce, C. J., ed. 1961. *Catullus: A Commentary*. Oxford.

Forsyth, P. Y. 1977a. "The Ameana Cycle of Catullus." *Classical World* 70: 445–50.

Forsyth, P. Y. 1977b. "Comments on Catullus 116." *Classical Quarterly* n.s. 27: 352–3.

Forsyth, P. Y. 1980–1. "Quintius and Aufillena in Catullus." *Classical World* 74: 220–3.

Forsyth, P. Y. 1986. *The Poems of Catullus: A Teaching Text.* Lanham, MD.

Forsyth, P. Y. 1987a. "Catullus 64.400–402: Transposition or Emendation?" *Échos du monde classique/Classical Views* 31: 329–32.

Forsyth, P. Y. 1987b. "*Munera et Musarum hinc petis et Veneris*: Catullus 68A.10." *Classical World* 80: 177–80.

Forsyth, P. Y. 1989. "Catullus 14 B." *Classical World* 83: 81–5.

Forsyth, P. Y. 1991. "Thematic Unity of Catullus 11." *Classical World* 84: 457–64.

Forsyth, P. Y. 1993. "The Fearful Symmetry of Catullus' Polymetrics." *Classical World* 86: 492–5.

Foster, J. 1994. "Poetry and Friendship: Catullus 35." *Liverpool Classical Monthly* 19.7–8: 114–21.

Foucault, M. 1977. "What is an Author?" In *Language, Counter-Memory, Practice.* Trans. D. F. Bouchard and S. Simon. Ithaca, NY. 124–7.

Foucault, M. 1978. *The History of Sexuality.* Vol. 1, *An Introduction.* Trans. R. Hurley. New York.

Foucault, M. 1986. *The Care of the Self.* Vol. 3, *The History of Sexuality.* Trans. R. Hurley. New York.

Fowler, D. 1991. "Narrate and Describe: The Problem of Ecphrasis." *Journal of Roman Studies* 81: 25–35.

Fowles, J. 1981. *The Aristos.* London.

Fraenkel, E. 1955. "*Vesper adest* (Catullus LXII)." *Journal of Roman Studies* 45: 1–8.

Fraenkel, E. 1957. *Horace.* Oxford.

Frank, R. I. 1968. "Catullus 51: *otium* vs. *virtus.*" *Transactions of the American Philological Association* 96: 233–9.

Frank, T. 1928. *Catullus and Horace.* Oxford.

Fraser, G. S. 1964. *The Modern Writer and His World.* Baltimore.

Frazier, A. 2000. *George Moore, 1852–1933.* New Haven, CT.

Fredrick, D. 1995. "Beyond the Atrium to Ariadne: Erotic Painting and Visual Pleasure in the Roman House." *Classical Antiquity* 14: 266–88.

Fredrick, D. 1999. "Haptic Poetics." *Arethusa* 32: 49–83.

Fredricksmeyer, E. 1965. "On the Unity of Catullus 51." *Transactions of the American Philological Association* 96: 153–63.

Freudenburg, K. 1993. *The Walking Muse.* Princeton, NJ.

Friedlaender, L. 1886. *M. Valerii Martialis Epigrammaton Libri mit erklärenden Anmerkungen versehen.* 2 vols. Leipzig. Rpt. Amsterdam 1961.

Fröhlich, J. 1843. "Über die Anordnung der Gedichte des Q. Valerius Catullus." *Abhandlung der königl. bayerische Akademie der Wissenschaften,* Philosophisch.-philologischen Kl. 3.3 (Munich). 691–716.

Frost, R. 1969. *The Poetry of Robert Frost.* Ed. E. C. Latham. New York.

Frost, R. 1995. *Collected Poems, Prose and Plays.* New York.

Fusillo, M. 1985. *Il tempo delle* Argonautiche. Rome.

Gaisser, J. H. 1992. "Catullus." In V. Brown, ed., *Catalogus Translationum et Commentariorum* 7. Washington, DC. 197–292.

Gaisser, J. H. 1993. *Catullus and His Renaissance Readers.* Oxford.

Gaisser, J. H. 1995. "Threads in the Labyrinth: Competing Views and Voices in Catullus 64." *American Journal of Philology* 116: 579–616.

Gaisser, J. H. 1999. *Pierio Valeriano on the Ill Fortune of Learned Men: A Renaissance Humanist and His World.* Ann Arbor, MI.

Gaisser, J. H. 2001. *Catullus in English*. London.

Gaisser, J. H. 2002. "Picturing Catullus." *Classical World* 95: 372–85.

Galán Vioque, G. 2002. *Martial, Book VII: A Commentary*. Trans. J. J. Zoltowski. Leiden, Boston, and Cologne.

Galinsky, K. 1996. *Augustan Culture*. Princeton, NJ.

Gamel, M.-K. 1998. "Reading as a Man: Performance and Gender in Roman Elegy." *Helios* 25: 79–95.

Garrison, D. H. 1992. "The *locus inamoenus*: Another Part of the Forest." *Arion*³ 2.1: 98–114.

Garrison, D. H. 2004. *The Student's Catullus*. 3rd edn. Norman, OK.

Garthwaite, J. 1978. "Domitian and the Court Poets Martial and Statius." Dissertation. Cornell University.

Gentili, B. 1988. *Poetry and its Public in Ancient Greece from Homer to the Fifth Century*. Trans. A. T. Cole. Baltimore.

Giardina, G. 1974. "La composizione del liber e l'itinerario poetico di Catullo: contributi alla sistemazione del problema." *Philologus* 118: 224–35.

Gigante, V. 1978. "Motivi gnomici nella poesia di Catullo." *Vichiana* 7: 257–67.

Ginsberg, E. S. 1986. "Peregrinations of the Kiss: Thematic Relationships between Neo-Latin and French Poetry in the Sixteenth Century." *Acta Conventus Neo-Latini Sanctandreani*. Binghamton, NY. 331–42.

Giordano, F. 1996. "Ricontestualizzazioni ovidiane in Mart. I 34." In G. Germano, ed., *Classicità, medioevo e umanesimo: studi in onore di Salvatore Monti*. Naples. 203–14.

Gleason, M. W. 1990. "The Semiotics of Gender: Physiognomy and Self-Fashioning in the Second Century C.E." In D. Halperin, J. Winkler, and F. Zeitlin, eds., *Before Sexuality*. Princeton, NJ. 389–415.

Gleason, M. W. 1995. *Making Men: Sophists and Self-Presentation in Ancient Rome*. Princeton, NJ.

Glenn, J. 1974. "The Blinded Cyclops: *lumen ademptum* (*Aen.* 3.658)." *Classical Philology* 69: 37–8.

Godman, P. 1988. "Johannes Secundus and Renaissance Latin Poetry." *Review of English Studies* 39: 258–72.

Godman, P. 1990. "Literary Classicism and Latin Erotic Poetry of the Twelfth Century and the Renaissance." In Godman and Murray (1990: 149–92).

Godman, P., and O. Murray, eds. 1990. *Latin Poetry and the Classical Tradition*. Oxford.

Godwin, J. 1995. *Catullus: Poems 61–68*. Warminster.

Godwin, J. 1999. *Catullus: The Shorter Poems*. Warminster.

Gold, B. K. 1993. " 'But Ariadne Was Never There in the First Place': Finding the Female in Roman Poetry." In N. S. Rabinowitz and A. Richlin, eds., *Feminist Theory and the Classics*. New York. 75–101.

Goldhill, S. 1991. *The Poet's Voice*. Cambridge.

Gonnelli, G. 1962. "Presenza di Catullo in Virgilio." *Giornale italiano di filologia* 15: 225–53.

Goold, G. P. 1969. "Catullus 3.16." *Phoenix* 23: 186–203.

Goold, G. P. 1973. "Interpreting Catullus." Inaugural lecture delivered at University College, London. London.

Goold, G. P., ed. and trans. 1983. *Catullus*. London.

Gotoff, H. 1986. "Cicero's Analysis of the Prosecution Speeches in the *Pro Caelio*: An Exercise in Practical Criticism." *Classical Philology* 81: 122–32.

Goud, T. 1995. "Who Speaks the Final Lines? Catullus 62: Structure and Ritual." *Phoenix* 49: 23–32.

Gow, A. S. F. 1965. *Theocritus Edited with a Translation and Commentary*. Vol. 2. Cambridge.

Gow, A. S. F., and D. L. Page, eds. 1965. *The Greek Anthology: Hellenistic Epigrams*. 2 vols. Cambridge.

Grafton, A. 1977. "Joseph Scaliger's Edition of Catullus (1577) and the Traditions of Textual Criticism in the Renaissance." *Journal of the Warburg and Courtauld Institute* 40: 150–88.

Grafton, A. 1983. *Joseph Scaliger: A Study in the History of Classical Scholarship*. Vol. I. Oxford.

Granarolo, J. 1982. *Catulle, ce vivant*. Paris.

Gratwick, A. S. 1991. "Catullus 1.10 and the Title of His 'Libellus'." *Greece & Rome* 38.2: 199–202.

Gratwick, A. S. 2002. "*Vale patrona virgo*: The Text of Catullus 1.9." *Classical Quarterly* 52: 305–20.

Graves, R. 1961. *Poems Selected by Himself*. Harmondsworth.

Graves, R. 2000. *Robert Graves: The Complete Poems in One Volume*. Eds. B. Graves and D. Ward. Manchester.

Green, P., trans. 2005. *The Poems of Catullus*. Berkeley, Los Angeles, and London.

Greenberger, J., ed. 2001. *Teacher's Guide: AP Latin*. New York.

Greene, E. 1994. "Apostrophe and Women's Erotics in the Poetry of Sappho." *Transactions of the American Philological Association* 124: 41–56.

Greene, E. 1995. "The Catullan Ego: Fragmentation and the Erotic Self." *American Journal of Philology* 116: 77–93.

Greene, E., ed. 1996. *Re-Reading Sappho: Reception and Transmission*. Berkeley, Los Angeles, and London.

Greene, E. 1997. "Journey to the Remotest Meadow: A Reading of Catullus 11." *Intertexts* 1: 147–55.

Greene, E. 1999a. "Re-Figuring the Feminine Voice: Catullus Translating Sappho." *Arethusa* 32: 1–18.

Greene, E. 1999b. *The Erotics of Domination: Male Desire and the Mistress in Latin Love Poetry*. Baltimore.

Greene, T. M. 1980. *The Light in Troy: Imitation and Discovery in Renaissance Poetry*. New Haven, CT.

Greig, C., ed. 1970. *Experiments: Nine Essays on Catullus for Teachers*. Cambridge.

Grewing, F. 1996. "Möglichkeit und Grenzen des Vergleichs: Martials *Diadumenos* und Catulls *Lesbia*." *Hermes* 124: 333–54.

Grewing, F. 1997. *Martial, Buch VI: Ein Kommentar*. Göttingen.

Griffith, R. D. 1995. "Catullus' *Coma Berenices* and Aeneas' Farewell to Dido." *Transactions of the American Philological Association* 125: 47–60.

Grimal, P. 1987. "Catulle et les origines de l'élégie romaine." *Mélanges d'archéologie et de l'histoire de l'école française de Rome, antiquité* 99: 243–56.

Gronewald, M., and R. W. Daniel. 2004a. "Ein neuer Sappho-Papyrus." *Zeitschrift für Papyrologie und Epigraphik* 147: 1–8.

Gronewald, M., and R. W. Daniel. 2004b. "Nachtrag zum neuen Sappho-Papyrus." *Zeitschrift für Papyrologie und Epigraphik* 149: 1–4.

Gruen, E. 1966. "Cicero and Licinius Calvus." *Harvard Studies in Classical Philology* 71: 215–33.

Gruen, E. 1974. *The Last Generation of the Roman Republic*. Berkeley, Los Angeles, and London.

Gunderson, E. 2000. *Staging Masculinity*. Ann Arbor, MI.

Habinek, T. N. 1998. *The Politics of Latin Literature: Writing, Identity, and Empire in Ancient Rome*. Princeton, NJ.

Habinek, T. N. 2005. *Roman Song Culture*. Baltimore.

Hale, W. G. 1910. "Benzo of Alexandria and Catullus." *Classical Philology* 5: 56–65.

Hallett, J. P. 1979. "Sappho and Her Social Context: Sense and Sensuality." *Signs* 4: 447–64.

Hallett, J. P., and M. B. Skinner, eds. 1997. *Roman Sexualities*. Princeton, NJ.

Halperin, D. M. 1990. *One Hundred Years of Homosexuality and Other Essays on Greek Love*. New York.

Hankins, J. 1990. "The Latin Poetry of Leonardo Bruni." *Humanistica lovaniensia* 39: 1–39.

Hardwick, L. 2000. *Translating Words, Translating Cultures*. London.

Hardwick, L. 2003. *Reception Studies*. Oxford and New York.

Hardy, T. 1902. *Poems of the Past and the Present*. London and New York.

Harmon, D. P. 1973. "Nostalgia for the Age of Heroes in Catullus 64." *Latomus* 32: 311–31.

Harris, W. V. 1985. *War and Imperialism in Republican Rome, 327–70 B.C.* Rev. edn. Oxford.

Harrison, E. 1915. "Catullus, LXXXIV." *Classical Review* 29: 198–9.

Harrison, S. J., ed. 1995. *Homage to Horace*. Oxford.

Harvey, E. 1989. "Ventriloquizing Sappho: Ovid, Donne, and the Erotics of the Feminine Voice." *Criticism* 31.2: 115–38.

Harvey, P. B. 1979. "Catullus 114–15: Mentula, Roman Agricola." *Historia* 28: 329–55.

Hausmann, F.-R. 1980. "Martialis." *Catalogus Translationum et Commentariorum* 4. Washington, DC. 249–96.

Havelock, E. 1967 [1939]. *The Lyric Genius of Catullus*. New York.

Heath, M. 2002. *Interpreting Classical Texts*. London.

Heck, B. 1951. "Die Anordnung der Gedichte des Gaius Valerius Catullus." Dissertation. Tübingen.

Heesakkers, C. L. 1976. *Praecidanea Dousana*. Amsterdam.

Hellegouarc'h, J. 1972. *Le vocabulaire Latin des relations et des partis politiques sous la République*. 2nd edn. rev. and corr. Paris.

Herrmann, L. 1930. "Le poème 64 de Catulle et Vergile." *Revue des études latines* 8: 211–21.

Herzfeld, M. 1985. *The Poetics of Manhood: Contest and Identity in a Cretan Mountain Village*. Princeton, NJ.

Heusch, H. 1954. *Das Archaische in der Sprache Catulls*. Bonn.

Heyworth, S. J. 1993. "Dividing Poems." In O. Pecere and M. D. Reeve, eds., *Formative Stages of Classical Traditions: Latin Texts from Antiquity to the Renaissance*. Spoleto. 117–48.

Heyworth, S. J. 2001. "Catullian Iambics, Catullian *iambi*." In A. Cavarzere, A. Aloni, and A. Barchiesi, eds., *Iambic Ideas: Essays on a Poetic Tradition from Archaic Greece to the Late Roman Empire*. Lanham, MD, Boulder, CT, New York, and Oxford. 117–40.

Hickson-Hahn, F. 1998. "What's so Funny? Laughter and Incest in Invective Humor." *Syllecta Classica* 9: 1–36.

Highet, G. 1957. *Poets in a Landscape*. New York.

Hinds, S. 1998. *Allusion and Intertext: Dynamics of Appropriation in Roman Poetry*. Cambridge.

Hinds, S. 2001. "Cinna, Statius, and 'Immanent Literary History' in the Cultural Economy." *Entretiens Fondation Hardt* 47: 221–57.

Hodge, R. I. V., and R. A. Buttimore. 1977. *The "Monobiblos" of Propertius: An Account of the First Book of Propertius Consisting of a Text, Translation, and Critical Essay on Each Poem*. Cambridge.

Hofmann, J. B. 1926. *Lateinische Umgangssprache*. Heidelberg.

Holland, T. 2004. *Rubicon: The Last Years of the Roman Republic*. New York.

Hollis, A. S. 1990. *Callimachus: Hecale*. Oxford.

Hollis, A. S. 1992. "The Nuptial Rite in Catullus 66 and Callimachus' Poetry for Berenice." *Zeitschrift für Papyrologie und Epigraphik* 91: 21–8.

Holmes, J. S. 1988. *Translated! Papers on Literary Translation and Translation Studies*. Amsterdam.

Holzberg, N. 2000. "Lesbia, the Poet, and the Two Faces of Sappho: 'Womanufacture' and Gender Discourse in Catullus." *Proceedings of the Cambridge Philological Society* n.s. 46: 28–44.

Holzberg, N. 2002a. *Catull: Der Dichter und sein erotisches Werk*. Munich.

Holzberg, N. 2002b. *Martial und das antike Epigramm*. Darmstadt.

Holzberg, N. 2004. "Impersonating the Young Vergil: The Author of the *Catalepton* and His *Libellus*." *Materiali e discussioni* 52: 29–40.

Holzberg, N. 2006. "Onomato-Poetics: A Linear Reading of 7.67–70." In J. Booth and R. Maltby, eds., *What's in a Name? The Significance of Proper Names in Classical Latin Literature*. Swansea. 145–58.

Hooley, D. M. 1988. *The Classics in Paraphrase: Ezra Pound and Modern Translators of Latin Poetry*. Selinsgrove, London, and Toronto.

Hooper, R. W. 1985. "In Defence of Catullus' Dirty Sparrow." *Greece & Rome* 32: 162–78.

Horsfall, N. 1979. "*Doctus sermones utriusque linguae*." *Échos du monde classique/Classical Views* 23: 85–95.

Howell, P. 1980. *A Commentary on Book One of the Epigrams of Martial*. London.

Howell, P. 1993. Review of Sullivan 1991. *Classical Review* 43: 275–8.

Howell, P. 1996. Review of Shackleton Bailey 1993. *Classical Review* 46: 36–8.

Hubbard, T. K. 1983. "The Catullan *Libellus*." *Philologus* 127: 218–37.

Hubbard, T. K. 1984. "Catullus 68: The Text as Self-Demystification." *Arethusa* 17: 29–49.

Hubbard, T. K. 1998. *The Pipes of Pan: Intertextuality and Literary Filiation in the Pastoral Tradition*. Ann Arbor, MI.

Hubbard, T. K. 2005. "The Catullan *Libelli* Revisited." *Philologus* 149: 253–77.

Hummel, F. H., and A. A. Brodribb, trans. 1876. *Lays from Latin Lyrics*. London.

Humphries, R. 1959. "Latin and English Verse: Some Practical Considerations." In Brower (1959: 57–66).

Hunt, L. 1849. *The Poetical Works of Leigh Hunt*. London.

Hunter, R. 1989. *Apollonius of Rhodes: Argonautica Book III*. Cambridge.

Hunter, R. 1991. "Breast Is Best: Catullus 64.18." *Classical Quarterly* n.s. 41: 254–5.

Hunter, R. 1993a. *The Argonautica of Apollonius: Literary Studies*. Cambridge.

Hunter, R., trans. 1993b. *Apollonius of Rhodes: Jason and the Golden Fleece*. Oxford.

Hunter, R. 1993c. "Callimachean Echoes in Catullus 65." *Zeitschrift für Papyrologie und Epigraphik* 96: 179–82.

Hurley, A. K. 2004. *Catullus*. London.

Hutchinson, G. O. 1988. *Hellenistic Poetry*. Oxford.

Hutchinson, G. O. 2003. "The Catullan Corpus, Greek Epigram, and the Poetry of Objects." *Classical Quarterly* n.s. 53.1: 206–21.

Hutton, J. 1946. *The Greek Anthology in France*. Ithaca, NY.

Irigaray, L. 1985. *This Sex Which Is Not One*. Trans. C. Porter. Ithaca, NY.

Irvine, J. 2001. " 'Style' as Distinctiveness: The Culture and Ideology of Linguistic Differentiation." In P. Eckert and J. R. Rickford, eds., *Style and Sociolinguistic Variation*. Cambridge. 21–43.

Itzkowitz, J. B. 1983. "On the Last Stanza of Catullus 51." *Latomus* 42: 129–34.

Jacobson, H. 1974. *Ovid's Heroides*. Princeton, NJ.

James, S. 2003. *Learned Girls and Male Persuasion: Gender and Reading in Roman Love Elegy*. Berkeley.

Janan, M. 1994. *"When the Lamp is Shattered": Desire and Narrative in Catullus*. Carbondale and Edwardsville, IL.

Janan, M. 2001. *The Politics of Desire: Propertius IV*. Berkeley.

Jaro, B. K. 1988. *The Key*. New York.

Jaro, B. K. 2002a. *The Lock*. Wauconda, IL.

Jaro, B. K. 2002b. *The Door in the Wall*. Wauconda, IL.

Jenkins, J. 1981. "A Commentary on Selected Epigrams from Martial Book 10." Dissertation. Cambridge University.

Jenkyns, R. 1982. *Three Classical Poets: Sappho, Catullus and Juvenal*. London.

Jenkyns, R. 1998. *Virgil's Experience: Nature and History: Times, Names, and Places*. Oxford.

Jocelyn, H. D. 1981. "Difficulties in Martial, Book 1." *Papers of the Liverpool Latin Seminar* 3: 277–84.

Jocelyn, H. D. 1999. "The Arrangement and the Language of Catullus' So-Called *polymetra* with Special Reference to the Sequence 10–11–12." In Adams and Mayer (1999: 335–75).

Johnson, M. 2003. "Catullus 2b: The Development of a Relationship in the '*passer*' Trilogy." *Classical Journal* 99: 11–34.

Johnson, W. R. 1976. *Darkness Visible: A Study of Vergil's Aeneid*. Berkeley and Los Angeles.

Johnson, W. R. 1982. *The Idea of Lyric: Lyric Modes in Ancient and Modern Poetry*. Berkeley.

Johnston, P. 1987. "Dido, Berenice, and Arsinoe: *Aeneid* 6.460." *American Journal of Philology* 108: 649–54.

Jones, J. W. 1998. "Catullus' *passer* as *passer*." *Greece & Rome* 45: 188–94.

Jonson, B. 1983. *Volpone*. Eds. B. Parker and D. Bevington. Manchester and New York.

Kaster, R. A. 1995. *C. Suetonius Tranquillus: De Grammaticis et Rhetoribus*. Oxford.

Kay, N. M. 1985. *Martial Book XI: A Commentary*. London.

Keil, H. 1874. *Grammatici latini VI*. Leipzig.

Keil, H. 1961. *Grammatici latini (GLK)*. 8 vols. Hildesheim. Rpt. of the 1855–80 Leipzig edn.

Kelley, W. K. 1891. *The Poems of Catullus and Tibullus . . . A Literal Prose Translation*. London.

Kemp, P., ed. 1999. *The Oxford Dictionary of Literary Quotations*. Oxford.

Kennedy, D. 1993. *The Arts of Love: Five Studies in the Discourse of Roman Love Elegy*. Cambridge.

Kennedy, D. 1999. " 'cf.': Analogies, Relationships and Catullus 68." In S. M. Braund and R. Mayer, eds., *Amor: Roman Love and Latin Literature*. Cambridge. 30–43.

Kenney, E. J. 1974. *The Classical Text: Aspects of Editing in the Age of the Printed Book*. Berkeley.

Kenney, E. J. 1982. "Books and Readers in the Roman World." In Kenney and Clausen (1982: 3–32).

Kenney, E. J., and W. V. Clausen, eds. 1982. *The Cambridge History of Classical Literature. Vol. II: Latin Literature*. Cambridge and New York.

Kerkhecker, A. 1999. *Callimachus' Book of Iambi*. Oxford.

Kidd, D., ed. 1997. *Aratus: Phaenomena*. Cambridge.

Kilroy, G. 1969. "The Dido Episode and the Sixty-Fourth Poem of Catullus." *Symbolae Osloenses* 44: 48–60.

King, J. K. 1980. "The Two Galluses of Propertius' *Monobiblos*." *Philologus* 124: 212–30.

King, J. K. 1988. "Catullus' Callimachean *carmina*, cc. 65–116." *Classical World* 81: 383–92.

Kinsey, T. E. 1965. "Catullus 11." *Latomus* 24: 537–44.

Klein, J. T. 2005. *Humanities, Culture, and Interdisciplinarity: The Changing American Academy*. Albany, NY.

Klingner, F. 1964. "Catulls Peleus-Epos." *Sitzungsberichte der Bayerischen Akademie der Wissenschaften. Philosophisch-Historische Klasse, Heft 6* (1956) = *Studien zur griechischen und römischen Literatur*. Zurich. 156–224.

Knight, V. 1995. *The Renewal of Epic: Responses to Homer in the Argonautica of Apollonius*. Leiden, New York, and Cologne.

Knight, W. S. J. 1944. *Roman Vergil*. 2nd edn. London.

Knox, P. E. 1998. "Ariadne on the Rocks." In P. E. Knox and C. Foss, eds., *Style and Tradition: Studies in Honor of Wendell Clausen*. Stuttgart and Leipzig. 72–83.

Knox, P. E. 2002. "Representing the Great Mother to Augustus." In G. Herbert-Brown, ed., *Ovid's Fasti: Historical Readings at its Bimillennium*. Oxford. 155–74.

Konstan, D. 1977. *Catullus' Indictment of Rome: The Meaning of Catullus 64*. Amsterdam.

Konstan, D. 1993. "Neoteric Epic: Catullus 64." In A. J. Boyle, ed., *Roman Epic*. London. 59–78.

Konstan, D. 2000/2. "Self, Sex, and Empire in Catullus: The Construction of a Decentered Identity." In V. Bécares Botas, F. Pordomingo, R. Cortés Tovar, and C. Fernández Corte, eds., *La intertextualidad griega y latina*. Madrid. 213–31. (Also available online at http://zeno.stoa.org/cgi- bin/ptext?doc=Stoa:text:2002.01.0005.)

Koster, S. 1981. "Catull beim Wort genommen." *Würzburger Jahrbücher* n.F. 7: 125–34.

Kranz, W. 1961. "SPHRAGIS: Ichform und Namensiegel als Eingangs- und Schlußmotiv antiker Dichtung." *Rheinisches Museum* 104: 3–46 and 97–124.

Krebs, C., unpublished. "Caesar Magnus: Alexander, Pompey, and Caesar in Catull. 11."

Kroll, W. 1924. *Studien zum Verständnis der römischen Literatur*. Stuttgart.

Kroll, W. 1968 [1923]. *C. Valerius Catullus, herausgegeben und erklärt*. 5th edn. Stuttgart. (1st edn. Leipzig.)

Krostenko, B. A. 2001a. *Cicero, Catullus, and the Language of Social Performance*. Chicago and London.

Krostenko, B. A. 2001b. "*Arbitria urbanitatis*: Language, Style, and Characterization in Catullus cc. 39 and 37." *Classical Antiquity* 20.2: 239–72.

Kühner, R. K., and C. Stegmann. 1976. *Ausführliche Grammatik der Lateinischen Sprache*. Hanover.

Kuttner, A. L. 1999. "Culture and History at Pompey's Museum." *Transactions of the American Philological Association* 129: 343–73.

Labov, W. 2001. *Principles of Linguistic Change: Social Factors*. Malden, MA.

LaFleur, R. A. 1997. "*Latina resurgens*: Classical Language Enrollments in American Schools and Colleges." *Classical Outlook* 74: 125–30.

LaFleur, R. A., ed. 1998. *Latin for the 21st Century: From Concept to Classroom*. Glenview, IL.

Laidlaw, W. A. 1968. "*Otium*." *Greece & Rome* 15: 42–52.

Laird, A. 1993. "Sounding out Ecphrasis: Art and Text in Catullus 64." *Journal of Roman Studies* 83: 18–30.

Landino, C. 1939. *Christophori Landini Carmina Omnia*. Ed. A. Perosa. Florence.

Landor, W. S. 1853. *The Last Fruit off an Old Tree*. London.

Lardinois, A. 1989. "Lesbian Sappho and Sappho of Lesbos." In J. Bremmer, ed., *From Sappho to de Sade: Moments in the History of Sexuality*. London. 15–35.

Lardinois, A. 1994. "Subject and Circumstance in Sappho's Poetry." *Transactions of the American Philological Association* 124: 57–84.

Laumonier, P. 1923. *Ronsard, poète lyrique*. 2nd edn. Paris.

Lawall, G. 1967. *Theocritus' Coan Pastorals: A Poetry Book*. Washington, DC.

Lawall, G. and E. Baer. 2004. *Catullus Supplement: The New Selections of the Advanced Placement Syllabus*. Amherst, MA.

Leach, E. W. 2000. " Cicero's Pro Sestio: Spectacle and Performance." In S. K. Dickison and J. P. Hallett, eds., *Rome and Her Monuments: Essays on the City and Literature of Rome in Honor of Katherine A. Geffcken*. Wauconda, IL. 329–97.

Lee, G., trans. 1990. *The Poems of Catullus*. Oxford and New York.

Leeman, A. D. 1963. *Orationis ratio*. 2 vols. Amsterdam.

Lee-Stecum, P. 1998. *Powerplay in Tibullus*. Cambridge.

Lefevere, A. 1975. *Translating Poetry: Seven Strategies and a Blueprint*. Amsterdam.

Lefèvre, E. 1991. "Was hatte Catull in der Kapsel, die er von Rom nach Verona mitnahm? Zu Aufbau und Aussage der Allius-Elegie." *Rheinisches Museum für Philologie* 134: 311–26.

Lefèvre, E. 2000a. "Alexandrinisches und catullisches im Peleus-Epos (64)." *Hermes* 128: 181–201.

Lefèvre, E. 2000b. "Catullus Parzenlied und Vergils vierte Ekloge." *Philologus* 144: 62–80.

Lehnus, L. 2000. *Nuova bibliografia callimachea (1489–1998)*. Alessandria.

Lieberg, G. 1958. "L'ordinamento ed i reciproci rapporti dei carmi maggiori di Catullo." *Rivista di Filologia e di Istruzione Classica* 36: 23–47.

Lightfoot, J. L. 1999. *Parthenius of Nicaea*. Oxford.

Lindsay, W. M., ed. 1913. *Festus: De verborum significatione*. Leipzig.

Lintott, A. 1999. *Violence in Republican Rome*. 2nd edn. Oxford.

Lipking, L. 1988. *Abandoned Women and Poetic Tradition*. Chicago.

Lloyd-Jones, H., and P. Parsons. 1983. *Supplementum Hellenisticum*. Berlin.

Loefstedt, B. 1911. *Philologischer Kommentar zur Peregrinatio Aetheriae: Untersuchungen zur Geschichte der Lateinischen Sprache*. Uppsala and Leipzig.

Loomis, J. W. 1972. *Studies in Catullan Verse: An Analysis of Word Types and Patterns in the Polymetra*. *Mnemosyne* Supplement 24. Leiden.

Lorenz, S. 2002. *Erotik und Panegyrik: Martials epigrammatische Kaiser*. Tübingen.

Lorenz, S. 2003. "Martial: 1970–2003. 1. Teil." *Lustrum* 45: 167–277.

Lorenz, S. 2004a. "*Nulla virtus dulcior esse potest*: 'Mannestum' und 'Männlichkeit' in der erotischen Kleindichtung." In G. Partoens, G. Roskam, and T. Van Houdt, eds., Virtutis imago: *Studies on the Conceptualisation and Transformation of an Ancient Ideal*. Louvain. 117–43.

Lorenz, S. 2004b. "Waterscape with Black and White: Epigrams, Cycles, and Webs in Martial's *Epigrammaton liber quartus*." *American Journal of Philology* 125: 255–78.

Lowrie, M. 1997. *Horace's Narrative Odes*. Oxford.

Lowry, M. 1979. *The World of Aldus Manutius*. Cambridge.

Luck, G. 1960. *The Latin Love Elegy*. New York.

Ludwig, W. 1986. "Kannte Lovato Catull?" *Rheinisches Museum* 129: 329–57.

Ludwig, W. 1989. "*Catullus renatus*: Anfänge und frühe Entwicklung des catullischen Stils in der neulateinischen Dichtung." In L. Braun, W. W. Ehlers, P. G. Schmidt, and B. Seidensticker, eds., *Litterae Neolatinae: Schriften zur neulateinischen Literatur*. Munich. 162–94.

Ludwig, W. 1990. "The Origin and Development of the Catullan Style in Neo-Latin Poetry." In Godman and Murray (1990: 183–98).

Lyne, R. O. A. M., ed. 1978a. *Ciris: A Poem Attributed to Vergil*. Cambridge.

Lyne, R. O. A. M. 1978b. "The Neoteric Poets." *Classical Quarterly* 28: 167–87.

Lyne, R. O. A. M. 1980. *The Latin Love Poets from Catullus to Horace*. Oxford.

Lyne, R. O. A. M. 1994. "Vergil's *Aeneid*: Subversion by Intertextuality, Catullus 66.39–40 and Other Examples." *Greece & Rome* 41: 187–204.

Lyne, R. O. A. M. 1995. *Horace: Behind the Public Poetry*. New Haven, CT.

Lyne, R. O. A. M. 1998. "Love and Death: Laodamia and Protesilaus in Catullus, Propertius, and Others." *Classical Quarterly* n.s. 48: 200–12.

Macleod, C. W. 1973. "Catullus 116." *Classical Quarterly* 23: 304–9.

Macleod, C. W. 1974. "A Use of Myth in Ancient Poetry." *Classical Quarterly* n.s. 24: 82–93.

Maïer, I. 1966. *Ange Politien: la formation d'un poète humaniste*. Geneva.

Maleuvre, J.-Y. 1998. *Catulle ou L'anti-César: perspectives nouvelles sur le "Libellus."* Paris.

Mantuan (B. Spagnoli). ca. 1490. *Contra poetas impudice scribentes carmen*. Paris.

Manzo, A. 1967. "Testimonianze e tradizione del 'liber' catulliano nella letteratura esegeticoscolastica antica." *Rivista di Studi Classici* 15: 137–62.

Marinčič, M. 2001. "Der Weltaltermythos in Catulls Peleus-Epos (*C*. 64), der kleine Herakles (Theokr. *ID*. 24) und der römische 'Messianismus' Vergils." *Hermes* 120: 484–504.

Marinone, N., ed. 1997. *Berenice da Callimaco a Catullo: testo critico, traduzione e commento*. Rev. edn. Bologna.

Marmorale, E. V. 1957. *L'ultimo Catullo*. Naples.

Martin, C., trans. 1990. *The Poems of Catullus*. Baltimore and London.

Martin, C. 1992. *Catullus*. New Haven, CT, and London.

Martindale, C. 2005. *Latin Poetry and the Judgement of Taste*. Oxford.

Marullo, M. 1951. *Michaelis Marulli Carmina.* Ed. A. Perosa. Zurich.

Massimilla, G. 1996. *Callimaco: Aitia, Libri Primo e Secondo.* Pisa.

Mayer, R. G. 1994. *Horace: Epistles, Book I.* Cambridge.

Mayer, R. G. 1995. "*Graecia Capta*: The Roman Reception of Greek Literature." *Papers of the Liverpool Latin Seminar* 8. Liverpool. 289–307.

McCullough, C. 1990.*The First Man in Rome.* New York.

McCullough, C. 1991. *The Grass Crown.* New York.

McCullough, C. 1993. *Fortune's Favorites.* New York.

McCullough, C. 1996. *Caesar's Women.* New York.

McCullough, C. 1997. *Caesar: A Novel.* New York.

McCullough, C. 2002. *The October Horse.* New York.

McEvilley, T. 1971. "Sappho, Fragment 94." *Phoenix* 25: 1–11.

McKay, A. G. 1975. *Houses, Villas and Palaces in the Roman World.* London.

McKie, D. S. 1977. "The Manuscripts of Catullus: Recension in a Closed Tradition." Dissertation. Cambridge University.

McNeill, R. L. B. 2001. *Horace: Image, Identity, and Audience.* Baltimore.

McPeek, J. A. S. 1939. *Catullus in Strange and Distant Britain.* Harvard Studies in Comparative Literature 15. Cambridge, MA. Rpt. 1972.

Mendell, C. W. 1935. "Catullan Echoes in the *Odes* of Horace." *Classical Philology* 30: 289–301.

Mendell, C. W. 1951. "The Influence of the Epyllion on the *Aeneid*." *Yale Classical Studies* 12: 205–26.

Mendell, C. W. 1962. *Latin Poetry: The New Poetry and the Augustans.* New Haven, CT.

Merrill, E. T., ed. 1893. *Catullus.* Rpt. 1951. Cambridge, MA.

Mette, H. J. 1956. Review of E. V. Marmorale, *L'ultimo Catullo. Gnomon* 28: 34–8.

Meyer, C. 1995. *Caesar.* Trans. D. McLintock. New York.

Meyers, T. L., ed. 2004. *The Uncollected Letters of Algernon Charles Swinburne. Vol. 3: 1890–1909.* London and Brookfield, VT.

Michie, J., trans. 1969. *The Poems of Catullus.* London.

Miller, P. A. 1994. *Lyric Texts and Lyric Consciousness: The Birth of a Genre from Archaic Greece to Augustan Rome.* London and New York.

Miller, P. A. 1998. "Catullan Consciousness, the 'Care of the Self,' and the Force of the Negative in History." In D. H. J. Larmour, P. A. Miller, and C. Platter, eds. *Rethinking Sexuality: Foucault and Classical Antiquity.* Princeton, NJ. 171–203.

Miller, P. A. 2002. *Latin Erotic Elegy: An Anthology and Reader.* London.

Miller, P. A. 2004. *Subjecting Verses: Latin Love Elegy and the Emergence of the Real.* Princeton, NJ.

Minyard, J. D. 1988. "The Source of the *Catulli Veronensis Liber*." *Classical World* 81: 343–53.

Moore, G. 1985. *Hail and Farewell.* Ed. R. A. Cave. Gerrards Cross.

Morrison, M. 1955. "Catullus in the Neo-Latin Poetry of France before 1550." *Bibliothèque d'humanism et renaissance* 17: 365–94.

Morrison, M. 1956. "Ronsard and Catullus: The Influence of the Teaching of Marc-Antoine de Muret." *Bibliothèque d'humanism et renaissance* 18: 240–74.

Morrison, M. 1963. "Catullus and the Poetry of the Renaissance in France." *Bibliothèque d'humanism et renaissance* 25: 25–56.

Most, G. 1981. "On the Arrangement of Catullus' *Carmina Maiora*." *Philologus* 125: 109–25.

Most, G. 1996. "Reflecting Sappho." In E. Greene (1996: 11–35).

Muecke, F., ed. 1993. *Horace* Satires II. Warminster.

Müller, V. 1941. "The Date of the Augustus from Prima Porta." *American Journal of Philology* 62.4: 496–9.

Mulroy, D., trans. 2002. *The Complete Poetry of Catullus*. Madison, WI.

Muret, M.-A. de. 1554. *Catullus et in eum Commentarius*. Venice.

Murphy, C. A., D. Thiem, and R. T. Moore. 2005. *Embers of the Ancient Flame*. 2nd edn. Wauconda, IL.

Murray, O. 1985. "Symposium and Genre in the Poetry of Horace." *Journal of Roman Studies* 75: 39–50.

Myers, R., and R. J. Ormsby, trans. 1970. *Catullus: The Complete Poems for American Readers*. New York.

Mynors, R. A. B., ed. 1958 (rev. 1960). *C. Valerii Catulli Carmina recognovit brevique adnotatione critica instruxit*. Oxford.

Mynors, R. A. B., ed. 1969. *P. Vergili Maronis opera*. Oxford.

Nadeau, Y. 1982. "*Caesaries Berenices* (or the Hair of the God)." *Latomus* 41: 101–3.

Nappa, C. 2001. *Aspects of Catullus' Social Fiction*. Frankfurt.

Nauta, R. R. 2002. *Poetry for Patrons: Literary Communication in the Age of Domitian*. Leiden, Boston, and Cologne.

Németh, B. 1974. "Zur Analyse von Catull, c. 40." *Wissenschaftliche Zeitschrift der Universität Rostock* 23.3: 237–43.

Neudling, C. L. 1955. *A Prosopography to Catullus*. Iowa Studies in Classical Philology 12. [London.]

Newman, J. K. 1990. *Roman Catullus and the Modification of the Alexandrian Sensibility*. Hildesheim.

Nichols, F. J. 1979. *An Anthology of Neo-Latin Poetry*. New Haven, CT, and London.

Nicolson, H. 1968. *Diaries and Letters 1945–1962*. London.

Nippel, W. 1995. *Public Order in Ancient Rome*. Cambridge.

Nisbet, R. G. M. 1978. "Notes on the Text of Catullus." *Proceedings of the Cambridge Philological Society* n.s. 24: 92–115 (= R. G. M. Nisbet, *Collected Papers on Latin Literature*, ed. S. J. Harrison [Oxford 1995] 76–100).

Nisbet, R. G. M., and M. Hubbard. 1970. *A Commentary on Horace's Odes: Book I*. Oxford.

Nisbet, R. G. M., and M. Hubbard. 1978. *A Commentary on Horace's Odes: Book II*. Oxford.

Nisbet, R. G. M., and N. Rudd. 2004. *A Commentary on Horace's Odes: Book III*. Oxford.

Nisetich, F. 2001. *The Poems of Callimachus*. Oxford.

Noonan, J. D. 1979. "*Mala bestia* in Catullus 69.7–8." *Classical World* 73: 155–64.

Norden, E. 1957. *P. Vergilius Maro: Aeneis, Buch VI*. 4th edn. Stuttgart.

Obermayer, H. P. 1998. *Martial und der Diskurs über männliche "Homosexualität" in der Literatur der frühen Kaiserzeit*. Tübingen.

O'Brien, F. 1967. *At Swim-Two-Birds*. Harmondsworth.

Oehler, K. 1961. "Der consensus omnium als Kriterium der Wahrheit in der antiken Philosophie und der Patristik." *Antike und Abendland* 10: 103–29.

Offermann, H. 1980. "*Uno sim tibi minor Catullo*." *Quaderni urbinati della cultura classica* 5: 107–39.

Offermann, H. 1986. "Catull-Martial: Dichtung im Vergleich." *Anregung* 32: 226–35, 316–25.

O'Higgins, D. 1990. "Sappho's Splintered Tongue: Silence in Sappho 31 and Catullus 51." *American Journal of Philology* 111: 156–67.

Oliensis, E. 1997. "The Erotics of *amicitia*: Readings in Tibullus, Propertius, and Horace." In Hallett and Skinner (1997: 151–71).

Oliensis, E. 1998. *Horace and the Rhetoric of Authority*. Cambridge.

O'Sullivan, N. 1993. "Allusions of Grandeur? Thoughts on Allusion-Hunting in Latin Poetry." *Electronic Antiquity* 1.5. http://scholar.lib.vt.edu/ejournals/ElAnt/V1N5/osullivan.html.

Otis, B. 1964. *Virgil: A Study in Civilized Poetry*. Oxford.

Owen, S. G. 1915. *P. Ovidi Nasonis Tristium Libri Quinque Ibis Ex Ponto Libri Quattuor Halieutica Fragmenta*. Oxford.

"Paedagogus." 2002. Contributions by H. Bender, J. P. Hallett, P. A. Miller, L. Pearcy, M. Skinner. *Classical World* 95.4: 413–38.

Palmer, L. R. 1954. *The Latin Language*. London.

Palmer, L. R. 1980. *The Greek Language*. Atlantic Highlands, NJ.

Papanghelis, T. D., and A. Rengakos, eds. 2001. *A Companion to Apollonius Rhodius*. Leiden.

Parker, H. N. 1993. "Sappho Schoolmistress." *Transactions of the American Philological Association* 123: 309–51.

Parker, H. N. 1997. "The Teratogenic Grid." In Hallett and Skinner (1997: 47–65).

Partenio, A. 1491. *Antonii Parthenii Lacisii Veronensis in Catullum Commentationes*. Venice.

Pasquali, G. 1951. "Arte allusiva." In *Stravaganze quarte e supreme*. 11–20. Venice. (Rpt. in *Pagine stravaganti*. Florence, 1968. II.275–83.)

Paukstadt, R. 1876. "De Martiale Catulli imitatore." Dissertation. Halle.

Perella, N. J. 1969. *The Kiss, Sacred and Profane*. Berkeley.

Perkins, J. 1981. "Literary History: H.-G. Gadamar, T. S. Eliot and Virgil." *Arethusa* 14: 241–9.

Perosa, A., and J. Sparrow. 1979. *Renaissance Latin Verse: An Anthology*. London.

Perrotta, G. 1931. "Il carme 64 di Catullo e i suoi pretesi originali ellenistici." *Athenaeum* 9: 177–222, 371–409.

Perry, D. J. 1998. "Using the Reading Approach in Secondary Schools." In LaFleur (1998: 105–16).

Perutelli, A. 1980. "L'episodio di Aristeo nelle *Georgiche*: struttura e tecnica narrativa." *Materiali e discussioni* 4: 59–76.

Petrini, M. 1997. *The Child and the Hero: Coming of Age in Catullus and Vergil*. Ann Arbor, MI.

Pfeiffer, R., ed. 1949. *Callimachus*. 2 vols. Oxford.

Pigman, G. W., III. 1980. "Versions of Imitation in the Renaissance." *Renaissance Quarterly* 33: 1–32.

Pizzone, A. M. V. 1998. "Memmio e i carmi catulliani contro Mamurra: una proposta di cronologia." *Maia* 50: 281–9.

Platter, C. 1995. "*Officium* in Catullus and Propertius: A Foucauldian Reading." *Classical Philology* 90: 211–24.

Pleck, E., and J. Pleck, eds. 1980. *The American Man*. Englewood Cliffs, NJ.

Poliziano, A. 1971. *Opera Omnia*. Ed. I. Maïer. 3 vols. Turin.

Pomeroy, A. J. 2003. "Heavy Petting in Catullus." *Arethusa* 36: 49–60.

Pontani, F. 1999. "The First Word of Callimachus' AITIA." *Zeitschrift für Papyrologie und Epigraphik* 128: 57–9.

Pontano, G. G. 1902. *Ioannis Ioviani Pontani Carmina*. Ed. B. Soldati. 2 vols. Florence.

Pontano, G. G. 1978. *Ioannis Ioviani Pontani, Hendecasyllaborum Libri*. Naples.

Pontano, G. G. 2006. *Giovanni Gioviano Pontano: Baiae*. Trans. R. G. Dennis. I Tatti Renaissance Library 22. Cambridge, MA, and London.

Port, W. 1926. "Die Anordnung in Gedichtbüchern augusteischer Zeit." *Philologus* 35: 280–308, 427–68.

Pöschl, V. 1983. *Catull*. Freiburg.

Pound, E. 1960 [1935]. *The Literary Essays of Ezra Pound*. New York and London.

Pound, E. 1970. *Ezra Pound*. Ed. J. P. Sullivan. Harmondsworth.

Pound, E. 1973. *Selected Prose of Ezra Pound 1909–1965*. New York and London.

Pound, E. 1979–80. "Arthur Symons." *Agenda* 17–18: 54–7.

Pound, E. 1982 [1950]. *Selected Letters of Ezra Pound*. Ed. D. D. Paige. New York and London.

Pound, E. 1984 [1963]. *The Translations of Ezra Pound*. New York and London.

Pound, E. 1987a [1970]. *The Cantos of Ezra Pound*. New York and London.

Pound, E. 1987b [1971]. Personae: *The Shorter Collected Poems of Ezra Pound*. New York and London.

Prins, Y. 1996. "Sappho's Afterlife in Translation." In E. Greene (1996: 36–67).

Pucci, P. 1961. "Il carme 50 di Catullo." *Maia* 13: 249–56.

Puelma-Piwonka, M. 1949. *Lucilius und Kallimachos: Zur Geschichte einer Gattung der hellen-istisch-römischen Poesie*. Frankfurt.

Pulbrook, M. 1984. "The Lesbia *Libellus* of Catullus." *Maynooth Review* 10: 72–84.

Putnam, M. C. J. 1960. "Catullus 66.75–8." *Classical Philology* 55: 223–8.

Putnam, M. C. J. 1961. "The Art of Catullus 64." *Harvard Studies in Classical Philology* 65: 165–205.

Putnam, M. C. J. 1970. *Virgil's Pastoral Art: Studies in the* Eclogues. Princeton, NJ.

Putnam, M. C. J. 1982. "Catullus 11: The Ironies of Integrity." In *Essays on Latin Lyric, Elegy, and Epic*. Princeton, NJ. 13–29.

Putnam, M. C. J. 1983. "The Future of Catullus." *Transactions of the American Philological Association* 113: 243–62.

Putnam, M. C. J. 1986. *Artifices of Eternity*. Berkeley.

Putnam, M. C. J. 1989. "Catullus 11 and Virgil *Aen.* 6.786–7." *Vergilius* 35: 28–30.

Putnam, M. C. J. 1994. "Elder, John Petersen." In Briggs (1994: 159–60).

Putnam, M. C. J. 1995–6. "The Lyric Genius of the *Aeneid*." *Arion* 3.2–3: 81–101.

Putnam, M. C. J. 1998. *Virgil's Epic Designs: Ekphrasis in the* Aeneid. New Haven, CT.

Putnam, M. C. J. 2006. *Poetic Interplay: Catullus and Horace*. Princeton, NJ.

Quinn, K. 1959. *The Catullan Revolution*. Melbourne. Rpt. Cambridge 1969; Ann Arbor, MI, 1971. 2nd edn. London 1999.

Quinn, K. 1968. *Virgil's* Aeneid: *A Critical Description*. Ann Arbor, MI.

Quinn, K., ed. 1972a. *Approaches to Catullus*. Cambridge.

Quinn, K. 1972b. *Catullus: An Interpretation*. London.

Quinn, K., ed. 1973a. *Catullus: The Poems*. 2nd edn. London and Basingstoke.

Quinn, K. 1973b. "Trends in Catullan Criticism." In H. Temporini, ed., *Aufsteig und Niedergang der römischen Welt*. Vol. I.3. Berlin and New York. 369–89.

Ramage, E. S. 1973. Urbanitas: *Ancient Sophistication and Refinement*. Norman, OK.

Rand, E. K. 1906. "Catullus and the Augustans." *Harvard Studies in Classical Philology* 17: 15–30.

Rankin, H. D. 1972. "The Progress of Pessimism in Catullus, Poems 2–11." *Latomus* 31: 744–51.

Raphael, F. 2003. *A Spoilt Boy: A Memoir of Childhood*. London.

Raphael, F., and K. McLeish, trans. 1979. *The Poems of Catullus*. Boston.

Rauk, J. 1997. "Time and History in Catullus 1." *Classical World* 90: 319–32.

Raven, D. S. 1965. *Latin Meter*. London.

Raven, S. 1967. *Fielding Gray: A Novel*. New York.

Rawson, E. 1985. *Intellectual Life in the Late Roman Republic*. Baltimore.

Ready, J. L. 2004. "A Binding Song: The Similes of Catullus 61." *Classical Philology* 99: 153–63.

Reece, B., ed. 1969. *Sermones Ratherii Episcopi Veronensis*. Worcester, MA.

Reitzenstein, R. 1912. "Zur Sprache der lateinischen Erotik." *Sitzungsberichte der Heidelberger Akademie du Wissenschaften* 12: 1–36.

Reynolds, L. D., ed.1983. *Texts and Transmission: A Survey of the Latin Classics*. Oxford.

Richardson, L., Jr. 1977. *Propertius:* Elegies *I–IV*. Norman, OK.

Richlin, A. 1981. "The Meaning of *irrumare* in Catullus and Martial." *Classical Philology* 76: 40–6.

Richlin, A. 1992 [1983]. *The Garden of Priapus: Sexuality and Aggression in Roman Humor*. Rev. edn. New York and Oxford.

Richlin, A. 2000. "Gender and Rhetoric: Producing Manhood in the Schools." In W. Dominik, ed., *Roman Eloquence: Rhetoric in Society and Literature*. London. 90–110.

Ricks, C. B. 1989. *Tennyson: A Selected Edition Incorporating the Trinity College Manuscripts*. Berkeley and Los Angeles.

Ridenour, G. M. 1988. "Swinburne's Imitations of Catullus." *Victorian Newsletter* (Fall): 51–7.

Roffia, E. 1997. "Sirmione, le 'grotte di Catullo'." In E. Roffia, ed., *Ville romane sul lago di Garda*. Brescia. 141–69.

Roffia, E. 2005. *Le "grotte di Catullo" a Sirmione: Guida alla visita della villa romana e del museo*. Milan.

Roller, M. B. 2004. "Exemplarity in Roman Culture: The Cases of Horatius Cocles and Cloelia." *Classical Philology* 99: 1–56.

Ronsard, P. de. 1928. *Oeuvres completes*. Ed. P. Laumonier. Paris.

Ross, D. O., Jr. 1969. *Style and Tradition in Catullus*. Cambridge, MA.

Ross, D. O., Jr. 1973. "*Uriosque apertos*: A Catullan Gloss." *Mnemosyne* 26: 60–2.

Ross, D. O., Jr. 1975. *Backgrounds to Augustan Poetry: Gallus, Elegy and Rome*. Cambridge.

Rothstein, M. 1979 [1920]. *Die* Elegien *des Sextus Propertius*. 2 vols. 2nd edn. New York.

Rudd, N. 1982. *The Satires of Horace*. Berkeley.

Rudd, N., and J. Foster. 1970. "Poem LI." In Greig (1970: 42–8).

Sabbadini, R. 1914. *Le scoperte dei codici latini e greci ne' secoli xiv e xv*. 2 vols. Florence.

Sandy, G. N. 1971. "Catullus 63 and the Theme of Marriage." *American Journal of Philology* 92: 185–95.

Santirocco, M. S. 1986. *Unity and Design in Horace's Odes*. Chapel Hill, NC.

Sarkissian, J. 1983. *Catullus 68: An Interpretation*. *Mnemosyne* Supplement 76. Leiden.

Sarkissian, J. 2004. "The Grading of the 2004 Advanced Placement Examinations in Latin: Vergil." *Classical Outlook* 82.1: 1–18.

Saylor, S. 1991. *Roman Blood*. New York.

Saylor, S. 1992. *Arms of Nemesis*. New York.

Saylor, S. 1993. *Catalina's Riddle*. New York.

Saylor, S. 1995. *The Venus Throw*. New York.

Saylor, S. 1996. *A Murder on the Appian Way*. New York.

Saylor, S. 1997. *The House of the Vestals*. New York.

Saylor, S. 1999. *Rubicon*. New York.

Saylor, S. 2000. *Last Seen in Massilia*. New York.

Saylor, S. 2002. *A Mist of Prophecies*. New York.

Saylor, S. 2004. *The Judgment of Caesar*. New York.

Saylor, S. 2005. *A Gladiator Dies Only Once*. New York.

Scaliger, J. 1577. *Castigationes in Valerii Catulli librum*. Paris.

Schäfer, E. 1966. *Das Verhältnis von Erlebnis und Kunstgestalt bei Catull*. *Hermes* Einzelschriften 18. Wiesbaden.

Scheid, J., and J. Svenbro. 1996. *The Craft of Zeus: Myths of Weaving and Fabric*. Trans. C. Volk. Cambridge, MA.

Scherf, J. 1996. *Untersuchungen zur antiken Veröffentlichung der Catullgedichte*. *Spudasmata* 61. Hildesheim, Zurich, and New York.

Scherf, J. 2001. *Untersuchungen zur Buchgestaltung Martials*. Munich.

Schmale, M. 2004. *Bilderreigen und Erzähllabyrinth: Catulls Carmen 64*. Munich and Leipzig.

Schmidt, B. 1914. "Die Lebenzeit Catulls und die Herausgabe seiner Gedichte." *Rheinisches Museum* 69: 267–83.

Schmidt, E. A. 1973. "Catulls Anordnung seiner Gedichte." *Philologus* 117: 215–42.

Schmidt, E. A. 1979. "Das Problem des Catullbuches." *Philologus* 123: 216–31.

Schmidt, E. A. 1985. *Catull*. Heidelberg.

Schmiel, R. 1979. "A Virgilian Formula." *Vergilius* 25: 37–40.

Schork, R. J. 1997. *Latin and Roman Culture in Joyce*. Gainesville, FL.

Schulze, K. P. 1887. "Martials Catullstudien." *Jahrbücher für Classische Philologie* 33: 637–40.

Schwabe, L. 1862. *Quaestiones Catullianae*. Vol. I. Giessen.

Schwabe, L., ed. 1886. *Catulli veronensis liber*. 2nd edn. Berlin.

Scott, R. T. 1983. "On Catullus 11." *Classical Philology* 78: 39–42.

Seager, R. 1974. "*Venustus, lepidus, bellus, salsus*: Notes on the Language of Catullus." *Latomus* 33: 891–94.

Sedgwick, E. K. 1985. *Between Men: English Literature and Male Homosocial Desire*. New York.

Segal, C. 1968. "The Order of Catullus, Poems 2–11." *Latomus* 27: 305–21.

Segal, C. 1970. "Catullan *otiosi* – The Lover and the Poet." *Greece &Rome* 17: 25–31.

Selden, D. L. 1992. "*Ceveat lector*: Catullus and the Rhetoric of Performance." In R. Hexter and D. Selden, eds., *Innovations of Antiquity*. New York and London. 461–512.

Sesar, C., trans. 1974. *Selected Poems of Catullus*. New York.

Seymour-Smith, M. 1983. *Robert Graves: His Life and Work*. London.

Shackleton Bailey, D. R. 1990. *M. Valerii Martialis Epigrammata*. Post W. Heraeum edidit D. R. S. B. Stuttgart.

Shackleton Bailey, D. R. 1993. *Martial: Epigrams. Edited and Translated*. 3 vols. Cambridge, MA, and London.

Sharrock, A. R. 2000. "Constructing Characters in Propertius." *Arethusa* 33: 263–84.

Sheets, G. A. 2001. "Rhythm in Catullus 34." *Memoirs of the American Academy in Rome* 46: 11–21.

Sherwin White, A. N. 1966. *The Letters of Pliny: A Historical and Social Commentary*. Oxford.

Shorey, P. 1960. *Horace: Odes and Epodes*. Chicago.

Silver, I. 1966. "Marc-Antoine de Muret et Ronsard." In R. Antonioli, R. Aulotte, M.-E. Balmas, et al., eds., *Lumières de la Pléiade*. Paris. 33–48.

Simpson, F. P., ed. 1879. *Select Poems of Catullus*. London.

Singh, K. L. 1998. "Grammar-Translation and High-School Latin." In LaFleur (1998: 90–104).

Sisson, C. H., trans. 1967. *The Poetry of Catullus*. New York.

Skinner, M. B. 1972. "The Unity of Catullus 68: The Structure of 68a." *Transactions of the American Philological Association* 103: 495–512.

Skinner, M. B. 1979. "Parasites and Strange Bedfellows: A Study in Catullus' Political Imagery." *Ramus* 8: 137–52.

Skinner, M. B. 1981. *Catullus' Passer: The Arrangement of the Book of Polymetric Poems*. New York.

Skinner, M. B. 1982a. "Pretty Lesbius." *Transactions of the American Philological Association* 112: 197–208.

Skinner, M. B. 1982b. "Supplementary Note on the Latin Sexual Language: Catullus 56.5–6." *Liverpool Classical Monthly* 7: 140.

Skinner, M. B. 1983. "Clodia Metelli." *Transactions of the American Philological Association* 113: 273–87.

Skinner, M. B. 1984. "Rhamnusia Virgo." *Classical Antiquity* 3: 134–41.

Skinner, M. B. 1987. "Cornelius Nepos and Xenomedes of Ceos: A Callimachean Allusion in Catullus 1." *Liverpool Classical Monthly* 12: 22.

Skinner, M. B. 1988. "Aesthetic Patterning in Catullus: Textual Structures, Systems of Imagery and Book Arrangements. Introduction." *Classical World* 81: 337–40.

Skinner, M. B. 1989. "*Ut decuit cinaediorem*: Power, Gender, and Urbanity in Catullus 10." *Helios* 16: 7–23.

Skinner, M. B. 1991. "The Dynamics of Catullan Obscenity: cc. 37, 58 and 11." *Syllecta Classica* 3: 1–11.

Skinner, M. B. 1993a. "Catullus in Performance." *Classical Journal* 89: 61–8.

Skinner, M. B. 1993b. "*Ego mulier*: The Construction of Male Sexuality in Catullus." *Helios* 20: 107–30 (= Hallett and Skinner 1997: 129–50).

Skinner, M. B. 1993c. "Woman and Language in Archaic Greece, or, Why is Sappho a Woman?" In N. S. Rabinowitz and A. Richlin, eds., *Feminist Theory and the Classics*. New York. 125–44.

Skinner, M. B. 2001. "Among Those Present: Catullus 44 and 10." *Helios* 28: 57–73.

Skinner, M. B. 2003. *Catullus in Verona: A Reading of the Elegiac* Libellus, *Poems 65–116*. Columbus, OH.

Skinner, M. B. 2005. *Sexuality in Greek and Roman Culture*. Malden, MA.

Skulsky, S. 1985. " '*Inuitus, regina . . .*': Aeneas and the Love of Rome." *American Journal of Philology* 106.4: 447–55.

Skutsch, O. 1969. "Metrical Variations and Some Textual Problems in Catullus." *Bulletin of the Institute of Classical Studies of the University of London* 16: 38–43.

Skutsch, O. 1970. "The Book under the Bushel." *Bulletin of the Institute of Classical Studies of the University of London* 17: 148.

Skutsch, O. 1985. *The Annals of Quintus Ennius*. Oxford.

Slater, D. A. 1912. "Was the Fourth *Eclogue* Written to Celebrate the Marriage of Octavia to Mark Antony? A Literary Parallel." *Classical Review* 26.4: 114–19.

Smith, R. A. 1993. "A Lock and a Promise: Myth and Allusion in Aeneas' Farewell to Dido in *Aeneid* 6." *Phoenix* 47: 305–12.

Smith, S. 1972. *Collected Poems of Stevie Smith*. New York.

Snyder, J. M. 1997. *Lesbian Desire in the Lyrics of Sappho*. New York.

Solodow, J. B. 1987. "On Catullus 95." *Classical Philology* 82: 141–5.

Spencer, D. J. 2005. "Lucan's Follies: Memory and Ruin in a Civil-War Landscape." *Greece & Rome* 52: 46–69.

Stahl, H. P. 1985. *Propertius: "Love" and "War": Individual and State under Augustus*. Berkeley.

Starr, R. J. 1987. "The Circulation of Literary Texts in the Roman World." *Classical Quarterly* n.s. 37: 213–23.

Statius, A. 1566. *Catullus cum commentario*. Venice.

Stehle [Stigers], E. 1977. "Retreat from the Male: Catullus 62 and Sappho's Erotic Flowers." *Ramus* 6: 83–102.

Stehle [Stigers], E. 1979. "Romantic Sensuality, Poetic Sense: A Response to Hallett on Sappho." *Signs* 4: 464–71.

Stehle [Stigers], E. 1981. "Sappho's Private World." In H. Foley, ed., *Reflections of Women in Antiquity*. New York. 45–61.

Stehle [Stigers], E. 1997. *Performance and Gender in Ancient Greece*. Princeton, NJ.

Stock, N. 1985. *The Life of Ezra Pound*. Harmondsworth.

Stoessl, F. 1977. *C. Valerius Catullus: Mensch, Leben, Dichtung*. Meisenheim.

Stoevesandt, M. 1994/5. "Catull 64 und die *Ilias*." *Würzburger Jahrbücher für die Altertumswissenschaft* n.s. 20: 167–205.

Stoppard, T. 1997. *The Invention of Love*. New York.

Stroh, W. 1990. "Lesbia und Juventius: Ein erotisches Liederbuch im Corpus Catullianum." In P. Neukam, ed., *Die Antike als Begleiterin*. Klassische Sprachen und Literaturen Band XXIV. Munich. 134–58.

Suits, T. A. 1976. "The Iambic Character of Propertius 1.4." *Philologus* 120: 86–91.

Sullivan, J. P. 1991. *Martial: The Unexpected Classic. A Literary and Historical Study.* Cambridge.

Summers, K. 2001. "Catullus' Program in the Imagination of Later Epigrammatists." *Classical Bulletin* 77: 147–60.

Süss, J. 1877. *Catulliana.* Erlangen.

Sutherland, C. H. V. 1984. *The Roman Imperial Coinage.* Vol. 1. Rev. edn. London.

Swann, B. W. 1994. *Martial's Catullus: The Reception of an Epigrammatic Rival.* Hildesheim.

Swann, B. W. 1998. "*Sic scribit Catullus*: The Importance of Catullus for Martial's Epigrams." In F. Grewing, ed., Toto notus in orbe: *Perspektiven der Martial-Interpretation.* Stuttgart. 48–58.

Sweet, D. 1987. "Catullus 11: A Study in Perspective." *Latomus* 46: 510–26.

Swinburne, A. C. 1912. *Poems and Ballads.* 6 vols. London.

Syme, R. 1939. *The Roman Revolution.* Oxford.

Syme, R. 1958. *Tacitus.* 2 vols. Oxford.

Syme, R. 1979. *Roman Papers.* Vols. 1–2. Oxford.

Syme, R. 1984. *Roman Papers.* Vol. 3. Oxford.

Syme, R. 1988. *Roman Papers.* Vols. 4–5. Oxford.

Syme, R. 1991. *Roman Papers.* Vols. 6–7. Oxford.

Symons, A. 1973. *The Collected Works of Arthur Symons.* 9 vols. Rpt. of 1924 edn. New York.

Syndikus, H. P. 1984. *Catull: Eine Interpretation. Erster Teil: Einleitung, Die kleinen Gedichte (1–60).* Darmstadt.

Syndikus, H. P. 1987. *Catull: Eine Interpretation. Dritter Teil: Die Epigramme (69–116).* Darmstadt.

Syndikus, H. P. 1990. *Catull: Eine Interpretation. Zweiter Teil: Die grossen Gedichte (61–68).* Darmstadt.

Tarrant, R. J. 1983. "Catullus." In Reynolds (1983: 43–5).

Tatum, J. 1984. "Allusion and Interpretation in *Aeneid* 6.440–76." *American Journal of Philology* 105.4: 434–52.

Tatum, W. J. 1993. "Catullus 79: Personal Invective or Political Discourse?" In F. Cairns and M. Heath, eds., *Papers of the Leeds International Latin Seminar 7.* Leeds. 31–45.

Tatum, W. J. 1997. "Friendship, Politics, and Literature in Catullus: Poems 1, 65 and 66, 116." *Classical Quarterly* n.s. 47: 482–500.

Tatum, W. J. 1999. *The Patrician Tribune: Publius Clodius Pulcher.* Chapel Hill, NC.

Tatum, W. J. 2006. "The Final Crisis, 69–49." In N. Rosenstein and R. Morstein-Marx, eds., *A Companion to the Roman Republic.* Oxford. 190–211.

Tennyson, A., Lord. 1899. *Poetical Works of Alfred Lord Tennyson.* London.

Theodorakopoulos, E. 2000. "Catullus, 64: Footprints in the Labyrinth." In A. Sharrock and H. Morales, eds., *Intratextuality.* Oxford. 115–41.

Thomas, R. 1983. *The Latin Masks of Ezra Pound.* Ann Arbor, MI.

Thomas, R. F. 1979. "New Comedy, Callimachus and Roman Poetry." *Harvard Studies in Classical Philology* 83: 179–206.

Thomas, R. F. 1982. "Catullus and the Polemics of Poetic Reference (Poem 64.1–18)." *American Journal of Philology* 103: 144–64.

Thomas, R. F. 1983. "Callimachus, the *Victoria Berenices*, and Roman Poetry." *Classical Quarterly* 33: 92–113.

Thomas, R. F. 1986. "Virgil's *Georgics* and the Art of Reference." *Harvard Studies in Classical Philology* 90: 171–98.

Thomas, R. F., ed. 1988. *Virgil:* Georgics. 2 vols. Cambridge.

Thomas, R. F. 1993. "Sparrows, Hares, and Doves: A Catullan Metaphor and its Tradition." *Helios* 20: 131–42.

Thomas, R. F. 1999. *Reading Virgil and His Texts: Studies in Intertextuality.* Ann Arbor, MI.

Thomsen, O. 1992. *Ritual and Desire: Catullus 61 and 62 and Other Ancient Documents on Wedding and Marriage.* Aarhus.

Thomson, D. F. S. 1961. "Aspects of Unity in Catullus 64." *Classical Journal* 57: 49–57.

Thomson, D. F. S., ed. 1978. *Catullus: A Critical Edition.* Chapel Hill, NC.

Thomson, D. F. S., ed. 1997. *Catullus, Edited with a Textual and Interpretative Commentary.* Toronto.

Tracy, S. V. 1977. "Catullan Echoes in *Aeneid* 6.333–36." *American Journal of Philology* 98: 20–3.

Tränkle, H. 1981. "Catullprobleme." *Museum Helveticum* 38: 245–58.

Traglia, A., ed. 1962. *I Poeti Nuovi.* Rome.

Traill, D. A. 1988. "Ring Composition in Catullus 63, 64, and 68b." *Classical World* 81: 365–9.

Treggiari, S. 1991. *Roman Marriage: iusti coniuges from the Time of Cicero to the Time of Ulpian.* Oxford.

Trypanis, C. A., trans. 1958. *Callimachus:* Aetia, Iambi, *Lyric Poems,* Hecale, *Minor Epic and Elegiac Poems, and Other Fragments.* Cambridge, MA.

Tuplin, C. J. 1981. "Catullus 68." *Classical Quarterly* n.s. 31: 113–39.

Ullman, B. L. 1908. *The Identification of the Manuscripts of Catullus Cited in Statius' Edition of 1566.* Chicago.

Ullman, B. L. 1955. "Hieremias de Montagnone and his Citations from Catullus." In *Studies in the Italian Renaissance.* Rome. 181–200.

Ullman, B. L. 1960. "The Transmission of the Text of Catullus." In *Studi in onore di Luigi Castiglioni.* 2 vols. Florence. II.1027–57.

Ullman, B. L. 1973. *Studies in the Italian Renaissance.* 2nd edn. Rome.

Untermeyer, L. 1964. *Robert Frost: A Backward Look.* Washington, DC.

Vance, N. 1997. *The Victorians and Ancient Rome.* Oxford and Cambridge, MA.

Vandiver, E. 1990. "Sound Patterns in Catullus 84." *Classical Journal* 85: 337–40.

Van Sickle, J. 1980. "The Book-Roll and Some Conventions of the Poetic Book." *Arethusa* 13: 5–42.

Van Sickle, J. 1989. "The Hellenistic Background." *Augustan Age* 9: 42–8.

Van Sickle, J. 1992. *Virgil's Messianic Eclogue.* New York.

Venuti, L. 1998. *The Scandals of Translation: Towards an Ethics of Difference.* London and New York.

Venuti, L., ed. 2000. *The Translation Studies Reader.* London and New York.

Verboven, K. 2002. *The Economy of Friends: Economic Aspects of* Amicitia *and Patronage in the Late Republic.* Brussels.

Veyne, P. 1983. "La folklore à Rome et les droits de la conscience publique sur la conduite individuelle." *Latomus* 42: 3–30.

Veyne, P. 1988. *Roman Erotic Elegy: Love Poetry and the West.* Trans. D. Pellauer. Chicago.

Vian, F. 1974–81. *Apollonius de Rhodes* Argonautiques. 3 vols. Paris.

Vine, B. 1992. "On the 'Missing' Fourth Stanza of Catullus 51." *Harvard Studies in Classical Philology* 96: 251–8.

Vox, O. 2000. " Sul genere grammaticale della *Chioma di Berenice.*" *Materiali e Discussioni* 44: 175–81.

Wallace-Hadrill, A. 1988. "The Social Structure of the Roman House." *Papers of the British School at Rome* 56: 43–97.

Wallace-Hadrill, A. 1997. "*Mutatio morum*: The Idea of a Cultural Revolution." In T. Habinek and A. Schiesaro, eds., *The Roman Cultural Revolution.* Cambridge. 3–22.

Walters, K. R. 1976. "Catullan Echoes in the Second Century A.D." *Classical World* 69: 353–60.

Warner, R., trans. 1972. *Plutarch: Fall of the Roman Republic.* London.

Watson, L. C. 1991. Arae: *The Curse Poetry of Antiquity.* Leeds.
Watson, L. C. 2003. *A Commentary on Horace's Epodes.* Oxford.
Watson, L. C., and P. Watson. 2003. *Martial: Select Epigrams.* Cambridge.
Watson, P. 1999. "Martial on the Wedding of Stella and Violentilla." *Latomus* 58: 348–56.
Watson, P. A. 1984. "The Case of the Murderous Father: Catullus 64.401–2." *Liverpool Classical Monthly* 9: 114–16.
Weber, C. 1983. "Two Chronological Contradictions in Catullus 64." *Transactions of the American Philological Association* 113: 263–71.
Weiss, M. 1996. "An Oscanism in Catullus 53." *Classical Philology* 91: 353–9.
West, M. L. 1974. *Studies in Greek Elegy and Iambus.* Berlin.
West, M. L. 1982. *Greek Metre.* Oxford.
Westendorp-Boerma, R. E. H. 1958. "Vergil's Debt to Catullus." *Acta Classica* 1: 51–63.
Westphal, R. 1867. *Catulls Gedichte in ihrem geschichtlichen Zusammenhange übersetzt und erläutert.* 2nd edn. 1870. Breslau.
Wheeler, A. L. 1934. *Catullus and the Traditions of Ancient Poetry.* Berkeley and Los Angeles.
Whigham, P., trans. 1966. *The Poems of Catullus.* Harmondsworth.
Whitaker, R. 1983. *Myth and Personal Experience in Roman Love-Elegy: A Study in Poetic Technique.* Göttingen.
Whitehouse, J. C., ed. 1997. *Catholics on Literature.* Dublin.
Whitman, C. H., trans. 1980. *Fifteen Odes of Horace.* Lunenburg, VT.
Wigodsky, M. 1972. *Vergil and Early Latin Poetry.* Wiesbaden.
Wilamowitz-Moellendorff, U. von. 1913. *Sappho und Simonides.* Berlin.
Wilamowitz-Moellendorff, U. von. 1924. *Hellenistische Dichtung in der Zeit des Kallimachos.* 2 vols. Berlin.
Wilder, T. 1961 [1948]. *The Ides of March.* Harmondsworth.
Wilkinson, L. P. 1969. *The Georgics of Virgil: A Critical Survey.* Cambridge.
Willett, S. J. 2001. "Recent Trends in Classical Verse Translation." *Syllecta Classica* 12: 221–63.
Williams, C. A. 1999. *Roman Homosexuality: Ideologies of Masculinity in Classical Antiquity.* New York and Oxford.
Williams, C. A., ed. 2004. *Martial, Epigrams: Book 2.* Oxford.
Williams, F. 1978. *Callimachus,* Hymn to Apollo: *A Commentary.* Oxford.
Williams, G. 1958. "Some Aspects of Roman Marriage Ceremonies and Ideals." *Journal of Roman Studies* 48: 16–29.
Williams, G. 1980. *Figures of Thought in Roman Poetry.* New Haven, CT.
Williams, G. 1985 [1968]. *Tradition and Originality in Roman Poetry.* 2nd edn. Oxford.
Williamson, M. 1995. *Sappho's Immortal Daughters.* Cambridge, MA.
Wills, G. 1967. "Sappho 31 and Catullus 51." *Greek, Roman, and Byzantine Studies* 8: 167–97.
Wills, J. 1996. *Repetition in Latin Poetry: Figures of Allusion.* Oxford.
Wills, J. 1998. "Divided Allusion: Virgil and the *Coma Berenices.*" *Harvard Studies in Classical Philology* 98: 277–305.
Wilson, E. 2005. "Sparrows and Scrubbers" (review of Green 2005). *New Republic* November 14: 30–3.
Wimmel, W. 1960. *Kallimachos im Rom. Hermes* Einzelschriften 16. Wiesbaden.
Winkler, J. J. 1990. "*Phallos politikos:* Representing the Body Politic in Athens." *differences* 2.1: 28–45.
Wiseman, T. P. 1969. *Catullan Questions.* Leicester.
Wiseman, T. P. 1974. *Cinna the Poet and Other Roman Essays.* Leicester.
Wiseman, T. P. 1979. *Clio's Cosmetics: Three Studies in Greco-Roman Literature.* Leicester.
Wiseman, T. P. 1985. *Catullus and His World: A Reappraisal.* Cambridge.

Wiseman, T. P. 1987. *Roman Studies Literary and Historical.* Liverpool.

Wiseman, T. P. 1994. "Caesar, Pompey and Rome, 59–50 B.C." In J. A. Crook, A. Lintott, and E. Rawson, eds., *The Cambridge Ancient History.* 2nd edn. Vol. IX. Cambridge. 368–423.

Witke, C. 1970. "Poem XXXI." In Greig (1970: 36–41).

Woodman, T. 2002. "*Biformis vates*: The *Odes*, Catullus and Greek Lyric." In Woodman and Feeney (2002: 54–64).

Woodman, T., and D. Feeney, eds. 2002. *Traditions and Contexts in the Poetry of Horace.* Cambridge.

Woodman, T., and D. West, eds. 1984. *Poetry and Politics in the Age of Augustus.* Cambridge.

Wormell, D. E. 1966. "Catullus as Translator (C. 51)." In L. Wallach, ed., *The Classical Tradition: Literary and Historical Studies in Honor of Harry Caplan.* Ithaca, NY. 187–201.

Wray, D. 2000. "Apollonius' Masterplot: Narrative Strategy in *Argonautica* 1." In *Hellenistica Groningana 4.* Leuven. 239–65.

Wray, D. 2001. *Catullus and the Poetics of Roman Manhood.* Cambridge.

Wyke, M. 2002. *The Roman Mistress: Ancient and Modern Representations.* Oxford.

Yardley, J. C. 1981. "Catullus 11: The End of a Friendship." *Symbolae Osloenses* 56: 63–9.

Yeats, W. B. 1953. *The Autobiography of W. B. Yeats.* New York.

Yeats, W. B. 1961. *Essays and Introductions.* New York.

Zaffagno, E. 1975. "L'epigramma di Benvenuto di Campesani: *de resurrectione Catulli poetae Veronensis.*" In *I classici nel medioevo e nell'umanesimo.* Università di Genova. Pubblicazioni dell'Istituto di filologia classica e medievale. Genoa. 289–98.

Zarker, J. W. 1967. "Aeneas and Theseus in *Aeneid* 6." *Classical Journal* 62.5: 220–6.

Zetzel, J. 1983. "Catullus, Ennius, and the Poetics of Allusion." *Illinois Classical Studies* 8: 251–86.

Zukofsky, L., and C. Zukofsky, trans. 1969. *Catullus* (Gai Valerii Catulli Veronensis liber). London.

General Index

Note: Except as an initial, C. = Catullus.

Abel, D. H., 386
Achard, G., 335
Achilles: in the *Argonautica*, 308–9;
 in poem 64, 79–80, 99, 310, 380
Acosta-Hughes, B., 155
Adams, J. N., 196, 532
Adams, R., 112
adaptation: of C., 469–70, 523, 537–8;
 distinguished from translation, 538;
 see also imitation; translation
addressees, of poems, 207–8; *see also*
 dedications
Adler, E., 251
Adrian VI, Pope, 453
adultery: Caesar accused of, 338, 342;
 contrasted with marital sex, 284; of Lesbia
 and C., 259, 267, 328, 411, 412; Mamurra
 accused of, 342; in political invective,
 76–7; of Paris and Helen, 411; Pompey
 accused of, 77
Advanced Placement syllabus, C.'s role in,
 2, 481–6, 488, 489, 491–2, 503,
 514, 516
Aeneas: compared to lock of hair, 387–8;
 shield of, 390–1; Theseus as model for,
 382–6
aesthetics: and the arrangement of the poems,
 35, 40–46; Catullan, 218, 239, 249;
 Callimachean, 153–5, 249, 250;

Ciceronian, 179–80; and eros, 318; and
 judgment, 94; neoteric, 242, 243, 258;
 and politics, 214–15, 216–18, 220–5,
 227; and style, 208–9; *see also* poetics;
 programmatic poetry
aggression: by C., 229; sexual, 283; *see also*
 competition; masculinity; violence
Alcaeus, as influence on Horace, 132, 364
Alcaic strophe, as Horatian meter, 361
Alexandria, Callimachus' residence in, 83,
 152
Alexandrian footnotes, 296
Alexandrianism, 1, 14, 92, 180, 220, 221,
 224, 405, 455; as obstacle to translation,
 523, 535–7
alienation, and desire, 139–40
Allen, W., 154
Allius, in poem 68, 315–16, 320–3, 410–11
Ameana, as foil for Lesbia, 263
amicitia, see friendship
amor, meaning of, 265–6; *see also* desire; love
Anacreon, on poetry, 318
Anchises, Aeneas' visit to, 393
Ancona, R., 2, 6–7, 50n18, 141, 503, 510;
 education of, 486–7
anthropology, and the reading of C., 121–2;
 see also competition; masculinity
Antimachus, 101–2
Antony, as target of Cicero's invective, 115

diminutives, C.'s use of, 195–6, 198–9, 242, 244, 256, 506

Dion, J., 42

Dixon, S., 3

doctus: C. as, 5, 93, 440; as term of approbation, 219; *see also* Alexandrianism; learning; wit

Dodds, E. R., 462

domina: meaning of, 267, 322, 411–12; Lesbia as, 322, 411–12

Domitian, 424, 430, 434

domus: of Allius, 322–3, 328, 410–11; of C., 325, 411; of Laodamia and Protesilaus, 324–5, 411; in poem 68, 410–12; in Roman ideology, 411; as site of married love, 327

Dover, K. J., 118

duBois, P., 148n23

duty: C.'s attitude toward, 138–9; and friendship, 335; and passion, 184

Dyson Hejduk, J. T., 3, 5, 425

Earl, D. C., 335, 341

ecphrasis, in poem 64, 101, 293, 295, 306–7, 308, 310

editing, *see* text, of C.

Edwards, C., 113, 141

Edwards, M. J., 289

effeminacy: of Antony, 115, 125; of Caesar, 115, 214, 226, 338, 342–3; of C., 116, 133, 139, 142, 145, 146, 247–8, 256, 266; of Cicero, 114–15; of the *concubinus*, 282–3; of Furius and Aurelius, 532; of grooms, 283; of Hymenaeus, 283; and leisure, 141; of Pompey, 115–16, 125; power of, 226; of Propertius, 407; *see also* castration; gender; masculinity

Elder, J. P., 157, 239, 240, 487

elegy: arrangement of in Catullan corpus, 48–9; C.'s influence on, 399–413; contrasted with epic, 400–1; generic expectations of, 200, 403–4, 406; poem 68 as, 410–13; self-presentation in, 410; as subgenre of lyric, 406; *see also* epigrams

Eliot, T. S., 461; disapproval of C. by, 474; obscene verse of, 474

elite, Roman: C.'s attitude toward, 8, 212–29, 372–3; C.'s audience as, 92; diction of, 195–6; Horace's attitude toward, 359, 372–3; and *virtus*, 341; *see also* equestrian order

Ellis, B., 489

Ellis, R., 25, 32, 38, 192, 299

emendation, *see* text, of C.

emotion, C.'s portrayal of, 357, 505; as lure for students, 488–9, 494–5

Ennius, 102, 156; Cicero's attitude toward, 175–6; as influence on C., 92; as influence on Vergil, 187, 393–4; neoteric attitudes toward, 177; style of, 178, 179, 180

epic: Apollonius' treatment of, 300; Callimachus' rejection of, 181, 238, 239; C.'s use of, 265, 294–5, 296–7, 299, 303–4, 305–6; contrasted with elegy, 400–1; influenced by neoterics, 187; opening lines of, 296–7

Epicureanism, as influence on C., 75

epigrams: arrangement of in Catullan corpus, 21, 36, 40; C.'s reputation as author of, 439–40, 441; epigrams, contrasted with elegies, 402; generic expectations of, 200, 404, 406–7, 423, 427, 430; Martial's preference for, 419, 430; obscenity as requirement of, 423, 427; and pederasty, 404, 406–7; *see also* elegy

epithalamium: in poem 61, 277; in poem 64, 186; as title of poem 62, 29–30; *see also* marriage; wedding

epyllion, 199, 293

equestrian order: C.'s membership in, 4, 348, 349, 351; and the nobility, 348, 349, 351; status of, 64, 75; *see also* elite, Roman

Ernout, A., 194

eros, *see* desire; homosexuality; passion; sexuality

Estaço, A., *see* Statius

ethics: and the term *vir*, 113; Catullan, 334

Euphorion, 175–6, 183

Evans-Grubbs, J., 491

exchange: among men, 125; and friendship, 236, 320; of gifts, 238, 241; of poetry, 14, 221, 236, 241, 243, 316–17, 320, 349

exile, and poetry, 321

Fabbrini, D., 431

Fabullus, 81, 96, 97, 261

facetiae, 215, 217, 219, 220; as desirable quality, 318; *see also* wit

facetus, as Catullan keyword, 212, 213, 219; as rhetorical term, 220

family, of C., 3, 59–67; *see also* brother, of C.; *domus*, of C.; father, of C.

Troy: associated with death, 99, 186, 323–6, 393, 411; associated with glory, 101; C.'s journey from, 392; as grave, 324; as model for Pompey, 98; and the Roman past, 324; as site of C.'s brother's death, 99, 186

Tynan, K., 464

Ullman, B. L., 24, 25, 28

United Kingdom, study of C. in, 481–2, 492–6

United States, study of C. in, 481–2, 484–92

Untermeyer, L., 524

urbanitas, of C., 95, 104; *see also* wit

Valeriano, P., 444–5, 450–4

Valerii Catulli: *domus* of, 411; evidence concerning, 59–65

Valerius Cato, P., 14, 106–7

Valerius Catullus Messallinus, L., 64, 65, 67–8

values, Roman: C.'s acceptance of, 412; C.'s rejection of, 225–7, 237, 244–5, 334; neoterics' attitude toward, 178

Van Sickle, J., 49n9

Vance, N., 461

variety: of C.'s meters, 526; of C.'s poems, as obstacle to translation, 523; as organizing principle in the Catullan corpus, 39, 40

Varro of Atax, 400

Varus, identity of, 225

Vatican MS of C., 25–6

Vatinius, P., 80–1, 82

Venus, power of, 283–4

venustus: as Catullan keyword, 212, 215–17, 219; in Cicero, 225; Crassus as, 318; and performance, 224; as political term, 216–17, 222–3; as rhetorical term, 213, 216, 220, 221–2, 225; simpler meaning of, 227–8; *see also lepidus*; wit

Veranius, 81, 96, 97; identity of, 68–9

Vergil: in the Advanced Placement syllabus, 481, 485; *Aeneid*, as influenced by C., 381–93; *Eclogues*, as influenced by C., 377–80; Eliot's approval of, 474; *Georgics*, as influenced by C., 380–1; on the Golden Age, 378–9, 381; influence of Callimachus on, 186; influence of C. on, 162–3, 304, 377–94; influence of neoterics on, 187; modern reception of, 462, 465, 466

Vermees, M., 496

Verona: C.'s withdrawal to, 314, 319–20, 321, 324, 325, 329; C.'s writing of poetry in, 82–3; as home of C., 70, 72, 103, 104, 347; as military stronghold, 57; in poem 68, 319–20; as site of the Verona codex, 14, 26

Veronensis (MS of C.), 14, 17, 22, 23–4, 26–7, 29, 439, 457

Veyne, P., 334, 399

Victorian era, reception of C. in, 461, 465–6

violence: of the First Triumvirate, 339, 341, 347–8, 350; and marriage, 279; sexual, 117, 277, 279, 286, 287, 289; sexual, and masculinity, 345–6; sexual, in Pound, 468

vir: definition of, 113–14; as opposed to *cinaedus*, 114; *see also* gender; masculinity

virginity, 145, 282; and beauty, 280–1, 287; *see also* defloration

virtus: acquisition of, 94; and aggression, 346; meaning of, 79–80, 113, 341

vocabulary, of C., as obstacle to translation, 527–9

Volusius, 101, 102, 158, 164–5, 179, 219, 221, 242–3, 245, 262

Vox, O., 163

Wallace-Hadrill, A., 85

Walters, K. R., 440

Warman, M. S., 495

Watson, L. C., 432

Watson, P., 426

wealth: C.'s rejection of, 133; and friendship, 105; and human worth, 135; and learning, 105; and literary culture, 105, 107; of Mamurra, 73–4, 75–6, 339–41; and *mollitia*, 118; and passion, 258; as source of corruption, 104–5

Weber, C., 299

weddings: color symbolism in, 282; Greek vs. Roman, 277; hair as significant in, 282–3; of Peleus and Thetis, 79, 80, 92, 99–103, 165–8, 295, 301, 304, 305–9; *see also* marriage

Weiss, M., 87n33

West, M. L., 201, 202, 338

Westphal, R., 37

Wheeler, A. L., 38, 45, 46, 49n2, 238–9

Wheelock, F., 487

Whitaker, R., 411

Whitehouse, J. C., 463

Whitman, C., 487

Whitman, W., 463

Wigodsky, M., 382

Index Locorum

20037939R00340

Printed in Great Britain
by Amazon